THE EVIDENCE OF CHILDREN

The Law and the Psychology

Books ... n or before

THE EVIDENCE OF CHILDREN

The Law and the Psychology

Second Edition

John R. Spencer, MA, LLB
Reader in Common Law,
University of Cambridge,
and Fellow of Selwyn College

Rhona H. Flin, BSc, PhD
Reader in Applied Psychology,
The Robert Gordon University
Aberdeen

BLACKSTONE
PRESS LIMITED

First published in Great Britain 1990 by Blackstone Press Limited,
9-15 Aldine Street, London W12 8AW. Telephone 081-740 1173

© John R. Spencer and Rhona H. Flin, 1990

First edition 1990
Second edition 1993

ISBN: 1 85431 218 9

British Library Cataloguing in Publication Data
A CIP Catalogue record for this book is available from the British Library

Typeset by Style Photosetting Ltd, Mayfield, East Sussex
Printed by Bell & Bain Ltd, Glasgow

Contents

Child witnesses who are not victims — Children as witnesses to crimes by children — Child abuse victims as witnesses – child abuse in general — Notes

Criminal proceedings in England — Criminal proceedings in Scotland — Civil proceedings in England — Civil proceedings concerning children in Scotland — Duty to report child abuse to the authorities — Note

(A) What matters must be proved by evidence — (B) The burden of proof — (C) The standard of proof — (D) How facts are to be proved: what does and does not amount in law to evidence — (E) Rules about how evidence is to be evaluated — Note

English law — English law: historical background — Criticism of the competency requirement: its curtailment and partial abolition — English law: the competency requirement today — The position in Northern Ireland — Scottish law — Compellability — Notes

Preface

In March 1989, the first author was about to abandon his plan to write a book on the law and psychology of children's evidence because he felt unable to handle the psychology. At the same time, the second author was about to abandon her plan to write a book on the psychology and law of children's evidence, because she felt she could not cope with the law. Each discovered the predicament of the other, and this joint book was the result.

The first purpose of the book is to explain the legal rules that govern the evidence of children. This we try to do in enough detail to be of use to lawyers, and — no simple task — with enough clarity to enable them to be grasped by people in other disciplines. In this respect the book is British rather than purely English, because we describe the law of evidence in Scotland as well as in England. We have done this with some trepidation, because although the second author has the advantage of being a Scottish psychologist, the first author has the disadvantage of being a purely English lawyer. We hope that lawyers in Scotland forgive the first author's errors with the thought that the stronger features of their system may get some publicity south of the Border. It is now almost 400 years since James VI of Scotland became James I of England, and nearly 300 years since the Act of Union: yet little knowledge about the Scottish legal system seems to have spread south of the Border. In Cambridge University Library there has been a copy of Dickson's classic treatise on the law of evidence in Scotland since 1864, and when the first author consulted it in 1989, he found that every page remained uncut!

In this second edition we have also included information about the law in Northern Ireland, in so far as it differs from the law in England.

Our second aim is a reformist one. We try to examine the legal rules in the light of modern psychological research in order to see if they are sensible, and we argue for the reform of those rules which seem to run counter to the insights this research provides. In recent years the evidence of children has been a matter of continuous public discussion. As the first edition went to press, the report of Judge Pigot's Home Office Advisory Group on Video Evidence had just been published, and so had the 125th Report of the Scottish Law Commission. Since then, various parts of the reforms proposed by these bodies have been enacted and whilst lawyers struggle to take on board the recent changes, there is continuing discussion about the need for more radical changes to be made. We hope this book may prove a useful contribution to the public debate.

Our thanks are due to a large number of people who have provided us with information: among them judges, magistrates, prosecutors, barristers, solicitors, Law Commissioners, psychiatrists, psychologists, paediatricians, social workers, police officers, and for the first edition Esther Rantzen, who shared with us a collection of correspondence from viewers of 'That's Life!' For the second edition, we gratefully acknowledge many useful comments which readers made to us about the first edition. We are grateful to Selwyn College, Cambridge, for funding the services of a research assistant, Miss Lindsay Yates, for part of the summer of 1989, and Miss Heleen Scheer for part of the summer of 1992. We owe our thanks to Blackstone Press for their help and encouragement. And we owe our particular thanks to Rosie Spencer and to David Flin, who bore our neglect of them with patience as we strove to finish the book before the contents were overtaken by events.

John Spencer
Rhona Flin

References

One problem we had to face in writing this book was how to harmonise the different methods of referencing which are used by lawyers and scientists. In the end we devised the following compromise. References to cases and statutes are made in the text as they occur: 'The Court of Appeal held these statements to be inadmissible in *H* v *H* [1989] 3 WLR 933; however, this ruling was rapidly overruled by Parliament (Children Act 1989, s. 96)'. Books and learned articles, whether legal or scientific, are referenced by putting the author's name and the date of the book or paper in the text — for example, 'In the USA there is a legal duty to report suspected child abuse to the authorities (Whitcomb 1990)' — and at the end of the book the documents are listed, in alphabetical order by authors, with full details.

Table of Cases

Table of Statutes

Table of Statutory Instruments

CHAPTER ONE
Introduction

The evidence of children is important mainly because the machinery of justice has to use it in order to deal with child abuse. Horrible as it is to contemplate, children are sometimes beaten, starved, neglected and sexually assaulted. When detected, this may give rise to civil proceedings brought by the State to remove the child from both parents, civil proceedings by one parent to remove the child from the clutches of the other, and criminal proceedings brought to punish the person responsible. Where a child has been abused, in the nature of things there will probably be only two eyewitnesses, one of whom is the offender and the other is the child. So it is vital—sometimes quite literally so—that the law should provide a workable means by which a child can tell his story to the court, and the court can evaluate it.

CHILD WITNESSES WHO ARE NOT VICTIMS

However, although the public perception of a child witness is that of a child who has been the victim of cruelty or a sexual offence, it would be wrong to think children never give evidence except in cases of child abuse. Children, no less than adults, are often bystander witnesses to crimes and other legally significant events in which they are not otherwise involved. A study of children aged between 11 and 15 living on a council estate in Scotland showed that 33% had seen a car broken into during the last nine months, 24% had witnessed a housebreaking, and 64% had seen someone injured in a fight (Kinsey and Loader 1990). Some children who witness crimes as bystanders have to give evidence in court. A leading case on sentencing for robbery reached the courts only because 'a very observant girl of 12' took the number of a car (*Attorney-General's References Nos 10 and 11 of 1990* (1990) 92 Cr App R 166). When Peter Hain was tried (and resoundingly acquitted) for a bank theft, the whole case turned on the evidence of two 12-year-old boys who appeared as witnesses for the prosecution, and one slightly older boy who gave evidence for the defence (Hain 1976). Sadly, the crimes children see are quite often acts of violence committed against their parents, and where these result in death the child may be the only person who can give an eye-witness account: a poignant example is the Hungerford massacre in August 1987, where the only witnesses to Michael Ryan's abduction and murder of one of his victims were her two children, aged two and four, with whom she was eating a picnic in a wood when he arrived on the scene with his gun (*The Times*, 26 September 1987). In the United States, it has been estimated that of 2,000 homicides committed in the Los Angeles area in 1982, no less than 200 took place in front of children (Pynoos and Eth 1984).

No equivalent study has been made in Britain. Nor is it possible to quote from any official statistics about child witnesses, because despite official concern about the plight of child witnesses, no one in authority seems to have thought of keeping any kind of record of the number of children who are called as witnesses in legal proceedings, let alone in what capacity they are called, or in what type of case. A recent study in Scotland, however, revealed the possibly surprising fact that considerably more children are cited to give evidence about offences they witnessed as bystanders than about crimes committed upon themselves. In Scotland it seems that the child abuse victim, although the popular stereotype, is in the minority (Flin et al. 1993). In England, on the other hand, it is frequently said that children rarely give evidence except where they are victims. This is borne out by a recent study of Crown Court cases where the live video link (see chapter 5) was used, where it was found that no less than 89% of child witnesses were victims (Davies and Noon 1991). The difference between the two jurisdictions is probably explained by the Scottish rule of evidence which requires every criminal offence to be proved by the evidence of at least two witnesses—which puts the prosecution in the position of having to use every piece of evidence they have got (see chapter 8).

CHILDREN AS WITNESSES TO CRIMES BY CHILDREN

As well as being victims of abuse, and bystander witnesses, children sometimes get involved with the law courts because they commit crimes themselves. Their offences are usually minor ones, but even the most serious offences are occasionally perpetrated by children. (The case of Mary Bell, who in 1968 at the age of 11 was convicted of the manslaughter of two little boys aged 4 and 3, is the most famous modern example: see *Re X* [1984] 1 WLR 1422). If prosecuted, a child defendant, like an adult, may elect to give evidence in defence, and in the nature of things children are often witnesses to crimes committed by other children. Hence this is another area where children's evidence is a matter of practical importance.

In England a child below the age of 10 incurs no criminal liability at all; a child between 10 and 14 may be convicted of an offence provided he or she is shown to have 'mischievous discretion'—which means that the child can be shown to have known that his or her behaviour was seriously wrong: a curious rule that has occasionally resulted in children being acquitted for extremely serious offences, like murder, where there is no doubt that they were the culprits (Mullins 1943); above the age of 14 a child incurs criminal liability for his or her acts according to the same principles that govern the criminal liability of adults. In recent years it has been official policy in England to caution young offenders wherever possible, and to divert them from the criminal courts; but the number of boys and girls under the age of 14 who go through the criminal courts in England is still quite large—nearly 5,500 in 1990 (as compared with over 21,000 in 1977). By the Criminal Procedure (Scotland) Act 1975, ss. 170 and 369, the minimum age of criminal responsibility north of the Border is eight: two years lower than it is in England. However, it is rarer for a child to be prosecuted for a crime in Scotland, because s. 31 of the Social Work (Scotland) Act 1968 forbids the prosecution of any child under 16 without the Lord Advocate's permission—consent which is refused unless the offence is serious. Where a child has committed an offence this is one of the grounds on which he may be referred to a children's hearing (see chapter 2), and this, rather than prosecution, is usually how a crime committed by a child is dealt with.

In practice, cases where children are accused of crimes are not usually bedevilled by the same sort of evidential problems which occur when children have to give evidence against adults. As far as England is concerned it is only children aged 10 and upwards who can be prosecuted, and by s. 24 of the Magistrates' Courts Act 1980 (as amended in 1991) all offenders under the age of 18 must be tried in youth courts—except in the rare cases where they are accused of very serious offences, or where they are tried jointly with an adult. The youth courts where most child defendants are tried are magistrates' courts specially adapted for dealing with children. The judges are magistrates who have been specially trained and selected; they always sit in private and they follow an informal procedure which is intended to make communication with the child defendant easier. Whilst the English youth (formerly juvenile) courts have their vigorous critics, there is no doubt that they are generally much better adapted for receiving the evidence of children than are the ordinary courts. As far as Scotland is concerned, children's crimes are usually handled by a children's hearing rather than an ordinary court of law. If the child admits the crime which is the ground of the referral, the children's hearing will deal with him under its general powers. If he disputes it, this issue, like any other disputed ground of referral, will be handed over to the sheriff court for proof. Where an alleged crime by the child is a disputed ground of referral, the sheriff is forbidden by statute to find it proved unless he is satisfied according to the criminal rather than the civil standard of proof (Social Work (Scotland) Act 1968, s. 42(6)). But in other respects he will handle the case as he would any other disputed ground of referral: which means that he sits in private, and hears the evidence informally. Thus in England and in Scotland the recent public concern about children's evidence has centred on children giving evidence against adults accused of subjecting them to physical violence or sexual abuse.

CHILD ABUSE VICTIMS AS WITNESSES—CHILD ABUSE IN GENERAL

Awareness of child abuse in the past

From what one reads in the newspapers one might think that child abuse was a wholly modern discovery. However, in Britain and elsewhere in the Western world child abuse has been a matter of intermittent public concern for over a hundred years.

Credit for first bringing cruelty to children to public attention must be given to the Frenchman, Auguste-Ambroise Tardieu (1818–1879), Professor of Forensic Medicine and Dean of the Medical School at the University of Paris, who published a paper entitled 'Étude médico-légale sur les sévices et mauvais traitements exercés sur des enfants' in 1860.

In the English-speaking world, it was child murder that first attracted public attention. In the 1860s concern about 'baby-farmers'—unscrupulous people who 'adopted' children in return for payment, and then actively killed them or let them die of neglect—led to some spectacular prosecutions, and changes in the law about registration of births, and the duty to support illegitimate children (Behlmer 1982). Public concern about physical cruelty short of death began in the USA. The first society for the prevention of cruelty to children was founded in New York in 1871, following a celebrated incident in which a little girl called Mary Ellen, who was being hideously ill-treated by her adopted parents, was rescued as a result of a prosecution brought under a law against cruelty to animals—a rescue which proved possible only because the judge conveniently interpreted the term 'animal' to include a child. The public revelation of Mary Ellen's sufferings (1), and of the fact that there was a statute against cruelty to animals but not one against cruelty to children, led to a society being founded to campaign against cruelty to children. The news spread across the Atlantic and the first such society in Britain was founded in Liverpool in 1882 (Allen and Morton 1961). Societies in other cities followed. The English societies eventually merged to form the National Society for the Prevention of Cruelty to Children (NSPCC); plans for a merger with the Scottish societies broke down in a dispute about finance, and since 1907 there has been a separate society in Scotland, the Royal Scottish Society for the Prevention of Cruelty to Children (RSSPCC) (Ashley 1985). The driving force behind the campaign against cruelty to children was Benjamin Waugh, the Congregationalist minister who founded the NSPCC, who devoted his life to exposing the problem. The difficulties he faced have a sadly modern ring to them. In his preface to the biography Rosa Waugh wrote of her father in 1913, Lord Alverstone wrote this:

> Mr Waugh discovered by personal investigation that the cases of cruelty to children—cruelty, inflicted in many cases by their own parents, relations, and persons who had charge of them—were far more numerous than the general public at that time supposed. . . . Persons of the most charitable and benevolent disposition declared that his efforts were to a large extent uncalled for: that cases of cruelty by parents were comparatively few and unimportant: and that the then existing law was strong enough to investigate and deal with such cases.

From the start the societies campaigned for changes in the law. One of their early successes was the Prevention of Cruelty to Children Act 1889, which first made child cruelty and neglect a specific criminal offence.

In Britain the sexual abuse of children became a public issue rather earlier than physical abuse, when it surfaced as a side-issue of a public campaign against prostitution. The London Society for the Protection of Young Females, which was founded in 1835, became concerned at the fact that girls were often lured into brothels at a very young age. As a counter-measure it began to agitate for the age of consent—which then stood at 12 in England—to be raised (Bristow 1977). In the 1880s a new purity group called the National Vigilance Association (NVA) came into being, and this joined forces with the NSPCC in a campaign to raise the age of consent. Their combined campaign received an enormous boost from the activities of the investigative journalist W. T. Stead, who made public the fact that a regular trade in the prostitution of young girls existed to satisfy the tastes of a particular type of Victorian debauchee. To get his information he posed as a debauchee himself, 'bought' a young girl of 13, obtaining her with a certificate of virginity from an abortionist, who also equipped him with a bottle of chloroform and a promise 'that if the child was badly injured Madame would patch her up to the best of her ability'. Then instead of taking her off to the house where the owner had assured him that he could 'enjoy the screams of the girl with the certainty that no one else hears them but yourself' he set her free and wrote a sensational article about what he had done in the *Pall Mall Gazette* (6 July 1885). Despite the fact that he had not used the girl for the purposes for which he had allegedly procured her, this led to him being prosecuted and jailed for his act of procurement (Bristow 1977). The resulting public outcry about the state of the law concerning sexual offences induced Parliament to pass the Criminal Law Amendment Act 1885, which not only raised the age of consent to 16, but also toughened up the law on homosexual offences.

These developments arose from public concern about the sexual abuse of children by those who were not members of the family: but the 19th century also saw the beginnings of public concern about intra-familial sexual abuse of children. Once again it seems to have been Ambroise Tardieu who first made the scientific world aware of this issue; in 1857 he published an important book on rape which discussed many cases where children had been sexually abused by their relatives. This went through six editions, and stimulated a series of studies by other French doctors, and a public debate about the extent to which allegations of sexual offences against children are true and false (Masson 1984). At the end of the 19th century Sigmund Freud took the matter further. He found that many of his patients told him how they had been sexually abused as children, and in a paper in 1896 he put forward the view, now widely accepted, that sexual abuse in childhood is a powerful cause of mental disturbance in later life. In the face of hostility and scepticism from his professional colleagues, however, Freud recanted: standing his original theory on its head, he then put forward the idea that children tend to fantasise about sexual relations with their parents. This theory has had a considerable effect on the view the law takes on the credibility of children, as we explain in chapter 11.

If 19th-century scientists were divided about whether incest was common, many influential people in late Victorian Britain seem to have had no doubt that it was widespread, at least among the poor. William Booth, the founder of the Salvation Army, said 'Incest is so familiar as hardly to call for a remark' (Booth 1890). Similar views were expressed by other Victorian evangelists and social reformers, who made much of the problem—which they commonly blamed on overcrowded conditions—in their fight to obtain better housing for the poor (Bailey and Blackburn 1979). Others drew attention to the fact that incest was common in order to produce a change in the law. In Scotland, incest was punishable as a serious crime in the ordinary criminal courts, and had been so since 1567 if not before. In England, however, incest as such was punishable only in the ecclesiastical courts. As these had long been moribund, in practice it was not punishable at all, unless some other sexual offence like rape or intercourse with an under-age girl was also committed. In the 1880s and 1890s the NVA and the NSPCC waged a joint campaign to have this changed. The NVA wanted all incest made criminal because it was immoral, and the NSPCC wanted it criminalised, even between consenting adults, because they felt that where incest took place between a father and his daughter over the age of consent this would almost certainly mean that he had started abusing her while she was under it, even if it was now impossible to prove this. The fruit of their endeavours was the Punishment of Incest Act 1908, the provisions of which are now codified as the incest provisions of the Sexual Offences Act 1956.

While the criminal law was being amended to deal with child abuse important changes were also made in the law governing children's evidence. The Act of 1885 which raised the age of consent also made it possible for children to give unsworn evidence in criminal proceedings in England (see chapter 4). The Prevention of Cruelty to Children (Amendment) Act 1894 first contained the provisions which in theory allow the evidence of a sick child to be taken before a magistrate in advance of trial (see chapter 5); and the Punishment of Incest Act 1908 contained a provision, later repealed, requiring all proceedings for incest to be heard in camera.

◊ In the 1920s there was another wave of public concern about child abuse. The government set up a Departmental Committee to look at sexual offences against young persons in England, which published a report in 1925 (Cmd 2561) pointing out many of the needless legal difficulties over the evidence of children which have been discussed again in recent years; but public concern seems to have died down again by the time the report appeared, because no action followed. The London stipendiary magistrate and law reformer Claud Mullins tried to raise public consciousness about the problems of children's evidence with a pungent chapter in a book he wrote a few years later (Mullins 1943); the British Medical Association and the Magistrates' Association tried to do the same in *The Criminal Law and Sexual Offenders* in 1949, and Glanville Williams sought to raise the matter again in the Hamlyn Lectures which he gave in 1955 (Williams 1963). But nothing was ever done to implement the Committee's recommendations.

Child abuse—current awareness
The present wave of concern about child abuse can be traced to the work of the American paediatrician, Henry Kempe, and his colleagues in the early 1960s. With the help of modern scientific methods, they conclusively demonstrated that a large number of the supposedly accidental injuries for which children

werc treated in hospital must have been deliberately inflicted—a finding which implied that physical violence to children was far more prevalent in the USA than was then generally supposed. Kempe's views were rapidly accepted in the USA and acted upon, an important result being the enactment in all States of 'reporting statutes' which oblige those who have professional dealings with children to report to the authorities any suspicion that a child is being abused. Kempe's views spread to Britain following a sabbatical visit he later made here. The NSPCC set up a battered child research department and a number of 'special units', and started a publicity campaign about battered children. Public attention was further aroused by a series of horrible incidents which would probably have passed without notice in earlier and harsher days—in particular, the brutal murder of the eight-year-old Maria Colwell by her parents, which led to an official enquiry in 1974 (DHSS 1974). As the result of various promptings from the Department of Health and Social Security, important changes were made in the way that local authority social services departments handle cases of violence and suspected violence to children. These were designed to ensure that information about battered children reached the right quarters, and that social services departments coordinated their efforts with the police and other agencies. They included area review committees, now called area child protection committees (ACPCs), for policy discussions, multi-disciplinary case-conferences over individual cases, and the creation in each area of a 'child protection register' where details of any child thought to be at risk could be officially recorded (see generally Jones, Pickett, Oates and Barbor 1987; Johnson 1990). Unlike what happened in the USA, however, in Britain it has not been made obligatory to report suspected child abuse or to enter cases on the local register.

Although the reporting laws in the USA were designed with cases of physical violence to children in mind, one incidental result they had was that the authorities began to hear of many more cases of sexual abuse. In the 1970s this prompted a number of people in the USA to undertake serious research into child sex abuse: among them David Finkelhor (1979 and 1984) and Diana Russell (1983). In brief, this work showed that child sexual abuse, like physical abuse, was much more frequent than previously recognised, and—even more disquieting—that serious sexual abuse in childhood is associated with psychiatric and personality disorders later on in life. (On this, see Glaser and Frosh 1988; Tong and Oates 1990.) These studies, like Kempe's earlier studies on violence to children, rapidly became known in Britain, where researchers replicated their studies with similar results (CIBA Foundation 1984; West 1985; Baker and Duncan 1985). In consequence, Freud's theory that children tend to fantasise about sexual behaviour with their parents was rapidly discarded by professionals concerned in child care, who now saw it as one of the more unfortunate mistakes in the history of science (see chapter 11). In the space of a few years it became widely accepted that when a child complains of sexual abuse he or she is likely to be telling the truth. In 1988 this was officially recognised by the DHSS. In *Working Together*, a guide to social services departments on the proper investigation of child abuse cases it said: 'A child's statement about an allegation of abuse, whether in confirmation or denial, should always be taken seriously. A child's testimony should not be viewed as inherently less reliable than that of an adult.' (DHSS et al. 1988) (2)

This new attitude towards the sexual abuse of children also stimulated paediatricians to study its physical symptoms. In 1986 two Leeds paediatricians, Dr Hobbs and Dr Wynne, published a paper which indicated that buggery was more commonly practised on young children than previously realised, and which also suggested that a physical sign called 'reflex anal dilation' is commonly associated with it (Hobbs and Wynne 1986). In Cleveland in 1987 two pediatricians, Dr Higgs and Dr Wyatt, took this message very seriously, and in the space of a few months diagnosed so many children as the victims of sexual abuse that the social services department and the court system broke down under the strain. This led to a public outcry, this time not against the problem of undetected child abuse, but against a perceived problem of official witch-hunts about imaginary cases of it. The government set up an official enquiry into the affair under Lord Justice Butler-Sloss, the results of which were eagerly awaited by those who hoped to be told precisely how many (if any) of their diagnoses had been false. This hope was disappointed, because the report (Cm 412, 1988) did not give this information (although it has since been said that out of 126 diagnoses, some 26 were eventually held by judges to be wrong (Campbell 1988)). The report criticised the doctors for the way they had gone about their work, but on the other hand it clearly reaffirmed that child sexual abuse is a major social problem, and refused to accept the idea that the whole business had been a groundless witch-hunt (Freeman 1989). The final conclusions of the Cleveland Report begin as follows:

We have learned during the Inquiry that sexual abuse occurs in children of all ages, including the very young, to boys as well as girls, in all classes of society and frequently within the privacy of the family. The sexual abuse can be very serious and on occasions includes vaginal, anal and oral intercourse. The problems of child sexual abuse have been recognised to an increasing extent over the past few years by professionals in different disciplines. This presents new and particularly difficult problems for the agencies concerned in child protection.

In 1991 Scotland had its equivalent of the Cleveland affair when social workers removed nine children from four families in Orkney, partly on the basis of what other children had said who had been removed earlier. The case was said to involve 'ritual' abuse, and attracted the widest publicity. When the families appealed against the 'grounds of referral' (see page 28 below) the Sheriff rejected the grounds of referral, and ordered the children home, without hearing the Reporter's evidence in support of the removal. The Reporter won his appeal, but promptly dropped the case. Amid growing public concern, Lord Clyde, a Scottish judge, was appointed to hold an official enquiry, the report of which appeared in October 1992 (Clyde 1992). This report contained criticisms of nearly everyone who had been officially involved, particularly about methods used for interviewing children (see chapter 12), but no attempt was made to ascertain the facts that remained in doubt as a result of the court proceedings being dropped. What had actually been going on, if anything, thus remains a mystery.

The frequency of child abuse

How common are the various forms of child abuse? This is a complicated matter with which many researchers have tried to grapple, and despite this—or possibly because of it—the public is often badly confused about it. One source of confusion is the different senses in which researchers try to measure whether something is 'common'. A given set of figures may be trying to record *prevalence*—that is, to how many people does it happen? Or they may try to measure *incidence*—how many cases are there per week, month or year? Another frequent source of confusion concerns the different definitions of what amounts to child abuse, and in particular, sexual abuse. Obviously, there is much more 'child sex abuse' around if the definition includes comparatively minor matters, like indecent exposure by men beyond the range of physical contact, than if it is limited to cases where physical contact took place. Here we have room for only a sketchy account of the available data, and readers who want further information should look elsewhere: for example, Birchall (1989), La Fontaine (1990), Gillham (1991), Mayes et al. (1993).

For information on physical abuse we have two sources: the official criminal statistics, and child protection registers. For sexual abuse we also have a third: various surveys compiled by questioning a sample of the adult population about their experiences as children.

The criminal statistics are of little help. In the first place, they only show the cases which enter the criminal justice system, which we now know to be a minority. And secondly, although the Departmental Committee on Sexual Offences against Young Persons recommended that official statistics should record the number of offences against children as long ago as 1925, the criminal statistics are still compiled by type of offence and offender, with no details about victims. Thus child abuse cases can only be detected insofar as the prosecutor charged a child-specific offence, like cruelty and neglect: a state of affairs which again received unfavourable comment in the report of the Pigot Committee (see below) in December 1989. Despite this difficulty, however, the Pigot Committee managed to find out that in England there were 3,229 prosecutions for offences against children in 1983, rising to 3,723 in 1987. Against a background of some 2,250,000 prosecutions in the criminal courts of England every year, the criminal statistics make child abuse look like a tiny problem.

The NSPCC holds the child protection registers in certain areas. It has tried to estimate the national incidence of child abuse by extrapolating from the number of cases entered each year on the registers in those areas (see table 1.1). These figures are difficult to compare in any meaningful way with what is shown by the criminal statistics. However, they certainly indicate the problem is much larger—indeed, some four times larger—than the criminal statistics suggest, and that the problem—or public awareness of it—is growing.

Self-report surveys, which try to detect the prevalence of child sexual abuse, suggest a rate which is enormously greater. The much cited and widely respected study carried out by Baker and Duncan for Mori and published in 1985 revealed that roughly one in 10—vastly more than the figures as suggested by the number of prosecutions and the number of children on child protection registers—reported some form of sexual abuse at the hands of an adult before the age of 16. Baker and Duncan used a wide definition of 'sexual abuse' which included not only indecent assault, but exposure, showing pornographic material, and talking about sexual matters in an erotic way. For about half of those who said they had been abused the 'abuse' was fairly mild, consisting of indecent exposure, or some other sexual behaviour not involving physical contact. For the other half—roughly one in 20—the abuse had involved at least some sexual touching. Roughly one in 200 of those questioned had suffered abuse consisting of full sexual intercourse, and for roughly one in 400 of the respondents there had been sexual intercourse with a blood relative: incest. To understand what these figures mean, it is helpful to compare them with the incidence of certain illnesses. Medical statistics show that roughly one child in 2,500 is born with cystic fibrosis, and roughly one person in 100 contracts diabetes at some stage in his life. On Baker and Duncan's figures the risk of a person's suffering serious sexual abuse in childhood falls somewhere between these two. Other studies suggest that the incidence rates put forward by Baker and Duncan are quite possibly too low (see Glaser and Frosh (1988), ch. 1).

Table 1.1 Estimates of national incidence per year (rounded)

Estimated number of children in England and Wales	1983	1984	1985	1986	1987	1988	1989	1990
0–14 Years								
Physically Injured	6,800	7,050	9,100	9,600	8,070	8,300	9,700	9,300
Sexually Abused	680	1,200	2,400	5,300	6,060	5,300	5,900	4,500
Registered	11,300	11,100	16,000	21,900	23,500	25,100	34,100	32,500
0–16 Years								
Physically Injured	7,100	7,500	9,800	10,400	9,000	9,100	10,500	10,100
Sexually Abused	900	1,560	3,000	6,400	7,200	6,200	6,600	5,300
Registered	11,900	11,800	17,100	23,900	25,700	27,000	36,300	34,700

Souce: *Child Abuse Trends in England and Wales 1983–87* (NSPCC 1989) and *Child Abuse Trends in England and Wales 1988–1990* (NSPCC 1992).

These and other studies have also given us useful information about the persons who sexually abuse children. First, the offenders are usually men. At one time, it was thought that the offence was almost exclusively an adult male one, but some offences are committed by females, and there are some indications that child sexual abuse by women may have been under-reported (La Fontaine 1990). Furthermore, 'It is now widely recognized that sexual abuse of children by other children takes place' (Home Office 1991, para. 123; Horne et al. 1991). Secondly, contrary to the public stereotype of the sex offender as the stranger with a long mac, very many of those who sexually abuse children are already known to them, and many are close relatives. In the Baker and Duncan study 49 per cent of abusers were previously known to the victim, and 14 per cent of all abuse took place within the family. Other studies suggest that the proportion of fathers and other close relatives involved increases with the more serious types of abuse. Paediatricians, who tend to see cases where the children have suffered injury—which usually means abuse by penetration—say that natural fathers are the perpetrators in as many as one-third of the cases which paediatricians see (Wynne 1989). Figures issued by ChildLine in 1987 showed that 97 per cent of the children who telephoned them about sexual abuse were being abused by someone from within the family circle: but the tiny number of cases involving strangers in this sample probably reflects the fact that children find it easier to discuss sexual abuse by strangers with their parents, and have less need of a telephone counselling service. In the last few years, a number of much-publicised prosecutions have made the public conscious of the fact that a certain amount of sexual abuse takes place in children's homes and residential schools; notably the scandalous case of Beck, convicted of a series of offences in Leicestershire committed over many years (*The Independent*, 27 November 1991). And there is increased concern about the abuse of children suffering from disability (Kelly 1992).

In the light of the modern self-report studies, almost everyone now believes that previous estimates of the prevalence of incest, which were based on other kinds of information, gravely underestimated the extent of the problem. Weinberg, for example, in his study of incest in 1954, showed that the criminal statistics in the English-speaking world reveal a detected rate of incest of around 1 per million of the population, and concluded that 'incest is very rare'. If the figure is really 1 in 400 rather than 1 in 1,000,000 incest is still not universal, but it can no longer be described as 'very rare'.

In recent years, important information has also become available about the attitude of offenders when they are detected. In the past, it was usually only those who confessed who were prosecuted, from which lawyers often had the general impression that those who sexually abuse children are pathetic individuals with a particular tendency to confess. In fact, the great majority of alleged abusers, including many against whom suspicion is extremely strong, deny the offence. In one English study, 86% of those accused denied the offence (Bexley Report 1987).

Child sexual abuse and changes in the laws of evidence

In the USA, the increasing number of child abuse cases going through the courts focused public attention on the unsatisfactory way in which the legal system then treated the evidence of children: in particular that it made the experience of giving evidence a frightening and distressing one, and that the law worked on the assumption that children who complain of sexual abuse ought not to be believed. In the early 1980s this led to pressing demands for changes in the rules governing the evidence of children. A number of important changes have now been made in many parts of the USA: changes which include toning down the rules of competency and corroboration, and the introduction of videotaped testimony and closed-circuit television. Many of these changes are discussed later in this book (see chapters 5, 7 and 14).

The same thing began to happen in Britain a few years later. In the late 1970s and early 1980s public opinion began to be roused by a number of studies which pointed out the indignities the legal system often heaps upon adult rape victims (e.g., Chambers and Millar 1983; see generally Temkin (1987), ch. 1). Then in July 1983 there was enormous press interest when the television actor Peter Adamson (Len Fairclough to those who watched 'Coronation Street') was tried for indecently assaulting two eight-year-old girls in a Lancashire swimming-bath. One of the girls was so distressed by the prospect of a court appearance that she attempted to commit suicide. This, and their obvious distress when giving evidence in open court, led the press to criticise the existing rules of evidence, and moved George Carman QC—whose cross-examination had reduced the girls to tears—to say in his closing speech for the defence: 'It may be that a case such as this may require the law to look again and reappraise the problem of how children may give evidence more informally and more privately rather than in the presence of the public and the press' (*The Sun*, 27 July 1983). From this point on, the problem of children's evidence has been rarely out of the newspapers. A particularly heavy barrage of press criticism was fired in March 1986, when the Director of Public Prosecutions declined to prosecute over the alleged rape of an eight-year-old girl by a doctor, and multiple offences of buggery by a clergyman, because of difficulties created by the law of evidence. Esther Rantzen—through whose efforts ChildLine was set up in 1986 to offer telephone advice to child abuse victims—made reform of the law relating to child witnesses one of her campaigning issues in her long-running television programme 'That's Life!'.

It is not only the press and the general public which have taken up the matter of children's evidence, however. Paediatricians, lawyers, psychiatrists, psychologists, policemen, social workers and civil servants have all begun to think seriously about it. In 1981 a team of workers at Great Ormond Street Hospital began to experiment with new techniques for interviewing child abuse victims (see chapter 9). Between 1985 and 1987 the Metropolitan Police and Bexley social services department carried out an experiment designed to humanise the investigation of child sexual abuse cases. An important element of the scheme was recording initial interviews with children on videotape, to avoid the need for repeated interviews (Bexley Report 1987). The scheme they devised, or parts of it, has now been introduced in many parts of the country. A similar experiment, funded by the Home Office, was carried out in West Yorkshire between 1987 and 1989 (West Yorkshire Police 1989). In Scotland in 1986 a group of psychologists, funded by the Scottish Home and Health Department, began the first British study of child witnesses (see chapter 13), and in England a year later the Home Office funded a study of child victims of crime at the Oxford Centre for Criminological Research (Morgan and Zedner 1992). In the legal press a campaign for change was vigorously led by the septuagenarian Professor Glanville Williams, who had first tried to raise interest in the matter in 1955 (Williams 1987 (a-d)). A number of important cross-disciplinary conferences were held to discuss the problems of children's evidence. A conference organised by the RSSPCC in 1985 (Irvine and Dunning 1985) was followed by one organised by the British Psychological Society in 1986 (Davies and Drinkwater 1988). Children's evidence formed a major element in an international conference on child sexual abuse at Glasgow in 1988 (Murray and Gough 1990). An international conference at Cambridge in 1989 was devoted entirely to the evidence of children, and the opening paper was given by the Lord Chancellor of Great Britain, Lord Mackay of Clashfern (Spencer, Nicholson, Flin and Bull 1990). It was also the subject of a NATO Conference in Italy in 1992, the proceedings of which are now in press (Peters 1993).

In England, the government responded to the pressure for reform by including several changes in the law relating to children's evidence in the Bill which eventually became the Criminal Justice Act 1988: live video link (closed-circuit television) for children giving evidence in the Crown Court (see chapter 5), and amendments to the rules on corroboration (see chapter 8). In response to pressure in Parliament for more radical changes in England, the government set up a Home Office Advisory Committee under Judge Tom Pigot, QC, to consider the possible use of videotapes, which produced a very radical report in December 1989. This proved too radical for the government, and only a watered-down version of the Pigot proposals found their way into the Criminal Justice Act 1991. The 1991 Act, however, does make videotaped evidence more readily admissible in criminal proceedings (see chapter 7), and attempts to abolish the competency requirement (see chapter 4). In Scotland, the Lord Advocate referred the law governing children's evidence to the Scottish Law Commission in 1986. A discussion paper was published in June 1988, and a number of important recommendations were made in its final report in February 1990. Some of these were implemented by the Law Reform (Miscellaneous Provisions) (Scotland) Act 1990, and others by the Prisoners and Criminal Proceedings (Scotland) Act 1993. For Northern Ireland, the government has introduced most of the same changes to the rules of children's evidence as have taken place in England. This has been done by issuing orders which copy the English statutes.

Similar developments have taken place elsewhere in the English-speaking world. In the Republic of Ireland, for example, the Law Reform Commission produced an impressively documented discussion paper in 1989. Important changes were then enacted by the Criminal Evidence Act 1992, some of which go beyond what has been done in England and Wales.

NOTES

1.   Happily, Mary Ellen's sufferings did not prevent her living to a ripe old age. She died in 1956, aged 92: Lazoritz (1990).

2.   The passage does not appear in the 1991 edition (Home Office et al. 1991).

CHAPTER TWO
An outline of the English and Scottish legal systems

This section is meant for readers who are not familiar with the British (1) legal system, and its purpose is to give them just enough background knowledge to understand the context in which the problems discussed in the rest of the book arise. It contains nothing about English law which English lawyers will not know already, nor anything about Scots law which is new to Scottish lawyers: but English lawyers may find it useful to read the section on the Scottish legal system, and vice versa.

In both jurisdictions there is a basic division between criminal proceedings, which are brought in the name of the Queen for the punishment of wrongdoers, and civil proceedings, which are brought to settle disputes between one citizen and another, or disputes between the citizen and the State.

Where children are concerned, a major difference between civil and criminal proceedings is the presence or absence of the 'welfare principle'. For most civil proceedings in which the rights of children are dealt with, or questions about the future of a child are decided, it is nowadays accepted that the welfare of the child must be the court's 'paramount consideration'. This is laid down by statute, notably by s. 1 of the Children Act 1989 in England, and by s. 3(1) of the Law Reform (Parent and Child) (Scotland) Act 1986 in Scotland. In criminal proceedings, whether against a child, or against an adult for an offence committed against a child, the welfare of the child is not the paramount consideration. In criminal proceedings against juveniles, the juvenile's welfare is only one factor which the court is obliged to weigh up together with others, such as the need to protect society. For criminal proceedings against adults in which children are incidentally involved, however, the court is under no obligation to consider the welfare of the child at all; though the court will sometimes take account of it, as when a Scottish court refused to order a criminal case to be retried to avoid a child witness having to give evidence a second time (*Kelly* v *Docherty* 1991 SLT 419). In a civil case, an English judge recently expressed the view that when making the decision whether or not to prosecute an alleged child abuser, 'the welfare of the children should be to the fore' (*Re S* (*Child Abuse Cases: Management*) [1992] 1 FCR 31, 32).

CRIMINAL PROCEEDINGS IN ENGLAND

In England, as in Scotland, the job of investigating criminal offences belongs to the police. Until recently, the police in England also had the job of conducting the prosecution. In 1986 this was changed, and the position is now that the police decide whether or not to start a prosecution, but once begun it is taken over and run (or dropped) by the Crown Prosecution Service, an independent body headed by the Director of Public Prosecutions, an official who is responsible to the Attorney-General. The idea of a Crown Prosecution Service was copied from Scotland, where prosecutions have long been carried out by independent officials called procurators fiscal; but the copy is a loose one, and the crown prosecutor is in a generally weaker position than his Scottish equivalent. In Scotland it is the procurator fiscal who makes the initial decision as to whether a prosecution shall be brought.

Although the vast majority of prosecutions are begun by the police and taken over by the Crown Prosecution Service, a striking feature of the English criminal justice system is that any private citizen has the right to start a prosecution. Thus a private citizen will sometimes launch a prosecution in a case where either the police or the Crown Prosecution Service refuse to act. This occasionally happens in cases involving children. In 1986 a mother brought a much-publicised private prosecution against a doctor whom she accused of raping her little girl aged eight. (2)

In England there are two different courts with jurisdiction in criminal cases, each with a different form of procedure. *Summary trial* takes place in the magistrates' courts, and *trial on indictment* is the form of trial in the Crown Court.

Summary trial in a magistrates' court takes place before a bench of magistrates, alias justices of the peace. In London and some other big cities the bench may be a single legally qualified professional, called a *stipendiary magistrate* (or 'stipe'), but it will usually consist of two or three lay justices (alias lay magistrates)—respectable citizens, who usually have no legal qualifications, but who have been selected with some care and given a certain amount of basic training. In legal matters they will be guided—and sometimes more than guided—by a professional clerk. The rules of procedure and evidence which the magistrates follow are in outline the same as those which apply in trials on indictment, but the atmosphere is less formal. There is no jury, the magistrates deciding all disputed matters, whether of fact or law. The courtroom contains fewer persons, robes are not worn, and instead of barristers appearing, the prosecution is usually represented by a member of the Crown Prosecution Service, and the defence by a solicitor. The powers of the court to punish are limited. In general, magistrates' courts may not impose more than six months' imprisonment, or a fine of more than £5,000 (although they can sometimes circumvent these limits by sending a defendant up to the Crown Court to be sentenced there). Magistrates' courts are organised and administered locally, with the disadvantage that the quality of justice tends to vary rather sharply from one area to another. On the other hand summary trial takes little time, and is usually available more quickly than trial on indictment in the Crown Court.

Trial on indictment takes place in the Crown Court before a professional judge. The kind of judge who presides is determined by the seriousness of the case. The heaviest cases are tried by High Court judges; run-of-the-mill cases are tried by circuit judges; and a large slice of the less serious work is handled by recorders and assistant recorders—part-time judges who spend the rest of their working life as barristers or solicitors. There is no formal specialisation among judges in criminal work, but some judges are known to be experts in particular matters, and in practice that type of case tends to be wafted in their direction. (In December 1989 the Pigot Committee formally proposed that offences against children should be tried by judges with experience of child abuse cases.)

Where the defendant pleads guilty the judge deals with the case alone. Where the defendant fights the case, the issue of guilt or innocence is decided by a jury of 12 citizens randomly selected, who must normally reach their decision by a majority of at least 10 to 2. (If they fail to reach the necessary majority, whether for acquittal or conviction, no verdict can be returned. This state of affairs is called a 'hung jury'—and it usually means that the case is retried. If the case involves sexual offences against young children, the consequence will be that they have to give their sordid evidence all over again: (for example, see *Henri* [1990] Crim LR 51). The sentence, if the jury convict, is decided by the judge.

At a trial on indictment, everything is much more formal than at summary trial. Prosecution and defence are almost always represented by barristers, who appear in wigs and gowns, and the judge wears a wig and a judicial robe. The courtroom is more crowded—especially in a contested case, where there is a jury. The pace of the proceedings is usually much slower than summary trial, and there is usually a greater delay before the case can be brought to trial. For these reasons, trial on indictment is usually thought to be much less suited to the needs of children, whether as witnesses or defendants—even if the quality of justice may be higher than at summary trial. (On the other hand, it is also said that judges are better at controlling advocates than magistrates are, and more likely to stop them bullying fragile witnesses.)

Part of the reason why a trial on indictment takes longer to arrange than a summary trial is that it must be preceded by *committal proceedings* in the magistrates' court. At committal proceedings magistrates examine the prosecution evidence in order to make sure that the elements of an offence triable on indictment are disclosed. Since 1967 the magistrates have usually done this by looking at the written statements the prosecution witnesses have given to the police, but the defence in principle retained the right to insist on the prosecution bringing their main witnesses to court to give their evidence orally. This procedure is officially known as 'old-style committal'—but the term is often corrupted to 'all-star committal', for obvious reasons. As those who give oral evidence at committal proceedings do so in the presence of the defendant, and are subject to adversarial cross-examination, this usually enabled the defendant in a child abuse case to inflict on a child witness a preliminary helping of both, and it was suspected that some defendants exploited this possibility simply to put pressure on the prosecution to drop the case in order to spare the child a double ordeal. Adopting a suggestion of the Pigot Committee, the Criminal Justice Act 1991 resolves this problem in two ways. First, where in a child abuse case there is an old-style committal, and a key witness is a child, the defence no longer have the right to make the prosecution call the child to give live evidence. Secondly, s. 53 gives the DPP the power, modelled on that which already exists in a serious fraud case, to issue a 'notice of transfer' which bypasses the committal stage altogether.

Whether a case is tried summarily or on indictment depends in part on the age of the defendant. Almost all offences by children and young persons (which by the Criminal Justice Act 1991 now means anyone under 18) must be tried summarily. The trial takes place in the youth court. This is a department of the magistrates' court, but it uses a panel of specially selected magistrates, and operates under a separate code of procedural rules, one of which is that the court sits in private. For people under 18, trial on indictment is possible for only the most serious offences, and also for cases, serious or otherwise, where they are tried jointly with an adult. However, the fact that the victim, rather than the defendant, is a juvenile, does not mean that the offence must be tried summarily in the juvenile court—as is the case in Germany, for example. In England, an adult defendant must always be tried in the ordinary criminal courts, irrespective of the age of the victim.

As a general rule there is no time-limit within which the prosecution must be started: in 1991, a man was jailed for raping his daughter in 1957 (*The Independent*, 30 November 1991). For summary offences there is a general limitation period of six months, and there are time-limits for certain indictable offences—notably unlawful intercourse with a girl under 16, which must be prosecuted within 12 months of the commission of the offence. Where there is no time-limit as such, the court has power to suppress a prosecution for a very stale offence as part of its general power to suppress anything which amounts to 'an abuse of process'.

In the case of an adult offender the mode of trial depends in part on the definition of the offence. A range of minor offences are classed as *summary offences*, and can only be tried summarily; and a number of serious crimes are *purely indictable offences* which must always be tried on indictment in the Crown Court. Examples of purely summary offences which may be committed in relation to children are common assault, giving alcohol to children under five, and selling tobacco to children under the age of 16; at the other end of the scale, purely indictable offences include homicide, rape, buggery, incest, and sexual intercourse with girls under the age of 13. In addition there is a third and very important category, consisting of offences that are in principle indictable, but which are capable of summary trial. These are known as *either-way offences*, and this class includes a large number of the moderately serious offences likely to have been committed against child victims of crime: indecent assault, indecency with children, assault occasioning actual bodily harm, malicious wounding, and child cruelty and neglect contrary to s. 1 of the Children and Young Persons Act 1933. With either-way offences, the magistrates decide the mode of trial at what are called *mode of trial proceedings*. Their decision in favour of trial on indictment is final, but if they propose a summary trial the defendant has the right to override their decision and insist on being tried with full formality in the Crown Court. Thus the prosecutor can sometimes decide the mode of trial by prosecuting for an offence which is triable only in one way or the other, but if he chooses an either-way offence—as often he must—the decision on mode of trial is out of his hands. In practice, any offence against a child that is more than trivial either must be tried on indictment, or may be at the defendant's option. This puts the English child abuser in a much better position to make life awkward for the prosecution than his counterpart in Scotland, where the procurator fiscal has the power to send most cases for summary trial.

An important feature of trials in England (and in Scotland) is that radically different procedures are followed, according to whether the defendant pleads guilty or not guilty. On a plea of not guilty, the case against the defendant must be proved by producing witnesses to give oral evidence. On a plea of guilty, however, no evidence is usually called at all. (This is very different from the position in many foreign legal systems, where the courts often refuse to punish merely on the strength of an admission by the accused, even one that he makes to the court.) Thus guilty pleas save time and money for the State, and for witnesses they also save the unpleasantness of having to give evidence in court. For these reasons they are officially encouraged in various ways—in particular, by the practice of giving lighter sentences to defendants who plead guilty.

Another significant feature, which the Scottish system also shares, is the lowly status of the victim of the offence. In principle the victim is nothing more than a potential witness for the prosecution. Unlike his counterpart in some countries, the English victim has no legal right to be represented at the trial, to be consulted about what charges are brought or dropped, or even to be told when the trial is taking place, or what its outcome was. In recent years, the criminal courts have been given the power to order a convicted defendant to pay compensation to the victim: but no one has thought to give the victim the right to ask the court to exercise it in his case. The publication in 1990 by the Home Office of a document optimistically called the 'Victim's Charter' has done nothing to alter the victim's legal position.

Other prominent features of the English criminal justice system are the adversarial nature of the trial, and a distinctly technical set of rules of evidence. Much of the rest of this book is devoted to examining these matters.

The practitioner's books are *Archbold's Criminal Pleading, Evidence and Practice* and *Blackstone's Criminal Practice*. The standard students' textbook is C. J. Emmins's *A Practical Approach to Criminal Procedure*. An overview for beginners is contained in *Jackson's Machinery of Justice*. The youth courts are described in Morris and Giller, *Understanding Juvenile Justice* (1987).

CRIMINAL PROCEEDINGS IN SCOTLAND

When viewed from Paris or New York the most obvious thing about the Scottish criminal justice system is its similarity to the system in England. When viewed from London, however, a number of differences seem very striking.

One of these is the position of the procurator fiscal. In outline the fiscal looks rather like the crown prosecutor. The fiscal service is organised in much the same centralised way as the Crown Prosecution Service, under an official called the Crown Agent, who is responsible to the Lord Advocate, and the fiscals perform a roughly similar task. But the status of the procurator fiscal is considerably higher than that of the crown prosecutor in England. No doubt this is partly because the office is centuries older, but the powers of the fiscal are considerably greater too. It is the fiscal who decides whether to institute criminal proceedings, not the police. The fiscal deals directly with the prosecution witnesses—unlike the crown prosecutor, who leaves such matters to the police. The fiscal has a limited power to summon the accused for questioning in the presence of a sheriff. And it is the fiscal, or an assistant called the procurator fiscal depute, who appears in person to prosecute at most jury trials—unlike the crown prosecutor, who must leave this to members of the Bar. Furthermore, as we explain below, he virtually decides the mode of trial. Another important difference concerns private prosecutions. Although these are possible in Scotland, they are much more strictly controlled, and in practice most uncommon.

In Scotland, as in England, there are two different modes of trial—*summary procedure*, and *solemn procedure*; but in Scotland there are three courts for trying criminal cases, not two.

At the bottom of the jurisdictional ladder is the *district court*. Like the magistrates' court in England it is staffed by magistrates, some of whom are stipendiaries, but most of whom are lay justices of the peace. Like its counterpart in England it conducts summary trials only. But it is much more limited in power and prestige. Normally the maximum penalty that a district court may impose is imprisonment for 60 days, and in practice it spends its time dealing with the easiest and most unimportant matters, like offences of drunkenness, minor breaches of the peace, and the more trivial traffic offences. However, it can punish more heavily, and sometimes takes more serious cases, when it is a stipendiary magistrate who is on the bench. It has no civil jurisdiction.

The middle, and in many ways the most important rung of the ladder is the sheriff court. In some ways this is similar to the Crown Court in England, but its powers are considerably wider: in particular, because it has an important civil jurisdiction. It is staffed by *sheriffs*, who are professional full-time judges with a status similar to that of an English circuit judge; there are also temporary sheriffs, who are similar to recorders and assistant recorders. It is organised regionally, each area headed by a sheriff principal, a senior sheriff with administrative responsibilities, and the power to hear appeals in civil cases. On the criminal side, the sheriff court handles the great majority of trials, both summary and solemn. In summary trials the sheriff deals with the case on his own, deciding questions of both fact and law. In trials under solemn procedure he sits with a jury. In either situation the advocates will usually be a procurator fiscal for the Crown, and a solicitor for the defence. In general, the sentencing power of the sheriff court is limited to six months' imprisonment in summary trials, and three years following a trial under solemn procedure. However, higher sentences can be imposed for some offences, and in solemn procedure the sheriff can remit the case for sentence to a High Court judge—whose sentencing powers are not limited.

The superior criminal court in Scotland is the High Court of Justiciary—usually known as the High Court. Its judges are the senior judges of the Scottish legal system, who also staff the Court of Session in Edinburgh, which is the superior civil court. As High Court judges they go on circuit to try heavy criminal cases in much the same way as the English High Court judges formerly took the assizes (and as they still go out in rotation to help staff the main Crown Court centres). High Court trials are by solemn procedure only, and rights of audience were until recently restricted to members of the Scottish Bar; the one who appears for the Crown being called the *advocate depute*. The High Court has exclusive jurisdiction over murder, treason and rape; over other matters its jurisdiction is shared with the sheriff court—but unlike the sheriff court, there are no general limits on the punishment it may impose.

In many respects, Scottish criminal procedure is similar to criminal procedure in England. Both systems share similar rules about guilty and not guilty pleas, both have adversarial systems, and both have a similar set of rather technical rules of criminal evidence. In both, the victim lacks any official standing; in 1989 a Scottish High Court judge tried to consult a rape victim as to her views on sentencing, and was roundly rebuked for his pains (*H. M. Advocate* v *McKenzie* 1990 SLT 28). In Scotland, as in England, some offences must be prosecuted within a time-limit of commission, and others can be prosecuted without limit of time; though the basis for deciding whether the time-limit applies to a particular offence is slightly different.

The two forms of trial in Scotland are roughly equivalent to the two forms in England. As far as the trial itself is concerned, the main difference between solemn and summary procedure is that in solemn procedure the case, if defended, is tried by a jury. The Scottish jury consists of 15, not 12 as in England, and unlike the English jury it decides by a simple majority. English lawyers usually regard this as very harsh. However, it is probably not much easier to convince eight persons of the defendant's guilt than 10, and the Scottish system is actually kinder to the defendant in that there is no such thing as a 'hung jury': if eight jurors will not vote to convict, the defendant is acquitted and cannot be retried (Maher 1983). A well-known feature of the Scottish system is that the jury may acquit by means of two different verdicts, being able to find 'not proven' as an alternative to 'not guilty'. This feature of the system looks strange to English eyes, and is criticised by some Scotsmen; those who defend it usually do so by relating it to the requirement for a verdict of guilty in Scotland to be reached on corroborated evidence (see chapter 8). Summary trial is broadly similar to summary trial in England, the main difference being that most summary trials are heard not by benches of lay magistrates, but before a professional judge.

A major difference between the two systems lies in the way in which the mode of trial is chosen. As in England, some offences can be tried by solemn procedure only, and others must always go for summary trial. But the class of 'either-way' offences is significantly bigger, and contains a number of offences which in England must always be tried on indictment: incest, for example. Furthermore, where the offence is triable either way, in Scotland the decision as to mode of trial is made by the procurator fiscal, whose word on the matter is final; there is no question, as in England, of the defendant being able to insist on jury trial. English libertarians may shudder at the thought that the Scottish prosecutor has the power to send almost any case for trial by judge alone in something that looks suspiciously like a 'Diplock court'; but where unsavoury offences against children are concerned this certainly has one big advantage, which is that it is usually possible, at least in principle, to arrange for the case to be tried in a court which can operate without too much intimidating formality. In England, the defendant accused of molesting children can almost always insist on being tried by a jury; in Scotland, the procurator fiscal can usually insist on his being tried by a judge sitting without one.

As was mentioned in chapter 1, there is a very big difference between the Scottish and English systems when it comes to dealing with juvenile offenders. In Scotland there is no separate system of youth courts, and if juveniles are tried for crimes they are tried in the same courts as adults—although when trying juveniles the courts operate under a slightly different set of procedural rules. However, as was mentioned in chapter 1, offences by juveniles do not always result in prosecutions in Scotland, and are very often dealt with civilly through the system of children's panels which is discussed below.

The standard Scottish practitioner's book in criminal procedure is Renton and Brown, *Criminal Procedure According to the Law of Scotland* (1984). More elementary books are A. V. Sheehan, *Criminal Procedure* (1990), and A. L. Stewart, *The Scottish Criminal Courts in Action* (1990).

CIVIL PROCEEDINGS IN ENGLAND

Almost all law governing civil proceedings to do with children is contained in the Children Act 1989, which came into force on 14 October 1991. This is a major piece of reforming legislation, which followed a series of official reports—the DHSS review of the child care law in 1985, the Government White Paper on the law on child care and family services in 1987, the Report of the Cleveland Inquiry in 1987, and the Law Commission's review of child law, guardianship and custody in 1988.

Before examining the rules in detail, two major aims of the Children Act 1989 should be noted. The first is to make the law simpler and more consistent. In the past, different procedures have been created piecemeal to deal with different situations, causing an unwieldy tangle of different remedies, some of which are available in one type of court but not in another. The Children Act 1989 introduced a regime under which the number of different procedures is reduced, the scope of each is widened, and there are fewer restrictive rules about which court can do what. A second major aim is to make all the available procedures subject to the same set of overriding principles. Section 1(1) of the 1989 Act provides that when a court determines any question with respect to the upbringing of a child, or the administration of a child's property, or the application of any income arising from it, the child's welfare shall be the court's paramount consideration. A third aim, which sits a little uneasily with the second, is to give greater rights to parents who are threatened by the State intervening in what it claims to be the interests of their children. In this respect, the Act attempts to answer a number of criticisms made of the law at the time of the Cleveland affair (see chapter 1).

In principle, the maltreatment of a child may result in any or all of four different types of civil proceedings.

Emergency protection

Procedures have long existed to protect a child in cases of emergency by removing him or her from a setting where he or she is in immediate and serious danger. Until recently the main piece of legal machinery was something called a 'place of safety order'. Emergency protection is now governed by Part V of the Children Act 1989, and instead of the place of safety order we have what is called an 'emergency protection order'. This order is available only where 'there is reasonable cause to believe that the child is likely to suffer significant harm' unless the order is made. If this condition is made out, an order can be made removing the child from home, for a period of no longer than eight days. The court has power to give directions about the child's contact with parents and others, and about medical or psychiatric examinations, during the period when the order is in force.

A criticism that was sometimes made about place of safety orders was that they were too easy to obtain. Any person could apply for one, and any single magistrate could validly grant it. In 1988 the Lord Chancellor's Department floated the idea of an 'office of child protection' on the model of the reporter in Scotland (see below) to scrutinise applications, but there was little support for this, and the idea was dropped. However, the Act does give the Lord Chancellor the power to designate particular courts as competent to make particular orders under the Act, and this could eventually be used to change the present situation, under which a place of safety order can be made by any single justice of the peace.

In the past, problems arose where social workers suspected that a child had been abused, and would have liked to have had the child medically or psychiatrically examined to see if their fears were correct, but the parents refused to allow this. Usually, the social workers would have had to obtain a place of safety order, take the child into care, or make the child a ward of court—but the evidence necessary for these legal steps to be taken might have been impossible to obtain without an examination. Because the Children Act 1989 tightened up the conditions for obtaining the emergency removal of a child from home, and also reduced access to wardship (see below), there was fear that this problem would recur more frequently in future. In the hope of meeting this difficulty, s. 43 of the Children Act 1989 created a new kind of measure called the 'child assessment order', under which those who have care of the child can be required to allow him or her to be examined or assessed.

When deciding whether or not to grant an emergency protection order, magistrates are not bound by the strict rules of evidence. Section 45(7) of the Children Act 1989 entitles the court to act on any evidence which it considers to be relevant.

As a supplement to the place of safety order, the police had a statutory power to remove a child to a place of safety in an emergency. Under s. 46 of the Children Act 1989 this power is retained: but the period for which a child may be detained under this procedure is reduced from eight days to 72 hours.

Care proceedings: public law

Care proceedings are civil proceedings brought by the public authorities in order to remove a child from the custody of his parents and to place him in the care of the local authority—or, as an alternative, to place him under local authority supervision. By s. 31(2) of the Children Act 1989:

A court may only make a care order . . . if it is satisfied —

(a)   that the child concerned is suffering, or is likely to suffer, significant harm; and
  (b)   that the harm, or likelihood of harm, is attributable to
    (i)   the care given to the child, or likely to be given to him if the order were not made, not being what it would be reasonable to expect a parent to give him; or
    (ii)   the child's being beyond parental control.

Since they were introduced in 1984, an increasingly important part in care proceedings has been played by guardians *ad litem*. These are independent persons, usually with a background in social work, whom the court appoints to safeguard the interests of the child. They investigate the case and make a report to the court, which in practice the court usually treats as an important source of information. The guardian *ad litem* was introduced to look after the interests of the child in cases where there was a conflict of interest in the proceedings between the child and his parents; but s. 41 of the Children Act 1989 requires the court to appoint one in all cases, unless it is satisfied that it is not necessary to do so to safeguard the interests of the child. In addition to the power to appoint a guardian *ad litem*, a court dealing with care proceedings has wide powers to order a probation officer, or a local authority social worker, to investigate and report. Sections 7 and 41 of the Children Act 1989 allow the courts to treat statements in these official reports as evidence, whether or not they would be admissible under the rules of evidence that normally apply. (Hearsay evidence is further discussed in chapter 6.)

Disputes between care-givers: private law

Where parents separate or divorce, disputes often arise as to whom the child should live with, who will have access to him or her, and other matters relating to the child's upbringing. At one time, the rules which were applicable varied according to how the dispute arose and in which court it was litigated.

Part II of the Children Act 1989 effects a drastic and much-needed simplification. A distinct set of rules is retained for adoption, but apart from this a standard procedure is created for dealing with such questions irrespective of the context or court in which the dispute arose. What is more, the Act has changed the concepts with which the courts must work. Formerly there existed a concept of 'custody', which was a composite collection of rights over a child, which the court awarded to one parent or the other as a bunch, and 'access', which was the right to see the child from time to time. In the 1989 Act these terms are abandoned. There is now a concept of 'parental responsibility', which s. 3(1) defines as 'all the rights, duties, powers, responsibilities and authority which by law a parent of a child has in relation to the child and his property'. This every parent has, and will usually retain, whatever the outcome of the dispute. But the operation of 'parental responsibility' may be limited by the court making any of the orders contained in s. 8: 'contact orders' (determining who shall and shall not have contact with the child), 'prohibited steps orders' (prohibiting certain things being done without the consent of the court), 'residence orders' (determining with whom the child shall live), and 'specific issue orders' (giving directions about any other specific question arising in connection with parental responsibility).

In private law proceedings the court has, as yet, no power to appoint a guardian *ad litem* for the child. However, the court has various powers to obtain reports from social workers, and from the court welfare officer (who is a probation officer allocated to the courts to handle these requests). These various powers are now conveniently brought together in s. 7 of the Children Act 1989, which also provides, for the avoidance of doubt, that these reports shall count as evidence for any relevant matters contained in them, irrespective of the normal rules of evidence. The courts treat these reports as a major source of information. In particular, they usually rely on the report for information about what the child has to say on the matter. Whilst the courts may hear evidence from the child in person—and, except in the magistrates' court, may even interview the child in private—they rarely do this, and prefer instead to leave this to the social worker or court welfare officer.

A large amount of information on these matters is contained in Andrew Bainham's *Children—the Modern Law* (1993).

Wardship

Wardship is an ancient institution, which began as a remedy concerned with the property of rich orphans, and changed its function over the years until it became a protective measure for children generally.

Any person may apply to the High Court to have a child made a ward of court, and where the child is made a ward custody of the child then vests in the High Court, with the consequence that a High Court judge must then supervise and authorise every major step that is taken in the child's life. Wardship jurisdiction is open-ended: there are (or were until recently) no restrictions on the types of case where a child may be made a ward, and few if any limits on the judge's powers when a child has been made one.

Before the Children Act 1989, when the law governing care proceedings was inadequate in many ways, local authorities widely resorted to wardship as an alternative to care proceedings. It was also used, to some extent, as a means of redress against local authorities who were not felt to be adequately carrying out their duties towards children in their care, and as an unofficial method of appeal in cases where, from care proceedings, there was no regular right of appeal. The widespread use of wardship for these purposes did not please the government, because wardship (like all High Court business) is expensive, and was thought to be consuming too large a slice both of High Court time and of the legal aid budget. Thus when the Children Act 1989 removed many of the existing deficiencies in care proceedings, the government at the same time engineered the passage of s. 100 of the Act, which greatly limits the use of wardship by local authorities, and in respect of children who have been taken into care. The government justified this by saying that care proceedings had been reformed, so removing the need to use wardship, and by pointing to the new statutory complaints procedure in s. 24 of the Act, which creates an extra-judicial way in which the decisions taken by local authorities about children in care can be challenged. At the same time, an extensive training programme was started for judges and magistrates who will handle the remodelled care proceedings, and provision was made for care proceedings that raised difficult issues to be transferred from the lower civil courts to the High Court. As a result, 'The conclusion seems irresistible that [wardship] will suffer a major decline' (Bainham 1990). We have yet to see what the practical consequences of this will be.

Wardship is a legal institution which has no equivalent in Scotland, and seems to be one of the few aspects of the English law relating to children which Scots are inclined to envy. 'The lack of such a procedure is perhaps one of the more serious defects in contemporary Scottish family law' (Thomson 1987). So it is ironical that the reforming Children Act 1989 should have placed major restrictions upon its availability and use.

In wardship the role played by the guardian *ad litem* in care proceedings is usually filled by a civil servant called the Official Solicitor, or in practice, the officers of his department. The Official Solicitor 'commands a team of extremely conscientious and experienced workers who investigate the circumstances and test the views of the relevant adults as well as the children themselves. He has access to the foremost forensic experts, especially child psychiatrists and paediatricians. He regularly instructs members of the Bar with specialist experience who he knows can be relied upon to put the interests of the child before the court dispassionately and without the taint of adversarial joinder' (Thorpe 1990). His involvement was always thought to be one of the advantages that wardship had to offer. So when wardship was made less readily available in public law cases, a Practice Direction ([1991] 2 FLR 471) was issued making his services generally available in care proceedings which are transferred up to the High Court. (For a comment, see Masson 1992.)

The courts with jurisdiction in civil cases involving children
In principle there are first-instance civil courts in England at two levels: the High Court with unlimited jurisdiction, and county courts, with limited jurisdiction, for smaller civil matters. Where child-care matters are concerned, however, the picture is complicated by the fact that a range of civil matters affecting children are handled by the magistrates' courts, although these are

primarily courts for criminal cases. The origin of this rather surprising state of affairs is historical. The office of justice of the peace (or magistrate) dates from before the county courts were created, and in those days the justices of the peace were seen as a useful dumping ground for civil law matters too trivial for the High Court. A sizeable part of this civil jurisdiction remains. Thus at present it is the magistrates who make emergency protection orders, and it is also the magistrates who handle care proceedings. As a result of a series of historical accidents, the magistrates' courts also have concurrent jurisdiction with the regular civil courts over certain private law disputes concerning children arising from separation rather than divorce. Most of this work, like juvenile justice, is handled by a special panel of magistrates. This was known as the 'domestic court', and is renamed 'the family proceedings court' by the Children Act 1989.

The fact that three sets of courts are involved can have some serious drawbacks. One is that the same child abuse case can easily result not only in the same matters being ventilated in both criminal and civil courts, but parallel proceedings in several different civil courts as well—with needless confusion, delay and expense. Another problem is inadequate expertise: matters concerning the care and custody of children are distributed in little bits among a range of courts, some of which are mainly concerned with other matters, instead of being concentrated in one court which is able to acquire specialist skills through experience in dealing with them. Until recently, the range of courts involved in family cases also involved complications over the rules of evidence, because, as we explain in the next chapter, one set of rules of evidence applied in the magistrates' courts, another set applied in the county court, and a third set in the High Court wardship jurisdiction.

In recent years this state of affairs has led to increasing pressure in England for the various jurisdictions to be rearranged to form a single, unified family court, as is found in a number of other countries. The government—or at any rate, the Lord Chancellor—now seem to accept this idea in principle: but they have taken the view that before deciding what sort of shape (if any) a family court should take, a preliminary step must be to enact a single set of uniform rules, and make them applicable in all the existing courts which at present exercise jurisdiction in family matters (Mackay 1988). The Children Act 1989 has gone a long way towards achieving this, and it now remains to be seen whether a family court will be the next big move. Meanwhile, the Children Act gives the Lord Chancellor power to redistribute the various types of child care business among the existing civil courts. This has already been used to achieve some useful rationalization, and the restriction of certain types of work to specialist judges and courts.

CIVIL PROCEEDINGS CONCERNING CHILDREN IN SCOTLAND

In part, the Scottish system is very different from the system in force south of the Border. The powers of the State to intervene where children are in need of care and protection were radically redesigned by the Social Work (Scotland)

Act 1968, which enacted the Kilbrandon Report in 1964. This introduced a new official and a new special tribunal, neither of which have an equivalent in England. There is a body called a *children's panel*, made up of specially selected independent lay persons, neither magistrates nor social workers, who have the task of deciding what measures of compulsory care shall be provided for the children who are referred to them. The members sit in teams of three to hold *children's hearings*, at which decisions on these matters are made. These hearings are informal, and the purpose of the hearing is to secure the welfare of the child, not to prove a disputed case; if the facts of the matter are in dispute, they are referred to the sheriff court for determination. The new official is the *reporter to the children's panel*. He or she is rather like a special kind of procurator fiscal whose job is to investigate cases brought to his or her attention, and to decide which ones shall be referred to the children's panel. Thus the reporter plays a crucially impotant role in the system of children's panels and, in addition, oversees and controls the machinery for emergency protection.

Emergency protection
As in England, there is a procedure for removing a child from a dangerous situation in an emergency. By s. 37(2) of the Social Work (Scotland) Act 1968, a police constable may remove a child to a place of safety if he believes that the child has been the victim of one of a number of specified criminal offences; and on similar grounds any other person may remove a child to a place of safety if he has been authorised to do so by a court or by a justice of the peace. However, when this is done the reporter must be informed at once, and the reporter can send the child back home and order no further action. If the reporter decides that the child must remain in a place of safety, a children's hearing—which the parents have the right to attend—must be convened as soon as possible, and within seven days at the latest. At this hearing the panel members decide whether the child must stay away from home. This procedure protects the child, whilst also protecting the parents from having their children taken away from them for a lengthy period without the chance of a hearing—an undesirable feature of the English place of safety order before the Children Act 1989.

Proceedings to secure compulsory care or supervision
As previously mentioned, children in Scotland may be placed in care, or put under the supervision of the local authority, by a decision at a children's hearing. The children's panel deals with cases which are referred to it by the reporter, and the reporter may only refer the case in one of the 11 situations specified as 'grounds of referral' in s. 32(2) of the Social Work (Scotland) Act 1968. The children's hearing may only proceed where the child and his or her parents accept the grounds of referral. If the grounds of referral are disputed the case is passed over to the sheriff court, where a sheriff resolves the issue by hearing the evidence. If the sheriff finds the grounds of referral are made out, he refers the case back to the children's hearing, which carries on as if the grounds had been accepted; if the sheriff finds they are not, the children's

hearing has no further jurisdiction. This division of functions was made in order to enable the tribunal to act as a welfare agency, free of the tension and formality which inevitably arise when someone trying a case has to make a finding that one of the parties before it has not been telling the truth. Although the system normally seems to work quite well, it seems to have broken down badly at this point in the Orkney case, when the sheriff held that the grounds of referral were not made out without first hearing the reporter's evidence—for which the sheriff was later castigated on appeal (*Sloan* v *Booth* 1991 SLT 530). In addition to deciding disputed grounds of referral, the sheriff also hears appeals by the parent or the child against the final decision of the children's hearing.

One possible 'ground of referral' is that the child has committed a criminal offence. In Scotland, a large proportion of juvenile crime about which official action is taken comes before a children's hearing under this provision, with a view to the child receiving compulsory care or supervision rather than punishment. If the child or his parents say that the child is innocent of the offence, the issue of guilt or innocence is decided by the sheriff in the same way as any other disputed ground of referral: only in this case, s. 42(6) of the Social Work (Scotland) Act 1968 requires the ground to be proved according to the more stringent rules of criminal evidence. It is still possible for a child to be prosecuted for an offence, but by s. 31 of the Social Work (Scotland) Act 1968 this can only be done where the Lord Advocate grants permission. Where this is done, the prosecution takes place in the ordinary criminal courts: as previously mentioned, there is no separate system of juvenile courts in Scotland.

In a case where there appears to be a conflict of interest between the child and the parents, the children's hearing or the sheriff has power to appoint a *safeguarder*, who does the same job as the guardian *ad litem* in care proceedings in England. However, the Scottish safeguarder, unlike the English guardian *ad litem*, has to operate on a rather low flat-rate fee, which obviously curtails the amount of work he or she is usually able to do in any given case.

The definitive account of the law and practice in these matters is Sheriff Brian Kearney's *Children's Hearings and the Sheriff Court*. A useful summary is contained in the final chapter of J. M. Thomson's *Family Law in Scotland*. Studies from a research angle have been published by Martin, Fox and Murray (1981) and by Martin and Murray (1982).

Disputes between care-givers: private law
In relation to these disputes, the Scottish system is broadly similar to the system in England. In this area, Scots law still uses the concepts of 'custody' and 'access', which as we have seen have been abolished in England. Apart from differences of terminology, the main difference is that in Scotland the court structure is simpler, because the magistrates have no civil jurisdiction.

In Scotland, most custody disputes are dealt with in the sheriff court, which is the main court for civil as well as for criminal cases. On the civil side, it occupies roughly the same place as the county court in England, only its jurisdiction is considerably wider. However, the Court of Session, which sits in Edinburgh and is the superior civil court in Scotland, has concurrent jurisdiction, so disputes about custody and access may also be handled there.

Disputes about parental rights most commonly arise in the wake of a divorce. By s. 9(1) of the Conjugal Rights (Scotland) Amendment Act 1861 a court which is dealing with divorce, judicial separation or nullity of marriage has the widest powers to resolve issues about custody of children, and access to them. The court has jurisdiction over disputes that arise outside the context of divorce by s. 3(1) of the Law Reform (Parent and Child) (Scotland) Act 1986, which gives the court equally comprehensive powers. This section provides that 'Any person claiming interest may make an application to the court for an order relating to parental rights, and the court may make such order relating to parental rights as it thinks fit'. Section 3(2) of this Act enacts the 'welfare principle', now also given pride of place in England in the Children Act 1989: in any proceedings relating to parental rights, the court is bound to treat the welfare of the child as the paramount consideration, and may not make any order relating to parental rights unless it is satisfied that to do so would be in the interests of the child.

There is a difference in practice between the Scottish and the English courts when it is a question of gathering information as the basis for deciding an issue of custody or access. In England, as we saw, judges make extensive use of the court welfare service in order to obtain background information about the case, and they usually let the welfare officer interview the child and report to the court in preference to trying to interview the child themselves. In Scotland there is no court welfare service. The judge has the general power to appoint a curator *ad litem* to safeguard the interests of the child, and if a Scottish judge wants the sort of information the welfare officer provides, he also has powers under several different statutes to commission either a local authority social services department, or any individual, to investigate for him. Social workers are sometimes used, and so are practising lawyers (Seale 1984); the practice seems to vary from court to court. Scottish judges, like English judges, sometimes get the information for themselves by interviewing the child in private, but this practice was criticised on appeal in 1985 (*McDonald* v *McDonald* 1985 SLT 244 (see page 98 below)). When they wish to hear what the child has to say about a disputed issue of fact, the Scots civil courts—unlike the English ones, which accept hearsay evidence—have no qualms at all about having the child brought to court to give evidence (see pages 156, 157 below).

Whilst many features of the Scottish system compare favourably with what goes on in England, the Scottish machinery for securing that the interests of children in custody disputes are properly investigated and presented to the court does not. In 1980 it was criticised by the Royal Commission on Legal Services in Scotland, but the changes therein proposed have never been enacted. In 1990 the Scottish Office published a Review of Child Care Law in Scotland, and in 1992 the Scottish Law Commission published a Report on parental responsibility and related matters: so there may be legislation before long.

Futher details are contained in J. M. Thomson's *Family Law in Scotland*.

DUTY TO REPORT CHILD ABUSE TO THE AUTHORITIES

Contrary to what most people seem to imagine, there is no general duty on the citizen of either part of Britain to report suspected crimes to the police. Specific duties have been created by statute from time to time—in respect of terrorist offences, for example. In a number of other countries, notably the USA, specific legal duties have been placed on various people to report their suspicions of child abuse to the authorities (Whitcomb 1990). From time to time, the question has been raised as to whether such a duty should be created in Britain, but the case for doing this has failed to convince those who are in a position to procure a change in the law. In England, the DHSS Review of Child Care Law examined the idea in 1985 and came out against it.

On the other hand, statutory duties are laid upon public authorities to investigate suspicions of child abuse that are brought to their attention. Section 47 of the Children Act 1989—building on a duty that already existed under the Children and Young Persons Act 1969—imposes on local authorities the duty to make enquiries wherever they have 'reasonable cause to suspect that a child who lives, or is found, in their area is suffering, or is likely to suffer, significant harm'. In Scotland, a statutory duty to investigate information suggesting that a child may be in need of compulsory measures of care and protection is laid upon the local authority by s. 37(1A) of the Social Work (Scotland) Act 1968—an addition to the original Act that was made in 1975.

When a local authority receives information suggesting that a child may have been abused, delicate questions sometimes arise over when and to whom they should pass on the information. In England, the courts have recognised that when passing on such information to others, or recording it in a child protection register (see chapter 1), the local authority's actions can be challenged in court by way of judicial review. The authorities are reviewed by Latham (1991).

NOTE

1. This chapter is only about England and Scotland. We do not deal separately with Northern Ireland, which also has a separate legal system. This is broadly the same as in England, as is most of the substantive law. Although statutes passed by Parliament for England do not usually have direct effect in Northern Ireland, they are generally copied for use there: by the Northern Ireland Parliament passing Acts in identical terms until 1972, more recently by the government making Orders under the Northern Ireland Act 1974. At the time of writing, Northern Ireland does not yet have an equivalent of the Children Act 1989, which means that there is at present a significant difference on the civil law relating to children in England and Northern Ireland. A difference more widely known is that in Northern Ireland there is no right to jury trial for a range of offences connected with terrorism ('Diplock courts').

For the benefit of foreign readers, we should also explain that the laws and the legal system in Wales are integrated with those of England: but that in the Welsh courts the Welsh language has official status together with English.

2.   The prosecution was unsuccessful, and the final result was a very heavy fine for the newspaper which had not only financed the proceedings, but had also published material about them so as to constitute contempt of court *Attorney-General* v *News Group Newspapers* [1989] QB 110.

CHAPTER THREE
The concept of evidence

'Do not expect to understand the law or rules of evidence! It is a whole legal minefield understood by very few' (Livesey 1988).

These despairing words from a solicitor in a book for social workers sum up what many lay people feel about the rules of evidence. Another lawyer felt the same. C. P. Harvey QC said:

> I suppose there never was a more slapdash, disjointed and inconsequent body of rules than that which we call the Law of Evidence. Founded apparently on the propositions that all jurymen are deaf to reason, that all witnesses are presumptively liars and that all documents are presumptively forgeries, it has been added to, subtracted from and tinkered with for two centuries until it has become less of a structure than a pile of builders' debris. (Harvey 1958, p. 79.)

These observations prompt two questions: (a) Why do we have rules of evidence—are they necessary? and (b) If we do, do they have to be incomprehensible to the intelligent lay person? To anticipate our conclusion, we think the answer to the first question is yes, and to the second one no.

In primitive legal systems there are laws, but no rules of evidence, because the concept of evidence is unknown. Disputed issues are resolved by an appeal to the supernatural. This appeal can take a number of different forms. In England a common method was to subject one of the parties to an ordeal. Another method, which was popular on both sides of the border, was to challenge one of the parties to gather a specified number of 'oath-helpers', who were prepared to risk their immortal souls by taking a formal oath that he was in the right. In place of the rules of evidence, there were rules of procedure to determine which of the parties had to undergo the test: although the judges officially believed these tests were bound to produce the just result, they were always careful to avoid a situation in which both parties were put to the test, because of the risk of a possibly embarrassing outcome. A very major step in the direction of rationality was taken when these superstitious methods were replaced by the court making an impartial examination of all the available evidence, weighing it up, and attempting to make a rational decision one way or the other.

Once any legal system reaches this stage, it is obvious that it needs some elementary rules to make sure that the court goes about its task in a fair, consistent and rational manner. Thus in every developed legal system, and not only in England and Scotland, we find a body of rules which bears on some or all of the following matters: (a) what matters must be proved by evidence; (b) who is to prove it (burden of proof); (c) what degree of proof is required (standard of proof); (d) how it must or may be proved—or in other words, what does and does not constitute evidence; and (e) how the evidence is to be assessed (the weight that is to be placed on different pieces of evidence) (Honoré 1981).

(A) WHAT MATTERS MUST BE PROVED BY EVIDENCE

The rules in this area are not complicated, nor is there much in them which would cause the intelligent layman any surprise. The basic rule is that all material facts must be established by evidence. If, for example, X is prosecuted under s. 1 of the Children and Young Persons Act 1933 for wilfully ill-treating a child aged under 16 of whom he has care so as to cause it unnecessary suffering, it must be proved by evidence (a) that X had custody, charge or care of the child, (b) the child is under 16, (c) that X ill-treated the child so as to cause it needless suffering, and (d) that X did so wilfully. There are no mystical requirements about the evidence having to be direct rather than circumstantial. In law, as in other areas of enquiry, any fact on which there is no direct evidence may be established by proof of other facts which point to its existence, as well as by direct evidence. Thus the fact that X ill-treated the child can be established not only by the child or a bystander witness saying they saw X hit the child, but by medical evidence of non-accidental injuries to the child which must have been inflicted whilst the child was in the care of X (*Farrer* v *Guild* 1991 SCCR 174). Nor, in the main, are there any mystificatory rules forbidding courts to draw the inferences which common sense suggests, or requiring them to draw inferences counter to it. By and large, if a reasonable person would draw a particular inference, the courts may draw it too.

The main exception to this is the rule in criminal cases that generally forbids the court to draw an adverse inference from an accused person's suspicious silence. Broadly speaking, the present position is that a criminal court is forbidden to infer that the accused did what he has been accused of doing from the fact that he refuses to answer police questions, or fails to explain suspicious circumstances where an innocent person would unquestionably have done so (see chapter 8).

This gives rise to some particular difficulties where the prosecution can prove that either D or E must have done it, and if we ignore suspicious silence, there is a 50 per cent chance that it was done by either D or E. The inferences the court may draw then cannot point to guilt in D or E on the balance of probabilities, let alone beyond reasonable doubt (see page 36 below), and if this is all the evidence that can be produced then logically the conviction of either is impossible. If the courts felt able to draw inferences of guilt from suspicious silence, then—as Professor Glanville Williams recently pointed out—it would sometimes be possible to convict in this sort of case if either of them failed to give an explanation where it would be reasonable to expect an explanation from the suspect if he had one to give (Williams 1989).

An acute form of this problem arises when parents are prosecuted for homicide of children. If D is accused of killing a child, the fact that the child died of serious non-accidental injuries suffered whilst in the care of D alone is obviously circumstantial evidence that points to D as the person responsible, upon which the court could properly convict D of homicide. But when a child dies at home from deliberate injuries it will often be the case that there were two parents, D and E, both of whom were supposedly looking after it at the time. If either of them could have done it, and the details of the injury make it equally likely that D did it without the help of E, or E did it without the help of D, then in principle the court cannot convict in the absence of other evidence (*Lane* (1985) 82 LGR 5; *Aston and Mason* (1992) 94 Cr App R 180); although the courts do sometimes manage to get around the difficulty by making maximum use of some slender piece of additional evidence (*Russell* (1987) 85 Cr App R 388). Even if the court could draw adverse inferences from suspicious silence this would not necessarily make it possible to convict a pair of suspiciously silent parents, because the court might well think the silence was as likely to be motivated by a desire to protect the other parent, who was guilty, as by the desire of the guilty parent to protect himself (Williams 1989). In 1987 a circuit judge and legal writer, Judge Fallon QC, proposed something even more radical than making it permissible to infer guilt from suspicious silence. If correctly reported in the newspapers, he suggested that the burden of proof should be reversed in this sort of case, so that both parents would be found guilty unless they proved they were not involved in the injury (*The Times*, 27 October 1987). The objection to this solution is that it would fly in the face of the presumption of innocence, which is an important principle of criminal justice. The problem under discussion has caused acute difficulties in the United States as well as Britain (*Michael* v *Alaska* (1988) 767 Pacific Reporter 2nd 193). In practice, it can sometimes be circumvented by prosecuting the parents with the statutory offence of cruelty to children, which is defined so as to include various forms of passive non-intervention or failure to help or protect a child for whom one is responsible, which both parents are likely to be guilty of, no matter which one inflicted the blows.

To return to the question of what matters must be proved by evidence. The rule that all material facts must be proved by evidence only applies to facts which are in dispute. Thus there is no need for evidence to support facts which the parties are prepared to admit. If this principle is easy to grasp, the rules about when one of the parties to a piece of litigation is taken to have admitted a fact are rather complicated, and differ as between England and Scotland, and also as between civil and criminal proceedings. In general the rules are quite rational and sensible. However, one aspect of them which many lay people find hard to swallow is that a party to litigation—usually the defendant in a criminal case—does not admit a fact by carefully failing to point out that his opponent has failed to prove it until after his opportunity to do so has gone by. For example, where the prosecution sought to identify the defendant as the criminal by means of his fingerprints, and forgot to bring formal proof that the set of fingerprints they were comparing with those of the criminal belonged to the defendant, it was open to the defendant to keep quiet about this at trial, and then successfully appeal on the ground that the prosecution had failed to prove a material fact (*Chappell* v *DPP* (1988) 89 Cr App R 82).

Nor does the rule that all material facts must be proved by evidence apply to certain facts which are so well known and obvious that it would be ridiculous to put the parties to the bother of having to prove them. In principle, where facts are obvious the courts are permitted to use their common sense, and where they are notorious they may rely on common knowledge. As an example of the first, a court may find that a child who looks much less than 18 is under 18 without the need for formal evidence of age (*Wallworth* v *Balmer* [1966] 1 WLR 16), and as an example of the second, the court does not need evidence before it can find that keeping a child without sufficient food, clothing or bedding is likely to cause it unnecessary suffering, or damage to its health (*Brenton* (1890) 111 Old Bailey Sessions Papers 309). The matter is a little more complicated than this, however, because over the years a sizeable body of case law has built up around the issue of what is obvious and notorious and what is not, some of which is less than wholly rational. Thus although the courts have been prepared to accept without evidence that boys have playful habits (*Clayton* v *Hardwicke Colliery Co. Ltd* (1915) 85 LJ KB 292), that cats are normally kept for domestic purposes (*Nye* v *Niblett* [1918] 1 KB 1) and that a fortnight is too short for a period for human gestation (*Luffe* (1807) 8 East 193), an English court once required evidence that 360 days was an impossibly long period for human gestation (*Preston-Jones* v *Preston-Jones* [1951] AC 391), and a Scottish court distinguished itself by requiring expert evidence before it would find that a woman of 81 was too old to conceive (*Rackstraw* v *Douglas* 1917 SC 284). Professionals, including professionals in child-care matters, are sometimes exasperated when the courts refuse to accept without evidence matters which seem very obvious to them: for example, that sexual abuse of children within the family is not extraordinarily rare. Conversely, judges are sometimes impatient when professionals from other disciplines fail to know the law; but judges have been able to fortify themselves against the problem by inventing a legal rule that everyone is presumed to know the law. (The question of expert knowledge is discussed in chapter 9.)

(B)   THE BURDEN OF PROOF

Under the umbrella phrase 'the burden of proof' are gathered the rules about two related but subtly different matters.

First, there are rules about which side must lead evidence on a particular issue in order to persuade the court to investigate it. Here, the basic rule is that the party who wishes an issue to be considered must put some evidence about it before the court; and if he fails to do so, he will not be heard to complain if the court fails to consider it. In a prosecution, for example, it is always up to the Crown to put before the court some evidence suggesting that the defendant committed the offence with which he is charged; and this usually means not only evidence suggesting that the defendant did the prohibited act, but also evidence suggesting that he did that act with any degree of fault which is an ingredient in the offence. On the other hand, it is up to the defence to lead evidence about general defences, like duress, self-defence, or insanity. The court will not give its mind to any of these defences without some evidence on the subject, and unless the prosecution are kind enough to volunteer such evidence the defence must call it. Where it is the job of one party to lead evidence about a matter in order to make it a live issue, lawyers usually say he bears the 'evidential burden' in relation to it.

Secondly, there are the rules that determine which side loses if there is a gap in the evidence on some vital point, or a conflict of evidence so severe that the court is unable to make up its mind who to believe. The side which loses is the one which bears the 'burden of proof', the other side being the one which gets the benefit of the doubt. In a civil case it is usually the plaintiff who bears the burden of proof in this sense, and in a criminal case it is nearly always the prosecution. In a criminal case the prosecution usually have the burden of proof on all matters, including those on which the defence had the 'evidential burden'. The accused gets the benefit of the doubt not only as to whether he did it and as to whether he meant to do it, but also as to whether the circumstances gave rise to some general defence, if he has made this an issue by calling evidence about it. There are some exceptional cases where the burden of proof is reversed and it is the prosecution rather than the defence which gets the benefit of the doubt (and it was another one of these that Judge Fallon was proposing, to deal with the problem of the two suspiciously silent parents of a murdered child). These exceptions form a complicated area of the law and fortunately this book is not the place to go into them.

By and large there is nothing in the rules about the burden of proof which the lay person is likely to find difficult or surprising.

(C)   THE STANDARD OF PROOF

The courts on both sides of the Border recognise two different standards of proof, one for criminal and one for civil cases. In a criminal case the defendant's guilt must be proved 'beyond reasonable doubt'—an idea which English judges often put to juries by telling them that they must convict only if they are 'satisfied so as to feel sure'. In civil cases the standard of proof is lower, and a civil case is usually proved if the court is satisfied 'on the balance of probabilities': in other words, if it is at least 51 per cent sure of the material facts.

It follows from the existence of these two different standards that on the same evidence a civil action may succeed in a case where a prosecution fails. In cases involving children this situation frequently arises. Civil proceedings are often taken to remove children from abusing parents in cases where a prosecution of the parent would almost certainly fail. And there have been a number of cases in England and in Scotland in which fathers or stepfathers have been prosecuted for abusing their children and acquitted, only to find that a civil court then takes the children away from them having reached a decision that the abuse did indeed occur: as in *Re G* [1988] FCR 440, [1988] 1 FLR 305, where both parents were acquitted of causing serious injuries to a little girl, and in wardship proceedings that followed the judge made a finding that the father was responsible. Conversely, it also follows that when someone has been convicted of an offence against a child in a criminal case, it will be rare for the judge in later civil proceedings to reach a decision that the offence did not take place. Although he is theoretically entitled to do so, he risks being overturned on appeal (*Re CB (A Minor) (Access)* [1992] 1 FCR 320).

Some people find this puzzling: but it is surely right that this dual standard of proof should exist. The object of criminal proceedings is to punish the offender, and as punishment is an evil it is right that society should not punish someone as an offender unless it is well and truly sure that he deserves it. Furthermore, if a guilty man escapes punishment, the harm this does is harm to society in general, which is of less concern than the immediate harm which is done to an individual by punishing him for something he did not do. The object of a civil case, on the other hand, is to resolve the dispute between A and B, and if the court reaches the wrong decision, one or other of two identifiable individuals is bound to suffer. By wrongly refusing to act, in other words, a civil court can do as great an injustice as by wrongly acting. This difference is particularly obvious where child abuse cases are concerned. If the criminal court wrongly fails to convict someone of harming a child, the civil courts can still remove the child from his clutches, and that victim is unlikely to suffer further harm, even if the culprit offends again; but a civil court which is asked to remove the child from the home of a parent who has allegedly abused him must balance the risk of unjustly depriving the parent of the child against the risk of leaving the child in a home where he may suffer more abuse if he stays.

Normally the standard of proof in civil cases is proof on the balance of probabilities: but the English courts have sometimes said that the matter is more complicated than this, and that a higher standard of proof may sometimes be required in certain types of civil proceedings (Cross 1990, p. 146 et seq.); and in Scotland similar views have also been expressed (Macphail 1991, sect. 760). In England, this notion formerly led to some confusion about the standard of proof in civil cases where the issue is whether or not a child has been abused, or is at the risk of it. On the one hand, there have been statements from some judges that it is higher than the balance of probabilities. In *R v Birmingham Juvenile Court, ex parte S* [1984] Fam 93 Sir John Arnold P suggested this was so in care proceedings for any matter which would justify the removal of a child into care, and in *Re G (Child Abuse: Standard of Proof)* [1987] 1 WLR 1461 Sheldon J suggested a higher degree of probability might be required to satisfy the court that a father has been guilty of some sexual misconduct with his daughter (but not for a finding that the child has been the victim of abuse by some unidentified person). On the other hand, other judges went to the opposite extreme and suggested they could reach a finding that a child has been sexually abused when they were satisfied according to a standard lower than the balance of probabilities—that is, when they thought that it was no more than 'a real possibility' (*Re F* [1988] 2 FLR 123). In *H v H* [1990] Fam 86, however, Croom-Johnson and Butler-Sloss LJJ condemned this last idea. There are, they said, two distinct matters: whether someone has done something to the child in the past, and whether there is a risk of harm to the child in the future. On the first question, they said that no judge should make a finding in a civil case unless he felt it was more probable than not that abuse had occurred (and, according to Butler-Sloss LJ, the converse applies: he ought always to make the finding if this degree of certainty is reached). But as to the second, the judge in deciding whether or not to continue a wardship, or to refuse someone access to a child, could properly base his decision on the possibility, rather than the probability, of future abuse. Here, it is a question of balancing the level of risk against the seriousness of the harm if it occurs. This approach was recently confirmed by the Court of Appeal in *Newham Borough Council* v *A-G* [1992] 2 FCR 119, where the court said that the judge was right to make a care order removing a two-year-old child from his mother, whose mental disturbance created a risk that she would kill or seriously injure him, even though there was a less than 50 per cent chance of her doing so. An equally slight risk of some lesser harm, on the other hand—like certain kinds of sexual abuse—might not justify removing an older child from a family where she was well settled (*Re H (Suspected Child Abuse: Interim Decisions)* [1991] FCR 736).

In child abuse cases in the civil courts, it is probably now safe to say that the standard of proof in respect of events that are said to have happened is the balance of probabilities, no more and no less. The matter is not wholly free from doubt, however, because in *Miles* v *Cain* (1989) *The Times*, 15 December 1989, Lord Donaldson MR, when dealing on appeal with a civil claim for damages brought by a woman alleging that the defendant had raped her, apparently resurrected the idea that sexual allegations made in civil proceedings must be proved to a level higher than the balance of probabilities. The criminal standard was also applied by a first instance judge who, in civil proceedings, had to decide if the defendants had murdered the plaintiff's daughter (*Halford* v *Brookes, The Independent,* 1 October 1991; and see [1991] 1 WLR 428).

(D)   HOW FACTS ARE TO BE PROVED: WHAT DOES AND DOES NOT AMOUNT IN LAW TO EVIDENCE

It is at this point that legal rules seriously part company with what the intelligent lay person considers to be common sense. When a lay person complains that the law of evidence is a nonsense it is usually this part of it that he or she has in mind.

In every other discipline where a reasoned conclusion has to be made on the basis of evidence, the only restriction that anyone recognises as to the evidence that may properly be used to support a conclusion is that it should be relevant. As far as the lawyer is concerned, however, evidence must satisfy not only the test of relevance, but a further one: (a) it must be relevant, and (b) it must be *legally admissible*.

As far as relevance is concerned, lawyers apply the same test as everyone else. According to the classic definition, which comes from J. F. Stephen's *Digest of the Law of Evidence* in 1876:

The word 'relevant' means that any two facts to which it is applied are so related to each other that according to the common course of events one either taken by itself or in connection with other facts proves or renders probable the past, present, or future existence or non-existence of the other.

To this one further point should be added. Relevance is a matter of degree, and the courts will sometimes exclude evidence which, though logically relevant, is relevant to such a small extent that it does not seem worth the trouble of hearing. They do this particularly in criminal cases where they think the question carries a risk of unfairly prejudicing the jury. In England, the criminal courts originally expressed this idea in terms of a *discretion to exclude evidence which is more prejudicial than probative*. Interestingly, in the first case where the idea was clearly articulated, the disputed evidence was an identification made by a child of five, and the defendant's reaction to it (*Christie* [1914] AC 545). In 1984, the discretion to exclude was put on a wider basis by s. 78 of the Police and Criminal Evidence Act, which enables the court to exclude any evidence the admission of which it thinks would make the trial unfair. In a recent case, the Court of Appeal raised the possibility of this discretion being used to exclude the evidence of children who, during an investigation, had been interviewed in such a leading way as possibly to contaminate their courtroom testimony (*H* [1992] Crim LR 516). In England, this discretionary power to exclude otherwise admissible evidence does not apply in civil proceedings (*Bradford City Metropolitan Council* v *K* [1990] Fam 140), and in Scotland it does not apply at all, even in the criminal courts.

Legal admissibility is partly a matter of relevance, because no evidence is legally admissible unless it is relevant. But admissibility is more than this, because no matter how relevant a piece of evidence may be, it may not be used in a court of law if it falls into one of a number of prohibited categories.

These excluded categories were originally invented by the judges, and the boundaries have fluctuated from time to time as judges have added to the list, and Parliament has passed Acts subtracting from it. Originally the rules were the same for both criminal and civil law, but in recent years there has been a tendency to abolish particular exclusions for the purpose of civil proceedings only. As a result of the Civil Evidence Act 1968 in England, and the Civil Evidence (Scotland) Act 1988 in Scotland, on both sides of the Border there are now two sets of rules, one for civil and one for criminal cases. In England the matter is more complicated still because, within the general scope of civil law, different rules have been made for different types of court. As far as children's evidence in civil cases is concerned there are now three sets of rules: (a) those applied in the High Court wardship jurisdiction, where there are no legal restrictions, and the only test of admissibility is relevance (see chapter 6), (b) those applied in civil cases heard in the ordinary civil courts, where the Civil Evidence Act 1968 is in force, and (c) those applied in civil cases heard in the magistrates' courts, where officially the rules are the rules of criminal evidence, with certain modifications. As all these courts are handling what are essentially the same issues, having three different sets of rules of evidence seems a wholly needless complication.

The most important categories of inadmissible evidence are the following.

The evidence of incompetent witnesses

Certain witnesses are disqualified from giving evidence. In various legal systems different people have been disqualified at different times, and often for reasons which now seem completely arbitrary. As Jeremy Bentham wryly said 165 years ago:

> On account of age, persons of tender years have been refused the right of giving evidence, being considered undeserving of confidence, and incapable of discernment; on account of their servile condition, slaves could not bear witness against free men, or domestics against their master; on account of propinquity, to allow a wife to depone against her husband, a child against its father, or one kinsman against another, was to violate a moral relation or a natural right; on account of sex, women were considered to be in perpetual childhood; on account of religion and worship, the enemies of the faith could not be heard against a believer, and those who refused a particular form of oath were worthy of no credit; on account of colour, a negro was held not to be a man, when he was to depose against a white; on account of personal dignity, a dispensation from rendering society a service was a privilege of honour; pecuniary interest in the cause, was a valid ground of exclusion, as if every interest, however small, must annihilate integrity; finally, a judicial condemnation, to which this forfeiture was arbitrarily attached, had the same effect; in a word, there is no pretext which has not been used, in some country or another, as a reason for excluding whole classes of witnesses. Combine all these pretexts, and there would no longer be any admissible judicial evidence. (Bentham 1825, b. 7, ch. 1.)

Since Bentham wrote, many of the exclusions then recognised in Scots and English law have been abolished. The most important class of legally incompetent witnesses that remains is little children. We discuss this in chapter 4.

Hearsay

To the lay person, hearsay implies rumour picked up at several removes from source, as when overheard in pubs and buses and from gossips in the street. To the lawyer it has a much stricter meaning, because the rule against hearsay renders inadmissible any evidence that an event took place which does not come directly from the mouth of someone who saw or heard it with his or her own eyes or ears. This means that a court will reject as 'hearsay' quite a lot of evidence which is not only relevant but which would be considered quite reliable enough to act on in other areas of life. If someone wishes to prove that a child has been assaulted or sexually abused, for example, it is not open to him to do so by calling a parent, doctor, or policeman to repeat to the court what the child has told them: the child must be produced as a witness to tell the court himself. In this situation the hearsay rule combines with the rule about the competency of witnesses to produce a very unfortunate result, because if the child is too young to be competent as a witness, the court cannot hear the child's account at all. For civil cases, this difficulty has been tackled in England by making several large breaches in the hearsay rule, and in Scotland by abolishing it altogether. In criminal cases the difficulty still largely remains. These issues are discussed in chapters 6 and 7.

Evidence of previous misconduct

In criminal cases, the prosecution are generally forbidden to prove that the defendant has a criminal record, or to put before the court any other evidence designed to show that he has a tendency to commit the offence charged. In many cases, the fact that the accused has a criminal record tells us little or nothing about whether he is likely to have committed the offence which the court is investigating, and it could be rejected on the ground that it is irrelevant. On the other hand, there are many situations in which the fact is highly relevant. If a child has been injured by one or other of its parents, each of whom blames the other, any paediatrician or social worker trying to decide who did it would think it highly significant if one of them has a couple of previous convictions for deliberately injuring other children in the family, and most intelligent lay people would agree. Yet in a criminal case this evidence, though highly relevant, would be legally inadmissible. (We discuss this in chapter 8.)

Evidence that was improperly obtained

In some situations the courts—particularly the criminal courts—will refuse to accept evidence because it has been obtained in an illegal or oppressive fashion. To take an extreme example, no court, whether in England or in Scotland, would nowadays receive as evidence a confession that had been obtained under torture. Quite often, as with confessions that have been improperly obtained, the manner of obtaining the evidence makes it inherently unreliable, and illegality aside the court could reject it on the ground that it seemed more prejudicial than probative. But the courts' powers to exclude improperly obtained evidence go wider than this, and enable them to exclude even pieces of highly cogent evidence. Whether it is sensible for cogent evidence to be excluded merely because it was obtained improperly is a contentious matter, but it has little to do with the evidence of children and no more need to be said of it here.

Privilege

There are some circumstances in which the court is willing to listen to evidence if it is offered, but allows the witness a privilege to withhold it. The best known example is the *privilege against self-incrimination*, which allows a witness to refuse to answer questions that might reveal him to be guilty of a criminal offence. In Britain this applies to any witness except for the defendant in a criminal case, who cannot refuse to answer questions for this reason if he chooses to give evidence (although he has the right to decline to give evidence at all).

An important derogation from the privilege against self-incrimination is contained in s. 98(1) of the Children Act 1989, which provides that in care proceedings and in proceedings to obtain emergency protection orders no witness may refuse to answer a question because the answer could incriminate him. Thus, for example, a parent could be required to answer a question like 'Did you beat your son?' However, s. 98(2) provides that the forced answer to such a question may not be used against a witness in later criminal proceedings.

A related privilege enables a party to refuse to disclose legal advice he has received, and, by an extension of this, other professional advice he has received in connection with a lawsuit, for example an expert report. Where the welfare of a child is at stake, however, the courts are sometimes prepared to overrule this privilege and order disclosure (*Re A* [1991] FCR 844).

There are also certain situations where a court will allow witnesses to refuse to answer questions, or even require them not to answer when willing to do so, because they think the greater public good requires it. This body of rules is usually called *public interest immunity*. In the leading case, the House of Lords held that in an action for damages for negligence the NSPCC could refuse to disclose the name of the person who had told the society of suspicions that a child was being abused (*D* v *NSPCC* [1978] AC 171). At one time, social work records were protected from disclosure under this principle, but the Court of Appeal had second thoughts about this in *Re M (Social Work Records: Disclosure)* [1990] FCR 485, and said that here too the court could order disclosure if the welfare of the child required it. A related point is that all evidence in wardship proceedings is confidential, and can only be used or disclosed for use in other proceedings with the consent of the wardship court.

When a new type of evidence is invented, it is considered fair game for lawyers to attack it as contravening one of the exclusionary rules. If none of these applies the courts may still be invited to condemn it, and in effect create a new category of inadmissible evidence to cover it. When print-outs from computerised machines first appeared they were unsuccessfully challenged as contravening the hearsay rule (*Wood* (1982) 76 Cr App R 23) and in the first case where robbers were photographed in the act by an automatic security camera they unsuccessfully appealed solely on the ground that the pictures should not have been put before the jury (*Dodson* (1984) 79 Cr App R 220). Nowadays such challenges usually fail, because the courts usually hold any new type of obviously relevant evidence to be admissible. But the fact that such challenges can be made at all tells us a lot about the attitude of lawyers to evidence.

On the face of it, to ask a tribunal to make an important decision shutting its eyes to a piece of relevant and cogent evidence sounds distinctly like inviting it to get it wrong. Generally speaking, the legal systems other than those in the English-speaking world know little or nothing of the concept of relevant but inadmissible evidence, and it is pertinent to ask when we acquired the idea, and why.

Traces of the exclusionary rules can be found several centuries earlier, especially in Scots law, but the main structure seems to have been built in the late 18th and early 19th centuries. As far as the criminal courts in England are conerned, the exclusionary rules date from the time when lawyers first began to appear for prosecution and defence in a process which had previously run largely without them (Langbein 1978). The reason why the rules were made have never been fully explored, but there seem to have been a number of them acting together. The most respectable one was a desire to shut out evidence that was felt to be inherently untrustworthy, lest in their innocence lay juries should be misled by it (Thayer 1898). Another factor was probably the fear of putting people in the witness-box who might be tempted to lie on oath, which to the superstitious seemed a dreadful evil compared with hanging the innocent, or letting the guilty go free. Another reason may have been that the courts had to cope with a rising case-load with fixed resources in time and manpower, and snatched at any chance to cut down on the time-consuming business of hearing evidence. And another factor may have been the lawyer's love of rules for the sake of rules, and of learning which enables him to be profitably learned. However respectable the reasons for which the rules were originally created, there is no doubt that many of the rules lost all contact with them many years ago. In the case of *Myers* v *DPP* [1965] AC 1001 the House of Lords held that cards on which the chassis and cylinder-block numbers of cars had been recorded in a factory were inadmissible as evidence because they technically amounted to hearsay, even though they were unquestionably reliable, and far more reliable than the subsequent recollections of the workers who had filled them in, even if anyone could have traced them (1). In other words, the hearsay rule no longer had a reason: it was a sacred cow, which could not be killed and had to be fed, simply because it was sacred.

As to whether rules that exclude logically relevant evidence can ever be justified, views differ. In his *History of the Criminal Law of England* the 19th-century judge and legal writer Sir James Fitzjames Stephen vigorously criticised some aspects of the rules, but was broadly in favour of them. In his view the absence of any such rules in earlier times was one of the factors that made a series of famous and terrible miscarriages of justice possible in the 17th century—notably the Titus Oates affair, where 14 innocent people were convicted and executed for treason on the strength of perjured evidence (Stephen 1883, vol. 1, ch. 11). The arrival of exclusionary rules on the scene was a big step in the direction of a satisfactory criminal justice system, a destination Stephen felt we were closer to reaching than our Continental neighbours. 'The essentially scientific though superficially technical rules of evidence which give their whole colour to English trials, and which grew up silently and very gradually in our courts, seem to me to be just what is wanted to bring French trials into a satisfactory shape' (Stephen 1883, vol. 1, pp. 548–9).

Jeremy Bentham, on the other hand, was enormously scathing about them in his *Treatise on Judicial Evidence* (1825). In his view, the rules of judicial evidence should conform as far as possible to the rules the intelligent head of a family would instinctively use in sorting out some dispute within the household:

> . . . in the bossom of his family, the lawyer, by the force of good sense, returns to this simple method from which he is led astray at the bar by the

folly of learning. No one is so deeply tainted with judicial practice, as to apply its rules to his domestic affairs. He takes up and lays aside his maxims with his gown. If you would represent madness—but a madness where all is melancholy and unintelligible—you have only to imagine an English barrister carrying into ordinary life the fictions, the rules, and the logic of the bar. (Bentham 1825, b. 1, ch. 3.)

He said that rules excluding logically relevant evidence can never be justified as helping the court perform its main task of reaching the truth, because a true conclusion can only be reached by considering everything that is logically relevant. Exclusionary rules are sometimes justifiable where they serve secondary purposes: the avoidance of delay, expense, and 'vexation'—such as serious inconvenience and embarrassment to the witness who must give it. But even then they are at best a necessary evil, and not to be tolerated if they frustrate the court in its main object of discovering the true facts as the basis upon which to do justice according to law. Most of the exclusionary rules, in his view, had been created for the wrong purpose:

Exclusion insofar as it is applied to prevent erroneous judgments, that is, to remove evidence which it is thought would mislead, has been admitted with remarkable prodigality. Exclusion, insofar as it is applied to prevent delay, expense, and vexations, has been admitted very sparingly, and almost never with this view. Thus, in cases where this medicine would certainly be efficacious, it is seldom used; and in cases where its effects are only more or less dangerous, it is frequently used. (Bentham 1825, 6.7, ch. 4.)

Over the years Bentham's views on evidence have had an impact. Many of the particular exclusionary rules which he attacked have been abolished, and Parliament has nibbled away at several of those that remain. Every time a change has been proposed a section of the legal profession has prophesied every kind of evil as a result. Yet it is hard to think of any bad result that has followed the abolition or curtailment of any exclusionary rule. Sometimes even the traditionalists who opposed the change—like Mr Justice Hawkins, who publicly opposed the abolition of the rule that made the defendant incompetent to give evidence in a criminal trial—have later admitted they were wrong (Williams 1963, p. 48).

(E)   RULES ABOUT HOW EVIDENCE IS TO BE EVALUATED

Most legal systems have rules that certain types of presumptively weak evidence must not be acted on alone, or acted on only with great caution, or may not prevail against evidence of some other type which is presumed to be more reliable. In Britain, the best known of these is the Scottish rule which forbids a criminal court to return a conviction in the absence of evidence from two separate sources. There is no such general rule in England, as several well-known unfortunate defendants seem to have discovered to their cost; but there are some specific rules that forbid courts to act on certain types of evidence if uncorroborated; until it was abolished in 1988 the best known one was the rule against convicting on the uncorroborated evidence of unsworn children. In England there are also rules requiring the courts to approach certain types of evidence with caution. Specific rules of this type are justified as long as they correctly identify the types of evidence upon which it is generally unsafe to act, which has not always been the case in the past. We discuss the rules about corroboration insofar as they relate to children in chapter 8.

NOTE

1. This particular decision was rapidly reversed by statute: see chapter 6.

CHAPTER FOUR

The competency requirement

ENGLISH LAW

In England, this area of the law has recently seen major changes: notably that, with effect from 1 October 1992, the Criminal Justice Act 1991 attempts to abolish the competency requirement for child witnesses in criminal proceedings altogether. This change, however, only applies to criminal proceedings, and in civil proceedings a competency requirement—surprisingly—remains. Thus, unfortunately, the section that follows still has practical relevance.

ENGLISH LAW: HISTORICAL BACKGROUND

In England, the rule since the eighteenth century has been that all witnesses must give evidence on oath (*Lee* [1988] Crim LR 525, *Bellamy* (1986) 82 Cr App R 222), or, if they have religious objections to taking oaths, after making a solemn declaration (Oaths Act 1978, s. 5). Those who take oaths must be competent to do so, and this means that they must understand the nature of an oath (*White* (1786) 1 Leach 430); and so presumably must those who wish to exercise the right to object to the oath and insist on a solemn declaration. Whilst adult witnesses are presumed to have this understanding, with children under the age of 14 the presumption has been the other way, and the judge has always had to question them on the subject before allowing them to give evidence. If judicial questioning shows the child does not understand the nature of an oath, it was not necessarily the end of the matter, because in a criminal case s. 38 of the Children and Young Persons Act 1933 permitted a child who does not understand the nature of an oath to give unsworn evidence 'if, in the opinion of the court, he is possessed of sufficient intelligence to justify the reception of the evidence, and understands the duty of speaking the truth'. A similar rule still applies in civil cases by s. 96 of the Children Act 1989. If the child does not give evidence through incompetency or any other reason, then in theory the hearsay rule prevents anyone else from repeating to the court what the child has said. In civil cases involving children the hearsay rule has now been abolished and the courts generally allow adults to repeat things said by children who would undoubtedly have been rejected as competent witnesses (see chapter 6). In criminal cases, however, the rule is strictly applied, and if the child does not give live evidence at trial the result will usually be that the court never hears the child's version of events.

This was not always so. Originally there were rules forbidding certain persons to take oaths, but no blanket rule against the acceptance of unsworn evidence, and the courts would listen to unsworn evidence from those who were ineligible to be sworn. Thus defence witnesses were barred from taking oaths until 1702 (Thayer 1898, p. 157, Stephen 1883, vol. 1, pp. 350–4, 416), and the defendant himself until the Criminal Evidence Act 1898: but both were permitted to make unsworn statements—an option the defendant retained until the Criminal Justice Act 1982. Similarly, it seems that the courts would formerly listen to unsworn evidence from children who failed the competency examination. In his *History of the Pleas of the Crown*, Sir Matthew Hale (1609–76) wrote this:

If the rape be committed upon a child under twelve years old, whether or how she may be admitted to give evidence may be considerable. It seems to me, that if it appear to the court, that she hath the sense and understanding that she knows and considers the obligation of an oath, tho she be under twelve years, she may be sworn. . . . But if it be an infant of such tender years, that in point of discretion the court sees it unfit to swear her, yet I think she ought to be heard without oath to give the court information, tho singly of itself it ought not to move the jury to convict the offender, nor is it in itself a sufficient testimony, because not upon oath, without concurrence of other proofs, that may render the thing probable; and my reasons are, 1. The nature of the offense, which is most times secret, and no other testimony can be had of the very doing of the fact, but the party upon whom it is committed, tho there may be other concurrent proofs of the fact when it is done. 2. Because if the child complain presently of the wrong done to her to the mother or other relations, their evidence upon oath shall be taken, yet it is but a narrative of what the child told them without oath, and there is much more reason for the court to hear the relation of the child herself, than to receive it at second-hand from those, that swear they heard her say so; for such a relation may be falsified. . . . But in both these cases, whether the infant be sworn or not, it is necessary to render their evidence credible, that there should be concurrent evidence to make out the fact, and not to ground a conviction singly upon such an accusation with or without oath of an infant. (Hale 1736, pp. 634–5.)

Elsewhere in his treatise Hale tells us that the same practice prevailed not only in rape cases, but also in cases of 'buggery, witchcraft, and such crimes which are practised upon children' (Hale 1736, p. 284). This is borne out by Professor Langbein's modern study of 17th and early 18th-century criminal trials (Langbein 1978), in which he describes the case of *Arrowsmith*, a rape trial that took place at the Old Bailey in 1678. In this case the court initially heard evidence from two girls aged eight and nine without requiring them to take an oath, and apparently without any sort of competency examination; they were recalled, questioned on their understanding of the meaning of an oath, sworn and re-examined, only when the jury, to the annoyance of the bench, expressed its reluctance to convict without hearing them give evidence on oath.

In England, the modern restrictive rules of evidence, including those relating to the evidence of children, took shape in the 18th century. Following a period of confusion during which different judges followed different practices—confusion which is fully described in East's *Pleas of the Crown* (1803) pp. 441–3—the old and more liberal rules about child witnesses were discarded in the case of *Brasier* in 1779 (East PC, 443). The defendant, a soldier, was tried at Reading Assizes for assaulting Mary Harris, a little girl of five, with intent to rape, the prosecution case being that he had attacked her as she went home from school. At the trial her mother and her mother's lodger repeated the account the little girl had given them as soon as she got home, which included the information that her attacker was a soldier; adult witnesses also told how she had described the soldier's lodgings correctly and had picked out the defendant at an identification parade, and a surgeon swore 'that she had received some hurt'. No attempt was made to call the child herself as a witness, and her story was put before the court entirely in the form of hearsay delivered by the mouths of others. This satisfied the jury, who convicted. But the case was referred to the judges in London—a procedure which in those days stood in for appeals in criminal cases—and they eventually condemned what had happened at the trial as improper:

> . . . all the judges being assembled, they unanimously agreed that a child of any age, if she were capable of distinguishing between good and evil, might be examined on oath; and consequently that evidence of what she said ought not to have been received. And that a child of whatever age cannot be examined unless sworn. (East PC, p. 444.)

The result was a pardon for the defendant.

The rule that the child must tell her story to the court herself, on oath, caused extreme difficulties in cases of child abuse. To give sworn evidence in those days it was not enough that the witness had a general idea of the difference between 'good and evil': the witness had to believe that God would damn his soul for ever if he lied. The flavour of the contemporary competency examination is conveyed by this examination by Judge Jeffreys (*Braddon* (1684) 9 St Tr 1127, 1148–9).

> Judge Jeffreys: Suppose you should tell a lie, do you know who is the father of liars?
> 13-year-old boy: Yes.
> Jeffreys: Who is it?
> Boy: The devil.
> Jeffreys: If you should tell a lie, do you know what will become of you?
> Boy: Yes.
> Jeffreys: What if you should swear to a lie? If you should call God to witness to a lie, what would become of you then?
> Boy: I should go to hell fire.

An 18th-century example, where the witness failed the test, is given at the end of this chapter. (1)

In those days many serious-minded people thought it quite in order to fill the minds of little children with thoughts of eternal torment. When John Wesley preached hell-fire and damnation to the children at Kingswood School, producing scenes of distress that were indescribably hideous, he wrote of 'the wonderful work of grace which God wrought in them' (Vulliamy 1931). Not all parents thought such ideas were fit for tiny children's minds, however, and to the extent that children were ignorant of the doctrine of eternal damnation they could, in effect, be beaten or abused with impunity. Troubled by this, some judges tried to get around the problem by adjourning cases where child witnesses failed the competency examination for the child to be given religious instruction. A note on p. 430 of vol. 1 of Leach's reports records that:

> Mr Justice Rooke, in a criminal prosecution that was coming on to be tried before him at Gloucester, finding that the principal witness was an infant who was wholly incompetent to take an oath, postponed the trial till the following assizes, and ordered the child to be instructed in the mean time by a clergyman in the principles of her duty, and the nature and obligation of an oath. At the next assizes the prisoner was put upon his trial, and the girl being found by the court, on examination, to have a proper sense of the nature of an oath, was sworn, and upon her testimony the prisoner was convicted, and afterwards executed. Mr Justice Rooke mentioned this at the Old Bailey in 1795, in the case of Patrick Murphy, who was indicted for a rape on a child of seven years old, and the learned judge added, that upon a conference with the other judges upon his return from circuit, they unanimously approved of what he had done.

This procedure became so common that in 1836 a barrister described it as 'every day's practice' (*Williams* (1836) 7 C & P 321), and it has even been resorted to in modern times when a judge was particularly anxious for a child to give evidence on oath (see *The Times*, 20 November 1976). But not all judges would allow it. In one case where a child of eight who had witnessed a murder had received two visits from a clergyman, and by the time of the trial had progressed as far with her religious studies as to believe that hell lay under the kitchen grate, Patteson J rejected her as a witness and said: 'The effect of the oath upon the conscience of the child should arise from religious feelings of a permanent nature, and not merely from instructions, confined to the nature of an oath, recently communicated to her for the purposes of this trial' (*Williams* (1836) 7 C & P 321: see also Alderson B in *Hall* (1849) 14 JP 25). Perhaps it was as well that not all judges would follow the practice, because it must have been exquisitely cruel. Not only did the child who had been battered and assaulted have a shocking memory to contend with: after a crash course of religious instruction the child had an eternity in hell to think about as well.

When the NSPCC was founded (see chapter 1) it quickly found the competency requirement as interpreted in *Brasier* an enormous obstacle to successful prosecutions for cruelty to children. A vivid example is given in the biography of the founder, Benjamin Waugh:

The counsel defending objected to the child's evidence being taken, on the ground that she was 'too young to understand the nature of an oath'. Thereupon the judge asked her to come closer to him, which she did with great reluctance. She was put on to the table just underneath him. Then from above he said in his kindest voice, 'What do you know, my child, about the Supreme Being?' The child looked for a moment at the most terrible-looking man she had ever seen in her short life, hesitated, and then, perhaps naturally, began to cry. 'I do not think I can take this evidence', said the judge. The counsel for the prosecution, anxious not to lose the evidence, obtained leave from the judge to try his hand—so, by way of making matters easier, said, also in his kindest voice, 'Now, my dear, who is God?' The child, being still unable to give any reply, satisfactory or otherwise, was put down. (Waugh 1913, p. 141.)

In 1885 the society tried to persuade the government to put a provision enabling young children to give unsworn evidence into its Criminal Law Amendment Bill. After an initial rebuff from the Home Secretary, who thought that such a change was inconceivable, the government eventually gave way in the face of a near rebellion from its supporters in the House of Commons, and because the Home Secretary made the remarkable discovery that the Scots courts (see below) had long permitted children to give evidence unsworn. Thus young children were allowed to give unsworn evidence by s. 4 of the Criminal Law Amendment Act 1885. The result is said to have been a rapid increase in successful prosecutions for assaults on children.

In a charge at the Old Bailey some time ago, Mr Justice Hawkins said he had tried 120 cases of assault upon women and children within the last six months. 'It does not follow', he continued, 'that dastardly acts, such as have been faintly described in reports of recent trials at the Central Criminal Court, are on the increase, but owing to a clause in the new Act, due to the Society for the Prevention of Cruelty to Children, a child can now give evidence without the necessity of taking and understanding an oath, and more criminals are arrested and convicted than was previously the case.' (*The Child's Guardian*, vol. 1, No. 1 (January 1887).)

At first this provision only applied to trials for unlawful sexual intercourse with girls under 13, but in the years that followed it was extended piecemeal to other offences, and in 1933 it was extended to criminal trials generally. Surprisingly, it was not until the Children Act 1989 that it was extended to civil proceedings.

Before 1 October 1992 the statutory provision about the unsworn evidence of children was s. 38 of the Children and Young Persons Act 1933, which, as amended by the Criminal Justice Act 1988, was as follows:

(1)   Where, in any proceedings against any person for any offence, any child of tender years called as a witness does not in the opinion of the court understand the nature of an oath, his evidence may be received, though not

given upon oath, if, in the opinion of the court, he is possessed of sufficient intelligence to justify the reception of the evidence, and understands the duty of speaking the truth.

Over the years, the rules about the competency of children to give sworn and unsworn evidence underwent two important changes.

The first was that the test a child had to pass before being allowed to give evidence on oath was greatly watered down. The statute that permitted children to give unsworn evidence originally carried the important proviso that the accused could not be convicted on such evidence unless it was corroborated by 'other material evidence', which was taken to mean evidence of some kind other than another piece of unsworn child evidence (*Director of Public Prosecutions* v *Hester* [1973] AC 296). Until this proviso was repealed in 1988 it was often necessary for at least one child to give sworn evidence in order to obtain a conviction in a child abuse case: and it seems to have been this that led to the threshold for sworn evidence being gradually lowered, even after children could in principle give evidence unsworn.

Before a child took an oath, he or she originally had to show that he 'understood the nature of an oath' in its original and ancient sense: as a conditional self-curse, under which the swearer calls upon God to damn his soul for all eternity if he fails to tell the truth. But during the 19th century there was growing scepticism about the idea of eternal damnation, as shown by the following exchange which is said to have taken place when Mr Justice Maule (1788–1858) had to examine a little girl on the nature of an oath.

Judge: And if you do always tell the truth, where will you go when you die?
Little girl: Up to heaven sir.
Judge: And what will become of you if you tell lies?
Little girl: I shall go down to the naughty place, sir.
Judge: Are you quite sure of that?
Little girl: Yes, sir.
Judge: Let her be sworn, it is quite clear she knows more than I do. (Parry, 1922.)

Accordingly, the judges took it as good enough if the witness believed in some kind of divine punishment, although it need not be as bad as hell-fire. As Brett MR said in *Attorney-General* v *Bradlaugh* (1885) 14 QBD 667:

. . . there is no necessity that the person taking the oath should believe that he will be liable to be punished in a future state. If there be any belief in a religion according to which it is supposed that a Supreme Being would punish a man in this world for doing wrong, that is enough.

After this the oath gradually became little more than a solemn promise to tell the truth with a reference to God attached. In the case of children this was officially recognised in 1963 when Parliament, enacting a proposal of the Ingleby Committee (Cmd 1191, 1960), changed the form of an oath that a child must take from the usual 'I swear by Almighty God' to 'I promise before Almighty God' (Children and Young Persons Act 1963, s. 28). Then in *Hayes* (1977) 64 Cr App R 194 the Court of Appeal held that a child could take an oath provided he or she could make a solemn promise, and it no longer mattered that the child had never heard of God. In this case the trial judge had permitted two boys aged 11 and 12 to give evidence on oath, although his questioning had revealed the fact that neither of them had heard of God, Jesus or the Bible—let alone of hell and eternal damnation, and on this evidence the jury had convicted. The defendant appealed, saying that both boys should have been required to give their evidence unsworn—which, as the law stood then, would have meant his acquittal because the boys' evidence was corroborated by nothing except other unsworn evidence. Upholding the conviction the Court of Appeal said that the judge had been right to let the boys give evidence on oath:

> It is unrealistic not to recognise that, in the present state of society, amongst the adult population the divine sanction of an oath is probably not generally recognised. The important consideration, we think, when a judge has to decide whether a child should properly be sworn, is whether the child has a sufficient appreciation of the solemnity of the occasion, and the added responsibility to tell the truth, which is involved in taking an oath, over and above the duty to tell the truth which is an ordinary duty of normal social conduct.

After this decision there was little real difference between the standard of competency for giving sworn and unsworn evidence (2). To give unsworn evidence a child had to show that he had 'sufficient intelligence to justify the reception of his evidence and understands the duty of speaking the truth', which differs little in any meaningful sense from 'appreciating the solemnity of the occasion, and the added responsibility to tell the truth, which is an ordinary duty of social conduct'. In theory a child had to appreciate no more than the general importance of telling the truth in order to give unsworn evidence, but had also to understand the particular importance of telling the truth in a court of law before giving evidence on oath. But as a practical matter this was almost a distinction without a difference, and no doubt this partly explains why in the Criminal Justice Act 1988 Parliament was content to abolish the only consequence that flowed from it—that on unsworn evidence there could be no conviction without corroboration.

The second change that took place was that for a period of about 30 years, the courts imposed an age limit below which children were forbidden to give evidence, even when not on oath. This was entirely the invention of the judges. The statutory provision (later s. 38 of the Children and Young Persons Act 1933) under which children gave unsworn evidence in criminal cases was undoubtedly intended to enable the English criminal courts to listen to child witnesses who satisfied the requirements of that section, however young, and at first this seems to have been the effect of it. Several reported cases from the early years of this century incidentally reveal that the courts were then in the practice of hearing evidence from children as young as five (*Murray* (1913) 9 Cr App R 248; *Christie* [1914] AC 545, 561; *Stanley* (1927) 20 Cr App R 58; *Southern* (1930) 22 Cr App R 6); the *Report of the Departmental Committee on Sexual Offences against Young Persons* in 1925 mentions a child who was called as a witness at the age of four (Cmnd 2561, para. 57); and in a book a London stipendiary magistrate described how he once received the evidence of a child of two (Mullins 1943, p. 195). In 1958, however, there was an abrupt change as a result of the decision in *Wallwork* (1958) 42 Cr App R 153. At a man's trial for incest with his daughter aged five, the prosecution had called the little girl as a witness, but had been unable to persuade her to say anything in the witness-box. The attempt to use her as a witness provoked the following comment from Lord Goddard CJ in the Court of Criminal Appeal:

> The court deprecates the calling of a child of this age as a witness. Although the learned judge had the court cleared as far as it can be cleared, it seems to us to be unfortunate that she was called and, with all respect to the learned judge, I am surprised that he allowed her to be called. The jury could not attach any value to the evidence of a child of five: it is ridiculous to suppose that they could. There must be corroborative evidence if a child of tender years and too young to understand the nature of an oath is called, but in any circumstances to call a little child of the age of five seems to us to be most undesirable, and I hope it will not occur again.

These words rapidly found their way into the practitioners' books, giving rise to a belief that no child can be competent to give even unsworn evidence until he has reached the age of six, and a practice of not usually attempting to call children until they reached the age of eight. As the Court of Criminal Appeal in *Wallwork* also reasserted the hearsay rule, and condemned the trial judge for allowing the child's grandmother to repeat to the court the little girl's account of what her father had done to her, the difficulty this case put in the way of prosecuting child molesters can hardly be exaggerated, as we explain below. Yet in 1987 the decision was resoundingly reaffirmed by the Court of Appeal in *Wright* (1987) 90 Cr App R 91 and extended, indeed, because in that case the child was six years old at the time of the trial.

Then in 1990, the Court of Appeal overturned the decision in *Wallwork*. In *Z* [1990] 2 QB 355 the Court of Appeal explained Lord Goddard's remarks in that case as stemming from two fears: first, that the evidence of a young child would always be unreliable, and secondly, that having to give evidence was a terrible ordeal which a little child should be spared. Developments in psychology, said Lord Lane CJ, had shown young children to be more reliable as witnesses than previously thought, and the introduction of the live link (see Chapter 5) had made giving evidence less stressful for them. Thus there was no arbitrary age below which a judge must reject a child as a witness: in every case he should decide for himself if the requirements of s. 38 of the Children and Young Persons Act 1933 are met. Notwithstanding Lord Lane's remark that a child of five would 'very rarely' be found competent, a later Court of Appeal approved in principle the fact that a judge had allowed evidence to be given by a child of four (*Selby* 24 May 1991, No. 90/1925/X4 (unreported). In a further judgment, delivered after the provision abolishing the competency requirement in criminal cases had been passed but before it had come into force, the Court of Appeal reaffirmed with some vigour what it had earlier said in *Z* (*N* (1992) 95 Cr App R 256).

CRITICISM OF THE COMPETENCY REQUIREMENT: ITS CURTAILMENT AND PARTIAL ABOLITION

If a child is too immature to understand the difference between truth and falsehood, or to explain it, common sense suggests that we should be cautious in believing anything that child tells us. But it does not suggest that we should simply refuse to listen altogether, particularly if the child appears to be the victim of a criminal offence and is the only witness except for the offender. Yet that is exactly the effect of the competency requirement.

By the age of two most children can talk a little, and by the age of three many children are talking fluently. Once they can talk, they can impart potentially useful information, whether or not they would satisfy a competency test. (Aged three the first author's daughter could describe an event in simple terms; but when asked what a 'liar' was she replied, 'A *liet* is when a fat lady has too much to eat'. Aged four her answer was, 'A liar is when you say you didn't do it': a definition some judges might secretly agree with, but on which, at least in England, they could hardly accept her as a competent witness.) No sane parent, or doctor, would treat a child's injury without asking him what happened, and no sane policeman would dream of investigating an offence against a child without at least trying to communicate with the child. Yet if a child is unable to grasp the distinction between truth and falsehood, or if he or she can but is unable to express it in a way that convinces the court that he or she does, no court that has to apply the traditional competency requirement will listen to a word the child has to say. In the words of the Pigot Committee, the competency requirement appears 'to be founded upon the archaic belief that children below a certain age or level of understanding are either too senseless or too morally delinquent to be worth listening to at all' (Home Office Advisory Group on Video Evidence 1989, para 5.12). This attitude is wholly at variance with what modern psychology has to tell us about the abilities and qualities of children, as we explain in chapter 11.

The practical consequences of the competency requirement, particularly as applied until recently in criminal cases in England, was often disastrous, and particularly so in sexual cases. Here the prosecution often have no medical evidence at all, and where they do have any, it will usually show no more than that someone committed the offence, and will rarely point unequivocally to the defendant as the culprit (Muram 1989; Heger 1990). By disqualifying the child as a witness the competency requirement often deprived the prosecution of their only clear piece of evidence. The result, as Jeremy Bentham explained as long ago as 1827, was that:

... the child may have been abused and mangled [but] the malefactor goes unpunished, laughing at the sage from whose zeal, so little according to knowledge, he has obtained a licence (Bentham 1827, b. 9, pt. 3, ch. 6).

To see that this was true it was only necessary to read the newspapers:

At Winchester Crown Court, [X] denied assaulting the girl, then aged six, in Southampton between Sept 2 and 5. Mr David Jenkins, prosecuting counsel, asked Judge Joanne Bracewell if she would hear the girl's evidence. He said he made the application in view of recent Appeal Court decisions which had criticised the use of evidence by little girls. . . . Judge Bracewell said she was 'troubled by the tender age of the witness' and needed time to consider the matter. She retired for 10 minutes before ruling: 'This little girl is too young to be called as a witness in this case.' . . . [X], married with a child, was formally found not guilty and released. He made no comment as he left. (*Daily Telegraph*, 10 May 1989.)

A man charged with raping a five-year-old girl walked free from court yesterday without having to stand trial. The case collapsed after a judge decided the alleged victim was too young to give evidence. . . . Mr Justice Macpherson warned the Crown Prosecution Service that in future cases it must think very carefully before bringing charges for sex offences against very young children. He then discharged without trial the man who, looking stunned, hurriedly left the court. (*Glasgow Herald*, 19 May 1989.)

An Aberdeen man was yesterday cleared of sexually abusing a five-year-old girl when a judge said he was not satisfied the girl could tell the difference between the truth and lies. (*Press and Journal* (Aberdeen), 6 March 1993.)

Like other exclusionary rules of evidence the competency requirement was sometimes justified by saying it is better that 10 guilty men should be acquitted than one innocent person should be convicted. But by shutting out the evidence of the one person who really knows what happened, the competency requirement can be as effective to secure wrongful convictions as false acquittals. In the leading case of *Sparks* v *R* [1964] AC 964, for example, it was one of the things which prevented a white man who was prosecuted for assaulting a three-year-old girl from calling evidence that the girl had originally described her attacker as black. There, the Privy Council managed to quash the conviction on other, unrelated grounds: but there has been at least one other case in which the defendant's conviction was allowed to stand, although he did not answer the description given by the children involved, neither of whom gave evidence (Sargant and Hill 1986, p. 4). In another case where the conviction was eventually quashed, a mentally handicapped man was convicted of abducting and assaulting a little girl of three, apparently on no hard evidence other than his confession (*Delaney* (1988) 88 Cr App R 338). It seems astonishing that the legal system could tolerate even the possibility of convicting the defendant in a case like that without knowing whether or not the victim said that it was him.

However gloomy a view we take of the abilities of children, surely the evidence of even the youngest child has some element of value, and as such is worth putting before the court—in the same way as the reaction of an animal may be information that has some element of value, even though an animal has no sense of the duty to speak the truth. If a tracker dog recognises a scent and tracks a suspect then this fact can be put before the court (McCormack 1985), and a court might also be told that a dog appeared to recognise someone if this was relevant—and there is obviously no question of submitting a dog to a competency examination. Yet if it is a small child and not a dog, a competency requirement might force the court to refuse to admit the evidence. The rules of evidence—or at least, the rules of criminal evidence in England—seemed to rate little children less than dogs.

Such thoughts led Jeremy Bentham to condemn the competency requirement in his *Rationale of Judicial Evidence* (1827) a century and a half ago. More recently Wigmore, the American writer on evidence, also condemned it. His words have been widely quoted:

> A rational view of the peculiarities of child nature, and of the daily course of justice in our courts, must lead to the conclusion that the effort to measure *a priori* the degrees of trustworthiness in children's statements, and to distinguish the point at which they cease to be totally incredible and acquire suddenly some degree of credibility, is futile and unprofitable. The desirability of abandoning this attempt and abolishing all grounds of mental or moral incapacity has already been noted, in dealing with mental derangement. The reasons apply with equal or greater force to the testimony of children. Recognising on the one hand the childish disposition to weave romances and to treat imagination for verity, and on the other the rooted ingenuousness of children and their tendency to speak straightforwardly what is in their minds, it must be concluded that the sensible way is to put the child upon the stand to give testimony for what it may seem to be worth. To this result legislation must come. To be genuinely strict in applying the existing requirement is either impossible or unjust; for our demands are contrary to the facts of child nature. (2 Wigmore, Evidence, sect. 509 (1940).)

Even if we believe that it could ever be sensible for a court to distinguish the children it is prepared to believe from those it is not prepared to believe before it has heard what they have to say, there is still a serious objection to the competency requirement, at least in its traditional English form: the line it draws between children who are competent and incompetent to testify seems to be little related to the likelihood that they will tell the truth.

What lies behind the competency requirement is the feeling that children are less reliable as witnesses than adults: that they remember less accurately, and are more prone to suggestion, even when they are trying to be truthful; and that because of their immaturity and dependence on adults they are more easily manipulated into telling deliberate lies. As a test of how reliable a child is likely to be when trying to be truthful we might expect the traditional competency test to tell us nothing, because it is designed to see if a child will undertake to tell the truth, not whether he will be reliable if he does so; and it is hardly surprising to learn that psychological research shows these kinds of questions shed no light on the question of reliability. The psychologist Gail Goodman and others questioned a group of children aged between three and six who had undergone venepunctures and immunisation about the experience, in order to discover how much they could remember and how suggestible they were about an incident which had caused them considerable stress. They also asked the children a number of questions that judges typically ask during a competency examination—and found their performance on these questions poor predictors of their ability to provide accurate information (Goodman, Aman and Hirschman 1987).

To require the court to reject a child who does not know the difference between a truth and a falsehood, and why it is wrong to tell lies, may be some safeguard that those children who do give evidence will at least attempt to tell the truth. But it obviously does little to guard against the problem of manipulative adults coaching pliant children to tell lies, because if an adult can coach a child to tell a lie, that adult can equally coach him to give the right answers in a competency examination. As Jeremy Bentham said:

> The mother of such a child forms a scheme for ruining a male enemy. She employs the requisite time and labour in impressing upon the mind of the child two lessons: the one, a false story of the supposed injury; the other, an appropriate catechism, such as may afford the requisite satisfaction to the pious anxiety of the judge . . . . The same artificial mark of trustworthiness . . . might even be imprinted upon the faculties, mental and vocal, of a naturally-accomplished and well-instructed parrot or magpie. (Bentham 1827, b. 9, pt. 3, ch. 6.)

Nor is this point lost on lawyers. As an American prosecutor once soothingly explained, 'Remember, the most important thing is to rehearse the competency questions before you go to court' (Morey 1985).

In most of the rest of the world the competency requirement is either unknown or, if known, is in the process of being demolished. The common law jurisdictions in the English-speaking world originally inherited the decision in *Brasier* (1779) East PC 433 and the requirement for all witnesses to give evidence on oath. All, or almost all, have subsequently enacted legislation along the lines of s. 38 of the Children and Young Persons Act 1933 to enable young children to give unsworn evidence in certain cases, and many have since gone much further, and have virtually eliminated the competency requirement altogether. In France, Germany and as much of the rest of the world as we have been able to look at, competency requirements in the sense in which English law knows them are unknown: the age and immaturity of the witness naturally affects the weight that is put upon the evidence, but there is no question of the court refusing to listen to children below a certain age or level of understanding. (The position in other countries is discussed in more detail in chapter 14.)

It is only recently, however, that these arguments have made headway in England. In 1972, indeed, the Criminal Law Revision Committee's 11th Report on Evidence (Cmnd 4991) actually put forward a proposal which, far from relaxing the competency requirement, would have stiffened it up. This was that all children under 14 should give evidence unsworn, and that before they were allowed to do so, they should understand not merely the general duty to speak the truth, but that there is a risk of miscarriage of justice if false evidence is given in a court of law. If children had been expected to understand that it is important to tell the truth in court for this reason, the change would have been restrictive. As we explain in chapter 11, when small children are asked why it is important to tell the truth in court, the reason they usually give is that they will be detected and punished, not that it will lead to a wrongful conviction.

In 1989, however, the Pigot Committee, using arguments of the sort that we have just explained, concluded that 'the competence requirement which is applied to potential child witnesses should be dispensed with and that it should not be replaced' (para 5.13). This was one of the Committee's recommendations which the Government—meaning the Home Office—was prepared to accept, and it promoted what is now s. 52 of the Criminal Justice Act 1991 to achieve this.

Unfortunately, this provision is doubly inept. In the first place it only deals with the competency issue in criminal proceedings. In civil proceedings the position therefore remains as we have tried to explain it in the preceding section. This makes still necessary the next section of this chapter, which explains the practicalities of how a competency examination is carried out. Secondly, the provision is clumsily drafted: for the reasons explained in the next section but one (page 63), it may not even succeed in its intended aim of abolishing the competency requirement in criminal proceedings.

ENGLISH LAW: THE COMPETENCY REQUIREMENT TODAY

Civil proceedings in England

For the first hundred years of its existence, the statutory provision that permits children to give unsworn evidence was never extended to civil proceedings. This had the half-baked consequence that a criminal court in England could use the unsworn evidence of a child too young to understand the nature of an oath in order to decide whether an adult should go free or go to prison, but a civil court in England could not receive the evidence in order to decide the fate of the child itself. In 1989, by a late government amendment to the Bill, s. 96(1) and (2) were added to the Children Act 1989, which are as follows:

(1)   Subsection (2) applies where a child who is called as a witness in any civil proceedings does not, in the opinion of the court, understand the nature of an oath.
(2)   The child's evidence may be heard by the court if, in its opinion—
    (a)   he understands that it is his duty to speak the truth; and
    (b)   he has sufficient understanding to justify his evidence being heard.

This enabled children to give unsworn evidence in civil proceedings on the same terms as they were then able to do in criminal proceedings under s. 38 of the Children and Young Persons Act 1933; and from 14 October 1991, when the Children Act 1989 came into force, until 1 October 1992 when s. 52 of the Criminal Justice Act 1991 came into force, the test of competency in civil and criminal proceedings was the same. Thereafter, the competency requirement was (we hope!) abolished in criminal cases altogether and the law on competency became lopsided as between civil and criminal proceedings once again.

In practice the stiffer competency requirement in civil proceedings matters little, because the difficulties to which it would give rise are usually avoided by the civil courts receiving hearsay evidence of what the child has said. However, for those rare cases in which a child does give evidence in civil proceedings it is necessary to know the practicalities of how the competency requirement is carried out.

As to age, the Court of Appeal has said that it is always necessary to conduct a competency examination where the witness is under the age of 14 (*Khan* (1981) 73 Cr App R 190). There is no official age below which a child may not give evidence on oath (*Khan; Brasier* (1779) East PC 433, 1 Leach 199), and whether a child between the ages of six and 14 gives sworn or unsworn evidence depends on the trial judge's view of which version of the competency test the child can satisfy. Where the child is under the age of 14, the judge, according to the older cases, must hold a kind of 'Dutch auction': first he must find out if the child understands the nature of an oath, and swear him if he does, and he should consider the question of unsworn evidence only if the child does not (*Southern* (1930) 22 Cr App R 6; *Surgenor* (1940) 27 Cr App R 175). In the first of these two cases the Court of Criminal Appeal obtusely quashed a conviction partly because the trial judge let a child give unsworn evidence without first seeing if she was competent to take an oath, but in the second they let the conviction stand, reasoning that if the jury had accepted the child's unsworn evidence they would hardly have rejected the same evidence given on oath.

Other decisions of the superior courts have clarified other matters of procedural detail concerned with competency examinations. Thus we know that it is the job of the court rather than the advocates to ask the questions (*Lyons* (1921) 15 Cr App R 144; *Southern* (1930) 22 Cr App R 6; *Surgenor* (1940) 27 Cr App R 175; *Norbury* (1992) 95 Cr App R 256), and also that where there is a jury the questioning must take place in their presence, to help them assess the credibility of the child if he or she is allowed to give evidence (*Reynolds* [1950] 1 KB 606). In *Reynolds* it was also held, rather grudgingly, that it is proper for the party putting forward a child as a witness to call other evidence—in that particular case, a school attendance officer—to give the court information about the child's education and general background—although in practice such evidence is rarely if ever called (see chapter 9). In Scotland, it has been held proper for a judge, even where a child is very young, to decide the competency issue on his own unaided observation (*KP v H M Advocate* 1991 SCCR 933).

As to the sort of questions that should be asked there was until recently no official guidance. As one judge explained to the authors, 'We navigate by common sense and the light of nature'. In the recent case of *Russell* (3 July 1992, No. 90/2468/22, unreported) the Court of Appeal provided guidance by approving the questions a judge had asked in one case, and condemning those asked in another. The approved questions (which were originally asked at the trial in *Z* [1990] 2 QB 355 where the child was aged six) were as follows:

Judge: Claire, can you see and hear me?
Child: Yes.
Judge: Do you go to school?
Child: Yes.
Judge: How long have you been going to school? Roughly?
Child: A year.
Judge: A year?
Child: Yes.
Judge: Do you get taught about God at school, or not?
Child: No.
Judge: Do you know the difference between telling the truth and telling lies?
Child: Yes.
Judge: And you realise how terribly important it is that you tell the truth and no lies at all?
Child: I do not tell lies.
Judge: Are you going to tell us about what happened with Daddy?
Child: Yes.
Judge: And it must all be true.
Child: Yes.
Judge: Was everybody able to hear what she said?

The judge then said that having seen a videotape of the child in conversation with a woman police officer, and having asked her the foregoing questions, he ruled her incompetent to take an oath but able to give evidence unsworn.
    The questions that the Court of Appeal disapproved of were these.

Judge: Hello Amy . . .
Child: Yeah.
Judge: That is better. We can see a bit more of you now. You can see me all right, can you?
(Child laughs.)
Judge: Can you hear me as well?
Child: Yeah.
Judge: In a minute, Amy, somebody is going to ask you some questions.
Child: Yep.
Judge: Will you listen very carefully?
Child: Yep.

Judge: And try and tell us the answers, and try and get the answers right. How old are you? You disappear when you bob down like that. That is better. How old are you?
Child: Six. [In fact she was five.]
Judge: When were you six? Long ago? When was your birthday? Do you know?
Child: My birthday's in April.
Judge: You are nearly seven, or are you just six?
Child: Just six.
Judge: All right. Do not keep bobbing away, we lose you. Somebody is going to ask you some questions, and I will leave it to them.
Child: Thanks.
Judge: All right. Good girl.

On this, the judge found her competent to give unsworn evidence.

Something that has never been clearly explained, however, is what such an examination is really supposed to be testing. One would have thought the main object of the examination was to find out if the child has a knowledge of the difference between truth and falsehood, and an awareness that telling the truth is right and telling falsehoods wrong; and where the child's fitness to give sworn evidence is in issue, there is the extra object of discovering whether he understands why it is particularly important to tell the truth in a court of law. It is one thing to understand these matters, however, and quite another to have the ability to explain them. In the case of a young child one can imagine one line of questioning which would result in a child's being accepted as a witness because his answers revealed he understood these matters, and another line of questions that led to his being rejected because he could not properly explain them. One hopes that judges would put questions that tested the child's knowledge rather than his ability to articulate it; but from what we have heard from those who are in practice, not all judges do approach the question with this in mind.

In some kinds of civil proceedings the formal rules of evidence do not apply, and in these the evidence of any child may be received without any competency examination. The most prominent of these is wardship, where the judge is free to question any child of any age informally if he wishes—although in practice he more commonly relies on reports of interviews by others. Nor is there any question of a competency examination where a judge in ordinary civil proceedings sees a child in private to discover his views and wishes on a question of residence or access (see page 96). Nor do the rules of evidence apply to emergency protection orders (see page 27 above). The coroner's court is another exception. Thus despite the competency requirement and the hearsay rule the coroner's court that sat on the Hungerford massacre was able to hear, from a police officer, a little girl of four's account of how Michael Ryan abducted and shot her mother (*The Times*, 26 September 1987): evidence which at the time would clearly have been inadmissible, even from the mouth of the child herself, if Ryan had survived and been on trial for murder.

Criminal proceedings in England

As already mentioned, the matter is now governed by s. 52 of the Criminal Justice Act 1991, which was passed with the avowed aim of abolishing the competency requirement in criminal cases. The section is as follows:

> **52.**—(1)   After section 33 of the 1988 Act there shall be inserted the following section —
> **Evidence given by children**
>   33A.—(1)   A child's evidence in criminal proceedings shall be given unsworn.
>   (2)   A deposition of a child's unsworn evidence may be taken for the purposes of criminal proceedings as if that evidence had been given on oath.
>   (3)   In this section 'child' means a person under fourteen years of age.
>   (2)   Subsection (1) of section 38 of the 1933 Act (evidence of child of tender years to be given on oath or in certain circumstances unsworn) shall cease to have effect; and accordingly the power of the court in any criminal proceedings to determine that a particular person is not competent to give evidence shall apply to children of tender years as it applies to other persons.

Regrettably, this is not a model of clear drafting. Not only is there the minor but tiresome point that as a result of the way it arranges things, the relevant law is now spread over no less than three different Acts of Parliament: the Criminal Justice Act 1988, the Criminal Justice Act 1991, and s. 38(2) of the Children and Young Persons Act 1933, which makes intentional falsehoods by children giving unsworn evidence criminally punishable. There is the more serious problem that it may in fact fail to achieve its intended object.

The formula it adopts to abolish the competency requirement was inspired by paragraph 5.13 of the Pigot Report, which said: '. . . we believe the competence requirement which is applied to potential child witnesses should be dispensed with and not replaced. Once any witness has begun to testify he or she may appear to be of unsound mind, become incoherent or fail to communicate in a way that makes sense. The judge is already able to rule such a witness incompetent and advise the jury to ignore any evidence that may have been given. We think that this power, applied where necessary at the preliminary hearing or trial, is all that is needed . . . '.

Section 52 of the 1991 Act tries to put these thoughts into effect in three stages.

(a)   All evidence from persons under 14 is henceforth to be given unsworn, so knocking out as much of the competency requirement as applies to sworn evidence.

(b)   Section 38(1) of the Children and Young Persons Act 1933 is repealed, so removing the requirement that the judge be satisfied that the child 'is possessed of sufficient intelligence to justify the reception of the evidence, and understands the duty of speaking the truth' before being allowed to give evidence.

(c)   So child witnesses are now in the same position as adult witnesses, who usually have to undergo no competency examination before they give evidence, but who may be stood down if they reveal themselves unable to communicate intelligibly.

The flaw in this scheme is the following. The power a court has to reject an adult witness, and which now governs the rejection of children as witnesses, is wider than a mere power to stand the witness down if he jabbers incomprehensibly. In theory, a judge is also supposed to reject an adult witness, irrespective of any ability to communicate intelligibly, if he or she turns out to lack an understanding of an oath: (*Archbold* para. 8–35; *White* (1786) 1 Leach 430; *Hill* (1850) 5 Cox 259; *Bellamy* (1985) 82 Cr App R 222). Thus on the face of it, s. 52 pushes the competency requirement out through the front door, only to unbolt the back door to let it in again.

At first sight this might seem a hopeless argument, because it defeats the part of the section which provides that 'a child's evidence in criminal proceedings shall be given unsworn'. However, it could be claimed that that part of the section only removes the necessity for a child to *take* an oath, because this is a needlessly daunting formality; and that the main thrust of the section is to make sure that child witnesses do not give evidence unless they have the same level of knowledge and understanding as is required of an adult witness when giving evidence on oath 'sufficient appreciation of the solemnity of the occasion, and the added responsibility to tell the truth which is involved in an oath over and above the duty to tell the truth which is an ordinary duty of normal social conduct' (*Bellamy* (1985) 82 Cr App R 222). On this view, far from relaxing the competency requirement, s. 52 would actually tighten it up: not a ridiculous argument to someone who is ignorant of the background to the provision, but aware that this is what the Criminal Law Revision Committee was proposing in its 11th Report twenty years before (see above, page 58).

If this argument failed, there is still room for a further argument. Oaths apart, it might be said, surely no court would allow an adult witness to give evidence if he did not at least understand the duty to speak the truth: therefore the court must examine the child and reject him as a witness if he does not have at least that level of understanding. The objection to that argument is that it sets at nought the repeal of s. 38 of the 1933 Act, which used to impose exactly that requirement. But an answer to the objection could be that s. 38 also imposed a further requirement that the child be possessed of sufficient intelligence to justify the reception of the evidence. Thus on this view the repeal of s. 38 is not completely without purpose, because it would at least get rid of that additional requirement.

There is, unfortunately, a real risk that the provision will indeed be interpreted as preserving or even raising the competency requirement. Some judges believe the law about competency should be revised in the direction which the Criminal Law Revision Committee once proposed, that is, tightened up (*Baines* v *DPP* [1992] Crim LR 795). And the 1992 edition of a well-known students' text on evidence examines the section and concludes that the test of competency is now indeed whether the child understands the duty of telling the truth in a court of law (Murphy 1992, pp. 434–5).

These difficulties were brought to the government's attention by the authors of this book when the Criminal Justice Bill was before Parliament (Spencer 1990). In Committee in the House of Commons, an amendment was introduced to redraft the provision as follows:

Notwithstanding any existing rule of law or practice to the contrary, any child of tender years shall be competent as a witness provided he is able to give coherent replies to questions that are put to him, and his level of understanding shall affect the weight of his evidence and not its admissibility.

— a formula rather like the one that has since been enacted in the Republic of Ireland (3). The government opposed this amendment, however, assuring the committee that the Home Office's chosen form of words was clear. The Home Office seems to have had second thoughts, however, because in paragraph 2.14 of its Memorandum of Good Practice on Video Recorded Interview (see page 178) it states, depressingly, that 'It is not possible to predict precisely how the courts will treat the question of competence', and the Home Office Circular (SP/1992) which explains the children's evidence provisions of the Act carefully avoids saying that the competency requirement has now been abolished. We can only hope that the fact that many people know what the section was meant to achieve will enable the courts to interpret it so that it does achieve it. The chances of this are increased by the House of Lords' decision that now officially allows the courts to look at Parliamentary debates in order to interpret statutory provisions that are ambiguous or absurd (*Pepper* v *Hart* [1992] 3 WLR 1032).

Assuming that s. 52 has managed to abolish the competency requirement, some further points arise. First, can the child still be asked questions designed to test his or her intelligence, and understanding of the duty to speak the truth? Common sense would suggest that the answer is yes. Although these are no longer matters which determine whether or not the child is permitted to give evidence, they are still highly relevant to the weight that the court will wish to put upon it. A possible difficulty, however, is once again the wording of s. 52(2), which appears to say that the court shall treat child witnesses for competency purposes in the same way as it treats adults. Questions of this sort, of course, are not usually put to adults. It is to be hoped that despite this, the courts still allow such questions to be put to children, or at any rate, to those who are very young.

If the child can still be asked such questions, there is the question of who should ask them. In the past, when such questions went to competency, they were always asked by the judge. Now that the competency requirement has been abolished, it could be argued that such questions, like any other question intended to bear on the credibility of a witness, should be put by counsel as part of their examination and cross-examination. Yet as the Court of Appeal said in *Norbury* (1992) 95 Cr App R 256, it can be better for the child if it is the judge who asks such questions, because then they are only asked once. Unless and until the Court of Appeal decides the question, the wise course would be for the judge to discuss the matter with counsel before the child gives evidence, in the hope of agreeing that one of the three of them should do it.

In addition there is the related question of whether evidence from other people, a child psychologist, for example, or someone who knows the child, would be admissible to shed light on the child's intelligence and understanding. The answer seems to be that it would be. (The reasons for this are discussed in chapter 9.)

Finally, assuming that there is no longer any threshold test of competency, has the judge any power to reject the evidence of a child he thinks so immature that it can carry no weight whatever? The answer once again seems to be yes. As explained in chapter 3 (page 39), English law gives the judge wide powers, both at common law and under s. 78 of the Police and Criminal Evidence Act 1984, to rule evidence inadmissible if he thinks admitting it would make the trial unfair. In one case the Court of Appeal thought that the trial judge should have used this power to reject evidence of an out-of-court identification by a young child made in circumstances likely to make it unreliable (*O'Leary* (1988) 87 Cr App R 387; and see *Christie* [1914] AC 545). These powers are virtually unlimited, and even before the Criminal Justice Act 1991 came into force the Court of Appeal suggested that s. 78 could in theory be used to refuse to admit a child as a witness who had been 'brainwashed' by excessive pre-trial interviewing (*H* [1992] Crim LR 516). In *Norbury* (1992) 95 Cr App R 256, however—another case decided shortly before the 1991 Act came into force—the Court of Appeal were hostile to the idea of a judge using s. 78 of the 1984 Act to suppress the evidence of a child of six, who had satisfied the competency test, simply because she was young. If s. 78 was too readily used in this sort of case, it would obviously defeat the whole purpose of abolishing the competency requirement, which is to let the evidence of a young child be heard, for as much or as little as it seems to be worth.

As 10 is the minimum age for incurring criminal responsibility in England, there is no question of any sanction against a child below that age who gives false evidence. If a child over 10 wilfully gives false evidence, then in theory he or she can be punished. Section 38(2) of the Children and Young Persons Act 1933, as amended by the Criminal Justice Act 1991, says:

> If any child whose evidence is received unsworn in any proceedings for an offence by virtue of section 52 of the Criminal Justice Act 1991 wilfully gives false evidence in such circumstances that he would, if the evidence had been given on oath, have been guilty of perjury, he shall be liable on summary conviction to be dealt with as if he had been summarily convicted of an indictable offence punishable in the case of an adult with imprisonment.

In practice, it goes without saying that the likelihood of prosecution is remote.

THE POSITION IN NORTHERN IRELAND

So far, the provisions of the Children Act 1989 have not been extended to Northern Ireland. Thus as far as civil proceedings other than wardship are concerned children have to testify on oath, which means that they must 'understand the nature of an oath'. In criminal proceedings, the law at the time of writing is as it was in England before the Criminal Justice Act 1991 was enacted; but the government has now produced a Draft Criminal Justice (Northern Ireland) Order 1993, which is intended to replicate the children's evidence provisions of the 1991 Act. In its present form, this contains a s. 20 which exactly copies the confusing competency provision in s. 52 of the Criminal Justice Act 1991. Unless this is amended before being brought into effect, it will put the law of Northern Ireland in the same state of obscurity as it is in England.

SCOTTISH LAW

The former law
Until the 19th century, the law of Scotland seems to have been even more restrictive than the law of England on the competency of child witnesses. All witnesses were bound to give evidence on oath, which disqualified all 'pupils'—girls under 12 and boys under 14—because pupils were forbidden to take oaths (Stair 1693, b. 4, tit. 43, sect. 7). There was a further rule, derived from Roman law and with no counterpart in the law of England, that children of whatever age were incompetent as witnesses in proceedings in which their parents were involved (Stair 1693), and for good measure, a further rule that banned the evidence of any female witness, old or young (Stair 1693, b. 4, tit. 43, sect. 9). In cases of domestic violence (McDouall 1752, b. 4, t. xx), and other 'occult or more private facts, where there must in most cases be a penury of unexceptionable witnesses' (Erskine 1773, b. 4, tit. 2, sect. 26), the court had some measure of discretion to admit witnesses who would otherwise have been incompetent. Nevertheless, in those days it must have been a very rare event for a court to listen to the evidence of a child.

The modern law
The rule disqualifying children from testifying for or against their parents was abolished by the Evidence (Scotland) Act 1840. By this time the courts themselves had rejected the rule that all witnesses must give evidence on oath. The development is described in detail in the 1844 edition of Hume's *Commentaries*, vol. 2, p. 341, where a collection of otherwise unreported decisions are briefly set out, including the case of *Janet White* at Jedburgh in 1782, where Lord Braxfield received the unsworn evidence of a girl of six. Thus it became possible for young children in Scotland to give evidence unsworn without the need for an Act of Parliament, and apart from the Evidence (Scotland) Act 1840 the Scottish rules on children's evidence are wholly based on the decisions of the courts. The modern Scottish rule which emerges from these decisions is that all persons capable of making themselves intelligible to the tribunal are competent as witnesses, oaths being required of those who have sufficient understanding, and dispensed with for those who do not. Thus in Scotland not only a child, but also a person who is mentally handicapped can give evidence unsworn (Wilkinson 1986, p. 138). (Thus there

is no need, as there is in England, to go through the farcical performance of making such a person take an oath, as was held necessary in the English case of *Bellamy* (1986) 82 Cr App R 222: with the unfortunate consequence that those who commit offences against the mentally handicapped in England sometimes quite undeservedly escape their just deserts (see *Richardson, The Independent,* 5 October 1989).)

In Scotland it is still the case—as it no longer is (we hope!) in criminal proceedings in England—that the child must undergo a competency examination before being allowed to give evidence. In recent years, the High Court has twice reminded first instance judges of this when hearing appeals (*Rees* v *Lowe* 1989 SCCR 664; *Kelly* v *Docherty* 1991 SLT 419). Nowadays the usual practice is that children over the age of 14 are sworn, children under the age of 12 give evidence unsworn, and children between the ages of 12 and 14 give sworn or unsworn evidence depending on their level of understanding: but this is a rule of practice rather than a rule of law, and in the last resort whether any child gives evidence on oath or not seems to be a matter of judicial discretion (Renton and Brown 1984, sect. 18-82; Scottish Law Commission 1988).

Unlike in England, however, in Scotland there has never been any question of the courts laying down an arbitrary age below which no child will be permitted to give evidence. In *Thompson* (1857) 2 Irv 747, a murder case, Lord Justice-Clerk Hope refused to hear evidence from a child of three who was said to have told her mother 16 days after the death of her aunt, that she had seen the defendant giving her aunt some poison just before she died; but the judge seems to have based this ruling on his general duty to maintain the fairness of a criminal trial, and because he was afraid the child might have been coached to make the accusation. 'Had she spoken out on hearing of the death,' he said, 'the case would have been different. . . . But we do not know what she may have heard in the meantime.' In the later case of *Millar* (1870) 1 Coup 430, the prosecution were allowed to call Mary Gillespie, a little girl of three and a half, to tell the court who it was that had stabbed her in the face and neck, inflicting serious injuries, and Lord Justice-Clerk Moncrieff and Lord Cowan overruled a defence objection that 'In no case hitherto had so young a child been examined as a witness'. On Mary's evidence the defendant was convicted. This was in 1870: and the courts seem no less willing to hear evidence from very young children today. The authors have been told about one recent case in Aberdeen where a baby-sitter was convicted of an indecent assault partly on the evidence of the victim, aged four, corroborated by the evidence of her sister, aged two, who had witnessed the assault.

In Scotland, as in civil proceedings in England, there is a competency requirement in the sense that a child will not be accepted as a witness, even unsworn, unless he or she 'understands the duty to speak the truth'. 'Only those persons ought to be admitted as witnesses, whose powers of observation and memory, and whose knowledge of the duty to speak the truth, are so far developed that they will be likely to give trustworthy evidence.' (Dickson 1887, sect. 1543.) As in England, it is a matter for the judge whether the competency requirement is satisfied, and—as was recently reasserted by the

High Court in a case involving a witness aged three—he is obliged to question the child before she gives evidence, and also to warn her to tell the truth (*Rees v Lowe* 1989 SCCR 664). As in England, no set form of questions is prescribed, and it is left to each judge to decide how he will approach the question. In his 19th-century treatise, W. G. Dickson expressed the view that a child ought to be rejected as a witness unless he could tell the judge it was 'a sin against God to lie'. Even then the case law, to his pain, was against him (Dickson 1864, sect. 1676); much less is any such religious test insisted on today. Although the competency requirement for unsworn child witnesses is theoretically the same as it is (or was) in England, in practice it usually seems to have been interpreted more liberally.

It is usually also said that in order to be competent the child must be able to 'give an intelligible account'. This aspect of the matter was considered by the First Division in *M and M* v *Kennedy* 1993 SCCR 69, which involved a child who was an 'elective mute', almost incapable of spontaneous communication. The Sheriff was upheld in admitting her as a witness, once he was satisfied that she understood the duty to speak the truth: the ability to give an intelligible account did not mean the ability to give a spontaneous one. In that case, as in others, the Scottish courts have been satisfied with a competency examination that was fairly rudimentary. In *P* v *H.M. Advocate* 1991 SCCR 933 the examination of a five-year-old boy, J, had gone as follows:

Judge: Hello.
J: Hello.
Judge: Do you go to school?
J: Yes.
Judge: Which school do you go to?
J. (Named school.)
Judge: The same as your sister, is it?
J: Yes.
Judge: How long have you been at school for?
J: Hundreds of times.
Judge: Pardon?
J: Hundreds of times.
Judge: Now, J, do you know what it is to tell the truth?
J: Yes.
Judge: Do you know what it is to tell fibs?
J: Yes.
Judge: Do you know you mustn't tell fibs?
J: Yes.
Judge: You know that, yes. Well, J, these gentlemen are going to be asking you some questions.
J: Right.
Judge: And when you answer the questions do you promise to tell the truth?
J: Yes.
Judge: And you mustn't tell any fibs, all right?
J: Yes.

Judge: Promise that?

J: Yes.

On appeal it was held that he had been correctly admitted as a witness.

An interesting question is whether 'ability to give a trustworthy account' includes anything else beyond an understanding of the duty to speak the truth, and if it does, then what that additional element is. In *McNair* v *H.M. Advocate* 1993 SLT 277 the High Court said that a boy with some mental problems should not have been rejected as a witness simply because of a doctor's certificate that he was likely to be an unreliable witness.

Whilst some Scottish books on evidence suggest that there is a presumption against a young child being competent to give evidence (Walker and Walker 1964, sect. 349) the Scottish Law Commission say in their Discussion Paper in 1988 that '... nowadays many judges tend to approach the question of competency from the other end. That is to say, they assume that a child is prima facie a competent witness but may, upon a preliminary conversation with the child, reach the conclusion that the child is either incapable of giving intelligible evidence or is not yet able to understand the difference between right and wrong, and so is unable to undertake to tell the truth' (para. 2.3). Scottish judges and practitioners have told the authors of occasions when a very young child has failed a competency examination—such as the notorious case of *Maine and McRobb*, where the judge felt obliged to reject as a witness a girl, by then aged three, who had been abducted and tortured (see page 160). (Another example is given on page 55 above.)

But most children who are tendered as witnesses seem to be accepted. It may be that the existence of a competency requirement affects the procurator fiscal in deciding which children he should cite as witnesses. But even here it does not seem to act as much of a restriction, because in Scotland the competency requirement seems to have given rise to little public criticism or debate.

The liberal Scottish interpretation of the competency requirement is probably due in part to the rule of Scots law that forbids a conviction based on any single piece of evidence (see chapter 8). This blunts the argument 'Surely you wouldn't convict a man on this piece of evidence' and makes the courts anxious to make use of every piece of evidence that is available. But the Scottish attitude also seems to reflect a more favourable view about the reliability of children's evidence among Scots lawyers that goes back many years. In a case in 1881 Lord President Inglis said:

I have found that when the question is as to what happened on a particular occasion the best witnesses are boys and girls. Their eyes are generally open and they are not thinking of other things and they are not talking to their neighbours. Everyone who has had experience in the criminal courts must know that when the question is as to what occurred at a particular time and a particular place the best evidence is often given by boys and girls. (*Auld* v *McBey* (1881) 18 SLR 312.)

And in his *Treatise on the Law of Evidence in Scotland* W. G. Dickson criticised the rules in England, adding:

An intelligent child is generally a good witness in matters within his comprehension. Being accustomed to observe more than to reflect, he tells what he has seen or heard without drawing inferences or preconceived opinion. The solemnity of the examination has a strong influence on his mind; while one who is daily examined at school is in a good training to answer questions as a witness. In cross-examination a young witness generally tells ingenuously whether he has been tutored, and (if so) what he was desired to say. (Dickson 1864, sect. 1679.)

In the past, this liberal attitude to competency has meant that the Scottish courts were able to handle with little difficulty a matter which was causing acute difficulty in England. This meant, however, that the competency requirement was a virtual non-issue in Scotland when the Scottish Law Commission was examining the law, and in its Report No. 125 in 1990 it did not propose its abolition, as did the Pigot Committee in England. Thus the competency requirement still exists in both civil and criminal proceedings in Scotland, whereas if the Criminal Justice Act 1991 has done for English law what it was intended to do, it has been abolished for criminal proceedings in England. For those who do not approve of the competency requirement, English law, originaliy behind, has now taken the lead.

COMPELLABILITY

This chapter has been about the rules that prevent children from giving evidence when they wish to do so. What about the converse of this problem: can a child who is competent as a witness be forced to give evidence when he or she is unwilling? To put the question in legal terminology, is a child witness, if competent, also compellable?

The first point that should be noted is that in Britain—unlike France, for example—there is in general no legal obligation on the citizen, whether child or adult, to give information to the police when they ask for it. Nor, for that matter, is there any general duty to answer questions put by social workers. To this principle there are important exceptions, some of them concerning children: for example, s. 48 of the Children Act 1989, under which a court can order any person to disclose the whereabouts of a child to someone—usually a social worker—who is seeking an emergency protection order. But there is no exception to the normal rule in connection with the scheme for video interviews under the Criminal Justice Act 1991 in England (see pages 176 and 341), and a child can lawfully refuse a request from the police, the social services or the Crown Prosecution Service to give such an interview. If the child refuses, could his parent or guardian override the refusal by giving consent on his behalf? In the context of medical treatment, the courts have ruled that parents can sometimes overrule a child's refusal to submit to treatment (*Re R (Wardship: Consent to Treatment* [1992] Fam 1). Theoreti- cally, the courts could decide that by analogy with this, a parent can overrule a child's refusal to be interviewed by the police. However, such a ruling would be practically meaningless: first, the fact that the parents gave consent to the interview would not turn the child's refusal to talk into a criminal offence, and secondly, if parental consent enables a doctor to administer treatment to a child who physically resists, it is inconceivable that parental consent to an interview would justify the police—or the parents themselves—in using physical force on the child to make him talk (4).

Secondly, if police officers or social workers cannot compel a child to answer their questions, nor, *a fortiori*, can anyone else. Thus in the run-up to a civil case, the lawyers for the parties have no right to require a child who is a potential witness to give them an interview. Not only has the child a right to refuse. In certain circumstances the court can intervene to protect a reluctant child from being pressed to give one. If a child in England is a ward of court, he or she may not be interviewed (whether with a view to civil or to criminal proceedings) without the consent of the court: *Practice Direction (Ward: Witnesses at Trial)* [1987] 1 WLR 1739; *Re K (Minors) (Wardship: Criminal Proceedings)* [1988] Fam 1; *Re R (Wardship: Criminal Proceedings)* [1991] Fam 56). Even where the child is not a ward, it may be possible, at least in England, to apply to the court for a 'specific issue order' under s. 8 of the Children Act 1989 prohibiting the interview from taking place (Cousins 1992). In addition, a child who is the subject of 'family proceedings' under the Children Act 1989 may not be subjected to a medical or psychiatric examination except by leave of the court (Family Proceedings Rules 1991, S.I. 1991 No. 1247, rr. 4.18; Family Proceedings Courts (Children Act 1989) Rules 1991, S.I. 1991 No. 1395, r. 18).

When it is a question of calling a child as a witness, however, then in theory at least a child may be compellable. The basic rule, in England and in Scotland, is that a witness who is competent to give evidence in court proceedings is also compellable. In both jurisdictions there are exceptions. In criminal proceedings, for example, the defendant's spouse is competent to give evidence, but not compellable to give evidence against him (or her). But, unlike the position in Germany, for example, none of these exceptions relates specifically to a child, even when called to testify against a parent.

In principle, both prosecution and defence in a criminal case, and any party to civil proceedings, can require the attendance of a child witness by getting the court to issue a formal order to attend. This may be called a citation, a subpoena, a witness order or a witness summons, depending on the jurisdiction and the court within it. Failure to obey such an order is punishable as a criminal offence, and, in addition, the courts have power to order an absconding witness to be arrested and brought to court by force. On both sides of the border a witness who, having entered the witness-box, refuses to answer a question which he is legally obliged to answer—as he will be, unless it is irrelevant, or he has a privilege not to answer it (see page 41)—can be punished for contempt of court. An example of the pressure that is sometimes put on young witnesses to make them talk is furnished by this passage from the judgment in the English case of *Thompson* (1977) 64 Cr App R 96, where a girl of sixteen was reluctant to give evidence against her father, who was accused of incest with her, and of other sexual offences against her sister:

. . . when counsel for the prosecution begins to ask her questions dealing with the merits of the case she said: 'I'm not saying nothing, I'm not going to give evidence'. The learned judge said: 'Oh yes you are'. She answered: 'I'm not'. The learned judge said: 'Unless you want to spend some time in prison yourself, do you?' to which she replied: 'No'. The judge continued 'You won't like it in Holloway I assure you. You answer these questions and behave yourself, otherwise you will be in very serious trouble. Do you understand that?' To which she replied: 'Yes' . . . [This witness then gave evidence reluctantly] . . . When it came to the turn of the [other] daughter . . . to give evidence she also refused as in the case of her sister, and the judge, who was no doubt getting a little tired of this sort of conduct in this case, gave an order that she should be detained overnight in a remand home. The result of that was that on the following morning when she was brought back into the witness box she agreed to give evidence . . .

More sympathetic treatment was given to a 15-year-old boy who recently refused to testify against two youths who were accused of assaulting and robbing him. The judge told him that:

. . . he was not entitled 'to just stand there and say you don't want to give evidence. You are not going to be thrown into a cell and tortured, but you have caused a great deal of public money to be expended and it is now your duty to give evidence'. He conditionally discharged him and ordered the jury to enter 'Not Guilty' verdicts . . . (*The Independent*, 29 March 1992.)

The compellability of a child witness is limited, however, in two ways. First, a witness, whether child or adult, is only 'compellable' in the limited sense that, once brought to court, his or her refusal to answer questions is punishable as a criminal offence. If a child is below the age of criminal responsibility—which is 10 in England, eight in Scotland—no sanction exists to punish his refusal. Secondly, the courts in both England and Scotland have the power to excuse a witness if they consider his or her attendance would not serve the ends of justice. In both jurisdictions there are decisions which permit this to be done where a litigant, wishing to create a diversion, attempted to call a long series of witnesses who knew nothing about the matter in hand (*Baines* [1909] 1 KB 258; *McDonald* v *H.M. Advocate* 1989 SCCR 165.

In England, recent case law goes considerably further. In one case, involving adult witnesses, it was held to be a proper ground for quashing a witness summons that the witness was hostile to the party trying to call him, and hence unlikely to say anything that would further his case (*R* v *Marylebone JJ ex parte Gatting and Emburey* (1990) 154 JP 549). And in *R* v *B County Council ex parte P* [1991] 1 WLR 221, the Court of Appeal upheld the refusal of magistrates to issue a witness summons at the behest of the father of a teenage girl who was the object of care proceedings. These had been begun because she had accused her father of sexually abusing her. The County Council were proposing to use hearsay evidence of what she had said to others, as is possible in civil proceedings (see page 146), and the father wanted her compelled to come to court to give oral testimony. The Court of Appeal said that the court below had a discretion to refuse to grant an order compelling a witness to attend if it considered it to be an abuse of process: and that the order in this case had been properly refused, partly because it was not necessary to call the girl when her account could be put before the court using hearsay evidence, and partly because, if her father were called, she would be his witness and he would therefore be unable to cross-examine her to try to get her to change her story. The Court of Appeal also thought the order was rightly refused in the light of the court's statutory duty, in this type of case, to consider the welfare of the child.

NOTES

1. From *White*, Old Bailey Sessions Papers, No. VIII Part II, 11 September 1786:

THOMAS ATKINS called.
Mr Garrow: How old are you?—Twenty-one.
   Does thee know the nature of an oath?—Yes.
   Can you read?—No, Sir, I be not no scholar.
   You do not know what an oath binds you to do?—No, I think not.
Mr Garrow: I object to him.
Court: Did you never learn your catechism?—No, Sir.
   Do you know whether it is a right or a wrong thing to tell stories?—Yes.
   What will become of you if you tell stories?—I shall come to the gallows.
   Have you never been taught any thing else if you are a bad boy and tell stories?—No, Sir.
   Was you never at school?—No never.
Mr Garrow: My Lord, it is the perception of moral good and evil that makes him a competent witness: he must be able to know what the solemnity of a Christian oath is.
Court: Did you ever hear whether there is another world?—No, Sir.
   Did you ever take an oath before a justice?—No.
   Do you know whether there is a God Almighty?—Yes.
   You believe there is?—Yes.
   Have you ever heard where people go to that live bad, and tell stories?—No.
   How many miles do you live from London?—Thirty six.
Mr Garrow: My Lord, I object to his being sworn, if a man says he is an Atheist, and does not believe that there is a God, but believes that we made ourselves, and that the world formed itself out of chaos, would your Lordship swear such a man on the Christian testament?
Court: I will hear some other witnesses; I may ask him some questions after the trial.

2. The decision in *Hayes* was affirmed by the Court of Appeal in 1983 (*Campbell* [1983] Crim LR 174) and again in 1989 (*X, Y and Z* (1990) 91 Cr

App R 36). Yet surprisingly trial judges sometimes overlook it. In a much-publicised case at Exeter Crown Court in 1988 a judge refused to allow a 10-year-old girl to give sworn evidence because of her lack of religious knowledge—with the result, as the law then stood, that the prosecution case collapsed (*The Times*, 2 March 1988).

3. The Irish provision is the Criminal Evidence Act 1992, s. 27(1): 'Notwithstanding any enactment, in any criminal proceedings the evidence of a person under 14 years of age may be received otherwise than on oath or affirmation if the court is satisfied that he is capable of giving an intelligible account of events which are relevant to those proceedings'. This provision is also superior to the English provision in that it goes on to provide that the same applies to adult witnesses who are mentally handicapped.

4. The converse of this question is whether the police can lawfully question a willing child whose parents refuse consent. It is suggested that they can. Parents, at least in England, have no right to sue for interference with parental authority (*F* v *Wirrall Metropolitan Council* [1991] Fam 69). But if a child who is too young to know what he is consenting to is taken to the police station, this might theoretically enable him, through his parents, to sue for false imprisonment.

CHAPTER FIVE

The accusatorial system

Part I

Accusatorial and Inquisitorial Systems

GENERAL

It is generally accepted that there are two main systems of trial in the civilised world: the accusatorial (alias adversarial) and the inquisitorial. In an accusatorial system each side presents a case before a court the function of which is limited to deciding who has won. The judges have nothing to do with the preliminary investigations, give no help to either side in presenting its case, and take no active steps to discover the truth, which emerges—or so the theory goes—from the clash of conflicting accounts. As Lord Justice-Clerk Thomson once said, 'Like referees at boxing contests they see that the rules are kept and count the points' (*Thomson* v *Glasgow Corporation* 1961 SLT 237). In an inquisitorial system, on the other hand, the court is viewed as a public agency appointed to get to the bottom of the disputed matter. The court takes the initiative in gathering information as soon as it has notice of the dispute, builds up a file on the matter by questioning all those it thinks may have useful information to offer—including, in a criminal case, the defendant—and then applies its reasoning powers to the material it has collected in order to determine where truth lies.

It is the accusatorial theory which predominates in both parts of Britain, and the British are conditioned to believe that the accusatorial system is self-evidently fair and rational, and the inquisitorial system is self-evidently wrong. Yet historically it was the accusatorial system that was the irrational method. The accusatorial system has its origins in the pre-rational world of ordeals, when the method of trial was for one of the parties to accuse the other, whereupon the court decreed that one or other should be floated in water, or burnt in the hand with a hot iron, or made to swallow a 'cursed morsel' with a feather in it, to enable God to show whose cause was just. When the Church withdrew its support for ordeals in 1215 this caused a general problem throughout Europe. The English and the Scots kept to the traditional pattern, but replaced the judgment of God with a group of neighbours called to give their *verdict* on the matter: that is, the neighbours were compelled to take an oath, and say whose cause was just, on the basis of their local knowledge if they had any, or their hunch if they did not. The Continental countries, on the other hand, moved from ordeals to a system under which the State appointed an inquisitor to find out the truth of the matter by asking questions and applying his powers of reason to the answers—on the face of it a far more rational way of doing justice. Over the intervening years, however, the accusatorial improved and became rational when the jury developed into an independent group of assessors who learnt the facts from witnesses called by the parties to tell them, and the inquisitorial systems degenerated when the inquisitors took to torturing defendants in order to overcome their reluctance to answer questions: a gruesome development which led many contemporary writers on the Continent to praise the humanity of our system by comparison with their own, so giving rise to the belief, still firmly held by Britons, that the accusatorial system is 'the envy of the world'.

The accusatorial system, as understood in England and Scotland, has given rise to a method of trial which has a number of distinctive features. As far as the defendant is concerned, the main one is that he is not subjected to an official interrogation at the hands of the court (although of course he may be interrogated by the police). As far as the witnesses other than the defendant are concerned the most important are the following:

(a)   The trial consists of a 'day in court', at which all the evidence must be produced orally and in one continuous presentation. In the inquisitorial systems, where it is seen as the job of the court to collect the evidence, there is no difficulty about the idea of the court gathering the evidence in little oral helpings over a period of time, and then sitting down to study the resulting file; but this notion fits ill with the idea of a court which takes no part in the collection of the evidence, and is presented with 'a case' which it is meant to evaluate with a fresh mind.

(b)   Witnesses are called and adversarially examined by the parties, and not by the court. The examination of each witness takes place in two stages: first he is 'examined in chief' by the party calling him, in the course of which that party tries to elicit evidence favourable to his case, and then he is 'cross-examined' by the other side, who try to elicit evidence damaging to it, and failing that, to dent his credibility. This is very different from what happens in France and Germany, for example, where the witnesses are called by the court, and examined by the presiding judge from what is—or is supposed to be—a position of neutrality.

(c)   The witnesses for each side are expected to give their evidence in the presence of the other. This must necessarily be so, because the other side must know what their opponent's witnesses said in order to know what questions to ask them in cross-examination. In criminal trials, where until comparatively recent times most defendants had to conduct their defence in person because they had no lawyers, this has traditionally meant that the prosecution witnesses must give their evidence in the presence of the accused. (In England, this rule depends on case law, but in Scotland it has had a statutory basis since 1587 (Macphail 1987, sect. 20.41).)

(d)   The trial takes place in open court, to which the public and the press have access. The origin of this was probably not so much high principle as the fact that the courts were originally also the local assemblies in which all kinds of public business were conducted; but nowadays the practice is usually said to be essential to preserve the quality of justice. 'It keeps the judge himself while trying under trial' (Bentham 1790). In 1913 the House of Lords ruled that all courts are bound to sit in public except where there is an explicit law permitting a particular court to do otherwise (*Scott* v *Scott* [1913] AC 417).

THE CONSTITUTIONAL POSITION

In some countries, certain minimum rights for litigants are guaranteed by the Constitution—and sometimes these are aspects of the accusatorial system. This is particularly so in the USA. The Fifth Amendment provides, among other things, that 'No person shall . . . be compelled in any criminal case to be a witness against himself', and among other guarantees the Sixth Amendment provides that in all criminal prosecutions the accused shall enjoy the right to a 'public trial, by an impartial jury' and the right 'to be confronted with the witnesses against him'. These constitutional rights are not absolute in the sense that there can never be any exceptions to them, because some exceptions must be made in the face of competing constitutional rights; but they are legal absolutes in the sense that it is not open to any US judge, or even to any US legislature, to make exceptions to them just because it seems sensible and fair to do so. If an exception is made, it is liable to be challenged as unconstitutional—as has happened a number of times where attempts have been made to protect child witnesses from the full rigour of the accusatorial system. Thus some attempts to exclude the public when children are giving evidence have fallen foul of the Sixth Amendment requirement of a 'public trial' (Myers 1987a, sect. 7.6), and over the years a number of attempts to alter the arrangement of the courtroom to spare a child witness in a sex case the ordeal of having to give evidence within sight of the defendant have been struck down as violating the defendant's Sixth Amendment right to 'be confronted with the witnesses against him'—as in the Californian case where a trial was overturned on appeal because a magistrate had allowed a five-year-old child to turn her chair away from the defendant (*Herbert* v *Superior Court* (1981) 117 Cal App 3d 661).

In recent years, the 'confrontation' issue has come before the US Supreme Court on no less than three occasions. In *Coy* v *Iowa* (1988) 108 S Ct 2798, at the defendant's trial for a sexual assault two 13-year-old girls were permitted to give evidence from behind a translucent screen which blocked out their view of him whilst giving him a rather fuzzy view of them. By a majority of six to two the judges of the Supreme Court quashed the defendant's conviction, holding that the defendant's right of 'confrontation' means confrontation face-to-face, in which the witnesses see him as well as he sees them; some of the majority judges were prepared to accept the possibility of an exception to the confrontation requirement in a case where it could be shown by evidence that 'confrontation' would cause undue distress to the particular child in question: others were not prepared to be flexible even to this limited extent. Two years later the Supreme Court back-tracked in *Maryland* v *Craig* (1990) 110 S Ct 3157, where it was held constitutional to allow a child to give evidence through a live video link, if it could be shown that giving evidence in the presence of the defendant would upset the child so badly that she would be unable to communicate. Once again it was a decision by a majority, this time of five to four. The judgments in these cases leave a number of matters in doubt, and have spawned a huge amount of legal commentary (e.g. Vaillancourt 1990, Cecchetini-Whaley 1992). Then in 1992 the Supreme Court—to the surprise of many lawyers—held that despite the 'confrontation requirement', in a case where the child did not give evidence the court could properly convict on the basis of a collection of hearsay statements, each of which was admissible under some exception to the hearsay rule (*White* v *Illinois* 116 S Ct L Ed 2nd 851). In Canada, too, there are doubts about how far the measures adopted to shield child witnesses from the worst rigours of the accusatorial system are compatible with the Canadian Charter (Graham 1990).

In Britain, by contrast, there is no question of rules of procedure and evidence being held unconstitutional, because there is no written constitution. In theory, any aspect of the accusatorial system could be swept away by Parliament, or even by the judges in a court decision if that feature of the system was based on previous court decisions rather than an Act of Parliament. In practice, however, any changes would have to conform to the European Convention on Human Rights, although this is not directly binding on our courts.

The European Convention does not give the same unqualified support to the accusatorial system as is provided by the Constitution of the USA. Thus Article 6(1) provides that everyone is entitled to a 'public hearing' for the determination of his civil rights and obligations and of any criminal charge against him, but qualifies the right as follows:

> Judgment shall be pronounced publicly but the press and public may be excluded from all or part of the trial in the interests of morals, public order or national security in a democratic society, where the interests of juveniles or the protection of the private life of the parties so require, or to the extent strictly necessary in the opinion of the court in special circumstances where publicity would prejudice the interests of justice.

Thus there could be no Convention-based objections to a rule requiring the court to be cleared when a child is giving evidence.

Article 6(3) guarantees the defendant in a criminal case a number of minimum rights, one of which is the right 'to examine or have examined the witnesses against him and to obtain the attendance and examination of witnesses on his behalf under the same terms as witnesses against him'. Several decisions of the European Court of Human Rights (ECHR) have condemned convictions obtained on the basis of out-of-court statements by witnesses whom the defendant had no chance to challenge (*Unterpertinger* v *Austria* (1986) Series A No 110; *Kostovski* v *The Netherlands* (1989) Series A No 166);

Delta v *France* (1990) Series A No 191). In the last of these, a French court was held to have violated the Convention by convicting a man of a robbery in the Paris metro on the basis of identifications made at the police station by the 16-year-old victim and her friend, neither of whom had later given evidence. However, the 'right to examine or have examined the witnesses against him' is plainly something very different from the right to 'eyeball' witnesses while they are trying to give live evidence at a public hearing. In the *Delta* case, reaffirming what the court had said in earlier cases, the ECHR emphasised that the Convention does not enable the defendant to insist on the witness being brought to court to give live evidence. The prosecution, they said, can make use of written statements obtained from witnesses pre-trial, provided the defendant had 'an adequate and proper opportunity to challenge and question [the] witness against him, either at the time the witness made his statement or at some later stage of the proceedings'. Furthermore, from remarks the ECHR made in another case, the Convention would probably not be broken if a court convicted partly on the out-of-court statement of a witness whom the defendant had had no opportunity to confront or question, if this had been genuinely impossible to arrange (*Asch* v *Austria* (1991) Series A No 203). It also seems likely that the right to 'examine or have examined the witnesses against him' under Article 6(3) of the Convention is satisfied not only by allowing the defendant or his counsel to put questions to the witnesses, as in Britain, but also by the system in many European countries under which the judge or some other court official puts questions to them at the request of the defence. (The full text of Article 6 is set out in Note (1) at the end of this chapter.)

In Britain, not only are the main features of the accusatorial system virtually unprotected by constitutional guarantees: the courts are ready, when they think it necessary, to permit significant departures from it. Thus although in the ordinary law-courts the parties usually call the witnesses and examine them, special tribunals sometimes adopt the inquisitorial method under which the chairman does the questioning (see *R* v *Commission for Racial Equality, ex parte Cottrell & Rothon* [1980] 1 WLR 1580). In England, a number of deviations from accusatorial practice are also made in wardship proceedings, which 'are really inquiries and not adversarial proceedings', as Hollings J put it in a recent case (*Re A (Minors: Child Abuse: Guidelines)* [1991] 1 WLR 1026). And even in the ordinary law-courts, where the parties examine the witnesses, the judge has the right to ask supplementary questions. In England (though not in Scotland) the judge in a criminal case even has the power, at one time widely used, to call witnesses whom the parties have failed to call. Indeed, as we explain below, there are big exceptions to all the main features of the accusatorial system.

When we look at the foreign systems that we class as 'inquisitorial' we find the converse of this is true. Many of them incorporate a number of the features commonly regarded as the hallmarks of the accusatorial system. In Germany, where the witnesses are usually examined by the presiding judge, it is possible for the defendant in a criminal case to conduct a cross-examination (although he very rarely does). In France and the other countries where the criminal courts take an active part in gathering the evidence at a session of pre-trial questioning conducted by a *juge d'instruction*, the tribunal that finally decides on guilt or innocence on the basis of the evidence so collected is separate from the one which carried out the collection process. In Scandinavia it is the parties, not the judges, who ask the questions—and for this reason Scandinavian lawyers, to the surprise of many British lawyers, usually consider themselves to have an accusatorial system.

From all this two things follow. First, it is an over-simplification to talk about accusatorial and inquisitorial systems as if they are mutually exclusive. In fact all systems have ingredients drawn from both ideas, the final flavour depending only on the mix. Secondly, it is not a convincing objection to any proposed reform to say that it 'flies in the face of the accusatorial system'. In each case the real question must be this: Given the other features of the system which remain untouched, would this proposal prevent the litigant getting a fair deal?

THE ACCUSATORIAL SYSTEM IN THE CASE OF CHILD WITNESSES

The author Anthony Trollope, who had experience of giving evidence in England, wrote this famous purple passage about the sufferings of a witness:

> A witness in a court of law has no protection. He comes there unfed, without hope of guerdon, to give such assistance to the State in repressing crime and assisting justice as his knowledge in the particular case may enable him to afford; and justice, in order to ascertain whether his testimony be true, finds it necessary to subject him to torture. One would naturally imagine that an undisturbed thread of clear evidence would be best obtained from a man whose position was made easy and whose mind was not harassed, but this is not the fact; to turn a witness to good account, he must be badgered this way and that until he is nearly mad; he must be made a laughing-stock for the court; his very truths must be turned into falsehoods, so that he may be falsely shamed . . . he must be made to feel that he has no friend near him, that the world is all against him; he must be confounded till he forgets his right hand from his left, till his mind be turned into chaos, and his heart into water, and then let him give his evidence. What will fall from his lips when in his wretched collapse must be of special value, for the best talents of practised forensic heroes are daily used to bring it about and no member of the Humane Society interferes to protect the wretch. (*The Three Clerks*; quoted in C. P. Harvey, *The Advocate's Devil*, 1958.)

Polemical as these words may seem, it is common to find similar feelings expressed by those who have gone through the experience of giving evidence. Many witnesses are embarrassed at having to tell their tale in open court, find the adversarial process of examination and cross-examination stops them telling their story fully and coherently, and are very upset when their cross-examiner accuses them of telling lies.

It is well known that the features of the accusatorial system that make it stressful and difficult for adult witnesses to give their evidence cause even greater problems when the witnesses are children. As long ago as 1925 a Departmental Committee said:

> We have had many cases brought to our notice in which a child or young person has been overcome with distress or fright in giving evidence at the trial and has broken down or even fainted. The result of this distress has sometimes been that no evidence could be obtained and the case has consequently been lost or has had to be withdrawn. (Departmental Committee on Sexual Offences against Young Persons 1925, Cmnd. 2561 para. 66.)

The first difficulty stems from the insistence on live evidence at trial, which inevitably means there is a period of waiting while the child has the prospect of giving evidence hanging over his head. A recent study of child sexual abuse trials in England showed that the period between the defendant's arrest and charge and the final trial ranged from four months to 26, with an average wait of $10\frac{1}{2}$ months (Davies and Noon 1991). (See also chapter 13.) If the child must wait for months to testify about something really serious, like being kidnapped, raped or buggered, or witnessing the murder of a parent this delay is very bad for the child. Common sense suggests, and psychiatrists confirm, that for a child to get over some horrible and highly traumatic event he or she must first be got to face up to what has happened—usually by talking it through with someone—and then be induced to put it behind him so that it no longer continues to occupy his mind (Bentovim et al. 1988). Yet if the child is waiting to give evidence about it, these are the very things he or she cannot be allowed to do. If he discusses the incident too much with others his evidence becomes contaminated, and if he forgets the incident he has no evidence to give at all. So he must keep it fresh in his mind, at the cost of what may be considerable psychiatric harm. The Scottish case of *Maine and McRobb* provides an extreme example. A child of two was abducted and tortured by sexual sadists, and an (unsuccessful) attempt was made to get her to give oral evidence at the trial of the offenders four months later. It was very harrowing. Her father told the court: 'Last night I spent six hours with my daughter. She went through the whole thing again last night. We were at the stage of calling a doctor.' (*Press and Journal*, 25 June 1979). In chapter 1 we described a case in which the stress of waiting to give evidence induced a girl of eight to make a suicide attempt. The delay may matter little from the child's point of view if the case is something minor like a none-too-serious motoring offence: but then there is the further problem that all witnesses' memories fade with the passage of time, and it is widely assumed, and is probably the case (see chapter 11), that children's memories fade faster than those of adults—at least for matters which fail to make much impact on them at the time. In recent years, the problem of delay has been officially recognised, but it is far from clear that the various official exhortations that have been issued have actually speeded these cases up (Plotnikoff 1990).

Secondly, the experience of an adversarial cross-examination is often especially stressful for children. Adults may (or may not!) be mature enough to see the need for their evidence to be tested by a defence lawyer 'putting it to them' that they are telling lies. For a young child it is often confusing and distressing: confusing, because she thought the adult world was on her side when the authorities at first believed her, and she now thinks the adult world has turned to disbelief; distressing, particularly for the truthful child, because for a child to be falsely accused of telling lies is one of the more stressful things that can happen to her (see chapter 13). The following account of her courtroom experience was sent to Esther Rantzen at 'That's Life!' by a woman who as a child was indecently assaulted in a cinema:

> However, this experience was not as frightening or as upsetting as the time I had giving evidence in the magistrates' court. I was accused of lying, fabrication and made to feel as though I was the accused and not an innocent nine-year-old victim. . . . The defence lawyer treated me roughly as though I was 19 instead of nine-years-old, shouting at me, muddling me, confusing me. I hated him and still do for the way he treated me. The trouble is that after 23 years I still have horrible dreams now and then—not about the incident at the cinema, but of the court appearance I made.

Thirdly, children are often very distressed by seeing the defendant:

> In a recent case when an accused exercised his right to question a small girl she appeared to realise his presence in court for the first time, and dived screaming under the clerk's desk where she remained for the rest of the proceedings (Magistrates' Association 1962).

> A little girl of 11 experienced a total breakdown when she was asked to point out the man who attacked her—the following day, the court was informed that psychiatric treatment had to be arranged for her (Adler 1987, pp. 51–2).

In this sort of situation the consequence is often that the child is unable to give any evidence at all:

> At the age of seven I was indecently assaulted by a lad who was known to our family. Trying to explain to my parents was hard but to stand up in court and explain was impossible. He sat there watching me all the time. Of course he got away with it like so many do. (Letter to 'That's Life!')

Fourthly, children, even more than adults, find it embarrassing and off-putting to have to tell their tale in front of a large crowd, including not only lawyers, court officials and the jury, but representatives of the press and the general public:

> It begins in a small room where one has the one-to-one chat with the first and only person you think you have to tell. Gradually you slowly, very slowly, tell all, of course the woman being caring and friendly makes it

easier. No one, but no one tells you that there are more people, hundreds more. Well that's what it seemed like and the devil himself there. . . . you just cannot speak the same in front of all those people as you did to one person. You aren't sure what's going on, there's one man that seems very nice, asking you quietly when, where and how. You try to do your best and answer him because he's nice, . . . but find it very hard. Oh, it's so embarrassing what he's asking you in front of all those people. (Letter to 'That's Life!')

Nor, for some, is the experience made easier when part of the crowd is clad in what to childish eyes is most peculiar dress (see chapter 13).

When, as all too often happens, something goes wrong during the trial, the proceedings may be aborted and the trial begun again. When this happens, our insistence on oral evidence means the child has to be put through the ordeal of giving evidence a second time. In a recent English case of which an MP sent us details, the first trial was stopped after the child had given evidence because it had become clear that the defendant should have been charged with buggery, not rape; the second trial had to be stopped because one of the jurors, perhaps understandably, collapsed; and in consequence, a nine year-old girl had to give her sordid and distressing evidence, in public, and in the presence of the defendant, three times over.

These difficulties with the adversarial system have led to its being modified in a number of ways in an attempt to make it more suitable for children.

Part II
Modifications to the accusatorial system to cope with children's evidence

TAKING EVIDENCE IN ADVANCE OF TRIAL

Criminal proceedings
In criminal proceedings in both England and Scotland children are usually expected to give their evidence live at trial.

In England, however, there is a little-used procedure which in theory permits the evidence of a child under 14 to be taken in advance of trial. It is laid down by ss. 42 and 43 of the Children and Young Persons Act 1933, the cumbersome terms of which are these:

42.—(1) Where a justice of the peace is satisfied by the evidence of a duly qualified medical practitioner that the attendance before a court of any child or young person in respect of whom any of the offences mentioned in the First Schedule to this Act is alleged to have been committed would involve serious danger to his life or health, the justice may take in writing the deposition of the child or young person on oath (2), and shall thereupon subscribe the deposition and add thereto a statement of his reason for taking it and of the day when and place where it was taken, and of the names of the persons (if any) present at the taking thereof.

(2)   The justice taking any such deposition shall transmit it with his statement —

(a)   if the deposition relates to an offence for which any accused person is already committed for trial, to the proper officer of the court for trial at which the accused person has been committed; and

(b)   in any other case, to the clerk of the court before which proceedings are pending in respect of the offence.

43.   Where, in any proceedings in respect of any of the offences mentioned in the First Schedule to this Act, the court is satisfied by the evidence of a duly qualified medical practitioner that the attendance before the court of any child or young person in respect of whom the offence is alleged to have been committed would involve serious danger to his life or health, any deposition of the child or young person taken under . . . this Part of this Act, shall be admissible in evidence either for or against the accused person without further proof thereof if it purports to be signed by the justice by or before whom it purports to be taken:

Provided that the deposition shall not be admissible in evidence against the accused person unless it is proved that reasonable notice of the intention to take the deposition has been served upon him and that he or his counsel or solicitor had, or might have had if he had chosen to be present, an opportunity of cross-examining the child or young person making the deposition.

[The words left out are 'the Indictable Offences Act 1848, or'. They add nothing to the meaning of the section because that Act has been repealed.]

An identical provision exists in Northern Ireland in ss. 61 and 62 of the Children and Young Persons (Northern Ireland) Act 1968.

In one sense these provisions are broad, because they apply in the magistrates' courts as well as in the Crown Court. But in other respects their scope is strictly limited. First, there is the obvious limitation that they may only be used where the defence were given the chance to conduct a cross-examination at the time the deposition was taken. Secondly, there is the less obvious limitation that the procedure is only available where someone is on trial for one of the offences listed in sch. 1 to the Children and Young Persons Act 1933. This list (which is set out in note (3) at the end of this chapter) covers most of the serious offences of which children are likely to be the victims, but fails to cover many crimes of which a child might be terrified to give evidence in open court—the murder of a parent, for example, or an arson attack which burnt the family home to the ground. Thirdly—and more seriously—the sections are limited to the case where a court appearance by the child would involve 'serious danger to his life or health'. Lastly, and most anomalously, they do not seem to apply where the child is unable to give evidence, not because his health is frail, but because he is actually dead.

Nowadays it seems to be generally assumed that 'serious danger to life or health' is limited to the risk of purely physical harm, and that the risk of psychiatric damage, however serious, will not do. This was the assumption of the Ingleby Committee on Children and Young Persons, which in 1960 recommended a change of wording to bring injury to mental health within the provisions (Cmnd 1191, para. 261). From their Parliamentary history, however, it seems that the sections were meant to cover the risk of mental as well as physical injury, and at the time they were enacted no one doubted this (Spencer and Tucker 1987). If the question came before a court today there is reason to think that psychiatric harm would indeed be held sufficient. In the notable case of *Bourne* [1939] 1 KB 687, Macnaghten J had to interpret the scope of a statute which permitted a foetus to be killed 'for the purpose of preserving the life of the mother', and he said this included the case where 'the probable consequence of the continuance of the pregnancy will be to make the woman a physical *or mental* wreck'.

Like various other changes in the law of evidence, ss. 42 and 43 are the result of public pressure brought to bear by the NSPCC. They were first enacted in the Prevention of Cruelty to Children (Amendment) Act 1894, and when introducing the provisions Sir Richard Webster—a prominent barrister and NSPCC supporter who later became Lord Alverstone, Chief Justice of England—explained they were meant to allow the evidence of a child who was too badly injured to come to court to be used at the trial of the person who had abused him. The original clauses in the Bill would have made the procedure available wherever a court appearance would be 'injurious or dangerous to [the child's] health', and would have made the child's deposition admissible whether or not the defence were given a chance to attend and cross-examine. The stricter formula of 'serious danger to his life or health', and the requirement that the defence be given the chance of cross-examining at the time the deposition is taken, were added to placate opposition to the clause which was led by a Member of Parliament who was a barrister (Spencer and Tucker 1987).

The procedure laid down by these sections has been very little used. We have found no written record of its use and we have been told of only one attempt to use it—and this failed because the child was young and the justices' clerk pointed out that he would fail the competency requirement as interpreted in *Wallwork* (1958) 42 Cr App R 153 (see chapter 4). At first sight this disuse seems odd, because, as we explain in chapter 14, broadly similar provisions are widely used in other jurisdictions, including many in the English-speaking world.

No doubt much of the problem is the stringent conditions that must be met before ss. 42 and 43 are available. But it is likely that an equally off-putting factor is the strength of the oral tradition of justice, and a feeling shared by advocates and judges that a written transcript of an interview is a poor thing indeed, because it does not enable the court to listen to the witness's tone of voice and see his or her demeanour when giving evidence. This view was echoed by the Departmental Committee in 1925, which said:

Save in . . . exceptional circumstances, we are convinced that it is necessary for the child to give evidence in court. A written statement is much less impressive than oral evidence. It is far less likely to carry conviction to the mind of the court or jury, especially when they know that the child could itself give evidence before them. (Departmental Committee on Sexual Offences against Young Persons 1925, Cmnd. 2561 para. 58.)

As might be expected in provisions that were enacted in 1894, ss. 42 and 43 are limited to depositions taken in writing, and do not provide for 'video-depositions'. It is possible that if they were amended to cover taped depositions, which would permit the court to see and hear the child, this would breathe some life into the procedure. With this in mind, in 1988 Mrs Llin Golding MP tried to amend the Criminal Justice Bill by adding a clause making the necessary alterations to ss. 42 and 43. It is difficult to see what rational ground there could have been for opposing this amendment, given that these sections already permit a written record of the judicial examination to be put in evidence, and that a videotape is obviously a much superior form of record: yet the government blocked the amendment (Parl. Deb., Standing Committee H, 22 March 1988, cols 753–6)—and did so when she tried again during the debates on what became the Criminal Justice Act 1991 (Spencer 1991).

As was explained in chapter 2, a trial on indictment in the Crown Court in England is preceded by committal proceedings, where the magistrates review the evidence and decide whether the prosecution have shown the defendant has a case to answer. Before 1967 the prosecutor always had to produce his witnesses for oral examination at this stage, which meant that child witnesses, like adults, always had to give their evidence in court not once but twice. This was very stressful for children, and in 1963 a section of the Children and Young Persons Act 1963 (now consolidated as s. 103 of the Magistrates' Courts Act 1980) made it possible for the child's live appearance at the committal proceedings to be replaced by a pre-prepared written statement of what he or she had to say. This was a toothless provision, because in its original form the child's out-of-court statement could not be used if the defence objected. In 1967 it was rendered virtually redundant by the enactment of a general provision—now s. 102 of the Magistrates' Courts Act 1980—permitting a written statement to replace the live evidence of any witness at committal proceedings if the other side does not object.

In 1989 the Pigot Committee said that:

In cases which involve children existing committal proceedings are irredeemably flawed. They enable defendants to subject child witnesses to all of the burdens which we have already discussed: delay, appearance in open court, cross-examination in open court, face-to-face confrontation with an alleged perpetrator and repeated and unnecessary worry about matters which may be extremely distressing or even traumatic. (Paragraph 6.6.)

Worse, they said that 'on occasions they are abused by the defence to deter witnesses from appearing at the subsequent trial or to undermine their evidence' (para. 6.4).

This was one part of the Pigot Report which the Home Office was prepared to act upon, and the Criminal Justice Act 1991 now contains two measures to avoid the need for children to give live evidence at committal proceedings.

First, where the defendant insists on having an old-style committal (see page 16 above), the defendant has now lost his right to force the prosecution to produce a child as a live witness instead of using the child's pre-recorded statement. This is achieved by s. 55(1), which amends s.103 of the Magistrates' Courts Act 1980 by removing the defendant's right to object. As amended, s. 103 applies where the witness is under 17 in a sex case, or under 14 in a case of cruelty or violence: age-limits that rise to 18 and 15 if video evidence is to be used (see chapter 6) and the witness was under 17 or under 14 when the recording was made. The 'statement' that can be used at committal can be either a written one, or a video-recording (Criminal Justice Act 1988, s. 32A(10); H (1991) 155 JP 561). However, the provision is limited to cases involving sex, cruelty or violence. Thus if the legendary Fagin were prosecuted for intimidating a gang of children to make them steal, for example, he could still insist on their making a live appearance at committal proceedings. (The text of s. 103 as amended is printed as note (4) at the end of this chapter.)

The second and more radical change is contained in s. 53 of the Criminal Justice Act 1991, which enables the Director of Public Prosecutions to issue a 'notice of transfer' which bypasses committal proceedings altogether, so that the trial starts, without preliminaries, in the Crown Court. The procedure for 'notices of transfer' is set out in Schedule 6 of the Act, and a Practice Direction ([1992] 1 WLR 838). The defendant who finds his case whisked straight into the Crown Court by this method has the right to ask a judge to review the case in advance of trial, and dismiss the proceedings if he thinks that 'the evidence would not be sufficient for a jury properly to convict him' (Sched. 6, para. 5(2)). When the judge hears such an application, oral evidence may be called if he grants leave: but leave to call a child victim or witness may not be given (Sched. 6 para. 5(5)), and the judge must decide on the basis of their out-of-court statements. The procedure for 'notices of transfer', like s. 103 of the Magistrates' Courts Act, is limited to cases of sex, violence and cruelty, and the age-limits are also the same. However, in one respect it is more restrictive, because whereas s. 103 applies to any child witness in such a case, the 'notice of transfer' procedure may be used only where there is ' . . . a child who is alleged (i) to be a person against whom the offence was committed; or (ii) to have witnessed the commission of the offence' (Criminal Justice Act 1991, s. 53(1)(b)). It is not difficult to think of circumstances where, because of this phraseology, the procedure would not be available to help a frightened child: for example, where D is prosecuted for murdering his child P, and his other children did not see him do it, but can give evidence of his brutality to P on earlier occasions. Not for the first time, fussy and over-detailed drafting ends up leaving tiresome holes.

In many other legal systems, including some within the accusatorial tradition, the evidence of children in criminal cases is taken in advance of trial: either routinely, or exceptionally in cases where a live court appearance would be difficult or impossible (see chapter 14). In civil cases this is also generally done, even in England—as we explain later in this chapter. Mindful of this, the Pigot Committee put forward as its main recommendation that this should become the practice in England. Video technology, they said, enabled this to be done in a way which ensured the virtues of oral evidence were preserved.

The scheme they proposed is most easily explained with the help of a diagram (Figure 5.1).

The Pigot Committee proposed that when an alleged offence comes to official notice, the child should be informally interviewed, once, under cooperative arrangements between the police and the local social services department. The interview would be carried out by a police officer, or a social worker, or both, or by some other suitable person, depending on the circumstances of the case. The interviewer should be trained, and follow an official code of practice. This interview should be videotaped. If the child at interview accused someone of an offence, and the police were thinking in terms of criminal proceedings, the next stage would usually be to invite that person to view the tape at the police station. At the subsequent trial, if there was one, the videotape of the original interview would be admissible in evidence, and would replace the child's evidence-in-chief, unless a judge ruled it inadmissible because he felt that it was 'more prejudicial than probative'. Thus if the police decided to prosecute having interviewed the suspect and shown him the tape, the next step would be to show the tape of the initial interview to a judge to determine the question of admissibility. The defence would be allowed to see the videotape, and would be able at this point to require a cross-examination. This would take place before a judge in chambers, and be done with as much informality as possible. The only people present would be the judge, prosecution and defence counsel, the child, and the child's 'support person'. The defendant would not be physically present, but would be able to watch the proceedings from an adjoining room by means of a one-way mirror or live video link, and to communicate with his lawyer through a microphone in the lawyer's ear. The cross-examination session would also be recorded on videotape, and the tape would be shown to the court in place of the traditional live cross-examination. The cross-examination would be carried out as early as practicable, in order to reduce the stress for the child and to combat the problem of fading memory caused by delay. If further matters then came to light which the defence wished to put to the child, the judge in charge of the case would have a discretion to hold a supplementary cross-examination, under similar conditions, the tape of which would also be admissible in evidence at trial. This scheme, the Pigot Committee said, would have two advantages. First, as the child would be able to drop out of the proceedings once the second videotape had been done, it would be better for the child. Secondly, a child examined earlier and in less stressful surroundings would often give a fuller and more accurate account, and this would be in the interests of justice.

The Pigot proposal attracted widespread support. Not only did child-orientated bodies like the NSPCC support it, but it attracted favourable reactions from the legal profession. The Law Society made its support for the scheme public. When the Criminal Justice Bill was debated in Parliament, it

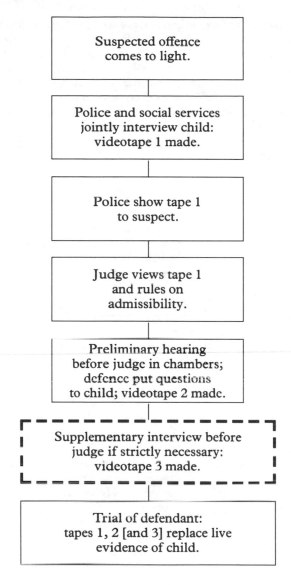

Figure 5.1 *The Pigot Committee Scheme*

was also revealed that both the Criminal Bar Association and the Council of Her Majesty's Circuit Judges were in favour of the scheme. Nevertheless, the government rejected it. The official reason given was that in practice the defence would always need to ask for a series of supplementary cross-examinations—the totality of which would be as stressful as a cross-examination live at trial. As the public debate progressed, however, it became clear that the real opponents of the scheme were in the Home Office: and that the main reason for their opposition was that they either agreed with, or were not prepared to argue with, a group of ultra-traditionalist barrister peers in the House of Lords who claimed it would undermine the position of the defendant. Their arguments were, first, that the defendant would be forced to disclose his defence ahead of trial, and secondly, a live cross-examination is more likely to force a child accuser to retract. The answer to the first objection should have been that the only defendant who stands to lose from disclosing his defence ahead of trial is the one whose defence will not stand investigation, and the answer to the second should have been that a traditional cross-examination can pressure a child to retract a true accusation as well as a false one. These points cut no ice with the Home Office, however, and in the Criminal Justice Bill 1990 it put forward an alternative scheme under which video-recorded interviews with children would be admissible in evidence in criminal proceedings, provided the child attends court for a live cross-examination. Despite the vigorous support of Lord Ackner, a Law Lord, an attempt to get the Criminal Justice Bill amended in the House of Lords so as to incorporate the whole Pigot scheme was narrowly defeated, and the Home Office scheme—explained in chapter 7—became law. So opposed was the Home Office to the idea of pre-trial examination that, as already explained, it even blocked the attempt to amend ss. 42 and 43 of the Children and Young Persons Act 1933 so that the deposition of a sick child can be video-recorded.

In addition to the little-used provisions in ss. 42 and 43 of the Children and Young Persons Act 1933, English law contains some general exceptions to the hearsay rule which could theoretically be used to enable a child's evidence to be taken in advance of trial for use in criminal proceedings. These are discussed in chapter 6.

Until recently, Scottish criminal procedure had no special power under which the evidence of a child could be taken in advance of trial. Since 1980, the High Court and the sheriff court (but not the district court) have had the power to take the evidence of any witness *on commission* in a criminal case. Where evidence is taken on commission the court of trial appoints some trusted person to act as a 'commissioner'. He or she then visits the witness together with the parties (or more probably their lawyers); each side asks the witness their questions while the commissioner presides, and a written transcript of the examination is then put before the court. In theory this procedure could be used to take the evidence of a child ahead of trial—but for various reasons (explained in the first edition of this book) in practice it is unlikely to be available. (Although in one case it was used for a witness who was extremely old: *Larry* 1991 SCCR 138.)

The Scottish Law Commission, like the Pigot Committee in England, thought there was a need to provide an effective means of enabling the evidence of a child to be taken ahead of trial. Their emphasis was different, because unlike the Pigot Committee they thought that Scottish court pro-cedure could be made sufficiently 'child-friendly' to make it unnecessary for most children to have their evidence taken out of court and in advance. However, they recognised that a live court appearance would not be possible in all cases, and they therefore proposed that 'it should be competent, as an alternative to adducing the child as a witness in open court, to take the evidence of that child on commission prior to the date of the trial or, exceptionally, during the course of the trial' (Scottish Law Commission 1990 para. 4.16). Like the Pigot Committee, they proposed that the evidence should be video-recorded. Unlike the Pigot Committee, however, they thought that such a session should normally take place later rather than sooner, and close enough to the date of the trial for the defence to know what matters they needed to put to the child in cross-examination. The Scottish Law Commission added, however, that 'There may be exceptional cases where the use of the procedure at an earlier stage might be advantageous, and we do not wish to exclude that possibility' (para. 4.13).

In 1993, this proposal was eventually enacted as section 33 of the Prisoners and Criminal Proceedings (Scotland) Act, which is as follows:

(1) . . . subject to section 35 of this Act, where a child has been cited to give evidence in a trial the court may appoint a commissioner to take the evidence of the child if —

(a) in solemn proceedings, at any time before the oath is administered to the jury;

(b) in summary proceedings, at any time before the first witness sworn;

(c) in exceptional circumstances in either solemn or summary proceedings, during the course of the trial,
application has been made to the court in that regard; but to be so appointed a person must be, and for a period of at least five years have been, a member of the Faculty of Advocates or a solicitor.

(2) Proceedings before a commissioner appointed under subsection (1) above shall be recorded by video recorder.

(3) An accused shall not, except by leave of the commissioner, be present in the room where such proceedings are taking place but shall be entitled by such means as seem suitable to the commissioner to watch and hear the proceedings.

This provision will come into effect on 1 January 1994.

Section 35 of the Act, to which this section is made subject, imposes the same limitation on this power as limits the power of the Scottish court to give permission for a child to give evidence by live video link. It may only be done:

. . . on cause shown having regard in particular to —

(a) the possible effect on the child if required to give evidence, no such application having been granted; and

(b) whether it is likely that the child would be better able to give evidence if such application were granted (Law Reform (Miscellaneous Provisions) (Scotland) Act 1990, s. 56(2)).

In considering whether to grant the application, this provision goes on to say that the court may taken account of the age and maturity of the child, the nature of the alleged offence, the nature of the evidence which the child will have to give, and the relationship (if any) between the child and the accused. The section does not expressly forbid the child to be examined a long time ahead of trial, but a very early examination is hardly possible. This is because the power to order one only arises 'where a child has been cited to give evidence'—something which happens at a fairly late stage in the preparation for the trial.

The possibility of a pre-trial examination for child witnesses in Scotland, fairly limited as it is, only came about because the government included it as part of its legislative programme to reform the law of Scotland: which is peculiar, because only the year before the same government opposed, as both impracticable and contrary to principle, the same idea when it was proposed for England.

It remains the case that children will almost always have to come to court to give their evidence live in both England and Scotland. When they do so, there is the further complication that the rules of criminal evidence on both sides of the border usually stop a party who calls a witness from putting before the court that witness's previous statements in order to explain, amplify or support what he or she succeeds in uttering in the witness-box. The rule against previous consistent statements ensures that if a child has been questioned in advance of trial, normally the only use to which this may be put is to prove her a liar if she says something different in the courtroom. This rule is subject to exceptions, however, and in England an important one is where the child's previous statement was recorded on videotape. (The rule against previous consistent statements is discussed in chapter 6, and the videotape exception in chapter 7.)

Civil procedure on both sides of the border lacks any express power for the evidence of children to be taken in advance. In theory the civil courts in both jurisdictions have almost unlimited powers to order evidence to be taken on commission for use in civil cases (Scotland: Macphail 1987, sect. 24–47 to sect. S24.48A; England: Cross 1990, p. 261). But in practice these powers are used rarely if ever for taking evidence from children. In England the problems of children having to give evidence in open court in civil proceedings—like those posed by the competency requirement—are largely avoided because the civil courts are usually willing to bend the hearsay rules in proceedings where the custody and welfare of the child is in issue, and they generally allow adults to tell them what the child has said (see chapter 6). Traditionally the civil courts in Scotland have been stricter about the hearsay rule, and in civil proceedings they usually expect to hear from the child in person. As will be explained in chapter 6, however, the hearsay rule was completely abolished for civil proceedings in Scotland by the Civil Evidence (Scotland) Act 1988; but as we also explain in chapter 6, the Scottish judges seem reluctant to follow the English practice.

In law a 'court' is a person or persons, not a building, and at common law there is no reason why the court cannot go to the witness instead of making the witness come to court. Whilst it is obviously not feasible to adjourn a full-blown jury trial and bus the participants to a child witness's home or hospital bed, a court that consists of a judge alone can occasionally take justice to the child and so relieve him of the need to attend a trial. In October 1987 there was considerable press interest when a Glasgow sheriff went to hospital to watch the behaviour of an allegedly abused child of four (*Aberdeen Evening Express,* 8 October 1987). In a similar case in February of that year, however, a sheriff refused to adjourn the court to the playroom of a children's hospital to watch and listen to a three-year-old child being talked to and played with by a child psychologist (Kearney 1987, p. 229).

AVOIDING ADVERSARIAL EXAMINATION

British lawyers generally regard the adversarial examination of witnesses as a fundamental feature of the system. Whilst it is permissible for the judge to ask supplementary questions in order to clear up ambiguities, he is usually forbidden to take over the job of examining the witnesses. If he does so, this will ground an appeal—not merely because he has demonstrated his bias by 'descending into the arena', as the saying is, but because he has deprived the parties of their basic right to have their counsel present their case in their own way. This is the position both in England (*Matthews* (1984) 78 Cr App R 23) and in Scotland (*Livingstone* 1982 SCCR 100), and the attitude prevails in civil as well as criminal cases (*Jones* v *National Coal Board* [1957] 2 QB 55). When the proposal to introduce the live television link for children (see below) was before Parliament Lord Silkin tried to move an amendment giving the court the power to nominate an examiner to question the child in place of counsel for the prosecution and defence. The government successfully resisted it: although Lord Silkin's proposal would have allowed the defence to use their own counsel for cross-examination if they wanted to, the government said that it would undermine the defendant's right to conduct an adversarial cross-examination in practice, because they might in practice feel inhibited in exercising their rights (Parl. Deb. (Lords) vol. 489 col. 267, 22 October 1987). The argument for Lord Silkin's proposal was that the traditional adversarial method of examining witnesses is inept for young and frightened children, and the objection to it amounted in effect to saying that the prosecution must continue to use this inept method lest the defence feel inhibited in using it too. When the Pigot Committee, by a majority, came out in favour of Lord Silkin's proposal it was, predictably, one of the proposals which the Home Office found unacceptable. It has nevertheless found favour in a number of other common law jurisdictions: notably in Ireland (Criminal Justice Act 1992, s. 14), and New Zealand (Evidence Act 1908, s. 23E(4)). In Italy, which went over to the adversarial examination of witnesses in the new Code of Criminal Procedure in 1988, child witnesses can still be non-adversarially examined by the judge (CCP para. 498(4)).

It is generally assumed that this tradition of examining witnesses is an ancient one, but in fact it is comparatively modern. At least in English criminal proceedings it was once the custom for the judge to examine all the witnesses,

because in most cases neither prosecution nor defence were legally represented, and there was nobody else in court competent to do it (Langbein 1978);
and it seems to have been their practice to let the witnesses tell their rambling
stories freely in their own words, rather than to ask them pointed questions
designed to get the answer the questioner desires, as is the case with adversarial
questioning today (Stephen 1883, p. 431). The modern practice grew up when
English criminal trials gradually became 'lawyerised' during the 18th century,
with barristers prosecuting and defending.

Sometimes one side will be unrepresented even today, and here the judge
still has the power to take over the examination of witnesses where one of the
parties is unrepresented and cannot play the role the adversarial system assigns
to him. Indeed he is sometimes under a duty to do so. When trying a young
defendant the youth court in England is bound by a rule that where an
unrepresented juvenile defendant starts making assertions when he should be
cross-examining, the court shall put his questions for him (Magistrates'
Courts (Children and Young Persons) Rules 1992, r. 8(3)); under this
provision, child witnesses are often examined by the court. A similar provision
in England applies in domestic proceedings in the magistrates' courts where
the parties are unrepresented (Magistrates' Courts Act 1980, s. 73). Furthermore, in any proceedings the court has the power to help out where a party is
legally represented, but the lawyer is unable to get his witness to talk. Where
the prosecution call a child witness who is dumb in the face of counsel's efforts
to examine him in-chief, the judge may try asking questions. In at least one
English trial of which we have been told, the judge allowed the prosecuting
solicitor, who was known to the child, to put questions to the child when she
was too shy to communicate with the prosecuting counsel, who was a stranger
to her; and Mr Justice Humphreys (1867–1956) used to get a woman juror 'to
let the child stand or sit next to her so that she can hold the child's hand and
then act as a sort of interpreter to and for the little one' (Humphreys 1946, p.
176). (In these situations, of course, the examination is still adversarial. The
court does not take over the whole job of examining the witness, but merely
helps one side to conduct their examination; the witness, whether child or
adult, will still be—or have been—examined by the other side as well.)

It is also worth noting that under the adversarial system in both parts of
Britain the right of a party to cross-examine his opponent's witnesses is not
absolute, but is limited in two important respects. In the first place, it is subject
to the control of the judge. In the words of Mr Justice Stephen:

The legitimate object of cross-examination is to bring to light relevant
matters of fact which would otherwise pass unnoticed. It is not unfrequently
converted into an occasion for the display of wit, and for obliquely insulting
witnesses. It is not uncommon to put a question in a form which is in itself
an insult, or to preface a question or receive an answer with an insulting
observation. This naturally provokes retorts, and cross-examination so
conducted ceases to fulfil its legitimate purpose, and becomes a trial of wit
and presence of mind which may amuse the audience, but is inconsistent
with the dignity of a court of justice, and unfavourable to the object of

ascertaining the truth. When such a scene takes place the judge is the person principally to blame. He has a right on all occasions to exercise the power of reproving observations which are not questions at all, of preventing questions from being put in an improper form, and of stopping examinations which are not necessary for any legitimate purpose. (Stephen 1883, vol. 1, pp. 435–6.)

Thus judges can, and usually do, intervene to stop child witnesses from being unduly browbeaten. (But as with all aspects of judging, some judges are better at doing this than others; and in England lay magistrates are widely said to be weaker in controlling the excesses of lawyers than are professional judges.) And secondly, there is no absolute rule that renders any and every statement inadmissible where the maker cannot be cross-examined on it. In both England and Scotland there are exceptions to the hearsay rule that permit the parties to put in evidence certain out-of-court statements made by people who cannot possibly be cross-examined on them. Furthermore, where a witness does testify at trial, what he or she said is not wiped out as evidence because it then proves impossible to cross-examine on it; as in the English case of *Stretton* (1988) 86 Cr App R 7, where the cross-examination of a mentally handicapped rape victim had to be discontinued when she began to have epileptic fits under the strain, or the Scottish case of *X* v *Y* 1945 SLT (Sh Ct) 2, where a witness under cross-examination made an even stronger implied comment on the adversarial system by dropping dead. This principle is obviously important where the witness is a young child who breaks down—as in the recent case of *Wyatt* [1990] Crim LR 343. (Of course, the fact that there has been no cross-examination is seen as affecting the weight of the evidence.)

In England and in Scotland, there is a statutory limit on how far witnesses in a sex case—whether children or adults—can be cross-examined about their sex-lives in general (Sexual Offences (Amendment) Act 1976, s. 2, *Blackstone's Criminal Practice* 7.13; Criminal Procedure (Scotland) Act 1975, ss. 141A, 141B, 346A, 346B; Macphail 1987 para. S16.10; Brown, Burman and Jamieson 1992). Although these provisions only apply to prosecutions for certain specified offences, judges tend to apply similar principles when trying sexual offences generally. There are limits, however, to how far judges feel able to protect witnesses without being unfair to the defendant. In *Funderburk* [1991] 1 WLR 587, for example, a girl of 13 gave a vivid account of losing her virginity to the defendant, who was accused of having unlawful sexual intercourse with her. The Court of Appeal said that the trial judge was wrong to refuse to allow her to be cross-examined as to whether she had had intercourse with other men; which, if she had, would have explained her sexual knowledge.

Particularly distressing for a child is where a defendant in a criminal case who is unrepresented insists on cross-examining her himself. There is no need for this to happen, because nowadays legal aid is routinely available in such a case, and accordingly the Pigot Committee proposed that unrepresented defendants should be forbidden to cross-examine child witnesses (para. 12.30). In England their recommendation was carried out by s. 55(7) of the Criminal Justice Act 1991. Like the other child-protective measures in this

Act, this provision is hedged about with detailed restrictions. It applies where (i) it is a trial for an offence of sex, violence or cruelty, (ii) the child is the alleged victim, or a witness to the commission of the offence, and (iii) the child is under 14, or in a sex case, 17: an age limit that rises to 15 or 18 if the videotape evidence is admitted under the rules explained in chapter 7. The Act does not say what is to happen if the defendant is offered counsel, but stubbornly refuses. Presumably, the judge would then offer to put the defendant's questions for him, or such as he thought it proper to be put. In Scotland, the unrepresented defendant's right to cross-examine child witnesses remains.

Civil proceedings: private law cases

Although as we have seen the normal rule is that child witnesses, like adults, are adversarially examined, some important exceptions exist in civil proceedings which are concerned with the care, welfare and upbringing of the child. Here, a contested issue is frequently what the child wants to happen next to him, rather than what someone has done to him in the past (although in practice these two issues may become entwined), and a major exception to the principle of adversarial examination is the procedures that are available to the courts to discover the wishes of the child.

At one time the courts regarded the wishes of the children as largely irrelevant, but during the course of this century their attitude radically changed. In England, s. 1 of the Children Act 1989 now lays down that in such proceedings the child's welfare shall be the court's paramount consideration, and, at the head of the list of matters which the court must consider in deciding what the child's welfare requires, puts 'the ascertainable wishes and feelings of the child concerned (considered in the light of his age and understanding)'. As Butler-Sloss LJ said in a recent case, 'In all family cases it is the duty of the court to listen to the children, ascertain their wishes and feelings and then make decisions about their future having regard to but not constricted by those wishes' (Re P (Minors) [1992] 2 FCR 681).

Usually, the judge informs herself about the wishes of children by getting the court welfare officer to interview them on her behalf (see chapter 2), but the judge has the power to question the child personally, and sometimes exercises it (Bevan 1989, sect. 3.11). Where she does so, she usually sees the child privately in chambers. This practice was first approved in wardship by the House of Lords (Re K (Infants) [1965] AC 201), and its use in other courts was approved by a decision in which the Court of Appeal said:

> It is of course often most desirable in matters of this sort that the judge hearing the case should see the children and should see them otherwise than in open court. One can well understand that in matters of this sort the children may be reluctant to express themselves freely and frankly where there is the possibility that what they say may be made known, particularly, perhaps, to their parents (H v H [1974] 1 WLR 595).

Although the judges allow themselves to do this, they have however forbidden magistrates to do the same (Re T (1974) 4 Fam Law 48). Despite the fact that one of the policy objectives of the Children Act 1989 was to unify the procedural rules which operate in the different courts that deal with family business, it seems that as a result of this decision, magistrates are still unable to see a child privately: although they can achieve nearly the same result by seeing the child in their retiring room, with the warring parents absent, provided—unlike the judge who sees a child privately—they allow the parties' lawyers to be there.

That this anomaly was not cleared up reflects the fact that there is some difference of attitude among English judges to the practice, and also between the civil servants of the various government departments who were involved in putting the Children Act together. There is a conflict here between the need to obtain the child's honest views and the usual principle in litigation that the parties should be told the evidence on which the judge decides the case, and have the chance to comment on it. Different people still have different views about which of these is more important, although Parliament might have been thought to have resolved the question by giving the 'welfare principle' pride of place in s. 1 of the Children Act. Statements of principle about when a child may be seen privately, and if so how, are conspicuously absent from the Children Act itself and from the Rules made under it; as indeed are any detailed rules about how the child's views are to be obtained (Wyld 1991). However, from the decided cases, and from discussions with a number of judges and practitioners, the following points emerge.

(1)   The judge has a discretion to see the child, not a duty. Thus in *Re R (a Minor) (Residence Order), The Times*, 3 November 1992, the Court of Appeal rejected an appeal brought against a residence order on the ground that the judge had refused to see the child.

(2)   Judges are officially discouraged from seeing children who are very young. In one case it was said that the judge should not interview children under eight (*Ingham v Ingham* [1976] LS Gaz 486).

(3)   Before seeing a child privately the judge is expected to tell the parties and the court welfare officer what he or she intends to do, and to consider their objections if they have any.

(4)   The judge is expected to see the child in chambers, with at least one other person—usually a court clerk of the same sex as the child—present; in one case, a judge was criticised by the Court of Appeal for going, on his own, to see the child at school (*L v L* [1991] FCR 547).

(5)   The judge must normally tell the parties—albeit in expurgated terms—what the child has said: and for this reason, he must not promise the child that what is said will go no further (*H v H* (1974) above); though the child's welfare remains the paramount consideration, and in very exceptional circumstances the judge can keep any information from the parties if he thinks the disclosure would be positively harmful for the child (*Re C* [1991] FCR 308; *B v B* [1992] 1 FCR 223; *Re B* [1992] 2 FCR 617; Kingham and Latham 1992).

(6)   An important question is how willing the child is to see the judge. An increasing number of judges now take the view that if a child has expressed the wish to see the judge, the child then should be seen.

In Scotland the 'welfare principle' also prevails in this area of the law by virtue of s. 3(1) of the Law Reform (Parent and Child) (Scotland) Act 1986. Although the courts are not as yet under any express statutory duty to take the child's wishes into account, they in practice try to do so. Sometimes they inform themselves of the child's wishes by exercising their various statutory powers to commission people to obtain reports (see chapter 2), but as in England, some judges will see the child privately (Macphail 1988 765–7). The practice continues despite the fact that in 1985 it was condemned as a method of resolving a dispute about a contested matter, the judges of the Second Division saying:

> . . . this departure from the recognised procedure (with its in-built rules and safeguards) of having issues of this nature determined by proof in open court . . . is fraught with difficulties, and there is no justification for substituting an inquisitorial procedure for an adversarial one even with the consent of the parties (*McDonald* v *McDonald* 1985 SLT 244).

Scottish judges who see children, like their English brethren, sometimes find that difficult questions of confidentiality arise (Ross 1991).

The judge's private interview with the child is mainly thought of as a means of informing the judge about the child's views and wishes. In practice, however, it sometimes ends up with the judge and the child discussing disputed matters of fact that lie at the heart of the case. (As it seems to have done in *Nottinghamshire County Council* v *P* [1993] 1 FCR 180. The judge, having said that one of the children in the case vehemently denied being sexually abused, added ' . . . and when I saw her in my room, equally passionately denied it'.)

Private law cases: care proceedings: children's hearings
In care proceedings in England, there is something of a movement away from the adversarial method of examining witnesses. Such proceedings were declared 'essentially non-adversary' by Lord Widgery CJ in *Humberside County Council* v *R* [1977] 1 WLR 1251, and in consequence:

> . . . the rules of evidence and procedure must be liberally construed, so that [the] court will have all the relevant information about a child necessary for making a fair and accurate decision. . . . In practice it is becoming more customary for the bench to pose its own questions, particularly to professional witnesses, and to adopt a more inquisitorial approach. (Graham Hall and Martin 1987.)

Thus if a child is called as a witness in care proceedings—which is rather unusual—the magistrates are likely to do some questioning. As well as the possibility of the child speaking to the court as a witness, there is a further opportunity for direct interaction between the child and the bench, because when the court makes or varies a care order the magistrates may wish to explain this to the child and invite questions.

In Scotland children frequently give evidence in civil proceedings when the sheriff has to resolve a dispute as to 'grounds of referral' to a children's panel (see chapter 2). In such proceedings, 'As the law now stands the adversarial framework must be accepted as being in force' (Kearney 1987, p. 217). Thus if the disputed grounds arise out of alleged cruelty to the child, for example, the theory is that the child will be examined in chief by the reporter, and then cross-examined by the parents if it is they who are opposing the referral, and the child's safeguarder (if any). But in practice sheriffs try 'to hold the balance between allowing the child's evidence to be adequately tested under cross-examination and avoiding unnecessary distress to the child' (Kearney 1987, pp. 230–1).

SUPPRESSING THE PRESENCE OF THE PERSON ACCUSED

If the child has to give live evidence at trial there are various ways of arranging things so that he or she is not oppressed by the defendant's physical presence. The court can be rearranged, by moving seats around or using screens, so that the child cannot see the defendant. A television link can be used to enable the child to give evidence from an adjoining room. Or—simplest of all—the person the child is frightened of can be removed from the court while the child gives evidence. At present, all of these methods are in use in various courts in Britain, and here it is England that has given the lead.

A particular difficulty obviously arises over identification: a child cannot, at the same time, both identify the defendant and avoid seeing him. In England this problem is avoided because the courts readily accept, as evidence that the defendant was the person involved, evidence that the victim picked someone out on an earlier occasion, plus evidence that the person then identified is the person in the dock. The Scots, however, have always felt it necessary for the victim to identify the defendant at the trial, whatever identification procedure took place beforehand. The Scottish Law Commission recommended that when fragile witnesses are involved, the Scottish courts should be permitted to follow the English practice. This recommendation was carried out to a limited extent by the Law Reform (Miscellaneous Provisions) (Scotland) Act 1990, which allows the English procedure to be used in cases where leave has been given for the child to testify using the live TV link (see page 106 below).

Screens
In England the courts held, over 70 years ago, that a judge may rearrange his court so that a child witness does not have to see the defendant. In *Smellie* (1919) 14 Cr App R 128 the defendant's 11-year-old daughter was a prosecution witness at his trial for cruelty to children, and when she gave evidence the judge made him sit on the stairs leading from the dock into the cells so that he was out of her sight. He appealed, arguing that:

> removing appellant from the dock during the hearing of the evidence of Frances invalidates the whole trial. First, because a prisoner is entitled at common law to be within sight and hearing of all the witnesses throughout

his trial; and secondly, because on a charge of this kind the effect on the minds of the jury of the removal of the prisoner from the dock . . . when his daughter is entering the witness-box is incalculable; and thirdly, that in this particular case the effect of his removal on the evidence of the little girl would be incalculable, because it was admitted that he had beaten her for stealing, and she might be inclined to say untrue things in his absence which she would not have said under the restraining influence of his presence.

Lord Coleridge J dismissed these arguments laconically:

If the judge considers that the presence of the prisoner will intimidate a witness there is nothing to prevent him from securing the ends of justice by removing the former from the presence of the latter.

At the much-publicised trial in 1986 of a doctor accused of raping an eight-year-old girl Judge Greenwood made a similar order at Chelmsford Crown Court. The child gave evidence sitting next to the judge, while the defendant left the dock and sat at the back of the court (*The Times*, 9 December 1986).

The first judge to permit the use of screens when children were giving evidence was the Common Serjeant, Judge Pigot QC, when a group of men were tried at the Old Bailey for serious sexual offences involving children in the autumn of 1987 (*The Times*, 10 October to 4 November 1987). The idea of using screens seems to have been prompted by their use at the trial of the terrorist Hindawi a year earlier (*The Times*, 10 October 1986). As screens had been used in Hindawi's case to protect the anonymity of an Israeli security officer, it is hardly surprising that defence counsel's objection that 'the defendants will be over-prejudiced in the eyes of the jury and at a grave disadvantage' was rejected when the prosecution asked for screens on the ground that five child witnesses, aged between seven and 13, would otherwise be too frightened to give evidence. In the following year, screens were used at the Old Bailey in some 100 cases (Morgan and Plotnikoff 1990), and the practice of using screens began to spread to Crown Courts outside London, and to certain magistrates' courts. At the Old Bailey an improved model was then perfected, with a television monitor and a microphone placed to enable the defendant to see and hear the child as she gave evidence on the other side of the screen (*The Independent*, 16 November 1988). Then the original case involving screens reached the Court of Appeal, where the decision in *Smellie* was followed, and the use of screens was given formal approval (*X, Y and Z* (1990) 91 Cr App R 36). From the tenor of the judgment, however, it is clear that screens are not to be used automatically, and the judge is required in each case to balance the risk of the children being too distressed to give evidence against the risk of possible prejudice against the accused arising from the fact that it has been found necessary to screen the witnesses from him. Shortly after this decision, the Home Office issued a circular encouraging magistrates' courts to make use of screens (61/1990).

Although the children who gave evidence behind the original Old Bailey screen in 1987 still broke down in tears, it seems to be generally accepted that screens considerably reduce the stress for child witnesses, and enhance the chance of getting them to tell a coherent story. However, it seems that the administrative arrangements leave something to be desired. At present it seems that some judges believe in screens and others do not, and in the absence of any court rules or practice directions on the matter it can be rather a matter of chance whether or not screens are permitted. '. . . in a case involving girls aged 11 to 14 who had been indecently assaulted, one judge granted an application for screens, but the case was then re-listed to another location where the newly assigned judge refused their use' (Morgan and Plotnikoff 1990). In 1991, a judge was vigorously criticised in the press for refusing a screen to a 16-year-old girl, the victim of a gang rape (*The Mail on Sunday*, 3 February 1991). It is also said that there is a shortage of screens, and some confusion as to whose job it is to supply them. Finally, it is left to the prosecutor to ask for them, and there are said to be some prosecutors who think that if the child is demonstrably upset at seeing the defendant this will actually strengthen their case. These teething troubles may never be sorted out, because the official position is that screens are a stop-gap measure to be used only until the live television link is more generally available (see below) (Morgan and Plotnikoff 1990).

In Scotland, as in England, the courts began to permit the use of screens without any legislative nudge from Parliament. The first case seems to have been a High Court trial in Glasgow in 1988, where Lord Murray summoned up some hospital screens from the court's first aid room after a 10-year-old girl had broken down in tears when called to give evidence against her father on a charge of attempted rape (*Glasgow Herald*, 7 October 1988). The Scottish Law Commission, however, thought that the matter should be regulated by statute (Scottish Law Commission 1990), and this was done by s. 34 of the Prisoners and Criminal Proceedings (Scotland) Act 1993, which is as follows:

> Subject to section 35 of this Act, where a child has been cited to give evidence in a trial, the court may, on application being made to it, authorise the use of a screen to conceal the accused from the sight of the child while the child is present to give evidence; but arrangements shall be made to ensure that the accused is able to watch and hear as the evidence is given by the child.

The effect of s. 35, to which this provision is subject, is to limit the power of the court to order screens—like the power to order the child's evidence to be given by live video link or on commission—to cases where it will be stressful for the child to give evidence in the normal way. For the details, see page 91 above, and page 106 below.

Live video links

A live video link, alias closed circuit television, is an arrangement under which the child is televised when giving evidence in a separate room, and the child's image and voice are transmitted to a series of television monitors in the courtroom. There are 'one-way' and 'two-way' systems. The 'one-way' merely enables the child to be seen and heard in the courtroom, whereas the 'two-way' system also televises the courtroom for the child to see and hear. In either case the communication link is 'live': the witness is televised in the act of giving evidence, and the court sees the witness's live performance, as distinct from a videotape of a previously conducted interview. The system makes no record of the evidence: although it can be adapted to do this if desired. In England, the live link was made available for child witnesses in criminal proceedings by the Criminal Justice Act 1988, in Northern Ireland by the Police and Criminal Evidence (NI) Order 1989, and in Scotland by the Law Reform (Miscellaneous Provisions) (Scotland) Act 1990. There is no legislation in either jurisdiction that expressly permits its use in civil cases, but in the absence of any law to forbid it, it could presumably be used. An English High Court judge has told the authors that he once used it in an unreported wardship case, and it has been used in several reported civil cases in which children were not involved (*Garcin* v *Amerindo Investment Advisors Ltd* [1991] 1 WLR 1140; *Henderson* v *SSB Realizations Ltd, The Independent*, 20 April 1992.

The live link originated in the USA, where the germ of the idea seems to have been the 'child-courtroom' David Libai put forward in a well-known law review article in 1969:

> The Child-Courtroom is designed to take a victim's testimony in an informal and relaxed manner, while the child can see only four persons around him: the judge, the prosecutor, the defence counsel, and the child examiner, who will all be seated in a 'judge's room', arranged in a way which contributes to the security and psychological comfort of the child. The accused, the jury and the audience should be seated behind a one-way glass, separating them from the judge's room, but enabling them to observe everything which occurs there. In this manner the defendant's right to trial by jury is secured and the jury can view the accused's demeanor while the child is testifying. In addition, the accused will have microphone and earphones by means of which he and his counsel, who is in the judge's room, will be able to communicate with each other. The proceedings are transmitted to the accused's box by suitable electronic methods which would not interfere with the accused's capacity to communicate with his counsel. (Libai 1969).

As this 'child-courtroom' would have been expensive, and when built would have prevented the room where it was from being used as a normal courtroom, it is hardly surprising that no jurisdiction in the USA adopted it. However, many of the presumed benefits of the Libai 'child-courtroom' could be obtained with less money and disruption by means of a live television link from an adjoining room, and in 1983 certain States took the lead in passing legislation to make this possible. By December 1989, the idea had been adopted in various forms in 32 States (Whitcomb 1992): although it seems that in practice it is used quite rarely, partly because of fears by prosecutors and judges that convicted defendants will challenge their outcome by invoking the 'confrontation' provision in the Constitution (see page 77 above) (Whitcomb 1992). Meanwhile a version of the scheme was introduced in Canada in 1987

(Wilson 1990), in New Zealand in 1989 (Geddis et al. 1990), and other versions have been, or are being introduced in various jurisdictions in Australia (Warner 1990, Cashmore 1990, Law Reform Commission of Western Australia 1991).

In 1986 the government introduced a Criminal Justice Bill for England. This was largely designed to implement the recommendations of the Roskill Committee (Fraud Trials Committee, 1986), one of the recommendations of which was an alteration in the law of criminal evidence to enable vital witnesses who were overseas to give their evidence in English courts by means of a live satellite television link. By then there had been widespread criticism of the rules of evidence relating to children as witnesses (see chapter 1), and in order to do something about this the government mounted a live link proposal for child witnesses upon the back of the clause which implemented the proposal for satellite links in fraud cases. The live link proposal had a mixed reception. Barbara Amiel, writing in *The Times*, feared that by indicating to the jury that the child could not face the accused in open court it would make the jury think he must have done something really dreadful, and so reverse the presumption of innocence—an argument that had already been rejected by courts in the USA (Myers 1987a, p. 406). However, most critics said the proposal did not go nearly far enough, and a determined group of Members of Parliament fought to extend the live link proposal beyond its rather narrow limits, and to have it coupled—as in the US jurisdictions which invented it—with a further reform making videotapes of pre-trial interviews admissible in evidence. The government resisted this pressure at the time, but commissioned the psychologists Graham Davies and Elizabeth Noon to study how the live link worked in practice, and also set up the Pigot Committee to consider the question of evidence by videotape. The information that Davies and Noon (1991) collected showed the live link to work quite well, and the government responded to this by introducing legislation to make it more widely available. As already explained (page 89), the government rejected the main recommendations of the Pigot Committee, but it did then introduce legislation—discussed in chapter 7—which makes videotape evidence admissible. Both changes are contained in Part III of the Criminal Justice Act 1991—which, confusingly to the reader, works by tacking new subsections on to the relevant parts of the Criminal Justice Act 1988.

The live link provision is contained in s. 32 of the Criminal Justice Act 1988, as heavily amended by s. 55 of the Criminal Justice Act 1991. In its new form, the operative part of s. 32 is as follows:

(1) A person other than the accused may give evidence through a live television link on a trial in proceedings to which subsection 1A below applies if —
(a) the witness is outside the United Kingdom; or
(b) the witness is a child, or is to be cross-examined following the admission under section 32A below of a video recording of testimony from him, and the offence is one to which subsection (2) below applies,
but evidence may not be so given without the leave of the court.

(1A)   This subsection applies —

(a)   to trials on indictment, appeals to the criminal division of the Court of Appeal and hearings of references under section 17 of the Criminal Appeal Act 1968; and

(b)   to proceedings in youth courts and appeals to the Crown Court arising out of such proceedings.

(2)   This subsection applies —

(a)   to an offence which involves an assault on, or injury or a threat of injury to, a person;

(b)   to an offence under section 1 of the Children and Young Persons Act 1933 (cruelty to persons under 16);

(c)   to an offence under the Sexual Offences Act 1956, the Indecency with Children Act 1960, the Sexual Offences Act 1967, section 54 of the Criminal Law Act 1977 or the Protection of Children Act 1978; and

(d)   to an offence which consists of attempting or conspiring to commit, or of aiding, abetting, counselling, procuring or inciting the commission of, an offence falling within paragraph (a), (b) or (c) above.

Further subsections enable trials to be moved from courts that do not have the equipment to ones that do, and provide for other matters to be regulated in greater detail by Rules of Court. (The relevant Crown Court Rule is printed as note 5 at the end of this chapter.)

It should be noted that even as amended, s. 32 of the Criminal Justice Act 1988 is still restrictive in a number of ways. First, and most obviously, it only applies to criminal proceedings (though as we have seen, the civil courts can use the live link under their more general powers). Secondly, by subsection (2) it may only be used in trials for sex and personal violence, or other offences (such as attempt) which may be connected with them. It is hard to see any sense in this restrictive complication; there seems little logic in a rule which prevents the use of the live link in any type of case where a young child may be able to give useful evidence, but may be afraid to do so: a trial of a separated parent for attempting to burn down the family home, for example, or of a Faginesque adult who has organised a group of children to steal. Sensibly, the Scottish provision (see below) is not limited in this arbitrary way, nor is the Northern Irish one, which explicitly extends to any case where 'the witness will not give evidence otherwise through fear' (Police and Criminal Evidence (NI) Order 1989, s. 81). Thirdly, it is only available in certain courts: for practical purposes, the Crown Court, and the youth court when dealing with an offence which would have been tried in the Crown Court except for the offender's age. In particular, it is not available in the ordinary magistrates' courts: a serious problem when Crown Court trials were preceded by committal proceedings in the magistrates' court, at which the defendant could force the prosecution to produce the child for a live cross-examination, but less serious now that ss. 53 and 55 of the Criminal Justice Act 1991 have taken this right away (see page 87 above).

There is also a restriction as to age. In its original form, s. 32 of the Criminal Justice Act 1988 only applied where the child was under 14. As amended, the age-limit is now 14 in a case of personal violence, and 17 in a sex case: the limits rising to 15 and 18 if videotape evidence is given (see chapter 7), and the child was under 14 or 17 when the video recording was made. The rule is easy to state, but difficult to discover from the way the section has been drafted—which one commentary on the Act has rightly described as 'labyrinthine' (Wasik and Taylor 1991). The age-limits derive from s. 32(1)(b), which (to reverse the order in which the phrases appear in the section) says that the live link can be used either (i) where the witness 'is to be cross-examined following admission under section 32A below of a video recording of testimony from him', or (ii)—even where no videotape evidence is called—if the witness 'is a child'. As for (i), video-recorded evidence can be given under s. 32A where the witness is a 'child' as defined for the purposes of that section by s. 32A(7), which defines 'child', in a violence case, as someone 'under 14, or, if he was under that age when the video recording was made, is under fifteen years of age', and in a sex case as someone who 'is under seventeen years of age or, if he was under that age when the video recording was made, is under eighteen years of age'. To be a 'child' for the purpose of route (ii) into the live link room, however, you have to fall under the definition contained in s. 32(6), which—with all the elegance for which English statutes on criminal procedure are so justly famous—says:

> Subsection (7) of section 32A below shall apply for the purposes of this section as it applies for the purposes of that section, but with the omission of the references to a person being, in the cases there mentioned, under the age of fifteen years or under the age of eighteen years.

— which is a very contorted way of saying 'under 14 if it is violence, or under 17 if it is sex'.

Section 32 expressly states that in order for a child to use the live link a judge must first grant leave. There is nothing in the Act, or in the Rules made under it, to indicate how the judge should exercise his discretion. In a case in Leeds Crown Court in December 1989 (*Guy*, 21 December 1989), however, His Honour Judge Herrod QC made a written ruling in which he laid down what he considered to be the correct principles, which were as follows:

(a) A judge should not grant permission for the live link automatically, but should balance the risk of harm to the child against the risk of creating prejudice against the defendant by allowing the live link to be used.

(b) In principle, if the prosecution want the live link to be used it is up to them to produce some evidence that it is likely to be harmful to this particular child to give evidence in the traditional way:

(c) In the case of a very young child, however, 'there must come a time when the very fact of the child's age is almost sufficient in itself to show that it would be detrimental for the child to have to give evidence in open court and to be cross-examined in the usual way'.

In practice, English judges seem very willing to grant leave, and need little if any evidence to persuade them. In 1990, Davies reported that out of 115 applications all but nine had been approved, and in their evaluation for the Home Office in 1991 Davies and Noon report that 98 per cent of applications succeed (Davies and Noon 1991, p. 30). A practical difficulty, however, is that the Crown Court Rules require an application to use the live link to be made in advance of trial, and within specified time-limits: but by Rule 23A(8) the judge has power to allow an application out of time.

The equipment now in use and its arrangement in the courtroom was described by the Lord Chancellor in a speech in Cambridge in June 1989 (Mackay 1990). The courtroom has three 'work-stations' which can both receive and transmit sound and pictures, and there is a fourth work-station in the room with the child. One of the courtroom work-stations is for the judge and others are for prosecution and defence counsel. In addition to the work-stations there are also three large television monitors positioned so that the child can be seen by the jury, the defendant and many of those in court. At present three different systems are on trial; in two the picture switches automatically between those speaking in the courtroom, while the third is manually operated by the judge. With all three systems, the judge has what is known as a 'panic button' which enables the transmission to be interrupted in the event, for instance, of an outburst from the dock.

Paragraph 23A(10) of the Crown Court Rules states that 'A witness giving evidence through a television link . . . shall be accompanied by a person acceptable to a judge of the Crown Court and, unless the judge otherwise directs, by no other person'. In October 1991 Deputy Lord Chief Justice Watkins issued a 'guideline' saying that as a general rule, only a court usher, selected and trained for the task, should be allowed to accompany the child; another person, such as a social worker or a police officer, could be chosen 'in very exceptional circumstances', provided the defence agree; and that in no circumstances should the child be accompanied by a social worker or police officer who has conducted an interview with the child which forms part of the evidence in the case.

The Scottish Law Commission, initially cool towards video links (Scottish Law Commission 1988), was later persuaded of the merits of the idea, and recommended the live link for Scotland in its Report on the evidence of children and other vulnerable witnesses in 1990 (Scottish Law Commission 1990). Its recommendation was put into effect by s. 56 of the Law Reform (Miscellaneous Provisions) (Scotland) Act 1990—a provision considerably clearer and simpler than its equivalent in England.

56.—(1) Subject to subsections (2) and (3) below, where a child has been cited to give evidence in a trial, the court may, on an application being made to it, authorise the giving of evidence by the child by means of a live television link.

(2) The court may grant an application under subsection (1) above only on cause shown having regard in particular to—

(a) the possible effect on the child if required to give evidence, no such application having been granted; and

(b) whether it is likely that the child would be better able to give evidence if such application were granted.

(3)   In considering whether to grant an application under subsection (1) above, the court may take into account, where appropriate, any of the following—

   (a)   the age and maturity of the child;
   (b)   the nature of the alleged offence;
   (c)   the nature of the evidence which the child is likely to be called on to give; and
   (d)   the relationship, if any, between the child and the accused.

Unlike the English provision, the Scottish one potentially applies wherever a child gives evidence, and is not limited by a fussy list of particular offences. By s. 59, it is available to any witness who is under 16, and can be used in the High Court, and also in the sheriff court—for summary trials as well as for trials on indictment—but not in the district court. As in England, the leave of the court is needed before the live video link may be used, but unlike the English statute, the Scottish provision gives guidance as to when permission to use the live link should be given. In Scotland, as in England, an Act of Adjournal (rule of court—the text of which is printed as note (6) at the end of this chapter) lays down a procedure for seeking judicial leave, including time limits for making the application. A decision of Lord Justice-Clerk Ross holds, however, that a refusal of an application does not ban the use of the live link in that case once and for all. In refusing leave the judge can state that the matter can be reopened later if it then becomes clear that the conditions mentioned in s. 56 are met, and even without this the trial judge has a discretion to order a child's evidence to be taken by means of a live television link if need arises, and the equipment is available to be used (*H.M. Advocate* v *Birkett* (1992) SCCR 850).

At the time of writing, however, the video link has scarcely made an impact in the Scottish courts. It is only available in Edinburgh and Glasgow. It was not until the spring of 1992 that it was first used—in a High Court trial in Glasgow—(*Glasgow Herald*, 24 April 1992), and by the autumn of 1992 there had only been some four cases. Meanwhile, the psychologist Kathleen Murray and colleagues at Glasgow University have been commissioned to carry out a study of the live link in Scotland, which will provide further information when it is completed, as it is hoped, in 1994.

How is the live link working out in practice?
Davies and Noon's study, which we mentioned on page 103, contains a large amount of information. To this, we have been able to add information provided by a similar but smaller study carried out by the psychologist Judy Cashmore in Australia (Cashmore and De Haas 1992), and a large amount of anecdotal information we have gleaned from our own informal discussions with judges, barristers, policemen and others who have been involved in cases where the apparatus was used. From all of these a number of points emerge.

First, it seems that the live link works well at a technical level. Despite initial misgivings most counsel seem to be able to examine the witnesses over the equipment without much trouble, and the most serious mechanical problem reported to date has been that the 'voice-activated' work-stations sometimes get activated by courtroom noises other than speech, like coughs and sneezes and scraping chairs. It has been said that the live link makes it difficult for the jury to get an idea of the child's physical size: but at least one judge has overcome this problem by letting the child be seen by the jury after giving evidence.

Secondly, the live link seems to have won the approval of most of those within the legal system who have worked with it.

A total of 74% of the judges who completed Davies's and Noon's questionnaires had formed a 'favourable' or 'very favourable' impression. This view was also endorsed by 83% of the sample of 78 barristers who had experience of the system with little difference in attitude depending on whether they represented prosecution or defence. Likewise, 12 of the 13 chief court clerks had formed a favourable impression of the innovation and an equally positive attitude existed among the sample of 15 police officers and social workers who were directly involved in preparing the child for, or accompanying the child at, court (Davies and Noon 1991, p. 131).

The reasons Davies and Noon were given for liking the live link included the fact that it saved the child from having to see the defendant, and other stressful features of the open courtroom, that it makes child witnesses more forthcoming in their evidence, and that it enables evidence to be given by children markedly younger than those who have traditionally appeared in court.

Davies and Noon were not able to speak to the children to get their reaction to the live link. This was done, however, in Cashmore's study in Australia, where 'The reaction of the children who did use the [live link] was generally very favourable' (Cashmore and De Haas 1992, para. 5.74). Nor were Davies and Noon able to compare the performance of children in English courts who did not use the live link with that of those who did. However, they were able to compare the apparent stress and fluency of English children giving evidence by live link with that of children giving evidence in open court as observed in a Scottish study (Flin, Bull and others 1993). There were limits to how far these groups could be compared in a meaningful way, as Davies and Noon themselves point out. But for what it is worth, the comparison suggests that children using the live link are less stressed, more resistant to leading questions, and more confident than those who give evidence in open court. They were not able to make a comparison between children giving evidence by live link, and those doing so in open court with the protection of screens. On this, the anecdotal evidence we have heard conflicts. Judge Pigot—of the Pigot Report—had used both systems, and had a preference for screens. However, another judge who had used both told us that he found the live link incomparably better.

The suggestion has been made that the live link is causing an increased number of defendants to plead guilty in child-abuse cases; but until someone compares the rate of guilty pleas at courts that have the live link with the rate at courts that do not this remains at the level of speculation.

Before any intelligent judgment is made on the success of live link, however, there is an important psychological issue that needs to be addressed about the impact of such evidence on the court. What is the effect on the jury, if any, of the fact that the child is giving evidence on a television monitor rather than in the flesh? As to this there are two theories, and each has its supporters. Some commentators, apparently working on the theory that people tend to believe anything if it is on television, claim that it enhances the impact of the child's evidence, with the risk of making it more credible than it deserves to be. 'Seeing an interview on a screen is a very powerful way of receiving an image in an age dominated by television' (Woodcraft 1988). This view, which has also been put forward by some judges in the USA (*Hochheiser* v *Supreme Court* (1984) 208 Cal Rptr 273, 278–9), has been expressed to us by some lawyers who have prosecuted and defended using the live link.

Other commentators, working on the opposite theory that nobody ever believes a thing they see on television, argue that the live link has exactly the opposite effect. A commentator who watched a rape trial conducted using the live link said that:

Something which emerged during this trial . . . is that Julie's evidence seemed impersonal and assumed a quality of unreality. It seems likely that the jury felt this same sense of unreality, because when Julie gave evidence of an intimate nature, which was obviously distressing for her, the jurors appeared to remain impassive and showed no signs of discomfort or even sympathy. It is possible that the same evidence given personally in court might have had a very different effect on the jury. Similarly, when Julie broke down, the screens were switched off, the jury filed out for a tea break, people began to chat and there was a feeling that we were having a 'commercial break'. . . . When the defendant's family were visibly upset they received sympathetic glances from several of the jurors, as did the defendant when he showed signs of emotion, which he did several times. (Sharp 1989.)

A study in the United States showed that many American lawyers believe the live link has this effect, and for that reason try not to use it if they think the child is capable of uttering in open court (Latham 1989). This particular problem is given as a disadvantage of televised testimony in an American prosecutors' manual (Toth and Whalen 1987, sect. VI–8). An English police officer shares this view. He told us that after the live link had been introduced at the local Crown Court, juries acquitted nine of the first 10 defendants. He believed the children's evidence had been rejected because it caused their evidence to lose immediacy and impact.

The merits of these two rival views have been widely discussed, but until recently no scientific study has been done which takes the matter beyond the area of hunch and speculation (Cashmore 1990, Davies and Noon 1991). As two American psychologists who tried to study the matter using adult witnesses concluded, it may be that both theories are true, because giving evidence by television screen improves the impact made by some witnesses, whilst reducing the impact made by others. Just as there are some actors who do well on stage but are a flop in the cinema or on television, and vice versa, so there are some witnesses who come over better on the screen, and others who come over worse (Miller and Fontes 1979, p. 75).

It may be significant, however, that none of the judges and barristers who took part in Davies's and Noon's survey seem to have mentioned 'status enhancement' as one of the drawbacks of video testimony, whereas there were a number who did mention loss of immediacy and emotional impact. That there is a reduction in emotional impact is borne out by a recent study in the USA, in which some groups of 'mock jurors' watched children give live evidence about a staged incident live, whilst others watched them do so on screen. They found that the 'jurors' were indeed less inclined to believe the child when they had not seen him in the flesh (Tobey et al., in press).

However, if it is true that with the live link emotional impact is reduced, it is not necessarily a bad thing if the emotional temperature of the courtroom is lowered.

A number of barristers, both for the prosecution and defence, emphasised what they saw as the value of affect, particularly tears, in convincing a sceptical jury of a child's story and believed that with the live link, such outbursts were less likely and when they occurred, might be hidden from the jury by the exercise of the judge's power to switch off the system . . . Judged from the standpoint of law, to exploit a witness's vulnerability and stress for the benefit of achieving a conviction seems a somewhat dubious procedure. As one judge noted, the oral tradition of English law is based on the objective evaluation of factual evidence and the emotional exploitation of witnesses by barristers is clearly incompatible with such an objective (Davies and Noon 1991, p. 135).

It all depends, of course, on whether a jury of inexperienced lay people will be clever enough to understand that a witness may be able to describe a horrible incident calmly because of preparation and self-control rather than because she is lying—and that a witness who gives an emotional account may do so because he has natural skills as an actor. (The power of juries in these matters are discussed in chapter 10.)

Another psychological question which is sometimes asked is whether, when witnesses give evidence on a television screen, this makes it harder to detect the fact that they are telling lies. The live link might sometimes make it harder for the court to see the witness's 'body language'. However, as we explain in chapter 10, 'body language'—contrary to general belief—is a bad guide as to whether a witness is telling the truth or not. If the live link makes a jury concentrate on what a witness is saying, rather than on what they look like, this is therefore unlikely to hinder them discovering the truth. In a recent experiment, one group of children was questioned about a genuine visit to the British Museum, and another was questioned about a visit the children were told to imagine. The questioning was video recorded, and groups of adults then watched the tapes and tried to say which accounts were true and which were false. The 'raters' overall accuracy of detection was 59%. This was about what would have been expected from other studies of adults' abilities to detect whether witnesses are being truthful (Westcott, Davies and Clifford 1991). This study does not enable us to make a direct comparison between video and live evidence, unfortunately, because all the raters saw all the children tell their tales on tape. The comparison was made in the study by Tobey et al., in press, previously mentioned. Their findings 'do not support the notion that factfinders' discernment abilities are impaired by the use of closed-circuit technology. Instead, mock jurors had difficulty discerning the accuracy of children's testimony whether or not closed-circuit technology was employed'.

Overall, the verdict on the live link in England seems to be that it is helpful. It enables more children to give more and clearer evidence, and whilst suffering less stress: though at the possible cost—if it is a cost—of reducing the emotional impact of their evidence. It would be a mistake, however, to think that with the live link all problems of children's evidence are solved. In the first place, what it cannot do is relieve the child of the stress involved in having to wait for the case to come to trial. Furthermore, such advantages as it does have at the trial can still be thrown away if the judge and lawyers are clumsy with the technology, the child is repeatedly cut off from contact with the court for no apparent reason, is ill-prepared for a court appearance and unsupported, and is examined and cross-examined in a clumsy, inept and overbearing manner: as still happens in some cases (Davies and Noon 1991, p. 126). As Professor Davies was heard to put it in a lecture, the live link is 'a reasonable sticking-plaster for a legal system which insists on children giving their testimony live'.

REMOVING THE PERSON ACCUSED

Of course the simplest and most obvious way to relieve a child witness of the oppressive presence of an adult is to remove the adult from the courtroom rather than the child. This can certainly be done in most civil proceedings involving children. In wardship, and in most custody proceedings on both sides of the Border, the judge has the power to see the child privately if he wishes, as previously explained (see pages 96–98). For certain proceedings in the English youth court the child's parents are normally entitled to be present, but r. 19 of the Magistrates' Courts (Children and Young Persons) Rules 1992 gives the bench the power to order them to withdraw while the child gives evidence or makes a statement. Similarly, in Scotland, r. 8(4) of the Sheriff Court Procedure Rules gives the sheriff power to do the same when a child is giving evidence in the sheriff court about a disputed ground of referral to the children's panel. (But, surprisingly, there is no power to hear the child in the absence of his parents at the initial panel hearing—a matter which sometimes causes difficulty (Scottish Office, *Review*, 1990, p. 40).) Quite apart from these specific provisions, it is likely that in any civil case a court could order any person (other than a party to the proceedings) to leave if their presence was intimidating a witness, as part of its general power to control its proceedings in the interests of justice. In *R* v *Willesden Justices, ex parte London Borough of Brent* [1989] FCR 1, it was held that this inherent power enables magistrates to order out even those persons whom s. 47 of the Children and Young Persons Act 1933 expressly permits to be present at care proceedings, if they are to be witnesses later in the proceedings and their presence while other witnesses are heard is likely to contaminate their future evidence. The same can hardly be less true if a person's presence in court is likely to contaminate the testimony of another witness.

In Britain it seems to be generally assumed that it would be quite out of the question to exclude the defendant in a criminal case while a witness is giving evidence against him. Where the defendant is not legally represented this would of course be grossly unfair to him, because it would prevent him hearing the evidence of that witness, and hence make it impossible for him to challenge it effectively. The argument becomes weaker, however, where the defendant has a lawyer to represent him who can listen to the evidence, cross-examine the witness, and look after his interests in his absence; and there are some entirely respectable legal systems in which a represented defendant can indeed be excluded from the court while witnesses give evidence who may be frightened of him. This is so, for example, in France, Holland, and Germany. In France and Holland the judge has an apparently unlimited power to do this, provided the defendant is told what the witness has said in his absence immediately afterwards. The German provision, which is more detailed, says the judge may do this both where it looks as if the witness will not tell the truth in the defendant's presence, and, where a witness is under 16, the welfare of the witness requires it. It is also possible in Denmark to remove the defendant while the witness is giving evidence (Andersen 1985). This is interesting, because criminal proceedings in Denmark, like those in Britain, are basically accusatorial (Hansen 1990). (For the texts, see note (7).) Equally interesting is a recent change in the rules of evidence in Queensland, Australia where the legal system is not only accusatorial but modelled directly on that of England. A court is given a number of options when hearing evidence from a child under 12, one of which is to exclude the defendant from the court while providing for the proceedings to be relayed to him by a television: a live link in reverse (Evidence Act 1977, s. 21A(2) and (4)). The idea of using the live link in reverse is clearly a good one, if it is really the case that the impact of a witness's evidence is reduced when it is relayed by television.

MODIFICATIONS TO 'OPEN COURT'

Removal of the public

The most sweeping exceptions to the 'open court' principle are found in civil proceedings. There is no power on either side of the Border to remove the public on the rare occasion when a child gives evidence in an ordinary civil case, like an action for damages for negligence or assault. But by law nearly all the various civil proceedings which are concerned with the child's welfare and upbringing have to be held in private, and the necessary consequence of this is that members of the public are not present if the child gives evidence. In Scotland, the Social Work (Scotland) Act 1968 requires children's hearings to be held in private (s. 35(1)). References to the sheriff to resolve disputed matters arising from children's hearings must also be held in private (s. 42(2)). In England, wardship cases are and always have been heard in chambers, and judges always sit in chambers to deal with custody questions, both in England

and in Scotland. In England, where magistrates have a wide jurisdiction over civil matters affecting children, statute requires them to sit in private when they exercise that jurisdiction (Magistrates' Courts Act 1980, s. 69; Children and Young Persons Act 1933, s. 47(2); Children Act 1989, s. 97(1)). In the cases where a statute deals with the matter by expressly providing for the court to sit in private it usually makes an exception in favour of representatives of the press. Thus press reporters have a right to be present at children's hearings in Scotland, and in England can attend sittings of the family proceedings court and the youth court. Where the matter is dealt with by providing for the case to be heard *in chambers* — i.e., in the judge's private room—a press reporter has no right to be there, and a judge would be most unlikely to let one in (Kearney 1987, p. 158).

In criminal cases the position is different. In England the youth court tries young offenders in private, but otherwise the basic rule is that all criminal trials are conducted in open court. However, in both England and Scotland the criminal courts have statutory powers to remove the public when a child is giving evidence. Whilst the provisions are similar on each side of the border, the practice in each jurisdiction is very different.

In Scotland the main provision is set out in ss. 166 and 362 of the Criminal Procedure (Scotland) Act 1975 (8).

(1) Where, in any proceedings in relation to an offence against, or any conduct contrary to, decency or morality, a person who, in the opinion of the court, is a child is called as a witness, the court may direct that all or any persons, not being members or officers of the court or parties to the case, their counsel or solicitors, or persons otherwise directly concerned in the case, be excluded from the court during the taking of the evidence of that witness:

Provided that nothing in this section shall authorise the exclusion of bona fide representatives of a newspaper or news agency.

(2) The powers conferred on a court by this section shall be in addition and without prejudice to any other powers of the court to hear proceedings in camera.

For the purposes of this provision, a 'child' includes any person under the age of 16 (9). This is fortified by s. 145(3) which gives the court a power to evict all members of the public, press included, when a witness, child or adult, is giving evidence in a trial 'for rape or the like': a provision with no equivalent in England, where there is no power to clear the court when an adult rape victim is giving evidence, and which is not a concession to modern feminism, but dates from an Act of 1693. These provisions are very widely used in Scotland, where the courts are nearly always cleared when children are giving evidence about sexual offences (Scottish Law Commission 1988, para. 2.26).

The English statute is s. 37 of the Children and Young Persons Act 1933, the words of which are the same as ss. 166 and 362 of the Criminal Procedure (Scotland) Act 1975, except that they refer to a 'child or young person' instead of to a 'child'. As a result of this the section applies to a slightly different range of witnesses, because in English law a 'young person' is anyone over 14 and under the age of 18 (Children and Young Persons Act 1933, s. 107, as amended by the CJA 1991). The main difference between England and Scotland on this matter, however, is one of practice. It seems that the English courts are as reluctant to clear the court when a child gives evidence as the Scots courts are willing (Morgan and Plotnikoff 1990). The reluctance of the English courts to use their powers to clear the courtroom of unnecessary people when children are giving evidence is nothing new, being the subject of complaint by the Departmental Committee in 1925 (Cmnd 2561, para. 64), the British Medical Association and the Magistrates' Association jointly in 1946 and the Magistrates' Association in 1962. The remedy these organisations suggest is to make it compulsory for the public to be cleared unless the court rules otherwise, instead of vice versa. Even where the child gives evidence by live video link, the need to clear the court remains. In some courts, child witnesses have had their evidence by video link interrupted while the judge tells visiting school parties to behave themselves, and in others, the public gallery is sometimes filled by seedy characters who sit there drinking in the details in child abuse trials—including such matters as the child's name and address (Davies and Noon 1991, p. 129). Even where the visitors behave themselves, the child may be inhibited in giving evidence merely because he or she knows that members of the public are present.

A notable limitation on these powers on both sides of the border is that they only apply to proceedings for 'offences against decency or morality'. Although in one sense it is as much of an offence against morality to batter a child as to bugger one, there can be little doubt that as a matter of law these words limit the scope of these powers to trials for sexual offences. There seems to be no sensible reason for this: if the presence of a crowd scares a child witness into silence this is bad for justice, and the court should surely be able to take counter-measures, whatever the nature of the offence (Macphail 1987, sect. 7.33).

Restrictions on publicity

On both sides of the Border a number of complicated provisions also limit what the newspapers may report about a child witness; and these provisions apply even where the press is permitted to be in court when the general public may not be present. The English statute is s. 39 of the Children and Young Persons Act 1933, which is as follows:

(1) In relation to any proceedings in any court, the court may direct that —

(a) no newspaper report of the proceedings shall reveal the name, address, or school, or include any particulars calculated to lead to the identification, of any child or young person concerned in the proceedings, either as being the person by or against, or in respect of whom the proceedings are taken, or as being a witness therein;

(b) no picture shall be published in any newspaper as being or including a picture of any child or young person so concerned in the proceedings as aforesaid;

except insofar (if at all) as may be permitted by the direction of the court.

As previously mentioned, a 'young person' is someone who is under the age of 18. This provision, which originally applied to newspapers alone, was later extended to broadcasting (Children and Young Persons Act 1963, s. 57; Cable and Broadcasting Act 1984, sch. 5). In applying it, the courts seem to start from the position that for juveniles, publicity should normally be restricted: thus in one case, the Divisional Court condemned a judge for allowing the name of a 12-year-old boy to be published who had set fire to an ambulance station causing £2.5m worth of damage (*R* v *Leicester Crown Court ex parte S* [1993] 1 WLR 111). In a later case, however, it refused to condemn a decision allowing the press to publish the name of a 14-year-old convicted of robbery (*R* v *Lee* [1993] 1 WLR 103). In certain respects the courts have interpreted the scope of the section narrowly. In *Ex parte Godwin* [1992] QB 190 the Divisional Court quashed an order banning the publication of the name of the adult accused of an offence against a child: as far as the adult defendant's name is concerned, the most a judge can do is to make an order banning in general terms 'anything calculated to lead to the identification' of the child, and say he hopes the press agrees that publishing the defendant's name should be avoided. (The case in question was a particularly sensitive one, where the prosecution led to reprisals against the child and his family, who were driven into hiding: see *Re C* [1991] FCR 1018; *The Times*, 12 August 1991.)

In Scotland, the position is more complicated (Macphail 1987 sect. 7.10 to 7.35). For criminal proceedings, the Criminal Procedure (Scotland) Act 1975, ss. 169 and 374 (as amended by the Criminal Justice (Scotland) Act 1980 and other Acts), empowers the court to ban the publication of any identifying details of a witness under the age of 16 who gives evidence against an adult. For civil proceedings, the Children and Young Persons (Scotland) Act 1937, s. 46 (as amended), enables the court to ban the publication of any details about any person involved in them who is under the age of 17, and the Fatal Accidents and Sudden Deaths Inquiry (Scotland) Act 1976, s. 4, makes a similar provision for the Scottish equivalent of inquests.

On both sides of the border, there are a number of exceptional circumstances in which the usual position is reversed, the rule is stricter, and the media are forbidden to publish any identifying details unless the court grants leave. In Scotland this is so where persons under 16 are prosecuted, when neither the defendant nor any witness under the age of 16 may be identified (Criminal Procedure (Scotland) Act 1975, ss. 169 and 174). It is also the case as far as witnesses involved in children's hearings are concerned (Social Work (Scotland) Act 1968, s. 58), and in England the same goes for children in any way involved in proceedings before the youth court (Children and Young Persons Act 1933, s. 49). Section 97(2) of the Children Act 1989 enacts a similar rule applicable to civil proceedings brought under the terms of that Act in the magistrates' courts. Where a judge hears a case in chambers, then the press are not admitted and have no story to report; and if a reporter does manage to find out what evidence a child (or any other witness) has given, publishing it would usually amount to a contempt of court (Administration of Justice Act 1960, s. 12(1)). Nor is this all: there are several other sets of statutory restrictions that apply to produce the same result in other types of proceedings (e.g., adoption). This tangled mass of overlapping provisions was condemned by Lord Justice Butler-Sloss in the Cleveland Report, which strongly recommends Parliament to enact a single rule, applicable to all civil proceedings involving children, that no identifying matter should be published. In 1990, this recommendation was repeated by the Calcutt Committee on privacy and the press (Calcutt 1990, para. 10.4), but without success, as was the case with most of its other proposals for changes in the law. Some foreign lawyers find our reluctance to protect the names of innocent people involved in litigation very odd. In Holland, for example, even the names of adults who are convicted in the criminal courts are normally withheld by the press (Scheer 1993). In Scotland, similar criticisms have also been made (*C* v *S* 1989 SLT 168; Macphail 1987 sect. 7.30).

REDUCING THE FORMALITY OF THE COURTROOM: REMOVING ROBES, COURTROOM REARRANGEMENTS, SUPPORT PERSONS, PREPARATION

It is widely recognised that part of the difficulty for a child who has to give evidence in court is the fact that a courtroom is a strange and intimidating place, which the witness has to face alone and unsupported. To some extent, these problems can be countered by making the courtroom less strange and intimidating, and allowing the child to be supported. A simple way to reduce the formality in those courts where wigs and robes are worn is for the judges and the lawyers to remove them. Another is to rearrange the court so that the child can make herself seen and heard without difficulty: as from a table in the well of the court instead of from the usual witness box. It is also possible to allow a child to have some trusted person sitting with her when giving evidence.

All these things are permissible, and indeed are sometimes done, in the courts of England and of Scotland. In the past, they have always been a matter of judicial discretion, with no guidance on the subject, either by statute, practice directions, or words of wisdom from appeal courts or in legal texts. In consequence, what is done (or not done) tends to depend on the views of the particular judge.

In England, this is still broadly the position; although the question of allowing the child a support person has now been discussed by the Court of Appeal, which gave it qualified approval in the following terms:

Plainly to have anyone sitting alongside a witness is a course of conduct which has to be undertaken with considerable care. When it happens the court must be astute to see nothing improper passes or no undue encouragement is given to the child witnesses which might make them say something other than the truth. But there is no suggestion here that the social workers did anything other than that which was perfectly proper when they were sitting alongside the witnesses.

The official position as regards support persons for children giving evidence by live video link has already been mentioned (page 106).

In Scotland, however, there has been an official attempt to regulate these matters. The provisional thoughts of the Scottish Law Commission, as explained in a Discussion Paper, were that these matters needed to be regulated by legislation (Scottish Law Commission, 1988). This provoked a mixed reaction. 'As one experienced Sheriff put it—"I would not like to see a rule which required me to disrobe and sit beside, if not actually hold hands with, a 15-year-old lout who was determinedly committing perjury in the interests of his 16-year-old friend who was on trial for assault".' (Scottish Law Commission 1990, para. 2.3). In their Report in 1990, they therefore thought that the reducing of courtroom formality was best left as a matter of discretion, and suggested that the Lord Justice General should issue a memorandum to the judges in order to encourage a coordinated approach, which he later did. This memorandum lists as measures to be considered:

(a)   the removal of wigs and gowns;
(b)   positioning the child at a table in the well of the court rather than in the witness box;
(c)   permitting a relative or other supporting person to sit with the child while giving evidence;
(d)   clearing the court.

It lists a series of factors to be considered in deciding whether to adopt these measures or not: the age and maturity of the child; the nature of the evidence the child is likely to have to give; the relationship (if any) between the child and the defendant; whether the trial is summary or on indictment—the latter being inherently more intimidating, with greater need to provide counter-measures; the disposition, health or physique of the child; and the physical possibilities of the courtroom in question—for example, the availability of amplification. (For the text, see Nicholson and Murray 1992.)

In some jurisdictions in the common law world, the process of putting informality on a formal basis has gone further, and some of these matters are regulated by legislation. In a number of jurisdictions in the USA, for example, a child has a statutory right to a support person (Whitcomb 1992). Under a Federal statute, the Victims of Child Abuse Act of 1990:

A child testifying at or attending a judicial proceeding shall have the right to be accompanied by an adult attendant to provide emotional support to the child. The court, at its discretion, may allow the adult attendant to remain in close proximity to or in contact with the child while the child testifies. The court may allow the child attendant to hold the child's hand or allow the child to sit on the adult attendant's lap throughout the course of the proceeding. An adult attendant shall not provide the child with an answer to any question directed to the child during the course of the child's testimony or otherwise prompt the child. The image of the child attendant, for the time the child is testifying or being deposed, shall be recorded on videotape.

There is also legislation on the matter in a number of jurisdictions in Australia (Law Reform Commission of Western Australia 1991).

In some civil proceedings where the rights of children are involved, the interests of the child are protected by a safeguarder or guardian *ad litem*, whose duties are to see that proper account is taken of the child's interests. From time to time, there are discussions about whether some such person should be introduced to look after the interests of child witnesses in criminal proceedings: as is already done in at least 15 jurisdictions in the USA (Whitcomb 1992, ch. 9). The Scottish Law Commission raised the matter in their Discussion Paper (Scottish Law Commission 1988), but later reported there was little enthusiasm for the idea (Scottish Law Commission 1990, pp. 75–76).

As will be explained in chapter 13, a large part of the difficulty child witnesses experience in giving evidence stems from unfamiliarity with the courts and fear of the unknown. Even wigs can present no terror for the child who is expecting them, as is shown by the following letter from a solicitor who once acted in adoption proceedings:

> The adoption order was duly made but, as we were leaving, I noticed that the small boy was about to burst into tears. Fearing that he was, perhaps, unhappy about the outcome, I inquired the reason. A few words between mother and son quickly brought the reply that he was bitterly disappointed that the judge was not wearing a wig. On hearing this, the kindly judge immediately donned his wig and mother and son went away happy (*The Independent*, 27 August 1992).

Unfamiliarity and fear of the unknown can often be countered effectively by giving the child some preparation. The difficulty about this, at least as far as England is concerned, is doubt both about what kind of preparation is permissible, and who is supposed to do it. We examine this in chapter 13.

Part III

A Critique of the Accusatorial System (10)

It is now time to assess the accusatorial (or adversarial) system insofar as it applies to the evidence of children. Our view on the matter is that at least in the full-blooded form it takes in criminal proceedings it is bad, and major changes are needed.

In the first place, the main features of the accusatorial system are bad for the child. The fact that the child must give evidence live at the trial often imposes severe stress on the child as a result of having to wait to give evidence; and when the time finally comes to give evidence, the fact that this must be done in public, in the presence of the defendant, and with the added bonus of an adversarial cross-examination, is also very upsetting. The question of stress is examined more fully in chapter 13, where we look at the evidence on whether this sort of stress has any permanent ill effects. Whether or not it does so, however, to put children through an experience which causes them tears and hysterics is an evil, and clearly should not be inflicted unless this brings about a compensating good.

According to one view, a certain measure of stress for witnesses is something that cannot be avoided:

> In discussing the subject of criminal trials and the procedure, as to evidence and otherwise, to be observed upon them, people are usually tempted to forget their real character. Cool, unexcited bystanders, often demand that a criminal trial should be conducted as quietly as a scientific inquiry, and are disgusted if any course is allowed to be taken which compromises the interests or character of third parties, or which leads to any sort of unseemly discussion. The truth is that litigation of all sorts, and especially litigation which assumes the form of a criminal trial, is a substitute for private war, and is, and must be, conducted in a spirit of hostility which is often fervent and even passionate. No man will allow himself to be deprived of character, or liberty, or possibly of life, without offering the most strenuous resistance in his power, or without seeking, in many cases, to retaliate on his opponent and his opponent's supporters. A trial of any importance is always more or less a battle, and one object of the rules of evidence and procedure is to keep such warfare within reasonable bounds, and to prevent the combatants fron inflicting upon each other, and upon third parties, injuries, the inflicting of which is not absolutely essential to the purposes of the combat. Such injuries, however, as are essential to the object in view must be permitted. Within its proper limits the battle must be fought with swords and not with foils. Unless this is clearly understood it is practically impossible to form a sound judgment upon the limits to be imposed upon cross-examination. (Stephen 1883, vol. I, p. 432.)

The assumption behind this is that the stress we inflict on witnesses, including witnesses who are children, is justified by the need that truth should out and justice should be done. But is it? The other objection to the adversarial system for child witnesses is that, like the competency requirement, it is actually truth-defeating.

> A mother and father accused of repeatedly sexually abusing their own four children and four others were acquitted on Wednesday on Judge Francis Petre's direction after their 10-year-old daughter broke down when she went to give evidence against them. The prosecution did not continue with the case because of the difficulties in presenting young children's testimony in court. The children's grandfather, who had also been charged, was also freed. (*The Times*, 25 September 1987.)

In this case the defendants were not 'cleared' because the children's evidence was discredited. The court was simply unable to go into the question of their guilt or innocence because the rigours of the adversarial system made it impossible for the children to give any evidence at all.

In fact the failure of justice is much greater than appears from cases where the child breaks down in giving evidence, because, as we explain further at the end of chapter 15, there are many more cases where the risk of harm to the child persuades the police and the Crown Prosecution Service to drop a prosecution, or not to prosecute at all.

> In a case at the Central Criminal Court, three charges of rape against the stepfather of a 12-year-old schoolgirl were dropped. 'Even if this child could brace herself to come to court to give evidence, the traumatic effects would be such as to leave her emotionally scarred for the rest of her life', Mr David Waters said as he announced the decision not to proceed. (*The Times*, 3 October 1987.)

As one commentator put it, 'Something, we feel, is rotten in the way that criminal trials are run if guilty men are allowed to go free because a nine-year-old girl breaks down in tears' (Woodcraft 1988).

Some lawyers who think the courts are too punishment-minded when dealing with child sexual abuse say it is a good thing that the rules of evidence make it impossible to prosecute in many cases. But the difficulty with this argument is that problems with the adversarial system prevent prosecutions not only in comparatively trivial cases, but also in some cases which are very serious indeed. If anything, our adversarial rules discriminate in the wrong direction. The more horrible the crime the more traumatised the child will be: and the less likely that he or she will be able to stand up to giving evidence under our present system. Even this might be acceptable if the evidence a child manages to give under the adversarial rules is of a quality so superior, and evidence obtained in any other way so inferior, that only what is obtained under the adversarial rules could be acceptable as the foundation for a conviction. We do not believe this is the case, for reasons we elaborate in chapter 10.

When we look at the matter broadly, two things are really striking. The first is how far we have already abandoned the adversarial method in civil proceedings involving children. And the second is how most other legal systems contrive to avoid using adversarial methods when dealing with the evidence of children even in criminal cases, usually by providing for some kind of pre-trial examination to take the place of evidence given live at trial. We discuss what happens in other legal systems in chapter 14, and in chapter 15 we examine the various proposals to make further inroads on traditional adversarial methods in Britain.

NOTES

1.   Article 6 of the European Convention on Human Rights is as follows:

> (1)   In the determination of his civil rights and obligations or of any criminal charge against him, everyone is entitled to a fair and public hearing within a reasonable time by an independent and impartial tribunal established by law. Judgment shall be pronounced publicly but the press and public may be excluded from all or part of the trial in the interests of morals,

public order or national security in a democratic society, where the interests of juveniles or the protection of the private life of the parties so require, or to the extent strictly necessary in the opinion of the court in special circumstances where publicity would prejudice the interests of justice.

(2)   Everyone charged with a criminal offence shall be presumed innocent until proved guilty according to law.

(3)   Everyone charged with a criminal offence has the following minimum rights:

(a)   to be informed promptly, in a language which he understands and in detail, of the nature and cause of the accusation against him;

(b)   to have adequate time and facilities for the preparation of his defence;

(c)   to defend himself in person or through legal assistance of his own choosing or, if he has not sufficient means to pay for legal assistance, to be given it free when the interests of justice so require;

(d)   to examine or have examined witnesses against him and to obtain the attendance and examination of witnesses on his behalf under the same conditions as witnesses against him;

(e)   to have the free assistance of an interpreter if he cannot understand or speak the language used in court.

2.   If the child is under 14 the deposition would now be taken unsworn: Criminal Justice Act 1988, s. 33A(2) (see page 62 above).

3.   As amended by later legislation, the Children and Young Persons Act (CYPA) 1933, sch. 1, comprises the following list: murder or manslaughter of a child or young persons, or aiding or abetting their suicide; infanticide; exposing children so as to endanger life (Offences against the Person Act (OAPA) 1861, s. 27) and child-stealing (OAPA) 1861, s. 56); common assault (OAPA 1861, s. 42) and aggravated assault (OAPA 1861, s. 43) where the victim is a child or young person; child cruelty or neglect (CYPA 1933, s. 1); allowing a person under 16 to be in a brothel (CYPA 1933, s. 3); causing or allowing a person under 16 to beg (CYPA 1933, s. 4); exposing a child to the risk of burning (CYPA 1933, s. 11); letting children take part in dangerous performances (CYPA 1933, s. 23); where the victim is under 16, offences against the Sexual Offences Act 1956, ss. 2–7, 10–16, 19, 20, 22–26, and 28, and attempt to commit offences against ss. 2, 5, 6, 7, 10, 11, 12, 22 or 23; indecency with children (Indecency with Children Act 1960) and taking, possessing, distributing or publishing indecent photographs of children (Protection of Children Act 1978, s. 1); and 'any other offence involving bodily injury to a child or young person'.

4.   Magistrates' Courts Act 1980, s. 103, now reads as follows:

(1)   In any proceedings before a magistrates' court inquiring into an offence to which this section applies as examining justices —

(a)   a child shall not be called as a witness for the prosecution; but

(b)   any statement made by or taken from a child shall be admissible in evidence of any matter of which his oral testimony would be admissible, except in a case where the application of this subsection is excluded under subsection (3) below.

(2)   This section applies —

(a)   to an offence which involves an assault, or injury or a threat of injury to, a person;

(b)   to an offence under section 1 of the Children and Young Persons Act 1933 (cruelty to children under 16);

(c)   to an offence under the Sexual Offences Act 1956, the Indecency with Children Act 1960, the Sexual Offences Act 1967, section 54 of the Criminal Law Act 1977 or the Protection of Children Act 1978; and

(d)   to an offence which consists of attempting or conspiring to commit, or of aiding, abetting, counselling, procuring or inciting the commission of, an offence falling within paragraph (a), (b) or (c) above.

(3)   The application of subsection (1) above is excluded —

. . .

(b)   where the prosecution requires the attendance of the child for the purpose of establishing the identity of any person; or

(c)   where the court is satisfied that it has not been possible to obtain from the child a statement that may be given in evidence under this section; or

(d)   where the inquiry into the offence takes place after the court has discontinued to try it summarily and the child has given evidence in the summary trial.

(4)   Section 28 above [use in summary trial of evidence given in what began as committal proceedings] shall not apply to any statement admitted in pursuance of subsection (1) above.

(5)   In this section 'child' has the same meaning as section 53 of the Criminal Justice Act 1991.

5.   Crown Court Rules, r. 23A (SI 1992 No. 1847)

23A.—(1)   Any party may apply for leave under section 32(1)(b) of the Criminal Justice Act 1988 for evidence to be given through a live television link where—

(a)   the offence charged is one to which section 32(2) applies; and

(b)   the evidence is to be given by a witness who is either—

(i)   in the case of an offence falling within section 32(2)(a) or (b), under the age of 14; or

(ii)   in the case of an offence falling within section 32(2)(c), under the age of 17; or

(iii)   a person who is to be cross-examined following the admission under section 32A of that Act of a video recording of testimony from him;

and references in this rule to an offence include references to attempting or conspiring to commit, or aiding, abetting, counselling, procuring or inciting the commission of, that offence.

(2)   An application under paragraph (1) shall be made by giving notice in writing, which shall be in the form prescribed in Schedule 5 or a form to the like effect.

(3)   An application under paragraph (1) shall be made within 28 days after the date of the committal of the defendant, or of the consent to the preferment of a bill of indictment in relation to the case, or of the service of notice of transfer under section 53 of the Criminal Justice Act 1991, or of the service of Notice of Appeal from a decision of a youth court or magistrates' court, as the case may be.

(4)   The notice under paragraph (2) shall be sent to the appropriate officer of the Crown Court and at the same time a copy thereof shall be sent by the applicant to every other party to the proceedings.

(5)   A party who receives a copy of a notice under paragraph (2) and who wishes to oppose the application shall within 14 days notify the applicant and the appropriate officer of the Crown Court, in writing, of his opposition, giving the reasons therefor.

(6)   An application under paragraph (1) shall be determined by a judge of the Crown Court without a hearing, unless the judge otherwise directs, and the appropriate officer of the Crown Court shall notify the parties of the time and place of any such hearing.

(7)   The appropriate officer of the Crown Court shall notify all the parties and any person who is to accompany the witness (if known) of the decision of the Crown Court in relation to an application under paragraph (1). Where leave is granted, the notification shall state—

(a)   where the witness is to give evidence on behalf of the prosecutor, the name of the witness, and, if known, the name, occupation and relationship (if any) to the witness of any person who is to accompany the witness, and

(b)   the location of the Crown Court at which the trial should take place.

(8)   The period specified in paragraph (3) may be extended, either before or after it expires, on an application made in writing, specifying the grounds of the application and sent to the appropriate officer of the Crown Court, and a copy of the application shall be sent by the applicant to every other party to the proceedings. The appropriate officer of the Crown Court shall notify all the parties of the decision of the Crown Court.

(9)   An application for extension of time under paragraph (8) shall be determined by a judge of the Crown Court without a hearing unless the judge otherwise directs.

(10)   A witness giving evidence through a television link pursuant to leave granted under paragraph (7) shall be accompanied by a person acceptable to a judge of the Crown Court and, unless the judge otherwise directs, by no other person.

6.   Act of Adjournal (Consolidation) 1988 rules 61A and 111A (SI 1991 No. 1916 (S.161)

61A.—(1)   An application to the court under section 56(1) of the Law Reform (Miscellaneous Provisions) (Scotland) Act 1990 for authorisation of the giving of evidence by a child by means of a live television link shall be made by petition in Form 28D(1) or Form 28D(2) of Schedule 1.

(2) An application referred to in paragraph (1) shall—

(a) where it relates to proceedings in the High Court, be lodged with the Clerk of Justiciary; and

(b) where it relates to proceedings in the sheriff court, be lodged with the sheriff clerk,

not later than 14 clear days before the trial diet (except on special cause shown).

(3) The court shall, on the application being placed before it—

(a) order intimation of the application to be made to the other party or parties to the proceedings; and

(b) fix a diet for hearing the application on the earliest practicable date.

(4) After hearing the parties and allowing such further procedure as the court thinks fit—

(a) the court may make an order granting or refusing the application; or

(b) where section 57 of the Law Reform (Miscellaneous Provisions) (Scotland) Act 1990 applies, the sheriff may make an order under that section transferring the case to another sheriff court in the same sheriffdom.

(5) Where the sheriff makes an order under paragraph 4(b) transferring the cause to another sheriff court (the 'receiving court') the sheriff clerk shall forthwith transmit the record copy indictment, the minute of proceedings, any productions and any relevant documents to the clerk of the receiving court.

111A.—(1) An application to the court under section 56(1) of the Law Reform (Miscellaneous Provisions) (Scotland) Act 1990 for authorisation of the giving of evidence by a child by means of a live television link shall be made by petition in Form 56A of Schedule 1.

(2) An application referred to in paragraph (1) shall be lodged with the sheriff clerk not later than 14 clear days before the trial diet (except on special cause shown).

(3) The sheriff shall on the application being placed before him—

(a) order intimation of the application to be made to the other party or parties to the proceedings; and

(b) fix a diet for hearing the application on the earliest practicable date.

(4) The sheriff may, after hearing the parties to the proceedings and allowing such further procedure as he thinks fit—

(a) make an order granting or refusing the application; or

(b) where section 57 of the Law Reform (Miscellaneous Provisions) (Scotland) Act 1990 applies, make an order under that section transferring the case to another sheriff court in the same sheriffdom.

(5) Where the sheriff makes an order under paragraph (4)(b) transferring the cause to another sheriff court (the 'receiving court') the sheriff clerk

shall forthwith transmit the complaint, the minute of proceedings, any productions and any relevant documents to the clerk of the receiving court.

7.   France: *Code de procédure pénale* art. 339. 'The president may, after or in the course of a witness's evidence, make one or more of the defendants withdraw, and examine them separately on certain aspects of the case; but he must not allow the debate to recommence until after he has informed each defendant of what has taken place in his absence, and what it has produced'.

Holland: *Strafvordering* (code of criminal procedure) art. 292. (i) In the manner prescribed in the previous article [i.e. on the application of one of the parties, or on his own initiative] the president may order one or more of the defendants to leave the courtroom, so that a witness may be heard out of his presence. (ii) In such a case the defendant must, on pain of nullity, be informed immediately of what has taken place in his absence, and only after that may the hearing be resumed.

Germany: *Strafprozeßordnung* (code of criminal procedure) art. 247. The judge can order the defendant to leave the courtroom if there is reason to think that a co-defendant or a witness will not tell the truth in his presence. He may do the same if there is reason to fear serious harm to the well-being of the witness if, being 16 he has to give evidence in the presence of the defendants, or if, in the case of any other witness there is a serious risk to his health, should he testify in the presence of the defendants . . . As soon as the defendants return, the president must inform them of the essence of what was said during their absence.

Denmark: *Lov om Rettens Pleje* (Criminal Procedure Act) art. 848. Details are given in Andersen (1985).

8.   The provision, like a number of others, appears in the Act twice: once in the code of rules for summary trials, and once in the code of rules for solemn procedure.

9.   The Criminal Procedure (Scotland) Act 1975, s. 462, adopts the definition of 'child' in the Social Work (Scotland) Act 1968, s. 30; this defines a child as including a person under 16 and—rather ineptly as far as child witnesses are concerned—a person under 18 who is the subject of a supervision order.

10.   See further McEwan (1992).

CHAPTER SIX
The rule against hearsay

The first part of this chapter explains what hearsay evidence is. Parts II to V attempt to explain how it affects the evidence of children in criminal and in civil proceedings in Britain. These sections are meant to be of practical use to those who must operate the rules as they are at present, as well as to set the scene for Part VI, in which the hearsay rule is critically examined. As the hearsay rule and its ramifications are complicated and technical, unfortunately much of the chapter will not be easy reading.

Part I
Definition of the rule; the proceedings in which it applies

The rule against hearsay is a prominent feature of the law of evidence in England, Scotland and Northern Ireland. In essence, it provides that a fact may not be established by calling A, who did not see or hear it, to tell the court that he heard B, who did, describe it; either B must be called to describe it to the court, or the incident must be proved by some other means. Where children are concerned, it means that if the child cannot or will not give evidence in person, no parent, teacher, doctor, psychiatrist, or social worker may repeat to the court what the child has told them. Thus in *Brasier* (1779) East PC 433, for example, it was not permissible for the little girl's mother, the lodger and the doctor to tell the court what she said the soldier had done to her on the way home from school (see chapter 4). A further example is *Sparks* v *R* [1964] AC 964, where a white man was prosecuted for indecently assaulting a little girl of three, and he could not call a witness to say that immediately after the incident she had described her attacker as black. This is a particularly interesting case, because it reminds us that the hearsay rule applies to both prosecution and defence.

Insofar as the ban on hearsay prevents a party from calling his own witness A to say he heard non-witness B say something, it also prevents him smuggling this in by the back door; when cross-examining his opponent's witness, he is not permitted to say 'A says that B said so-and-so—what do you say to that?' (*Re P* [1989] Crim LR 897).

The orthodox reason for excluding hearsay is that it is inherently unreliable. The original speaker may have told a false tale, not having been on oath, and if he did his lies cannot be exposed by cross-examination; furthermore, even if his tale was true there is the risk that it has been changed in the telling:

> The rule is so firmly entrenched that the reasons for its adoption are of little more than historical interest but I suspect that the principal reason that led the judges to adopt it many years ago was the fear that juries might give undue weight to evidence the truth of which could not be tested by cross-examination, and possibly also the risk of an account becoming distorted as it was passed from one person to another. (Lord Havers of St Edmundsbury in *Sharp* (1988) 86 Cr App R 274, 278.)

These are powerful reasons for being sceptical about hearsay evidence, but less powerful reasons for refusing to listen to it altogether, particularly if the original speaker is not available. For this reason critics of the law often say that the hearsay rule is thoroughly misconceived, and the fact that a piece of evidence is hearsay ought to affect its weight rather than its admissibility. This view now prevails in Scotland as far as civil proceedings are concerned, and at one time it was the accepted view in both civil and criminal proceedings in England. In England, the ban on hearsay evidence seems to have been invented during the early 18th century, and it never became universal, because there have always been some legal proceedings, like coroners' inquests, and wardship, where it has never applied. Twenty years ago it was cut down to size by the Civil Evidence Act 1968, which makes a lot of hearsay evidence admissible in civil proceedings in England when direct evidence is not available. In Scotland the hearsay rule seems to be much older (Dickson 1864, p. 75; Wilkinson 1982); and in Scotland it has been much more thoroughly cut back, because the Civil Evidence (Scotland) Act 1988 abolishes it in civil proceedings altogether, as we explain later. In consequence the hearsay rule is nowadays largely confined to criminal proceedings. Even within the criminal justice system the hearsay rule does not apply everywhere; for example, the courts dispense with it in bail applications, and when gathering information about a defendant for the purpose of sentencing him. But in that part of a contested criminal trial in which the prosecution try to show the defendant guilty the hearsay rule survives with almost unabated vigour.

Where it does apply, the hearsay rule applies to statements contained in documents as well as to oral statements repeated from memory. To establish an incident took place, a witness may not produce a letter from B in which B describes it—as in *Re P* [1989] Crim LR 897, where the prosecutor tried to use in evidence a letter a child had written accusing the defendant of committing a sexual offence against her; and this is so whether or not there is any doubt about whether the document is authentic. Of much greater importance where children are concerned is that tape recordings, whether audio or video, are treated in the same way as documents: A may not play the court a tape of B describing the incident any more than he may read the court B's letter (see chapter 7). The law, it seems, views a tape recorder not as a means by which a non-witness may speak directly to the court, but as a person who has heard someone speak and is now repeating what he heard from memory. It is curious that the hearsay rule should apply to documents, because where B's words are preserved on tape or in a document he wrote there can be no risk of distortion, as there is when someone tries or purports to remember the words B told him, and one of the risks the hearsay rule is intended to guard against is missing. But the statement was still made without oath or cross-examination, and the law views this as sufficient objection on its own. (As we explain later, however, there are extra exceptions to the hearsay rule where documentary hearsay is concerned.)

The hearsay rule applies not only to attempts to relay the spoken words of others. It also prohibits evidence of their non-verbal communications, if the maker was trying to assert something by means of gestures instead of words: as where someone's throat is cut, rendering them incapable of speech, and they makes signs to show who did it (see *Chandrasekera* v *R* [1937] AC 220). But does the hearsay rule apply to evidence of words or gestures which are not meant to assert a fact, but which nevertheless imply one? In the course of a police raid on D's house, for example, the telephone rings and a voice is heard to ask 'Have you got any more cannabis?'. The speaker neither said, nor meant to say 'D sells drugs', but his words and conduct imply this. Can his statement be used as evidence that D was dealing in drugs? In England, the House of Lords has recently held that such a statement does fall within the hearsay rule, and is inadmissible for this reason (*Kearley* [1992] 2 AC 228). In Scots law, this important point of principle has yet to be finally settled (Wilkinson 1986, p. 37). A hearsay rule with such a wide scope obviously shuts out a lot of evidence which is likely to be reliable (Spencer 1993a), and for this reason, the Federal Rules of Evidence in the United States restrict it to words and behaviour which are meant to be assertive.

A particular difficulty arises where a young child, on being confronted with a suspect, reacts in some way that shows hostility or terror. Is this admissible as a piece of real evidence, or, assuming the hearsay rule does cover implied assertions, is it an implied assertion by the child that the suspect did something to her? In the USA the child's reaction is said to fall outside the hearsay rule, and thus to be admissible (Myers 1987a, p. 268, *Re Penelope B* (1985) 104 Wash 2d 643, 709 P 2d 1185). In Scotland the point arose dramatically in the unreported case of *Maine and McRobb* (*Press and Journal* (Aberdeen), 27 June 1979), which involved a little girl of two who had been abducted and tortured. There the judge apparently admitted the evidence of her reactions, although he had earlier declined to accept her as a competent witness. In that case, it seems that the defence did not object. It is not clear what the answer would be in England (1).

The hearsay rule only prohibits a witness from repeating other people's assertions, and a witness may repeat in evidence the words he heard a non-witness utter if those words were not an assertion. If B is on trial for inciting a child to commit an indecent act with him, for example, it is obvious that the child may tell the court what he or she was asked by D to do, and quote D's very words, because D's words were an invitation to do something, not a statement that something was so or that an event had happened. Furthermore, the hearsay rule only prohibits A from giving evidence of B's assertion where the purpose of A's doing so is to establish that the thing B said happened did happen. If the fact that B made an assertion is relevant for some other purpose in the trial then evidence of B's assertion may be given (*Subramaniam* v *Public Prosecutor* [1956] 1 WLR 965). Thus evidence of what a child told his father that X had done to him would not be admissible at the trial of X for indecently assaulting the child; but if the father was on trial for murdering X, and ran a defence of provocation, the father could give or call evidence of what the child had told him—not to show that X did assault the child, but to show that the father thought he did, and therefore had reason to lose his self-control. Similarly, if a little boy of three says, 'Uncle Bill showed me how he makes white stuff come out of his willy', this would be clearly inadmissible as evidence that Uncle Bill had committed an indecent act with the child, but it would be admissible as evidence to show that the child had a certain level of sexual knowledge. (For a case that illustrates this principle, see *S* v *Kennedy* (unreported, Kearney 1987, p. 276).) Unfortunately it is not always clear whether the reason for calling evidence of a statement is to establish a fact contained in it, or some other purpose, and very subtle distinctions are sometimes drawn.

Something which usually surprises non-lawyers is that the hearsay rule prohibits not only evidence of out-of-court statements by those who do not themselves appear as witnesses at the trial, but also evidence of any previous out-of-court statements made by those who do. This subdepartment of the hearsay rule is sometimes given the honour of a separate title, and is variously known as 'the rule against narrative', 'the rule against previous consistent statements', and 'the rule against self-corroboration'. Previous statements by the witnesses in the case are never open to the main objection to hearsay evidence, which is the absence of oath and cross-examination; by definition the maker will go into the witness-box at trial, where he may be cross-examined on oath as to whether his previous statement was the truth. Yet they are inadmissible, and remain so even where the other risk with hearsay—inaccurate reporting—is absent, as it will be if the earlier statement is recorded on video or audio tape. As with documentary hearsay, however, the law recognises extra exceptions for hearsay evidence of previous statements by witnesses. The main one is that where the witness contradicts his earlier statement by what he says in the witness-box, evidence may be given of the earlier statement to undermine the credibility of what he has said in court (see page 137 below). The wisdom of the rule against narrative, and the proposals that have been made to abolish it, are discussed elsewhere in this book (pages 142 and 269).

Part II
Exceptions to the hearsay rule in criminal proceedings

As already mentioned, the hearsay rule is mainly applicable in criminal proceedings, and in this section we shall examine the chief exceptions to the hearsay rule as it applies there. Of these there are a very large number: a

Scottish writer discusses 20 (Wilkinson 1986), an American double that number (Binder, *Hearsay Handbook*, 2nd ed 1983; quoted by Myers 1987a, 326). Here we shall only take a brief look at the exceptions most relevant to the evidence of children, and for a full account readers must consult the standard British works on evidence, of which the hearsay rule accounts for a sizeable part. Conveniently, the law on both sides of the Border is sufficiently similar to enable the Scots and English rules to be treated together.

HEARSAY STATEMENTS ADMITTED BY CONSENT

In England s. 9 of the Criminal Justice Act 1967 enables a written statement to be read in place of live evidence from a witness where one side gives advance notice of their intention to do this, and neither their opponents nor the court object. To be admissible under this section the statement must be signed by the maker, who must declare that he believes it to be true. Where the maker is over 14 he must also declare that he knows he is liable to prosecution if it is false; if under 14 he merely declares that he 'understands the importance of telling the truth in it'. This useful provision enables many witnesses, including children, to be relieved of a court appearance where their evidence is not likely to be controverted. In Scotland there is no such provision, and the only way in which a witness may be relieved of giving oral evidence in criminal proceedings is where the other side—unusually—are prepared to make a formal admission that the things he would say in evidence are true: something a party does not do when he consents to a written statement being used under Criminal Justice Act 1967, s. 9, in England. At the time of writing a proposal to make it easier to prove undisputed facts is under discussion in Scotland (Scottish Law Commission 1992).

CONFESSIONS

Where the defendant has admitted the offence his confession, though hearsay, is admissible in evidence against him at the trial. In England the subject is now governed by ss. 76 to 78 of the Police and Criminal Evidence Act (PACE) 1984 (provisions mirrored in Northern Ireland by the Police and Criminal Evidence (NI) Order 1989). The dangers of false confessions, and the wider problem of heavy-handed police tactics when dealing with suspects, are well known, and these provisions try to deal with them by means of a triple layer of protection. By s. 76 the judge must exclude a confession unless he is satisfied that it was not obtained by oppression, or under circumstances likely to make a confession unreliable. Secondly, by s. 78 the judge has a discretion to exclude a confession if he thinks that admitting it in evidence would make the trial unfair. This discretion enables him, if he wishes, to exclude a confession on the ground that the accused was not cautioned before he was questioned, or was denied any of the other rights that PACE 1984 confers on suspects, either directly, or indirectly through the codes of practice drawn up under s. 66. PACE 1984 and the codes give juveniles more extensive protection than adults, and hence there are more grounds upon which the confession of a juvenile may be excluded. Thus, for example, under Code C a juvenile must usually be questioned with a supporting adult present, and a confession was held rightly excluded where a girl of 16 was questioned without one (*Director of Public Prosecutions* v *Blake* [1989] 1 WLR 432). Thirdly, by s. 77 the judge is sometimes under a duty to give a warning about the danger of accepting a confession made by a person who is mentally handicapped—although, surprisingly, there is no explicit duty to warn of the equal danger of accepting a confession by a child.

In Scotland the law is broadly comparable, but depends on case law rather than statute. Confessions made to the police or other people in authority are inadmissible if made in response to threats or promises, and also if extracted by over-zealous questioning that the judge feels was unfair to the suspect:

> The ultimate test in the admission of confessions and other statements against interest by accused persons is fairness to the accused. In judging fairness, three matters require to be taken into account: 1 the nature of the charge; 2 the physical and mental capacity of the accused; and 3 the circumstances in which the statement was made. (Wilkinson 1986, p. 48.)

Confessions are a hearsay exception that is mainly relevant to defendants, and hence of limited importance as far as children are concerned. It is worth noticing, however, that where an adult has confessed, this may have the indirect result of enabling the court to hear the hearsay statement of a child. Sometimes a defendant's 'confession' consists of an accusation which somebody else made to his face, which he then admits to be true. In such a case the court must hear the accusation in order to understand what was admitted. Where the defendant was confronted with a child who accuses him—or more probably, with the videotape of a child making an allegation against him—and he accepts what the child has said, the court would necessarily hear the statement the child had made (see *Christie* [1914] AC 545).

RES GESTAE

In America this exception is known as 'excited utterances'. In its original form it applied to statements uttered at the very moment the crime was being committed, and not to those uttered afterwards; thus in the extraordinary case of *Bedingfield* (1879) 14 Cox CC 341 the prosecution could not use it to admit evidence that when a woman emerged from the room where her husband was with her throat cut, she said 'See what Harry has done!' In its modern form it also covers a statement made in response to some startling event, provided it was made very soon afterwards. Thus in the leading case of *Andrews* [1987] AC 281 it enabled a court to hear a statement identifying his attackers made by a man a few minutes after he had been stabbed, and who had died before the trial. According to Lord Ackner in that case, the test for admisssibility is whether the statement was made so close to a startling event that the judge can answer yes to the question: Can the possibility of concoction or distortion be disregarded? In deciding this he must consider how startling the event was, and how long after it the statement was made. A risk of accidental error, as against deliberate distortion, affects the weight to be put upon the statement but does not make it inadmissible. The law of Scotland seems to be the same (Macphail 1987, sect. 19.69; Macphail 1991, sect. 710).

In some jurisdictions in the USA this exception to the hearsay rule has been stretched to cover statements made as long as several hours after the incident, provided they were spontaneous, and consequently 'excited utterances' has become a usual vehicle for putting children's hearsay statements before the court (Myers 1987a, p. 329; Yun 1983). But, at least at present, the British *res gestae* exception is clearly limited to statements made in the immediate aftermath of the event—as was held by Mr Justice Otten in *Bradford City Metropolitan Council* v *K (Minors)* [1990] Fam 140.

In principle, the *res gestae* exception applies whether or not the witness gives evidence at trial. However, the courts dislike the prosecution trying to use it to let in the statement of someone they could have called as a witness had they chosen to do so (*Andrews* [1987] AC 281; *Tobi* v *Nicholas* (1988) 86 Cr App R 323).

Where the child gives evidence at trial a statement that falls outside the *res gestae* exception may nevertheless be admissible as what Scots lawyers call a *de recenti* statement, and English lawyers a 'recent complaint'. This is discussed below, together with the other hearsay exceptions which only operate where the maker testifies in court (page 137).

STATEMENTS REGARDING PHYSICAL OR MENTAL CONDITION

This hearsay exception, which applies in both jurisdictions, is explained by a Scottish writer as follows:

> Evidence is admissible of statements regarding the physical or mental condition of the maker in the sense of physical sensations experienced or the content of the mind at the time the statement was made. Such statements are admitted as being the ordinary indications of state of mind or physical sensation. In many cases physical symptoms and sufferings and the content of the mind cannot otherwise be ascertained. (Wilkinson 1986, p. 41.)

As proof of mental condition it would be possible to lead evidence that a child said 'I'm scared of daddy' in order to prove that the child was in fear of his or her father. As proof of physical sensations it would be possible to give evidence that a child said, 'I am hungry', in order to prove that he was: as was held in the sad case of *Conde* (1868) 10 Cox CC 547, where a little child had died of starvation and neglect, and his parents were prosecuted for manslaughter.

According to the English case law, the exception concerning physical sensations permits a witness to recount how a patient described his symptoms, but not how he said he got them. So although a witness could say in evidence, 'Johnny told me that his head hurt', the witness could not say, 'Johnny told me that his head hurt *where Uncle Bill had hit it with the poker'* (*Aveson* v *Kinnaird* (1805) 6 East 188; *Gloster* (1888) 16 Cox CC 471). Most jurisdictions in the USA also refuse to admit evidence of who the child said was responsible for his symptoms, but there are some States where the courts now seem willing to admit the entire statement, at any rate where it was made in order to get medical treatment (Myers 1987a, pp. 359–60). There seems to be no case law on this point in Scotland.

WHERE THE ORIGINAL MAKER OF THE STATEMENT IS UNAVAILABLE

This is a misleading heading, because there is no general principle in either English or Scots law that makes hearsay admissible wherever the original maker is unavailable to testify. However, it is a convenient rubric under which to group a series of scrappy exceptions applying to particular statements by particular people, the common thread between them being that the witness is not available. Here the rules differ significantly on each side of the border.

By the common law of Scotland, there is a limited hearsay exception for statements made by witnesses now unavailable. This applies where the original speaker is now dead, insane or a prisoner of war (Wilkinson 1986, 49–51; Scottish Law Commission 1988(b)). The exception does not apply to *precognitions* — what English lawyers would call proofs of evidence—the theory being that it is unfair to allow these in evidence because they are often moulded around what the procurator fiscal or defence agent wanted the witness to say.

The equivalent hearsay exception under the common law of England is much narrower. South of the border it is not enough that the original maker of the statement should be insane or a prisoner of war. The speaker must be well and truly dead, and even that is not enough, because in addition to this, one of a number of supplementary criteria must also be met. Of these, the best known is that the statement amounts to a 'dying declaration'. To make it count as a dying declaration there must be evidence that the maker of the statement was under a 'settled, hopeless expectation of death' (Archbold 1993, sect. 11–26; Cross 1990, p. 653). Dying declarations, it should be noted, are only admissible in trials for homicide—which is most peculiar, because the rationale for the requirement of a settled hopeless expectation of death is that no one would wish to die with a lie upon his or her lips, and it is hard to believe there are many dying men willing to face eternity with a lie on their lips about a robbery or a rape, but not about a manslaughter or murder. As child deaths are fortunately rare these days, and dying children are not usually told they are dying even if they are, no more need be said here about dying declarations.

In England, statements by deceased persons may also be admissible if they were made against financial interest, or in the course of a duty; but these conditions are even less likely to apply to the words of children.

In England, these preposterously inadequate common law exceptions are supplemented by two complicated statutory provisions which let in the statements of certain witnesses who are unavailable for reasons other than death.

The first is s. 13 of the Criminal Justice Act 1925, which makes a *deposition* admissible at a Crown Court trial if the person who made it 'is proved at the trial by the oath of a credible witness to be dead or insane, or so ill as not to be able to travel, or to be kept out of the way by means of the procurement of the accused or on his behalf'. When this was first enacted, committal proceedings were always oral, and when a witness made a deposition he took an oath and was examined and cross-examined in the usual adversarial fashion. So in those days this was not so much an exception to the hearsay rule as a case where a witness gave his formal evidence in advance of trial. But the Criminal Justice Act 1967 made it possible for magistrates to commit for trial on the basis of witness statements, and s. 2(7) of that Act (now s. 102(7) of the Magistrates' Courts Act 1980) deems those witness statements to be 'depositions' for the purpose of s. 13 of the Act of 1925. Witness statements, unlike genuine depositions, are statements made to the police by people who are not on oath and at a time when the defence does not have a chance to cross-examine, so the effect of the 1967 Act was to turn s. 13 of the 1925 Act into a genuine exception to the hearsay rule. Up to now the English courts have been wary of these provisions, and in 1983 the Court of Appeal urged judges to use their discretion to reject any statements tendered under them except where they contained evidence that was formal and non-controversial (*Blithing* (1983) 77 Cr App R 86). However, a recent case sanctions their wider use (*Scott* v *R* [1989] AC 1242). (This case was an appeal from a murder conviction in Jamaica, where the key prosecution witness was himself shot dead in the interval between deposing at the committal and trial.) A similar approach was taken in the later case of *Henriques* v *R* (1991) 93 Cr App R 237.

The second is the documentary hearsay provisions of the Criminal Justice Act 1988, ss. 23 to 26—reproduced for Northern Ireland as Part II of the Criminal Justice (Evidence etc.) (NI) Order 1988.

These provisions are of mind-numbing complexity. In an attempt to make them more comprehensible, we have drawn a map (see figure 6.1, page 138). The reason for the complication is that they began life as provisions intended to serve one purpose, and were extended in the course of enactment to serve another. As their title in the Act—'documentary evidence'—suggests, their origin was a proposal of the Fraud Trials Committee in 1986, which wanted the hearsay rule amended to make it easier to admit company records, letters and so forth as evidence in fraud trials. The Home Office, however, seized the chance to draw up a series of clauses which went far beyond this, and would have made admissible in evidence the statements which witnesses absent from the trial had earlier given to the police: a matter which raised very different policy considerations. This did not please the Bar, and this led to a row when the relevant Bill reached the House of Lords, at the end of which the Home Office hurriedly had to redesign its Trojan Horse on less ambitious lines (Wolchover 1987, 1988). The saw-marks of hasty Parliamentary carpentry are all too obvious (Birch 1989).

According to the marginal note, s. 23 of the Criminal Justice Act 1988 covers 'first-hand hearsay'. This section makes a statement contained in any document admissible if the person making the statement was giving first-hand information: for example, if he says in the document 'I saw D expose himself'. Section 24, according to its marginal note, is concerned with 'business etc. documents'. This section makes statements admissible in evidence where they are contained in documents 'created or received by a person in the course of a trade, business, profession or other occupation, or as the holder of a paid or unpaid office'. Under s. 24, the statement is admissible even where the information is second-hand rather than first-hand: 'X told me that he saw D expose himself', rather than 'I saw D expose himself'. In principle, a document recording a child's description of a criminal offence to a policeman or a social worker (or a tape-recording, video or audio) could fall within either s. 23 or s. 24.

To become admissible under either of these sections, however, one of a number of further requirements must usually be met. No statement can be admitted under s. 23 (first-hand hearsay in documents) unless one of the following conditions are met, which are set out in s. 23(2) and (3). All of them presuppose the maker of the statement is unavailable to give evidence in person:

(a) the original maker of the statement ' . . . is dead, or by reason of his bodily or mental condition unfit to attend as a witness' (s. 23(2)(a)); or

(b) he is outside the UK and it is not reasonably practicable to secure his attendance (s. 23(2)(b)); or

(c) he has vanished and all reasonable steps have been taken to find him (s. 23(2)(c)); or

(d) — by section 23(3)—'that the statement was made to a police officer or some other person charged with the duty of investigating offences or charging offenders; and that the person who made it does not give oral evidence through fear or because he is kept out of the way'.

Statements that fall under s. 24 (the so-called 'business etc. documents') are normally admissible whether or not these conditions are met. However, if they were made post-crime and with a view to criminal proceedings, then one of these conditions must once again be present—or the following extra one:

(e) that the maker cannot reasonably be expected to have any recollection of the matters dealt with in the statement.

One vital question for readers of this book is whether these sections would enable the prosecution (or the defence) to produce in evidence the witness-statement of a child who was too frightened to come to court, or too frightened to give coherent evidence having got there. The answer is 'yes, in principle' (McEwan 1989). The terms of s. 23(3)—which we have set out above and called 'condition (d)'—are met *either* when the witness fails to give evidence through fear *or* when he or she has been 'kept out of the way'. So they are met when, through fear, the witness either refuses to come to court, or where he gets there but is too frightened to go into the witness-box (*R* v *Acton JJ, ex parte McMullen*; *R* v *Tower Bridge Magistrates' Court ex parte Lawlor* (1991)

92 Cr App R 98), or where she goes into the witness-box but is then tongue-tied with fear (*R* v *Ashford Magistrates' Court ex parte Hilden* [1993] 2 WLR 529). Another equally important question is whether these provisions also apply where the child's appearance would be very upsetting for him. Once again, the answer seems to be 'yes, in principle', at any rate where the court appearance would involve real danger to his mental health. Such circumstances would seem to fall within the words of s. 23(2)(a)—which we have set out above and called 'condition (a)': 'that the person who made the statement is . . . by reason of his bodily or mental condition unfit to attend as a witness'. This condition might also cover the case of the child who suffers from severe communication problems, as a result of which it is not feasible to get him or her to give live evidence in court.

The answer to these questions is only 'yes, in principle', however, because even where one of the conditions (a)–(e) is satisfied the hearsay statement is not admissible automatically, but only subject to the judge's discretion. Under s. 25 the judge has a general discretion to exclude any statement which would be admissible under either of these sections. Furthermore, if the statement came into existence post-crime and with a view to criminal proceedings—like the statement a witness gives to the police—the position is stricter, because in that case s. 26 provides that:

the statement shall not be given in evidence in any criminal proceedings without the leave of the court, and the court shall not give leave unless it is of the opinion that the statement ought to be admitted in the interests of justice; and in considering whether its admission would be in the interests of justice, it shall be the duty of the court to have regard —

   (i)   to the contents of the statement;
   (ii)   to any risk, having regard in particular to whether it is likely to be possible to controvert the statement if the person making it does not attend to give oral evidence in the proceedings, that its admission or exclusion will result in unfairness to the accused or, if there is more than one, to any of them; and
   (iii)   to any other circumstances that appear to the court to be relevant.

Unfortunately these three clauses do not resolve the central question, which is this: can it ever really be 'in the interests of justice' to admit against a defendant in a criminal case a hearsay statement like a police witness-statement, which was made without his having any chance to confront the maker with his side of the story? The case-law on the section to date, which is listed in note (2) at the end of this chapter, does not involve children, although there have been several cases about the analogous problem of witnesses who are fragile because of old age rather than youth. It shows that some judges feel it is proper to admit such evidence, whilst others do not: so that whether it is admitted depends on the tastes of the judge who tries it, and if there is a conviction, those of his brethren who hear the appeal. All the more surprising, therefore, that the Royal Commission on Criminal Justice (1993) felt able so confidently to recommend the wider use of these provisions where fragile witnesses are concerned (Report, page 129).

This seems no way for the law to resolve a major question of principle, particularly one on which the European Convention on Human Rights has something to say (see chapter 5). A better way to tackle the problem would surely be to devise a way under which the evidence of fragile witnesses could be taken in private ahead of trial at a questioning-session where the defence were represented: as indeed the Pigot Committee proposed (see chapter 5). Yet, for reasons which they have never explained, the Home Office have so far been firmly opposed to this idea.

For the purpose of these sections, 'document' is defined to include video and audiotapes (see page 173). Thus where a written witness-statement would be admissible, so would an interview that was tape-recorded.

In Scotland the hearsay rule has also been changed recently to make documents more readily admissible in evidence in criminal cases. However, the Prisoners and Criminal Proceedings (Scotland) Act 1993, which does this, carefully excludes from the new provisions any statements which were given in contemplation of criminal proceedings. A wider reform of the hearsay rule in Scotland is now under discussion (Scottish Law Commission 1988(b)).

Before leaving this section it is worth mentioning the limited provisions under which the evidence of certain fragile witnesses can be taken ahead of trial. The provisions for children, contained in ss. 42 and 43 of the Children and Young Persons Act 1933 and in s. 33 of the Prisoners and Criminal Proceedings (Scotland) Act 1993, were discussed in the previous chapter. In addition there is, in England, s. 105 of the Magistrates' Courts Act 1980, which enables a magistrate to take a deposition from a witness who is dangerously ill. This is rarely used—but in 1992 it seems to have enabled someone dying of AIDS to give evidence that secured the conviction of a man for sexual offences against a six-year-old boy (*The People*, 13 December 1992). Section 32 of the Criminal Justice (Scotland) Act 1980 makes a similar provision.

THE HEARSAY RULE AND THE PREVIOUS STATEMENTS OF WITNESSES WHO GIVE EVIDENCE IN CRIMINAL PROCEEDINGS

As was mentioned earlier, a branch of the hearsay rule sometimes called the 'rule against previous consistent statements', the 'rule against narrative' and the 'rule against self-corroboration' extends to bar a party from giving evidence of the previous out-of-court statements that a witness has made. With child witnesses, this means that where a child gave a full and convincing account of abuse to the police, and gives a faltering and incomplete one in the witness-box, the court may not be told about the statement to the police in order to supplement the child's weak account in court.

Although the previous consistent statements of a witness may not be used to bolster up his testimony, full use may be made of his previous inconsistent statements in order to destroy it. Sections 147 and 349 (see note (3)) of the Criminal Procedure (Scotland) Act 1975 provide:

Figure 6.1   Flow chart: documentary hearsay provisions of the Criminal Justice Act 1988, ss. 23 to 26

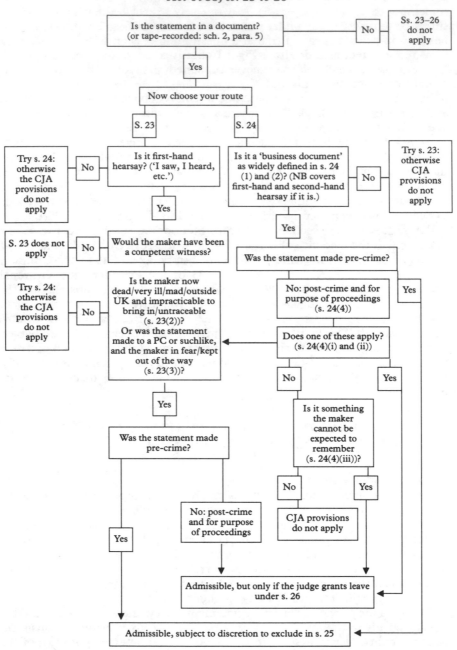

In any trial, any witness may be examined as to whether he has on any specified occasion made a statement on any matter pertinent to the issue at the trial different from the evidence given by him in such trial; and in such trial evidence may be led to prove that such witness has made such different statement on the occasion specified.

In England the same rule is laid down by the somewhat less crisp provisions of the Criminal Procedure Act 1865, ss. 4 and 5 (note 4). Thus where a child is called as a prosecution witness, and gives live evidence in-chief, he or she can expect to be cross-examined to show up any discrepancies between what was said in the witness-box and any earlier statement to the police. If the original interview was tape-recorded, then he can of course be questioned about the differences between his courtroom testimony and his earlier statements on the tape. As we explain in chapter 7, in England the child's interview with the police, if video-recorded, can now be used as a substitute for the child's live evidence in-chief. Where this is done there can obviously be no cross-examination on the discrepancies between the police interview and the evidence given live in-chief: but the child could be cross-examined about the discrepancies between the videotape and any earlier account that he or she has given.

It sometimes happens that in the course of an investigation a witness is interviewed several times, and on one of those occasions gives an account of events which conflicts with his courtroom testimony. This quite often happens in child-abuse cases. For example, following a medical examination which reveals clear evidence that a girl has been sexually abused she is questioned and denies this, but the next day gives a full and circumstantial account of a rape committed by her stepfather, which she repeats in evidence at trial; or a child whose evidence of acts of incest committed with her over a period of several years is revealed in a series of interviews, in which she tells more on each occasion, at the first interview saying that only minor indecent acts took place; or a child who has told a mainly consistent story may have retracted it briefly at some point. In such cases the effect of the law is that the child's one inconsistent story may be used to destroy her as a witness, but her other consistent ones may not be put in evidence to rehabilitate her. In England this was held to be the case in *Beattie* (1990) 89 Cr App R 303. On July 16 a girl gave a muted account of sexual misconduct by her father, and on July 19 made a full and detailed account of incest. The Court of Appeal quashed his conviction because when defence counsel attacked her credibility on the ground that the first statement conflicted with her courtroom evidence, the judge had let them see her second statement.

Where a cross-examiner proves his opponent's witness made a previous inconsistent statement he is supposed to prove all of it, and not just selected parts of it. This is so that the court can judge for itself whether taken as a whole the earlier statement really does contradict what the witness said at trial (*Riley* (1866) 4 F & F 964). In strict law, however, nothing contained in the earlier statement counts as evidence except insofar as it bears on the credibility of what the witness said in court. If a child is called as a prosecution witness, and the defence put in her earlier statement because it contradicts part of her courtroom testimony, it may be that the earlier statement contains a gem or two of information which is useful to the prosecution case. If it does, however, these extra pieces of information have not, strictly speaking, been proved by admissible evidence, and the judge ought to tell the jury to disregard them.

The same point arises where a witness unexpectedly deserts the party calling him and retracts his original statements when giving evidence in chief. For example, a child who has consistently alleged that her stepfather had sexual intercourse with her is called as a prosecution witness, and when examined by prosecuting counsel she now tells the court that nothing happened at all. Although the right to use the previous inconsistent statements of a witness is normally reserved for the opposing side, here the judge may allow them to treat their own witness as if she was a witness for the other side, and to use her previous inconsistent statements against her. If she then turns round, retracts her retraction, and says her original statement was true, the court now has legally admissible evidence from her that the act of incest did take place (although it may not be thought very convincing). If she persists in her denial, even when confronted with her original statement, then in law the situation is very different. Although the court has heard her original statement, it does not amount to legally admissible evidence that the sexual intercourse took place. Although the jury will have heard what she originally said, the judge will have to tell them to disregard it, and his failure to do so will be a serious misdirection. This was held in the English case of *Birch* (1924) 18 Cr App R 26, the facts of which were exactly these, and the rule is the same in Scotland (*Paterson* v *H.M. Advocate* 1974 JC 35). In such a case as this, however, the judge will probably have to go further than warning the jury and stop the case for want of enough admissible evidence to justify a conviction.

The previous consistent statement of a witness is admissible if one of the exceptions to the hearsay rule already mentioned, like *res gestae*, applies to it. And in addition there are three further cases where the previous statements of a witness may be put in evidence. These are limited exceptions to the hearsay rule because, unlike the other exceptions discussed earlier, they only apply where the original maker of the statement gives evidence at trial.

Rebutting an allegation of previous fabrication

Where a witness gives oral evidence at trial, and in cross-examination it is alleged that the story is all a recent fabrication, his or her previous statement (whether recorded in writing, video-recorded or purely oral) can be proved to show that it is not (Blackstone 1993, sect. F6.16; Wilkinson 1986, 47; Macphail 1987, sect. 19–38 to 19–44). Thus if defence counsel tries to say 'Mary only made this accusation against her father after she had been given a new bike for Christmas by her stepfather', the prosecution can use her previous statement to prove that in fact she first made the accusation long before.

In theory the previous statement is not evidence of the matters it contains, but merely something that bears on the credibility of the evidence the witness has given in court. The practical implication of what may appear to be a distinction without a difference is that it therefore cannot amount to corroboration (*Burns* v *Colin McAndrew & Partners Ltd* 1963 SLT (Notes)

71)—something which is particularly important in Scots criminal law where the court may not convict of any offence on a single piece of uncorroborated evidence (see chapter 8).

Recent complaints in sex cases: *de recenti* statements

Where the alleged victim of an offence made a complaint about it very soon after, the terms of the complaint may be put in evidence. Statements that qualify under this exception are known as 'recent complaints' in English law (Blackstone 1993, sect. F6.14; Archbold 1993, sect. 8.90–8.93), and '*de recenti* statements' in the law of Scotland (Wilkinson 1986, pp. 59–60). Here there are some subtle differences between the rules in the two jurisdictions, the main one concerning the type of case in which the exception is available. In England, recent complaint only applies to complaints of sexual offences, or so it is assumed in the modern law (*Camelleri* [1922] 2 KB 122, *Jarvis* [1991] Crim LR 374; such authority as there is for saying it applies to non-sexual offences in England is discussed in Cross, 6th ed. 1985, pp. 258–63). In Scotland, on the other hand, it seems that *de recenti* statements are in principle admissible in any kind of trial (Walkers 1964; Dickson 1864, sect. 95; but Field 1988, p. 324).

In both jurisdictions the complaint must be a fresh one. Whether it is fresh or not is a matter of fact for the judge in the case, so reported cases give us limited guidance. However, it seems clear that the test is not how great a span of time elapsed between the incident and the complaint, but whether the complaint was made at the first reasonable opportunity. In one English case a 15-year-old girl's complaint was held admissible although she made it eight days after her father had raped her (*Hedges* (1909) 3 Cr App R 262), and in an old Scottish case a complaint was admitted in evidence although nearly a month had elapsed (*M'Millan* (1833) Bell's Notes 288). But in an English case the court ruled that an interval of one day made the complaint too late where there had been a good opportunity to complain earlier (*Rush* (1896) 60 JP 777; and for Scotland, see *Hill* v *Fletcher* (1847) 10 D 7). Where young children have been the victims of sexual abuse within the family, and have been subjected to threats, they often fail to disclose until a long time after-wards—quite often only when they have been moved to a new home where they feel secure. In the light of this, a New Zealand court held that the complaint of a seven-year-old girl had been made at the first reasonable opportunity when it was after a delay of six months (*S* (1990) 5 CRNZ 668); but the opposite result was reached where the delay was 16 months and the child was older (*S* (1991) 7 CRNZ 135). The English (but not the Scottish) case law also holds that to qualify as a recent complaint the statement must have been made spontaneous-ly, and not in response to leading questions. According to Ridley J in the leading case of *Osborne* [1905] 1 KB 551, neutral questions like 'What's the matter?' or 'Why are you crying?' do not prevent the complaint from being spontaneous, but questions like 'Did (so-and-so) assault you?' or 'Did he do this and that to you?' would make the complaint inadmissible. He added that if the circumstances indicate that but for the questioning there would probably have been no voluntary complaint, the answer is inadmissible.

In both jurisdictions recent complaints are only admissible to reinforce the credit of the complainant as a witness at the trial, and are not regarded as independent evidence of the matters they contain. Thus it was held in *Wallwork* (1958) 42 Cr App R 153 (see chapter 4) that where a child did not give evidence, no evidence of her recent complaint could be given. It has also been held that where the child does give evidence, a recent complaint does not amount to corroboration (*Evans* (1925) 18 Cr App R 123; *Coulthread* (1933) 24 Cr App R 44). The law is the same in Scotland (*Morton* v *H.M. Advocate* 1938 JC 50). In the past the same approach has been taken in the USA and in the other parts of the common law world. However, a number of jurisdictions in the USA now admit a child's recent complaint as a piece of substantive evidence (Myers 1987a, p. 280), and the same is true in South Australia (*Corkin* (1989) 50 SASR 580; Warner 1990).

The law of recent complaints contains much that is strange and anomalous. First, why in England should it be limited to sexual cases? It seems very odd that a child's recent complaint is admissible where the defendant is accused of putting his hand up her skirt, but not when he is accused of starving her or torturing her or beating her within an inch of her life. Secondly, why should it be limited to *recent* complaints? Speaking in the context of rape, Dickson said that *de recenti* statements are admitted because of 'the importance of sifting the woman's whole conduct and explanations regarding the charge' (Dickson 1864, sect. 98). In other words, it is admitted because it is important for the court to know, among other things, the terms in which the victim complained. But if this is the reason it justifies more than *de recenti* statements, because it is equally informative for the court to be told the terms of the alleged victim's complaint, no matter whether she made it soon or late. In England the rule probably had its origin in the idea that where an adult or child is really the victim of a sexual offence his or her natural reaction would be to tell somebody about it at once; so where he or she did so, the complaint is more likely to be true. Sir Matthew Hale (1609–76) said:

> The party ravished may give evidence upon oath, and is in law a competent witness, but the credibility of her testimony, and how far forth she is to be believed, must be left to the jury, and is more or less credible according to the circumstances of fact, that concur in that testimony.
>
> For instance, if the witness be of good fame, if she presently [immediately] discovered the offence made pursuit after the offender, shewd circumstances and signs of the injury, whereof many are of that nature, that only women are the most proper examiners and inspectors, if the place, wherein the fact was done, was remote from people, inhabitants or passengers, if the offender fled for it; these and the like are concurring evidences to give greater probability to her testimony, when proved by others as well as herself. (Hale 1736, p. 633.)

Similarly in *Brown* (1910) 6 Cr App R 24, where a man had been tried for raping his 15-year-old daughter, whom he had allegedly threatened to kill if she told, the Court of Criminal Appeal said: 'In the absence of any complaint by a girl of 15 ravished by her father, where no caution is given to the jury, in our opinion the trial is not satisfactory'.

Even in the 17th century it seems improbable that the natural reaction of an adult woman who had been raped was to rush out and tell the world about it. Modern studies on rape victims show that it is very common for them to delay reporting the matter because of shock, fear and feelings of irrational guilt—and that many never report the offence (Temkin 1987, ch. 1). Where children have been sexually abused this is just as true, and probably even more so. Paediatricians with experience in dealing with sexually abused children say that:

> Disclosure may be made before, during, or after the examination and sometimes follows months or years after the event. Children may indicate they have a secret, cannot talk to you, or say 'I can't remember' or 'I was asleep'. (Hobbs and Wynne 1987a.)

Psychiatrists who work with sexually abused children say the same.

> Children are likely to reveal all types of sexual acts quickly if the offender has been a stranger. However, with family acquaintances and family members the disclosure may come about only after many years. (Mrazek amd Mrazek 1985.)

These facts are well known to the police: in a study of 177 cases of incest that were reported to the Metropolitan Police, in 44 cases the victim had made no attempt to disclose the offence at all (Gorry 1986). Community surveys of adults reveal that where they were sexually abused as children usually no one told the police, and that in many cases the child never told anyone about the incident (Finkelhor 1979, Russell 1983, Russell 1986). One little girl, who was badly sexually assaulted by a stranger in the toilets at her school, was so scared that she told no-one for two weeks (*The Independent*, 1 November 1990). The reasons for this are explained in the Report of the Cleveland Inquiry:

> Many children who have been subject to sexual abuse are put under pressure from the perpetrator not to tell; there may be threats of violence to the child or that the perpetrator will commit suicide, of being taken away from home and put into care, threats that someone they love will be angry with them, or that no one would believe them. Children may elect not to talk because of a genuine affection for the perpetrator and an awareness of the consequences to the perpetrator, to the partner, to the family unit, or for an older child an understanding of the economic considerations in the break-up of the family and the loss of the wage-earner. The secretive element persists. Professor Sir Martin Roth in evidence said 'There is a powerful disincentive to disclosing the fact that one has been subject to sexual abuse. The person who discloses this has fears that he may be regarded as having permitted himself, as having collaborated in it, as having been lastingly damaged in a sexual way. He is likely to fear ridicule, humiliation, obloquy and so on'. (Cleveland Report 1988, para. 17.)

In Canada and in New South Wales statutes have been enacted to reverse the law's official preference for sexual allegations that are made at the first opportunity (5). Until recently this idea had not penetrated the minds of lawyers in Britain, but it has now begun to do so. In a recent case, Beldam LJ remarked that indecent assault was an offence 'which, as is commonly known, even mature women may be reluctant to come forward and complain of' (*R v Sheffield Stipendiary Magistrate, ex parte Stephens* (1992) 156 JP 555).

Not only is the psychology behind the doctrine of recent complaints very unconvincing, there is also a piece of hypocrisy embedded in it. Although the jury or magistrates may not always be told the terms of the child's complaint, they are likely to find out that the police were sent for because of something that she said, from which they will assume that she accused the defendant, even if she in fact did not. Indeed in *Wallwork* (1958) 42 Cr App R 153, where Lord Goddard CJ said the five-year-old girl's complaint should not have been admitted, he added:

> There would have been no objection to the grandmother saying: 'The little girl made a complaint to me' and she could have been asked: 'In consequence of that complaint what did you do?'—and the answer would have been 'I took her to the doctor and later to the police'. One realises that, although the terms of the child's statement must not be given, any jury could see at once that as a consequence of the complaint the grandmother took the child to the doctor and the police and that the terms of the complaint would mention her father.

There is not much to be said for a rule that forbids a jury to be told the truth, but allows it to guess, and possibly guess wrong.

Previous identifications
Where a witness identifies the defendant at trial, evidence may be given that the witness earlier identified the defendant somewhere else. Evidence of the previous identification may be given by the witness personally, or by someone else who saw the witness make the identification, or both. This exception to the rule against previous consistent statements was put beyond all doubt as far as England was concerned in the House of Lords decision in *Christie* [1914] AC 545. At trial a small boy identified the defendant as the man who had indecently assaulted him, and it was held to be quite proper for his mother and others to give evidence that a few minutes after the incident, when confronted with the defendant, the boy had said, 'That is the man, mum'. This evidence was said to be admissible 'to show that the boy was able to identify at the time and to exclude the idea that the identification of the prisoner in the dock was an afterthought or a mistake'. On this point the law of Scotland has long been the same (Macphail 1987, sect. 19.60). In *Christie* the previous identification was at a confrontation, but nowadays it will usually have been at an identification parade. In England, evidence may also be given that an identifying witness had constructed a Photofit portrait which looked very much like the accused (*Cook* [1987] QB 417), or guided a police artist to make a sketch of him (*Smith* [1976] Crim LR 511).

The courts also allow evidence of a previous identification which goes beyond what the witness is able to reproduce in court. Where at trial the witness remembers that he previously identified the culprit, but cannot now remember who it was, or re-identify him in court, the courts on both sides of the border have also long allowed those who saw the original identification to say who was then picked out (*Burke* (1847) 2 Cox CC 295; *Muldoon v Herron* 1970 JC 30). More recently they have gone even further. In *Osbourne* [1973] QB 678, where two women who had witnessed an armed robbery at a Co-op were quite incoherent with fear at the trial and could give no intelligible evidence either about what they had done at the identity parade or about the identity of the defendants in the dock, the Court of Appeal said it was proper for a policeman to have given evidence that they in fact picked out the defendants at a parade held a few days after the robbery. In *Muldoon v Herron* the Scottish courts went still further, and held that evidence of an earlier identification could be given where at trial a witness actually claimed that the defendant was not the person she had picked out. The earlier identification was a piece of evidence in its own right, and capable of corroborating other evidence in the case. (On this see also page 99 above.)

A very important legal question about children's evidence is whether evidence of an early identification by the child can be given in a case where the child does not give evidence at trial. Logically, it ought to follow from *Osbourne* and *Muldoon v Herron* that the answer is yes. In those cases the witnesses gave no coherent evidence of identification in court, and in admitting the evidence of earlier identification the courts necessarily accepted it as something which did more than merely render more credible evidence of identification give by a witness at trial. They therefore treated it as evidence with a validity of its own, and if this is what it is, it ought to be admissible whether or not the person who made the identification gives evidence. The courts might say that this is unfair to the defendant, who has no opportunity to cross-examine the person who identified him; but in a case where the witness can remember nothing about the identification the defendant does not have a lot to lose in this respect. As yet there is no clear decision on the matter, however. The point arose in the unreported case of *Maine and McRobb* (*Press and Journal* (Aberdeen), 27 June 1979), where the prosecution led evidence of an identification made by a two-year-old child whom the judge had earlier rejected as a competent witness. It is not clear on what basis the evidence was admitted, however—and as far as we have been able to discover, the defence raised no objection to it, because by the time of the trial identification was no longer a major issue (1). The point under discussion has arisen repeatedly in the USA, where the courts in most jurisdictions have rejected the evidence where the child was not called at trial (Myers 1987a, p. 286); but in New Jersey it was admitted in a case involving an adult deaf-mute with a mental age of seven who, like the child in *Maine and McRobb*, did not merely identify the defendant, but reacted with spontaneous agitation when confronted with him (*State v Simmons* (1968) 52 NJ 538, 247 A 2d 313; (1969) 395 US 924).

In England s. 78 of the Police and Criminal Evidence Act 1984 gives the courts a general discretion to reject evidence if admitting it would make the trial unfair. In *O'Leary* (1988) 87 Cr App R 387 the Court of Appeal said that a judge should consider using this power to reject evidence of a previous identification made minutes after the crime by a little girl of nine who had been indecently assaulted and was still very frightened and upset at the time, if he thought her state created a serious risk of false identification.

Videotaped interviews
In England, the Criminal Justice Act 1991 has created an important new exception to the rule against previous consistent statements. Provided the child comes to court as a witness, the court can hear (any) previous statement (whether admissible under the rules explained above or not) provided it was recorded on videotape. This is discussed in the following chapter.

Part III
Hearsay in civil proceedings in England

When the first edition of this book came out, the English law about hearsay in civil cases involving children varied between one court and another, and was so complicated that it had to be explained with the help of a table. Fortunately, this is one part—perhaps the only part—of the law on children's evidence where efforts at reform have actually made it simpler. Broadly speaking, any civil court that is concerned with the welfare of a child may now receive and act on hearsay evidence. The fact that it is hearsay affects its weight, naturally, but no longer makes it inadmissible.

This was always the position in wardship. It was confirmed by the important House of Lords decision in *Re K* [1965] AC 201, where two children had been made wards of court in a dispute between their separated parents over custody. The Official Solicitor, acting as the children's guardian *ad litem*, submitted a written report to the court which seemed to cast doubt on the mother's fitness to look after the children, and this the judge took into account in reaching his decision. The mother appealed, raising, among other objections, the fact that the report contained hearsay. The House of Lords accepted that it contained hearsay: indeed, Lord Devlin even said the entire report was technically hearsay, because the Official Solicitor had transmitted his findings to the judge in writing instead of giving oral evidence on oath and submitting himself to cross-examination. Nevertheless the House of Lords said that the evidence was properly admitted. In wardship, they said, the court has a duty to act in the child's best interests, and what these are can only be discovered by listening to all the evidence available, hearsay included. As Lord Devlin put it, 'The [wardship] jurisdiction itself is more ancient than the rule against hearsay and I see no reason why that rule should now be introduced into it'.

The case for admitting hearsay evidence in other civil proceedings involving the welfare of children is the same as the case for admitting it in wardship, and not surprisingly, the other civil courts quickly started following where the House of Lords had led. In 1989 they had a rude shock in *H* v *H*; *K* v *K* [1990] Fam 86, when the Court of Appeal told them that the right to dispense with the hearsay rule was the exclusive prerogative of the High Court in wardship cases. In so holding, the Court of Appeal reversed county court decisions refusing fathers access to their children, partly because they were based on findings of sexual abuse made on hearsay evidence from social workers about what the children had told them had been going on. The decision was heavily criticised, and in response to this, the government moved a last-minute amendment to the Children Bill, which later became law as s. 96(3) to (7) of the Children Act 1989. This gave the Lord Chancellor power to make orders permitting hearsay evidence to be used in civil proceedings concerned with the upbringing, maintenance or welfare of children.

It was generally expected that this would be followed by an order making hearsay generally admissible in civil proceedings concerned with children. There was amazement, therefore, when the Lord Chancellor made an order making hearsay admissible in some proceedings but not in others—and in particular, made different rules for different parts of the magistrates' courts. The Children (Admissibility of Hearsay) Order 1990 (SI 1990 No. 143) allowed hearsay to be used in the juvenile (now youth) court when dealing (as it then did) with care proceedings, but failed to do the same for the domestic court, where the same justices might have to examine the same allegations in the context of a dispute between the parents over custody or access. The explanation is said to have been a dispute between the Lord Chancellor's Department, which is responsible for civil law and the court system, and the Home Office, which at that time shared responsibility with the Lord Chancellor's Department for the magistrates' courts. The Lord Chancellor's Department wanted to make hearsay generally available, but the Home Office opposed the change, and this ridiculous compromise was the result. The Order caused immediate difficulty in the courts (*Re B (Appeal to Crown Court: Evidence)* [1992] FCR 153), and in the legal press it attracted the derision it deserved (White 1990). This persuaded the Lord Chancellor to think again. The following year he issued the Children (Admissibility of Hearsay Evidence) Order 1991 (SI 1991 No. 1115), which revoked the earlier order, and permitted hearsay evidence to be used in all family proceedings in a magistrates' court. And in 1993 he replaced this with an even wider provision, which covers proceedings under the Child Support Act 1991 as well. This, the Children (Admissibility of Hearsay Evidence) Order 1993, provides as follows:

In (a) civil proceedings before the High Court or a county court; and (b) (i) in family proceedings, and (ii) civil proceedings under the Child Support Act 1991 in a magistrates' court, evidence given in connection with the upbringing, maintenance or welfare of a child shall be admissible notwithstanding any rule of law relating to hearsay.

This has the effect of allowing a child's account of an event to be received in the form of hearsay evidence in virtually any civil case involving children. In the magistrates' courts there is some limit, because it is plain from the words of the Order that (child support proceedings aside) it only applies to 'family proceedings'. At first sight, this appears to mean 'family proceedings' as listed in s. 8(2) of the Children Act 1989, where they are defined to include proceedings under Parts I, II and IV of the Children Act, and a range of other statutes. However, in *Oxfordshire County Council* v *R* [1992] 2 FCR 310 it was held that proceedings under any part of the Children Act were within the scope of the Order: hence hearsay was admissible in proceedings brought to determine whether a local authority should keep a child in care in 'secure accommodation'—which are under Part III of the Act. Notwithstanding this ruling, however, there are still some civil proceedings in magistrates' courts where the Order does not apply. For example it would not enable a magistrates' court to receive a hearsay account of a child's evidence when hearing an application for a liquor licence, or condemning a dangerous dog. In the High Court and in the county court the Order applies to any 'civil proceedings'. Section 96(7) of the Children Act, under which the Order is made, defines 'civil proceedings' as having the same meaning as in s. 18 of the Civil Evidence Act 1968, which defines 'civil proceedings' in a way that is open-ended. Thus in the High Court and the county court there is, in effect, no limit as to the type of proceedings to which the Order applies, and a hearsay account of what a child has said can be received wherever it is put forward 'in connection with the upbringing, maintenance or welfare of a child'. Obviously, such evidence will normally be put forward only in proceedings brought to determine the future of the child; but it could also be put forward, at least theoretically, in civil proceedings of other kinds—for example, a claim for damages against someone who was responsible for the child's welfare and neglected or abused him. In *Re C (Minors) (Contempt Proceedings)* [1993] 1 FCR 820 the Court of Appeal said that it was potentially applicable in proceedings for contempt of court.

In addition to this Order there are several other statutory provisions which potentially allow a child's account to be given by way of hearsay evidence in civil proceedings. Section 7(4) of the Children Act makes admissible hearsay which is contained in a court welfare officer's report, ss. 41(11) and 42(2) make hearsay admissible which is contained in a report from a guardian *ad litem*, and s. 45 allows a court dealing with an emergency protection order to receive and act on any kind of evidence. Obviously, these provisions are narrower than the 1991 Order, and add little to the law since that Order came into force.

In this section we have discussed these provisions in order to show how far they allow a court to receive in evidence a hearsay account of what has been said by a child, but they are not limited to children's evidence. In so far as they make admissible a hearsay account of what a child has said, they do the same for what has been said by an adult.

Now that hearsay evidence is in principle admissible in civil cases involving children, a further question arises. How much weight are the courts prepared to put upon it?

In deciding *Re K* in 1965, Lord Devlin said that he thought that in practice judges would be reluctant to act on hearsay evidence alone if serious misbehaviour was alleged. However, judges have not been able to avoid acting on hearsay in serious cases. In civil proceedings, the more serious the allegation the greater the risk to the child if the court refuses to act on it, should that allegation turn out to be true. As Waite J said in *Re W (Minors) (Child Abuse: Evidence)* [1987] 1 FLR 297:

> [These] are all cases of exceptional difficulty, because they bring into stark contrast two principles that everyone would acknowledge as fundamental to our society. One is the basic requirement of justice that nobody should have to face a finding by any court of serious parental misconduct without the opportunity of having the allegations against him clearly specified and cogently proved. The other is the public interest in the detection and prevention of parental child abuse as conduct which is liable, if persisted in, to do serious damage to the emotional development of the victim and to his or her capacity to form stable and satisfying relationships in adult life.

The suggestion is sometimes made that hearsay evidence may justify a finding that a child has been abused by somebody, but not a finding that the person who did it was X or Y. In *Re W (Minors) (Wardship: Evidence)* [1990] FCR 286 this question was discussed by the Court of Appeal. One of the three judges took this view. The majority, however, accepted that such a finding could in principle be made on the basis of a hearsay account of what a child had said, if the court found it sufficiently convincing. Butler-Sloss LJ put it cautiously:

> Grave allegations of sexual abuse made in a statement by a child naming a perpetrator present considerable problems. Such allegations would, unsupported, rarely be sufficiently cogent and reliable for a court to be satisfied, on the balance of probabilities, that the person named was indeed the perpetrator.

But she added that the child's statement might be supported by the 'manner in which he or she gives the description and in other aspects of his or her behaviour', and also said that the court could sometimes order the removal of the child from the family without expressly naming a particular member of the family as responsible for the abuse. Neill LJ put the matter more bluntly:

> . . . the court will be very slow indeed to make a finding of fact adverse to a parent if the only material before it has been untested by cross-examination. Morever, it will examine with particular care the evidence of the person who communicates the hearsay material to it. But as the welfare of the child is the paramount consideration I see no escape from the conclusion that in some cases a court, in assessing the risks to which a child may be exposed, may be obliged to reach conclusions of fact which in other circumstances and in other proceedings it would not be free to do.

These remarks were made in a wardship case: but there is no reason why the position should be any different in other civil proceedings, now that hearsay evidence can be used there too. As section 1 of the Children Act 1989 states very clearly, the child's welfare is to be the court's paramount consideration in any proceedings where the question is the upbringing of a child.

The law reports now contain a number of cases where courts, clearly influenced by hearsay evidence of what the child had said, have made findings that a particular person had sexually abused a child (6).

It goes without saying, however, that the fact that the evidence is hearsay makes the courts rather cautious about acting upon it. Hearsay, as against direct evidence, potentially presents two difficulties: (i) did the child really say it?—there is a risk of errors of transmission; (ii) did she mean it?—a hearsay account is usually made without the usual tests and safeguards by which the courts try to ensure that witnesses tell the truth. The less a particular piece of hearsay evidence is affected by these problems, the more weight the court is prepared to give it. Thus, as we explain in the next chapter, judges give more weight to a child's out-of-court statement that has been tape-recorded than to one to which a witness speaks from memory. And where the child's statement was made in the course of an interview, the courts give less weight to a child's statement if it was given under pressure, or as the result of suggestive questioning. The need for video-recording, the need for trained interviewers, and the undesirability of pressured interviewing were among the points made in the Cleveland Report; since when a number of judges (7) have stressed the importance of the 'Cleveland Guidelines' when deciding what weight to put on hearsay evidence (see chapter 12). Other important matters are obviously the age of the child, the length of time that has elapsed between the interview and the events the child is asked to describe, and how likely it is that the child's account has been influenced by coaching or by the questions asked in previous interviews (*Re M (Minors) (Sexual Abuse: Evidence)* [1993] 1 FCR 253. In the end, the judge has to weigh up the various factors relating to the interview, and then decide the case on the totality of the evidence. In *Re M* a judge found that a father had sexually abused his little daughters partly on what one child, aged only four, had told a psychiatrist in a diagnostic interview, six months after the incident, and after the child had already been exposed to questioning and the possibility of coaching. The Court of Appeal upheld his finding. Although these matters obviously weakened the evidence, the interview was competently done, and had been video-recorded. There was in addition a certain amount of other evidence, including the father's suspicious behaviour when the mother originally confronted him with what the child had told her he had done.

In deciding whether to act on a piece of hearsay evidence the courts obviously consider whether it stands alone, or is backed up by other evidence. As we explain in chapters 8 and 9, the civil courts are much less restricted than the criminal courts in the matters they can treat as evidence, and hence as corroboration of a hearsay account. They can, for example, treat as evidence the character and tendencies of the person whom the child accuses, and (as in the case described in the previous paragraph) his or her suspicious failure to answer the accusation when questioned by the police. The civil courts also regularly hear opinion evidence from experts which no-one would usually think of adducing in a criminal case.

In general, English judges are reluctant to hear direct evidence from children in civil proceedings, and prefer to rely on hearsay accounts. The following passage from a recent judgment illustrates this attitude:

> . . . When this trial began an indication was given to me that M wished to give evidence. I confess to showing my anxiety about that course of conduct to be adopted by the local authority. I took the view that I had no real power to prevent them calling evidence in support of their case, this evidence being tendered by a girl nearly 17, suffering though she may be from the disability of her learning difficulties, but I did not like the course proposed . . . In this Division as elsewhere one has both to grapple with the necessary process of ascertainment of truth, but here one is always mindful of the consequences that flow from the findings that are made and from the manner and the conduct of the forensic process of examination, cross-examination and re-examination . . . In the ordinary course, their voice is usually heard properly and sufficiently through their guardian and if there is a real need to see the judge, he can agree to see them in his room if that is necessary . . . (Ward J in *Nottinghamshire County Council* v *P* [1993] 1 FCR 180, at 188.)

HEARSAY IN CIVIL PROCEEDINGS TO WHICH THE CHILDREN (ADMISSIBILITY OF HEARSAY EVIDENCE) ORDER 1993 DOES NOT APPLY

It will be unusual for anyone to wish to put a child's evidence before a court as hearsay except where the 1993 Order applies. It could happen, however—for example if a child was a key witness to an accident which gave rise to a damages claim, and for some reason it was undesirable to insist on his or her giving live evidence. So the rules are explained here for the sake of completeness.

In any civil proceedings in these courts other than those covered by the Children (Admissibility of Hearsay Evidence) Order 1993—personal injury claims, for example—hearsay evidence is admissible under the Civil Evidence Act 1968, but generally not otherwise (see the Civil Evidence Act 1968, s. 1).

The main provision of the Civil Evidence Act 1968 is s. 2(1), which is as follows:

> In any civil proceedings a statement made, whether orally or in a document or otherwise, by any person, whether called as a witness in those proceedings or not, shall, subject to this section and to rules of court, be admissible as evidence of any fact [see note (8)] stated therein of which direct oral evidence by him would be admissible.

At first sight this appears to abolish the hearsay rule altogether, but in fact its effect is much more limited than this.

In the first place, there is the phrase 'of which direct oral evidence by him would be admissible', which makes it plain that if the statement would not have been admissible in evidence coming from the mouth of the original maker it cannot be relayed under this section second-hand by someone else. Thus this section clearly cannot be used to admit a statement from a child who would have been too young to pass the test of competency as still required in civil cases (see chapter 4).

Secondly, s. 2 is considerably restricted by subsection (3), which effectively limits it to first-hand hearsay. 'B may prove what he heard A say, but C may not prove what B told him A said. A's written statement that he saw X hit Y is clearly admissible as evidence of that fact, and B's written statement that A told him that he saw X hit Y is equally clearly inadmissible as evidence of the assault.' (Cross 1990, p. 548.)

Thirdly, by s. 8 of the Act, s. 2 operates subject to rules of court. The relevant rules (RSC, Ord. 38, rr. 21–31 in the High Court, CCR, Ord. 20, rr. 14–24 in the county courts) set up a system under which a party who wishes to call hearsay evidence under s. 2 must give advance notice to the other side, which then has the right to insist that they call the original maker of the statement, unless he is:

> dead, or beyond the seas, or unfit by reason of his bodily or mental condition to attend as a witness, or cannot with reasonable diligence be identified or found, or cannot reasonably be expected (having regard to the time which has elapsed since he was connected or concerned as aforesaid and to all the circumstances) to have any recollection of matters relevant to the accuracy or otherwise of the statement.

Presumably a child who has been seriously traumatised by the event about which he would have to testify would count as 'unfit by reason of his bodily or mental condition to attend as a witness', but—as Croom-Johnson LJ said in *H* v *H* [1990] Fam 86—not one who is just too young. The rules do give a judge a discretion to admit hearsay statements although the rules have not been complied with. However, according to Croom-Johnson LJ in *H* v *H*, this merely permits the judge to admit a statement where the procedural steps required by the rules could have been followed, but were forgotten; it does not permit him to let in hearsay where the witness is unavailable for some reason other than those listed in the rules.

Section 4 of the Civil Evidence Act 1968, which makes statements in records admissible, will sometimes let in hearsay evidence of a child's statement which fails to meet the requirements of s. 2. Section 4(1) is as follows:

> . . . in any civil proceedings a statement contained in a document shall, subject to this section and to rules of court, be admissible as evidence of any fact stated therein of which direct oral evidence would be admissible, if the document is, or forms part of, a record compiled by a person acting under a duty from information which was supplied by a person (whether acting under a duty or not) who had, or may reasonably be supposed to have had, personal knowledge of the matters dealt with in that information and which, if not supplied by that person to the compiler of the record directly, was supplied by him to the compiler of the record indirectly through one or more intermediaries each acting under a duty.

This provision is wider than s. 2 in two respects. First, it is not limited to 'first-hand' hearsay. Secondly it does not seem to be a requirement of s. 4 that the person who originally made the statement would have been competent to give evidence in person. Where s. 2 makes hearsay evidence of what a person said 'admissible as evidence of any fact stated therein of which direct oral evidence *by him* would be admissible', the equivalent words in s. 4 are 'admissible as evidence of any fact stated therein of which direct oral evidence would be admissible'. Here the words 'by him' are left out. So, as long as the fact mentioned in the statement was one which somebody could have given evidence about, it should not matter that the person who actually made the statement was a child too young to be a competent witness.

However, s. 4 is narrower than s. 2 in one important respect, because it only applies where the statement is contained in a 'document' forming part of a 'record' compiled by someone who is under a 'duty' to keep it. In construing these requirements, the courts have tended to limit the section to files of information gathered for general purposes, and to exclude files started for the specific purpose of investigating the matter about which the parties are now suing one another (*Savings & Investment Bank Ltd* v *Gasco Investments (Netherlands) BV* [1984] 1 WLR 271; but see *Taylor* v *Taylor* [1970] 1 WLR 1148).

Like s. 2, s. 4 is also subject to the rules of court about notice and counternotice.

The Civil Evidence Act 1968 has also reversed in civil proceedings the strange common law rule that prevents the court from having access to the previous statements of witnesses who do give evidence at trial (see page 137 above). By s. 2(2) of the Act these may be put in evidence to supplement a witness's testimony provided the court grants leave. Where such evidence is admitted its legal effect is not merely to support the witness's fractured utterances in court: it amounts to independent evidence of all that it contains. Furthermore, s. 3 of the Act provides that where in cross-examination a witness in civil proceedings is proved to have made a previous statement that is inconsistent with his courtroom testimony, this earlier statement now counts as positive evidence of the facts that it contains, and no longer merely disembowels the evidence the witness gave orally in court.

Section 20 of the Civil Evidence Act 1968 gives the Lord Chancellor power to bring the Act into force by stages in the various courts that exercise civil jurisdiction, but for reasons that remain obscure he has never brought it into force in the magistrates' courts. Thus unless the case is 'family proceedings' and thus within the 1991 Order (see above), hearsay in civil proceedings in magistrates' courts is still basically governed by the common law rules which operate in criminal proceedings: as a number of councils discovered painfully when they found they could not use computer records in the magistrates' courts to prove that people still owed poll tax, and it was necessary to call the officials to give evidence (*R* v *Coventry JJ ex parte Bullard* (1992) 142 NLJ 383). The common law rules were explained in the section of this chapter on criminal proceedings (see pages 129-146 above) and it is not necessary to say any more about them here. In civil cases in the magistrates' courts the common law rules operate minus a number of statutory exceptions, like the documentary hearsay provisions of the Criminal Justice Act 1988, which apply to criminal cases only. However, they are supplemented by the Evidence Act

1938: which should have been repealed and replaced by the Civil Evidence Act 1968, but which carries on a ghost-like existence in the magistrates' courts because of the failure of successive Lord Chancellors to implement the Civil Evidence Act 1968 for use there.

Section 1(1) of the Evidence Act 1938 provides:

In any civil proceedings where direct oral evidence of a fact would be admissible, any statement made by a person in a document and tending to establish that fact shall, on production of the original document, be admissible as evidence of that fact if the following conditions are satisfied, that is to say —

    (i) if the maker of the statement either —
      (a) had personal knowledge of the matters dealt with by the statement; or
      (b) where the document in question is or forms part of a record purporting to be a continuous record, made the statement (insofar as the matters dealt with thereby are not within his personal knowledge) in the performance of a duty to record information supplied to him by a person who had, or might reasonably be supposed to have, personal knowledge of those matters; and
    (ii) if the maker of the statement is called as a witness in the proceedings: Provided that the condition that the maker of the statement shall be called as a witness need not be satisfied if he is dead, or unfit by reason of his bodily or mental condition to attend as a witness, or if he is beyond the seas and it is not reasonably practicable to secure his attendance, or if all reasonable efforts to find him have been made without success.

These provisions, which at first sight look quite wide, are narrowed by two overriding limitations. The first is that they are restricted to statements contained in 'documents'. The definition contained in s. 6 seems to restrict these to papers, and tape recordings do not appear to be covered. The second limitation is contained in s. 1(3), which excludes 'any statement made by a person interested at a time when proceedings were pending or anticipated involving a dispute as to any fact which the statement might tend to establish'.

Subject to these two limitations, the Evidence Act 1938 lets in hearsay evidence of children's statements in the following three situations.

First, where the witness (child or adult) gives live evidence, his previous written statements can be put in evidence to supplement his courtroom testimony (s. 1(1)(ii)).

Secondly, where a witness (child or adult) would have given evidence about some matter within his personal knowledge but cannot do so for any of the reasons specified in s. 1(1), his written statement must be admitted in evidence despite his absence. (In addition to this, s. 1(2)(a) gives the court a discretion to admit the written statement of such a witness who is absent for some other reason, if 'undue delay or expense' would result from insisting on his live appearance.) To be admissible under this part of the Evidence Act 1938 the statement, if made by an interested party, must have been made before the dispute arose. It must also be contained in a document; and what is more, the document must either be written in the witness's own hand, or else 'signed or initialled by him or otherwise recognised by him in writing as one for the accuracy of which he is responsible' (s. 1(4)). A hearsay statement from a child that satisfies all these complicated requirements is conceivable, but will be a rarity indeed.

Thirdly, where a person in the course of official duties makes a written 'record', and includes within it information supplied by third parties from their personal knowledge, this record can sometimes be put in evidence, the third parties' hearsay statements included. For such a record to be admissible, the person who compiled it must give evidence, or be unable to do so for one of the reasons mentioned in the preceding paragraph (or be excused from doing so by the court in its discretion under s. 1(2)). The record must consist of a document, and be in the writing of the person who compiled it, or else signed or acknowledged by him or her: but these formalities do not apply to the person who supplied the information. Where, for example, a person saw a road accident and described it to a policeman, who recorded this account in his police notebook without getting the witness to sign it, the statement was held admissible (*Simpson* v *Lever* [1963] 1 QB 517). This 'record' part of the Evidence Act 1938 clearly has the potential to let in hearsay evidence of what children have told official people such as doctors, psychologists, psychiatrists, police officers, and social workers; but it is limited, of course, by the general prohibition against statements made by interested parties after the dispute arose.

Where the 'record' provision in the Evidence Act 1938 lets in a child's (or adult's) hearsay statement, that statement is then admissible not only as evidence that the statement was made—should that fact be relevant in itself—but also as evidence that the incidents described took place. This is implicit in the case law on the subject (e.g., *Simpson* v *Lever*).

For further details of the Evidence Act 1938 readers should consult a pre-1968 book on evidence, such as the 3rd edition of *Cross on Evidence* (1967).

THE POSITION IN NORTHERN IRELAND

In Northern Ireland, as in England, hearsay evidence is freely admissible in wardship (*Re B* [1986] NI 88). There is, however, no equivalent as yet of the Children Act 1989 or of the Order making hearsay admissible generally in civil proceedings concerning children in England. Outside wardship, therefore, hearsay evidence of what a child told someone happened is theoretically admissible in civil proceedings only under the limited statutory exceptions to the hearsay rule that apply to civil proceedings generally, which are the Evidence Act (NI) 1939 and the Civil Evidence Act (NI) 1971. In practice, the civil courts in Northern Ireland bend the rules a little to admit hearsay in children's cases. At the time of writing, reform of the hearsay rule in civil proceedings in Northern Ireland is under discussion (Law Reform Advisory Committee for Northern Ireland 1990).

Part IV
Hearsay in civil proceedings in Scotland

Fortunately, this section can be mercifully brief.

Until 1988, the same common law rules of evidence applied in civil as in criminal proceedings in Scotland. There was a slight tendency to bend them a little in order to admit hearsay evidence in proceedings where the welfare of the child was in issue, as when disputed grounds of referral had to be determined by the sheriff (*W* v *Kennedy* 1988 SLT 583). Nevertheless, the hearsay rule was generally applied, and the civil courts were not usually able to accept second-hand accounts of children's descriptions of events. As in England this sometimes caused problems in civil cases; however, the more relaxed Scottish attitude to the competency requirement (see chapter 4), and the fact that Scottish children could always give unsworn evidence in civil proceedings, meant that it was easier than in England to call the child to give direct evidence.

There was discontent with the hearsay rule in general, however, and in 1986 the Scottish Law Commission published its 100th report which recommended that for civil proceedings it should be abolished. The Scottish Law Commission favoured copying the scheme in the English Civil Evidence Act 1968 under which a party wishing to call hearsay evidence must give advance notice, giving his opponent the chance to insist on his calling the original maker of the statement if available. However, this idea did not find favour with the government law officers, who thought it was an undesirable complication, and s. 2(1) of the Civil Evidence (Scotland) Act 1988 simply abolishes the hearsay rule in civil proceedings as follows:

In civil proceedings —

(a) evidence shall not be excluded solely on the ground that it is hearsay;

(b) a statement made by a person otherwise than in the course of the proof shall be admissible as evidence of any matter contained in the statement of which direct oral evidence by that person would be admissible;

(c) the court, or as the case may be the jury, if satisfied that any fact has been established by evidence in those proceedings, shall be entitled to find that fact proved by the evidence nowithstanding that the evidence is hearsay.

The only Scottish civil proceedings in which the common law hearsay rules survive are referrals to children's hearings where the ground alleged is that the child has committed an offence. By s. 9 of the Civil Evidence (Scotland) Act 1988 the Act does not apply here, and the offence must be proved not only according to the criminal standard of proof—beyond reasonable doubt—but also according to the rules of criminal evidence, the rule against hearsay included. For all other proceedings the rule is completely abolished; and it is not only hearsay that is now admissible, but 'hearsay upon hearsay', because s. 9 also contains a definition of hearsay, which is that '"hearsay" includes hearsay of whatever degree'. Thus

It follows, strictly, from this provision that what the social worker tells the court about what mum told her as to what the child said is capable of being regarded as evidence as to the truth of what the child is said to have said (Kearney, 1990).

In cases involving children this Act has enabled the Scottish courts to receive as evidence accounts of interviews that police officers and social workers have had with children, and where these interviews were recorded, to see and hear the tapes. If the child later gives live evidence retracting what was said at the interview, the judge is also legally entitled to believe the original statement rather than the oral evidence, if the earlier statement is the one that he or she finds more convincing (*K* v *Kennedy* [1992] SCLR 386).

An important limitation on the admissibility of hearsay, however, are the following words in s. 2(1)(b): 'a statement made by a person otherwise than in the course of the proof shall be admissible as evidence of any matter contained in the statement *of which direct oral evidence by that person would be admissible*'. This raises the question of how you show that the child who made the statement would have been competent as a witness. The problem arose in *F* v *Kennedy* [1992] SCLR 139, where a child of six had told a social worker about 'lewd and libidinous practices' of which he had been the victim, but when he appeared before the sheriff he refused to talk, and the sheriff was unable even to carry out a competency examination. On appeal it was held that in these circumstances the sheriff was not entitled to treat the child's earlier statements as evidence under the Act. This decision appeared to mean that if anyone wants to introduce evidence of a child's hearsay statement in a civil case in Scotland, the child must be called as a witness, if only for a competency examination: a situation which would shut out possibly useful evidence in certain cases, and would prevent the hearsay evidence being used, as it is in England, to relieve the child of the need to come to court. In the later case of *M and M* v *Kennedy* [1993] SCLR 69, however, *F* v *Kennedy* was qualified. The new case concerned a 12-year-old girl who was an 'elective mute': someone who is physically able to speak, but through psychological disturbance usually refuses to speak to others. To a psychiatrist she had given an oral account of sexual abuse, but to a very patient sheriff, who saw her at length, she had communicated little, and that by signs and drawings. On appeal it was held that the sheriff's rudimentary communication with the child was enough to justify his decision that the child was competent (see chapter 4). But the court also said that it would have been permissible for him to make a finding that the child would have been a competent witness on the basis of what the psychiatrists had told him, if they had asked the right questions, and could explain why the child herself could not communicate with the sheriff. The courts raised, but did not answer, a further question: what is the position if a witness makes a statement at a time when he or she is clearly competent, but by the time of trial something had happened to render him or her incompetent? The purpose of the competency requirement is supposed to be to shut out evidence that is likely to be unreliable, and reliability obviously depends on the state of the witness when the statement was made. So in principle such a statement surely ought to be admissible.

Part V
Competency and hearsay statements

This leads on to a general question. Where a child's statement may be repeated, does it usually matter whether or not the child himself would have been competent to give evidence? The matter has been discussed at length in the USA (Myers 1987a, sect. 5.39), but there is very little authority on the point in Britain, and the matter must be approached from first principles.

In the first place, where the child's statement is put in evidence not in order to establish the facts contained in it, but merely to establish that the statement was made, it is admissible without trespassing upon the hearsay rule, because it is irrelevant whether the child spoke the truth or lied. If the child's father is prosecuted for murdering X, for example, and he runs a defence of provocation based on his belief that X had raped his child, the court would undoubtedly receive evidence that the child had told her father that she had been raped: and the purpose of admitting it would not be to show that she had been raped, but merely to show that the father believed that this was so. In such a case as this it is obviously irrelevant whether the child would have been competent as a witness. The same should be true in the more likely case where the child's statement is put in evidence because the defendant incorporated it into his confession: where the police told him what the child had said about him, and he promptly admitted that it was true. Here the purpose of telling the court the child's statement is to show what the defendant has confessed to, not as direct proof of the facts contained within it.

Some statutory exceptions to the hearsay rule are created by statutes which make it plain that they only apply to the statements of those who would have been competent witnesses. This is the case with the Civil Evidence (Scotland) Act 1988, as we have seen. It is also the case with s. 13 of the Criminal Justice Act 1925 which makes depositions given in committal proceedings admissible at the subsequent trial in certain cases (page 134 above), and it is also the case with ss. 42 and 43 of the Children and Young Persons Act 1933, which cover depositions taken from children who are too sick to come to court (page 83). It is also the case in s. 23 of the Criminal Justice Act 1988, which admits first-hand documentary hearsay (page 135). Other statutory provisions leave the matter obscure. One of these is s. 24 of the Criminal Justice Act 1988, which, as we have seen, makes admissible most hearsay statements contained in records, and another is s. 2(7) of the Criminal Justice Act 1967, which deems unsworn witness statements taken by the police to count as depositions in certain circumstances, so rendering them admissible under the statutory provisions concerned with depositions in committal proceedings (page 134).

Turning now to common law exceptions, it seems that 'dying declarations' are inadmissible if the maker would not have been competent as a witness. This was held in the 19th-century English case of *Pike* (1829) 3 C & P 598, where the judge rejected the dying declaration of a little girl of four because there was no evidence that she had any idea of a future state, adding: 'from her age, we must take it that she could not possibly have had any idea of that kind'.

As far as the other common law exceptions are concerned, and the st
exceptions where the point is not expressly covered in the legislatid
courts would presumably look to the purpose behind the exception. *Res gestae*
statements, alias excited utterances, are admitted on the theory that people are
unlikely to lie in the immediate aftermath of some overwhelmingly exciting
event which they have just experienced. Before a judge admits a statement
under this exception to the hearsay rule he must ask himself: Can the
possibility of concoction or distortion be disregarded? (page 131.) As these
statements are only admitted where the judge thinks they are inherently
reliable, the competency requirement would seem to serve no useful purpose.
Thus in the Scottish case of *Murray* (1866) 5 Irv 232 Lord Ardmillan held a
mentally handicapped girl incompetent to be a witness, but admitted hearsay
evidence of what she had said immediately after the defendant had allegedly
raped her. The American courts also admit evidence of excited utterances by
children whether or not they would satisfy the competency requirement
(Myers 1987a, sect. 5.39) and it is probable that the English courts would do
the same.

We have already seen that it is uncertain whether evidence can be given that
a child identified a suspect if the child does not then give evidence in court
(page 145 above). If this can be done, the problem of competency might then
be raised. In the *Maine and McRobb* case (page 145 above) such evidence
seems to have been admitted, without objection, where the child herself, aged
three, was held incompetent as a witness. Whether the evidence, if objected to,
would be held admissible in either jurisdiction is a doubtful matter.

Insofar as the English civil courts admit hearsay evidence of children's
statements they seem to do so even where the child would not have been
competent as a witness under the English rules; for an example, see *S v S*
[1988] FCR 219. The position is otherwise in civil proceedings in Scotland, as
we saw in the previous section.

In reading the preceding paragraphs, it should be remembered that the
competency requirement for child witnesses probably no longer exists for
criminal proceedings in England (see pages 62–65 above).

Part VI
A critical look at the hearsay rule concerning
children's evidence

If anyone has succeeded in reading the preceding pages he is unlikely to have
enjoyed the experience. A lay person will probably be puzzled, confused and
angry at such a complicated, muddled and often apparently pointless set of
rules. Even the most uncritical of lawyers may have had some trouble in
grasping such a quantity of detail both so intricate and involved.

The first thing that is obviously wrong with the body of rules and exceptions
which we call the rules about hearsay is that it is very complicated, and that
many of the complications are pointless. In civil proceedings in England, for
example, different rules apply for different courts and different types of

proceedings—and for no better reason than that successive Lord Chancellors have failed to extend the Civil Evidence Act 1968 to the magistrates' courts. In criminal proceedings the hearsay rule has a mass of complicated exceptions, and the complications are often pointless, because they conflict with both the rules of human psychology, and the reasons why the exceptions were originally created: the tiresome minutiae of dying declarations, and of 'recent complaint', are good examples. And at a more basic level, the rules about hearsay are needlessly complicated because they lack any coherent unifying principle. Some exceptions to the hearsay rule seem to have been created because there was felt to be something about a particular type of hearsay which made it as reliable as evidence on oath: dying declarations, and *res gestae*, for example. Others were created solely because in the circumstances to which the exception applies the witness is unavailable, and without the exception the court would have to do without his evidence: like statements from deceased persons in Scotland. But if the fact that the witness is unavailable can justify any specific exception to the hearsay rule, it justifies a single, simple, general exception, in which all the tiresomely complicated detailed rules could be swallowed up.

The second criticism of this body of law is that it is silly.

There is a grain of sense at the bottom of the hearsay rule *stricto sensu* — the part of it that applies to out-of-court statements by non-witnesses. Broadly speaking, what vegans say about food is true of evidence: 'first-hand is first-rate'. It is obviously sensible for the law to insist on hearing a story from a first-hand source when a first-hand source is available. But it is not at all sensible to take the next step, and to say that if there is no first-hand source available then in principle the story cannot be told at all. Furthermore, there seems to be no sense whatever in that part of the rule which suppresses the previous statements of those who do appear as witnesses at trial. The orthodox reasons for refusing to listen to hearsay evidence are two: (i) how can we tell that he really said it? (ii) how can we be sure that he meant it? Both vanish when the person who originally made the statement is there in court. Furthermore, by making the court ignore every account he gave of the incident before he got there, and accept nothing save what he says in court, this rule requires us to accept the following two propositions of psychology as valid: (a) that memory improves with the passage of time; (b) that stress improves the process of recall. (We return to this point in chapter 10.)

When taken in combination with the other rules of criminal procedure and evidence the hearsay rule is a disaster for justice in cases where children are concerned. The competency requirement and the rigours of the adversarial system often prevent children giving evidence in court themselves; and the hearsay rule makes it impossible for other people to repeat in court the accounts the children gave them. In consequence, the courts have to deal with offences committed against children without being able to hear the child's version of what happened. In the case of *Maine and McRobb* (see page 145 1979 above), for example, the three-year-old torture victim was unable to give evidence in person, and the hearsay rule prevented her father from telling the court what she had said had been done to her.

[The father] was about to tell the court of what his daughter said when Mr Cameron objected on the grounds that it would be hearsay evidence. From the witness-box [the father] said to Mr Cameron 'How could it be hearsay—my daughter is only three'. Lord Kincraig warned [the father] that he would have to leave the court if he continued interrupting. (*Press and Journal* (Aberdeen), 27 June 1979.)

The result is usually that the guilty are improperly acquitted—or more probably, not even prosecuted. But as *Sparks* v *R* [1964] AC 964 reminds us, the resulting gap in evidence can have the opposite result. There, it will be recalled, a white man was prosecuted for indecently assaulting a child of three, and the defendant was not allowed to lead evidence that immediately after the incident she had described her attacker as black. Nor is this the only case where hearsay evidence from a young child has been excluded where it was favourable to the defence: for a striking modern example, see *Field* [1993] Crim LR 456.

Not surprisingly, most other legal systems manage to avoid these absurd and mischevous results.

In the USA, which inherited the hearsay rule together with the rest of the English law of evidence, the Federal Rules of Evidence—which many States have copied—list the various exceptions to the hearsay rule, and add a 'general residual exception' under which other hearsay statements are admissible if they possess 'comparable circumstantial guarantees of trustworthiness'. Children's hearsay statements have often been admitted under this exception (Myers 1987a, sect. 5.37; Yun 1983).

In 1982 the State of Washington went further and enacted a special statutory exception to deal with child abuse, which is as follows:

A statement made by a child when under the age of ten describing any act of sexual contact performed with or on the child by another, not otherwise admissible by statute or court rule, is admissible in evidence in dependency proceedings . . . and criminal proceedings in courts of the State of Washington if:

(1)   The court finds, in a hearing conducted outside the presence of the jury, that the time, content, and circumstances of the statement provide sufficient indicia of reliability; and
(2)   The child either:
    (a)   Testifies at the proceedings; or
    (b)   Is unavailable as a witness: *provided*, that when the child is unavailable as a witness, such statement may be admitted only if there is corroborative evidence of the act.

A statement may not be admitted under this section unless the proponent of the statement makes known to the adverse party his intention to offer the statement and the particulars of the statement sufficiently in advance of the proceedings to provide the adverse party with a fair opportunity to prepare to meet the statement. (Washington Revised Code Ann. s. 9A.44.120.)

A number of other States have copied this provision (Myers 1987a, s. 5.38, Yun 1983), and similar provisions have been enacted in some jurisdictions in Australia (Warner 1990). They have been advocated in New Zealand (Geddis Report 1988), and in Canada a similar exception has been created by a decision of the Supreme Court (*Khan* v *R* (1990) 79 CR (3d series) 1). In *White* v *Illinois* (1992) 116 S Ct L Ed 2nd 851 the United States Supreme Court held that, despite the 'confrontation clause' in the Constitution (see page 78 above), a conviction could be based on hearsay evidence admitted under such exceptions to the hearsay rule.

Many legal systems outside the common law go further, and have no hearsay rule at all, in civil or in criminal proceedings. There is no hearsay rule, as such, in France or Holland. Nor is this a peculiarity of the so-called 'inquisitorial systems'. The hearsay rule is also unknown in criminal proceedings in Scandinavia—where a system of criminal procedure is used which is broadly modelled on ours; and in Norway and in Denmark, as in Britain, juries are used to try serious cases (Andenaes 1990). In these jurisdictions there is obviously no legal problem about the court being told what the child said someone did to him.

Surprisingly, perhaps, this relaxed state of affairs at one time prevailed in criminal trials in England (Langbein 1978). Explaining why he would listen to the evidence of a young child, whether competent to take an oath or not, Sir Matthew Hale (1609–76) gave this as one of the reasons:

> Because if the child complains presently of the wrong done to her to the mother or other relations, *their evidence upon oath shall be taken, yet it is but a narrative of what the child told them without oath*, and there is much more reason for the court to hear the relation of the child herself, than to receive it at second-hand. (Hale 1736, pp. 634–5; emphasis added.)

In our view, the proper approach to children's hearsay evidence should depend, in the first place, on the nature of the proceedings. In civil proceedings brought to determine the future of the child the dominant consideration is the welfare of the child, to which all other considerations—for example, the need for the accused to confront his accuser—are secondary. Furthermore, these cases are not tried by juries, so there is not the risk of an inexperienced tribunal giving excessive weight to slender evidence, which is commonly used to justify the exclusionary rules of evidence in criminal trials. In criminal cases the matter is more complicated. A major concern is to avoid convicting the innocent, and there is also the widespread feeling, reflected in (among other places) the European Convention on Human Rights (see pages 120–1), that it is unfair to allow a person to be convicted without giving him the opportunity to put his side of the case to his accuser. This makes us uneasy about simply abolishing the hearsay rule in criminal cases—and even about allowing a defendant to be convicted solely on a piece of hearsay evidence admitted under some limited exception to the hearsay rule, as in *White* v *Illinois* (see above). The way forward, we believe, is not to treat hearsay as an issue on its own, but to tackle it together with other matters. In our view, the solution is to make a series of interconnected changes designed:

(a)   to alter the competency requirement and to modify the adversarial system to enable more children to give their evidence as first-hand witnesses—in particular, by developing a procedure by which the child can give her evidence, and answer defence questions, privately and ahead of trial;

(b)   to abolish the 'rule against narrative', so that wherever a child (or other witnesses) gives evidence, her previous statements are admissible to supplement her formal testimony (whether given at the trial, or beforehand); and

(c)   to permit hearsay evidence wherever the original maker is genuinely unavailable, but with a restriction that convictions must not be based on such evidence alone.

The proposals of the Pigot Committee in 1989, or those of the Scottish Law Commission in its 125th Report, if fully implemented, would go a long way to solve the problem. They are discussed in chapter 15.

For civil proceedings—or at any rate, for those which concern the welfare of children—there seems much to be said for the Civil Evidence (Scotland) Act 1988.

NOTES

1.   We should like to thank Lord Kincraig, Lord Morton, Alistair Cameron QC, John Cameron QC, and Colin McEachran QC for helpfully providing us with information about this case.

2.   *Neshet* [1990] Crim LR 579; *Cole* (1990) 90 Cr App R 478; *Price* [1991] Crim LR 707; *Samuel* [1992] Crim LR 189; *R* v *Acton JJ, ex parte McMullen; R* v *Tower Bridge Magistrates' Court ex parte Lawlor* (1991) 92 Cr App R 98; *Kennedy* [1992] Crim LR 37; *R* v *Ashford Magistrates' Court ex parte Hilden* [1993] 2 WLR 529); *Moore* [1992] Crim LR 882; *McGillivraly* [1993] Crim LR 530. These sections have also generated a number of articles: Birch (1989), McEwan (1989), Munday (1991), Ockleton (1992).

3.   The provision, like a number of others, occurs twice: once in the code for solemn procedure, and again in the code for summary procedure.

4.   Criminal Procedure Act 1865, ss. 4 and 5:

   4.   If a witness, upon cross-examination as to a former statement made by him relative to the subject-matter of the indictment or proceeding, and inconsistent with his present testimony, does not distinctly admit that he has made such statement, proof may be given that he did in fact make it; but before such proof can be given the circumstances of the supposed statement, sufficient to designate the particular occasion, must be mentioned to the witness, and he must be asked whether or not he has made such statement.

   5.   A witness may be cross-examined as to previous statements made by him in writing, or reduced into writing, relative to the subject-matter of the indictment or proceeding, without such writing being shown to him; but if it is intended to contradict such witness by the writing, his attention must, before such contradictory proof can be given, be called to those parts of the writing which are to be used for the purpose of so contradicting him: Provided always, that it shall be competent for the judge, at any time during the trial, to require the production of the writing for his inspection, and he may thereupon make such use of it for the purposes of the trial as he may think fit.

5.   Section 405B(2) of the New South Wales Crimes Act 1900 provides:

Where on the trial of a person for a prescribed sexual offence evidence is given or a question is asked of a witness which tends to suggest an absence of complaint in respect of the commission of the alleged offence by the person upon whom the offence is alleged to have been committed or to suggest delay by that person in making any such complaint, the judge shall —

(a)   give a warning to the jury to the effect that absence of complaint or delay in complaining does not necessarily indicate that the allegation that the offence was committed is false; and
(b)   inform the jury that there may be good reasons why a victim of a sexual assault may hesitate in making, or may refrain from making, a complaint about the assault.

6.   *Re W (Minors) (Child Abuse: Evidence)* [1987] 1 FLR 297; *Re A (A Minor) (Child Abuse: Evidence)* [1989] 1 FLR 30: *Re W (Minors) (Wardship: Evidence)* [1990] FCR 286.

7.   *Re F* [1990] FCR 793; *Re A* [1991] 1 WLR 1026; *Rochdale BC* v *BW and others* [1991] FCR 705; *KVS* v *GGS* [1992] 2 FCR 23; *Re C* [1992] 2 FCR 65. Similar remarks, but without explicit reference to the Cleveland Report, are to be found in *H* v *H: K* v *K* [1990] Fam 86 and in *Re W (Minors) (Wardship: Evidence)* [1990] FCR 286—where Butler-Sloss LJ's judgment contains a list of earlier authorities.

8.   By the Civil Evidence Act 1972 'fact' is to be construed to include matters of opinion.

CHAPTER SEVEN
Videotapes

Part I
Introduction

It was Thomas Edison who first showed that speech could be stored and reproduced in 1877. To the amazement of his colleagues, he turned the handle of the strange machine he had constructed whilst he recited 'Mary had a little lamb', turned the handle again, and his phonograph played back his very words (Dickson and Dickson 1894). Mechanical recording was clumsy, however, and it was not until the invention of magnetic tape in the middle of the 20th century that it occurred to anyone that this technology had obvious possibilities for use in court. The discovery that magnetic tape could be used to store images as well as sounds gave us the videotape, with the added benefit that the court could see the speaker as well as being able to hear him.

In Britain, recording technology was first applied to interviews with suspects. For years there was an intermittent public debate about the methods the police used when questioning, whilst in the criminal courts much time was consumed by disputes about what the suspect really said when he was at the police-station. In 1960 Glanville Williams pointed out that if police interviews with suspects were audiotaped these problems could be largely avoided, and he led the intellectual battle for the next 20 years (Williams 1960; Williams 1979). At first the police were very hostile to the idea, and the Home Office loyally backed them up. An oft-repeated claim was that if interviews were taped, the moment the machine was switched on every suspect would start to punch himself audibly and shout, 'Stop torturing me and I'll tell you anything!'—although many people suspected the real point was that the police did not want too much made public about their interrogation techniques. During the next 25 years, however, the general public was converted to the idea and the pressure for change grew more than even the police and the Home Office could resist. In England, the Royal Commission on Criminal Procedure (Cmnd 8092) came down in favour of taping in 1981, and their recommendations led to s. 60 of the Police and Criminal Evidence Act 1984. This required the Home Secretary to draw up a code of practice for making sound recordings of interviews with suspects, and then to implement it. Field trials were begun, and the police, to their surprise, found tape recording was a help rather than a hindrance to them (Baldwin 1985). A code came into force in July 1988, and in England tape recording is now being used everywhere. A parallel development has taken place in Scotland, where, following a recommendation of the Thomson Committee in its second report in 1975, an experiment began in four police stations in 1980, on the strength of which a working party recommended a national scheme in 1985 (Scottish Home and Health Department 1985; Macphail 1987, sect. S20.14). As in England, tape recording is now wide-spread. These developments led to experiments with video-recording inter-views with suspects (Baldwin 1992), but for the present, wider use of video-recording for this purpose has been shelved on account of cost (Home Office Circular No. 6 of 1993).

In Britain, it also seems to have been Glanville Williams who first advocated the use of tape recording to preserve accurate accounts of interviews with victims (Williams 1963, p. 388). By the 1960s the Scandinavians had already started to use tape technology for this, and in his influential article which appeared in the USA in 1969, David Libai commented favourably on the fact that police interviews with abused children were recorded on audio tape in Denmark and Sweden. Libai advocated tape recording, and added that a videotape would provide a much superior record, because it would enable those who saw it to appreciate the child's appearance and demeanour as well as to hear his or her words (Libai 1969). During the 1970s Libai's suggestion was widely taken up in the USA, and it became usual for police and social workers to video-record their interviews with child victims of sexual abuse. At that time, this was done merely to help the original interviewers remember what the child had said, and to enable other agencies who had to deal with the child to learn about his or her experiences first-hand without the need to carry out a further, probably stressful interview; the tapes were not then made with a view to use in court. But this was the next development.

It was a natural step for the Americans to take, because their courts had warmly embraced video technology in other contexts almost as soon as it was available. By the early 1970s, some jurisdictions had already changed their rules of evidence to permit their courts to see video depositions taken from witnesses who were unavailable to give live evidence at trial, and some courts were even experimenting with the 'pre-recorded video trial', or 'PVT', where all the evidence is recorded on videotape in advance, a judge launders out all the inadmissible parts, and the jury is shown what it is permitted to see without repeated interruptions of 'Objection, your Honour' (McCrystal 1977). The first PVT trial in a criminal case is said to have taken place in 1972 (Armstrong 1976). By 1976, the subject had already generated a literature of some 40 articles (Armstrong 1976), and a psychological study of the relative merits of videotaped and live testimony was published in the USA in 1979 (Miller and Fontes). In 1977 Montana was the first State of the Union to enact a law making a videotape of an interview with a child admissible in a criminal case, and a number of other States quickly followed (Anon. 1985). In 1982 the American Bar Association pronounced itself in favour of videotapes being used to a limited extent in court proceedings involving children (Graham 1985) (1). Then two years later the sufferings of child witnesses in court became headline news throughout the USA as a result of a *cause célèbre* in California, the McMartin preschool case (Crewdson 1988) (2). Following allegations that young children had been sexually abused at a preschool in Los Angeles there was a massive police investigation, and criminal proceedings were started against a number of defendants, all of whom were separately represented. In consequence:

> . . . one 10-year-old was on the stand every day for over a week. Seven defence attorneys questioned him. He was only one of many child witnesses to be called to testify. Worse yet, this seven-day ordeal occurred during preliminary hearings. The trial itself had not yet begun! (Goodman and Helgeson 1985, p. 202.)

At once, everyone turned to the idea of using videotapes in court as a means of solving the problems of stress for child witnesses, and by 1986 at least 27 States had enacted laws making videotaped testimony admissible as evidence (Eatman and Bulkley 1986).

These laws vary greatly from State to State in what they permit to be put in evidence. Some merely provide for a videotape of an early investigative interview to be played to the court to supplement the child's live testimony at trial. As the child must still be available to give live evidence at trial, and undergo an adversarial cross-examination, this does little to alleviate the problem of stress, but it is of some benefit to prosecutors, because it is an insurance policy against the child whose testimony at trial is hesitant and incomplete. Under legislation of this type, the problem of courtroom stress is usually addressed by allowing the child to give live evidence by means of a 'live link', alias closed-circuit television (see chapter 5 above). The legislation in some States goes further and provides for some form of *video deposition*. Here there is an official pre-hearing in advance of trial at which the child gives evidence in front of an officer of the court, before whom the defence cross-examination also takes place. This evidence-taking session is videotaped, and a showing of the video deposition takes the place of live testimony from the child at trial. In many States, both possibilities are provided for. In some jurisdictions there is a third possibility, because some legislation also provides that where a child gives evidence at the preliminary hearing—or committal proceedings, as they would be called in England—this evidence can sometimes be put on videotape and used to replace a further courtroom appearance by the child at trial (Myers 1987a, sect. 6.2). Since the Supreme Court case of *Coy* v *Iowa* (1988) 108 S Ct 2798, however, a cloud has hung over these developments, because of possible incompatibility with the 'confrontation requirement' in the US Constitution (see page 77 above).

When this rush of statutes was being enacted in the USA, many people seem to have thought that videotapes were the technological panacea by which all problems concerning child witnesses could be cured. Ten years later, everyone is much more cautious. If it has solved some problems it has not solved all of them, and it has brought some new ones of its own.

A number of the difficulties in the USA stem from attempts to avoid infringing the 'confrontation requirement'. To this end, a number of statutes try to preserve the right of the defendant to confront the child except where it is clear that a confrontation would make it impossible for the child to give evidence at all, and this results in features which largely cancel out the good the legislation is meant to achieve. Thus, for example, a number of the US laws about video depositions permit the suspect to be present with the child in the room where the video deposition is being taken—which puts the child in even closer proximity to the defendant than he or she would be in an ordinary courtroom, and makes the video deposition as much or more of an ordeal than giving evidence in open court. Others try to meet the confrontation point by making it possible to use videotapes only when there is evidence that the child is 'unavailable' to give evidence in court in the presence of the defendant—and this has sometimes resulted in children being subjected to a new form of stress in the form of a battery of medical and psychiatric tests by examiners for prosecution and defence (Whitcomb et al. 1985, p. 65). Similar problems are raised by the Canadian legislation (Graham 1990). Furthermore, where the legislation permits a videotape of an early interview with the child to be put in evidence, the result in some jurisdictions has been costly and time-consuming battles between rival experts: defence experts, called to say that the interviews were unfair and tendentious, versus prosecution experts called to say that on the contrary, they were fairly and properly done. Many prosecutors, fearful that any videotaping legislation might fail a constitutional challenge, steer clear of using videotape if they think the child can be persuaded to utter live in open court. Meanwhile, psychologists and psychiatrists have been pointing out that all the US videotaping legislation has been something of a leap in the dark. By and large it was enacted before there had been any solid research into what parts of the trial process children find distressing—and therefore without any real idea about whether the legislation would put the problem right.

That is not to say that everyone in the USA now thinks that videotaping is a wash-out. In a manual for prosecutors the authors put the matter thus:

> There is no consensus among prosecutors regarding the desirability or utility of videotape and closed-circuit technologies in child-abuse cases. Many prosecutors have found that their detriments outweigh their benefits and have chosen not to use them despite their availability through special statutes in their jurisdictions. Many of these same prosecutors have been able to demonstrate impressive success in prosecuting child abuse nonetheless.
>
> On the other hand, there are many prosecutors whose experience with videotape or closed-circuit television has been positive, and they are committed to continuing their use. In deciding whether to advocate the passage of special legislation authorising such procedures or whether to use these aids if available, prosecutors need to weigh their advantages and disadvantages within the context of their own jurisdictions. (Toth and Whallen 1987, ch. V–1; see also Macfarlane 1985.)

There can be no doubt that some forms of videotaping legislation have enabled justice to be done in desperately serious cases where it would otherwise have failed. We describe one such case at the end of this chapter (Jones 1987).

Other parts of the common law world then began to copy what the Americans were doing—but they moved more cautiously. In 1987, Canada enacted a package of reforms to do with child witnesses, one of which has made videotapes of early interviews admissible, but only where the child is available for cross-examination live at trial; though Canadian informants tell us that it has been very little used. In New Zealand, a law was passed in 1989 which, among other things, enables the court to order a videotape of an interview with the child to replace the child's evidence in-chief, and in addition, gives it a discretion to order the cross-examination to be held out of court and videotaped. A similar law exists in Queensland. In other parts of Australia the use of videotape evidence is under discussion (Warner 1990; LRC of Western Australia 1991).

In Britain, the issue of videotapes of children as evidence arose in two separate ways.

The first was in wardship proceedings in the High Court in England, where videotaping arrived as a by-product of expert evidence from child psychiatrists. Since the 1960s it has been common for High Court judges in wardship to admit expert evidence from psychiatrists and other professionals (see chapter 9). Where it is suspected that a child has been neglected, ill-treated or abused, but the matter is not clear, the judge in wardship often orders a child to be psychiatrically examined by an expert nominated by the court, who will give his opinion on the matter. (This is evidence which would not be permitted in criminal proceedings—but as has already been explained, the High Court in wardship is not bound by the rules of evidence which apply in ordinary civil cases, let alone by the rules of criminal evidence. Nor, at first, would such evidence probably have been admitted in civil proceedings other than wardship—although the practice that began in wardship has now spread to other civil jurisdictions hearing children's cases.)

In the early 1980s child psychiatrists found that more and more children were being referred to them by doctors, social services departments and the courts, for their expert opinions on whether they had been sexually abused, and if so by whom. Confronted with an ever rising load of problematical cases, many involving children who were very young, or very reluctant to talk, or both, psychiatrists at the Great Ormond Street Hospital made an effort to sharpen up their interview techniques. As part of this effort they began to videotape their interviews: not in order to show in court, but to give interviewers the means of reviewing their interviews at leisure, to enable them to ask their colleagues for advice, and as a source of training material for newcomers to the profession. However, when the psychiatrists appeared in court to present their reports it then came out that their interviews had been video-recorded, and the parties who wished to dispute the psychiatrists' evidence began to ask for the tapes to be shown in court, as a means of getting behind the psychiatrists' conclusions. The judges were prepared to allow this, and it became usual practice for judges in the High Court to see videotapes of assessment interviews in the course of proceedings concerning the welfare of children.

At first, some judges were distinctly unhappy with what they saw and heard. In the course of 1986 a series of High Court judges gave judgment in open court in seven cases, in four of which the Great Ormond Street techniques were seriously criticised for what the judges thought was improper pressure on the child to say that sexual abuse had taken place (*Re E* [1987] 1 FLR 269; *Re N* [1987] 1 FLR 280; *Re G* [1987] 1 FLR 310; *C* v *C* [1987] 1 FLR 321). These cases were reported in a special edition of the Family Law Reports, and generated adverse comment in the legal press.

As a body, child psychiatrists were mortified by these criticisms. Some psychiatrists are said to have given up seeing children, and others, remembering that the courts were prepared to accept their expert assessments without argument before the days of viedotaping, are said to have decided to carry on interviewing as before, but to abandon videotaping (Vizard 1987). However, the Great Ormond Street team took a more constructive approach, and immediately overhauled their interview techniques in order to cut out as far as possible the features which the judges objected to (Bentovim and Tranter 1988). Twelve months later their revised techniques were receiving favourable comments from judges:

I have seen videotape recordings of a number of these diagnostic interviews undertaken both at Great Ormond Street and several other hospitals in the past. In some of those in the past I would agree that adjectives such as 'coercive' and 'relentless' are appropriate. I do not agree that such descriptions are appropriate to the interview of A in this case. To my mind and observation it was gently and sympathetically conducted. Certainly there were some leading questions. Certainly there was questioning on an hypothetical basis. But has anyone, in this country or elsewhere, yet found a way of leading a child along without use of these methods? It is how it is done that matters, and then the interpretation to be put on the answers and reactions of a child. The fact is in this case that a good deal of what was elicited from A was spontaneous. (Latey J in *C* v *C* [1988] FCR 458, [1988] 1 FLR 462.)

When the original criticisms were being made, some people took them as an argument against videotapes ever being admissible in legal proceedings involving children, whether criminal or civil. The judges who deal with civil proceedings involving children took the opposite view: in their courts, the rules of evidence permit a person to report to the court what a child has said in the course of an interview (see chapter 6), and therefore

. . . there should always be a video recording. The reason is this: where there is a dispute whether there has or has not been abuse the court is anxious whether it should accept the *ipse dixit* of the interviewer or interviewers, however skilled and experienced. This is because cases have shown . . . that the precise questions, the oral answers (if there are any), the gestures and body movements, the vocal inflection and intonation, may all play an important part in interpretation. Where there is a dispute, there should be an opportunity for another expert in the field to form a view. Often, no doubt, he would reach the same interpretation and conclusion. In other cases he might not, and in the interest not only of justice between the parties but of doing its best to arrive at the truth of the matter in the interest of the child, the court should have the benefit of such evidence, so informed. (Mr Justice Latey in *Re M (A Minor) (Child Abuse: Evidence)* [1987] 1 FLR 293, 295).

This view has been repeated in many subsequent judgments (3), and the desirability of videotapes was one of the points made in the Cleveland Report in 1988.

The practice of viewing videotapes of diagnostic interviews began in wardship proceedings in the High Court in London, where the usual rules of civil evidence—and in particular, the hearsay rule—have never applied. Now that the hearsay rule has been virtually abrogated in civil proceedings concerned with children (see chapter 6), there are no legal difficulties about a videotape being viewed by any civil court, and they are sometimes shown in children's proceedings in the lower civil courts—in Scotland and in England.

The second manifestation of videotaping in Britain was the 'Bexley experiment'. The background to this was the problem of repeated interviewing, particularly in cases where criminal proceedings are started. Children who have been sexually abused would often find themselves interviewed by social workers, police surgeons, police officers, psychiatric social workers, child psychiatrists—and sometimes others too—all of whom would have to see the child. The child would have to tell the story to each one in turn, repeating it over and over again. If the story is a harrowing one, such repeated interviews are obviously bad for the child. And harm to the child apart, repeated interviewing tends to undermine the quality of any evidence the child eventually gives in court—partly because the child's memory tends to get corrupted by false details which each questioner accidentally implants in the child's mind, and partly because endless repetition kills all spontaneity so that the child's courtroom evidence sounds unconvincing and rehearsed. In an attempt to solve this problem, in 1985 the Metropolitan Police and the social services department of the London Borough of Bexley set up a pilot project under which children who were allegedly the victims of sexual abuse were interviewed once by a joint team acting on behalf of both agencies, and the interview was videotaped for anyone else who needed to hear the child's account of what had taken place. In 1987 a full report on the project was published (Metropolitan Police and Bexley London Borough 1987). The general feeling was that the experiment had been a great success, and steps were immediately taken to copy the scheme elsewhere. The Metropolitan Police began to introduce the Bexley procedure throughout the Metropolitan Police area. In 1987 West Yorkshire Police began a similar experiment with help from the Home Office (Lawrence 1988; West Yorkshire Police 1989). And in July 1988 the Home Office issued a circular (52/1988) to all English police forces in which it recommended them to set up joint investigation schemes with the local social services departments, with interviews recorded on videotape.

Like the Great Ormond Street tapes of diagnostic interviews, the Bexley tapes were not made with a view to use in court. However, they rapidly led to a campaign for the law to be changed to make tapes of this sort admissible in criminal proceedings in England (4). When the government introduced the legislation which eventually became the Criminal Justice Act 1988, and which introduced the 'live video link' (see chapter 5), this was the signal for a group of Members of Parliament to push for a further provision which would make videotapes of earlier interviews with children admissible to supplement their live evidence at trial. The government, beset with the Cleveland affair (see chapter 1), was not prepared to concede this. It reacted first by issuing a consultative paper on the subject (Home Office 1987), and then by setting up the Home Office Advisory Group, alias the Pigot Committee. As we described in chapter 5, this came up with proposals far more radical than those which the government was fending off when it set up the committee (Pigot Committee 1989). The Pigot Committee condemned the present system under which children have to give their evidence at trial, and proposed a wholly new scheme under which child witnesses in serious cases would give their evidence—both examination-in-chief and cross-examination—ahead of trial, and at trial the court would then see videotapes of these earlier questioning sessions instead of hearing the child as a live witness. Although this proposal attracted widespread public support (page 88 above) it was too radical for the Home Office, which responded by introducing legislation to make possible the more limited scheme which it had fought off several years earlier: a change in the law of evidence to make a videotape of an earlier interview with a child admissible in criminal proceedings, but only where the child comes to court to undergo a cross-examination (either in open court, or using the live video link). Despite the vigorous efforts by the supporters of the Pigot scheme to get the Bill amended (page 90 above), the government's limited scheme was enacted in the Criminal Justice Act 1991, and this came into effect on 1 October 1992. It is explained in detail below (pages 176–185).

In Scotland there was a parallel development. The whole issue of children's evidence was referred to the Scottish Law Commission in 1986. This reference led to a discussion paper, supplemented by a research paper from Kathleen Murray, in 1988, and then to the Commission's Report No. 125 in 1990. Among other things, this proposed that where a child (or adult) witness gives evidence, that witness's previous statements should be admissible in evidence, provided they were recorded in some permanent form; this would, of course, have had the effect of making videotapes of earlier interviews admissible where the child later gave evidence as a witness. It also proposed a scheme to enable the whole of a child's evidence to be taken 'on commission' in advance of trial, a videotape of this then replacing the child as a live witness: in essence the Pigot Committee's proposal, but intended for use in exceptional cases, rather than as the routine procedure. Parliament has since enacted various parts of this Report piecemeal, tagged on to other pieces of legislation. The proposal for taking evidence on commission in exceptional cases became law by the Prisoners and Criminal Proceedings (Scotland) Act 1993, as we explain above (page 90). The proposal to admit evidence of previous statements (including ones on video), however, has not so far been enacted. Thus Scotland is in the paradoxical position of having adopted the more radical proposal, but not the more conservative one which the Scottish Law Commission intended to go with it. There is the further paradox that what is now possible with videotapes in England is still impossible in Scotland, and what is possible with videotapes in Scotland is not possible in England. In England, a videotape can supplement the child's live testimony, but not replace it; in Scotland, it can replace it but not supplement it.

Part II
The admissibility of videotapes of children under the law today

The problem about videotapes as evidence in legal proceedings to which the strict rules of evidence apply is that they are usually inadmissible because of the hearsay rule. A person usually wishes to put a tape recording in evidence because it would enable the court to hear someone who has been taped describing an event which the person in possession of the tape needs to prove as an essential element in his case, and, as we saw in chapter 6, the hearsay rule prevents this. In proceedings where the hearsay rule applies, a fact may not be established by calling A, who did not see or hear it, to tell the court that he heard B, who did, describe it. The rule also unquestionably prevents A from reading to the court a letter which B wrote to him describing the event, and everyone assumes that the rule also prohibits A from playing a tape recording (whether audio or video) which he made of B describing it. Surprisingly there seems to be no decided case, either English or Scottish, that expressly holds this. But every lawyer takes it for granted that tape recordings count as documents for the purpose of the hearsay rule, and Parliament has made the same assumption on several occasions when, in the course of enacting statutes to exempt various types of documents from the hearsay rule, it has included a provision that the new exceptions for documents apply to audiotapes and videotapes as well (5).

To the lay person, the extension of the hearsay rule to documents and tape recordings does not look particularly sensible. One reason for the hearsay rule is the risk that B never really said what A proposes to tell the court he said, and this risk is absent if there is a videotape which enables us to see and hear B in the very act of saying it. The other reason is that it is not possible to cross-examine B to test the truth of his statement; and this reason is absent too in cases where the defence were given the chance to put their questions at the time the tape was made, or where the child is available for cross-examination at the trial. To the lawyer, however, it makes no difference whether there is any doubt about what B said, or whether B has been or can be cross-examined, because whether or not the result is sensible or silly is an irrelevant consideration. In *Myers* v *DPP* [1965] AC 1001 the House of Lords ruled, first, that hearsay must be rejected simply because it is hearsay, and irrespective of whether the piece of hearsay in question offends against the spirit of the rule, and secondly, that it is not open to the courts to make any fresh exceptions to the hearsay rule, however strongly common sense requires them; and in the recent case of _Kearley_ [1992] 2 AC 228, furthermore, this costive attitude was reaffirmed. It is true that despite this prohibition the English courts have since managed to invent some further small exceptions on the quiet (Ashworth and Pattenden 1986); and it is also true that _Myers_ v _DPP_ was an English appeal and the Scots courts are theoretically free to invent major new exceptions to the hearsay rule, and with a fanfare of trumpets if they feel inclined. But as a practical matter, it is certain that the courts on either side of the Border would think a new exception to the hearsay rule for videotapes was far too serious a matter to be introduced by precedent alone. Any further changes must come, as they have come already, by legislation.

TAPES AS REAL EVIDENCE

Generally speaking, it is only when a tape recording contravenes the hearsay rule that it is inadmissible as evidence.

If what is on the tape is a record of the disputed event taking place, rather than a person describing it afterwards, there is no problem whatever about its admissibility. The courts treat such tapes in the same way as photographs and other automatic records, which are admissible as 'real evidence'. Thus the criminal courts on both sides of the Border have accepted as evidence videotapes that television crews have made of riots (_Kajala_ v _Noble_ (1982) 75 Cr App R 149; Macphail 1987, sect. S13.12), and in recent years the criminal courts have often seen videotapes of thefts and robberies made by security cameras. Audio as well as video recordings are admissible where they record the offence as it takes place. Thus where two policemen were on trial for conspiracy to pervert the course of justice the court heard a tape recording of their voices as they tried to make a suspect pay a bribe (_Robson_ (1972) 56 Cr App R 450), and in a prosecution for cruelty to animals a court heard an audio recording of two men putting a budgerigar in a microwave oven (_The Times_, 19 October 1985). Where it is proposed to put such a tape in evidence the court will usually expect some supporting evidence to show that the tape is authentic, and has not been tampered with (Blackstone 1993, sect. F.130). But where there are problems about producing the original tape the courts are willing to see or hear a copy (_Kajala_ v _Noble_), and in 1986 the Court of Appeal in England held that where the tape of an incident taking place has been erased the court may hear a description of the tape from those who saw or heard it played. Such evidence, the court said, was as legally valid as if the witnesses had been describing an event which they had seen with their naked eyes, or heard with their own unaided ears (_Taylor_ v _Chief Constable of Cheshire_ [1986] 1 WLR 1479).

Where a person is taped in the act of committing an offence against a child, it follows that this is admissible in evidence against him. In 1987, a hidden video camera in a hospital ward was used to record two mothers as they tried to smother their baby children (Southall et al. 1987). Confronted with the tapes, the mothers confessed and eventually pleaded guilty; had they denied their guilt the tapes could have been used to prove it—as was done in a similar case in 1991 which was contested (*The Independent*, 30 October 1991). It is common knowledge that Brady and Hindley, the Moors Murderers, were convicted partly on the strength of audio tapes they had made of themselves torturing one of the children they had abducted (Goodman 1973). A pornographic film or videotape showing indecent acts with children is unquestionably admissible evidence both as to what took place, and who was involved in it.

VIDEOTAPES IN PROCEEDINGS WHERE THE HEARSAY RULE DOES NOT STRICTLY APPLY

In proceedings where the hearsay rule does not apply a tape recording is of course admissible in evidence even where it does not count as real evidence, but consists of an interview with a child (or adult) in the course of which the interviewee describes an event.

In civil proceedings about child care matters in England the hearsay rule has now been abolished, from which it follows that videotapes of interviews with children are admissible.

In proceedings of this sort, the argument is not about whether the videotape is legally admissible in evidence, but—as with other pieces of hearsay evidence—how much weight the court can properly put upon it. The question of weight arises in two forms. First, there is the question of whether there are any legal limits to the kind of finding the court is entitled to make on the basis of hearsay evidence alone. Is it entitled on hearsay evidence to reach a finding against a named person that he sexually abused a child, for example? This was discussed in the previous chapter (page 149 above), where it will be recalled that the courts have said that in principle hearsay evidence can be used as the basis for any finding. Secondly, there is the specific question that arises in every case of how much reliance the court should put on a particular videotape (or other piece of hearsay evidence). This is a question of fact, rather than a question of law. In reaching a decision, the courts take into account a number of matters. They do, of course, give more weight to tape recordings of children actually saying things than they do to oral acounts of what witnesses say children told them. High on the list of other factors is the skill of the interviewer, and the extent (if any) to which the child was pressured, or subjected to leading questions. Other relevant matters are the age of the child, and the length of time that has elapsed between the incident—if there was one—and the interview. In civil proceedings (unlike in criminal proceedings in England) the court has no discretion to suppress relevant evidence because it thinks it is unfairly prejudicial (*Bradford City Metropolitan Council v K* [1990] Fam 140). Thus the civil courts will look at a videotape of a diagnostic interview which would certainly be rejected if tendered as evidence in criminal proceedings—even one where every one of the Cleveland guidelines (see chapter 12) has been ignored—and draw from it such conclusions (if any) as they think justified.

The position in Scotland is similar; except for the complication, already explained (page 157), that a civil court in Scotland may only receive hearsay evidence of a child's statements if it is satisfied that the child would have been competent as a witness.

In Northern Ireland videotapes are less readily admissible than they are in Scotland or in England, because (at least in theory) hearsay evidence is still less freely admissible in civil proceedings (see page 155 above).

For a fuller discussion of hearsay in civil cases readers are referred back to chapter 6. Techniques of interviewing children are discussed in chapter 12.

VIDEO TAPES IN PROCEEDINGS WHERE THE HEARSAY RULE DOES APPLY

As was explained in chapter 6, the hearsay rule still flourishes in criminal proceedings, with the result that a tape recording of a child describing something that has happened is generally inadmissible in a criminal trial. To this there are a number of important exceptions, however. First, there is now the special statutory exception, created for England by the Criminal Justice Act 1991 and about to be extended to Northern Ireland by an Order in 1993, under which videotapes of earlier interviews are admissible where children give live evidence in those jurisdictions. Secondly, there is now the special statutory exception created by the Prisoners and Criminal Proceedings (Scotland) Act 1993, under which Scottish courts may hear the whole of a child's evidence on videotape where it has been taken 'on commission'. Then there are the established exceptions to the hearsay rule, discussed in the previous chapter, under most of which videotapes are potentially admissible. Confusingly, however, there are one or two hearsay exceptions which do not extend to videotapes: these are discussed at page 189 below.

In the section that follows, we have arranged the matter into two groups: the cases where the videotape may be shown provided the child comes to court (exceptions to the rule against narrative), and the cases where the tape is admissible although he does not (exceptions to the hearsay rule).

Videotapes in criminal proceedings: where they are admissible provided the child comes to court

Videotapes under the Criminal Justice Act 1991 (Criminal Justice Act 1988, s. 32A), and under the Criminal Justice (Northern Ireland) Order 1993, Part III

As already mentioned, these provisions make a videotape of an earlier interview with a child admissible in criminal proceedings in England and in Northern Ireland—provided the child comes to court to undergo a live cross-examination. They were originally enacted for England in the Criminal Justice Act 1991. The English provisions are about to be replicated for Northern Ireland by a Criminal Justice (Northern Ireland) Order 1993, which is in draft form at the time of writing, and which is likely to come into force shortly. In the explanation which follows, we shall refer to the relevant sections of the English statute.

The English provision is s. 54 of the Criminal Justice Act 1991, which —perhaps to show that the Home Office would only accept changes already under discussion three years earlier—works by inserting a new section 32A into the Criminal Justice Act 1988. (Although theoretically neat in putting all the law on videotechnology and children's evidence into one Act, in practice it means that the 1988 Act is now spread over two documents, and sections printed in one cross-refer to sections printed in the other. To ease the reader's task we have set out ss. 32 and 32A together at the end of this chapter together with rule 23C of the Crown Court Rules.)

It is important to note that this provision is *in addition* to the existing cases under which videotapes were already admissible. Section 32A (12) provides:

Nothing in this section shall prejudice the admissibility of any video recording which would be admissible apart from this section.

Field of application
Like the live video link (chapter 5), the new videotape exception cannot be used in any and every case involving children. Section 32A limits its availability, first, in respect of the courts which can use it. It is not generally available in the magistrates' courts: by section 32A(1) it can only be used in trials on indictment (i.e. in the Crown Court), in the youth court when trying offences which would have to be tried in the Crown Court if the defendant were over 18, and in the Court of Appeal on the rare occasions when evidence is heard there. Secondly, s. 32A (1) restricts the new videotape provision with reference to the type of offence: it may only be used at trials for the same fixed list of offences for which the live video link is available—crimes of sex, violence and cruelty to children. (The details of this list, and the policy of having one, are discussed on page 104 above). Thirdly, it only applies to witnesses below certain ages. In rather convoluted language (Wasik and Taylor 1991, p. 131), section 32A (7) says that the videotape exception applies in cases of violence and cruelty provided the witness was under 14 when the tape was made, and is still under 15 at the date of trial—limits which rise to 17 and 18 if it is a sexual offence.

If an age-limit geared to how old the child was when the tape was made is sensible, the same is not true of the additional limit relating to the age of the child at trial. Much of the justification for admitting videotapes of early interviews with children is that memories are corrupted with time, and what a child said when the incident took place is likely to be fuller and more accurate than what he can remember at trial. If this is true where the witness is still under the age-limit at trial, it is even truer if the trial has been so delayed that the child is over the age-limit by the time it happens. Memories do not improve with time—even when you have reached your fifteenth or eighteenth birthday.

In discussing the sections of the Criminal Justice Act 1991 that prevent children having to give evidence at committal proceedings, we saw that these were limited to children who would give, in effect, eye-witness evidence of the offence taking place (page 87 above). This particular restriction does not apply to the videotape provision.

It should go without saying that section 32A creates a rule which makes videotapes available as evidence in criminal proceedings to both prosecution and defence; although in the nature of things, it is more likely to be the prosecution that use them.

What kinds of videotape?
The Pigot Committee put forward a scheme under which the videotape was to be the vehicle by which the child gave evidence. It therefore proposed an official procedure for interviewing children, to be set out in a Code of Practice. Videotapes so made were to be admissible provided the judge gave leave, and 'in making this decision the court should have regard to the Code of Practice for the conduct of such interviews'. As explained below, when drafting what became the 1991 Act the government resolutely refused to allow it to contain any reference to a Code of Practice—although it was in fact planning to draw up some sort of official guidance on interviewing children, and eventually produced the 'Memorandum of Good Practice' (see chapter 12). Because the word 'Code' could not appear in the Act it could hardly limit the admissibility of tapes by reference to one, and s. 32A(2) is drafted in the following terms, which are open-ended:

> In any such proceedings a video recording of an interview which —
> (a)   is conducted between an adult and a child who is not the accused or one of the accused ('the child witness'); and
> (b)   relates to any matter in issue in the proceedings,
> may, with the leave of the court, be given in evidence in so far as it is not excluded by the court under subsection (3) . . .

This means that potentially any videotape of any interview with a child who later gives evidence is admissible: not only ones made with a view to criminal proceedings by police officers and social workers following the Memorandum of Good Practice (Home Office 1992), but tapes of diagnostic interviews done by psychiatrists, psychiatric social workers and psychologists (whether or not they have read the Cleveland Guidelines), and even home videos made by warring spouses as weapons in their custody disputes. The only limit on admissibility is the fact that the judge must give leave for a videotape to be used in evidence under these provisions, and as we are about to see, section 32A(3) gives the judge quite a wide discretion.

The preconditions for admissibility: judicial discretion
The Crown Court Rules, rule 23C (5), requires a person who wishes to use these provisions to put a videotape in evidence to apply for leave within 28 days of committal for trial (or notice of transfer—see page 87 above). Rule 23C (6) gives the court power to entertain applications that are made late. If one of the parties objects to the tape as evidence, there is a hearing before the judge.
In deciding whether or not to admit the tape, the judge is governed by s. 32A (3), which provides that:

> Where a video recording is tendered in evidence under this section, the court shall (subject to the exercise of any power of the court to exclude evidence which is otherwise admissible) give leave under subsection (2) above unless—

(a)   it appears that the child witness will not be available for cross-examination;

(b)   any rules of court requiring disclosure of the circumstances in which the recording was made have not been complied with to the satisfaction of the court; or

(c)   the court is of the opinion, having regard to all the circumstances of the case, that in the interests of justice the recording ought not to be admitted;

The first of these 'unless' conditions ties in with s. 32A(5)(a), which says that 'Where a video recording is admitted under this section, the child witness shall be called by the party who tendered it in evidence'. These provisions remind us of the limited nature of the reform, which only allows videotapes in evidence where the child makes an appearance as a live witness at the trial. Surprisingly, perhaps, nowhere in the Act does it say what is to happen if leave is given on the basis that the child will be available for cross-examination, the tape is played, the child is duly called as a witness—and is then too frightened to talk, or refuses to cooperate. If some sort of cross-examination had taken place, presumably the judge would proceed as he does in other cases where a cross-examination has to be abandoned: he would leave the evidence to the jury with a warning not to give too much credence to witnesses who have not been fully cross-examined (see page 95 below). If there had been no cross-examination at all, however, the judge might then decide that the tape was admissible under some other exception to the hearsay rule—for example, documentary hearsay (see page 187 below). Failing that, he would presumably have to direct the jury to disregard the tape. If it was a crucial piece of evidence, and a warning could hardly wipe out the effect of it, he would presumably feel obliged to stop the case.

The second 'unless' condition—s. 32A(3)(b)—requires the party putting forward the tape to have complied with the Crown Court Rules requiring him to describe the circumstances in which the tape was made. Crown Court Rule 23C(4), which deals with this, is as follows:

The statement of the circumstances in which the video recording was made . . . shall include the following information, except in so far as it is contained in the recording itself, namely —

(a)   the times at which the recording commenced and finished, including details of any interruptions;

(b)   the location at which the recording was made and the usual function of the premises;

(c)   the name, age and occupation of any person present at any point during the recording; the time for which he was present; his relationship (if any) to the witness and to the defendant;

(d)   a description of the equipment used including the number of cameras used and whether they were fixed or mobile; the number and location of the microphones; the video format used and whether there were single or multiple recording facilities;

(e)   the location of the mastertape if the video recording is a copy and details of when and by whom the copy was made.

Something the other side will often want to know more urgently than these technical details is how the complaint first came to light, what questioning the child underwent before the tape was made, and what answers were then given. Although these are not among the matters which rule 23C requires to be disclosed, they are matters which, if they affect their witness's credibility, the prosecution would now be expected to reveal under the rapidly-developing case law on advance disclosure (Grindrod 1992; *Berry* v *R* [1992] 2 AC 364; *Ward* (1993) 96 Cr App R 1). A refusal to do so would probably lead to the judge's refusing leave to admit the tape 'in the interests of justice', as mentioned in s. 32A(3)(c), and failure to do so, if undetected at the time, might be a successful ground of appeal. Doctors, psychologists, or social workers who interviewed the child earlier may reasonably object to disclosing what was said at those interviews on grounds of 'public interest immunity' (page 42 above). If that happens, the judge must see the evidence himself, and decide whether the light it sheds on the credibility of the witness is enough to justify ordering its disclosure, despite any breaches of confidentiality involved (*R* v *K* [1993] Crim LR 281).

For what other reasons might the judge decide to invoke s. 32A(3)(c) and refuse leave to use the videotape because he thinks that 'in the interests of justice the recording ought not to be admitted'?

The most likely one is that he thinks the interview was done in a pressured and slanted manner, using leading questions of a sort which the questioner would not be allowed to ask if he was examining the child in-chief at trial. In deciding whether the interview was fairly conducted, judges are certain to be guided to some extent by the Memorandum of Good Practice which the Home Office and the Department of Health issued on making videotapes for use in evidence under the Criminal Justice Act 1991—the 'Code that dare not speak its name'. This document—the contents of which are discussed in chapter 12—was designed in the hope of ensuring a high standard of interviewing when the police (usually aided by social workers) take video statements from children with a view to such statements being used as prosecution evidence in trials for offences against children. This is what the Pigot Committee hoped to achieve by their proposed official Code of Practice—so it is odd that the government (meaning the Home Office) strenuously opposed any reference to a Code of Practice in the Act. The reasons for their refusal seem to have been two. First, if the Act had mentioned a Code of Practice it would also have specified a procedure for making and amending it, whereas a document informally issued by a government department can be made and altered as it chooses. Secondly, they seem to have thought that judges would be less concerned about failures to comply with an 'informal' document of this sort than they would if it was a Code of Practice made under an Act of Parliament: and hence would provide less ammunition for defence counsel who wanted to prevent a videotape being used in evidence. However, as the Memorandum contains what nearly everyone agrees is sensible guidance on how to interview children without putting words into their mouths, it is inconceivable that judges will not be influenced by it when making decisions on admissibility.

This thought worries some people, who fear that judges will take an over-rigid attitude towards the Memorandum. A particular concern is the repeated emphasis in the Memorandum on the need to interview early: which makes sense from every point of view where a child has been assaulted on a single occasion by a stranger, but which can present obvious difficulties where a child has been subjected to a long history of abuse within the family, and discloses it in a series of ever more horrifying instalments after she has been moved out of the family, and gradually gains confidence in her new care-givers (Wattam 1993). It is to be hoped—and expected—that judges will treat the Memorandum as a set of flexible guidelines, to be followed as far as it is sensible and practicable to do so, and departed from when circumstances so require: which is the attitude they have generally taken in civil cases to the guidelines contained in the Cleveland Report. As Mr Justice Hollings said in *Re A (Minors) (Child Abuse: Guidelines)* [1991] 1 WLR 1026, 1029, these are:

> only what they say, guidelines, and there can be variation and flexibility to meet the needs of a particular case provided regard is paid to the principles underlying the guidelines.

The concluding words of s. 32A(3) make it plain that when granting leave the court may order the tape to be edited, so that the jury sees only part of it. Section 32A(4) tries to encourage judges to admit the whole tape where possible by saying that

> . . . the court shall consider whether any prejudice to the accused, or one of the accused, which might result from the admission of that part is outweighed by the desirability of showing the whole, or substantially the whole, of the recorded interview.

(On editing, see further the Practice Direction (1992) 95 Cr App R 354.)

Procedure at trial
Section 32A(5) provides that:

> Where a video recording is admitted under this section —
> (a)   the child witness shall be called by the party who tendered it in evidence;
> (b)   that witness shall not be examined in-chief on any matter which, in the opinion of the court, has been dealt with in his recorded testimony.

Thus the scheme is that the videotape should not merely supplement the child's oral evidence at trial, but should as far as possible replace his evidence in-chief.

For this provision there seem to be two reasons. The first is to deal with the argument that making the videotape admissible in evidence would make the situation worse for the child, because at trial he would undergo a harassing cross-examination on all the trivial differences between the account he had just given in examination-in-chief, and the account contained in the videotape—an argument the Home Office was using against changing the law to make videotapes admissible when other people first proposed it several years earlier. At that time it was scarcely a valid argument against changing the law to make videotapes more readily admissible in evidence, because the defence were already entitled to cross-examine on a previous videotape in so far as it contained statements inconsistent with the child's examination-in-chief: indeed, there had already been one well-publicised case where the effect of cross-examining a girl in this sort of way had caused her to have hysterics, as a result of which the trial had had to be adjourned (*Chatham News*, 23 October 1987). The government understandably wanted to reduce the scope for it happening in future, however, and s. 32A(5)(b) achieves this, in as much as where there is no examination-in-chief, there is no second telling of the story with which the earlier one can be microscopically compared. The second reason for the provision seems to have been to provide an answer to those who were saying 'This scheme is no good because, unlike the Pigot scheme, it does nothing for the child'—the answer, feeble but faintly plausible, 'Well, it does save the child from having to undergo an examination-in-chief'.

There is a difficulty about the way the section is drafted, however, and this is that it does not merely *enable* the party calling the child to use the videotape as the means by which the child tells his tale to the court, but—where he chooses to use the tape as evidence at all (see page 185)—actually *requires* him to use it as a substitute for a live examination-in-chief about the matters covered in it. This is not sensible, because interviews can be more or less competently conducted. If the video-interview is well done, and the child tells the tale clearly and distinctly, the tape can usefully replace the examination-in-chief: but if the opposite is true, forcing the party calling the child to use the tape as a substitute for examination-in-chief makes him the prisoner of the blunders that the interviewer made. Unfortunately, however, that is just what the section seems to do. It does not say that the party *may* so use it, or even that he shall, unless the judge grants leave to ask the child further questions. It says 'that witness shall not be examined in-chief on any matter which, in the opinion of the court, has been dealt with in his recorded testimony'. In Parliament this problem was pointed out, and an amendment was moved to make 'has been dealt with' into 'has been *adequately* dealt with': but the government resisted the amendment, arguing that 'dealt with' necessarily implies 'adequately dealt with' (HL Deb. vol. 528 col. 52)—which of course it does not, any more than 'fed' necessarily implies 'adequately fed'. Since the Act came into force, we have already heard of cases where counsel wanted to ask the child supplementary questions, and the judge, interpreting the section literally, refused to allow them: although other judges are prepared to strain the words to allow the questions to be asked.

There is a further inconvenience. Before being cross-examined, a child will obviously need to be reminded about what he or she said at the video-interview. Often this can be done by letting the child view the tape, either before the trial, or as the court is viewing it. However if the child is young, and the tape is long, it may be very tiresome for the child to have to view the tape, when a much better preliminary to cross-examination would be to administer a succinct examination-in-chief. Yet according to the terms of the Act, this sensible course is precluded.

Like the equally inept provision on competency (page 62 above), this section looks destined to make an early appearance in the Court of Appeal. Meanwhile it is to be hoped that judges take a robust approach to it. This they can fairly do, because it is difficult to see what the defendant has to complain about if a judge allows an examination-in-chief where the section arguably forbids it, since the provision was designed to protect not the defendant, but the child.

The Act does not lay down in detail what procedure is to be followed when, as the Act requires, the child is called by the party who tendered the videotape in evidence. Presumably it will be necessary for him to ask the child if she stands by what she said on the tape (Birch 1992). If the child is to answer this question meaningfully—and if she is to make any sense of the cross-examination—she must (in the absence of an examination-in-chief) have had a recent opportunity to see the tape. She could watch the tape at the same time as it is shown to the court, or equally properly, see it some time before the trial.

The legal effect of the videotape
As a matter of law, the videotape is as valid as oral evidence. Section 32A(6) provides:

> Where a video recording is given in evidence under this section, any statement made by the child witness which is disclosed by the recording shall be treated as if given by that witness in direct oral testimony; and accordingly —
> (a)   any such statement shall be admissible evidence of any fact of which such testimony from him would be admissible.

So where the child says something on the video which he or she later retracts in cross-examination, the court, if it believes the assertion and not the retraction, would be entitled to accept the video statement and reject the evidence given live in court. But obviously, in so far as corroboration is still needed (see chapter 8), a video recording of a child saying something cannot in law amount to corroboration of that child's oral evidence to that effect. Section 32A(6) continues by saying:

> (b)   no such statement shall be capable of corroborating any other evidence given by him.

Section 32A(6) concludes with the following words:

> and in estimating the weight, if any, to be attached to such a statement, regard shall be had to all the circumstances from which any inference can reasonably be drawn (as to its accuracy or otherwise).

— a piece of advice which most courts, one hopes, will hardly find necessary.

A possible difficulty might arise with s. 32A(6) over the question of competency. The Act makes the video 'evidence of any fact of which such testimony from [the child] would be admissible'. It may be that the oral evidence of young children is still only admissible where they pass some competency requirement (see page 62 above), and oral evidence from children between 14 and 17—to whom the videotape provisions apply in sex cases—is certainly admissible only when given on oath. Does this mean that for the tape to be admissible, the person conducting the video interview must put the child through the same procedures as the judge must when the child gives oral evidence?

This is surely not the case. Section 32A(6) says that when a video recording is given in evidence under this section, 'any statement made by the child witness which is disclosed by the recording shall be treated as if given by that witness in direct oral testimony': *the court* must treat *the video-interview* like evidence given live—not that *the interviewer* must treat *the child* as if he were giving live evidence in court. (Obviously not: the whole idea was to enable children's evidence to be put before the court without the stresses and strains of a normal court appearance.) There is an analogy, too, with the other exceptions to the 'rule against narrative'—like recent complaint (see page 141)—where there is no question of the earlier statement having to be given on oath. Nor is there any practical need for the child to be put on oath. Where a tape is used in evidence under these provisions the child must come to court as a live witness, and in so far as competency is still an issue, it should be sufficient for it to be examined in court.

How useful are these provisions?

Where children are likely to give incoherent evidence at trial, these provisions should give the prosecution a useful extra piece of evidence. As far as the child is concerned, however, they do little to help. Two particularly stressful things for child witnesses are often waiting for weeks or months for the case to come to court, and the live cross-examination when they get there. The video provisions of the 1991 Act—unlike the Pigot scheme—preserve these problems, because they require the child to come to court for a live cross-examination. Indeed, if being able to use the video enables the police and the Crown Prosecution Service to prosecute in cases they would otherwise have dropped, the effect of the Act on children generally may be to inflict the stress of giving live evidence on a larger number of them. Worry has also been expressed about the over-rigidity of the provision (s. 32A(5)(b)) forbidding the person calling the child who has been video-interviewed from conducting an examination-in-chief. How will it be for them when, instead of initial questioning from counsel for the side which is calling them, they are plunged straight into cross-examination? In one respect the child may benefit, however, and this is where therapy is needed to enable him or her to get over the incident. If the child must later give live evidence, therapy presents a danger for the prosecutor, because the defence may try to discredit the child's evidence by saying his or her recollection has been tainted by suggestive questioning from the psychiatrist. For this reason, prosecutors have often tried to prevent future child witnesses from having therapy until after the prosecution has wended its leisurely way through the courts. With a video interview, however, the child's account as given on that day is preserved for the court to see and hear: if on 1 March she said that X raped her, the psychiatrist cannot have put this into her mind by counselling that took place on 2 March. So the Act should make it easier for some child abuse victims to be given counselling.

How the Act works will only be discovered by experience, however. So it is reassuring to note that the Home Office has commissioned Professor Graham Davies, of the Department of Psychology at Leicester University (who earlier did the study on the live link—see page 103 above) to monitor progress.

Pending a final judgment on the success of the scheme, two final questions arise.

First, now that the possibility of using video evidence exists, is the prosecution bound to use it? Clearly, the videotaping scheme contained in s. 32A and the Memorandum of Good Practice is optional. Even the Home Office, which is encouraging the police to use it, is exhorting them not to use it unless and until they are confident they can use it properly. If the scheme turns out to be a success, however, and it becomes the accepted method of putting a child's account before the court, failure to use it might eventually lead to criticisms from the defence or from the judge: on the ground that they have failed in their duty to put forward the most reliable evidence available—the child's account in its earliest and least corrupted form.

Secondly, if an interview is videotaped under the Memorandum of Good Practice, and it is then clear that the interview was badly done and will be less effective as a means of putting the child's account before the court than live evidence in-chief, is it possible to scrap the tape and simply call the child as a live witness? In a prosecution, both sides have a discretion as to what evidence they call. Neither side would be obliged to put the videotape in evidence having made it, and they could certainly decide, on reflection, to abandon the tape and call the child for a live examination-in-chief. If the party with the tape is the prosecution, however, they cannot simply wipe the tape or put it in the bin, because presumably their general duty of disclosure would require them to tell the defence about it, and to give them access to it, in case at trial they should want to use it to show the child has previously said something inconsistent with his courtroom testimony.

We now consider four further cases where videotapes are admissible provided the witness comes to court to give live evidence.

Recent complaint; de recenti statement

For a statement to count as a recent complaint, alias a *de recenti* statement, it must have been made at the earliest possible opportunity after the offence. Where enough time has passed for a videotaping session to be organised, this condition will probably not be met. However, the condition might be met where a complaint is made to the police as soon as the child is assaulted, and the police happen to have video equipment in the station waiting to be used. In such a case it would not matter that the child had told her parents, or some other person, before the video interview took place: an English case holds that a recent complaint is one made quickly after the offence, whether or not the victim of the offence made an even earlier statement to someone else (*Wilbourne* (1917) 12 Cr App R 280).

Previous identifications

In both England and Scotland the courts have said that witness A may give evidence that witness B picked out a suspect at an identification parade, and in England the courts also permit evidence that after the crime a witness helped the police to make a Photofit or a drawing of someone who looks suspiciously like the accused (see page 144 above). If a witness may describe a person making a Photofit or drawing, or identifying the culprit at an identification parade, he may undoubtedly play the court a videotape of that person actually doing it. Here it is quite likely that the incident will be preserved on videotape, and that the prosecution will seek to use it.

To rebut an allegation of previous fabrication

Just as the suggestion that a witness's evidence is a recent fabrication can be rebutted by oral or written evidence to show that he or she has told the same tale from the start, so it could be rebutted by a videotape of the witness actually telling it. So if defence counsel tries to say 'Mary only said her father assaulted her after her stepfather gave her a new bike for Christmas', the prosecution could show a videotape of her describing the assault many months before.

Previous inconsistent statements

As explained in chapter 6, a witness may be confronted with a previous inconsistent statement in the course of cross-examination, and if the witness denies having made it the previous statement may then be proved. Thus for as long as anyone can remember, barristers cross-examining children have taken them through the written statements they originally gave the police in order to bring out any discrepancies between what they said then and their evidence in court. The same can undoubtedly be done if the previous statement is preserved on videotape. This rule, it must be stressed, enables the tape to be put in evidence quite independently of the Criminal Justice Act 1991, and without any need to follow the procedures under it. Indeed, as we mentioned above (page 182), there were cases in England where children were cross-examined on videotapes containing previous inconsistent statements several years before that Act came into force.

Videotapes in criminal proceedings: where they are admissible although the child does not give evidence at trial

Scotland: evidence on commission

In Scotland, the court has power to order the whole of a child's evidence—cross-examination as well as examination-in-chief—to be taken ahead of trial before a commissioner. The examination is video-recorded, and at trial the tape completely replaces a live appearance by the child. This was made possible by the Prisoners and Criminal Proceedings (Scotland) Act 1993. It was discussed in the section of this book on methods of taking the child's evidence in advance of trial (pages 91–92 above).

England: tapes as 'documentary hearsay'

In England, a videotape of an interview with a child could be admissible under the documentary hearsay provisions (ss. 23 and 24) of the Criminal Justice Act 1988. This is because the word 'document' is defined for the purposes of the 1988 Act to include video and audio tapes: a fact which the Parliamentary draftsman has done his best to disguise by teasingly referring the reader from the relevant sections of the Act to a Schedule 2, and thence to Part II of the Civil Evidence Act 1968—where, at the end of the treasure-hunt, the intention of Parliament is finally revealed.

The 'documentary hearsay' provisions are explained in chapter 6 (pages 134–137 above), to which readers are referred for the details. Here it is sufficient to say that these sections of the Criminal Justice Act 1988 allow a hearsay statement to be put in evidence where (a) one of a number of possible pre-conditions are met, and (b) the judge in his discretion grants leave. Among the possible conditions are where the maker of the statement is dead, or too ill to come to court, or does not give evidence at the trial 'through fear': which has been interpreted to cover the case where the witness is tongue-tied with fright in the witness-box, as well as the more obvious one where he fails to come to court at all. On the face of it, there might be quite a lot of cases in which videotapes of interviews with absent children could be put before the court under these provisions.

The Home Office clearly believes they should be used in this way. It used this possibility as an argument against the specific proposals to make videotape evidence admissible that were made during the debates that led up to the Criminal Justice Act 1988, and it used the argument again when critics said the videotaping provisions of the 1991 Act were insufficient because they fail to allow for the case where the child is too young, too ill or too traumatised to be cross-examined live at trial. The possibility of using the documentary hearsay provisions for videotapes of absent children is explained in the Memorandum of Good Practice, Appendix G (Home Office 1992).

From the point of view of the defendant, however, there is a serious objection to putting his main accuser's evidence before the court in the form of a hearsay statement under these provisions, because he will usually have had no chance to put his side of the story to the witness at the time the statement was taken. Indeed, it is questionable whether this would be compatible with the European Convention on Human Rights (page 78 above). No such difficulty attends any scheme which, like the Scottish provision for taking evidence on commission or the Pigot proposals, provides for this.

Taped confessions

The confession of a child or young person, like that of an adult, is admissible against him in criminal proceedings where he is the defendant. As we explained earlier in this chapter, it is now common practice for the police to audio-record interviews with suspects, and there is no question but that the audio (or video) recording of a confession is admissible to the same extent as a written transcript, or one repeated by a hearer from memory.

Adult suspects sometimes confess to abusing children after being shown videotapes of children describing what they did to them, and this situation could result in the videotape of the child being admitted as part of the defendant's confession. Where it is necessary to know what was said to the suspect in order to understand what he has confessed to, the court is ready to listen to the accusation as well as to the suspect's reply (*Christie* [1914] AC 545), and there is no legal reason why this should not apply where the accusation happens to have been contained in a videotape. This very point arose, and was put to a judge for decision, in one criminal trial that followed one of the Bexley interviews: but a last-minute change of plea meant that the judge did not have to make a ruling (Bexley Report 1987, p. 28).

Tapes of *res gestae* (excited utterances)
As we saw in chapter 6, this exception admits evidence of a statement made immediately after some startling event by a person who had no opportunity to start inventing falsehoods about it. In the nature of things it is unlikely in practice to cover a videotape, but it does not require too strong an imagination to think of cases where it would.

Tapes of statements regarding physical or mental sensations
Under this hearsay exception the courts admit evidence of what a person said about his bodily sensations as evidence of what his bodily sensations were. Thus, for example, a doctor could give evidence that a child told him 'my head hurts' as evidence that the child did have a headache at the time. If the doctor had videotaped the medical examination in the course of which the child said this, the tape would be no less admissible than the doctor's oral evidence. As was explained in chapter 6, however, this exception only extends to admit what a patient said when describing his symptoms, and does not render admissible his explanation of how he got them. In a child-abuse case, the child is quite likely to have told the doctor, 'My head hurts where daddy hit it'—and if he did, the admissible part of his statement would be so inextricably mixed up with what was inadmissible that a judge would probably find the videotape too unfairly prejudicial to be shown at trial.

Tapes of statements of persons now dead
As we explained in chapter 6, Scots law makes an exception to the hearsay rule where the maker of the statement is now dead—and indeed, where he is unavailable because he has gone mad or been taken prisoner of war. It follows that in a criminal trial in Scotland a videotape of an interview with a child would be admissible if the child had subsequently died. In England, as we saw, the equivalent exception is more limited, and applies only where the statement amounts to a 'dying declaration' made by someone under a 'settled, hopeless expectation of death'. This condition is obviously rather unlikely to be satisfied in the case of a videotape of an interview with a child; but

interestingly, the law reports do contain several cases where the prosecution sought to put in evidence dying declarations taken from children (*Pike* (1829) 3 C & P 598; *Perkins* (1840) 9 C & P 395). (It is also interesting to note that when Thomas Edison invented the phonograph in 1877 he foresaw that one of the future uses of voice recording would be to preserve 'the last words of dying persons' (Dickson and Dickson 1894).)

Hearsay exceptions which do not apply to tapes
By a curious freak of English law, there are four cases where an exception to the hearsay rule lets in a child's out-of-court statement if it is recorded in writing—but *not* if it is preserved on tape. The first of these is s. 9 of the Criminal Justice Act 1967, which allows either prosecution or defence to use a written statement to replace a personal appearance by the witness provided the other side consent (page 130). The second case is s. 13 of the Criminal Justice Act 1925 and s. 102(7) of the Magistrates' Courts Act 1980, which allow a deposition to be put in evidence in certain cases where the person who made the statement is unavailable to give evidence at trial (page 134 above). The third is s. 105 of the Magistrates' Courts Act 1980, which allows a deposition to be taken from a witness who is dangerously ill, for future use at trial. And the fourth is ss. 42 and 43 of the Children and Young Persons Act 1933, which allow a deposition from a sick child to be put in evidence where a court appearance would involve a serious risk to life or health (page 83 above).

The reason why these exceptions do not apply to tapes is the way the provisions happen to be drafted. For each, there must be a 'written' statement. Although the word 'document', which is used in some other exceptions to the hearsay rule, can be defined to include a tape, there is no way this extensive construction can be put on the words 'statement in writing'. The reason for this wording is that when these sections were first drafted, nobody in England had yet thought of using tape recordings in the legal process, and everyone assumed that a statement could be preserved in no way other than by writing it down. In the civil courts depositions, where permitted in evidence, can be and sometimes are recorded on videotape (*J. Barber & Sons* v *Lloyd's Underwriters* [1987] QB 103), and it is obviously absurd beyond words that the criminal courts should be able to receive written depositions, but not ones that are tape-recorded. Yet twice when there was a move in Parliament to extend ss. 42 and 43 of the Children and Young Persons Act 1933 to cover tape-recorded statements, it was successfully opposed by the government (see page 86 above).

Part III
The advantages and disadvantages of videotapes

In recent years there has been much public discussion about the merits and demerits of videotapes (4), and quite a campaign to provide for their wider use in evidence. It is convenient to end this chapter with a brief summary of the debate. Before launching into this discussion one or two general points need to be made.

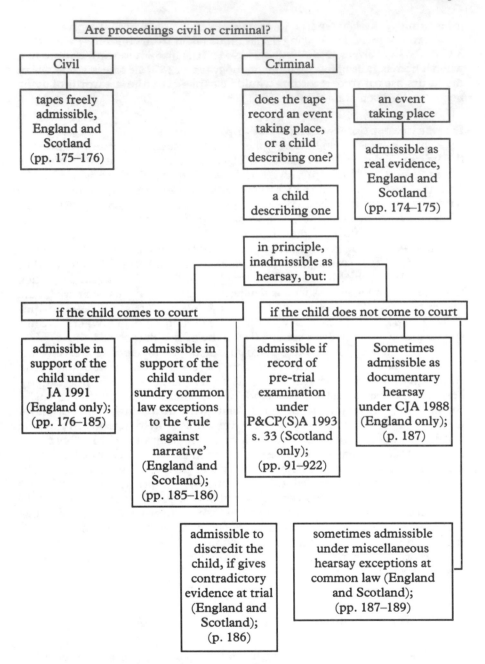

Figure 7.1   Flow chart: admissibility of videotapes

The first is to remind readers that videotapes are already widely admissible in legal proceedings under the law as it stands. There are virtually no restrictions on their admissibility in civil proceedings, and in criminal cases they may now be used in the situations which we discussed in the last section.

The second is that videotapes may be used either to supplement a child's oral testimony at trial, or as a substitute for it, and the arguments for and against making them more widely admissible in criminal proceedings are different according to which proposal we are talking about.

ARGUMENTS AGAINST VIDEOTAPES

At least eleven different arguments have been put forward against videotapes as evidence in criminal proceedings.

* First, there is what may be described—with considerable injustice to the pyschiatrists concerned, as the 'Great Ormond Street argument'. Influenced by the fact that some Family Division judges criticised some of the earlier Great Ormond Street tapes because they contained too many leading questions, some lawyers have said that it is unfair to admit videotapes of interviews with children in criminal cases, because the children's answers might have been extracted by leading questions, or other unfair techniques. Among those who have said this are Sir John Arnold, a former President of the Family Division (*The Times*, 21 December 1987), and Lord Hailsham, a former Lord Chancellor, in the course of Parliamentary debate (HL Deb., vol. 489, col. 281). More recently, this argument has been used in a well known textbook on evidence against the videotaping provisions of the Criminal Justice Act 1991.

> . . . In practice, the adult is likely to be a non-lawyer who is sympathetic to the child. The implications of this for the defendant are grim. The slant of the recording will be against him, and experience in the USA has shown that, in general, the impression made by the recording on the jury is so powerful that cross-examination is ineffective to uphold the defendant's interests . . . It is to be hoped that trial judges will give full consideration to the possible exercise of their discretion in these extremely critical cases. (Murphy 1992, p. 427.)

Murphy cites no sources in support of what he says is happening in the USA, which does not correspond with our impression of what is going on there. Nor do we agree with him that videotapes of interviews with children have an overwhelmingly powerful effect on juries. As we explained earlier (page 110) the research shows that they have, if anything, rather less emotional impact than live evidence from children.

In our view, the argument that videotape evidence should be banned because interviews can be unfairly conducted is a muddled one.

In the first place, it confuses two different types of videotape made for two different purposes: tapes of diagnostic interviews by psychiatrists, often with children unwilling to say anything and needing to be coaxed to talk, and tapes of interviews specially made with a view to criminal proceedings, where the child is almost by definition prepared to communicate. Secondly, it fails to recognise that interviews can be conducted fairly as well as unfairly, that non-lawyers can be trained to interview, and that it is possible to weed out the bad ones and prevent them being used in evidence—as the Criminal Justice Act 1991 attempts to do. That it is possible to conduct a bad video interview is no reason for a rule which requires us to reject a good one. Nor are lawyers being consistent when, in the same breath, they complain about slanted interview techniques and praise cross-examination: since one of the big criticisms of cross-examination, particularly where young children are concerned, is that cross-examiners are permitted to ask leading questions.

Finally, the fact that the child may have been questioned in a pressured and leading manner is, to some extent, an argument *in favour* of admitting videotapes of interviews, rather than a reason for excluding them. A child who gives live evidence at trial may well have been questioned in advance in a manner likely to put all sorts of ideas into his head, but this fact will usually be hidden from us. If the interview was not video-recorded, the most we usually have is a written statement which the police took at the interview, and from which the questions that produced the assertions in the statement may well have been laundered out. If the interview was videotaped the questions will be accurately preserved, and so if the tape is admissible in evidence the court can discover not only what the child said, but what was said or done to him to make him say it.

& * The second argument against making videotapes more generally admissible in criminal trials is that it would prejudice the defendant by allowing accusations to be made against him by witnesses whose evidence he is unable to challenge by cross-examination.

Whether this argument is valid or not depends on the details of the scheme proposed. It would be a valid objection to a scheme which allowed the prosecution to put in evidence the tape of an interview where the defence were given no opportunity to put their questions, and allowed it whether the child appeared as a witness at the trial or not. But it is obviously not a valid objection to a proposal to make a videotape of a previous interview admissible in a case where the child gives live evidence at trial, as under the Criminal Justice Act 1991 in England, because where the child is present in court it is possible to conduct a cross-examination about what he or she said on the tape.

If what is proposed is a video deposition with a right of defence questioning built in, the 'no cross-examination' objection falls to the ground unless it is reformulated as follows: it is unfair to the defendant to receive evidence from a witness whom he cannot cross-examine *at trial in the presence of the jury*. But this cannot be supported. First, there are already a number of well-known cases where the court can receive evidence from a source which the defendant could not cross-examine *in the presence of the jury*; ss. 42 and 43 of the Children and Young Persons Act 1933, discussed on pages 83–86, are one obvious example. Secondly, the real question must be whether a system that removes the defendant's right to cross-examine a child *at trial and in the presence of the jury* would prevent him getting a fair deal. It would undoubtedly weaken his position, because it would enable the prosecution to put before the court evidence it would otherwise be unable to hear. But that is not an objection in itself. The true issue is whether this would expose him to a greater risk of a miscarriage of justice. To believe this is so, we have to accept that in the case of a young or highly traumatised child, a cross-examination conducted by an advocate in open court months or even years after the event has a greater chance of extracting the truth than the alternative method of testing the evidence by questioning at the time the video deposition is taken. This proposition we find difficult to accept—for reasons we discuss when we examine cross-examination in greater detail in chapter 10.

* The third objection to making videotapes more readily admissible in evidence in criminal proceedings is that it would lead to increased stress for children giving evidence. Child witnesses, it is said, have a hard time as it is being adversarially cross-examined on the discrepancies between what they have said in their evidence in the witness-box and the written statement they earlier gave to the police. If a videotape of their previous examination was put before the court they would have an even worse time in the witness-box, because the videotape would give the defence a lot more detail about what the child originally said, and hence enable them to grill the child even more severely.

Clearly this is not a valid argument against a proposal to introduce a video deposition, rather than a proposal to admit a videotape where the child gives live evidence at trial. Where there is a video deposition this would replace the child's live evidence at trial, and there would be no question of the child undergoing an in-court cross-examination. Nor is it a valid argument against changing the law, as it has already been changed in England, to make videotapes admissible in criminal proceedings to supplement the testimony of children who give evidence live, because it has always been possible to cross-examine an opponent's witness about previous statements he has made that conflict with his courtroom testimony (though it could be an argument against videotaping interviews, as against making written notes of them).

In so far as this is a problem, it is possible to reduce it to some extent by enabling the party calling the child to use the videotape to replace the child's live evidence in-chief. If this is done, there is only one telling of the story, and not two stories for the cross-examiner minutely to compare, as there will be if the court hears both a videotape of an early examination, and in addition the child has to retell the tale in court months later, under stress. As we saw earlier (page 182), this is the technique which the Criminal Justice Act 1991 adopts—although unfortunately it does so too inflexibly, and so creates as many problems as it solves.

* A fourth and related objection is put forward by Toth and Whalen in an American prosecutors' manual. They say that videotapes may preserve a series of interviews in the course of which the child told divergent stories, or even

recanted at some point—and this can make a prosecution harder than where the only evidence is a live child in the witness-box (Toth and Whalen 1987, sect. VI–7). But this, like the last objection, is not an objection to changing the present law, because the present law would already allow the defence to put such tapes to devastating use if they existed. Furthermore, if the child has told contradictory stories in the course of the investigation this is surely a piece of information which the court should know. If it is a drawback to videotapes as far as prosecutors are concerned, for justice it is an advantage.

* A fifth objection to videotapes in evidence is the risk that they distort the impact of the evidence. According to some critics, juries tend to give videotaped evidence too much weight because of an effect called 'status enhancement', whilst according to others, they give it too little weight because it seems unreal to them. The same points are made about the 'live link' (closed-circuit television), and we examine such evidence as there is on the matter in chapter 5 (pages 109–110). Whether or not there is anything in this objection in either of its contradictory versions, it is not a strong objection to make if it would not be feasible to get the child in question to give live evidence, and the choice is between hearing the child on videotape or not hearing the child at all.

* A sixth and related objection some people have made is that videotapes would make it easier for children to tell lies, or harder to detect their lies, or both. Whether or not a child would find it easier to tell lies on tape than in the courtroom depends in part on how effective our traditional courtroom procedures are at extracting truthful evidence from live witnesses, and, as we explain in chapter 10, it may be that much of our confidence in these methods is misplaced. As to the question of lie detection, we are aware of no psychological research suggesting that observers are worse at detecting lies told on television screens than lies told in the flesh. Indeed, it could easily be the case that lies are easier to detect when video-recorded, because recorded evidence can be viewed several times over, which live evidence cannot. As an American writer said 17 years ago, the arguments in this area are highly speculative (Shutkin 1973).

* A seventh point that is made against videotapes in evidence is that the process of making them may be unsettling for the child.

Children are often uncomfortable with recording equipment and may be nervous about revealing abuse. Young children may become involved or distracted by it and want to play rather than concentrate on the alleged abuse. (Toth and Whalen 1987, sect. VI–7.)

This is not everyone's experience. One child psychiatrist writes: 'In my own clinical experience . . . children, and particularly young children, are very much more at ease with video equipment . . . than are the adult therapists who interview them' (Vizard 1989). Furthermore, would a child find making a videotape more troublesome than giving evidence in court, if one was an alternative to the other? Even if it would, this may be a practical argument against making a videotape, but it is hardly an argument against the admissibility of the tape in court if it is eventually made.

* An eighth objection to making videotapes more generally admissible in criminal proceedings is that it might lead to longer criminal trials. Until recently we have just had live evidence from the child—but if there is a videotape we can now have that too, and in the case of a young child particularly, the interview on videotape may well be considerably longer than the child's evidence in court. There are several points that can be made in reply to this. First, it would not matter if contested cases took longer, if—as may be the case—the greater availability of videotaped evidence resulted in a larger proportion of guilty pleas. Secondly, a longer trial is a weak objection if the reason the trial takes longer is that more information is put before the court, and that information is reliable and useful: to adapt a saying of Lord Atkin, 'Speed is a good thing, but justice is better'. Thirdly, this objection, if it is a valid one, is only an objection if the proposal is to admit videotapes of early interviews to supplement live evidence from the child at trial. If, as under the scheme proposed by the Pigot Committee, the proposal is for a video deposition, this objection would not apply. The video deposition would replace the child at trial: one piece of evidence would be offered in place of another instead of in addition to it.

* As a ninth objection, some people, looking over their shoulders at the United States and at some wardship cases where videotapes have been put in evidence, have said that videotapes in criminal trials would mean a lot of courtroom argument about whether the interviewer had used proper questioning techniques. This, it is said, will waste time, cost money, lead to the indecorous spectacle of professionals slandering one another in the witness-box, and divert what is meant to be a trial of the defendant for molesting the child into a trial of a policeman or social worker for conducting a negligent interview (see Toth and Whalen, sect. VI–8). If there is no agreement as to what are the appropriate ways of questioning children, and interviews are done by people with no training who follow nothing but the light of nature, this sort of problem might well occur. On the other hand, if—as is meant to be the case in England with the Criminal Justice Act 1991 and the Memorandum of Good Practice—there is an official code of practice for interviewing children, and children are interviewed by people who know the code and have been trained to follow it, this problem is less likely to arise. (It is also worth pointing out that an objection based on the 'battle of the experts' is also an objection to the way our adversarial system deals with expert evidence—a subject we examine further in chapter 9.)

* A tenth objection concerns confidentiality. Fears have been expressed about copies of tapes getting into the wrong hands, to the embarrassment of the child in later life (MacFarlane 1985, MacFarlane and Elias 1990, Myers

1992). This is of course a risk: but the risk arises from taping interviews with children, not from making those tapes admissible as evidence in court. (Obviously, access to such tapes needs to be strictly controlled. The Pigot Committee said that the defence should come to the police station to view the tape, and should not be allowed to borrow it, let alone be given a copy. Regrettably, in some people's view, this was another of its recommendations that was not carried out. The Memorandum of Good Practice says that copies may be made and given to defence solicitors—though not to defendants in person—provided they undertake to store them safely, and to return them after the case is over.) (This and other ethical issues arising from videotaping are discussed in a pamphlet by Murray (1993).)

   * Lastly, there are those who say that greater use of videotapes in trials would undermine the oral tradition of justice. To some extent it would have this effect. But that, without more, is hardly a sensible objection. As Lord Denning said during a debate on videotapes in the House of Lords in 1987, 'Let me say that in all criminal cases and in other cases the search is for truth and justice'. The question is whether this particular derogation from the oral tradition would hinder that search, or help it. For the reasons that follow, we believe that it would help.

ADVANTAGES OF VIDEOTAPES

Advantages of tapes of early interviews where the child gives evidence at trial

* The first and most obvious advantage of a videotape of an early interview is that it enables the court to hear an unquestionably accurate record of what the child was saying about the incident at the time it first came to light, before time wiped certain details from her mind, and prompting or questioning by adults implanted others. This is important, in order to secure the acquittal of innocent defendants as much as to secure the conviction of those who are guilty. It has become all the more important as the delay between a complaint being made and the eventual trial has grown in recent years. (In the 1950s the average time between committal proceedings and trial in London was a little over four weeks. According to the annual Judicial Statistics in 1991 (Cm 1990) it was nearly 16 weeks in London, and over 12 weeks in England as a whole.)

   As well as telling us exactly what the child said, an early tape would tell us how he said it. In the course of being questioned, little children often pick up the adult words for sexual acts. They then use these when giving evidence in court, which often leads to the suggestion that they have been coached. When an eight-year-old says, 'And then he ejaculated over me', defence counsel will immediately ask, 'Did your mummy teach you that word?', to which the answer will probably be yes—with the resulting suspicion that the child's knowledge of such things also comes from what her mother told her rather than from witnessing an indecent act. If when she first described the incident her words were 'And then he kind of flicked white wee from his willy', a videotape would often reveal that she originally used words appropriate to her age and understanding.

* Secondly, a tape of an early interview will tell us how the child was questioned as well as what the answers were. Early interviews may have been conducted in such a way as to put answers in the child's mouth, which a fluent witness then incorporates with apparent spontaneity into his or her courtroom testimony. What has happened may never be revealed if the court only sees the child when giving evidence live; but a videotape of an early interview might bring this to light. Conversely, when a child eventually comes to court under present conditions, it is likely that he or she will have been asked the same questions several times over by a number of different adults, and this sometimes means that the evidence in court will be given in a dull, parrot-like way which creates the false impression that coaching has taken place. Seeing an early interview on videotape would correct this impression.

* Thirdly, a suspect can be shown a videotape of an interview with a child witness in the course of an investigation, when he cannot so easily be confronted with the child himself. If he is innocent, an early sight of the videotape gives him an earlier and better opportunity to contest the accusations and produce counter-evidence than he has under the present rules governing advance disclosure of the prosecution case (6). If he is guilty, on the other hand, seeing the videotape may precipitate an admission, probably followed by a plea of guilty.

It may be said that both of these benefits are present merely because the interview has been videotaped, and neither are affected by whether or not the tape is admissible in evidence. This may be true of giving the defendant advance notice of what the child has said—but as far as inducing guilty pleas is concerned, the videotape is surely much more likely to have this effect if it is admissible in evidence, and the defendant and his lawyers know this. In England, where until recently everyone knew that videotapes were not usually admissible for the prosecution, those who have tried confronting suspects with videotapes say that it has not prompted admissions. This is mentioned in the West Yorkshire study (West Yorkshire Police 1989), and is confirmed by personal communications from several other sources. In the USA and Canada, on the other hand, where the prosecution generally can put these tapes in evidence, there is a certain amount of anecdotal evidence that it does precipitate guilty pleas. In their study, Whitcomb et al. (1985) say (at p. 60):

Many prosecutors have observed an unanticipated, yet welcome side effect of videotaping a child's early statement: it tends to prompt a guilty plea when viewed by defendants and their attorneys. Apparently the defense reasons that a child who performs well on videotape will perform equally well in court—an assumption that has not been empirically tested. This effect was reported to us in telephone interviews with prosecutors across the country.

A news item from the *American Bar Association Journal* (April 1984, No. 70, p. 36) is as follows:

Minneapolis police report success in their two-year programme of video-taping interviews with victims of child abuse. They haven't lost a case, and no child has been called by the defence to testify. Last year videotaping was used in 75 cases, and about 60 defendants pleaded guilty as soon as they saw the interviews. If a defendant doesn't plead guilty, the tapes are shown in court.

A similar claim has been made by Stephen Chaney, a District Attorney in Texas, in an article he wrote and also during a BBC 'Panorama' programme entitled 'Family Secrets' on 8 September 1986, where he appears to have said that out of 235 suspects confronted with videotape interviews with children, 221 pleaded guilty after seeing the tape. A noticeable increase in guilty pleas in Canada was reported by the psychologist John Yuille in a lecture he gave at Leeds on 12 January 1990. In their manual for prosecutors, Toth and Whalen (1987) list this as one of the potential advantages—but add '. . . the authors are not aware of any studies documenting a higher number of guilty pleas in jurisdictions using videotaped interviews' (sect. VI–6).

* Fourthly, if a videotape of an early interview can be used in evidence, this can supplement the evidence of a child who is inarticulate or forgetful at the trial. If a child is questioned in relaxed surroundings, this is likely to produce a much fuller story than the child is able to tell in open court (Hill and Hill 1987). In the words of a New Zealand judge, who had seen a videotape in a civil case:

Without seeing the videotape, it might well have been impossible for the court and counsel to have formed a true impression of the degree of shame and disgust which A felt as she told her story, or of the obvious and patent truthfulness of what she said. Child abuse cases often raise difficult questions of who is to be believed. It seems to me that if the court is to do its job effectively in placing the welfare of the child as the first and paramount consideration and in searching for the truth, it must make use of the technological aids that are available. In the present case the videotape . . . has, I believe, taken the court closer to the truth than would have been possible by any other more traditional means. (Judge Inglis QC, *Department of Social Welfare* v *H* (1987) 4 NZFLR 397, 402.)

This, it may be said, is not just an argument for videotapes, but an argument for admitting any previous statement of a witness who gives evidence at trial. This is true—and in chapter 10 we examine the case for abolishing the rule against previous consistent statements, whether they are preserved on tape, in writing, or by any other means. (The details of this rule are set out in chapter 6.)

In these four ways, a wider use of videotapes would be advantageous for justice, mainly because the courts would have more information to go on. However, except to the extent that they produced more guilty pleas, none of the points mentioned above are advantages for the children who give evidence. If the case was contested, the child witness would still have to go to court, and so endure both the stress of waiting for the trial, and the stress of actually giving evidence (see chapter 13): criticisms that have been made of the changes in England under the Criminal Justice Act 1991. In terms of children generally, these advantages could even prove harmful. More prosecution evidence would probably mean more prosecutions, and more prosecutions would mean more children stressed and upset through having to give evidence in court.

Advantages of video depositions (which replace the child at trial)
The great advantage of a system under which the whole of the child's examination takes place in advance of trial, and a tape of this is shown as a substitute for producing the child in court, is that it does reduce the problem of stress. A video deposition is not the only way of arranging to take the child's evidence pre-trial, of course, because the pre-trial examination could also be recorded in writing, as has always been the case in France and certain other jurisdictions. But of all the available methods, the video deposition seems by far the best, because it gives the court the fullest and most accurate account of what was said. It shares most of the advantages of the tape of an early interview used to supplement a live appearance by the child at trial. Thus like a tape of an early interview, a video deposition could be used to confront the suspect. And like the tape of an early interview, the video deposition has the potential for giving us a reliable account of what the child said at an early stage, and how he or she was induced to say it. In practice, it may sometimes be that the child told the story at an initial interview, and the video deposition was recorded later on, after a rehearsal, so to speak. But in this case, there seems to be no good reason why the court should not be given details of the original interview—including a tape recording if there is one—as a supplement to the video deposition.
The video deposition has other advantages as well.

* First, it is possible to examine a video deposition of a child telling a story much more closely than it is possible to study a child giving live evidence in the witness-box. A tape can be replayed, or made to pause while a particular detail or nuance is carefully studied. When a child gives live evidence, obviously this is quite impossible.

* Secondly, a video deposition, unlike a live child witness, does not go stale with time. As long as we depend on live evidence for prosecutions, the defendant has to be prosecuted while the child can remember, or else not prosecuted at all. So, as the law stands, it would be very difficult to devise any scheme under which, without a conviction, a person who had abused a child was diverted into treatment, with the threat of a prosecution hanging over him if he failed to behave himself. By the time he has dropped out of treatment, or misbehaved again, a prosecution is no longer possible. But a video deposition, unlike a live child witness, stays fresh until it is erased.

  * Finally, and most important, the video deposition offers a practical means of putting before the court the evidence of a very young or highly traumatised child, which the court would otherwise be unable to hear at all. At present, if a child of three or four is kidnapped, or raped, or buggered, or tortured, or witnesses the murder of a parent, or suffers some other terrible ordeal, a combination of the competency requirement, the hearsay rule and the rigours of open court often ensure that a criminal court is forced to do justice without hearing the child's version of events. Even if we altered the competency requirements, expedited the trial, stripped all the wigs from lawyers' heads, and gave the court the best live television link in the world, it is hard to believe that we would ever get a child like this to give satisfactory live evidence at trial. We have already described the harrowing Scottish case of *Maine and McRobb*, which shows what happens if you try to make a three-year-old torture victim give evidence in court (pages 145, 160).

  In this sort of case, however, the video deposition provides a possible solution to the problem. Dr David Jones describes a case in Colorado where a three-year-old girl was kidnapped, sexually abused, and dumped in a cesspit to drown. She survived the ordeal and was rescued 70 hours later. She was then interviewed by a child psychiatrist and a paediatrician together, when she described her ordeal, and repeatedly picked out the suspect from photographs and videos which she was shown. The interviews were recorded on videotape. She was later interviewed again, when the suspect's lawyer was permitted to put his questions to her through the mouth of the same examiners. This too was videotaped. The video deposition, as well as the tapes of the earlier interviews, would have been admissible in evidence at the eventual trial—and it seems that they would have been used, except that at the last moment the defendant admitted his crime and pleaded guilty. (In later interviews with the child psychiatrist, the defendant confirmed that the child's account of what he had done to her was in all material respects correct.) (Jones and Krugman 1986; Jones 1987.)

  Obviously, videotapes are not a magic solution to every problem with child witnesses. But they do offer a very greatly improved method of setting up a system under which the evidence of young or highly traumatised children is taken in advance of trial—a topic to which we return in chapter 15.

NOTES

1.   The ABA Resource Center published a pamphlet entitled *Recommendations for Improving Legal Intervention in Intrafamily Child Sexual Abuse Cases* (1982), which among other things proposed the use of videotapes to replace a live appearance by the child before the grand jury and preliminary hearings. In 1985 the ABA agreed a set of guidelines entitled *Guidelines for the Fair Treatment of Child Witnesses in Cases where Child Abuse is Alleged*, which includes the statement: 'where necessary, the court should permit the child's testimony at a pre-trial or noncriminal hearing to be given by means of a videotaped deposition'.

2. The case, which began with allegations made in August 1984, eventually ended in January 1990 with the acquittal of the defendants on 52 counts and the failure of the jury to agree on a further 13 (*New York Times*, 24 January 1990).

3. *H* v *H*: *K* v *K* [1990] Fam 86 (CA); *Re E (Child Abuse: Evidence)* [1990] FCR 793; *Re Z (Minors) Child Abuse: Evidence* [1989] FCR 440; *R* v *Hove Justices, ex parte W* [1989] FCR 286; *Re C (A Minor) (Care: Balancing Exercise)* [1992] 2 FCR 65.

4. The following are some of the articles on videotaping which appeared in the legal press in Britain: Spencer (1987a, 1987b, 1987c, 1987d, 1988; Glanville Williams (1987a, 1987b, 1987d). A number of legal and psychological papers are collected in Davies and Drinkwater (1988). See also Murray (1988).

5. Criminal Evidence Act 1965, s. 1(4): '... "document" includes any device by means of which information is recorded or stored'; *cf* Civil Evidence Act 1968, s. 10(1):

> ... 'document' includes, in addition to a document in writing —
> (c)   any disc, tape, sound track or other device in which sounds or other data (not being visual images) are embodied so as to be capable (with or without the aid of some other equipment) of being reproduced therefrom; and
> (d)   any film, negative, tape or other device in which one or more visual images are embodied so as to be capable (as aforesaid) of being reproduced therefrom.

This definition of 'document' is incorporated into the Police and Criminal Evidence Act 1984 (s. 118) and into the Criminal Justice Act 1988 (sch. 2, para. 5).

6. In their prosecutors' manual Toth and Whalen 1987, sect. VI–8, say 'Testimony videotaped prior to trial enables the defence to prepare its case with prior knowledge of crucial testimony', and give this as one of the *disadvantages* of videotaping. Nothing more clearly illustrates how much more adversarial prosecutions are in the USA than they are in Britain, where no prosecutor—at least in public—would think of saying this was a drawback to them!

APPENDIX

Criminal Justice Act 1988, ss. 32 and 32A, and Rule 23C of the Crown Court Rules

32. (1)   A person other than the accused may give evidence through a live television link on a trial in proceedings to which subsection (1A) below applies if—

(a)   the witness is outside the United Kingdom; or

(b)   the witness is a child, or is to be cross-examined following the admission under section 32A below of a video recording of testimony from him, and the offence is one to which subsection (2) below applies,

but evidence may not be so given without the leave of the court.

(1A)   This subsection applies —

(a)   to trials on indictment, appeals to the criminal division of the Court of Appeal and hearings of references under section 17 of the Criminal Appeal Act 1968; and

(b)   to proceedings in youth courts and appeals to the Crown Court arising out of such proceedings.

(2)   This subsection applies —

(a)   to an offence which involves an assault on, or injury or a threat of injury to, a person;

(b)   to an offence under section 1 of the Children and Young Persons Act 1933 (cruelty to persons under 16);

(c)   to an offence under the Sexual Offences Act 1956, the Indecency with Children Act 1960, the Sexual Offences Act 1967, section 54 of the Criminal Law Act 1977 or the Protection of Children Act 1978; and

(d)   to an offence which consists of attempting or conspiring to commit, or of aiding, abetting, counselling, procuring or inciting the commission of, an offence falling within paragraph (a), (b) or (c) above.

(3)   A statement made on oath by a witness outside the United Kingdom and given in evidence through a link by virtue of this section shall be treated for the purposes of section 1 of the Perjury Act 1911 as having been made in the proceedings in which it is given in evidence.

(3A)   Where, in the case of any proceedings before a youth court —

(a)   leave is given by virtue of subsection (1)(b) above for evidence to be given through a television link; and

(b)   suitable facilities for receiving such evidence are not available at any petty sessional court house in which the court can (apart from this subsection) lawfully sit,

the court may sit for the purposes of the whole or any part of those proceedings at any place at which such facilities are available and which has been appointed for the purposes of this subsection by the justices acting for the petty sessions area for which the court acts.

(3B)   A place appointed under subsection (3) above may be outside the petty sessions area for which it is appointed; but it shall be deemed to be in that area for the purpose of the jurisdiction of the justices acting for that area.

(4)   Without prejudice to the generality of any enactment conferring power to make rules to which this subsection applies, such rules may make such

provision as appears to the authority making them to be necessary or expedient for the purposes of this section.

(5) The rules to which subsection (4) above applies are—

Magistrates' Courts Rules, Crown Court Rules and Criminal Appeal Rules.

(6) Subsection (7) of section 32A below shall apply for the purposes of this section as it applies for the purposes of that section, but with the omission of the references to a person being, in the cases there mentioned, under the age of fifteen years or under the age of eighteen years.

32A.(1) This section applies in relation to the following proceedings, namely —

(a) trials on indictment for any offence to which section 32(2) above applies;

(b) appeals to the criminal division of the Court of Appeal and hearings of references under section 17 of the Criminal Appeal Act 1968 in respect of any such offence; and

(c) proceedings in youth courts for any such offence and appeals to the Crown Court arising out of such proceedings.

(2) In any such proceedings a video recording of an interview which—

(a) is conducted between an adult and a child who is not the accused or one of the accused ('the child witness'); and

(b) relates to any matter in issue in the proceedings, may, with the leave of the court, be given in evidence in so far as it is not excluded by the court under subsection (3) below.

(3) Where a video recording is tendered in evidence under this section, the court shall (subject to the exercise of any power of the court to exclude evidence which is otherwise admissible) give leave under subsection (2) above unless—

(a) it appears that the child witness will not be available for cross-examination;

(b) any rules of court requiring disclosure of the circumstances in which the video was made have not been complied with to the satisfaction of the court; or

(c) the court is of the opinion, having regard to all the circumstances of the case, that in the interests of justice the recording ought not to be admitted; and where the court gives such leave it may, if it is of the opinion that in the interests of justice any part of the recording ought not to be admitted, direct that that part shall be excluded.

(4) In considering whether any part of a recording ought to be excluded under subsection (3) above, the court shall consider whether any prejudice to the accused, or one of the accused, which might result from the admission

of that part is outweighed by the desirability of showing the whole, or substantially the whole, of the recorded interview.

(5)   Where a video recording is admitted under this section—
   (a)   the child witness shall be called by the party who tendered it in evidence;
   (b)   that witness shall not be examined in chief on any matter which, in the opinion of the court, has been dealt with in his recorded testimony.

(6)   Where a video recording is given in evidence under this section, any statement made by the child witness which is disclosed by the recording shall be treated as if given by that witness in direct oral testimony; and accordingly—
   (a)   any such statement shall be admissible evidence of any fact of which such testimony from him would be admissible;
   (b)   no such statement shall be capable of corroborating any other evidence given by him; and in estimating the weight, if any, to be attached to such a statement, regard shall be had to all the circumstances from which any inference can reasonably be drawn (as to its accuracy or otherwise).

(7)   In this section 'child' means a person who—
   (a)   in the case of an offence falling within section 32(2)(a) or (b) above, is under fourteen years of age or, if he was under that age when the video recording was made, is under fifteen years of age; or
   (b)   in the case of an offence falling within section 32(2)(c) above, is under seventeen years of age or, if he was under that age when the video recording was made, is under eighteen years of age.

(8)   Any reference in subsection (7) above to an offence falling within paragraph (a), (b) or (c) of section 32(2) above includes a reference to an offence which consists of attempting or conspiring to commit, or of aiding, abetting, counselling, procuring or inciting the commission of, an offence falling within that paragraph.

(9)   In this section—
   'statement' includes any representation of fact, whether made in words or otherwise;
   'video recording' means any recording, on any medium, from which a moving image may by any means be produced and includes the accompanying sound-track.

(10)   A magistrates' court inquiring into an offence as examining justices under section 6 of the Magistrates' Courts Act 1980 may consider any video recording as respects which leave under subsection (2) above is to be sought at the trial, notwithstanding that the child witness is not called at the committal proceedings.

(11) Without prejudice to the generality of any enactment conferring power to make rules of court, such rules may make such provision as appears to the authority making them to be necessary or expedient for the purposes of this section.

(12) Nothing in this section shall prejudice the admissibility of any video recording which would be admissible apart from this section.

Crown Court Rules 1982 rule 23C (as inserted by the Crown Court (Amendment) Rules 1992, S.I. 1992 No. 1847)

23C.—(1) Any party may apply for leave under section 32A of the Criminal Justice Act 1988 to tender in evidence a video recording of testimony from a witness where—
    (a)   the offence charged is one to which section 32(2) of that Act applies;
    (b)   in the case of an offence falling within section 32(2)(a) or (b), the proposed witness is under the age of 14 or, if he was under 14 when the video recording was made, is under the age of 15;
    (c)   in the case of an offence falling within section 32(2)(c), the proposed witness is under the age of 17 or, if he was under 17 when the video recording was made, is under the age of 18; and
    (d)   the video recording is of an interview conducted between an adult and a person coming within sub-paragraph (b) or (c) above (not being the accused or one of the accused) which relates to any matter in issue in the proceedings;
and references in this rule to an offence include references to attempting or conspiring to commit, or aiding, abetting, counselling, procuring or inciting the commission of, that offence.

(2) An application under paragraph (1) shall be made by giving notice in writing, which shall be in the form prescribed in Schedule 7 or a form to the like effect. The application shall be accompanied by the video recording which it is proposed to tender in evidence and shall include the following, namely —
    (a)   the name of the defendant and the offence or offences charged;
    (b)   the name and date of birth of the witness in respect of whom the application is made;
    (c)   the date on which the video recording was made;
    (d)   a statement that in the opinion of the applicant the witness is willing and able to attend the trial for cross-examination;
    (e)   a statement of the circumstances in which the video recording was made which complies with paragraph (4) below;
    (f)   the date on which the video recording was disclosed to the other party or parties.

(3) Where it is proposed to tender part only of a video recording of an interview with the witness, an application under paragraph (1) must specify

that part and be accompanied by a video recording of the entire interview, including those parts which it is not proposed to tender in evidence, and by a statement of the circumstances in which the video recording of the entire interview was made which complies with paragraph (4) below.

(4) The statement of the circumstances in which the video recording was made referred to in paragraphs (2)(e) and (3) above shall include the following information, except in so far as it is contained in the recording itself, namely—

(a) the times at which the recording commenced and finished, including details of any interruptions;

(b) the location at which the recording was made and the usual function of the premises;

(c) the name, age and occupation of any person present at any point during the recording; the time for which he was present; his relationship (if any) to the witness and to the defendant;

(d) a description of the equipment used including the number of cameras used and whether they were fixed or mobile; the number and location of microphones; the video format used and whether there were single or multiple recording facilities;

(e) the location of the mastertape if the video recording is a copy and details of when and by whom the copy was made.

(5) An application under paragraph (1) shall be made within 28 days after the date of the committal for trial of the defendant, or of the giving of a notice of transfer under section 53 of the Criminal Justice Act 1991, or of consent to the preferment of a bill of indictment in relation to the case, or of the service of Notice of Appeal from a decision of a youth court or magistrates' court, as the case may be.

(6) The period of 28 days in paragraph (5) may be extended by a judge of the Crown Court, either before or after it expires, on an application made in writing, specifying the grounds of the application. The appropriate officer of the Crown Court shall notify all the parties of the decision of the Crown Court.

(7) The notice under paragraph (2) or (6) shall be sent to the appropriate officer of the Crown Court and at the same time, copies thereof shall be sent by the applicant to every other party to the proceedings. Copies of any video recording required by paragraph (2) or (3) to accompany the notice shall at the same time be sent to the court and to any other party who has not already been served with a copy or in the case of a defendant acting in person, shall be made available for viewing by him.

(8) A party who receives a copy of a notice under paragraph (2) shall, within 14 days of service of the notice, notify the applicant and the appropriate officer of the Crown Court, in writing—

(a)   whether he objects to the admission of any part of the video recording or recordings disclosed, giving his reasons why it would not be in the interests of justice for it to be admitted; and

(b)   whether he would agree to the admission of part of the video recording or recordings disclosed and if so, which part or parts; and

(c)   whether he wishes to be represented at any hearing of the application.

(9)   After the expiry of the period referred to in paragraph (8), a judge of the Crown Court shall determine whether an application under paragraph (1) is to be dealt with—

(a)   without a hearing, or

(b)   where any party notifies the appropriate officer of the Crown Court pursuant to paragraph (8) that he objects to the admission of any part of the video recording and that he wishes to be represented at any hearing, or in any other case where the judge so directs, at a hearing at which the applicant and such other party or parties as the judge may direct may be represented,

and the appropriate officer of the Crown Court shall notify the applicant and, where necessary, the other party or parties, of the time and place of any such hearing.

(10)   The appropriate officer of the Crown Court shall within 3 days of the decision of the Crown Court in relation to an application under paragraph (1) being made, notify all the parties of it in the Form prescribed in Schedule 8 or a form to the like effect, and, where leave is granted, the notification shall state whether the whole or specified parts only of the video recording or recordings disclosed are to be admitted in evidence.

CHAPTER EIGHT
Corroboration

INTRODUCTION

'Whilst the victim needs a witness—INCEST REMAINS LEGAL.'

This public statement in 1988 by a group called Survivors of Child Sexual Abuse (1) reflects an attitude which is rapidly spreading. In England and those countries of the world where the law of evidence is based on English law, there were formerly corroboration requirements relating to the evidence of children and of complainants in sexual cases, and in the last few years these countries have largely abandoned them. Yet surprisingly in Scotland there exists in criminal law a rule that the evidence of every type of witness must be corroborated—something much wider than has ever been known in English law and the systems based on it—and at present there seems to be no serious move to get rid of it. But perhaps this is not surprising. A corroboration requirement, as such, is neither good nor bad: it all depends on what sort of evidence needs corroboration, what sort of evidence is acceptable as providing it, and precisely what the legal consequences are if corroboration is not forthcoming. If feminists and incest survivors have found the English corroboration rules infuriating because of their underlying assumption that women and children tell more lies than men, foreign observers are sometimes amazed to discover that in English law it is possible to convict a defendant on nothing but his uncorroborated confession (2). And in England, too, there have recently been calls to introduce a corroboration requirement in respect of confessions following a series of scandalous cases in which people were convicted on the basis of confessions that were false or fabricated (Pattenden 1991)—calls which the Royal Commission on Criminal Justice, in its Report of July 1993, has now rejected. In the next section of this chapter the Scottish and English rules on corroboration will be examined in their application to the evidence of children. In a final section we shall consider proposals for reform.

Part I
Corroboration in Britain today

CORROBORATION IN SCOTS LAW

The rule in criminal proceedings in Scotland is that no one may be convicted on the evidence of a single witness. The requirement is a general one. It applies, in principle, to all types of offence, and protects the defendant whether he is charged with a sexual offence, or a theft or a robbery or a breach of the peace. It applies, in principle, to all types of evidence. Thus a defendant cannot be convicted on his uncorroborated confession, nor on the evidence of a single eye witness, however credible it may seem. The corroboration requirement is not limited, as in England, to certain types of presumptively unreliable witness. A defendant may not be convicted on the sole word of the Moderator of the Church of Scotland, any more than on the sole word of a mentally subnormal recidivist perjurer. One result of the rule is that it is impossible for a court to convict on the sole word of a child witness, or of an adult who complains of a sexual offence, and to this extent the Scottish rule has much the same effect as the corroboration rules in English law which are (or used to be) specific to children and sexual complainants. However, because the Scots corroboration requirement is a general one the emphasis is very different. In English law, where the usual rule is that a court may convict on one person's word against another's if the court believes it, the word of a child or a sexual complainant are exceptions to the rule: and judges have often found it necessary to explain these exceptions to juries by telling them that they exist because women and children lie more than men do, or because the word of any person is not to be trusted if he or she complains of a sexual offence. It is these remarks, in some of their cruder versions, which in recent years have led to headlines in the English press, and campaigns for the corroboration rules to be abolished. A general rule that there may not be a conviction where it is only one person's word against another seems much more rational, and can be explained without denigrating the word of any particular group. This probably explains why the corroboration rule in Scottish criminal law has not come under much public attack.

It is not true that in Scotland the whole of the evidence must be corroborated in every criminal case, because the courts have invented a category called 'procedural facts' (Macphail 1987, sect. 23.01B; Wilkinson 1986, p. 9; Walker and Walker 1964, sect. 390), which may be proved by uncorroborated evidence. Procedural facts seem originally to have been matters of pure procedure, like whether a private prosecutor was someone who was legally entitled to bring a prosecution; but the category has been extended to include certain background matters to the offence itself, like who originally owned the goods the defendant is accused of stealing.

In Scotland, what must be proved by corroborated evidence is (a) that the offence took place, and (b) that the accused did it. There must be corroboration as to both of these matters and not merely one or other of them. If a child complains that X has raped her, for example, medical evidence that she had been raped would provide corroboration that the offence had taken place, but before X could be convicted there would have to be some further evidence to corroborate the child's statement that X was the culprit: like a confession, or fibres from his clothing on her body, or—best of all—a 'genetic fingerprint' which proves the defendant is the person who had intercourse with her.

Frequently, the fact that an offence took place involves the proof of several separate elements. In a rape, for example, it is necessary to show (a) that sexual intercourse took place, and (b) the victim did not consent. Where an offence consists of distinct elements like this, it is usually said that each of these must be proved by corroborated evidence—that is to say, there must be evidence about both these elements coming in each case from two distinct sources (Macphail 1987, sect. 23.04; Wilkinson 1986, pp. 206–207); but some court decisions say it is enough if a single witness gives evidence about each one, provided the witnesses are different (ibid.). Whichever of these views is right, it goes without saying that the need to corroborate each element in the offence is in addition to the need to corroborate the evidence that the accused was the person who committed it, and not a substitute for it.

Apart from the requirement that it must come from a source other than the witness to be corroborated, there is no particular magic in Scots law about what kind of evidence will be acceptable as corroboration. It may consist of an admission or confession by the defendant, or the direct evidence of some eyewitness other than the defendant and the victim. Where the witness to be corroborated is a child, there has never been any problem about another child providing the necessary corroboration. In this respect the Scottish courts have escaped the hole which the English courts dug for themselves, when they ruled that one child may not corroborate another (see page 209). Corroboration may also consist of a piece of circumstantial evidence—such as the defendant's fingerprints at the scene of the crime, and if the offence consists of several distinct elements, a different piece of circumstantial evidence may be corroboration for each one. Here again the Scots courts seem to have avoided a pitfall which trapped the English courts at one time, because there has never been any suggestion in Scots law of the rule against cumulative corroboration (see page 212). Thus if a child gives evidence of incest committed by her father, corroboration might consist of (a) medical evidence that someone had had sexual intercourse with her within the last six hours, and (b) the fact that during that period her father was the only man who had a realistic opportunity (3). For a piece of circumstantial evidence to amount to corroboration it is, of course, sufficient that the word of a single witness should prove it. Thus when a sheriff had to consider whether there was corroboration of evidence that a little boy had been beaten up, he could find it in the evidence of a single doctor that the injuries were consistent with this (*Kennedy* v *F* 1985 SLT 22).

The three points which give rise to some difficulty are complaints, previous convictions, and suspicious behaviour by the person accused. These are discussed later in the chapter (page 219 onwards).

Until recently, the corroboration requirement applied in civil cases in Scotland too. It was abolished for personal injury claims by the Law Reform (Miscellaneous Provisions) (Scotland) Act 1968. In the years that followed, the civil courts became increasingly restive about it in cases where the welfare of children was involved. In some cases where a child said she had been abused, they were prepared to find corroboration in distinctly tenuous pieces of circumstantial evidence (see *Baxter* v *Kennedy*, Kearney 1987, p. 263). Then, following a report (No. 100) from the Scottish Law Commission in 1986, which doubted whether the corroboration requirement was really compatible with a standard of proof in civil cases which was no higher than the balance of probabilities, the corroboration requirement was completely abolished for all civil proceedings by the Civil Evidence (Scotland) Act 1988.

The Scottish corroboration requirement is as old as the law of Scotland, and seems to have its distant roots in both Civil Law and the Bible (Stair 1693, b. 4, tit. 43; Dickson 1864, sect. 2038). Many other legal systems in the same intellectual tradition used to have it too, but most have discarded it (4). It is thus an antique survival, and not—like its English counterpart—a rule invented in modern times to deal with a perceived problem. Nevertheless, most modern Scots lawyers staunchly defend it as a vital safeguard against the risk of wrongful conviction (Macphail 1987, sect. 23.02). There is no doubt, however, that it puts considerable difficulties in the way of prosecuting for sexual offences generally, including those committed against children, and it is a matter for debate whether the difficulties it causes outweigh the risk of injustice through wrongful conviction. Fortunately, the difficulties seem to be less than those formerly encountered in English law because the Scots courts are less technical in what they will accept as providing corroboration. In particular, the Scots courts, as we have seen, are much readier to accept the evidence of young children, and have never seen any difficulty about the evidence of one child corroborating that of another. (For a striking example, see *P* v *H.M. Advocate* 1991 SCCR 933.) One result of the corroboration rule, of course, is that more children end up having to give evidence. The corroboration requirement probably also explains why, in Scotland, children quite often give evidence about crimes which they witnessed as bystanders (see page 2 above): because of the corroboration requirement, the prosecution have to put in all the evidence they have got. As to this, two views are possible. On the one hand, it makes for a just result that the courts hear from all witnesses who are able to provide relevant and reliable information; but on the other hand, if giving evidence is stressful for children (see chapter 13) it is a pity that so many children have to do it. In 1990 the Scottish Law Commission reconsidered the corroboration rule in relation to the evidence of children, and decided that no change in the law was either necessary or desirable (Report No. 125, p. 23).

There are some offences for which the corroboration requirement has been abolished by Act of Parliament, 'principally those in which, by the nature of the offence, there is liable to be a paucity of evidence, such as offences against the game and freshwater fisheries laws, and those in which the requirement of corroboration involves an extravagant use of resources, particularly police resources, such as certain road traffic offences' (Macphail 1987, sect. S23.31). A further feature of these offences is that none of them are punishable very severely, or carry a high degree of moral stigma. Thus although sexual offences against children are another obvious class of case where 'there is liable to be a paucity of evidence', here the corroboration requirement still firmly stands.

If the prosecution fail to provide corroboration it does not necessarily mean that the accused goes free without a stain on his character thanks to a technicality, because as well as the corroboration requirement, Scots law has another characteristic device—the verdict of 'not proven'. If the prosecution fail to provide any evidence capable of amounting to corroboration then the judge will direct an acquittal. But if the prosecution call a child whom the jury believe as their main witness, fortified by corroborative evidence which the jury do not accept, the result might well be a 'not proven' verdict rather than a straight acquittal.

CORROBORATION IN ENGLISH LAW

Although English law has never known a general requirement of corroboration, various specific corroboration requirements have been created at one time or another by statute. Some were made in response to a particular *cause célèbre*, like the Treason Act 1695, forbidding a conviction for treason except on the evidence of two witnesses (5). Others were enacted to overcome the argument that if some new offence was created it would expose the innocent to blackmail and unfounded prosecutions. The corroboration requirement that applied to the unsworn evidence of children until October 1988 first appeared in the Criminal Law Amendment Act 1885, when it was made an offence to have sexual intercourse with a girl under the age of 16, and children were allowed to give unsworn evidence in a trial for the offence (see chapter 4). Although the main reason for including the requirement seems to have been to defuse Parliamentary opposition to unsworn evidence, the thinking behind it may not have been purely political. Two centuries earlier Sir Matthew Hale had written that he allowed young children to give evidence unsworn, but would not accept a conviction based solely upon it; and the idea of allowing children to give unsworn evidence in England was borrowed from Scots law, where there is of course a general corroboration requirement (see above). When the provision allowing children to give unsworn evidence was extended to criminal proceedings of all sorts, the provision that there could be no conviction on the unsworn evidence of a child without corroborating evidence was extended with it.

While it lasted, the corroboration requirement for the unsworn evidence of children operated in the same way as the Scottish corroboration rule: if the prosecution could not produce any corroborating evidence then the judge was bound to stop the case. It was much more limiting than the Scottish rule in one crucial respect, however, because the English courts put the astonishing gloss on the provision that the evidence of one unsworn child could not corroborate that of another (*Director of Public Prosecutions* v *Hester* [1973] AC 296). This produced disastrous results for justice, because it meant that a person could indecently assault a series of young children, or a collection of them each in the presence of the others, and no matter how credible the tale they told, he was usually beyond the reach of the criminal law, provided they were all too young to take an oath.

The corroboration requirement which applied to the unsworn evidence of children was fortified by a *duty to warn* in the case of sworn evidence from children. Where there is a duty to warn, it means that the judge must warn the jury that it is dangerous to convict on a particular type of evidence unless it is corroborated—and if the case is tried by a bench of magistrates, they must go through the form of issuing such a warning to themselves. A duty to warn is less stringent than a corroboration *requirement*, because the jury or magistrates are free to convict in the absence of corroboration if they find the uncorroborated evidence sufficiently convincing; but the warning is meant to discourage them from doing so. Nobody knows if it really does have this effect, and a study on simulated juries published in 1973 actually suggested, most surprisingly, that corroboration warnings might actually have the *opposite* effect (LSE Jury Project 1973). We are unlikely to discover whether this is really true, however, because any attempt to check the matter by taking the obvious step of questioning jurors in England would involve an offence under the Contempt of Court Act 1981. However, practising lawyers and child-care workers usually seem to think the warnings do have the effect they are meant to have, and public debate about corroboration and the duty to warn assumes that this is so.

At common law, a duty to warn arose in three circumstances. The first involved the evidence of accomplices, where the courts first imposed the duty in the 18th century as an attempted safeguard against the risk of perjury by those who had 'turned King's evidence' (Langbein 1983). The second, which the courts began to impose towards the end of the 19th century, involved the evidence of a witness (of any age or sex) who claimed to be the victim of a sexual offence. The third category, which was the evidence of children, was the most recent, and grew out of cases where children were accomplices to adults and cases where children were allegedly the victims of sexual offences. It became a separate category as a result of some sexual cases early in the 20th century, where the courts based the need for a warning on the fact that the witness was a child rather than on the fact that it was a sexual offence (*Brown* (1910) 6 Cr App R 24; *Graham* (1910) 4 Cr App R 218; *Cratchley* (1913) 9 Cr App R 232). From here the courts went on to hold that a corroboration warning was needed even where the offence against the child was a non-sexual one—like cruelty (*Hatton* (1925) 19 Cr App R 29)—and even where the offence the child had witnessed was committed against someone else—as where a nine-year-old girl gave sworn evidence that she had seen the defendant steal another adult's watch (*Buck* [1981] Crim LR 108).

In recent years these rules were increasingly criticised as technical and silly. Part of the trouble was some strange decisions about what is and is not capable of amounting to corroboration—notably the 'rule against cumulative corroboration' (see below). Worse was the requirement that the judge should warn the jury against the evidence, and include in it the vital word 'dangerous', merely because a witness of a given type had given evidence (*Davies* v *Director of Public Prosecutions* [1954] AC 378). Where the prosecution case consists of the evidence of a child, sexual complainant or accomplice and nothing else, such a warning might be seen as a sensible precaution; but where the prosecution case is knee-deep in corroboration such a warning disparages a witness's evidence unnecessarily, and may confuse the jury, who could take it as a hint from the judge that he knows more than they do, and he thinks they had better acquit. On the other hand, if the duty to warn involves an overkill because it makes the judge tell the jury it is dangerous to convict in cases where it is not, it is open to graver criticism from the opposite direction: if, on the totality of evidence given in the case it really would be dangerous to convict, a warning to the jury is surely insufficient.

What [the judge] is entitled to tell them, according to the standard formulation, is that it is dangerous to convict on uncorroborated evidence, *but that the jury are entitled to convict on uncorroborated evidence if they think fit.* As it stands, a direction of this kind seems self-defeating; it appears to tell the jury that they are entitled to do what the experience of generations shows to be dangerous. (Williams 1963, pp. 152–3.)

In such a case, what the judge really needs is not a duty to warn the jury, but a power to stop the trial—such as he now has where the only evidence the prosecution produces is an identification by a witness who had no more than a fleeting glance (*Turnbull* [1977] QB 224).

In the 1970s and 1980s the English-law rules about corroboration were also fiercely attacked on another ground. They were said to be offensive in singling out particular groups of witnesses for disbelief and denigration. Of all the various types of suspect evidence, why, it was said, should accomplices, sexual complainants and children head the list? There is no duty, and has never been any duty to warn about the 'danger' of convicting on the evidence of madmen (*Spencer* [1987] AC 128), convicts, or recidivist perjurers. What justification can there be for a rule that seems to rate an insane adult above a rational child? These points were forcibly made by many critics (Dennis 1984). In the case of children, their attacks gained strength from studies which showed that sexual misconduct with children was far more common than had previously been supposed (see chapter 1)—indicating that children were not so likely to lie about sexual matters as we used to think—and psychological research suggesting children are capable of providing much more reliable evidence than was generally assumed when the corroboration rules were invented (see chapter 11).

In the face of this, virtually all the countries of the common law world either modified their English-based rules about corroboration, or else completely abandoned them. Most jurisdictions in the USA abolished the rules about corroboration for children and sexual complainants in the 1970s (Myers 1987a, sect. 4.21). Some Australian jurisdictions abolished the mandatory corroboration warning in relation to children, or sexual complaints, or both, during the 1980s (Warner 1990, Law Reform Commission of Western Australia 1991). Other jurisdictions have gone further, and have actually prohibited judges from issuing any generalised warning not to believe a witness because how or she belongs to a certain category. New Zealand did this for child witnesses in 1989, and in 1991 the Australian state of Victoria enacted a similar provision which also applies to mentally handicapped adults. In Canada the corroboration rules were first nibbled at by a series of Supreme Court decisions (*Warkentin* [1977] 2 SCR 355; *Murphy* [1977] 2 SCR 603; *Vetrovec* [1982] 1 SCR 811); then in 1987 the Canadian Criminal Code was amended to abolish the corroboration requirement for a wide range of sexual offences against children, and in these cases to forbid any general warning that it is unsafe to act without corroboration.

In England, where the rules were originally invented, they are proving more durable than in most other places. Even here, however, important changes have been made by the Criminal Justice Act 1988.

When the Criminal Justice Bill was before the House of Lords a group of peers moved an amendment to alter the corroboration rules concerning children. At this point the Home Secretary ordered a review of recent psychological research bearing on the reliability of children, which was undertaken by the Home Office Research and Planning Unit (Hedderman 1987). The broad conclusion of this review was that a special corroboration requirement was unnecessary, at least for children over the age of five. On the strength of this the government introduced an amendment to the Bill to abolish the corroboration rules concerning children, which was enacted as s. 34 of the Criminal Justice Act 1988. This did three things:

(a) It repealed the statutory rule forbidding courts to convict on the unsworn evidence of children without corroboration.

(b) It abolished the judge-made rule requiring warnings about the danger of acting on the uncorroborated evidence of children, sworn or otherwise.

(c) It made it clear that henceforth one child giving unsworn evidence can corroborate another (6).

As far as the unsworn evidence of children is concerned this section makes a major change, because it gets rid of the rules that there can be no conviction on the unsworn evidence of children, and that one unsworn child cannot corroborate another: a major step in the direction of rationality. Indeed, it is now in theory possible for an English court to convict an adult on the word of one unsworn child and nothing else besides—although it is perhaps difficult to imagine one doing so.

As regards judicial warnings, however, the change is largely cosmetic. Section 34 abolishes the duty to warn where the witness is a child, but does nothing to alter the rule that an official warning must be given that it is dangerous to act on the uncorroborated evidence of a sexual complainant. Although children quite often give evidence about non-sexual offences in the youth courts, in practice it is rare in England for children to give evidence against adults except where they are the victims of sexual offences. Thus where an adult is on trial, if a child gives evidence a warning will usually have to be given that his or her evidence is unsafe (7).

Although there is still a duty to give a corroboration warning in sex cases, the judges have recently begun to wage a war on the technicalities of the matter.

To amount to corroboration, evidence must satisfy what is known from the case which established it as 'the *Baskerville* test' (*Baskerville* [1916] 2 KB 658). This says that to amount to corroboration, evidence must come from a source independent of the witness to be corroborated, and must confirm not merely the general truthfulness of the complainant's evidence, but the truth of that part of it which implicates the accused in the offence. This itself is quite restrictive. Much more restrictive was a gloss on the *Baskerville* test called the 'rule against cumulative corroboration', which formerly required the corroboration to consist of one single piece of evidence, and said that corroboration could not consist of two separate pieces of evidence, one of which confirmed the general truth of the complainant's evidence, and the other of which implicated the accused (*Thomas* v *Jones* [1921] 1 KB 22; Cross, 6th ed. 1985, p. 226). This curious notion was summarily dispatched by the words of Lord Lane CJ in *Hills* (1987) 86 Cr App R 26:

> Corroboration is not infrequently provided by a combination of pieces of circumstantial evidence, each innocuous on its own, which together tend to show that the defendant committed the crime. For example, in a rape case, where the defendant denies he ever had sexual intercourse with the complainant, it may be possible to prove (1) by medical evidence that she had had sexual intercourse within an hour or so prior to the medical examination, (2) by other independent evidence that the defendant and no other man had been with her during that time, (3) that her underclothing was torn and that she had injuries to her private parts. None of those items of evidence on their own would be sufficient to provide the necessary corroboration, but the judge would be entitled to direct the jury that if they were satisfied so as to feel sure that each of those three items had been proved, the combined effect of the three items would be capable of corroborating the girl's evidence.

Two years later, the Court of Appeal reaffirmed this approach in *McInnes* (1990) 90 Cr App R 99. The defendant was convicted of kidnapping and sexually assaulting a little girl of seven, and it was held that her evidence that it was the defendant who drove off with her was corroborated by evidence that the interior of his car had a number of detailed features, which she had described to the police, and of which she could hardly have been aware unless she had been inside it.

Another restrictive technicality was the theory that the judge should tell the jury they must first decide if they believe the complainant, and throw the case out if they do not, before they give any thought to the corroborating evidence. This notion was rejected in *Attorney-General for Hong Kong* v *Wong Muk Ping* [1987] AC 501, where the Privy Council said the proper direction is to tell the jury to decide whether they believe a witness by looking at that witness's evidence in conjunction with the evidence offered to corroborate it. Similarly, if D is accused of assaulting step-daughters A and B, the jury does not have to be satisfied that B is telling the truth before considering whether B's evidence corroborates the evidence of A: it should consider the combined effects of both accusations in order to decide if either or both are true (*S* [1993] Crim LR 293).

As well as abolishing some of the technical rules, the judges have also tried to narrow the situations where the warning must be given. In *Simmons* [1987] Crim LR 630, the Court of Appeal said that a woman did not count as a 'sexual complainant', and therefore did not have to be the subject of a corroboration warning, where she complained, not that the defendant had raped or indecently assaulted her, but that he had locked her in his flat with the apparent intention of doing so. And in two later cases the Court of Appeal contrived to minimise the need for a corroboration warning even where the witness was indisputably a 'sexual complainant'. At one time the jury had to be told it is dangerous to believe the word of a sexual complainant even where there was no dispute that somebody had sexually abused the victim, and the issue was solely whether she had correctly identified the defendant as the culprit (*Trigg* (1963) 47 Cr App R 94). This was irrational, because the courts had invented the corroboration warning to guard against the perceived risk that women, children, and perhaps men, had a tendency to fantasise and make wholly false complaints. In *Atkinson* (1988) 86 Cr App R 359 and in *Chance* [1988] QB 932 the Court of Appeal condemned the practice of giving a warning where there had undoubtedly been an offence committed as adding an insult to the victim's injury. According to these new cases the judge must follow the rules laid down in *Turnbull* [1977] QB 224 for dealing with disputed identifications where there is a dispute about the identity of the offender, but need not confuse the issue by giving a corroboration warning as well. In *Feltrin, The Times*, 5 December 1991 (hearing 8 November 1991), the Court of Appeal said that it was sufficient for the judge when giving the corroboration warning to mention the danger of accepting one person's word against another's, and that it was no longer necessary for him to hold forth on the supposed tendency of women and children to make false allegations of sexual assault.

Unfortunately *Atkinson* and *Chance* leave it uncertain whether there must always be a warning where the victim of a sexual offence is a child, and the dispute is about who committed it rather than about whether anyone did anything at all. In between these two cases the Court of Appeal decided *Willoughby* (1989) 88 Cr App R 91, which involved a girl of nine who had unquestionably been the victim of an indecent assault, and once again the only issue was the identity of the attacker. There, the court was clear that the usual corroboration warning had to be given, in addition to the *Turnbull* direction about identification—although the court seems to have made this ruling in ignorance of *Atkinson*. And in *Chance*, where the Court of Appeal said that judges are not invariably bound to give the corroboration warning in sex cases where the issue is identity, it did say it would be wise to give the warning sometimes: and it added 'It should in any event always be given where the complainant is a child' (at page 943). It may be that the court only said this because at that time the general duty to give a corroboration warning wherever there was a child witness was still in existence—and if so, now that s. 34 of the Criminal Justice Act 1988 has abolished it, this part of *Chance* can be forgotten. Until the Court of Appeal pronounces on the subject again, however, the matter is uncertain. Trial judges are therefore likely to err on the side of safety and give the corroboration warning in any sex case where the victim is a child, even where the only issue is identity.

Whilst most of the recent Court of Appeal decisions show a willingness to take a common-sense approach to corroboration, there are some which do not and which are hard to reconcile with the cases discussed above. In the unreported case of *Selby* (24 May 1991), for example, the Court of Appeal seems to have said that medical evidence of assault, plus fibres from the defendant's clothes on the child's clothes, plus evidence that the defendant had been with the child, did not corroborate the evidence of a four-year-old that the defendant had assaulted him: which seems impossible to reconcile with *Hills* and the other cases on 'cumulative corroboration'. In *Goss* (1990) 90 Cr App R 400 admissions that the defendant and his wife had behaved lewdly in front of a girl before taking her to bed with them, and again when they were in it with her, were held not specific enough to corroborate her evidence that when in bed the defendant had indecently assaulted her by touching her vagina. In *Griffiths* (1992) (Archbold, 1993 Criminal Appeal Office Index para. E-2) D's admission to indecent behaviour with his daughter when over 16 was held not to be corroboration of her evidence of incest with her when under 13. And in *Izard* (1993) 157 JP 58 the Court of Appeal ruled that a trial judge was indeed obliged to mention the specific risk of fabrication when giving the corroboration warning in a sex case: which seems inconsistent with *Feltrin*—a decision by a different group of judges, which was not cited. So confusion about the nature of corroboration still remains, and there is mileage yet for unmeritorious defendants.

Despite the fact that the English rules on corroboration have now been purged of some of their technicalities, there is still discontent about them. Because the requirement to warn arises merely because the witness is a member of a particular group they are thought to be too rigid; and because it is a matter of law, rather than a matter of fact, whether a given piece of evidence amounts to corroboration, they are thought to be over-complicated. Nor does it seem very sensible that the requirement to utter a corroboration warning about child witnesses has been abolished, only for it to be perpetuated in the requirement to utter a warning about the danger of believing children who are sexual complainants.

In December 1989 the Pigot Committee criticised the corroboration rules, or what is left of them, in resounding terms in its report (paras 5.23 to 5.31). The basis of the rule—that sexual complainants are more likely to lie than other witnesses—it said was wholly unsound. Of the set of directions the judge is required to give the jury, it said: 'We suspect that many jurors find the whole exercise quite impenetrable.' The danger of weak evidence, said the committee, could be adequately covered by the existing power of a judge, where evidence is weak, to point this fact out to the jury. Thus it recommended that the duty to give a corroboration warning in sexual cases should be abolished. In September 1991 the Law Commission produced a report recommending that the existing corroboration rules be abolished without replacement (Law Commission 1991). This proposal came too late to be incorporated in the Criminal Justice Act 1991: but it has since been endorsed by the Royal Commission on Criminal Justice (1993).

No requirement that a child's evidence be corroborated, or received with special caution, has ever existed in English civil law (8). In one case the Court of Appeal said that a court should 'look for corroboration' before making a finding of a serious misbehaviour against one party to a marriage on the word of the other (*Alli* v *Alli* [1965] 3 All ER 480). But these were words of caution about believing what spouses said of one another, not what children said about their parents; and even if they were meant to apply to children as well they are hardly limiting, because in the next breath the Court of Appeal added: ' . . . it is, nevertheless, open to a court to act on the uncorroborated evidence of a spouse if it is in no doubt where the truth lies'.

Part II

Specific aspects of the corroboration rules: complaints, evidence of character and disposition, and suspicious behaviour

These three kinds of evidence raise acute problems with the rules about corroboration. The first is difficult because although complaints are often admissible in evidence the law does not accept them as amounting to corroboration. The second and third are troublesome for the more fundamental reason that they are usually not admissible as evidence at all.

COMPLAINTS

As we have seen, the fact that the victim of a sexual offence complained of it immediately afterwards is admissible in evidence notwithstanding the rule against hearsay and the rule against previous consistent statements—and this is so on both sides of the Border (pages 114–17 above). However, in both jurisdictions it is black-letter law that the victim's recent complaint, alias *de recenti* statement, does not amount to corroboration. The reason is that corroboration must come from a source independent of the witness to be corroborated, and if we accepted the previous complaint as corroboration this would be permitting the witness to corroborate herself (*Whitehead* [1929] 1 KB 99; *Morton* v *H.M. Advocate* 1938 JC 50). This reasoning has been criticised by Professor Glanville Williams:

> The reason is only pseudo-logical, for it misses the whole point of the rule. Surely the jury should be entitled to take account of any evidence which is persuasive to show that the charge is not a fabrication. Now the circumstances of a complaint made by the prosecutrix shortly after the occurrence complained of may be most potent in this respect. If a young girl runs to her mother in overpowering distress, complaining of a sexual attack; if it is evident that she has been attacked, and if she names the defendant as the culprit, a man with whom she is acquainted so that there is no possibility of a mistake on her part in identifying him, the risk of deliberate falsity in the charge—that she has spitefully substituted the name of the defendant for that of her real attacker—is surely negligible. Much greater risks of false evidence are accepted as part of the everyday course of the administration of justice. (Williams 1963, p. 163.)

The English courts have gone some way to meet this point by holding that although the previous complaint does not amount to corroboration,

corroboration may be found in the victim's distressed state immediately after the incident. This was held in *Redpath* (1962) 46 Cr App R 319, where, on her return home, a little girl of seven had complained to her mother that the defendant had indecently assaulted her on the moor, where a bystander witness had earlier seen her in a state of great distress. The fact that in that case the complaint was heard by one witness and the distress was witnessed by another, gave rise to a theory that before distress can be given any weight as corroboration it must be sworn to by someone other than the witness who testifies about the complaint (*Knight* (1966) 50 Cr App R 122); but the more recent English cases have accepted evidence of distress as capable of amounting to corroboration although it came from the witness to whom the victim made her complaint (*Chauham* (1981) 73 Cr App R 232; *Dowley* [1983] Crim LR 168).

After some initial uncertainty (Macphail 1987, sect. S23.01A), it is now clear that distress can also amount to corroboration in Scotland. In 1987, the Scots courts twice held that the complainer in a rape case was corroborated by her state of distress, if the jury believed it to be genuine (*Gracey* v *H.M. Advocate* 1987 SCCR 260; *Stephen* v *H.M. Advocate* 1987 SCCR 570), and in 1991 they held that a man's appearance at a farm, white and worried, and oblivious to the unfriendly attentions of a fierce alsatian farm-dog, corroborated his evidence that he had just escaped from the clutches of the defendants, who had abducted him (*Horne* v *H.M. Advocate* 1991 SCCR 249). Unsurprisingly, however, it was held not to be corroboration where a girl showed distress on reporting an incident twelve hours afterwards, having seen her boyfriend in the interval (*Moore* v *H.M. Advocate* 1990 SCCR 586).

Whether or not previous complaints and the distress of the complainant ought to be acceptable as corroboration ultimately depends on the policy and philosophy behind the corroboration requirement. If the idea behind the requirement is that evidence of a certain type is likely to be false, then it is sensible to accept as corroboration anything which suggests that it is true—including evidence of distress at the time of complaining, and even evidence of the complaint itself. If the underlying philosophy is that it is always unsafe to convict on the word of a single witness, however convincing, then it is rational to refuse to accept either complaint or distress as sufficient to satisfy the corroboration requirement.

In civil proceedings in England, and in Scotland, evidence of a witness's previous statements (including complaints) are now generally admissible by statute (chapter 6, Parts III and IV above). In neither jurisdiction are there now any corroboration requirements in civil proceedings. In the light of this it is odd that the English provision that makes previous statements admissible—s. 6 of the Civil Evidence Act 1968—takes the trouble to say that where evidence of a previous statement is admitted under that section it does not satisfy a corroboration requirement.

BAD CHARACTER: EVIDENCE OF TENDENCY

In criminal proceedings

In England and Scotland it is also black-letter law that the fact that the accused has a criminal record may not be used in evidence against him, nor evidence that merely shows he has a tendency to commit an offence. As it will usually be a criminal record that shows a tendency to crime, these two categories largely overlap with one another. But in fact they are distinct, and the prosecution may not produce evidence of tendency even if it is shown by something other than a previous conviction: as illustrated by the peculiar case, the source of much hilarity to law students, where a man was convicted of burgling a woman's house with intent to rape, and his conviction was quashed because evidence had been admitted that he had also entered another woman's house by climbing down the chimney, there to have intercourse with her consent (*Rodley* [1913] 3 KB 468).

On neither side of the Border is the ban on evidence of bad character a total one. There is a general exception in favour of evidence which incidentally reveals the defendant's bad character, provided it shows something more directly relevant as well. The rule, in outline, is that evidence of bad character is not admissible against the defendant if it merely shows that he is someone who is likely to break the criminal law; nor even where it shows he has a tendency to break this particular part of it; but it is admissible, although it happens to show this too, if it also shows his guilt by some other and more direct chain of reasoning. The range of ways in which this may be so is almost infinite, and the following are some of the best-known examples.

Previous misbehaviour may show motive for the crime in hand. Thus the fact that the defendant had been sexually abusing his stepdaughter was admissible against him at his trial for murdering her, because it showed he had a motive to kill in his fear that she would tell (see the trial of Ronald Barton for murdering Keighley Barton: *The Times*, 8 October 1986). Previous misbehaviour may be admissible because it shows the defendant's attitude towards a particular person. Thus where the defendant is charged with a sexual offence, previous sexual offences against that victim may be put in evidence to show his lust towards that person (*Ball* [1911] AC 47, *Flack* (1969) 53 Cr App R 166); and conversely, previous acts of violence against a particular victim may be used to prove he hated him (*Williams* (1987) 84 Cr App R 299). Sometimes previous misconduct is admissible because it shows that behaviour which could have been unintentional was really done on purpose: as where a sailor on trial for indecent assault said he touched his shipmate's penis by accident, at which the prosecution were allowed to prove a similar 'accident' to another shipmate earlier (*Sanders* (1962) 46 Cr App R 60; cf. *Makin* v *Attorney-General for New South Wales* [1894] AC 57). In some cases the previous misconduct may be admissible because it shows that a crucial witness is truthful. In one such case the prosecution were permitted to prove that a clergyman on trial for indecently assaulting a girl called Sheila had previously assaulted another girl called Judy; Sheila said the clergyman had described his exploits with Judy whilst making sexual advances to her; and as Sheila could not have heard of the goings-on with Judy except from the clergyman, the fact that they had actually happened proved Sheila was telling the truth (*Mitchell* (1953) 36 Cr App R 79). A more usual situation of this type is where a series of independent witnesses give accounts of what the defendant has done to them, all of which are similar. If the witnesses are truly independent this is explicable only on the assumption that all have invented identical fantasies about him—which is grotesquely unlikely—or on the much more likely assumption that he is a repeat offender who operates in a particular way; in this sort of case the evidence of A and B is admissible to corroborate the evidence of C, because once again it rebuts the suggestion that C has told a lie (*Moorov v H.M. Advocate* 1930 JC 68; *Director of Public Prosecutions v Boardman* [1975] AC 421). In some cases the defendant's previous misconduct has some unusual and highly characteristic feature or 'hallmark' which is also present in the case in hand. If this is so it is admissible to show that it was the defendant who committed the present offence, if the identity of the culprit is in dispute. In one case, for example, a woman alleged that a man she identified as the defendant abducted her in his car, drove her to a lonely spot in the country, and there forced her to go through a series of bizarre perverted sexual acts. The prosecution were permitted to call as a witness the defendant's ex-girl-friend, who swore that he sometimes drove her to the same place, where he would persuade her to go through the same peculiar routine. This showed that the defendant shared with the abducter a knowledge of the scene of the crime, and a taste for a particular assortment of perversions—so greatly increasing the chances that the two people were the same (*Butler* (1987) 84 Cr App R 12). Similar in principle is the well-known English case of *Straffen* [1952] 2 QB 911. A little girl was strangled, without any apparent sexual motive, and left by the roadside where her body was certain to be discovered. Straffen was in the area at the time, having just escaped from Broadmoor where he had been sent for committing two identical, equally motiveless murders of little girls. His earlier two murders were admissible to help prove that he was the author of the third.

Quite apart from the cases where previous misconduct is directly relevant in one of these sorts of ways, there is a statutory rule that the defendant's bad character may be put in evidence by cross-examining him about it if he has attacked the character of the prosecutor or the prosecution witnesses in the course of his defence (England: Criminal Evidence Act 1898; Scotland: Criminal Procedure (Scotland) Act 1975, ss. 141 and 346).

Here two points of general criticism must be made.

The first is that the rule against evidence of bad character is uneven in the protection it affords defendants. Evidence that shows the defendant has a tendency to commit crimes does not cease to show his tendency to commit crimes because it shows something else as well. Thus wherever such evidence is admitted the jury necessarily learn that the defendant has a tendency to break the criminal law. The judge may tell them to ignore this aspect of the matter, but it is hard to believe such warnings have any real effect, and such research as there is indicates that they do not (Doob and Kirshenbaum 1972). So the defendant is not just worse off, but very much worse off if evidence revealing his criminal tendencies shows something else about the case as well.

The second is that the rule as to when evidence of bad character is admissible is easy enough to state, but quite exceptionally difficult to apply. It is one thing to say that such evidence is admissible wherever it shows more than a mere criminal tendency, but it is quite another to say whether this condition is met in any given case. In practice the matter is often not clear-cut, but rather a question of degree. A large slice of the English and Scottish textbooks on evidence is devoted to exploring the ramifications of the rule, and attempting to reconcile the large and multiplying mass of case law that has grown around it.

A crucial area of doubt is how far the prosecution can prove the defendant has paedophile tendencies when he is on trial for a sexual offence against a little child. At one time the courts seem to have taken the view that a tendency to commit paedophile offences is so peculiar and specific that by definition it shows something of particular relevance to the case, and thus it is always admissible to corroborate the word of the child. In the leading Scottish case of *Moorov* v *H.M. Advocate* 1930 JC 68 Lord Justice-General Clyde said this:

> It is now a settled point in the law of evidence in this country that if, in cases of this sort, one child after another speaks to separate acts committed on him or her, material for the corroboration of each child's statement may be found in the statements of the others. Conduct of this sort differs from that normally produced by human lust or passion; and, if it is a necessary inference from the repeated acts spoken to individually by a number of children that the accused has, during the period covered by the separate acts spoken to, made a practice of getting himself into privacy with them for no purpose that can reasonably be suggested except a sinister one, it becomes possible to find circumstantial corroboration of each child's statement, in the same way as before— that is to say, in the same way as if there had been independent evidence to that effect. The peculiar and perverted character of the accused's conduct is an important element in this class of case; although no doubt the length of time elapsing between the separate acts spoken to may—especially if considerable—be of great importance against the corroborative effect of the separate statements.

Similar views were expressed by four of the other six judges in that case. At one time the same robust view seems to have been taken in England. In *Ailes* (1918) 13 Cr App R 173 a cinema attendant who had been convicted of indecent assault on a girl of 10 appealed because another young girl had been called to describe a similar assault he had committed on her. The Court of Criminal Appeal said the evidence was given 'quite rightly, to show that the appellant was a man with distorted sexual passions, and that he was addicted to such acts of indecency'. In the Scottish cases, the evidence admitted has always consisted of a series of similar acts committed by the accused. But at one time the English courts would go further, and admit evidence of abnormal sexual tendencies in general. In *Thompson* [1918] AC 221, a man convicted of gross indecency with boys appealed because the prosecution had used evidence that he possessed powder-puffs and indecent photographs of naked boys. The House of Lords affirmed the conviction, Lord Sumner remarking that:

> Persons . . . who commit the offences now under consideration seek the habitual gratification of a particular perverted lust, which not only takes

them out of the class of ordinary men gone wrong, but stamps them with the hallmark of a specialised and extraordinary class as much as if they carried on their bodies some physical peculiarity . . . The photographs . . . tend to show that the accused had this recognisable propensity, which it was shown was also the propensity of the criminal. (p. 235.)

In the English case of *Director of Public Prosecutions* v *Boardman* [1975] AC 421, however, where the defendant was on trial for homosexual offences against youths of 16, 17 and 18, the House of Lords made it very clear that evidence of other homosexual acts he had committed were not admissible against him merely because they showed that he had homosexual tendencies. They said that here the usual rule applies, and such evidence must point to his guilt by some more direct line of reasoning. Where, as there, the issue was whether the evidence of boy A could be used to support the evidence of boy B, it was not enough that both boys described homosexual acts he had committed: the evidence of each boy must be 'strikingly similar'.

In *Boardman* the defendant was charged with homosexual offences against post-pubertal youths. Thus the case was about ordinary male homosexual-ity—not paedophilia, sexual tendencies towards the pre-pubertal children, something which is clinically distinct (Groth and Birnbaum 1978), and which is generally assumed to be much rarer. From the fact that the Law Lords referred to the *Moorov* case with much approval it might be thought that for paedophile offences the position remained as before, and that evidence of previous paedophile incidents would still have been admissible on a paedophile charge. However, in *Clarke* (1977) 67 Cr App R 398 the Court of Appeal (at pp. 402–3) expressly rejected the idea that offences against children fell outside the *Boardman* rule, notwithstanding the approving remarks the House of Lords made in *Boardman* about the decision in *Moorov*. Thus even in cases involving little children the evidence had to be of something 'strikingly similar'.

In requiring the other incidents to be 'strikingly similar', the English courts initially set off on a path which led them far away from the rule in *Moorov* as applied in Scotland. North of the Border, the courts have always treated the other incidents as corroboration if they showed no more than a broadly consistent pattern of behaviour. In one case, for example, they held that A's evidence that D had indecently exposed himself to her was corroborated by B's evidence that he had done the same to her six days earlier, neither incident having any strikingly peculiar detail about it (*Pettigrew* v *Lees* 1992 SLT 320), and in another, it was held that a little girl's evidence that D had induced her to masturbate him was corroborated by her sister's evidence that he had indecently touched her (*Russell* v *H.M. Advocate* 1992 SCCR 257). The phrase 'strikingly similar' in the *Boardman* decision, on the other hand, gave rise to the idea that for the evidence of one alleged victim to corroborate the evidence of another, the adult's sexual behaviour must be not merely peculiar, but peculiar by the standards of peculiar behaviour. If what he had done was nothing more than the normal 'stock in trade of the seducer of small boys' (or girls), then it was not admissible against him (*Inder* (1978) 67 Cr App R 143,

149). In *P* (1991) 93 Cr App R 268, for example, the Court of Appeal held that on charges of rape and incest against daughter A, the prosecution should not have used evidence of his rape and incest against daughter B—because there was nothing about his behaviour which singled out his conduct from the 'normal' routine of any brutal father who repeatedly rapes his daughters over a period of years. The Court disliked the rule it felt itself legally bound to apply, and gave the Director of Public Prosecutions leave to appeal to the House of Lords.

In the House of Lords, a panel consisting—most unusually—of three Scotsmen and two Englishmen overturned the Court of Appeal decision and reinstated the defendant's conviction (*DPP* v *P* [1991] 2 AC 447). In doing so they condemned the English case law, and said that the Scottish approach should henceforth apply in England too. In a speech in which the other four Law Lords agreed, Lord Mackay, Lord Chancellor, said that 'striking similarity' might be necessary where the issue was one of identity and the prosecution were trying to prove that the defendant was the man who did it because of his 'hall-mark' on the crime; but where, as here, the issue was whether the witness is telling the truth or has invented the incident, general similarity is enough.

> In the present case the evidence of both girls describes a prolonged course of conduct in relation to each of them. In relation to each of them force was used. There was general domination of the girls with threats against them unless they observed silence and a domination of the wife which inhibited her intervention. The defendant seemed to have an obsession for keeping the girls to himself, for himself. The younger took on the role of the elder daughter when the elder daughter left home. There was also evidence that the defendant was involved in regard to payment for the abortions in respect of both girls. In my view these circumstances taken together gave strong probative force to the evidence of each of the girls in relation to the incidents involving the other, and was certainly sufficient to make it just to admit that evidence, notwithstanding any prejudicial effect.

In the first edition of this book we criticised the law as it stood after the *Boardman* case and before the decision in *DPP* v *P*. We said that the 'striking similarity' requirement was too restrictive, and gave rise to arbitrary decisions. It was in practice very uncertain when evidence of other misconduct could be given, and in consequence prosecutors tended not to call it even when it was cogent, and judges, to be on the safe side, often ruled it inadmissible even when they tried. In our view, therefore, *DPP* v *P* is to be welcomed. It is true that some English barristers and judges have been heard to grumble about the decision, but we suspect that this may have more than a little to do with the fact that it is Scotsmen who have had the nerve to blow upon the house of cards so lovingly built by English legal hands. Cases reported since the decision suggest that it has caused a real change of practice (*Roy* [1992] Crim LR 185; *Smith* [1992] Crim LR 445). But a recent Court of Appeal decision cuts down its effect rather radically by ruling that if a judge thinks there is 'a real possibility of collusion' between the witnesses to the different incidents, he should not allow the 'similar fact evidence' to be led (*Ryder* [1993] Crim LR 601).

There are two questions to which the case law has not yet given us an answer.

The first is whether, in the *DPP* v *P* type of case, where the issue is whether the alleged victim is telling the truth or fabricating, the prosecution can use as corroborating evidence a similar complaint by another victim which has already resulted in a conviction. In all the reported cases of this type, the other complaints seem to have been from victims whose allegations have not yet been tested in court, and whose cases the prosecution usually wanted tried at the same time. But logically this is irrelevant. The question is whether the earlier incident is close enough in time and place to suggest a consistent course of conduct: and this is so, or is not so, irrespective of whether the defendant has previously been tried for the other complaint. Obviously, where the defendant has already been tried and convicted over the previous complaint the earlier incident is more likely to have taken place a long time before. But this problem aside, there are reasons why the earlier complaint may be the more credible where there has already been a conviction. Where the earlier complaint has already been tried it is more likely to have been investigated by someone other than the person who questioned the child over the incident with which the court is now concerned. This means that there is less of a risk that child A is telling a similar story to child B, not because both happened, but just because both children were questioned in the same sort of inappropriate and overbearing way: a risk which may be present when the defendant is tried for a series of incidents which have been investigated by the same team of people (Bissett-Johnson 1993b). (There is also the common-sense point that we know that another court has already been convinced beyond reasonable doubt that the earlier complaint is true: although as a matter of law, the later court is not supposed to be influenced by this.)

The second is whether it is ever possible for the prosecution to use as corroborating evidence the fact that the defendant has paedophile tendencies, as against the fact that he has behaved in a similar way in the past.

As we saw earlier, some of the older English cases, like *Thompson* [1918] AC 221, suggest that this may sometimes be done. The modern cases, however, generally suggest the opposite. In *Wright*, *The Times*, 27 April 1989, where a headmaster had been convicted of buggering his pupils, the Court of Appeal said that the court should not have heard evidence that he was in possession of a videotape of men committing buggery, plus a guide to the homosexual hot spots of Paris. It is suggested, however, that such evidence ought on principle to be admissible in one kind of case. That is where there is overwhelming evidence that the defendant has behaved suspiciously, and knowledge of his tendencies really clinches the case against him (Elliott 1983); as where a single man is found in bed with a runaway child he admits having picked up at a public lavatory, for example, and explains himself by saying that he offered the child a bed as an act of charity—his own to share, because there was only one bed in the house (*King* [1967] 2 QB 338). In *Lewis* (1982) 76 Cr App R 33 evidence of a paedophile tendency was allowed, apparently on this sort of reasoning, where the defendant accused of indecent offences against his landlady's 10-year-old twin girls had admitted appearing naked in front of them, urinating in their presence, and drying them after a bath—although obviously they were old enough to bath and dry themselves.

The rule against evidence of previous bad character and tendency in criminal cases is well-established, and lawyers throughout the common law world are conditioned to believe it is essential. A full-scale attack on it is beyond the scope of this book, but not a passing salvo.

Why, it may be asked, do we have this rule? In one case Devlin J said such evidence is irrelevant, because the fact that he has committed an offence on one occasion does not in any way show that he is likely to commit an offence on any subsequent occasion (*Miller* (1952) 36 Cr App R 169). But this is plainly wrong, because there is no doubt at all that those who have criminal records are statistically more likely to offend than those without them. It is thought that perhaps as many as one in three of adult males may have a criminal record (Farrington 1981; *Social Trends* 16, 1986, p. 189). Yet the criminal statistics show that men with criminal records account for many more than one in three of those whom the courts convict of the more serious offences—a fact which strongly suggests that those with criminal records are more likely to commit such offences than those without.

A more plausible reason for rejecting evidence of previous convictions is that a criminal court, and particularly one with a jury, is likely to give it undue weight. Studies with mock juries suggest, as we might expect, that juries are indeed influenced by knowledge of previous convictions (Doob and Kirshenbaum 1972; Sealy and Cornish 1973). But if the fact of a criminal record has some degree of relevance, showing that juries are influenced by it is obviously not the same as showing that they are *unduly* influenced by it. Although the rule against evidence of bad character is accepted as self-evidently necessary throughout the English-speaking world, it is largely unknown in other legal systems, whether they use juries or professional judges. In France the first question asked of a defendant at his trial is often '*Avez-vous des condamnations?*' The rule against evidence of previous convictions is also unknown among the Danes and the Norwegians, who—unlike the French—use a system which is broadly accusatorial like in Britain. Essential as the rule may seem to us today, it may be that future generations will see it as a needless and truth-defeating complication.

Even if we accept that the general rule excluding evidence of bad character is right, the way it is now applied in paedophile cases, or was until recently in England, is remarkably favourable to the defence. Only a person who has the lust for sex with children is likely to abuse a child sexually, this lust is unusual, and the fact that the defendant has it makes it much more likely that he did indeed commit the offence. If the court is not told this they may well assume in his favour that his sex drive is normal, and deduce from this that he, like any normal person, is unlikely to have committed such an offence. Without this evidence, furthermore, the facts of a case often appear in a false light. Take for example the case of Colin James Evans, a child assaulter with a terrible record who managed under cover of his connection with a charitable organisation to set up as a provider of baby-sitting facilities for problem families, and who in due course was prosecuted for indecent assaults on the little girls left in his care. Without the information that he was a compulsive and persistent child molester, the case as it unfolded inevitably suggested the possibility of a kind and concerned individual who had given up his spare time to do voluntary social work, only to be framed by a problem family for another person's misdeeds. He was, of course, acquitted: and when he was later arrested for murdering another child he had abducted, and his house was thoroughly searched, the police found indecent photographs he had taken of himself in the course of indecently assaulting the very children he had been acquitted of assaulting (9).

If evidence of general bad character is normally excluded on the basis that criminal courts ought to reject evidence which is more prejudicial than probative, can this really justify excluding such evidence as this? In the nature of things, evidence of paedophilia in a paedophile case tells us something much more important than evidence of previous dishonesty in a trial for theft or of previous violence in a trial for common assault, and this should justify its being admitted. Before venturing an opinion on whether a child had been sexually abused, and if so by whom, a psychiatrist would certainly wish to discover all he or she could about the track records of other members of the family (Vizard 1987). In civil proceedings a judge would do the same. It seems extraordinary that such evidence may not be given in a criminal case.

Of course there are dangers. The child may have been told of the defendant's past misdeeds and invented a fantasy about them, or where the child did not know his molester the police may have picked up the defendant because of his record, and accidentally led the child into believing that he was the guilty man. But the answer here, surely, is to give the courts a discretionary power to reject such evidence in such inherently weak cases. It is not a sensible reason for rejecting evidence in case A, where it would not work injustice, that it would work injustice in case B, which is different. If a child accuses a known person of a sexual offence against her, whose paedophile tendencies were previously unknown to the child, the risks just mentioned are absent, and the court should surely know about his paedophilia, because it is a remarkable coincidence that a child should choose a genuine paedophile as the target for a false accusation. The only argument for the present near-total ban on such evidence is that juries, being composed of ordinary people, will be so inflamed by the information that the defendant is a paedophile that they will convict him of the offence charged not because they think he did it, but because they think he deserves extra punishment for his lust. But defenders of the legal status quo cannot have it both ways. Either a jury is a tribunal capable of trying sexual offences against children in a rational way, or it is not. If it is, we should not construct rules of evidence on the assumption that a jury is a bunch of prosecution-minded morons who can only be restrained from convicting innocent people by keeping relevant evidence away from them. If it is not, then it is high time we handed these child-abuse cases over to a different sort of tribunal.

What goes for evidence of sexual tendencies towards young children should surely go for evidence of sadistic tendencies towards them too. If it seems wrong that the jury could not be told of the fact that Colin James Evans was a compulsive child-molester, it seems equally extraordinary that a stepfather should be tried for kicking and biting a little girl to death without reference to the fact that he had been convicted of blinding her little brother the year before (*The Times*, 26 July 1985).

A proposal that the criminal courts should be able to receive evidence of this sort is not completely original, or revolutionary. Evidence of paedophile tendency was admissible in England earlier this century, as we saw. And in Queensland a serious attempt was made to make it admissible by statute in 1988. At present there is not much sign of this happening in Britain, however. In its recent Report No. 125 the Scottish Law Commission proposes leaving the *Moorov* rule alone, and in England the Pigot Committee rightly pointed out that the question of character evidence fell outside its terms of reference.

Evidence of bad character and tendency in civil proceedings

Broadly speaking, evidence of character and disposition is rarely an issue in the civil courts, and how far it is admissible is rather obscure. It seems that the civil courts on both sides of the Border would normally reject evidence that someone had done something in the past merely to show that he was likely to have done the same thing again (Macphail 1987, sect. 16.02; *Thorpe* v *Chief Constable of Greater Manchester Police* [1989] 1 WLR 665). But it also seems that the civil courts on both sides of the Border are willing to accept such evidence in some civil cases where they would reject it in a criminal case (Macphail 1987, sect. 16.03; *Mood Music Publishing Co Ltd* v *De Wolfe Ltd* [1976] Ch 119). In particular, there seems to be no doubt that the civil courts are willing to consider a person's previous behaviour towards children in cases concerned with the welfare of a child. The civil courts do not usually have to look at a person's previous record in order to decide whether or not he abused or hurt a given child. The issue that usually arises in the civil court is whether a particular person should be permitted to have continued contact with a child, given they are proved to have abused a child in the past; and once this fact is proved, the civil courts are usually very willing to find that there is an unacceptable risk of the same thing happening again. In *Re P* [1987] 2 FLR 467, for example, the Court of Appeal reversed the decision of a judge and ordered the removal of a ward of court aged one from her family where the other children had been sexually abused. Stephen Brown LJ said:

> It must always be borne in mind that in these cases, which are difficult and anxious, the court is not trying the parents in the sense of trying an allegation of a criminal offence, it is assessing the needs of the court's ward.

Indeed, before 1989 it was an express ground for making a care order in England that the child will probably suffer harm, 'having regard to the fact that a person who has been convicted of an offence mentioned in Schedule 1 to the Act of 1933 . . . is, or may become, a member of the same household as the child' (Children and Young Persons Act 1969, s. 1(2)(bb)), and this is still a 'ground of referral' under s. 32 of the Social Work (Scotland) Act 1968. The courts show the same attitude if the person in question shows sadistic tendencies. In *W* v *L* [1974] QB 711 a man who had treated animals with sadistic cruelty was about to return to a home where there was a baby, and the Court of Appeal took the risk to the baby into account in arranging his continued detention in a mental hospital. There seems little doubt that a civil court would also look at evidence that a given person had hurt or abused a child in the past if it had to decide the question whether or not he had hurt or abused the child in question on a particular occasion. In *Re G* (*A Minor*) (*Child Abuse: Standard of Proof*) [1987] 1 WLR 1461 the judge in a wardship case decided that a father had been sexually abusing his little girl in the light of various pieces of evidence, one of which was his previous convictions for sexual offences. (For a view on the position in care proceedings, see Graham Hall and Martin (1987), sect. 6.16).

SUSPICIOUS BEHAVIOUR

If the person the child accuses behaved suspiciously during the investigation or the trial, does this count as evidence against him? And if it does, does it satisfy the technicalities of corroboration in a criminal case? At present the law provides no simple answer to this, and the result depends on the type of suspicious behaviour, and whether the case is tried in England or in Scotland.

If the defendant told a lie, and it is firmly nailed by independent evidence, this will usually be the subject of acid comments from opposing counsel and the judge. To this extent his lies will count against him on either side of the border. The English criminal courts go further and are prepared to treat the defendant's lies as something which is capable of amounting to corroboration. They first did so with lies told out of court, as in *Credland* v *Knowler* (1951) 35 Cr App R 48, where a man told the police that he had never seen two little girls, but later said 'All right, I did just walk to the top of the hill with them, but I didn't do anything'—and this was held to corroborate their story that he had indecently assaulted them. In *Lucas* [1981] QB 720, a case which concerned accomplices, the Court of Appeal went further and said that lies could corroborate whether told in court or out of court, provided the following conditions are met:

> To be capable of amounting to corroboration the lie told . . . must first of all be deliberate. Secondly it must relate to a material issue. Thirdly the motive for the lie must be a realisation of guilt and a fear of the truth. . . . Fourthly the statement must be clearly shown to be a lie by evidence other than that of the accomplice who is to be corroborated, that is to say by admission or by evidence from an independent witness. (See Spencer 1982.)

In Scotland, however, it seems that the defendant's lies can never satisfy the corroboration requirement. At one time the Scottish courts were willing to hold that 'false denials' could corroborate the mother's evidence in affiliation proceedings, but in *Wilkie* v *H.M. Advocate* 1938 JC 128 the doctrine was criticised, and the court refused to extend the notion to criminal proceedings—a position they affirmed in 1990 (*Quin* v *H.M. Advocate* 1990 SCCR 254). Following the recommendation of the Scottish Law Commission, Parliament formally abolished the doctrine of corroboration by false denial in Scotland at the same time as it removed the corroboration requirement in civil cases by the Civil Evidence (Scotland) Act 1988.

In a criminal case the defendant's behaviour is often suspicious in that he refuses to give an explanation in circumstances where an innocent man would almost certainly have done so. In England, such a failure to explain is treated as evidence against him where he was challenged out of court by someone with whom he stood on equal terms, and insofar as his silence counts as evidence it amounts to corroboration (*Cramp* (1880) 5 QBD 307). However, it is now well established that, as a matter of law, no adverse inferences should be drawn from a person's suspicious silence when questioned by the police (*Hall* v *R* (1971) 55 Cr App R 108; *Gilbert* (1977) 66 Cr App R 237). Thus in English law the defendant at present has a right of silence, not only in the sense that he cannot be punished for refusing to answer questions put to him by the agents of the State, but also in the wider sense that no adverse inferences are to be drawn from his exercise of it. As suspicious silence to the police does not count as evidence against the defendant, obviously it cannot amount to corroboration. If the defendant suspiciously declines the opportunity to give evidence at trial, the Criminal Evidence Act 1898 forbids prosecuting counsel from making any adverse comment, but the judge is permitted to do so, within limits (Cross 1990, pp. 384–386). In fact the usual modern practice is for judges either to say nothing, or else to say that no adverse inference should be drawn, and a recent case seems to suggest that such a direction must now be given (*Forbes* [1992] Crim LR 593). But even if the judge tells the jury that adverse inferences may be drawn, it has been held that these inferences may not satisfy a corroboration requirement (*Jackson* (1953) 37 Cr App R 43). Cutting sharply across the judge-made rules which prevent an accused person's non-cooperation with the authority amounting to corroboration, however, is s. 62(10) of the Police and Criminal Evidence Act 1984. This expressly enacts that a suspect's unreasonable refusal to give an intimate body sample is not only evidence against him, but evidence capable of amounting to corroboration.

Thus the position in England about suspicious silence is a complicated one. In recent years, however, it has been criticised not so much for this as for being too generous to the guilty. In 1972 the Criminal Law Revision Committee recommended the law be changed to allow adverse inferences to be drawn from suspicious silence, and their view has been echoed by certain judges (*Allardice* (1988) 87 Cr App R 380), and by a Home Office working party (Home Office 1989). But such proposals are contentious. They divided the Royal Commission on Criminal Procedure in 1981. The Royal Commission on Criminal Justice, in its Report of July 1993, has now suggested that there should be no change in the law about adverse inferences from suspicious silence at the police station or at trial, but that if the defendant suspiciously fails to disclose his defence in the period leading up to trial, the judge should be allowed to make adverse comments in his summing up: a majority recommendation, and one which bears the signs of being the only thing that even a majority of a divided committee could agree upon.

In Scotland, as in England, suspicious silence in the face of accusations may in principle be treated as implied admissions; but there too, in deference to the right of silence, adverse inferences are not to be drawn from suspicious silence in the face of questioning by the police (*Robertson* v *Maxwell* 1951 JC 11). Some sort of judicial comment is permitted on his failure to put forward a defence at a pre-trial judicial examination, if there is one (*McEwan* v *H.M. Advocate* 1992 SLT 317) and the position about the accused's suspicious absence from the witness-box is uncertain to much the same extent as it is uncertain in England (Macphail 1987, sect. 5.20–5.28). It is quite clear, however, that absence from the witness-box, however suspicious, does not amount to corroboration (*Stewart* v *H.M. Advocate* 1980 SLT 245, 252; Macphail 1987, sect. 5.28)—which is as one would expect, bearing in mind that his presence in it telling lies is not enough. There is no special rule about corroboration in the form of refusal to give intimate body samples: nor is there any need for one, since in Scotland, unlike in England, the courts can order intimate body samples to be taken (Macphail 1987, sect. 25.32).

In Northern Ireland the government can change the law by decree, and without debates with civil libertarians. In consequence, the law there on suspicious silence is very different. The Criminal Evidence (Northern Ireland) Order 1988 allows adverse inferences to be drawn from suspicious silence both in the police station and at trial, and in either case this can amount to corroboration (Jackson 1989, 1991).

The reader will have noticed that the law on the subject of an accused person's suspicious behaviour is complicated, and in some ways strangely restrictive. It is hard to see why a suspect's lies do not corroborate the victim's evidence in Scotland, bearing in mind that they always come from a source independent of the witness to be corroborated, and are often strongly indicative of guilt. It also seems extraordinary to many lay people that a refusal to answer an accusation when any innocent person would unquestionably have answered it may not be taken to suggest that the accusation is well founded, no matter who put it to the suspect. This, of course, raises the question of the right to silence, a full discussion of which is beyond the scope of this book: but two points will be made. The first is that it sometimes causes great difficulties in cases of child abuse. A child is battered when it was in the care of A, or B, or both, and neither offers any explanation. If the child dies there is no case to answer against either of them (see page 34 above). If a child was indecently assaulted, and says that A did it, A may refuse to give any explanation, and decline to give evidence, and if the case proceeds to trial it will turn on the evidence of an uncorroborated child witness. The second point is that if there are good policy reasons for refusing to accept suspicious silence under police questioning as evidence and potential corroboration, these reasons are largely absent if what is in issue is a suspicious absence from the witness-box at trial. The police may be questioning the suspect on the basis of some slender piece of evidence not nearly serious enough to justify putting him on trial, and if we accept silence in the face of police questioning as evidence of guilt we are in danger of making something out of almost nothing. But if the defendant is on trial the prosecution will have made out a prima facie case against him that consists entirely of things other than his suspicious silence to persons in authority. At this stage it is hard to see why adverse inferences should not be drawn from his failure to answer it. When Colin James Evans shuns the witness-box, it seems absurdly generous for the judge to say, as he did, 'You must not, under any circumstances, members of the jury, infer or deduce from the fact that the defendant has not gone into the witness-box that he is guilty of the offence with which he is charged'.

These difficulties over suspicious silence do not extend beyond the criminal courts. In the civil courts, the inference is readily drawn that a person who fails to give an explanation, in the witness-box or out of it, has no explanation to give, and arguments based on the right of silence have been given short shrift in civil cases: as when put forward in unfair dismissal proceedings by employees who refused to explain the suspicious circumstances which led to their getting sacked (*Harris (Ipswich) Ltd* v *Harrison* [1978] ICR 1256; *Oxide* v *E. F. Kay Ltd* (1983) 133 NLJ 989). A dramatic example occurred when a civil judge, in a damages claim brought by a mother, found two men to have murdered her daughter—of whose murder one of them had earlier been acquitted in criminal proceedings. In reaching his decision the judge relied, as against one of the men, on both his failure to give evidence and his known disposition to acts of violence against women (*Halford* v *Brookes, The Independent*, 1 October 1991; and see [1991] 1 WLR 428).

Part III
A criticism of the rules about corroboration

Most of what we wish to say against particular aspects of the rules relating to corroboration has been said in the earlier sections of this chapter, but there are some general points to make by way of conclusion.

First, it is doubtful whether any corroboration rules on the English model can ever be satisfactory, even stripped of the more futile technicalities that surround them. A mandatory duty to warn of the danger of convicting on the evidence of a particular type of witness necessarily involves suggesting to the jury that a witness of particular type ought to be disbelieved, which is not only insulting to that type of witness, but undermines their evidence quite needlessly in a strong case where there is plenty of other evidence to back it up; and a duty to warn the jury that it is dangerous to convict seems insufficient protection for the defendant in a case where the judge believes from his experience that a conviction would indeed be dangerous. If we must have any rule about corroboration there is much to be said for the Scottish one, which does not discriminate against any particular kind of witness, and makes a conviction on the evidence of any single witness impossible.

The drawback with the Scottish rule, however, is that this particular safeguard against wrongful convictions is very rigid, and makes no allowance for the fact that certain types of wrongdoing—notably sexual assaults on children—are likely to happen in situations where no corroboration will be forthcoming. While it applies there is a certain amount of truth in the remark from the incest survivors' group with which this chapter began. (For a practical example, see the Scottish case of *Morrison* v *Allan* 1988 SCCR 74 where a nine-year-old persuaded a sheriff beyond reasonable doubt that the defendant had indecently assaulted her, and she withstood a cross-examination: but there could be no conviction because her evidence was uncorroborated.)

If any kind of special safeguard is needed against the risk of convictions based on unreliable evidence there is much to be said for the suggestion made by Glanville Williams, which is that the corroboration rules should be scrapped, and replaced with a rule requiring the trial judge to review the whole evidence at the close of the defence case, directing an acquittal if he feels that a conviction would be unsafe (Williams 1987c). This would be a considerable change in the present practice of withdrawing cases from juries, under which the judge reviews the evidence not at the close of the defence but at the close of the prosecution case, and he does so not on his own initiative but where the defence make a submission of no case to answer, and in deciding whether to stop the trial he is expected only to consider whether evidence covering all the elements of the offence charged has been called, not whether any of it is credible (*Galbraith* [1981] 1 WLR 1039). It is not completely without precedent, however, because it is what the English Court of Appeal said the judge should do when dealing with identification evidence when it laid down the guidelines for handling that kind of evidence in *Turnbull* [1977] QB 224. And it is not so different from what occasionally takes place in practice, for strong-minded judges do sometimes stop a case where they think that no reasonable jury would convict on the evidence heard (for example, see *Shippey* [1988] Crim LR 767).

When a group of peers first sought to move an amendment to the Criminal Justice Bill to alter the corroboration requirements concerning children's evidence in England, their draft incorporated the safeguard Glanville Williams proposed. When the Home Office took up the matter and produced its own clause, which was enacted, this safeguard was omitted. In 1989, as we saw, the Pigot Committee raised the matter of corroboration again, proposing the abolition of the mandatory corroboration warning in sexual cases too. Their solution to the problem of weak evidence, as we saw earlier (page 218), was for the judge to *advise* the jury to acquit where he thinks the evidence is weak: which in practice would be nearly the same as directing them to do so. The English Law Commission later took a similar line (Law Commission 1991). But the Royal Commission on Criminal Justice, in its Report of July 1993, has come down firmly in favour of the Glanville Williams approach—advocating a role 'that a judge may stop a case if the prosecution evidence is demonstrably unsafe or unsatisfactory, or too weak to be allowed to go to the jury' (page 195).

If we reject the idea of corroboration requirements as far as children are concerned, the courts clearly need all the help they can get in order to determine how far an uncorroborated child's evidence can be relied on. That brings us to the question of expert evidence, which is the subject of the next chapter.

NOTES

1. Part of a statement they màde at the First International Conference on Incest and Related Problems held at Irchel University, Zurich, 10–12 August 1988. See *Feminist Review*, **28** (1988), 3.

2. As well as Scotland, there are restrictions on convicting merely on the defendant's confession in countries as diverse as West Germany (Frchsee 1990), and China: see Yang Cheng (1988), p. 204.

3. As this book is about the evidence of children, we have talked in terms of evidence to corroborate the direct evidence of a child. But there is no reason why the entire case against a defendant should not consist of circumstantial evidence, as long as one piece of circumstantial evidence is corroborated by another, and it does not all emanate from a single source. For some striking examples, see Dickson (1964), Part I, tit. 7.

4. A notable exception is Holland, which has also kept a corroboration requirement: see *Strafvordering* (Sv.) (Code of Criminal Procedure), arts 341, 342 and 344.

5. This was enacted in response to the trials of Lord Russell and Algernon Sidney in connection with the Rye House plot (1683) 9 St Tr 577. This in turn was not long after the Titus Oates affair, in which 14 innocent people were convicted and executed on the strength of perjured evidence. See Stephen (1883), vol. 1, ch. 11. The 1695 Act has been repealed, and with it the requirement of corroboration in treason trials generally; but the Treason Act 1795 still requires the evidence of two witnesses for certain forms of the offence.

6. In order to tie in with s. 52 of the Criminal Justice Act 1991 (see page 62 above), s. 34 of the Criminal Justice Act 1988 was later amended by the Criminal Justice Act 1991, sch. 11, para. 37 and sch. 13; but these amendments do not alter the effect of it.

7. Section 34(2) of the Criminal Justice Act 1988 provides that 'Any requirement whereby at a trial on indictment it is obligatory for the court to give the jury a warning about convicting the accused on the uncorroborated evidence of a child is abrogated in relation to cases where such a warning is required by reason only that the evidence is the evidence of a child'. In *Pryce* [1991] Crim LR 379 a defendant tried to argue that the words of s. 32(2) abolishing the duty to warn 'where such a warning is required by reason only that the evidence is the evidence of a child', meant that where the judge was obliged to give a corroboration warning for some other reason—e.g. because the child was a sexual complainant—the duty to warn because the witness was a child still survived, and he had to give a double warning. Not surprisingly, the Court of Appeal rejected this contorted argument.

8.   Until recently, the requirement that the complainant had to be corroborated before a court could make an affiliation order prevented the court from
acting on the evidence of certain children; but this corroboration requirement
disappeared when affiliation proceedings, as such, were abolished by the
Family Law Reform Act 1987.

9.   Information about this case is taken from transcripts of his trials at
Aylesbury Crown Court in November 1982 and November 1983, and a range
of national newspapers on 18 December 1984 reporting on his conviction for
murdering four-year-old Marie Payne (when the judge recommended that he
serve a minimum of 30 years' imprisonment).

CHAPTER NINE
Expert assistance

Part I
Introduction

The courts in Britain are very ready to resort to experts when the word of a child is said to be confirmed or disproved by a piece of solid physical evidence. Thus there is no legal problem, whether in the criminal or the civil courts, about the admissibility of expert evidence from forensic scientists on matters like the matching of fibres, or blood-grouping, or 'genetic fingerprints' (DNA profiling) (Alldridge 1992). Nor are there problems of admissibility about expert evidence from paediatricians about the nature and possible cause of injuries suffered by the child.

In cases of sexual abuse, however, medical evidence is of limited value, and lawyers, psychologists and other professionals need to be aware of this.

In the first place, the absence of medical evidence cannot be taken as 'negative proof'. This is because many sexual offences against children leave no medical signs. Obviously, most of the less serious sexual offences against children are not of the nature to do so. Less obviously, even the more serious abuse, involving penetration of the vagina or the anus, will sometimes leave no signs: either because so little physical damage was done, or because what there was had healed before the medical examination. A report by the Royal College of Surgeons in 1991 says 'A substantial proportion of sexually abused children have no abnormal physical signs (para. 1.9) . . . It must be remembered that there may be no physical findings in as many as two-thirds of the children seen for suspected sexual abuse (para. 4.12)'. Surprisingly, it seems that even vaginal penetration of pre-pubertal girls can sometimes leave no signs, according to one study of victims where the offender had confessed to this (Muram 1989).

Secondly, the presence of physical signs, when there are any, is rarely conclusive. Many are supportive, in the sense that the signs in question are more commonly found in abused than non-abused children—but are easily capable of an innocent explanation. This is now generally reckoned to be the case with the 'reflex and dilation' sign which figured so prominently in the Cleveland affair (Butler-Sloss 1987, p. 193; Royal College of Physicians 1991). Others, like certain scars and tears, and various venereal diseases, are 'diagnostic' in the sense that they give grounds for stronger suspicion, but these too are capable—if less readily so—of innocent explanation. An official government publication (DHSS 1988) warns, in bold type, that 'It cannot be emphasised too strongly that no physical sign can at the present time be regarded as uniquely diagnostic of child sexual abuse'. This may be over-cautious. If the child has semen, or blood from another blood-group, in one of the bodily orifices, this is virtually conclusive: but even then there may be argument as to what substance was really found there. Furthermore, where medical signs are found that strongly suggest sexual abuse has taken place, they will rarely do more than corroborate the child's evidence about what act was done, and it will be unusual if they prove that some particular person did it. They will do this if body tissues are found on which DNA profiling can be used, but otherwise they will only amount to corroboration in conjunction with other pieces of evidence, such as opportunity—which raises the problem of 'cumulative corroboration' discussed in chapter 8. (Useful summaries of the medical knowledge in this area are contained in the Cleveland Report (Butler-Sloss 1987), in a DHSS publication *Diagnosis of Child Sexual Abuse: Guidance for Doctors* (1988), in *Physical Signs of Sexual Abuse in Children* by the Royal College of Physicians (1991) and in a paper by Bays and Chadwick (1993).) Thus despite advances in forensic science, the word of the child usually remains our most important source of information about what happened—or what did not.

Traditionally, the courts in Britain have been more reluctant to turn to help from behavioural scientists. We feel this is a pity, because the courts could surely get a lot of help from experts in these areas if only they were prepared to listen to them.

In his book, *Proof of Fact in Criminal Trials* (1984), the Scottish judge Sheriff Marcus Stone takes a tour around the kind of expert evidence that might be supplied by psychologists and comes to a wholly negative conclusion about its value:

> In any event . . . there is no body of specialist knowledge which can be brought to bear on questions of credibility. In this situation, the view of the law is the only one which is possible. It is that decisions about credibility can only be based on common sense, ordinary human intuition, and practical judgment based on experience of life. Nothing better has been shown to exist. The process is not vulnerable to the criticism that it is not scientific. Science has, so far, proved to be inadequate to the task.

His main point is that much of the work that psychologists have done on the reliability of evidence is statistical and general, and that even where the experts agree—which sometimes they do not—such information is of little or no use in a specific case. To be told, say, that in an experiment designed to test eye-witness memory 20 per cent of the subjects made a given observational error, or that 40 per cent of children aged eight correctly recognised a face after a six-week interval, does not tell the court a great deal that is of immediate use in deciding whether a particular witness, in the real world rather than the laboratory, made a similar mistake.

In this point there is obviously some force. But there are three qualifications that must be made.

First, it does not follow that information of this sort is therefore wholly useless. If it is of little practical use in the courtroom, general statistical information about the reliability of certain types of evidence is obviously of enormous importance when it comes to testing the wisdom of legal rules that are based on the assumption that certain forms of evidence are reliable or unreliable. A good example is the report of the Departmental Committee on Evidence of Identification in Criminal Cases in 1976, which drew on some of the published research of psychologists when proposing a rule of official caution in cases turning on eyewitness identification, and recommended further psychological research. We saw another example of the practical influence of psychological research in chapter 8: it was a survey of the current psychological literature on the reliability of children's evidence that induced the government to introduce an amendment to the Criminal Justice Bill to alter the rules about corroboration. Similarly, psychological studies designed to discover what aspects of giving evidence children find stressful are obviously of relevance to those who plan to alter the rules governing how and when children must give their evidence. We take up these matters in chapter 13.

Secondly, it may be that psychological evidence would often give a court nothing more than it could derive from 'common sense, ordinary human intuition, and practical judgment based on experience of life', as Stone suggests. But it is probable that 150 years of psychological research have had a considerable impact on the contents of common sense, and the common sense of lawyers in particular. That many lawyers now appreciate the fact that eyewitnesses can get things wildly wrong, for example, is probably due in part to Glanville Williams's influential book, *The Proof of Guilt*, which has informed the minds of several generations of budding lawyers since it first appeared in 1955, and in which the author discusses the matter with reference to the psychological literature. In Germany it is said that the judges have now begun to learn the principles of psychological assessment from the psychologists, and refer fewer cases to psychological experts for assessment as a result (Wegener 1989).

Thirdly, contrary to what Stone suggests, there are certain forms of expert evidence which courts would probably find helpful in deciding whether or not to believe a particular child witness.

First, there is evidence directed to the question of a particular child's intelligence, suggestibility, and understanding of the need to tell the truth. At present, judges investigate these matters in the course of a competency examination which, as the examples given in chapter 4 show, are usually crude and cursory in the extreme. It should be obvious, beyond all argument, that a child psychologist is much better placed than a judge both to gauge the intelligence of a child, and to explain what his intelligence means he should be capable of. The point is made by the unreported civil case of *Scaine* v *Ainger* which is described by the psychologist Lionel Haward:

> . . . a 14-year-old boy cycling along a country lane was knocked down by a passing car and sustained head injuries. The defendant pleaded contributory negligence on the part of the plaintiff, on the sole grounds that the latter

was not very bright. . . . The judge administered a two-item unstandardised intelligence test of dubious validity, first by asking the lad what was the time by the court clock, which the plaintiff was unable to answer, and then by asking him the date of the Battle of Hastings. The plaintiff confused this famous event with a more local and topical battle at Brighton between rival gangs of youths, so that his reply, 'last Tuesday week', did nothing to elevate his position on the judicial scale of intelligence. Indeed it so damned his chances of obtaining fair compensation that the clinical role had to be assumed by the psychologist in order to ascertain the boy's cognitive abilities in a more scientific fashion. This assessment certainly raised him from the cerebral discard in which the judge had obviously placed him, but it still showed him to be some 20 per cent below average and therefore vulnerable to the implication that his road sense was similarly lacking. Hurried consultations . . . led to the decision to carry out a field experiment at the site of the accident into the association between intelligence and cycling behaviour. This demonstrated that a group of boys, reasonably matched for age, intelligence and cycling experience with the plaintiff, performed equally as well as cyclists of average intelligence. . . . actuarial evidence on the probabilities of the plaintiff being at various distances off the road edge was then called for, as a result of which the case was then quickly settled out of court (Haward 1981b).

Teachers, who usually know more about the capabilities of children than most people, even the most experienced judges, regularly resort to educational psychologists for help in these matters. It would surely be sensible if the courts were willing to listen to child psychologists, both when deciding whether a young child is competent to give evidence at all, and in deciding what weight to put on its evidence if it does. 'That is a subject on which judges need, and should have, expert assistance from a clinical psychologist and not be left to flounder through what may be an ill-informed and perfunctory form of inquisition before the child gives evidence' (Cocks 1989).

Secondly, child psychologists and psychiatrists can tell us much about the behaviour of children which ordinary people are unlikely to know. An example concerns the state called 'post traumatic stress disorder'—a disorder now well recognised within the psychiatric profession (American Psychiatric Association 1987, sect. 309.81; Scott and Stradling 1992). When persons are exposed to some overwhelming event which makes them helpless in the face of intolerable danger, anxiety and arousal—as where they are forcibly raped, or buggered, or tortured, or forced to witness some hideous occurrence like the murder of a friend or parent—they commonly show some or all of a number of symptoms afterwards. They are unable to drive the incident from their minds, whether waking or sleeping, failing to concentrate on their normal acitivites by day and having nightmares and bouts of sleepwalking at night. Children often become incontinent, and have bursts of inexplicable violence and other anti-social behaviour where they were previously well-behaved, or periods of moodiness where previously they were cheerful and outgoing. Children (and adults) also tend to experience irrational fears, and feelings of extreme guilt which are even more irrational, as if they blame themselves for what someone else has done to them. Thus a child who has suffered some traumatic assault will often keep it to herself like a guilty secret, and only reveal it when the odd behaviour has prompted questioning (Jones and McQuiston 1992). Jurors are most unlikely to know this; the judge may know it, but equally he may not. As we saw in chapter 6, a substantial slice of the hearsay rule concerned with 'recent complaint' was constructed by judges on the assumption that those who have suffered sexual assaults will immediately disclose (see page 142). When judge or jury hear that a child began to behave very strangely, and then, after questioning, accused some person of assaulting her earlier, they may well accept defence counsel's invitation to treat the case as the fabrication of a child who is obviously mentally disturbed. Any competent child psychologist or psychiatrist will know that this is turning the evidence on its head. '. . . the episodes seized upon to discredit the child . . . are in fact the consequence of the abuse itself' (Ferguson 1985). Surely the experts should be able to tell the court that cause and effect are as likely, or even more likely, to be the other way around.

A particular subclass of post traumatic stress disorder is rape trauma syndrome (RTS), (Burgess and Holmstrom 1974; Burgess 1983). Studies on rape victims, initially carried out in the USA, reveal various things about the typical behaviour of those who have been raped. One of these is that quite a number of them go through a period of apparent self-control immediately after the rape in which they suppress their reactions and carry on as if nothing untoward has happened. To many people this would seem surprising. You would expect a genuine rape victim to fall into a state of instant collapse, and unless told otherwise, many jurors would probably think that the initial calm discredited the later distress and complaint.

Post-traumatic stress disorder is a comparatively straightforward example: but there are other more controversial areas where psychiatrists and psychologists could correct a widespread false impression about human behaviour which may be used to discredit a child witness. There is a group of behavioural symptoms which Roland Summitt has called the 'child abuse accommodation syndrome' (Summitt 1983). In his well-known paper Dr Summitt describes five features which are characteristic of child sexual abuse when it involves a member of the family or other trusted adult. They are: (a) secrecy; the child typically tells no one, either because of threats by the abuser, or for fear that no one will believe her; (b) helplessness; typically the child does not scream and cry out, but passively accepts what is done to her; (c) entrapment and accommodation; the child discovers that if the abuse is disclosed there will be dreadful consequences, not only for the abuser, but for the child and the whole family, and the child learns to adjust her life to cope with the continued fact of repeated abuse; (d) delayed, conflicting and unconvincing disclosure; for example at the high point of a family row, often precipitated by the arrival of a boy-friend on the scene and attempts by the jealous abusing adult to remove him from it, the child tells what has been going on; (e) retraction; terrified at the strength of the social forces she has released, the child now retracts the disclosure and denies the abuse. If the abuser is prosecuted in such a case as this the defence are likely to point to each of these features in turn as showing that the child's evidence is implausible: it stands to reason that if a family member really makes sexual advances to a child she will resist them, tell everyone about them at the first available opportunity, and not let him near her again; telling such a story in the course of a family row shows that she is clever and manipulative, and her retraction is proof positive that she lied. Sometimes, of course, the obvious explanation is the right one, but those with experience of these cases know that the truth can often lie in the opposite direction. In the USA, where expert evidence about child abuse accommodation syndrome has sometimes been admitted, some lawyers have argued that it should be excluded because of the risk that the courts will give it more weight than it is worth (Levy 1989). Others, however, argue that it can serve the ends of justice if used as a shield rather than a sword.

> The accommodation syndrome has a place in the courtroom. The syndrome helps explain why many sexually abused children delay reporting their abuse, and why many abused children deny that anything happened. When the syndrome is confined to these rehabilitative purposes, the accommodation syndrome serves a useful forensic function (Myers 1992, p. 128).

There are also widespread misconceptions about offenders which experts could show to be false. It is widely believed that paedophiles (who are attracted to pre-pubertal children), pederasts (who are attracted to teenage adolescents) and ordinary male homosexuals (who are attracted to adult males) are all part of one single group—'queers'—who by definition have no sexual interest in women. Some judges evidently believe it, because these groups have usually been treated as one when the courts are dealing with evidence of character and tendency (see chapter 8). Some defendants clearly hope the court will believe this, and when accused of child molesting try to counter the child's allegations by evidence that they are not homosexuals, or that they are married men, or have normal sexual relations with women—and conversely, the risk that the child will be abused is sometimes used as an argument in custody disputes where marriages have broken up because one parent has formed a romantic attachment to a person of the same sex (Green 1992). Yet psychiatrists and psychologists know very well that those who are sexually attracted to pre-pubertal children are rarely if ever ordinary homosexuals, and that some have (or have had) apparently normal sexual relations with women (Groth and Birnbaum, 1978; West 1977) (1).

Thirdly, there is the possibility of expert assessments from those who are used to dealing with abused children. There are two possible types of assessment.

The first is expert evidence from psychiatrists and paediatricians who have extensive experience with children who have been abused. These must regularly decide, for clinical purposes, whether their patients have been, or may have been, sexually or physically abused. They reach their decisions by weighing up a range of factors: medical signs, what the child says, the child's behaviour—and in cases where the abuse is said to have come from another member of the family, the behaviour of the family, and the past record of the various family members. How they go about their job is well documented in the professional literature (2).

The work of the team at Great Ormond Street Hospital, and how they modified their techniques in the face of constructive criticism from the judges, has already been described in chapter 7. They recently attempted to do a small-scale study to test the ability of members of various professional groups involved with children to judge, from watching videotapes of interviews, whether children were likely to have been abused or not. Among their conclusions was that '. . . those with more experience dealing with sexual abuse cases were better at identifying high likelihood cases' (Wiseman et al. 1992). Common sense, indeed, suggests that an expert, who spends much of his or her professional life examining such cases, is better placed than any but the most experienced judge—and infinitely better placed than the average juror—to say whether a child who claims to have been abused has actually been abused or not. Would it not be sensible to allow such an expert to give the court his or her view on the matter? At present this is certainly not permitted in criminal cases on either side of the border, and many lawyers would be outraged at the suggestion that it should be done. Yet it is exactly what is done, and done every day, by the civil courts when dealing with child-care matters. In the Continental legal systems it is extensively done in criminal proceedings as well.

The second is the procedure, so far used mainly in the German-speaking countries and in Scandinavia, called 'statement reality analysis', 'statement credibility analysis', or 'statement validity analysis' (3). The theory behind this is that truthful accounts by children typically show certain characteristics which untruthful accounts do not—and vice versa. With knowledge of these characteristics, and the opportunity to search for them, it is possible to make a more intelligent assesment of whether the child is telling the truth than by the usual process of hunch and intuition. So where the case turns crucially on the evidence of a child the matter is referred to a psychological expert who is trained in using this technique for his opinion on the matter. The expert analyses the child's statement looking for certain tell-tale signs: a procedure English-speaking psychologists now elegantly call 'criteria-based content analysis' or 'CBCA'. The expert then makes a general assessment of the child's credibility, making use of this and any other information about the case he or she has from other sources. The whole evaluation process, of which the CBCA forms part, is usually known as 'SVA'—for 'statement validity analysis'—and that is what we shall call it here. The court still makes the ultimate decision as to whether the child is to be believed, but the report from the expert is usually an important factor in the decision. (Although in practice it seems that the courts do generally accept the psychologist's evaluation of the witness (Wegener 1989).)

The origins of SVA lie in Europe in the early years of the 20th century, and the general fear of false accusations in sexual cases (see chapter 11). An international conference in Berlin in 1921 recommended that in any sex case turning on the evidence of a child or young person the court should seek an expert opinion from a specialist (Gorphe 1927, p. 164). This call was taken up in Germany, where it began to be usual to use a psychological expert in cases which turned on the uncorroborated evidence of a minor (and where it was eventually made obligatory in such a case by a decision of the German Supreme Court in 1954). At first the experts seem to have concentrated on general statements about the risk of errors and falsehoods in children's testimony, and assessments of the child's background and character. The first of these was of little use to the courts because it was too general, and too negative. As the courts are forced to act on human testimony for want of anything better, there is not much point in telling them that human testimony is inherently fallible. And the second was of little use because of the obvious fact that persons of bad character sometimes tell the truth, and persons of good character sometimes lie. SVA was the psychologist's attempt to devise a method of showing whether this particular statement by this particular child was true, based on the premise that true statements by children commonly contain a number of features which are commonly absent from false ones. The technique is associated with the names of two world-famous psychologists, Arne Trankell (d. 1984) in Sweden and Udo Undeutsch (b. 1917) in Germany. More recently their work has been further developed by the German psychologist Max Steller and his colleagues. In the English-speaking world it has attracted, in North America, the attention of the psychologists John Yuille, David Raskin and Phillip Esplin. The technique has also attracted attention in Britain, where experiments were conducted with it in the course of the West Yorkshire Police project (Lawrence 1988; West Yorkshire Police 1989). (A number of accounts of this technique have now been published in English, some of which are listed in note (3) at the end of this chapter.)

The German psychologist Günter Köhnken gives the following description of what takes place (Köhnken 1990):

[The expert] will get a complete copy of the case file. This includes documents of previous investigations, protocols of witness statements, and other pieces of evidence. Furthermore, he or she has the right to examine the child outside the courtroom using any legal psychodiagnostic methods he or she may wish to apply.

The analysis of the statement is conducted according to certain criteria applied to the content, the so-called *reality criteria*. These reality criteria or content criteria reflect specific features of the statement that differentiate truthful from invented testimonies.

The analysis of the quality of a statement by means of reality criteria is made against a background of the individual's personality and cognitive and verbal competencies. Most of the reality critieria can be evaluated properly only by taking into account the cognitive abilities of the witness. Therefore, some kind of analysis of the individual is included in assessing the veracity of the statement.

Usually, other persons who know the child witness (e.g., parents and teachers) are interviewed to obtain information about the biography and on the general level of cognitive and social development of the child. Furthermore, a test of general intelligence will be applied. Together with the results of a personality questionnaire, this information serves as background knowledge about the witness's personality and general cognitive abilities.

The main part of the investigation is a well-prepared interview of the witness. This interview provides the material for the analysis of possible motives for truthful or deceptive accounts and for the analysis of the quality of the statement itself. During this interview, the non-verbal and speech behaviour of the witness will be carefully observed and evaluated for possible clues to deception.

Concerning criteria-based statement analysis, the assessment of the witness's general verbal competence is of crucial importance. For example, the *quantity of details* as a reality criterion of testimony has to be judged with regard to the child's cognitive and verbal abilities. With a high degree of verbal competence we would require more details than we would do with a less intelligent child before we consider the given amount of details as an indicator of credibility. To obtain appropriate material for a comparison, statement analysis requires to allow the child to describe experiences which are of similar complexity as the (alleged) event under investigation. Sometimes the witness is asked to invent a story which refers to a few cue-items or to a picture. Sometimes it is sufficient to let the witness describe general topics like school career, friendships, hobbies, or other daily life occurrences.

The *reality criteria* by which the expert then assess the statement are many: in his account Köhnken refers to 16. They include the way in which the story is told. False stories are usually presented in a continuous, sequential and chronological order, because it is easier to learn a story that way. True stories, however, are often told in a disorganised manner with fragments of the event scattered throughout the statement out of proper chronological order. Hence *unstructured production*, where present, is one indicator of credibility. Another is *superfluous details*. Vivid but irrelevant details are something which the lying child would be unlikely to learn, unlss she or the person who coached her was herself an expert in SVA: as where a nine-year-old child, describing an indecent assault that took place in the kitchen, started off her account by saying: 'He came into the room, pinched two tomatoes from the fruit-bowl, ate them, and then . . . '. Another indicator of truthfulness that Köhnken mentions is *accurately reported details misunderstood*: as where a child gives sexual details the significance of which he or she clearly fails to grasp.

Further practical information is contained in a recent paper by Steller and Boychuk, which includes the transcript of an interview (Steller and Boychuk 1992).

The principles of SVA were developed empirically, by psychologists who at first used common sense and a measure of intuition, and until recently its critics have been able to point out that its validity has never been demonstrated by any kind of rigorous scientific research. The pioneers like Udo Undeutsch answered this criticism by saying that it seems to work in practice, and the courts are willing to accept its results.

Although this method has been applied in many thousands of cases during the last decades, there is not a single case to be found in the literature, or otherwise documented, in which the analysis of the statement, if applied by a competent expert and according to generally accepted rules, led to the clear finding that the statement had to be considered as the truthful account of a personally experienced real event, and which later in the criminal proceedings or afterwards turned out to be in conflict with other relevant evidence. (Undeutsch 1984.)

Recently psychologists have been trying to remedy this. Attempts have been made to set out the rules in a scientific fashion (Köhnken and Steller 1988). And research is in progress to show whether SVA is really any better than common sense and gut reaction in telling true stories from false ones. For this, two methods are being used. The first is controlled experiments, in which one group of children witnesses a staged incident, and another is told about one or invents one, and interviewers who do not know which child belongs to which group apply the SVA technique in an attempt to find this out. The second is field studies, in which 'blind' testers try to do the same using transcripts of interviews with children made in the course of real investigations, half the cases being ones where other evidence makes it almost certain that the person accused was guilty, the other half consisting of cases where all the other evidence strongly points the other way. The studies that have been done so far were recently reviewed by Max Steller (1989). The work that has been done has been said to suggest three things: first, that true and false accounts by children do in fact have different features to them; secondly, that SVA is generally more reliable than untutored common sense in telling which is which; and thirdly, that the technique seems slightly better at identifying true stories as true than at identifying false stories as false. However, the research has not yet shown this conclusively. In the case of the field studies, how sure can we be that the accusations the experimenters selected as false were really false, and vice versa? And if we can be sure, are they the kinds of case in which the courts would need to resort to expert help? (Wells and Loftus 1991.)

Is it sensible to propose that expert evaluations using SVA should be used in courts in Britain? Clearly, the key question remains whether the SVA technique has any real diagnostic value or not: and on this, psychologists who have examined it are divided. In Holland, where some use has been made of it in court proceedings, it has recently come under heavy criticism: 'The diagnostic worth of opinion by experts, even when armed with special instruments, is slight. Their contribution to the debate about sexual abuse of children solves little. In a number of cases the expert's contribution has even been a negative one, because it has led to evidence being destroyed.' (Crombag et al. (1992), p. 389). In the common law world, too, both lawyers and psychologists have expressed serious doubts about the wisdom of permitting the use of this sort of evidence in court (Bulkley 1989; Wells and Loftus (1991))—particularly in the light of the distorting effect that the adversarial process can have on any kind of expert evidence, even one the scientific basis of which is not in doubt (see Part II of this chapter). A well-known Canadian psychologist who has studied SVA, and who does think that it has value, believes that for the present it should be used by social workers, policemen and prosecutors for evaluating the statements of children out of court, but not necessarily by the courts themselves (Yuille 1989). With advances in psychological research, or a retreat from adversarial methods, these attitudes might change.

Sheriff Stone points out—quite rightly—that SVA involves applying general guidelines rather than making clear-cut and infallible scientific tests. This being so, he suggests that if there is really anything in the technique, judges and juries should be able to carry it out as satisfactorily as psychological experts (Stone 1984, p. 198). This may be true of judges, but as far as juries are concerned it is impossible to accept. Apart from the obvious point that people who have practice in doing something tend to make a better job of it than people who do not, the process of analysis as described by Köhnken and others involves a lot of quiet, patient and unhurried work (4). It is inconceivable that 12 untrained and randomly selected Englishmen, or even 15 untrained and randomly selected Scotsmen, could do this, even badly, in the course of a traditional 'day in court'.

Another possible area of expert knowledge which may eventually prove useful in evaluating the credibility of children is 'forensic linguistics': analysing speech patterns with the help of computers (Butler et al. 1991). But so far, this is no more than a possible idea for the future.

Part II
Methods of Giving Expert Assistance to a Court

If we assume that there is a body of expert knowledge that courts would find helpful in deciding whether or not a child witness is telling the truth, how is the court to equip itself with it? For the British lawyer, the immediate answer will be: expert witnesses. But in fact the position is more complicated than this, because there are five different methods by which the courts can equip themselves with expert knowledge, of which permitting the parties to call expert witnesses is only one. The full range of options is as follows.

JUDICIAL TRAINING

In England and in Scotland judges are appointed from the ranks of the legal profession, and it has not been the tradition to give them any extra training for their judicial role. Thus on appointment a British judge would have no knowledge of children as witnesses beyond what he had managed to pick up in practice, which would often be next to nothing. And as the appearance of a child witness in court is quite rare—at least in England—it would take most judges many years before they acquired much practice in dealing with child witnesses on the bench.

In England (but not yet in Scotland) a certain amount of initial training for newly appointed judges is now provided by the Judicial Studies Board, and

English judges below the rank of High Court Judge are now expected to attend periodic refresher courses as well. The amount of training so provided is to be measured in days rather than in weeks, however, and has necessarily been limited to rather basic topics, among which the psychology of children's evidence and the prevalence of child abuse used not to be included. However, one of the recommendations in the Cleveland Report (Cm 412) in 1988 was that 'All lawyers engaged in this type of work including judges and magistrates should have a great awareness of and inform themselves about the nature of child abuse and the management of children subjected to abuse and in particular sexual abuse' (p. 252), and the training-programme for civil judges which was laid on to prepare them for the Children Act 1989 was constructed with that recommendation in mind.

Lay magistrates and jurors also play a vital part in the British system of justice. For many years magistrates have been required to undergo a period of training on appointment. As magistrates are lay people, broadly speaking all the time available to train them is taken up with giving them the minimal information necessary to enable them to do the job at all. In recent years, however, extra training has been introduced in England for magistrates who sit in the family proceedings or the youth court. As for jurors, training is quite out of the question. Although in the past there could sometimes be 'special juries' consisting of people who were likely to have particular knowledge or expertise (5), juries are now selected at random, with none of the complicated selection procedure for juries that is found in parts of the USA. A positive bias against knowledge or experience is created by rules which give certain professional people, and those who have served on a jury recently, the right to be excused from jury service.

SPECIALIST COURTS

For the last hundred years the main way in which specialist knowledge has been applied to the process of resolving legal disputes has been through the creation of special tribunals. A typical arrangement, as with industrial tribunals, is a legal chairman sitting with two non-lawyers with appropriate specialist experience.

In England, some use of specialist courts is already made in proceedings that can turn on the evidence of children. Since 1908, almost all prosecutions for offences committed by juveniles have come before the juvenile courts, now called youth courts. The youth courts are staffed by magistrates who are specially selected, who have undergone a certain amount of extra training, and who then specialise in this type of work. A range of civil work involving children is handled in the magistrates' family proceedings court, where the magistrates are also specially selected and trained. Wardships are mainly dealt with by High Court judges of the Family Division. Although these receive no special training in matters relating to children, many are appointed from the family law Bar, and all acquire some expert knowledge through specialisation after being appointed to the Bench. The level of expertise among wardship judges is generally high, and the judges who handle child-care cases other than wardships will now usually have had a certain amount of training: an improvement over the position only a few years ago. Criticisms of judicial skills are, however, sometimes made: an experienced social worker told us: 'Some wardship judges don't believe in child abuse, like some children do believe in Santa Claus'. Some practical examples are given in a recent paper in *Family Law* (Weyland 1989; see also chapter 11). In Scotland, most child-care matters are handled by children's panels (see chapter 2); but although these are spcialised, this is of no help when it comes to assessing children's credibility, because disputed issues of fact have to be passed on to the sheriff court, where the judge who resolves them will not usually be a specialist in dealing with children.

It is only in criminal proceedings for offences committed by adults against children that there has so far been no move towards any kind of specialist court in Britain. Indeed, as these cases often involve jury trial, they are frequently tried before the least experienced tribunal of all. This is not the case in all legal systems, some of which do have offences against children tried before specialist courts. In West Germany the juvenile courts try offences committed against juveniles as well as offences committed by them (Frehsee 1990), and in France the *Tribunal Correctionnel* for Paris has now been organised with a special division for dealing with cases of child abuse. In England, a joint committee of the British Medical Associaton and the Magistrates' Association once proposed that sexual offences against children should be removed from the ordinary criminal courts and tried before a special court consisting of a judge and two youth court magistrates (British Medical Association and Magistrates' Association 1949, p. 14), and the suggestion has been resurrected in recent years (McEwan 1988). The bad public reception given to the Roskill Committee's proposal for a specialist tribunal to try serious commercial fraud cases suggests that any proposal to remove child-abuse prosecutions from the ordinary courts would raise considerable opposition (6). The Pigot Committee proposed that child-abuse cases should be tried before judges who were spccially selected—but this proposal, like much of the rest of the Report, has not been implemented.

ASSESSORS

An assessor is a neutral expert selected by the court to sit with the court as an adviser to the judge. Nautical assessors are widely used, on both sides of the border, in civil actions that turn on maritime matters—such as damages claims arising from collisions at sea; they are also used in civil cases concerning patents and in claims under the Race Relations Act 1976. In England the civil courts have wide powers, and in Scotland slightly narrower powers, to appoint assessors in other cases too, but in practice they rarely exercise them. In criminal cases the power does not even exist, at least as far as trial courts are concerned. A power to involve assessors was given to the Courts of Criminal Appeal in England and in Scotland when they were created. The English court refused to exercise it (*Thorne* (1925) 18 Cr App R 186), and it was allowed to lapse when the court was reconstituted as the Court of Appeal (Criminal

Division) in 1966. The Scottish Court still has the power, but according to
Sheriff Macphail it has never once been used (Macphail 1987, sect. 17.24,
n. 81).

COURT EXPERTS

A court expert, like an assessor, is appointed by the court to give neutral
advice, but unlike an assessor he does not sit with the court, and his job is
limited to giving his opinion (either orally or in writing) on some particular
aspect of the case.

The power to seek the opinion of a neutral expert has always been part of the
inherent jurisdiction of the civil courts in Scotland, where the procedure was
traditionally called *remit to men of skill*. It still exists, but nowadays it is rarely
used (Macphail 1987, sect. 17.23). Since 1934 the High Court in England has
had a similar power, and a more limited power belongs to county courts; but
in England, as in Scotland, these powers are rarely used.

Although the civil courts make little use of their own powers to appoint
court experts, in child-care cases the court often does receive expert information from a neutral expert, although this happens in a rather roundabout
fashion. In wardships, a guardian *ad litem* (usually the Official Solicitor) will
often be appointed to safeguard the interests of the child, and it is quite usual
in a contentious case for him to apply to the court for the child to undergo a
medical or psychiatric examination, a report of which is then put before the
court. Thus although the court does not itself appoint a neutral expert, an
expert is appointed by someone who is technically an officer of the court, and
who is thus in a neutral position. Similarly, in care proceedings in the juvenile
court the child will often have a guardian *ad litem*, whose statutory duties
include carrying out such investigations as may be necessary to safeguard the
interests of the child—and if the court grants permission, this could include
getting a medical or psychiatric report. In custody proceedings the equivalent
person is the court welfare officer, to whom the court has a discretionary power
to turn for a report. In the course of compiling his report the welfare officer
may speak to the child's doctor, and expert information from a neutral source
may reach the court via the welfare report. (In Scotland, however, the
equivalent persons play a more subordinate role—see pages 28–29 above—and
are less likely to be a source of independent reports.) As we explain below, the
willingness of the civil courts in child-care cases to listen to expert evidence of
a kind that would be rejected in a criminal case is undoubtedly connected with
the fact that by these means the evidence is usually drawn from a source
independent of the parties in the case.

The criminal courts have the widest powers to call for expert reports when
it comes to sentencing offenders, and they use them extensively. In deciding
whether someone who has been convicted of abusing a child shall go to prison
or be put on probation the court will very probably have a report from a
court-appointed doctor or psychiatrist to help it make up its mind—or a report
from some other agency that draws on information derived from them. This is
particularly the case when young persons are sentenced by the English youth

courts. Thus although it is sometimes said that the idea of independent court-appointed experts is wholly foreign to the traditions of British criminal justice, this is not in truth the case.

However, what is true at present is that the criminal courts in Britain have no explicit power to refer to neutral experts questions that arise before the sentencing stage. This is sharply different from the position in the Continental legal systems, where the normal pattern is for expert evidence on any matter arising in the course of a criminal trial to come from neutral experts appointed by the court. In England the judge in a criminal case has in theory the power to call any witness whom he thinks could give relevant evidence; but the power is rarely used, and there would be much raising of judicial eyebrows if a judge used it to call an expert witness whom neither prosecution nor defence had thought to call. The Scottish criminal judge, by contrast, does not even have the power to call a witness. Thus in a criminal case in Britain all expert evidence that bears on guilt or innocence is called on behalf of either prosecution or defence.

EXPERT WITNESSES (7)

The general rule is that the parties to a civil or a criminal case may call expert evidence on any matter which is likely to be outside the knowledge and experience of the judge or jury. But how far this enables the parties to a civil or a criminal case to call expert evidence that bears on the credibility of a child witness is a complicated matter. There are three points of some difficulty.

(i) Can an expert witness give evidence about the capabilities or veracity of a particular child?

Here the rules are different according to whether the child is an ordinary witness, or gives evidence as the defendant.

As far as victims or bystander witnesses are concerned there are two legal difficulties with this sort of expert evidence. One is the general reluctance of the courts to allow any witnesses—expert or otherwise—to give their opinions about the credibility of other witnesses; the other is the general reluctance of the courts to admit expert evidence on the question of how a normal (as against an abnormal) person is likely to behave, this being a matter which judges think lay people are capable of deciding without expert help. Both of these attitudes are closely bound up with the idea, fervently believed in by many lawyers, that juries are particularly adept at discovering whether witnesses are telling the truth—an idea we examine further in chapter 10.

It is open to the party against whom a witness is called to attack his general veracity in one of three different ways. First, he may do so by asking questions in cross-examination to show he is of bad character—leaving the court to draw the inference that because of his bad character he is likely to tell lies in court. This inference may or may not be a sensible one to draw. At one time it was something every writer on evidence took for granted: 'Une bonne moralité est la meilleure garantie de sincérité' (Gorphe 1927, p. 120), though modern writers, particularly the proponents of SVA, have seriously doubted the wisdom of it (Undeutsch 1989). Sensible or not, the inference may certainly be drawn; and in some circumstances—notably where the alleged bad character consists of a criminal record—the party cross-examining the witness can go further and prove the bad character if the witness denies it. Thus if a child witness had a criminal record this could be brought out in court. Secondly, there is in England the ancient rule in *Rowton* (1865) 10 Cox CC 25, according to which you may attack the veracity of your opponent's witness, X, by calling as a witness Y, who knows him, and asking Y two questions (and no more): 'Do you know X?' and 'From your knowledge of X would you believe his evidence on oath?' In fact this is rarely done, but it does happen occasionally; and *Rowton* would seem to enable the person against whom a child witness gives evidence to call his teacher or close relative and put these two questions to him—with possibly devastating effect. (In Scotland, however, it seems the rule in *Rowton* does not apply (Wilkinson 1986, p. 32).) Thirdly, it is permissible to attack the veracity of a witness by leading psychiatric or other medical evidence that he is abnormal. This was held by the House of Lords in the English case of *Toohey* v *Commissioner of Police of the Metropolis* [1965] AC 595, where a conviction was quashed because a judge refused to admit medical evidence that someone who had claimed in evidence to be the victim of an assault was mentally subnormal, prone to hysteria, and in a hysterical state at the time he first made the complaint. The same is true in Scotland, where on an appeal against conviction the court heard evidence from a psychiatrist that a girl who claimed to have been raped 'had an inordinate interest in sex, and was prone to making unwarranted accusations of rape and sexual interference on the part of various men of ages ranging from 90 downwards. She was also inclined to react to compromising situations in an hysterical way.' (*Green* v *H.M. Advocate* 1983 SCCR 42). In England, however, the Court of Appeal put a brake on this development in *MacKenney* (1983) 76 Cr App R 271. At a murder trial the defence were refused permission to call Barry Irving, a psychologist on the research staff at the Tavistock Institute of Human Relations, to say that he had observed the chief prosecution witness giving evidence, and from this had formed the opinion that he had a psychopathic personality which made him prone to tell all sorts of lies. The Court of Appeal upheld the rejection of this evidence, first because Irving was not medically qualified, and secondly, because the evidence he proposed to give did not show the witness to be mentally ill.

In principle, what a party may not do to attack the credibility of his opponent's witness he may not do in reverse to enhance the credit of his own. Indeed, the rules are even stricter here, because it has been said that 'in general evidence can be called to impugn the credibility of witnesses but not led in chief to bolster it up' (*Turner* [1975] QB 834, 842). There is little case law on calling evidence to enhance the credibility of one's own witnesses, but such as there is discourages it firmly. The issue was discussed in *Turner*, where the point at issue was slightly different from the one we have been discussing. The defendant, who had battered his girlfriend to death with a hammer, was prosecuted for murder and pleaded the partial defence of provocation. He sought to call a psychiatrist to give evidence that his personality, taken with the depth of his relationship with the girl, made it particularly likely the girl's behaviour had provoked him to lose his self-control. One reason for calling this evidence was that 'it helped to show that the appellant's account of what had happened was likely to be true'. The Court of Appeal in England held the evidence had been rightly rejected, saying: 'The jury in this case did not need, and should not have been offered, the evidence of a psychiatrist to help them decide whether the appellant's evidence was truthful'. Refusing to follow the earlier Privy Council case of *Lowery* v *R* [1974] AC 85, where psychological evidence had been admitted on behalf of a defendant in an attempt to show that his story was likely to be true, Lawton LJ added:

> We do not consider that [*Lowery*] is an authority for the proposition that in all cases psychologists and psychiatrists can be called to prove the probability of the accused's veracity. If any such rule was applied in our courts, trial by psychiatrists would be likely to take the place of trial by jury and magistrates. We do not find that prospect attractive and the law does not at present provide for it.

In 1991, the Court of Appeal reaffirmed this approach when it said a trial judge was right to refuse to admit expert evidence that the defendant, though sane, had a histrionic personality, which might have led her to make a false confession to attract attention (*Weightman* (1991) 92 Cr App 291).

Where does this leave us when it comes to calling expert evidence about the intelligence and capabilities of a particular child?

Although hardly encouraging, this body of case law does not close the door on expert evidence to assess the credibility of a child. What the courts are reluctant to accept is expert evidence about the credibility of a *normal adult*.

Thus the courts are prepared to accept expert evidence that bears on the credibility of abnormal adults. Not only will they admit the evidence of psychiatrists that the witness is mentally ill, as in the appeal cases we have mentioned. In practice, judges sometimes admit expert evidence that witnesses are mentally handicapped rather than mentally ill, and allow the expert to describe the degree of handicap, and to give his view of how far this affects the witness's ability to give a truthful account; and sometimes the expert has been a psychologist rather than a psychiatrist. In one case, for example, the defendant had allegedly raped a woman who was mentally subnormal. Two experts who had examined her at the request of the Director of Public Prosecutions—one a senior clinical psychologist and the other a professor of forensic psychiatry—gave the court their expert views on her level of intelligence and ability to give reliable evidence (Gudjonsson and Gunn 1982). And the Court of Appeal has now decided that judges can, and should, hear psychological evidence bearing on the defendant's mental state at the time he made the confession, in order to help him decide whether it should be excluded under s. 76 of the Police and Criminal Evidence Act 1984 as inherently unreliable (*Silcott, The Independent*, 5 December 1991)—a decision not particlarly easy to square with *Weightman*.

Furthermore, there are several reported cases in which the courts have accepted the evidence of non-experts about the truthworthiness of a particular child. In the English case of *Reynolds* [1950] 1 KB 606 the Court of Appeal said that it was in order for the prosecutor to call a school attendance officer to give evidence about a child's education and background in order to help the judge decide whether or not she satisfied the competency requirement (see chapter 4). In the Scottish cases of *Buchan* (1833) Bell's Notes 293 and *M'Lean* (1829) Bell's Notes 294, the prosecutor was allowed to ask the mother of a child witness whom he called whether the child was veracious and spoke the truth; although in another Scottish case permission to ask such questions was denied to the defence (*Galloway* (1836) 1 Swin 232).

If the courts are prepared to accept expert evidence about the credibility of adult witnesses who have the mental age of children, and evidence about the credibility of child witnesses from non-experts, there ought to be no problem about expert evidence on the mental capabilities of a particular child: although it is not at present the practice for such evidence to be offered.

Where the witness is the defendant the rules about evidence of credibility are different, and, in principle, more favourable to him. The normal rule that permits the other side to discredit their opponent's witnesses by evidence of bad character does not apply where the witness is the defendant, and the normal rule that forbids the side that calls a witness to lead evidence of character intended to enhance his credibility does not apply to the defendant as a witness either. Thus the defendant may—and very often does—call evidence of his good character. If he does 'put his character in issue' in this way, however, the prosecution may then lead evidence of bad character to rebut it. As we saw in *Turner*, the courts are reluctant to allow the defendant to call psychological or psychiatric evidence designed to enhance his credibility if he is mentally normal; but if he is abnormal he may call such evidence if it makes his line of defence more credible (*Masih* [1986] Crim LR 395; Beaumont 1987). In principle, the prosecution could presumably call psychiatric or other medical evidence in order to undermine the defendant's credibility as a witness, but in practice such evidence would usually fall foul of the rule against evidence of bad character and tendency (see chapter 8).

(ii)   Is expert evidence admissible about the behaviour of children (post-traumatic stress disorder etc.)?

In civil cases concerned with the welfare and custody of children this sort of evidence often comes before the court as part of a psychiatric assessment of the child (see below). At present it is not usually tendered in criminal cases, where a stricter version of the rules of evidence applies. Is it admissible under the strict rules of evidence or not?

The basic rule is that expert evidence may be called about matters which are likely to be outside the knowledge and experience of the judge or jury, but not about matters which are likely to fall within it.

Where the question is one about the mental functioning of normal adults the courts usually say that the judge or jury are quite capable of evaluating this without expert help. As Lawton LJ said in *Turner* [1975] QB 834, 841:

> If on the proven facts a judge or jury can form their own conclusions without help, then the opinion of an expert is unnecessary. In such a case if it is given

dressed up in scientific jargon it may make judgment more difficult. The fact that an expert witness has impressive scientific qualifications does not by that fact alone make his opinion on matters of human nature and behaviour within the limits of normality any more helpful than that of the jurors themselves; but there is a danger that they may think it does.

What, in plain English, was the psychiatrist in this case intending to say? First, that the defendant was not showing . . . any evidence of mental illness . . . ; secondly, that he had had a deep emotional relationship with the girl which was likely to have caused an explosive release of blind rage when she confessed her wantonness to him; thirdly, that after he had killed her he behaved like someone suffering from profound grief. The first part of his opinion was within his expert province and outside the experience of the jury but was of no relevance in the circumstances of this case. The second and third points dealt with matters which are well within ordinary human experience. . . . Jurors do not need psychiatrists to tell them how ordinary folk who are not suffering from any mental illness are likely to react to the stresses and strains of life. It follows that the proposed evidence was not admissible to establish that the defendant was likely to have been provoked. The same reasoning applies to its suggested admissibility on the issue of credibility. The jury had to decide what reliance they could put upon the defendant's evidence. He had to be judged as someone who was not mentally disordered. This is what juries are empanelled to do. The law assumes they can perform their duties properly. The jury in this case did not need, and should not have been offered, the evidence of a psychiatrist to help them decide whether the defendant's evidence was truthful.

The idea that judges and juries can evaluate the workings of a normal human mind unaided has also led the House of Lords to rule that psychologists may not give evidence about the effect on adults of reading pornographic books (*Staniforth* [1977] AC 699); and as we saw earlier it also led the English Court of Appeal to reject psychological evidence about the credibility of a witness who—though sane—appeared to suffer from a personality disorder (*MacKenney* — page 252 above).

How would the criminal courts in Britain react to evidence about the behaviour of children who are, or claim to be, the victims of sexual offences? As yet there has been no clear decision on the matter. The judges might decide that the combination of children and sexual offences takes the matter outside the ordinary knowledge of the jury, or might apply the usual rule banning expert evidence of normal human behaviour. The case law, such as it is, conflicts. In *Camplin* [1978] AC 705—a case about the defence of provocation in murder—four Law Lords remarked in passing that expert evidence would not be admissible on whether a 15-year-old boy who had been forcibly buggered would be provoked to lose his self-control and kill his attacker. However, the courts have sometimes been prepared to accept psychological evidence about the behaviour of children which they would reject in the case of adults. In *Director of Public Prosecutions* v *A and BC Chewing Gum Ltd* [1968] 1 QB 159 the Divisional Court held that psychological evidence was admissible on the likely effect of violent pictures on the minds of children. Lord Parker's words are apposite:

> ... I can quite see that when considering the effect of something on an adult an adult jury may be able to judge just as well as an adult witness called on the point. Indeed, there is nothing more that a jury or justices need to know. But certainly when you are dealing here with children of different age groups and children from five upwards, any jury and any justices need all the help they can get, information which they may not have, as to the effect on different children.

This case was distinguished in the later decisions where the courts disapproved of psychological evidence about the mental functioning of adults.

A case could certainly be made for saying that expert evidence about the behaviour of children who have been sexually abused is potentially admissible in a criminal case in Britain. In 1988 the Scottish Law Commission 'was unaware of any authority which would expressly prohibit it', and two years later thought that legislation to clear up any doubt about the matter was neither necessary nor desirable (Scottish Law Commission 1988, Scottish Law Commission 1990, para. 5.6). In England the case of *Morley* [1989] Crim LR 566 is a straw in the wind the other way. From the meagre report, it seems that the Court of Appeal held evidence of a four-year-old's sexualised behaviour inadmissible at the trial of an adult for abusing her. If the child's behaviour itself is not admissible in evidence, much less is expert evidence explaining it. On the other hand, the Court of Appeal did recently approve of evidence being given that a woman was suffering from a type of post-traumatic stress disorder known as 'battered woman syndrome' (Emery and Hedman, Archbold Criminal Appeal Office Index 1993, E-48).

This point has already come before the courts elsewhere in the common law world, where different courts have come to different conclusions. In the USA the courts in a substantial number of jurisdictions admit this sort of evidence freely, whilst some reject it altogether, and others have found a middle way—allowing the prosecution to call it where the defence argue that the child's peculiar behaviour shows her story is not to be believed, but not otherwise (8). An added complication with expert evidence in some jurisdictions in the United States is what is called the '*Frye* test' (after the leading case of *Frye* v *United States* (1923) 293 F 1013). In this case a rule was laid down forbidding the use of expert testimony based on any new scientific principle except where it has 'gained general acceptance in the particular field to which it belongs' (Hanson 1989): an approach which, perhaps surprisingly, has been decisively rejected in England (*Robb* (1991) 93 Cr App R 161). In States where this rule applies, there is room for a lot of argument about whether any type of psychological evidence satisfies this test (Bulkley 1989). In Canada different decisions have been reached in the courts of different provinces. In Australia and New Zealand there is a trend towards regulating the matter by statute. In New Zealand, for example, the law was changed in 1989 when the Evidence Act was amended to provide that in criminal proceedings certain designated kinds of psychiatrist and psychologist shall be permitted to give evidence about the mental capacities and emotional development of child complainants in sex cases, and whether the behaviour of the child in question is consistent or inconsistent with the behaviour of sexually abused children within the same age group. Similar changes were made in Queensland in 1988 (Warner 1990). In the Republic of Ireland, a change in this direction was provisionally proposed by the Law Reform Commission (Irish Law Reform Commission 1989, p. 118).

In the legal systems of France, Germany and many other countries, the courts have long been willing to receive the opinions of experts on such matters, in criminal and in civil cases; but there the source of the information is a neutral court-appointed expert, and not an expert witness called by prosecution or defence, as would at present be the case in England or in Scotland (9).

(iii) Is expert opinion admissible on whether a particular child is telling the truth?

In civil cases, it is now a well-established practice for the court to accept in evidence the opinion of a psychiatrist who has examined the child in order to help the court decide whether or not a child has been abused; and if the child spoke of the abuse, the psychiatrist's evidence will include an assessment which bears on the question whether or not the child is telling the truth.

In England, the practice began in the wardship jurisdiction of the High Court. At first the purpose of the expert evidence was usually to help the judge to decide whether a child would make better educational progress with one parent or the other (*Re S* [1967] 1 WLR 396). Since then it has become quite usual for the wardship court to hear the evidence of child psychologists or psychiatrists who have examined the child in cases where the disputed issue is whether or not one parent has been guilty of sexual abuse. In *Re G* [1987] 1 WLR 1461, for example, Sheldon J considered the opinions of three experts who had either spoken to the child, or watched a videotape of another expert speaking to the child, in the course of reaching the decision that the father of a four-year-old girl had 'been guilty of an over-familiar and sexually inappropriate relationship with her, amounting in the present context to sexual abuse'. The practice has since spread to the lower civil courts when dealing with child custody cases. *R v Hove Juvenile Court, ex parte W* [1989] FCR 286, [1989] 2 FLR 145 arose out of care proceedings which the local authority had instituted before the juvenile court on the ground that the child, a little girl of four, was being sexually abused by her father. The local authority called as witnesses the doctor who had carried out a physical examination, a social worker and a policewoman, each of whom had interviewed the child, and the child's guardian *ad litem* called Dr Vizard, a consultant child psychiatrist, who had studied the records of the physical examination and the interviews, and gave her opinion that the girl had indeed been sexually abused. The parents objected to Dr Vizard's evidence, and tried to get the proceedings quashed because it had been admitted. In the Divisional Court Waterhouse J held that it was rightly admitted, and the care order was upheld (10). In a case in 1991, the Court of Appeal, in a slightly conservative mood, said that in civil proceedings concerned with accusations of sexual abuse an expert who had examined a complainant could be asked whether her behaviour was consistent with that of victims of abuse—but should not be asked, point blank, if in the expert's opinion the complainant was telling the truth (*Re S and B* [1991] FCR 175). They upheld the decision below although the forbidden question had been asked, however: and from the questions which are permitted the court will usually have little doubt about what the expert's personal opinion is.

At present it is not the practice to call the sort of evidence which Dr Vizard gave in *R* v *Hove Juvenile Court, ex parte W* in criminal cases in Britain, and it would almost certainly be rejected if either prosecution or defence tried to do so. On both sides of the Border a feature of the rules of criminal evidence is the *ultimate issue rule*, which prohibits any witness from giving his opinion about a matter if it is the very question which the court is called upon to determine (Cross 1990, p. 499 et seq.; Wilkinson 1986, ch. 4). In a prosection for sexually abusing a child, whether the child was abused or not is the ultimate issue, and the rule would seem to pevent an expert saying 'in my opinion this child has been abused'. Obviously, there is an exception to the ultimate issue rule where the ultimate issue is something which the court is incapable of discovering by itself: for example, if someone is accused of possessing dangerous drugs, an expert may state his opinion that the substance the police found in a secret compartment in that person's suitcase is a certain type of drug. Furthermore, where the ultimate issue is something which the court can resolve by applying common sense to the relevant evidence, an expert can give his opinion that a certain fact—which a lay person might not notice, or if he did might not see the significance of—is in fact a piece of relevant evidence. Thus in a prosecution for incest a paediatrician would be allowed to describe the state of the girl's vagina, and give his opinion that this was consistent with penetration having taken place. But he would not be allowed to add 'and in my opinion, this child is the victim of incest'. If the jigsaw is capable of being assembled by the court on its own, the expert must leave the magistrates, judge or jury to do it: he can hand them the pieces, but may not put the pieces together for them, even if he could do it quicker and more accurately than they could.

In recent years the 'ultimate issue' rule has been attacked as highly inconvenient (Carson 1992). In England it was abolished for civil cases by the Civil Evidence Act 1968, s. 3, and its abolition in criminal proceedings was recommended in 1972 (Cmnd 4991, paras. 266–71). In some jurisdictions in the common law world it has been abolished altogether (Jackson 1984). If the 'ultimate issue' rule was abolished, however, evidence of the sort we are discussing might still fall foul of other exclusionary rules: for example, the rule that expert evidence is not admissible on matters which the court is competent to decide without it (see above), or, if called by the prosecution, the rule that the judge must reject evidence that is unduly prejudicial. In the USA, where the ultimate issue rule has been abolished in many jurisdictions, there is still a lot of judicial disagreement about whether it is permissible for experts to give opinion evidence on whether a child they have examined has been sexually abused (Myers 1987a, sect. 4.17; Myers 1990; Baker 1990).

In the Continental legal systems, on the other hand, the courts—criminal as well as civil—routinely permit psychiatrists and psychologists who have examined children to give their opinions on whether or not those children are the victims of abuse. But there the expert is usually appointed by the court, and is not as in Britain an expert witness appearing on behalf of the prosecution or defence.

Part III
Conclusion

There is no doubt that our courts tend to distrust expert evidence in general, and the evidence of psychologists and psychiatrists in particular. Why is this?

In part it is probably because lawyers, like other kinds of specialist, tend to be sceptical about areas of expertise other than their own; and all the more so if it is a comparatively new one. To some extent this attitude is understandable. Even the best of experts can get things wrong. In the Cleveland affair (see chapter 1), part of the trouble seems to have been that the two well respected paediatricians involved developed a view about medical evidence of child abuse which led to false positive diagnoses, in at least a proportion of the cases (Jones 1989). Not only can an individual expert get things wrong: there may be a flaw in the entire theoretical basis upon which the experts of the day are working—as with Freud's theory about the tendency of children to fantasise about sexual abuse, for example (see chapter 11), or the idea, cherished by Victorian doctors, that masturbation is highly unusual and leads to physical decay. More worrying still, there have sometimes been whole areas of expert 'knowledge' which eventually turned out to be completely bogus. At the Bury St Edmunds witch trial in 1665 one of the key witnesses was one Sir Thomas Browne, an 'expert' in demonology, who gave his opinion that the children had been bewitched, and added that 'in Denmark there had lately been a great discovery of witches, who used the very same way of afflicting persons by conveying pins into them, with needles and nails'; and he thought that the Devil, in such cases, 'did work upon the bodies of men and women by a natural inundation' (*Rose Cullender* (1665) 6 St Tr 687; Geis and Bunn 1981). No wonder lawyers prefer to follow common sense where they feel they safely can.

But a general healthy scepticism clearly does not explain everything, because there is no doubt that British judges turn their backs on expert help which their brethren on the Continent—and in some other parts of the English-speaking world—seem glad to accept.

The true reason for the reluctance of our courts to accept such expert evidence, it is suggested, lies within our version of the adversarial system. In Britain, expert knowledge is typically put before the court by opposing expert witness called by the parties, and is not supplied by neutral court-appointed experts, as it usually is in the legal systems on the Continent. Naturally, a judge's willingness to listen to experts increases in proportion to the expert's neutrality in the matter. In English child-care cases, as we have seen, psychological and psychiatric experts are mainly selected by the guardian *ad litem,* who is in the position of an officer of the court: and there, the judges willingly listen to expert evidence that would be ruled inadmissible if it was called by the prosecution or the defence in a criminal case. And even the criminal courts are happy to listen to psychological and psychiatric evidence at the sentencing stage, where the court may have called for the report.

It is quite understandable that the judges should be sceptical of evidence from expert witnesses who are called by the parties under the adversarial system, because there can be no doubt that where such evidence is concerned the adversarial system has a deeply corrupting effect.

The main problem is that the adversarial system ensures that much of the expert evidence the court receives is unreliable through bias.

The first and most basic rule of scientific research is that you must examine all the evidence dispassionately and search for the truth, whatever that may be. This rule is as relevant to scientific work that is undertaken for the courts as it is for scientific work undertaken for any other purpose. Indeed, it is if anything more relevant, because to a large extent a law court must take what an expert says on trust: this evidence is not readily capable of being checked for accuracy by the methods designed to uncover untruthfulness in other witnesses. The need to be neutral and impartial is recognised by every expert who has any shred of professional integrity:

> As a medical witness your role is to serve neither the prosecution nor the defence but the court. When the court is considering child abuse your duty is to the welfare of the child. On this basis a doctor should be above any partisan feelings and not influenced by any matter other than the welfare of the child. All questions should be answered with this in mind. (Mitchels and Meadow 1989.)

But because the expert is called by one of the parties, this detachment is difficult to achieve.

To begin with, the expert will often have been chosen not because his opinions are respected, but because he is prepared to give the evidence the party calling him wants the court to hear. In principle, both sides in the adversarial process are free to shop around from expert to expert, tearing up one inconvenient report after another, until they eventually find an expert who will say what they want the court to hear. In a criminal case the prosecution are under some restraint, because they are expected to pass on pieces of evidence which may prove helpful to the defence (although there have been a series of shocking cases in which this did not happen—the case of *Ward* (1993) 96 Cr App R 1 to name but one). But no such ethical constraints apply to the defence in a prosecution, or to either side in a civil action (11). This produces a particular breed of 'defence expert'—someone who never or very rarely gives evidence except for the defence, and whose scientific integrity is compromised as a result. An American legal writer tells us that:

> . . . mental health professionals now regularly provide expert testimony for the defence in child sexual abuse cases. It appears, however, that some have

gone beyond merely being advocates for a particular side, and have distorted or exaggerated research findings in articles or testimony regarding children as witnesses or false allegations of child sexual abuse, particularly in custody cases. (Bulkley 1989.) (See also Davies 1991.)

In the USA the derisive term for these is 'saxophones', or 'hired guns'. Even if the expert so selected tries to take the most elevated and detached view of his task, the very fact that he has been called by one side is likely to warp his evidence. This fact is well recognised, both by lawyers, and by experts. As a Scottish legal writer put it:

> There is, perhaps, no kind of testimony more subject to bias in favour of the adducer than that of skilled witnesses; for many men, who would not knowingly misstate a simple fact, can accommodate their opinions to the wishes of their employers, and the connection between them tends to warp the judgment of the witnesses without their being conscious of it. (Dickson 1864, sect. 1999.)

Or, as an eminent psychologist put it, there is 'conscious or unconscious identification on the part of the psychologist or psychiatrist with the party which employs him' (Haward 1981a, p. 177). And even if the expert can get over the problem of unconscious bias, the impartiality of the opinion will often be undermined by the fact that the side which has instructed him or her has provided information that is partial or incomplete (Gee 1987). In *Turner* [1975] QB 834, for example, a psychiatrist described the defendant as 'a placid, rather quiet and passive person who is quite sensitive to the feelings of other people . . . even-tempered . . . not in any way aggressive . . . he seems always to have displayed remarkably good impulse control'—an assessment which was a little difficult to square with his convictions for possessing an offensive weapon and assault with intent to rob, as the Court of Appeal acidly pointed out. Is it conceivable that any psychiatrist, not himself in need of psychiatric treatment, would have written this if he had known all the facts?

Even if the expert shares Olympian detachment with a total grasp of all the basic facts, in our adversarial system he will not be allowed to tell the court his conclusions in the way he wants to tell them, but will be examined by two counsel, each of whom is trying to get him to say what suits his case—no less, and definitely no more. When guidance is given to those who must give expert evidence, it usually includes something like this:

> The cross-examining advocate may use the 'yes/no' technique. So, for example, you may have said that the bruise is, beyond reasonable doubt, in the circumstances the result of a punch to the face. You may be asked to agree that it is possible that that could be caused by a fall from bed. If you simply answer yes without going on to qualify that statement by saying that in this case it is possible but not in the least bit likely (because of specific facts), then your simple yes answer will be built on by the advocate in his closing speech. . . . You may have to fight to get in your qualification to the

yes answer. If before you have finished giving your answer, the next question is asked, just carry on with your answer to the first question. You cannot be interrupted. (Boyle 1989.)

Even if counsel for both sides are scrupulously fair, and avoid the dirtier tricks of the trade, the fact that each expert is called and examined by a rival side who wants them to say what suits their case causes a more fundamental problem. Broadly speaking, most reputable experts agree with most other reputable experts on a wide range of the most important matters: but under the adversarial system the method of examination ensures that it is the areas of disagreement which are most obvious. The result is a courtroom 'battle of experts', at the end of which those who have to decide the case must often feel inclined to think that nothing either expert said is worthy of belief.

Obviously, the expert witness's position as a partisan within the adversarial system undermines the reliability of this evidence, and by this discredits the area of expertise in the eyes of the judges:

> . . . when he adopts the role of expert witness [the scientist] is immediately handicapped by the nature of the judicial proceedings, like a pianist trying to perform while wearing gloves. Indeed, a real danger lies in the possibility that the scientist could become more concerned to be an effective and acceptable witness than a conscientious scientist, and if he gave evidence frequently the courts might become accustomed to the performance with gloves, and be unaware of what it actually should sound like. (Gee 1987.)

In addition, it means that expert evidence cannot be used without causing serious practical inconveniences at the trial, and beforehand. If the prosecution are permitted to call a psychiatrist or a psychologist to give an expert opinion that a child has been sexually abused, the defence must then be permitted to call another—who may be reliable, or may have been selected as the only person in the world prepared to give this evidence—to state her or his expert opinion that the child has not been sexually abused. Furthermore, when it comes to deciding between two apparently well qualified experts, a jury of butchers, bakers and candlestick makers is not well placed to tell the genuine expert from the mountebank. If at the end of the prize-fight between rival experts the truth eventually prevailed, the trial would be greatly prolonged, its cost would be greatly increased, and—last but not least—the child would probably suffer the trauma and upset of not one but a whole series of expert examinations. For these reasons our judges, already overburdened with expert evidence in civil cases (*Re P* [1990] FCR 147), would probably reject this kind in criminal cases, even if they were convinced that it was valuable.

There is surely much to be said for a system under which an expert or experts are appointed by the court. The mechanics of the French system are described in a recent article by a psychiatrist who is an expert appointed by the Paris Court of Appeal (Bardet 1990). The Court of Appeal in each area maintains an official list of experts, membership of which is controlled by a committee, and is something of a professional honour. Once on the list the expert is obliged to undertake the tasks the court assigns, and at a fixed rate of payment which is fairly low. The need for an expert opinion usually becomes apparent in the early stages of the case, when the *juge d'instruction* will ask an expert on the list to provide it. The report may be acceptable to all parties. If not, either side may ask the judge to obtain a further opinion from another accredited expert—or experts: in a really difficult case as many as five court experts may be called in. Where more than one expert is involved they are expected to collaborate and produce a joint report. If they are unable to agree, and one expert submits a supplementary report, the main report is invalidated and the judge starts the procedure once again. It is sometimes possible for the defence to bring forward an expert witness of their own, but this runs counter to the usual way of doing things, and very rarely happens. According to Dr Bardet some conflicts between experts do occasionally take place: but even allowing for the fact that the grass always looks greener on the other side of the Channel, it does seem a much more satisfactory way of doing things than the adversarial system in operation here (12).

The French system, of course, is broadly inquisitorial. But their method of using experts is not limited to the inquisitorial systems. A system of court-appointed experts is also used in Norway and Denmark, which operate an accusatorial system broadly modelled on ours. In the USA, where on the whole methods are more fiercely adversarial than they are in Britain, Rule 706 of the Federal Rules of Evidence enables a neutral expert to be appointed in criminal proceedings by the judge.

A possible objection to the idea is that if either side did not like the opinion of the court-appointed expert they would immediately call their own as well, and we should have battles between three experts instead of two. But it would not be unthinkable for the law to impose some restriction on the use of further expert witnesses where a neutral expert (or experts) had been employed. The civil courts have already done this to some extent in child-care cases (Masson 1988). In criminal cases, as we have seen, they have taken the considerably more drastic step of holding certain types of expert evidence inadmissible altogether.

Various steps have been taken to improve the rules relating to expert evidence over the years, including, in England, a recent rule requiring each side in a prosecution to disclose their expert evidence in advance (Police and Criminal Evidence Act 1984, s. 81), in order to avoid the risk of 'trial by ambush'—and further changes of this sort have now been proposed by the Royal Commission on Criminal Justice (1993). But experts usually say these tinkering changes within the adversarial system are no use:

> The basic problem still remains, of the difficulty of squeezing the scientific process of obtaining and evaluating evidence, designed for one purpose, through the legal adversarial procedure till it emerges, bruised and mangled, and possibly unrecognisable (Gee 1987).

NOTES

1. Groth and Birnbaum (1987), pp. 175–81 suggest that paedophiles and ordinary homosexuals are mutually exclusive groups. West (1977), pp. 214–17 takes the view that they are distinct groups, but says that a small number of sexual psychopaths have an equal taste for violent sexual offences against men, women and children.

2. The following is a small selection. From paediatricians: Hobbs and Wynne (1986, 1987a, 1987b, 1989). From psychiatrists: Bentovim, et al. (1988); Vizard (1987, 1988); Jones (1992).

3. For accounts in English, see the following: Undeutsch (1982, 1984, 1989); Wegener (1989); Steller (1989); Köhnken (1989, 1990); Steller and Köhnken (1989); Köhnken and Steller (1988); Steller and Boychuk (1992). Arne Trankell described his techniques in his *Reliability of Evidence* (1972).

4. In Germany, a psychologist's opinion for use in court would probably consist of 20 closely typed and closely reasoned pages. We are grateful to Professor Dr Max Steller for providing this information.

5. In England, a 'special jury' consisted, in the main, of people who were above a certain rank in society. In the 18th century Lord Chief Justice Mansfield managed to collect a regular panel of experienced city men for trying commercial cases, to whom he turned for knowledge about commercial matters. 'One, in particular . . . who always wore a cocked hat . . . had almost as much authority as the Lord Chief Justice himself' (Campbell 1849, vol. 2, p. 407).

6. Fraud Trials Committee (1986). Most of this committee's proposals were enacted in the Criminal Justice Acts 1987 and 1988, but conspiciously not this one.

7. This is an area with rapidly expanding literature. Hodgkinson (1990) is the major text for legal practitioners; Graham Hall and Smith (1992) is a guide for experts; and there is now a specialist journal, *Expert Evidence*.

8. Roe (1985); Myers (1987a), sect. 4.12–4.19; Myers et al. (1989); Myers (1990); Myers (1992), chapter 5; Younts (1991); Hanson (1989).

9. In *Miles* v *Cain* (1988) *The Independent*, 26 November 1988, a civil action in which a woman claimed damages against a man who had raped her, the judge seems to have heard expert evidence about the psychological effects of being raped, and the extent to which women make false complaints, but from information kindly supplied by the judge, and from reading the transcript of his summing-up, it seems that both sides wished to call expert evidence, and neither therefore objected to the evidence being called by the other.

10. The main thrust of the parent's argument was that the expert evidence could only be admitted where the psychiatrist had seen a videotape of the original interview, rather than that it was not admissible at all: but from the tone of Waterhouse J's remarks he seems to have had no doubt that this sort of evidence is generally admissible in civil proceedings concerned with the custody and welfare of children.

11. Rules of Court made under the Children Act 1989 require the permission of the courts before a child the subject of legal proceedings can be medically or psychiatrically examined. Judges not infrequently give leave subject to the condition that the report be disclosed to the other side.

12. A system of court-appointed experts has its own potential problems, and in countries that use this system complaints are sometimes heard. But as far as we are aware the criticism is usually at the level of detail, and nobody wishes to abandon the basic idea that the expert is the expert of the court. For recent proposals in France, see Spencer (1992). For Holland, see Crombag et al. (1992, p. 472).

CHAPTER TEN

A criticism of the basic rules of evidence

In this section of the book we shall try to examine the underlying assumptions of the rules of evidence in the light of what the behavioural sciences can tell us. The meat of the section is the next chapter, chapter 11, which looks at the particular assumptions which underlie the rules of evidence in relation to children.

This present chapter is concerned with the broader assumptions which underlie the rules of evidence in general. This is a much wider subject—indeed one so broad that a whole book could be devoted to it—and the treatment we can give it here is in outline only. Various aspects of the matter, such as the rule against evidence of past misconduct, have been dealt with in other parts of the book as they arose. Here we shall consider four related matters only: (a) the primacy of oral testimony, (b) the value of cross-examination as an instrument for discovering the truth, (c) the need to confront a witness with the person he accuses, and (d) the idea that juries are particularly good at detecting lies.

THE PRIMACY OF ORAL EVIDENCE

One of the fundamental assumptions behind the rules of evidence in the English-speaking world is that the oral testimony of live witnesses at trial is greatly superior to any other type of evidence. From this a number of the best-known rules of evidence flow. First, and most obviously, there is the rule that hearsay evidence is generally inadmissible. Secondly, there is the absence of any regular procedure by which a witness may give his evidence to the court in advance of trial, and the unwillingness of the courts to act on it even in the rare situations in which this may be done (*Collins* (1938) 26 Cr App R 177—(1)). And thirdly, there is the rule that even where a witness gives oral evidence at trial his previous statements are not legally admissible in evidence, except for the limited purpose of showing that his evidence in court is not trustworthy because at some earlier point he gave a different version of events. Any proposal to modify these rules of evidence is always met with the objection that it undermines the primacy of oral evidence. As we explain elsewhere in this book, much of the stress that child witnesses suffer stems from the fact that at present they must give their evidence orally at trial. The argument about the primacy of oral evidence would no doubt be used against any proposal to alter this.

Although British lawyers automatically assume that oral testimony at trial is the highest form of evidence, our preference for oral evidence seems to be a purely cultural one. This preference is not shared by all lawyers outside the English-speaking world. By and large, the French and French-based systems have a preference for documentary evidence, and look on oral testimony as a second-best, to be accepted with caution when (as often) there is nothing more reliable to hand. A French criminal court makes extensive use of written transcripts of pre-trial interviews with witnesses which are carried out by an official called a *juge d'instruction*; these supplement the oral testimony of witnesses at trial, and sometimes replace it altogether. In civil law the French even go so far as to make documentary evidence a compulsory requirement for certain types of case (Honoré 1981).

In truth, there is nothing about oral evidence which makes it inherently better than evidence of any other type. Like other forms of evidence it has its advantages, and its drawbacks too.

The advantages of oral testimony at trial are six.

(a) It is free from errors of transmission. Where a witness gives oral evidence at trial there is no room for doubt about what he said, or about what he said it in response to.

(b) The court is able to 'observe the demeanour of the witness'; as well as discovering what the witness has to say the court can hear how convincingly or otherwise the witness gives his evidence, and can see his 'non-verbal communication' as he does so.

(c) The evidence is given on oath or, if not on oath, in solemn circumstances which are likely to impress at least some witnesses with the need to tell the truth.

(d) The honesty of the witness can be tested by cross-examination; which is a great advantage, at least in the eyes of those who believe with Wigmore that cross-examination is 'the greatest legal engine ever invented for the discovery of truth' (see below).

(e) If the witness makes an accusation, he is usually forced to make it in the presence of the accused; which is an advantage in the eyes of those who believe that if cross-examination is the greatest legal engine ever invented for the dicovery of truth, 'confrontation' is second greatest.

(f) The presence of the witness at the trial makes it possible to question him about aspects of the case which no one previously thought were relevant or important—something it is by definition impossible to do where evidence is the record of an examination conducted in advance of trial.

Whilst oral testimony at trial invariably has these advantages, only (f)—possibility of asking impromptu questions at trial—is actually exclusive to it. Whilst evidence that is not given live at trial may lack advantages (a) to (e) as well, it will not necessarily do so. If the evidence consists of a written record of an earlier interview it will lack advantages (a) (freedom from transmission errors) and (b) (seeing the demeanour of the witness); but features (c), (d) and (e) may be present, because a written statement can be made on oath with great solemnity, the maker can be subjected to a traditional cross-examination, and all this can be done in the presence of the accused. If the evidence consists of a videotape of an earlier interview rather than a written record, advantages (a) and (b) are provided too, because all doubts are at once resolved about what the witness actually said, and the court is also able to 'observe the demeanour of the witness'. And whilst advantage (f)—the possibility of questioning an oral witness about matters not previously considered relevant—is exclusive to oral evidence, it is sometimes possible to compensate for its absence where other kinds of evidence are used instead. If a witness's evidence consists of an interview recorded in advance of trial, there is nothing in principle to prevent the court adjourning the trial for the witness to be subjected to a supplementary interview, although it would often be inconvenient to do this.

Against the obvious advantages of evidence given orally at trial there must be set two equally obvious disadvantages. First, it is nearly always given a long time after the event in question. Secondly, when giving evidence live at trial a witness is usually suffering from stress. If there are two scientific facts about the psychology of human memory which are clear beyond any doubt, one is that memory for an event fades gradually with time, and the other is that stress beyond a certain level can impair the power of recall (see chapter 11). These rules of psychology will hardly come as a surprise to anyone who has practical experience of the courts, because there you see them in operation every day. A well-known problem for the advocate is the witness who gave a full and detailed account of an incident shortly after it occurred, and whose memory for some crucial detail fails him in the witness-box. Car registration numbers are the classic example, which have given rise to a number of cases over the years (*Kelsey* (1982) 74 Cr App R 213; cf. *McLean* (1968) 52 Cr App R 80). An equally common problem is the victim or other eyewitness who is so scared at having to give evidence as to be completely incoherent, and unable to utter any sense at all. These problems quite commonly arise with adult witnesses. With children they are considerably worse. As far as stress is concerned, there is no doubt that children are more easily frightened than adults. As far as lapse of time is concerned there is a widespread belief, for which there is a certain amount of scientific evidence, that young children foget more quickly than adults (see chapter 11); and the longer the delay, the greater the likelihood that they will have been repeatedly questioned about the incident by people who are concerned with their welfare rather than with the legal process—something which inevitably involves the risk of distorting their recollections, as psychologists like Elizabeth Loftus have demonstrated beyond all doubt (see chapter 11). The great advantage of pre-trial interviews as evidence is that these problems are avoided.

We could counteract the main disadvantages of oral testimony if we allowed the previous statements of oral witnesses to be put in evidence to supplement as much of their recollection as they can be persuaded to utter in the court. If we could do this we would enjoy the advantages of oral testimony, and the advantages of pre-trial interviews as well. However, this obvious course is forbidden, at any rate in the criminal courts. When giving evidence a witness may prompt himself from a contemporary note, in the unlikely event that he made one. If, as is more likely, he made a written statement after the event, he is not allowed to have it with him, and—amazingly—at one time was not even allowed to refresh his memory from it before the trial (*Yellow and Thay* (1932) 96 JPN 826.) In England, but not in Scotland, this much is now permitted (*Richardson* [1971] 2 QB 484)—whence the edifying sight at Crown Courts in England of witnesses frantically learning their witness-statements outside the door of the court, in order to give evidence from memory—and, if he did not look at the statement before giving evidence, he is now permitted to look at it during a break in the proceedings (*Da Silva* [1990] 1 WLR 31). Otherwise, as we explained in chapter 5, the basic rule is that the only use that may be made of a witness's previous statement is to undermine his oral testimony if it shows he said something different before the trial.

It is surely impossible to justify this rule: yet there has been no shortage of lawyers ready to defend it.

In England, when the Criminal Law Revision Committee recommended its abolition in its 11th Report in 1972, the English Bar put up a vigorous opposition (General Council of the Bar 1973). They said the proposal was 'unnecessary and dangerous': unnecessary, because a witness's earlier statement would either be the same as what he said at the trial, when it would be redundant, or else it would differ from it, in which case the two statements would cancel each other out; and dangerous, because it would be easy for dishonest third parties to allege that witnesses had previously said things they had not said, and thereby pervert the course of justice. These objections missed the main point, which is that the majority of witnesses are honest, and where a witness is honest the previous statement will usually neither duplicate nor contradict his courtroom testimony, but be a fuller and more complete version of it, because when he made the statement he could then remember details which he has since forgotten. As the Criminal Law Revision Committee said, '. . . what [the witness] said soon after the events in question is likely to be at least as reliable as his evidence given at the trial and will probably be more so' (Cmnd 4991, para. 239). If the witness is dishonest—whether by repeating in court the lies he has previously put on paper, or by falsely claiming that an honest witness previously told a different tale—we still have the chance of exposing his lies by cross-examination. This reasoning has now convinced the Scottish Law Commission, which now proposes that the previous statements of a witness should usually be admissible where they have been preserved in permanent form (Report No. 125, 1990: see chapter 15 below: a proposal that is yet to be acted upon).

The other objection to admitting previous statements made by oral witnesses in evidence is this. Where the previous statement was made to the police, it will probably have been extracted by leading questions, although this will not appear on the face of the statement—and to that extent the statement will be unreliable. Insofar as this is a valid objection, then the growing practice of the police in taping interviews with potential witnesses should answer it. If the statement to the police is recorded on tape the court will know the questions as well as the answers, and will be able to make up its own mind about how far the police put words into the witness's mouth.

Oral evidence has another disadvantage, which has nothing to do with its weight. This is that giving oral evidence at the trial can be a shattering experience for the witness. We take this matter up in chapter 13.

CROSS-EXAMINATION: 'THE GREATEST LEGAL ENGINE EVER INVENTED FOR THE DISCOVERY OF TRUTH'

Among English-speaking lawyers no belief is more deeply held than the value of cross-examination. It has been the subject of fervent professions of faith in so many speeches and writings that a collection of them would fill a sizeable book. The best known comes from the American writer Wigmore:

> Not even the abuses, the mishandlings, and the puerilities which are so often found associated with cross-examination have availed to nullify its value. It may be that in more than one sense it takes the place in our system which torture occupied in the mediaeval system of the civilians. Nevertheless, it is beyond any doubt the greatest legal engine ever invented for the discovery of truth. However difficult it may be for the layman, the scientist, or the foreign jurist to appreciate this its wonderful power, there has probably never been a moment's doubt upon this point in the mind of a lawyer of experience. . . If we omit political considerations of broader range, then cross-examination, not trial by jury, is the great and permanent contribution of the Anglo-American system of law to improved methods of trial procedure. (5 Wigmore, Evidence, sect. 1367 (Chadbourn rev. 1974).)

When changes in the rules of evidence are proposed, lawyers invariably attack them if they seem to undermine the right of cross-examination. It was to meet this criticism that the documentary hearsay provisions of the Criminal Justice Act 1988 had to be revised into their present complicated form (see chapter 6). The point was repeatedly made in the Parliamentary debates about the children's evidence provisions of what eventually became the Criminal Justice Acts 1988 and 1991.

British lawyers often say that cross-examination is a feature of our system that foreign lawyers envy and admire. The Anglo-American method of cross-examination was used at the Nuremberg Tribunal: and it is part of the folklore of the English Bar that the foreign lawyers assembled there were deeply impressed by it, all thinking it much superior to their own methods of getting at the truth. Indeed, English lawyers are so proud of this story that they have sometimes used it as an argument against proposals to change the rules of evidence about child witnesses. It is strange that they should do so. Apart from the point that techniques suitable for extracting the truth from major Nazi war criminals might seem a little excessive where children are concerned, the Anglo-American method of cross-examination in fact provoked mixed reactions from lawyers from other systems, some of whom thought it unfair (Wiliams 1963, p. 80). If we really want to know what foreign lawyers think of cross-examination we should read what a distinguished French judge and legal writer, François Gorphe, had to say about it:

The Anglo-American system has grave faults which cry out for it to be abolished. In the first place, it over-uses the right of questioning, to which it attributes an exaggerated efficiency in the case of suspect witnesses, whilst paying insufficient respect to witnesses who are sincere. Even more deplorably, it takes absolutely no precautions against the witness being influenced, or even badgered, and it takes no account of the distorting effect of suggestive questions, which get worse as the case is more bitterly contested. This, as Schneikert [see note (2)] says, is 'the best means of working upon witnesses and leading them astray'. Wouldn't the wretched witness have to be made of marble to stay calm and unruffled under the cross-fire of interrogation and counter-interrogation, examination, cross-examination, and re-examination which he must endure at the hands of the two adversarial opponents? Just think of a frightened witness, a weak one, or a child having to give evidence under such conditions! In reality, truth and justice cannot see the light of day except in an atmosphere of calmness and serenity. (Gorphe 1927, p. 90.)

Gorphe's first objection to cross-examination is hard to accept: it is hardly a valid criticism of cross-examination that it gives both sincere and suspect witnesses the same rough treatment, because the object of the exercise is to find out whether the witness is one or the other. But his second objection, that cross-examination bends and distorts the evidence by means of suggestive questions, seems incontrovertible.

All the work that psychologists have done on suggestibility and questioning shows that the more the questioner suggests a particular answer, the less reliable the answer is likely to be (see chapter 11). This is not particularly surprising: indeed it is something that lawyers have long known, at least in general terms, without the benefit of psychological research. It is the reason why lawyers are forbidden to ask 'leading questions'—that is, questions that suggest the answer required, or assume the existence of some disputed fact—when examining their witnesses in chief. Lawyers have also shown their awareness of it by attacking the leading style of questioning some child psychiatrists have used at interviews, videotapes of which were later shown in wardship cases. Indeed, the legal profession got so cross about psychiatrists asking children leading questions that some lawyers have used the risk of leading questions being put during interviews as an argument against any legislation to permit the use of videotapes as evidence in the criminal courts (see chapter 7). Yet asking leading questions is exactly what lawyers are permitted to do when they carry out a cross-examination. As one lawyer writes, with apparent approval, in a book on the subject:

Leading questions, i.e., those which suggest the answer, are the normal form in cross-examination; in effect, the advocate asserts the facts, and the witness agrees or disagrees.

One form of cross-examination is to lead the witness forcefully on one point after another, keeping maximum control over him and his testimony with a view to excluding harmful statements. Any deviation from the point of the question, or evasiveness, may be countered by warnings, reminders, repetition of questions, and insistence on proper answers. Non-compliance exposes the witness's partiality or reluctance. Restricting the witness by narrow questions and small steps, prevents him from dealing with the whole issue.

The cross-examiner would avoid open-ended questions, e.g. 'How?'; 'Why?'; 'What did you see then'; 'How did that happen?'. He would avoid general questions seeking explanations or reasons which would open the door to wide and harmful statements.

Alternatively, a comprehensive leading statement covering a whole incident may be put for acceptance or denial, which prevents the witness from disputing the details, one by one.

But any kind of forceful leading will be less effective if it gives the impression that the evidence is coming from the cross-examiner, not the witness. Thus, it is desirable to conceal the extent of control and leading, so far as possible, while maintaining it to the necessary extent. (Stone 1988.)

All this is most extraordinary. If rule number one of the lawyers' manual of psychology seems to be that memory improves with the passage of time, and rule number two that stress improves recall, rule number three seems to be that suggestive questions produce unreliable information *except* when asked by lawyers in cross-examination.

If leading questions can distort the evidence of adult witnesses, with child witnesses the damage they can do is worse. Psychological research on the suggestibility of children shows that children are more likely to give unreliable information in response to suggestive questioning than are adults, and the younger the child the more pronounced this effect becomes. A group of psychologists recently conducted an experiment where children watched an incident, after which they were first questioned about it 'in chief' without the use of leading questions, and then cross-examined using leading questions. The answers they gave under cross-examination were less accurate than the ones they gave under examination in chief, and in the case of the younger children, much less accurate. This is worrying enough: but the next phase of the experiment is even more so. Videotapes of the examinations were then shown to mock juries, who gave their views on the accuracy of the children's answers, and 'although actual accuracy of the witnesses' testimony varied with age, subject-jurors' estimates of accuracy did not' (Luus and Wells 1992).

Examples of the distorting influence of cross-examination can be drawn from reports of decided cases as well as from studies carried out by psychologists. In *Willoughby* (1989) 88 Cr App R 91, a girl of nine was abducted and indecently assaulted by a stranger. She picked the defendant out at an identity parade some two weeks later. At trial the defence suggested that she had identified Willoughby because the police had led her to believe that the man who attacked her would be present on parade. The police said they had told her that 'a suspect' would be there. In cross-examination, defence counsel asked the child, 'Did they tell you the attacker would be there?'—to which she answered 'Yes'—so giving him a handle to use against her evidence, and eventually, a ground on which to take the case to the Court of Appeal. But what are the chances that a little girl of nine would appreciate the significance of the word 'attacker' rather than 'suspect' in this context? It seems fair to guess that if asked, 'Did they tell you that the suspect would be there?' she would have answered 'Yes' to that as well. The only way of getting her to give a reliable account of what she remembered would have been to ask her open questions: 'Were you expecting to recognise anyone on the parade?', 'Do you remember exactly what the police said about who would be there?' etc. As we have not read the transcript of the whole examination, we do not know exactly what defence counsel said by way of build-up to the crucial question in this case. But whether or not he actually did so here, it would have been quite in order for him to put this question to the child out of the blue.

A particularly truth-distorting effect is produced by cross-examination when leading questions are put to the witness about details of peripheral matters. As we shall see in chapter 11, psychological research suggests that it is harder by leading questions to get children to give false answers about the features of an incident that seemed to them to be of central importance, than it is about matters which seemed unimportant to them at the time. Yet it is considered as proper for counsel to put leading questions to witnesses about peripheral matters—the colour of an attacker's shoes, for example—as it is to put them about the central question of what that person did. There can be little doubt that a cross-examination that presses for details of peripheral matters, far from being an engine for the discovery of the truth, produces a large amount of unreliable information.

Another and more fundamental psychological objection to the traditional cross-examination as an instrument for the discovery of truth is that it pursues two conflicting objects to the detriment of at least one of them. In cross-examining a witness a lawyer will have two things in mind. One is to test the sincerity of the witness by exploring his honesty and his motivation to lie. The other is to extract further details from the witness which he hopes will be helpful to his client's case—either because they are directly relevant to it, or because they conflict with other details the witness has given, and show him up as unreliable. In the course of testing the witness's sincerity, counsel is allowed to put certain 'questions' that are not really questions at all, but dressed-up ways of calling the witness a liar: 'You don't like your stepfather, do you Mary?', 'You've invented all this, haven't you Mary, in order to get him out of the house because you don't like him?', or even more bluntly, 'I put it to you that you have told the court a pack of lies'. Calling truthful people liars to their face is usually very upsetting to them (see page 81 above and 371 below). It will make an adult very angry, and a common effect on a child is to reduce it to tears. This puts the witness in a state of stress, in which he is often unable to collect his thoughts; and when counsel starts asking detailed questions designed to extract more information the witness then gets into a hopeless muddle and contradicts himself, not because he is unreliable, but merely because he is in such a state that he hardly knows what he is saying. A justices' clerk told the first author about a case where a man was prosecuted for indecently exposing himself to a woman from his car. Towards the end of the woman's cross-examination defence counsel asked her 'Did he have an erection?', to which she answered, 'No, it was a Cortina'. Such are the truths which the greatest legal engine ever invented is capable of extracting from the mouths of flustered witnesses.

This tendency of cross-examination to produce confusion in the place of truth would be reduced if cross-examiners had to keep questions designed to test the honesty and sincerity of the witness separate from questions designed to elicit further information in two distinct phases of the examination. But this is not the case. Far from it, in fact, because it is considered quite legitimate for a cross-examiner to hop from one point to another with the speed of a sword-dancer if he thinks this will produce the effect he wants; and this itself can be a fertile source of embarrassment and confusion to witnesses, which also undermines the value of cross-examination as an instrument for the discovery of the truth. In an interesting study two Australian psychologists, Mark and Roslin Brennan (1988), examined a number of transcripts of children under cross-examination and pointed out the various ways in which the questioning was likely to be confusing to children. They found rapid jumps from topic to topic to be a usual feature, and make this comment on it:

> In every day interactions the unspoken conventions for changing topics of conversation are accepted. There is generally an obvious link between what has just been discussed and the new item of conversation on the agenda. It is common to hear people say '. . . speaking of such and such . . . did you read about . . . have you seen . . .' If these cues are left out communication becomes disjointed and frustrated. Someone is inevitably left stranded by the privacy.
>
> In court there is no provision within the language to establish these linkages. The cross-examiner jumps from topic to topic and the child witness is expected to keep pace. The juxtaposition of questions seems inexplicable as topics are jostled randomly. The effects of this are most critical when intimate details of the child's alleged sexual assault are questioned, and juxtaposed with general and more objective questions.
>
> The technique of juxtaposing unrelated topics excludes the possibility of any transition time. Without this accommodation time it is likely that the child will become disorientated, confused and unclear about the general line of questioning. The greater the frequency of these shifts from the personal to the objective, the greater the cumulative effect of the confusion will be.

They give the following actual example.

Q. That was after he had stripped you?
A. Yes.
Q. And then you said he tried to put his finger in your vagina. Did he put his finger on your vagina or in your vagina?
A. In my vagina, in my vagina?
Q. Inside, you felt it inside did you?
A. (No verbal answer.)

Q. Did he do anything else to you?
A. No.
Q. Do you know Frank Murphy? (Suddenly mentioning a character who has not been mentioned previously, and whose identity is not established subsequently either.)

The Brennans do not say what happened next. If the girl had met Frank Murphy, and counsel could prove it, but still reeling from questions about vaginal penetration she mistakenly answered no, the greatest engine for the discovery of truth would have scored a direct hit, because counsel could then suggest the witness is a liar.

Nor is this the limit of the ways in which the traditional cross-examination tends to distort the truth rather than expose it (see Myers 1987b). In the discussion of expert evidence in chapter 9 we explained the cross-examiner's trick of extracting half an answer to a question, and then moving on to something else before the witness has time to utter the vital qualification which gives a wholly different flavour to his words. This only fails to work if the witness stands up to the cross-examiner and insists on having his full say. An adult witness may have the courage to do this, but it would be a rare child who was sufficiently assertive. Far from being a dirty trick of which the legal profession is ashamed, this particular device is actually commended to barristers in books about the techniques of advocacy (Harvey 1958, p. 128)—usually with a hilarious anecdote of some inconvenient cat that was let out of the bag when counsel unwisely asked 'one question too many' (Cecil 1972, p. 181; Du Cann 1964, p. 116). When members of other professions discover this, they sometimes wonder if lawyers are really being sincere when they quote Wigmore's eulogy on cross-examination at them.

By now it should be clear, first, that the traditional cross-examination has a number of features which tend to distort the truth, and secondly, that these operate more strongly where the witness is a child. In addition to this, it is also clear that the traditional cross-examination can be such a damaging experience for a child that prosecutors often drop cases against offenders who well deserve to be prosecuted in order to spare the child the ordeal (see chapter 13). On these grounds, many informed people have criticised it severely.

On the first page of the first edition of *The Child's Guardian*, Benjamin Waugh, the founder of the NSPCC, complained that 'A father with but a pound in his pocket can provide himself with legal ability to cross-question and perplex the injured little witness against him in the witness-box' (vol. 1, No. 1, 1 January 1887). A century later, in a letter to the press Dr Eileen Vizard, a child psychiatrist, said this:

As an experienced expert witness, I can confirm that there is not the slightest chance of a traumatised sexually abused child surviving cross-examination by a barrister. That is not to be unduly critical of lawyers but simply to state plain common sense. (*The Independent*, 30 October 1987.)

Two years later the Canadian psychologist, John Yuille, wrote:

One only needs to witness a single instance of the cross-examination of a child witness to realise that the procedure is ill suited to children. It is easy to confuse a young child with the use of age-inappropriate language, long and circuitous questions, and a confrontational style. The adversarial system creates as many problems as it solves in the area of child abuse. (Yuille 1989, p. 191.)

In the same year these words were echoed by an American judge, in a case where a man who had been convicted of indecently assaulting his four-year-old daughter appealed because he had not been given the chance to cross-examine her:

Events conspired to prevent [him] from having a chance to cross-examine his principal accuser. He was convicted on hearsay evidence. But we should not allow labels and lawyers' pieties to delude us into believing that cross-examination of a four-year-old child concerning sexual abuse by her father a year earlier is a more effective method of discovering the truth than listening to and weighing the testimony of a competent psychologist who interviewed the child over a period of many months in a setting designed to elicit truthful communcation. (Judge Posner in *Nelson* v *Farrey* (1989) 874 F 2d 1222.)

Some thoughtful British lawyers have also come to question the value of the traditional cross-examination where children are concerned. A serious problem is that young children quite often 'dry up' in cross-examination, so preventing the cross-examiner either testing their sincerity, or extracting any further information from them, true or false.

In examination-in-chief, unless a certain amount of leading is allowed with defence consent, it might often be impossible to obtain any coherent account at all. But the quality of the evidence given by a child in response to leading gives a court very little guidance, since the evidence is often limited to 'Yes' or 'No' answers. The defence have to conduct a cross-examination in these difficult conditions, and usually in an atmosphere which is unsympathetic to any possibility of harassing or upsetting the child. . . . This is not an ideal forum in which the art of cross-examination can flourish. (Stone 1988.)

With this difficulty in mind, sometimes defence counsel do not even make an attempt to cross-examine a child witness.

Obviously, justice cannot be done in a criminal case unless the defence version of events can be put to the witness by somebody at some point, and unless some examination can be made of the witness's intelligence, honesty and motivation to tell the truth. But it is foolish to pretend that in the case of a child this can only be done by the method of subjecting him or her to a traditional live cross-examination, in open court, on the day of trial—or even that it is the best method of doing so.

THE TRUTH-ENHANCING VALUE OF CONFRONTATION

It is a widely held belief among lawyers in the English-speaking world that confronting the accuser with the person he accuses ensures he tells the truth.

The strongest expressions of this viewpoint come from the USA, where the Constitution gives the defendant a right 'to be confronted with the witnesses against him', which the courts have interpreted as a right to look them in the eye whilst they do so (see chapter 5). When setting aside a conviction for sexual offences on a little girl of five whom the judge had allowed to turn her chair out of the defendant's line of vision, a judge in California said:

> By allowing the child to testify against the defendant without having to look at him or be looked at by him, the trial court not only denied defendant the right of confrontation but also foreclosed an effective method for determining veracity (*Herbert* v *Superior Court* (1981) 117 Cal App 3d 661 per Carr J).

In the Supreme Court case of *Coy* v *Iowa* (1988) 108 S Ct 2798 (see chapter 5) Scalia J said:

> It is always more difficult to tell a lie about a person 'to his face' than 'behind his back'. In the former context, even if the lie is told, it will often be told less convincingly. . . . The [prosecution] can hardly gainsay the profound effect upon a witness of standing in the presence of the person the witness accuses, since that is the very phenomenon it relies upon to establish the potential 'trauma' that allegedly justified the extraordinary procedure in the present case. The face-to-face presence may, unfortunately, upset the truthful rape victim or abused child; but by the same token it may confound and undo the false accuser, or reveal the child coached by a malevolent adult. It is a truism that constitutional protections have costs.

Similar views are occasionally heard in Britain. The following exchange took place between the presenter of a television programme and a QC eminent at the criminal Bar:

> Presenter: And do those ultimate safeguards involve necessarily cross-examining a child in open court?

> George Carman QC: I fear they must. It is important the jury be able to observe the demeanour of the child. It is important the defendant is able to give immediate instructions to his counsel as and when the child is giving evidence. And it is equally important that he, himself, is confronted with the child *and, unfortunately, the child is confronted with him.* (BBC 'Panorama', 8 September 1986.)

So far, this idea has not cut a lot of ice in Britain. Here there is no constitutional right of confrontation, and as we saw in chapter 5, the criminal courts have been prepared to allow vulnerable witnesses to give evidence out of sight of the accused, and Parliament has legislated to allow the same end to be achieved by closed-circuit television. We think that this is right.

It should be obvious that it makes it harder rather than easier to tell the truth about another to have the other person there, particularly if the truth is unpleasant. If nothing else it is embarrassing. If the accused is thought to be dangerous, or to have dangerous friends, fear becomes an added inhibition. And if the accused is someone in authority who has forbidden the accuser to talk, the accuser may be torn between his duty to the court and his duty to the accused.

Some years ago the first author was part of a small committee enquiring into allegations of theft and fraud that had been made against a catering manager. When questioned in his absence, the manager's subordinates spoke confidently and coherently, and provided a large amount of useful information. They were then questioned again in the presence of their 'boss'. They were all virtually incoherent with embarrassment; some were literally sweating with fear; and one of them retracted her earlier statement. If we had not had their earlier statements, as well as some damaging admissions from the manager himself, we would not have had enough information to justify dismissing him. After his dismissal, further enquiries more than confirmed that what his subordinates had told us in his absence was the truth. Far from helping truth to out, it was obvious that the presence of the accused produced the opposite effect.

These witnesses were adults. The same difficulties, only worse, are likely to arise wherever a child is called as a witness. If the child is called upon to give evidence againt a stranger he or she will often be afraid of him, and if the accused is a friend or a member of the family there will be feelings of embarrassment and conflicting loyalties as well. If the accused is physically present, these feelings are reinforced.

In chapter 5 we saw that when child witnesses are confronted with the defendant at a trial, quite often the effect is literally to scare them speechless. Of those who do succeed in giving evidence, many will be to some extent afraid, and as we have already seen, psychological research makes it plain that stress beyond a certain point makes it harder for witnesses to order their thoughts and produce accurate information from memory. Studies by Dent and Stephenson shed interesting light on the likely effect of confrontation on the accuracy of honest children's evidence. Children who had seen a workman enter their classroom were later asked to identify the man, some from a live parade, and others from slides. The children did significantly better from the slides than from the live parade, where a number showed significant signs of nervousness, and some refused to participate at all (Dent and Stephenson 1979a). Dent and Stephenson found a similar effect when the experiment was repeated using adults, but the effect of the suspect's presence was less marked. Once again, the assumptions that underlie the rules of evidence, if valid at all, are distinctly less valid where the witnesses are children (see further chapter 11).

If it is clear that confrontation makes it harder for honest witnesses to tell the truth, is there any validity in the common belief that it makes it more difficult for dishonest ones to lie? This could be so, at least in some cases. If a false accuser's conscience is already pricking, it is possible that the sight of the person he has wronged may give him the necessary psychological shove to return him to the path of righteousness. However, we are unaware of any psychological research that suggests it is generally harder to tell unpleasant lies about someone in their presence than unpleasant truths. It may be that the notion that confrontation generally causes liars to retract is false; and if it is, psychology provides a possible explanation for the unfounded belief. Studies with mock juries have shown that people tend to think that confidence in a witness is a sure sign of truthfulness—although in fact it is anything but this (see page 280 below). Confrontation will make many witnesses feel uncomfortable, and in this state they will seem unconfident. If lawyers and lay people are inclined to confuse confidence with truthfulness, the fact that confrontation makes some witnesses more unconfident than others might give rise to a false belief that confrontation enables the court to tell which witnesses are telling lies. Alternatively, the idea may be no more than a crude and confused notion that if someone can stick to a story through some unpleasant experience then that story is probably the truth. In ancient Rome, the evidence of slaves was tested by subjecting them to torture, and the theory that confrontation ensures truthfulness may be a similar idea.

Thus confrontation, in the sense of making the accuser give evidence in the presence of the accuser, is not only worse than useless as a truth-producer; it is also a lie-detector of very uncertain value.

Despite this, 'confrontation' in the wider sense of the word can still be a useful implement in the search for the truth. It shows us what one person's reaction is to another, which may be a useful piece of information. When done informally, and accused and accuser are not scared stiff of one another, it is a quick and easy method of putting one person's story to the other, and vice versa. In this sense, *la confrontation* is widely used by the *juge d'instruction* in the French system, and those based upon it. And where the defendant has no counsel to represent him, it is of course essential that he be 'confronted' with the witnesses against him, because otherwise he has no idea what they have said, and cannot defend himself against their accusations. Even if the defendant is legally represented, it is some advantage for the defence if the defendant as well as counsel can see and hear the witnesses.

'. . . WHEN ONE OR OTHER OF THE PARTIES MUST BE DELIBERATELY LYING, THEN TRIAL BY JURY HAS NO EQUAL' (3)

This theory consists of two ideas. The first is that where witnesses give oral evidence, it is possible to tell whether or not they are lying from their appearance and behaviour—their 'demeanour', as lawyers call it, or 'nonverbal communication' in the language of psychologists. The second is that juries are much better at doing it than judges. In combination, these ideas produce an argument which is used against both legal changes which would dispense with the child's appearance as a live witness at the trial, and proposals to transfer prosecutions for offences against children from the ordinary criminal courts to some specialist tribunal.

Judges have sometimes voiced the first of these ideas in judgments quashing convictions obtained by using written evidence. In *Collins* (1938) 26 Cr App R 177 Humphreys J said:

> The result . . . was to deprive the jury of the inestimable advantage—the one great advantage to which those who uphold the system of trial by jury always point—of the opportunity of not only seeing the witnesses who give evidence and hearing what they have to say, but also of observing their demeanour in the witness-box.

But when speaking off the bench, judges have often poured cold water on the idea that the demeanour of a witness is a sound guide to whether or not he is telling lies. In a public lecture, Mr Justice MacKenna said this:

> I question whether the respect given to our findings of fact based on the demeanour of the witnesses is always deserved. I doubt my own ability, and sometimes that of other judges, to discern from a witness's demeanour, or the tone of his voice, whether he is telling the truth. He speaks hesitantly. Is it the mark of cautious man, whose statements are for that reason to be respected, or is he taking time to fabricate? Is the emphatic witness putting on an act to deceive me, or is he speaking from the fullness of his heart, knowing that he is right? Is he likely to be more truthful if he looks me straight in the face than if he casts his eyes on the ground, perhaps from shyness or a natural timidity? For my part I rely on these considerations as little as I can help. (MacKenna 1974, p. 10.)

Similar views have been expressed in their writings by judges as diverse as Sheriff Marcus Stone (1988, p. 80), Judge Leon (alias Henry Cecil) (Cecil 1975, pp. 179–80), and Lord Devlin (1979, p. 63).

Psychologists would undoubtedly agree with those judges who doubt whether it is possible to tell the truthfulness of a witness from his or her demeanour. At the risk of over-simplification, the conclusions of a large body of psychological research may be summed up as follows. In tests designed to discover how good people are at telling whether another person is lying, subjects rarely manage a success rate that is much above chance level, or what they would achieve by shutting their eyes and ears and making a guess (Ekman 1986; Köhnken 1990). This is because the signs that are frequently associated with lying—like hesitancy, blushing, and a reluctance to look the questioner in the eye—are signs, not of lying, but of stress. And if a witness is under stress, this may be either because he is lying, and finding it embarrassing and awkward to do so, or because he is finding it embarrassing and awkward to tell the truth (Ekman 1986). Sometimes surrounding circumstances may make it obvious that the embarrassment of the witness must stem from one source rather than from the other, but often—as with a child who has to give evidence about suffering an indecent assault allegedly committed by a relative, for example—the stress could as easily come from one source as the other. The most that can be said for the value of the demeanour of a witness as an indicator of the truth is that it is one factor, which must be weighed up together with everything else. It would be quite wrong to promote it to the level where we use it to accept or reject the oral testimony of a witness in the face of other weighty matters all of which point the other way. The realisation that we have overvalued demeanour evidence in the past seems to be spreading among lawyers (Wellborn 1991). As Sheriff Marcus Stone says, 'For practical reasons, and in the interests of justice, it is submitted that the status of non-verbal communication in court should be limited to colouring evidence which is assessed on some other reliable basis' (Stone 1988, p. 61). Many psychologists would not even rate it as highly as this.

In the experiments that show how hard it is to detect lying from the demeanour of the witness, the subjects have been groups of ordinary people, selected more or less at random. As juries also consist of groups of ordinary people, selected more or less at random, the claim that juries have extraordinary powers in this respect seems most implausible. And yet this claim is made, and some of those who have made it have been judges. How can anyone, let alone a judge, suggest that a jury of untrained and inexperienced lay people, who see witnesses giving evidence only two or three times in a lifetime, is better at lie detection than a judge, who sees and hears them doing so nearly every day of his professional life?

On reflection, however, the idea that juries might be better at lie detection than judges is not quite so preposterous as at first appears.

First, it is questionable how much better judges really get at detecting lies as a result of practice. To begin with, the sort of practice they get is not the sort from which one readily learns. Judges see many witnesses giving evidence, and make many decisions about which ones are truthful and which ones are telling lies. But unlike participants in laboratory experiments they rarely have the opportunity to discover whether their assessments were correct, because they do not see the witnesses again once the case is over, and rarely hear any more about it. So their practice is of the kind which may build up their self-confidence, but which is unlikely to improve their skill. Secondly, there is reason to think that detecting lies from the demeanour of a witness is such a hit-and-miss business anyway that no one can raise his performance much above the average, even if his practice includes an objective assessment of the results (Bull 1989). On this view, the very most that a judge is likely to learn from experience about lie detection is the negative lesson that the demeanour of witnesses is an uncertain guide, of which too much notice should not be taken. This lesson, if the judge learns it, will put him or her in a slightly better position than most lay people, because studies show that lay people tend to overestimate their ability to detect other people's lies (Köhnken 1990). From experience judges will probably also learn other lessons that are helpful in lie detection, in particular, how improbable or otherwise certain stories are. They may learn, for example, that it is quite usual for children who have been sexually abused to say nothing about it until some time afterwards. We should probably conclude that judges are likely to be a bit better at detecting lies than jurors, but not so very much; and if they are better, it will not be because they acquire superior skills at reading lies from body language.

If juries are composed of individuals each a little worse at lie detection than a judge, juries do consist of 12 or 15 different people, and it may be said that this gives them an advantage over judges to the extent that two heads are better than one. This is the main reason that Lord Devlin gives for preferring them:

> I am myself convinced that the jury is the best instrument for deciding upon the credibility or reliability of a witness and so for determining the primary facts. Whether a person is telling the truth, when it has to be judged, as so often it has, simply from the demeanour of the witness and his manner of telling it, is a matter about which it is easy for a single mind to be fallible. The impression that a witness makes depends upon reception as well as transmission and may be affected by the idiosyncrasies of the receiving mind; the impression made upon a mind of 12 is more reliable (Devlin 1956, p. 140.)

Psychologists and lawyers would agree about part of this. Judges are human, and often have their irrational prejudices like the rest of us. In the last century Mr Justice Byles said he distrusted advocates who wore brown trousers (Harvey 1958, p. 34), and more recently Henry Cecil heard Mr Justice Macnaghten say, 'How can I believe either of these parties? They have admitted living together when they were not married'. (Cecil 1975, p. 67.) Within a group, there is a good chance that prejudices of this sort will be diluted and cancel one another out. There is also the related point that in Britain judges are nearly always middle-aged to elderly males, who, irrespective of their origins, are now firmly middle-class, and a jury will provide a wider range of age and recent life experience. If a tribunal is to judge the credibility of young children, for example, it is probably a good thing that some members of it are likely to be mothers and fathers with young children still at home.

However, on the idea that a group must necessarily reach a sounder decision than an individual, lawyers and psychologists part company. That a group is likely to do better than one individual who is biased or eccentric there is little doubt, but that groups will always do better than sensible and competent individuals is questionable.

The dynamics of group decision-making is a subject of great practical importance upon which psychologists have conducted a lot of research, with some rather surprising results. When experiments are conducted in which random groups of people are set to solve practical problems, one would expect them to produce bland and middle-of-the-road decisions: but instead they tend to produce decisions that are polarised towards extremes of risk or caution. The same effect has been found much less frequently when psychologists have studied real-life decision-making by groups who meet regularly for this purpose (Brown 1988, pp. 143–64). Unless we accept the extreme position that what people do in psychological experiments is bound to be different from what they do in real life, it does appear that where a group is selected at random, has never worked together before, and is set to solve a one-off problem without previous experience, it does have a tendency to plump for extreme positions. Relating this to juries, it means that they are likely to err from time to time, either by acquitting in the teeth of the evidence, or by convicting despite its virtual absence. Research in this area also suggests that where a group is required to solve a problem, the optimum size for a productive discussion leading to a rational decision is between three and six (Argyle 1989; Luft 1984)—which suggests that a jury is likely to be inefficient because of its size as well as its method of composition. All in all, the psychological research seems to back up the heretical view of one lawyer, Professor Brian Hogan, in a letter he wrote to *The Times* (3 May 1982);

> Of course trial by jury is one of our sacred cows. But, you know, if we'd long had trial by judge in criminal cases and I were now to suggest that his reasoned and professional judgment as to facts and inferences should be replaced by the blanket verdict of pretty well any 12 men and women placed in a cramped box and holed up there for days or even weeks at a time you would rightly think I had taken leave of my senses.

One of the main arguments for juries is that jurors can bring not only the common sense but also the collected life experience of a group of ordinary citizens to bear on the human problems which come before the courts. If this makes sense in run-of-the-mill cases, like shop-lifting and dangerous driving, it makes little sense in cases of child abuse. Although we know that child sexual abuse is more common than once thought, it is still unlikely that the majority—or even any—of the jury will have had practical experience of it. This leads to various unfortunate consequences. It creates a risk that jurors will disbelieve the evidence for bad reasons for example because the child did not report the offence at once (see chapter 9). It also creates a risk that they will judge the witnesses according to their stereotyped ideas of how such witnesses should behave. Police officers sometimes say—and some research confirms (Borgida et al. 1992)—that jurors think witnesses who claim to have been sexually assaulted ought to be emotional and distraught, and hence may disbelieve ones who are calm: so that, paradoxically, preparing child witnesses for court appearances may actually reduce the chance that they will be believed. Defence lawyers, for their part, often fear that juries will over-react in cases involving children, and will convict a defendant on insufficient evidence in horror at their discovery of what one human being is capable of doing to another: a fear echoed by the Court of Appeal when it spoke of the need 'to counteract any temptation on the part of the jury, albeit subconsciously, to succumb to emotional feelings about such things being done to a child' (*Bowditch, The Times*, 22 July 1991; [1991] Crim LR 831). An extreme form of this view which is heard occasionally is that little children should never be allowed to give evidence at all, so great is their emotional impact on a jury. Though intended as a criticism of children as witnesses, it is of course a damning criticism of juries if it is true. It amounts to saying, in effect, that because our tribunals of fact are so given to convicting against the evidence, crimes against the weakest members of society must be left without redress.

NOTES

1.   Section 13 of the Criminal Justice Act 1925 allows the earlier deposition
of a witness to be used in place of live evidence from the witness if he is unable
to attend the trial for various stated reasons. In *Collins* (1938) 26 Cr App R 177
the whole of the evidence consisted of such depositions, and for this reason the
conviction was quashed on appeal. In the case of *Scott* v *R* [1989] AC 1242,
however, the Privy Council departed from the traditional approach and
upheld a murder conviction which was largely based on evidence contained in
depositions.

2.   Hans Schneikert (chief prosecutor of Berlin), (1904), p. 24.

3.   This is a quotation from Lord Denning MR in *Ward* v *James* [1966] 1 QB
273. In fairness it should be pointed out that he said this in the course of a
judgment which limited the availability of jury trial, and also that he is one of
those who has spoken out in favour of altering the rules about the evidence of
children.

CHAPTER ELEVEN

The child witness: ingenious or ingenuous? A review of the psychological evidence

The rules of evidence outlined earlier have been designed in accordance with lawyers' beliefs about children's fitness to act as witnesses. In this chapter we consider the scientific validity of these assumptions in the light of modern psychological research into child development.

An English lawyer, Heydon (1984), (1) provided a neat summary of the specific reasons which were, until recently, often adduced to justify legal suspicion of children's testimony:

> First, a child's powers of observation and memory are less reliable than an adult's. Secondly, children are prone to live in a make-believe world, so that they magnify incidents which happen to them or invent them completely. Thirdly, they are also very egocentric, so that details seemingly unrelated to their own world are quickly forgotten by them. Fourthly, because of their immaturity they are very suggestible and can easily be influenced by adults and other children. One lying child may influence others to lie; anxious parents may take a child through a story again and again so that it becomes drilled in untruths. Most dangerously, a policeman taking a statement from a child may without ill will use leading questions so that the child tends to confuse what actually happened with the answer suggested implicitly by the question. A fifth danger is that children often have little notion of the duty to speak the truth, and they may fail to realise how important their evidence is in a case and how important it is for it to be accurate. Finally, children sometimes behave in a way evil beyond their years. They may consent to sexual offences against themselves and then deny consent. They may completely invent sexual offences. Some children know that the adult world regards such matters in a serious and peculiar way, and they enjoy investigating this mystery or revenging themselves by making false accusations. (Heydon 1984, p. 84.)

His catalogue of children's fallibilities echoed statements from English judgments:

> . . . small children are possibly more under the influence of third persons—sometimes their parents—than are adults, and they are apt to

allow their imaginations to run away with them and to invent untrue stories (*Dossi* (1918) 13 Cr App R 158 at 161, CCA, per Atkin J).

Children who, although old enough to understand the nature of an oath and thus competent to give sworn evidence, may yet be so young that their comprehension of events and of questions put to them, or their own powers of expression, may be imperfect (*Spencer* [1987] AC 128 per Lord Ackner).

When lawyers expressed such opinions as these, they usually did so without any reference to the views of doctors or social scientists. In fairness to lawyers, however, it must be said that the traditional legal view did accord, broadly speaking, with beliefs that have been widely held in society about children in the past (Aries 1962; De Mause 1974; Dziech and Schudson 1991; Stainton-Rogers 1992), and with what earlier generations of doctors and psychologists had to say about their abilities and characteristics as witnesses. Those lawyers who looked outside their own discipline—like Glanville Williams in *The Proof of Guilt* (1963)—found plenty of material in the writings of doctors and psychologists from the earlier years of this century to support the notion that children are highly suggestible and prone to fantasy.

The studies from the beginning of this century which support this gloomy view of the unreliability of children have now been widely criticised (see Goodman (1984)), and, as we explain below, modern psychological and medical research shows that children are much more reliable as witnesses than previously thought. However, legal thinking has not always kept apace with the evolution of the social sciences. The reasoning behind the former restrictions placed on children's evidence was out of line with modern scientific knowledge of children's intellectual capabilities and the typical behaviour patterns of child victims. 'Courts still prefer to rely on the accumulated wisdom of the past and have not absorbed or applied the fruits of modern research into child psychology' (Judge Pigot 1990).

Legal awareness of social science research now appears to be increasing in the 1990s as two recent dicta from Lord Lane illustrate:

It seems to us that Parliament, by repealing the proviso to section 38(1) [of the Children and Young Persons Act 1933, which said a court could not convict on an unsworn child's evidence without corroboration], was indicating a change of attitude by Parliament reflecting in its turn a change of attitude by the public in general to the acceptability of the evidence of young children and of increasing belief that the testimony of young children, when all precautions have been taken, may be just as reliable as that of their elders (*Z* [1990] 2 QB 355).

Is he [the judge] obliged to go further and to suggest possible reasons why the victim may be lying? . . . It was not so long ago . . . that a woman or girl who was shown to have indulged in extra-marital sexual intercourse was regarded with some degree of social disfavour, however hypocritical that view may have been. In those circumstances there was undoubtedly a possibility sometimes that she might cry 'rape' in order to protect her reputation. It seems to this court that at the present time, when social attitudes towards sexual intercourse have undergone such great changes, that this is a possibility for which, in the absence of any relevant evidence, the judge need not cater ... We do not take the view that it is a requirement that the judge should give these reasons in every case involving a sexual allegation as the appellant contends in this case (*Feltrin, The Times,* 5 December 1991).

Until recently, psychologists' theories of intellectual development like those of lawyers had also focused on the child's inabilities and weaknesses. Skolnick (1975) says of developmental research: 'by definition, these theories set up a polar opposition between child and adult nature. If the adult end of the scale is defined as logical and rational, then the child is by definition, autistic, irrational, emotional and lacking in perceptual and cognitive structures' (p. 57). In a similar vein, Donaldson et al. (1983) noted: 'Much of the research carried on in the first half of this century seems to have been curiously preoccupied with young children's incapacities'. This traditional assumption of childhood incompetence may have stemmed from a historical predisposition to regard infancy and childhood as a general period of weakness and incapacity, and to treat children almost as if they were a different species.

To some extent these beliefs were subsequently compounded by reports of developmental research from the 1950s and 1960s based on what nowadays seem rather meaningless laboratory experiments which younger children did not understand (e.g., learning lists of nonsense words), and in which predictably they demonstrated very poor performance. Later, more realistic work showed that these studies had tended to underestimate the true extent of children's mental abilities (Bronfenbrenner 1974; Donaldson 1978; 1992).

During the past 20 years, the enormous upsurge of interest in cognitive psychology and in child development (for general reviews see Flavell et al. 1993; Kail and Wicks Nelson 1993; Smith and Cowie, 1991) has permitted a reappraisal of the child's intellectual strengths. This is not to say that children are simply miniature adults: but we can say that their cognitive skills, particularly those relevant to giving evidence (e.g., perceiving and remembering people, places and events) may have been undervalued. Recent forensic research has also highlighted the ubiquitous imperfections of adult testimony, showing that mature witnesses' memories can be fragile and susceptible to the distorting influences of suggestion and misinformation (Loftus 1979; Loftus et al. 1989). In sum, the presumed gulf between the eyewitness abilities of children and adults has been seriously exaggerated.

The principal objections to children's evidence will be considered under six category headings which have been based on the scheme used by Heydon (1984) in the passage previously quoted.

(a) Children's memories are unreliable.
(b) Children are egocentric.
(c) Children are highly suggestible.

(d) Children have difficulty distinguishing fact from fantasy.
(e) Children make false allegations, particularly of sexual assault.
(f) Children do not understand the duty to tell the truth in court.

As the following discussion will demonstrate, most of the relevant psychological research bears on the question of reliability; whereas in practice, the legal concern is more commonly the child's honesty, an issue which until recently has been less fashionable as a topic for developmental research.

In the following chapter we examine the importance of interviewing skills and review the techniques currently favoured for gathering children's evidence.

(A) UNRELIABILITY

. . . a child's powers of observation and memory are less reliable than an adult's (Heydon 1984).

The development of memory

The lay person thinks of memory as a large box in which items are stored and pulled out when wanted. Unfortunately for the courts, the brain does not in fact work like a video recorder. Psychologists believe that memory is a complex network of interacting systems which operate in a reconstructive and subjective fashion. They conceptualise memory function as a three-stage process: (a) encoding—when new information is acquired and coded for retention; (b) storage—when the coded information is retained; (c) retrieval—when the stored information is accessed and brought to consciousness, usually by recognition or recall.

Using laboratory experiments it is relatively easy to demonstrate age differences in memory capacity, however, these experiments also show that children's memories can be very powerful and that developmental trends in memory performance can be reversed. For example, if children have superior knowledge of the subject-matter (e.g., chess or prehistoric monsters) they can remember more information than adults in a standard memory test (Chi and Ceci 1986). The same would be true of an eyewitnessing situation where, for example, a child who has a detailed knowledge of cars is likely to give a better vehicle description than the average adult (Davies and Robertson 1993).

One final point should be made in this general introduction, which is that in any given memory task there will be a broad range of performance even within a single age level. The ability to remember information is a function not only of memory capacity but also of prior knowledge, mnemonic techniques, contextual cues, motivation and emotional state. Consequently memory development is not simply an increase in 'the size of the memory box' and age is only one of a number of important factors to be taken into consideration when evaluating a witness's competence (Goodman and Schwartz-Kenney 1992). (For a readable introduction to the psychological research into human memory see Baddeley (1983).)

This section contains a lot of material and it is divided in the following way: the development of memory; children's memory for witnessed events;

children's memory for strangers; stress at the time of the crime; the effects of long delays on children's memory.

Children's memory for witnessed events

In the past 10 years there has been a flurry of research activity directed at the issue of children's ability to remember witnessed events. It is generally believed by researchers in this area that live experiments have superior validity to eyewitness tests based on pictures, stories or films of events. As experimental situations fail to capture the dynamics of serious offences (see Pynoos and Nader 1989), the extent to which one can generalise from data based on unrealistic laboratory-type tasks is very limited and can be potentially misleading (Flin 1991; Yuille 1988). For this reason the following discussion will be based on data derived from investigations which have attempted to be as realistic as possible. The standard experimental paradigm is to stage an incident in front of different age groups or to arrange an interaction between the child and an unfamiliar adult and then subsequently to test the children on their memory for events and their ability to identify the participants. Typical scenarios include children witnessing staged thefts (Brigham et al. 1986; King and Yuille 1987; Ochsner and Zaragoza 1988; Peters 1991) or adult arguments (Flin et al. 1992; Poole and White 1991; Saywitz and Snyder 1993) or children interacting with an unfamiliar adult (Davies et al. 1988, 1989; Farrar and Goodman 1992; Hudson, 1990; Leippe et al. 1991; Moston 1987; Price and Goodman 1990; Rudy and Goodman 1991; Saywitz and Nathanson in press; Tobey and Goodman in press) or children receiving routine medical treatment (Goodman et al. 1991; Merlin 1989; Oates and Shrimpton 1991; Ornstein et al. 1992; Saywitz et al. 1991; Steward 1989; Tucker et al. 1990). The subjects are usually unaware that there will be a subsequent interview.

The main developmental issues addressed are: children's ability to give an accurate and complete account of the events witnessed; susceptibility to leading questions, to test suggestibility, malleability, compliance; ability to describe and identify unfamiliar adults. Additionally, such studies permit an analysis of specific questioning techniques which may maximise, minimise or distort children's memory; for example, free recall ('Tell me what you saw'); general questions ('Was the man carrying anything?'), specific questions, ('Was he carrying a knife?') or leading questions, ('He was carrying the knife, wasn't he?'). The following section deals with age differences in the ability to remember events and strangers. A more detailed review of questioning techniques is presented in chapter 12.

Free recall

To date, research has shown clearly that the most salient and consistent age difference in witnessing is found when the memory test is free recall. This means that the subject is asked to recount everything he or she remembers without prompting, such as 'Describe everything you saw'. In response to this type of questioning, younger children typically report less information than older children and adults, but most significantly, the information they do recall is generally accurate (Davies et al. 1989; Dent 1991; Goodman et al. 1990,

1991b; King and Yuille 1987; Leippe et al. 1991; Poole and White 1991; Rudy and Goodman 1991).

Thus there appear to be age differences in the *quantity* of freely recalled details but not in the *quality* (accuracy). In one of the first studies of this genre (Marin et al. 1979), an interruption was staged during a testing session with each subject (five to 25 years). A male confederate entered the room and had an argument with the experimenter. Subjects were later asked to describe this incident and it was found that the youngest children could provide an accurate statement but that the older children and adults reported more information. In fact, some of the five- and six-year-olds failed to volunteer any information at all. All witnesses, and children in particular, remember more details than they spontaneously report, but young children can be prepared for interview in such a way as to increase the amount of detail in their reports (Saywitz and Snyder 1993). This seems an eminently sensible idea as children may hesitate to report peripheral observations, personal reactions or unfamiliar occurrences, which are the very details that can enhance the credibility of a child's statement.

Responding to questions

In a typical forensic context, free recall and very general questions are of limited use and interviews need to use more specific questions in order to elicit the maximum amount of information. In this type of interview, younger children do tend to respond less accurately than older children and adults (Brigham et al. 1986; Davies et al. 1989; Leippe et al. 1991), although the magnitude of any age differences may be dependent on the precise form of the question or the type of detail sought (Goodman et al. 1987; Goodman and Schwartz-Kenney 1992; King and Yuille 1987).

While most witnesses, irrespective of age, tend to remember central actions and familiar events better than peripheral information, younger children may find particular difficulty in reporting precise details of time (Friedman 1991; Tobey and Goodman in press), temporal order (Price and Goodman 1991), or estimates of distance or speed. Younger children may also have difficulty in differentiating specific episodes of a frequently repeated event (Farrar and Goodman 1992; Hudson 1990) a finding which has obvious implications for the investigation of long-term sexual abuse cases. Some studies have suggested that when child witnesses make errors they are more frequently errors of omission (not reporting something that did happen) rather than errors of commission (recounting events that did not occur). This is particularly relevant in the context of abuse allegations. Saywitz et al. (1991) found that children who had been touched by a paediatrician during a medical which included a genital examination, frequently reported that this touching had not taken place. (See also Leippe et al. 1991.)

There is little doubt that the quality of a witness's report is dependent on the communication skills of the interviewer. Any specific questioning will increase the likelihood of incorrect responses and the rate of error appears to be directly related to the complexity of the questions posed. But even with simple sentence constructions, the power of language is easily demonstrated, asking

'Did you see a knife?' is less suggestive than 'Did you see the knife?' and even small children may be responsive to the change from indefinite to definite article (Dale et al. 1978). It is well known that leading questions can be particularly hazardous and the risk of suggestibility is discussed in more detail as a separate topic at page 302.

It should be emphasised that, although there are developmental differences in recall, the youngest children can still be performing at a perfectly acceptable level and several studies have now demonstrated that three- and four-year-olds can recall witnessed events and, if carefully interviewed, they can provide valuable information (Goodman et al. 1990; Jones 1987; Ornstein et al. 1992; Poole and White 1991). Suitable interviewing techniques are considered in the final section of this chapter.

Identification: Children's memory for strangers

In the majority of sexual abuse crimes, the perpetrator will be a familiar adult (La Fontaine 1990) but Davies and Noon (1991) found that in as many as 22% of prosecuted abuse cases, the accused was unknown to the child prior to the offence. And serious cases occur, such as abductions or crimes committed on others which the child happens to see, where he or she will be required to assist the police by identifying the perpetrator. In 1989 there were allegedly 140 attempted abductions of children by motorists in the UK, an increase of 40% in five years (*Sunday Correspondent*, 18 November 1990).

Various well-known methods are used to gather identification evidence such as verbal descriptions, Photofit, Videofit, photograph albums and identification parades, and a number of studies have examined children's performance with these techniques.

Identification: Descriptions

In general, witnesses tend to remember details of the event (i.e., what happened) better than descriptive information (Cole and Loftus 1987), and this should be borne in mind when assessing a child's competence. If children are asked to give an unprompted description of a stranger, they typically give limited but accurate information and both the amount of information and the overall accuracy tend to increase with age (Davies et al. 1989; Goodman et al. 1990; Yuille et al. 1986). Facial descriptions tend to include details of hair more frequently than of other features (Davies et al. 1989; King and Yuille 1986), as the upper parts of the face are more salient than the lower.

Even adults tend to offer rather sketchy accounts of a stranger's appearance, and this makes it necessary to prompt for a fuller description. Questioning increases the amount of detail recalled but with a concomitant increase in errors: for example, colours are often poorly recalled. Younger children tend to produce proportionately more incorrect answers than older children in response to questioning about identity information (Brigham et al. 1986; Davies et al. 1989; King and Yuille 1986; Leippe et al. 1991; Yuille et al. 1986).

Children find it especially difficult to make accurate judgments of an adult's age (Ellis 1992; Saywitz et al. 1991; Tobey and Goodman in press), height and weight (Brigham et al. 1986; Goetze 1986), and may be reluctant to offer estimates (Davies et al. 1988; Dent 1982). Rudy and Goodman (1991) found that when asked the age of an actor in an experiment, 88% of four-year-olds said 'Don't know', but when given magazine photographs of men of different ages, 70% of them could point to a photograph in the correct age range. It appears that children are more willing to make relative estimates (e.g., in comparison to the interviewer's height) and these are more accurate than their absolute judgments ('What height was he?') (Davies et al. 1988). Experienced police officers regularly use this type of anchoring device with adult witnesses who can also be very poor judges of physical characteristics such as height, weight and age (Cutshall and Yuille 1989; Flin and Shepherd 1986).

There are cases where a child's descriptive information has proved crucial for the apprehension of an assailant. A ten-year-old girl who had been abducted and sexually assaulted while walking home from school in Banff was abandoned in a desolate moorland culvert where her head was smashed with a boulder until, as she told the police, 'she fell asleep' (*Glasgow Herald*, 1 October 1986). From hospital and with the help of a female detective, she was not only able to describe the man but provided precise details of an oil rig motif printed on his sweatshirt which was immediately published (*Press and Journal*, (Aberdeen) 28 June 1986). She also gave an accurate description of the vinyl on the rear seat of the man's car which proved to be the vital clue. The police were amazed by the quality of the information she supplied and her attacker (who had no previous convictions) was arrested on a North Sea oil rig within a week of the assault.

Identification: Face construction systems

Specialist forensic techniques, such as the face reconstruction systems, Photofit, Identikit and Videofit, are used to help witnesses recall a suspect's face, and children may be asked to produce a Photofit likeness, sometimes with resounding success. A nine-year-old girl who saw her baby sister (aged six months) being abducted, compiled one of the two Photofits which led to the arrest of the kidnappers (*Daily Express*, 9 May 1988). A laboratory study of children's Photofit ability (Flin et al. 1989) found clear age differences between eight-year-olds, 11-year-olds and adults, which suggested that children's Photofits should be regarded with a degree of caution. In a second study using a live event which children witnessed (Davies et al. 1989), there was no difference between the performance of eight- and 11-year-olds. Again, the general level of children's competence was not high, although there were marked individual differences and some children constructed excellent likenesses. (But here it should be emphasised that adult witnesses are not particularly good at this task, and can create composite faces which bear no resemblance whatsoever to the perpetrator (Davies 1981).)

Photographic identification

Laboratory experiments of children's ability to recognise strangers from photographs typically show that face recognition generally improves with age, although surprisingly there is a slight decline in this ability around puberty (Flin and Dziurawiec 1989). However, most studies which have staged live encounters with a stranger have shown younger and older subjects to be equally good at picking out the target's face from an array of photographs (Davies et al. 1988, 1989; Goodman et al. 1986; Marin et al. 1979; Soppe 1986; Steward 1989) although some report age differences here as well (Brigham et al. 1986; King and Yuille 1987; Leippe et al. 1991). Very young children (three years) may experience difficulty with photographic identifications, especially following a delay (Goodman et al. 1987; Goodman and Reed 1986; Peters 1987). In these experiments the target face was always shown in the array, whereas in a real investigation the criminal's face will not always be included. Studies using blank arrays (where the target face is absent) have suggested that extra care needs to be taken when younger children are asked to make an identification from photographs, because younger children are more likely to pick a face from a blank array than older subjects. The first study to include blank arrays found that 74% of eight- to 11-year-olds made a false positive identification when the target face was absent, compared with 36% of 12- to 14-year-olds (King and Yuille 1986). Peters (1987) reported a false identification rate of 71% by three- to eight-year-olds from a blank array (compared with 31% if the target face was included). This was despite explicitly instructing the children to respond 'no idea' rather than to guess. It was possible that younger children were demonstrating a social compliance effect rather than a memory deficit. Why would a large adult go to the bother of carefully laying out an array of photographs, if there was no right answer to the puzzle? Adults do not spend a great deal of time setting tasks for children for which the correct answer is 'I don't know', and the younger children may have been complying with an assumed suggestion, namely that if photographs are shown then the suspect must be present. Davies et al. (1988) attempted to overcome this problem by giving children who had witnessed a staged incident, practice with a mini array (in which the experimenter's face was present or absent), before they were asked to select the actor's face from photographs. This practice made no difference and children were still showing fairly high false alarm rates in the 'target absent' array. Error rates were higher for the seven- to eight-year-olds (87 per cent) than for nine- to 12-year-olds (53 per cent): clearly the urge to help the experimenter by selecting a face is very strong. (See also Davies et al. 1989 and Goodman et al. 1991 for reports of other techniques designed to reduce this effect.)

To put this into perspective, however, in one of the few studies of real witnesses to crimes, Cutshall and Yuille (1989) commented on the high false identification rates made by *adults* who are asked to look at photographs. Computer-based systems which show a sequence of faces rather than simultaneous display (e.g., Ellis et al. 1989) may help to reduce the frequency of these errors for both adults and children.

These studies underline the importance of understanding the demands the child perceives in any interview situation. Nevertheless, if sufficient care is taken, there is no reason why small children should not be asked to undertake photographic identificatons. In one real case described by the psychiatrist, David Jones (1987), a three-year-old who was abducted, sexually abused and abandoned in a cesspit, was able not only to make an identification but also to reject a sequence of photographs from which the suspect's face was missing, 'She studied the photographs in a matter of fact manner, then firmly stated he was not among the photographs'. When his photograph was introduced into the series, she gasped when she encountered it saying, 'He want to put me in the hole—he got a car'. Finally, when shown the 12 photographs in an array format and told that the interviewer had 'lost' the photograph of the bad man, she was reported to be exasperated and irritated and again picked out the suspect's photograph 'and held it up to emphasise it to the interviewer' (p. 678).

Identification parades

If the police have a suspect, the witness may be asked to view a live identification parade and children seem to find this task difficult. In a study by Dent and Stephenson (1979a) children (10 to 11 years) witnessed a 'workman' inspect the doors and windows in their classroom for two minutes and one week later they were asked to select the man from a live parade or a colour slide version of the parade. In the live parade, only 12% of the children correctly recognised the workman, compared with 29% from the slides. Incorrect selections were approximately equal (32%) in both formats, and their scores are similar to those of an adult group who viewed a live incident and who were also tested on live and slide parades. The poorer performance at the live parade may have been due to the stress experienced by the children. 'The majority of those who went in front of the live parade were nervous, embarrassed and even frightened. Two children were so afraid that they were unable to attempt the task at all. Children had to be coaxed to walk up and down the line at all and even then they were unwilling to look at the men.' (Dent and Stephenson 1979a, p. 199.)

Peters (1991) examined the effects of stress on children's ability to make identifications from live parades. He staged a simulated theft in front of 96 children (aged five to 10) while they were waiting alone in a room. The children were then asked to identify the culprit from photographs or from a live parade. Those who saw the parade were rated as more anxious than those who looked at photographs. Moreover, the poorest performance was found for those children who had to walk in front of the live parade which did include the target. In this condition, seven of the 12 subjects (58%) failed to identify the man: but four of these seven children later told their parents that they recognised the thief but were afraid to identify him in case 'something bad might happen or that someone would get into trouble'. Peters had also taken the trouble to film all the children as they walked down the line-up, and he found that adult subjects asked to observe these videotapes could frequently identify which man was the target by watching the child's behaviour, even though the child failed to make an identification. Certainly Peters's preliminary results would seem to endorse the need for careful intructions for children viewing live parades and the use of devices, such as screens or videotaped line-ups, to shield the child from the gaze of the parade members.

Adult witnesses do not relish the prospect of making identifications by walking down a live line-up and also find this to be stressful (Dent 1977). Some American police departments are now recording videotapes of suspects and have used these to create videotaped line-ups (Cutler et al. 1989). This technique has also been successfully used at least twice by English police forces with young child witnesses (both aged seven years) (Nottingham Constabulary 1987; *The Times*, 7 February 1990) and the new version of Code E now provides for video parades (Home Office 1991). In Scotland, the police routinely use one-way screens for identity parades, which allow the witness to view the parade without being seen by the parade members, but at present screens are only used in England by certain police forces.

As with 'mug-shot' identification, care must be taken to see the task demands from the child's perspective: literally, as the following Scottish case demonstrated. A girl aged eight years, was asked by the police to view an identification parade (which was of course behind a one-way screen) and if she saw the person she had mentioned in her statement, to indicate the number. The numbers were on cardboard squares positioned at the feet of the parade members. After viewing the parade the girl merely shook her head and said she could not give the number. A statement was taken from her at the conclusion of the parade, in accordance with normal practice, and it was at that stage discovered that she could not see any numbers. It was then realised that from her lowly position, the angle was such that she could not see the feet nor the numbers of the parade—a situation that was subsequently remedied by the introduction of a raised platform for children to view a parade through the one-way screen (Jessop 1988).

Even very young children have made identifications from parades which have been tailored to suit the needs of the child. In the case of *Maine and McRobb* in 1979, a two-year-old girl was abducted from Aberdeen market and taken to a house where she was tortured and sexually assaulted (see page 28 above). After 10 days of a major police investigation, two suspects were asked to take part in an identification parade. The police ingeniously adapted the formal line-up by seating the parade members around tables in a café-type arrangement. The child was carried into the room by her father and had therefore a clear view of the parade members. She was reported to be terrified when identifying the woman who had abducted her, but she was still able to return and confirm the identification by pointing out the suspect's chair once the room had been cleared (*Press and Journal*, (Aberdeen) 27 June 1979). For a more detailed review of children's ability to provide identification evidence see Davies (1993, in press).

Stress at the time of the crime: effects on reliability

It was customary when it was wished to retain legal testimony of any ceremony, to have it witnessed by children, who then and there were flogged with unusual severity; which it was supposed would give additional weight to any evidence of the proceedings they might afterwards furnish (Thrupp 1862).

The impact of fear and anxiety on eyewitness memory interest both lawyers and psychologists, given the violent nature of many crimes. However, experimental studies of arousal and memory in adults have not produced consistent results. Does high anxiety enhance or impair eyewitness memory? Deffenbacher (1983) reported that a majority of American criminal court judges believed that high arousal aids perception and thus enhances witness memory. Brigham found that American prosecutors shared this view, but not defence attorneys or police officers who tended to think that high arousal leads to poorer recognition memory (Brigham and Wolfskeil 1983). That lawyers generally believe people observe stressful events accurately is suggested by the fact that the English and Scottish rules of evidence make an exception to the hearsay rule in respect of 'excited utterances' (see chapter 6).

The accurate measurement of psychological stress and its effects are problematical, and there are obvious ethical constraints on laboratory studies, particularly where children are concerned. Nevertheless, there have been several investigations which have taken advantage of naturally occurring sources of stress in children's lives. Gail Goodman tested children (three to seven years) who had been scheduled for routine blood sampling (Goodman et al. 1986) or for inoculations (Goodman et al. 1987) and assessed their memory of the procedure. The children's stress levels were assessed by parents' and experimenters' ratings and there was no evidence that the more stressed children had inferior memories of the events or of the medical staff. Similar findings were reported by Goodman et al. (1991a); Ornstein et al. (1992); Tucker et al. (1990). Oates and Shrimpton (1991) found no effect of stress on the memory of children (4–12 years) who had a blood sample taken compared with a control group who interacted with a friendly stranger. A similar investigation was carried out by Peters (1987) who conducted face and voice recognition tests with children aged three to eight years after a visit to the dentist for a check-up or teeth cleaning. The level of each child's stress was based on ratings given by the dentist and parents, but there was no clear relationship between the ratings of stress and recognition accuracy.

It would be premature to conclude on the basis of these results that children's memories are not sensitive to stress; but those researchers who have reported effects of anxiety do not agree on their direction. Goodman et al. (1991b) argued that stress can have a facilitative effect on children's memory. 'Across the four studies stress was never associated with a reliable negative effect on memory. In contrast, when stress was very high and children became nearly hysterical with fear, stress was associated with enhanced memory.' (p. 145.)

This conclusion has been challenged by Peters (1991) who reported a contradictory finding from an experiment which managed to record a physiological measure of children's anxiety while they were witnessing an event during a stressful situation. A sample of 64 children (aged six to nine years) took part in the experiment which was ostensibly to study physical attributes and skills. In the first phase of the experiment, the children had their weight, blood pressure and pulse recorded, they played a card-sorting task and answered a few questions. In the second phase, their blood pressure and pulse were being recorded, when suddenly an extremely loud fire alarm began to ring in the room. (A videotape showed clearly the children's discomfort and anxiety.) At this point a stranger entered the room to deliver a message and after she left the fire alarm stopped, and each child was asked to complete the card task and then was given a memory test regarding the stranger's appearance and behaviour. (For the control group, a radio was played instead of the fire alarm.) The results showed that the children in the alarm condition were more stressed, and they performed more poorly than the control group on all the memory tests (objective questions, suggestive questions and photo identification) with the exception of the free recall test.

From this, Peters concluded that high arousal during event witnessing can at times impair the eyewitness performance of children and that 'heightened arousal never increased the recognition or recall accuracy of our subjects'. However, given the lack of a time delay in Peters's study it is not clear whether this experiment is actually measuring stress at encoding (at the time of the crime) or at test (during the recall task), because his subjects may well still have been aroused during the memory test. (Goodman (1991) raises several other methodological queries about this experiment.)

The experimental studies of stress which typically assess memory for unpleasant medical procedures vary in so many methodological aspects that it is difficult to formulate any firm predictions from their combined results (see Davies (in press) for a more detailed discussion of this problem in relation to identification evidence.) What is apparent is the lack of any simple correlation between anxiety and memory and it is likely that if there is a relationship, it is complicated by other interacting factors, such as physiology, personality, experience and context (Vandermass et al. 1993). This conclusion is strengthened by psychiatric case studies of child victims of traumatic crimes which reveal a complex pattern of reactions.

The effects of stress on child witnesses have been evaluated in a retrospective fashion by psychiatrists who have studied child victims of traumatic crimes. For example, in the Jones (1987) case of a three-year-old girl who had endured a most dreadful abduction, the child was able to give a detailed description of her experience and to identify the suspect (see pages 200 and 294 above). In a Californian mass kidnapping, 26 children (five to 14 years) were abducted with the driver of their school bus and 'buried' in an articulated lorry for 16 hours. Terr interviewed the children several months after the event and concluded: '. . . even though the children may misperceive who did it and in what order it occurred, all the incidents are remembered. There is no amnesia. In this respect, children make better witnesses than adults who often employ massive denial when traumatised.' (Terr 1986, p. 213.)

In a subsequent study, Terr (1988) interviewed 20 children several years after they had been traumatised, at the age of two or three years, typically by sexual abuse or accidents. She only used events which had been independently documented in some way. She found that traumatic events created lasting visual images and that there was a 'general accuracy of early verbal memories of trauma despite individual tendencies to add to or delete from these memories over time'. Of particular relevance to sexual abuse victims is her conclusion that 'the probability [is] that short, single events from early childhood will better be recalled in words than will extended, multiple or variable events' (p. 103), but she found that even here there are usually behavioural memories of such events which the child can demonstrate. These demonstrations 'remain quite accurate and true to the events that stimulated them' (p. 96).

The American psychiatrist Robert Pynoos has conducted a series of studies of children who witnessed horrific crimes. In the first study Pynoos and Eth (1984) interviewed over 40 children who had witnessed the murder of their mother or father and concluded, 'The dramatic nature of a parent's death causes multiple enduring effects on memory content and function. In our opinion, child witnesses to homicide remember certain details vividly.' (Pynoos and Eth 1984, p. 95.) In a later study Pynoos and Nader (1988) interviewed 10 children who had watched their mothers being raped. For some children there was evidence of memory distortions, which appear to have a protective function, insulating the child from intolerable emotion (e.g., one boy who had been next to his mother, claimed that he was in the next room). In contrast, other children were able to remember precise information about the rapists. In one case a seven-year-old whose mother was raped and murdered gave 'eye-witness testimony which was critical to the assailant's conviction' and in another family, the children aged seven and 11 years provided the police with detailed descriptions whereas their mother could only remember that the man was 'approximately six feet tall and pot-bellied'. (See also Black, Kaplan and Harris-Hendricks (1993) for a British study of children bereaved by the death of one parent at the hands of the other (usually the father)).

Pynoos and Nader (1989) studied the memories of 133 primary school children in California, who were involved in a sniper attack on the school playground. 'Scores of children were pinned under gun-fire, one child and a passer-by were killed, and 13 other children and one playground attendant were injured. Some children ran screaming across the yard trying to get out of the line of fire, some hid behind trees or trash cans, and others dropped to the ground and remained motionless. The bullets shattered windows, pierced metal doors at the far side of the school yard, and left holes in the nearby monkey bars. In several classrooms, teachers put groups of children in closets or directed them to hide under tables.' (Pynoos and Nader, p. 236.)

The children were interviewed between six and 16 weeks after the shooting and were asked to free recall what they remembered, and they were also asked to draw, dramatise, review the event in slow motion or to walk through the scene of the crime. Pynoos and Nader's major finding was that the child's proximity to the violence influenced his or her recall. For example, those children who were most exposed to the danger apparently remembered being further away from the direct line of fire than they actually were, while non-exposed children's recall was of increased proximity to the danger. Pynoos and Nader believe that for those who were seriously threatened, this effect minimises the renewal of traumatic anxiety. However, they point out that in cases of sexual molestation where the degree of the child's involvement may be a critical issue, such distortion could complicate an assessment of the child's statements.

They also found that the children's recall was not organised as a single episode, and instead was focused around memory markers which they call 'anchor points'; these included worst moments, actions of adults, sight of victims, injury or blood, hearing victims cry for help. Some children reported imagined actions such as fantasising that they had been able to rescue victims. This type of research provides a unique insight into the influence of extreme stress on children's memory and it demonstrates that while children often retain vivid memories, these may be structured in particular ways and with identifiable distortions; such effects serving to protect the child's fragile emotional state. Interviewers need to be aware that memories of traumatic events can be stored as verbal, visual or behavioural representations which may require non-verbal interviewing techniques (e.g., drawing, demonstrating) in order to facilitate their retrieval from the child's memory.

These investigations suggest that although memory distortions and losses can occur, child victims (even as young as three years) do appear to retain accurate and, sometimes, surprisingly detailed memories of central events and characters even many months after a traumatic crime. The same seems to be true for adults; Cutshall and Yuille's (1989) study of witnesses to violent crimes found that 'stress does not necessarily impair performance'.

In summary, the effects of stress on eyewitnesses' memory are complex and idiosyncratic. However, there is now increasing scientific evidence to suggest that if skilfully interviewed, children do remember a significant amount of information about traumatic events. Furthermore, there is no reason to suppose that their reactions to stress are essentially different to those of adult witnesses.

The effects of stress on children's ability to retrieve memories during testimony are discussed in chapter 13.

The effects of long delays on children's memory

Children frequently have to wait many months between observing or experiencing a crime and being asked to recall the details of the events in court. From a sample of over 200 child witnesses in Aberdeeen, the average delay between the witnessed incident and the trial was six months (Flin et al. 1988); in a sample of 1,800 child witnesses in Glasgow the average time was seven months (Flin et al. 1993); and Davies and Noon (1991) reported that 154 children waited on average for 10½ months to give evidence by live link in England. How do such delays affect a child's ability to remember the perpetrator and the events that occurred? Are children's memories disproportionately affected by delay in comparison with their elders? These are important issues, because if children do forget information more quickly than adults it is essential to ensure that their statements are recorded, or that their evidence is tested, as soon as possible following the alleged crime.

Both adults' and children's memories are highly sensitive to the passage of time. Although some knowledge and experiences are stored for decades, a great deal of information is lost or becomes inaccessible due to decay or interference (Baddeley 1983). Dent and Stephenson (1979a) tested 10- and 11-year-olds' memory of a film of a theft and found that after a delay of up to two months, although the level of accuracy was maintained, the overall amount of information recalled was diminished. Hudson and Fivush (1991) found that while a long delay reduced the amount of information recalled, 11-year-olds could still remember details of a museum trip which they had made six years previously.

Studies of three- and six-year-olds (Goodman et al. 1987; Ornstein et al. 1992; Peters 1987) show surprisingly good memory for events and for strangers after several weeks, although three- and four-year-olds remembered less following the delay. Psychiatric case studies of children involved in traumatic incidents show that even pre-school children can retain accurate memories of these events for a very long time, although memory for detail is not always preserved (Jones 1987; Terr 1988). Gail Goodman has retested some of the children who participated in her eyewitness experiments following delays of one year (Goodman et al. 1991b) and four years (Goodman et al. 1990). Not surprisingly, children do show significant memory loss after these intervals, although there does not seem to be an increase in the amount of incorrect information recalled. Her results indicated that suggestive questioning may be especially problematical after long delays. These unique experiments, although small scale at this stage, are important because sexual-abuse victims sometimes wait for months or years before they decide to report the offences. Thus there appears to be little doubt that while children can retain long-term memories of witnessed events these will be sensitive to the passage of time.

Judges are well aware of the importance of taking statements at the earliest opportunity from witnesses, especially when the witness is a child. Lord Denning said: 'If we are to obtain truth and justice, the sooner the child's statement is taken the better. I have tried many cases and have always found that a statement made to the police immediately after an incident is more likely to be true than a statement made weeks or months later.' (HL Deb. vol. 185, col. 158, 17 November 1987).

The Pigot Committee (1989) concurred with his view, stating, 'Evidence which we received from practitioners, psychiatrists, social workers and the police suggested that if an interview takes place shortly after the child's first allegation or disclosure it will usually provide the freshest account least tainted by subsequent discussions and questioning' (2.16).

It is clear that memories fade with time: but are children's memories less robust than adults? Lawyers generally assume that children's memories fade faster than those of adults. 'It is now widely accepted that children, including very young children, can be as reliable in their recollections of events as adults. However, it also seems to be generally accepted that a child's capacity for recall, especially on points of detail, may deteriorate more rapidly over time than would that of an adult. This seems to be particularly the case with young children.' (Scottish Law Commission 1990, p. 3.) There is not, in fact, an abundance of psychological research on age differences in forgetting rates over very long delays. Goodman and Helgeson, in a review of children's testimony said cautiously: 'The fact that children may not testify until months or years after the assault increases the chances that they will have forgotten part of what occurred. We do not know whether children's memories fade more quickly than adults' memories but if so, children will be at a relative disadvantage.' (Goodman and Helgesen 1985, p. 203.)

The received view from developmental psychology has traditionally been that there are no age differences in forgetting rates and therefore this factor was not responsible for observed differences in children's and adults' memory capacity. This consensus has recently been challenged by Brainerd who argues (on the basis of laboratory studies) that forgetting rates are not developmentally invariant and that younger children do forget information faster than older children (Howe and Brainerd 1989). Unfortunately few of the more realistic tests of children's eyewitnessing ability have included adults as well as children. One reason for this is the difficulty in designing and staging an incident that is both convincing for adults and comprehensible for children. Yet unless children and adults view the event under identical conditions, it is impossible to ensure that the context for encoding the event or the information content is identical across all subjects. Flin et al. (1992) tested children's (six and nine years) and adults' memories for a staged argument between two actors either the following day and/or after a five month delay. Their results showed that there was a significant reduction after five months in the accuracy scores of the six-year-olds and nine-year-olds, but no apparent reduction in the scores for the adults. Furthermore, the six-year-olds' performance levels had fallen significantly more than the nine-year-olds. Only the nine-year-old group gave more inaccurate responses following the five month delay. Poole (1992) has recently reported that children's (six to ten years) memories of a staged argument were disproportionately affected compared with adults' memories when interviewed after a two year delay. These two sets of results are consistent and provide empirical support for the special importance of videorecording children's evidence as soon as possible after an offence is alleged. There is also psychological evidence which suggests that the initial interview (if skilfully conducted) will help the witness to consolidate his or her memory and this may help to inoculate it against ravages of time (Brainerd and Ornstein 1991).

From this discussion it should be plain that the ability of children to remember accurately is a complex matter about which it is misleading to generalise. However, we think it is safe to say two things. First, the reliability of children's evidence depends crucially on how they are questioned. Secondly, if this has been done properly, there is no reason why their evidence should not be regarded as competent and evaluated by the court like that of any other witness.

(B) EGOCENTRICITY

In addition to the suspicion that children's memories are poorer or less reliable than adults', a second doubt is sometimes voiced about their competence, namely that children are egocentric.

This criticism appears in two guises: (a) egocentricity as a moral weakness, as a lack of concern for the impact of one's actions (e.g., lying) on others; and

link ToM

(b) egocentricity as a cognitive weakness, an inability to appreciate another person's point of view, and a selective memory for information that has personal significance.

(a) 'They [children] are egocentric, and only slowly learn the duty of speaking the truth.'

Thus wrote Glanville Williams (1963, p. 178) when outlining the rationale for treating children's evidence with caution. He cited Gorphe (1927) in support, who in turn referred to a catalogue of research on children from the beginning of the 20th century, most of which is now regarded as scientifically flawed (see Goodman 1984).

However, there is evidence that very small children's emotional frame of reference is egocentric and that their interpretation of cause and effect is primarily self-centred. Garbarino and Stott (1989) suggest that 'the ability to make simple but reasonable inferences about what other people feel, intend and think develops somewhat later, generally between four and five' (p. 50). Obviously an appreciation of this developmental trend should be taken into account when interviewing pre-school children or when interpreting their statements, but whether this kind of egocentrism has any effect on veracity is far from clear. The question of children's honesty and their understanding of the 'duty to tell the truth' are discussed in later sections of this chapter.

(b) 'They are also very egocentric, so that details seemingly unrelated to their own world are quickly forgotten by them' (Heydon 1984).

In the second sense, egocentricity is used to define a cognitive deficit in the sense that children show a failure to remember details that do not directly interest them. This is certainly true—children do pay more attention to events or details that hold personal significance. However, so do adults, and there is no evidence for a developmental difference. Perception and memory are highly subjective processes and each individual retains a unique memory of the world. What is central and what is peripheral in any given situation are entirely in the eye of the beholder, irrespective of the beholder's age. As Donaldson, a developmental psychologist, says, 'We are all egocentric through the whole of our lives in some situations and very well able to decentre on others' (Donaldson 1978, p. 25. See also Cox (1991) for a robust challenge to the criticism that children are egocentric). Finally, Glasgow et al. (1993), discussing this issue, make the pertinent observation that the real danger of egocentrism may be the egocentricity of the adult who is unable to appreciate fully the child's perspective in an interview or in child protection work.

(C) SUGGESTIBILITY

. . . because of their immaturity they are very suggestible and can easily be influenced both by adults and other children. One lying child may influence others to lie; anxious parents may take a child through a story again and again so that it becomes drilled in untruths. Most dangerously, a policeman taking a statement from a child may without ill will use leading questions so that the child tends to confuse what actually happened with the answer suggested implicitly by the question. (Heydon 1984.)

Lawyers seem to believe that children are particularly suggestible witnesses, in the sense that their testimony can easily become distorted by leading questions or by misinformation introduced deliberately or unwittingly during an interview. This argument has been frequently used as a further caution against relying on children's evidence. Lord Paget, an English lawyer said, 'Children do not speak the truth naturally. In the normal way children live so much in the world of their imagination. Another point is the tremendous and emotional suggestibility of children.' (Debate on the Criminal Justice Bill, House of Lords, 22 October 1987.)

These attitudes are derived from cultural and legal mythology, but in modern times lawyers may also have been influenced by early psychological research which concluded that children were highly suggestible and therefore should be regarded as the most dangerous category of witnesses In 1911, the Belgian psychologist Varendonck asked 'When are we going to give up, in all civilised nations, listening to children in courts of law?' (See Goodman 1984 for a historical review.) These early experimental studies rarely used adults as a control group against which to measure children's performance. Whilst there is no doubt that children can be influenced by suggestion, it must be emphasised that adults too are notoriously susceptible to suggestive and leading questions (Gudjonsson 1992; Loftus et al. 1989).

The fundamental questions to be considered are two:

(a)   Are children suggestible? That is, are their reports of witnessed events likely to be influenced or distorted by suggestive or leading questions, and if so, under what conditions is this most likely to occur?
(b)   Are child witnesses more or less suggestible than adult witnesses?

The question of children's suggestibility has attracted a significant degree of attention from psychologists and several detailed reviews of this literature are available (Baxter 1990; Ceci and Bruck 1993a; Doris 1991). The most useful research studies are those which have examined the influence of suggestive questioning when children are asked to give an account of a real event which they have witnessed. While attempts to measure children's susceptibility to suggestion when being questioned on their memory for a story or pictures may have theoretical value, these laboratory experiments represent too few of the relevant characteristics to be of real forensic significance. There are, however, more realistic investigations, but these have predictably shown mixed effects indicating that children (five years) are no more susceptible to leading questions than adults (Marin et al. 1979) or that younger children (three to six years) can be more easily misled than adults (Ceci et al., in press; Goodman and Reed 1986; King and Yuille 1987). Ceci and Bruck (1993a) argue that there is more evidence to support the view that young children are particularly susceptible to leading questions and suggestive interviewing. The explanation for the discrepant results is that children (like adults) are more likely to be influenced by leading questions in some circumstances than in others. For example, we know that children are less suggestible when the information concerns unambiguous events and central rather than peripheral information (Goodman and Reed, 1986), but here it must be emphasised that central and peripheral should be defined in terms of the *child's* perception of the events and not the adult's (King and Yuille 1987); the child's view of a given situation may be different from an adult's, both from a psychological perspective and a purely physical one—as with the little girl who could not see the numbers at an identity parade.

We also know that children are more influenced by leading questions: (a) when being asked about descriptions of people or things, rather than events; (b) when they are pressed to provide additional details; (c) when they do not have a good memory of the information in question; (d) after a long delay; (e) when the interview is stressful, and (f) when the interviewer lacks appropriate skills (Dent 1991).

Dent (1982) gives an excellent example of the effect of constant probing for details, when S.K., a police officer (in an experiment) was interviewing a child about a woman's appearance:

S.K.: Wearing a poncho and cap?
Child: I think it was a cap.
S.K.: What sort of cap was it? Was it like a beret, or was it a peaked cap, or—?
Child: No, it had sort of, it was flared with a little piece coming out (demonstrates with hands). It was flared with a sort of button thing in the middle.
S.K.: What—sort of—like that—was it a peak like that, that sort of thing?
Child: Ye-es.
S.K.: Like a sort of orange segment thing, like that, do you mean?
Child: Yes!
S.K.: Is that right?
Child: YES.
S.K.: That's the sort of cap I'm thinking you're meaning, with a little peak out there.
Child: Yes, that's top view, yes.
S.K.: That sort of thing, is it?
Child: Yes.
S.K.: Smashing. Um—what colour?
Child: Oh! Oh—I think it was um black or brown.
S.K.: Think it was dark, shall we say?
Child: Yes—it was dark colour I think, and I didn't see her hair.

The woman was not wearing anything on her head, nor was she wearing a poncho. (Dent 1982, p. 291.)

The American psychologist Gail Goodman argues persuasively that the most important issue is not simply whether children are suggestible, but whether children are easily led when questioned about personally significant events, such as sexual abuse. She and her colleagues have conducted a series of experiments that have demonstrated clearly that children as young as four years of age can be remarkably resistant to suggestive questions when they concern potentially abusive actions (Rudy and Goodman 1991).

In one set of experiments, they assessed children's suggestibility in situations which are both personally significant and stressful, by interviewing children after they have received routine medical procedures, such as inoculation (Goodman et al. 1991a), giving a blood sample (Goodman et al. 1987, 1991b), or a full medical including a genital examination (Saywitz et al. 1991). When these children (three to eight years) are later asked questions about what took place, several suggestive questions of the type that would be asked of a suspected victim are included: Did he kiss you? She took your clothes off didn't she?; Did he ask you to keep a secret about your private parts?; How many times did he spank you? Their results suggest that even following delays of a year (Goodman et al. 1991b) children are unlikely to make false reports of abuse in response to leading questions. In fact, in her studies the children made many more errors of omission than of commission, and frequently denied they were touched or examined when these events did take place. (As discussed below, false denials of sexual abuse are nowadays regarded as more common than false accusations.)

If Goodman's experiments show that children are less likely to accede to suggestion where the events in question are significant ones in which the child is personally involved, they do not prove that this can never happen. Ceci and others conducted a similar experiment, except that the 5-year-old children were subjected not to a single questioning session, as in the earlier studies, but to a series of them. As in Goodman's studies, the children proved quite resistant to misleading questions about what had gone on at the medical examination during the initial questioning. However, 'In the fourth interview, when asked to tell what had happened to them when they visited the doctor one year previously, approximately 45% of the misled children (vs. 22% of the control children) reported that the paediatrician showed them the poster, gave them treats and read them a story. For children who were falsely told that the research assistant had given them the shot and the vaccine, 38% of their reports (vs. 10% of the control children's) were consistent with this suggestion' (Ceci and Bruck 1993b). In the same paper, Ceci and Bruck report another experiment which suggests that young children become more susceptible to questions falsely suggesting people did things if, before the occasion on which they allegedly did them, the children had been led to expect them to do them.

When attempting to devise interviewing techniques which will minimise the risk of suggestibility, it is important to distinguish between cognitive effects which involve a memory distortion and the effects of compliance which may appear to produce the same result, but are actually a 'social dominance phenomenon'. King and Yuille (1987) reported that 'on several occasions we received unprompted admissions from children that they had "gone along" with a misleading suggestion', despite evidence that the child had correctly recalled the information. In certain circumstances it appears that young children are susceptible to leading questions because the child bows to the superior social status of the adult and submissively complies with any suggestions that the interviewer appears to make. This can happen because the child is unfamiliar with the social rules of a formal interview and, in an attempt to make sense of the situation, is very sensitive to the cues given by the adult (including the adult's non-verbal behaviour). The child's aim may be to please the adult or to terminate the interview as quickly as possible, or the children may simply believe the adult has superior knowledge and therefore must be correct. In our society, children are taught that adults know best, not to contradict adults, to be polite to strangers and that it is wiser to hazard a guess rather than to admit ignorance. This powerful constellation of social rules can make children compliant in all but the most carefully conducted interviews.

Hughes and Grieve (1980) demonstrated that children (five to seven years) have a very strong propensity to answer adult questions, even if the questions are bizarre and do not permit direct answers without clarification, such as, 'Is milk bigger than water?' or 'Is red heavier than yellow?' Only one five-year-old answered 'I don't know' to these questions, the others in this age group gave direct and unqualified answers, by attempting to impose their own context on the question. In response to another question, children who had initially answered 'I don't know', subsequently gave answers when the question was repeated. Similarly, Moston (1987) found that repeated questioning reduced the number of children's (six to 10 years) correct responses and he suggests that this may partially explain why children appear to be suggestible: 'The child may well mistake a request for confirmation as an indication that their first answer was wrong and, consequently, offer a new one' (p. 77).

Recent research has attempted to pin-point the principal sources of such effects in order to minimise the risks of suggestibility and compliance. Laboratory studies have shown that if the status of the interviewer is reduced by having the child questioned by another child rather than an adult then the impact of misleading questioning is reduced (Baxter 1988; Ceci et al. 1987): an interesting observation but hardly a practicable solution. Other applied studies have analysed the styles of adult interviewers in order to identify which behaviours are likely to influence suggestibility. Dent (1990) advises the following tactics: (a) the interviewer explicitly telling the child that the interviewer does not know what occurred; (b) giving the child unambiguous and comprehensible instructions at the start of the interview; (c) explictly instructing the child to say 'I don't know' if unsure of the answer to a question; (d) to avoid repeating questions; (e) while generally avoiding leading questions, if these are necessary, knowing how and when to use them; (f) to interview the child on 'home ground' if possible (see also MacFarlane 1985).

Goodman et al. (1991b) assessed the relative influence of more or less intimidating interviewing styles with three- to seven-year-olds and found that the younger children were more resistant to suggestive questioning in the less intimidating condition (see also Tobey and Goodman in press). Providing support and giving specific permission to disagree with the interviewer or to admit not knowing the answer appear to be important factors. King and Yuille

(1987) recommend that, 'Children need to understand that the interviewer is only interested in what the child remembers and that admissions of memory failures and memory gaps are expected' (p. 32). Warren et al. (1991) found that warning subjects that questions could be 'tricky', and the instruction to answer with 'only what you really remember', increased resistance to leading questions in seven- and 12-year-olds and adults.

The likelihood that a given witness will be susceptible to suggestion is probably a function of the witness's personality characteristics and the pressure of the situation. Ceci and Bruck (1993) argue on the basis of an extensive review of the psychological research that because suggestibility is influenced by situational factors, it is essential when judging the credibility of a child's evidence to know as much as possible about the context of their initial allegations and of the ensuing investigation. 'It seems particularly important to know the circumstances under which the initial report of concern was made, how many times the child was questioned, the hypotheses of the interviewers who questioned the child, the kinds of questions the child was asked, the consistency of the child's report over a period of time. If the child's disclosure was made in a non threatening, non suggestible atmosphere, if the disclosure was not made after repeated interviews, if the adults who had access to the child prior to her testimony are not motivated to distort the child's recollections through relentless and potent suggestions and outright coaching, and if the child's original report remains highly consistent over a period of time, then the young child would be judged to be capable of providing much that is forensically relevant. The absence of any of these conditions would not in and of itself invalidate a child's testimony, but it ought to raise cautions in the mind of the court.' (p. 434). Some interviewing techniques have built-in checks which are designed to gauge the witness's resistance to leading questions (Jones and Seig 1988; Steller and Köhnken 1989; see also Gudjonsson's 1992 work on the suggestibility of defendants). It is important to remember that witnesses, both children and adults, will vary in the degree to which they are suggestible in a given interview (or identification task); and beyond the pre-school years, age *per se* is not a particularly useful predictor of suggestibility (Hedderman 1987).

In essence, the psychological research shows that children, like adults, can be suggestible but that this risk can be minimised by the use of sensitive questioning techniques in the hands of a skilled interviewer.

To what extent are lawyers aware of these findings?

Certainly American attorneys believe children to be highly suggestible witnesses (Brigham and Spier 1992; Leippe et al. 1989), and British lawyers seem to be extremely concerned with the dangers of leading questions being posed by social workers, doctors or police officers during the early stages of a criminal investigation. Paradoxically, they do not seem to be in the least bit concerned about their own use of leading questions in cross-examination and the effects this may have on the quality of a child's evidence. The characteristics of a typical interview conducted during cross-examination appear to violate all the principles of best practice, with the predicted outcome of maximising the risk of contaminating the evidence (see chapter 10).

Repressed memories—implanted memories

So far, our discussion of suggestibility in children has centred around the situation where an incident is thought to have happened, a child is questioned about it once by someone acting in good faith, and there is later concern as to whether the style of questioning may have induced the child to provide information that is false.

A related and harder question, which sometimes arises in legal proceedings, is whether it is possible for a person or persons regularly in contact with a child (or an adult) to behave in such a way as to implant a wholly false 'memory' in his or her mind. For example, if a mother continually told a child about the time the child's father had indecently exposed himself—though he had not—might the child come to believe that he had?

The issue has arisen in the USA over a series of 'repressed memory' cases, where adults claim suddenly to have remembered witnessing or being victims to criminal offences during childhood. The most famous case is from California in 1990, where one Eileen Franklin in her early thirties alleged that she had seen her father rape and murder her friend in a camper van 20 years earlier. The father was convicted on her evidence (Loftus et al., in press; MacLean, 1993).

Is it possible that in at least some of these cases the witness, far from remembering a genuine incident, regurgitated a false memory accidentally or deliberately implanted by the activities of others—for example, during long sessions with a therapist who was convinced that the incident occurred? Some people think so, and in the USA a False Memory Syndrome Foundation has been set up to publicise the issue. This group represents parents who claim that their children (often as adults) have made false allegations of sexual abuse against them, and some eminent American psychologists have added their names to its 'Scientific and Professional Advisory Board'. A similar organisation called Adult Children Accusing Parents has apparently been established in Britain (*Sunday Times*, 20 June 1993).

At present, psychologists and mental health professionals disagree about how likely it is that such 'repressed memories' are genuine. On the one hand, there is ample evidence that memory is a constructive process which can be subject to influence and distortion, even to the extent of wholly false memories occasionally being implanted (Loftus 1993). On page 305 we described the experiments in which Ceci and Bruck, by repeatedly questioning young children in a misleading manner, caused them to make serious errors about what had taken place at a medical examination. The Swiss psychologist, Piaget, tells how he grew up with a vivid memory of an attempt to abduct him as a child from his pram: which years later he discovered to be false when the nursemaid who had supposedly saved him from abduction returned the watch which Piaget's parents had given her as a reward, confessing that she had made the incident up (Piaget 1965). On the other hand, it is also true that cases of total or partial amnesia following traumatic events such as sexual abuse are well documented (Briere and Conte, 1993). Thus on the face of it, 'repressed memories' for events long ago—and even ancient memories not said to have been repressed—could be true or could be false, irrespective of the honesty of the witness, and the courts that must decide whether they are true or not are in a difficult position. To tackle the job sensibly they need to know whether any event taking place between the 'incident' and the recollection—certain types of psychotherapy, for example—might have affected the recollection. If there is some corroborating evidence dating from the time of the alleged event, of course, their task is considerably easier.

In response to increasing claims and counter-claims, the American Psychological Association has now formed a special working group to review and evaluate the literature on recovering repressed memories of childhood abuse (APA Monitor, May 1993) (5).

Meanwhile, the courts in England have reacted unfavourably to attempts to litigate about allegations of child abuse that are many years old. Attempts to prosecute have been sometimes halted as an 'abuse of process' (*R v Telford JJ, ex parte Badham* [1991] 2 QB 78), and the House of Lords has blocked attempts to sue civilly by a strict interpretation of the Limitation Act 1980 (*Stubbings v Webb* [1993] AC 498).

(D) INABILITY TO DISTINGUISH FACT FROM FANTASY

Children are prone to live in a make-believe world, so that they magnify incidents which happen to them or invent them completely (Heydon 1984).

Over the years it has been found that children can invent or imagine things that in fact may not have happened at all (Judge Pickles, BBC 'Panorama', 8 September 1986).

This section examines the question of fantasy from three angles: witchcraft; ritualistic satanic and cult abuse allegations; children's imagination.

Witchcraft

Legal concern about children fantasising probably stems in part from the fantastic evidence given by some children in the witchcraft trials of the 16th and 17th centuries. In his *Encyclopedia of Witchcraft and Demonology* Robbins (1959) writes:

During the centuries of witch hunting, hundreds of people were sent to their death because of the wanton mischief of undisciplined youngsters. England was especially afflicted with such little monsters, and American children copied their antics (p. 94; see also Seth 1969).

In 1989, the Salem witch trials were still being cited as a caution to those who would unquestioningly accept children's complaints of sexual abuse (*R v Norfolk County Council Social Services Department, ex parte M* [1989] QB 619).

It is true that there were some cases where people were convicted of witchcraft mainly or exclusively on the testimony of children. In the trials at Salem, Massachusetts in 1692, which resulted in 20 people being hanged for witchcraft, key prosecution evidence was given by children (see Boyer and Nissenbaum 1977). In Scotland, seven people were executed for witchcraft in 1697, largely upon the testimony of one girl about 11 years old (6 St Tr 656 n). Similar events occurred in England, such as the trial at Leicester in 1619 where nine women were tried for witchcraft and hanged on the testimony of a single child. 'The King on a visit to the town a month after the trial personally examining the boy, discovered and exposed the imposture, but too late to save the unfortunate victims' (Foss 1870, p. 748).

However, when we look at these particular cases we need to remember two things: first that they took place in a society where nearly everyone from the King down believed in witchcraft, thought it common, and believed that it posed a serious social danger; and secondly, that the cases involving children as the main accusers were only a small part of a very much larger whole.

The fact that almost everyone then believed in witchcraft does not make the children's evidence less untrue, of course, but it does make some of it rather less fantastic. If some of the evidence that children gave in those cases seems bizarre to us, it was often only what everyone at the time said and believed happened. The children were retailing what was common rumour and gossip, rather than demonstrating that children have superbly fertile imaginations.

Furthermore, where really bizarre evidence was given in these cases it did not come exclusively from children. At the Bury St Edmunds trial in 1665, where two widows were found guilty and hanged for bewitching a number of children, the evidence came not from the children but from their parents, one of whom described his children's afflictions thus:

> At other times they would fall into swoonings, and upon the recovery of their speech they would cough extremely, and bring up much phlegm, and with the same crooked pins, and one time a twopenny nail with a very broad head, which pins (amounting to 40 or more) together with the twopenny nail were produced in court, with the affirmation of the said deponent, that he was present when the said nail was vomited up, and also most of the pins (*Cullender* (1665) 6 St Tr 687, 692).

As to the part that was played by children's accusations, Macfarlane's classic study of witchcraft prosecutions in Essex shows that it was comparatively small. 'Not only do the pamphlets, and witness' names on the indictments, show that the majority of cases were tried without child witnesses, but it also seems apparent that such witnesses were only brought in to give added proof. They did not start suspicions, but were persuaded to give testimony' (Macfarlane 1979, p. 170).

Where children did give evidence against alleged witches, furthermore, they were often far from the 'little monsters' described by Robbins (1959): they had often been dragged into the proceedings unwillingly, and gave their evidence after long interrogations and under pressure. A number of sixteenth and seventeenth century treatises on witchcraft stress the importance of interrogating young children, in order to get evidence in cases where—as usual—anything in the nature of solid evidence was lacking. A typical passage is found in Jean Bodin's treatise of 1593. After describing the usual gruesome methods used in France to make a 'witch' confess, he said that if these fail

> . . . it is necessary to take the witches' little daughters. For it is very often found to be the case that they have been instructed by their mothers, and taken to the sabbaths: and at their tender age it is easy by promises of immunity to persuade and re-educate them away from the things that their age and the instruction of their mothers will have led them into. Then they will provide the names of the people involved, the times and places of the meetings, and what went on there (Bodin 1593, p. 319).

To what extent did those who gave evidence in witchcraft prosecutions do so with the conscious intention to deceive? There were certainly cases where the accusation began because a child (or an adult) told deliberate lies to get another into trouble, or to get himself out of it. Thus the Lancashire witch trial of 1634 began because a boy invented 'a fantastic story, to save himself a whipping for playing truant instead of bringing home his father's cattle' (Thomas 1971, p. 645). But modern scholars like Keith Thomas (1971) and Alan Macfarlane (1970), who have taken into account the work of anthropologists among primitive people, suggest that many of the accusations were made in good faith. The typical evidence that started a prosecution for witchcraft would usually consist of three things: first, that the defendant was 'by common fame' a witch, secondly, that she (or sometimes he) had made some threat or curse against the 'victim' or his family, and thirdly, that some misfortune had then befallen them. Whether the witness was a child or an adult, the whole of such evidence might well have been true, and given in good faith. This might even have been partly so in Salem: it has been suggested that some of the witchcraft allegations might have been the result not of childish fantasy or malice, but of ergotism—poisoning by a fungus which contaminates rye and makes those who eat it suffer hallucinations (Goodman 1984). In other words, many of the witnesses were probably describing what were to them real events, which they explained in the terms in which they understood them. Where this was so, the falsity lay not in the facts to which the witnesses deposed, but in the deductions they and others then drew from them: the investigators, who then proceeded to question the 'witches' in order to get confessions out of them—using torture routinely and openly in Scotland where, as in the rest of Europe, it was legally permitted (Larner 1981) (and in England where it was supposedly forbidden, quietly and on the side)—and the courts, which thought that rumour plus curse plus misfortune proved the witch to be guilty. Furthermore, as almost everyone believed in witchcraft, and in the effectiveness of curses, is likely that at least some of the 'witches' were 'guilty', to the extent that they had been trying to do what people said they had been doing.

Before leaving the subject of witchcraft accusations, it is also worth pointing out that children were often themselves the victims of the belief. Although most witches were the ugly old women of the stereotype, witchcraft allegations were made against all kinds of people, including sometimes children. In the witch-hunt in Mora, Sweden, fifteen children were executed, and several dozen more were sentenced to public beatings (Horneck 1682). Children were accused in Britain, too. Macfarlane gives a case from Northampton that involved a boy of nine (Macfarlane 1970, p. 162)—though British child-witches do not seem to have been dealt with so severely. Children also became the indirect victims of the belief in various ways. They were sometimes used to get evidence against their parents. The most hideous example is the case of Alison Balfour of Orkney in 1594, whose whole family, including a little girl of seven, was tortured before her eyes 'to this efect that hir husband and bairnis beant swa tormentit besyde her mycht move hir to mak ony confessioun for their relief' (Pitcairn 1833 vol. 1, pp. 375–7). Children sometimes suffered in another way. On the Continent (and to some extent in Britain) it came to be widely believed that people became witches by making a pact with the Devil (Cohn 1975), the pact being sealed by sexual intercourse with the Devil in human form: as a male *incubus* to service his female apostles, and as a female *succubus* to seduce his male ones. From time to time, children who had been sexually abused found themselves diagnosed as having had intercourse with the Devil—and hence of course as witches. The sixteenth-century French inquisitor Nicholas Remy gives a striking example involving a child who was already being held on suspicion of witchcraft. After saying that the Devil tries every means of intimidating those of this servants whom he fears are likely to confess, Remy adds:

> Thus, although Catharina Latomia of Manche, at Haraucourt, February 1587, was not yet of an age to suffer a man, [the Devil] twice raped her in prison, being moved with hatred for her because he saw that she intended to confess her crime; and she very nearly died from the injuries she received by that coition (Remy 1595, p. 166).

A recent examination of the concepts of evil, witchcraft and sexual abuse in England can be found in La Fontaine (1992).

Ritualistic, satanic and cult abuse allegations
The issue of fantasy is sometimes raised in connection with allegations of 'ritualistic', 'satanistic' or 'cult' abuse. Children have sometimes said—or are said to have said—that they have been abused in ways which are 'at the very reaches of human imagination' (Jones 1991). Their accounts include perverse or sadistic sexuality, with objects inserted into vagina, anus or penis, and smearing, or swallowing urine, excrement or blood; multiple abuse by whole groups of people; and allegations that the children, or their abusers, dressed up in 'robes' or other unusual clothes. Even more extraordinary allegations are sometimes made of animals, and sometimes even babies or children, being sacrificed, or tortured. And in some cases it is said that all these elements were blended into some kind of ritual, associated apparently with a religious belief—usually devil-worship (2).

In the United States, and to a lesser extent in Britain, such claims have given rise to acute controversy. For some, the fact that these accounts are so bizarre and horrible proves that they are true: how could children ever invent such terrible things? For others, they are obviously false, and the fact that children give them merely proves once and for all that children should never be believed. This is a murky area, where—despite the fact that many people claim to speak with authority—there is really little in the way of solid information. In this book, all we can do is briefly review some of the things that are and are not established (3).

First, as to group involvement, there is no doubt that 'child sex rings' do indeed exist. 'Adults can and do organize themselves into conspiratorial networks to pursue the abuse of children and young people for sexual gratification, and to avoid detection' (Directors of Social Work in Scotland 1992, para. 5.1.3). Such rings have given rise to a number of successful prosecutions. (For a graphic example, see 'Operation Hedgerow' which resulted in four men—one of whom was a barrister—receiving a total of 34 years imprisonment; *The Independent*, 4 February 1989.)

Secondly, if the allegations seem improbable, it should be borne in mind that there seems to be no conduct so bizarre and unspeakable that some abnormal person has not derived sexual pleasure from it. One leading case on the criminal law involves a group of sado-masochistic homosexuals who, with everyone consenting, inflicted genital torture on one another—practices which came to light when they made a videotape of their sessions which fell into the hands of the police (*Brown* [1993] 2 WLR 556)—and another leading case involves a man who forced his wife to commit bestiality with an alsatian dog (*Bourne* (1952) 36 Cr App R 125). Several years ago a Welsh Methodist minister was jailed for mutilating the corpses of his dead parishioners by cutting off their genitals (*Owen, The Times*, 27 March 1985), and the first author remembers when a Dorset farm labourer was once jailed for wandering the countryside at full moon, sexually mutilating cows. More recently, a series of bizarre mutilations of horses in Hampshire and Dorset has featured in the national press (*The Independent*, 13 August 1992). Other strange perversions which are well-documented, if comparatively rare, include eating excrement, necrophilia, and obtaining sexual pleasure from the sensation of being suffocated or hanged.

Thirdly there are also well-attested cases of people sexually abusing children in sadistic ways. The Scottish case of *Maine and McRobb* is described elsewhere in this book (see page 128). Worse, there are some well-documented cases of people abducting children and actually torturing them to death for the sadistic pleasure it gave them. The historical archetype is of Gilles de Rais (1404–1440), the French nobleman, who, with some associates, confessed to, and was executed for abducting and sadistically murdering a large number of children. Estimates of the number of his victims range from several dozens to an astonishing 800, and he is said to be the origin of the story of Bluebeard (Berents 1982; Bossard and De Maulde 1886). Nobody really knows if Gilles de Rais was guilty, and there is a school of thought that he was framed (Hernandez 1921): but in modern times the Moors murderers are a hideous example, the details of whose crimes, unlike those of Gilles de Rais, are not obscured by historical doubt and controversy (Goodman 1973)).

Fourthly, some people who have sexually abused children have behaved in ways which could have been interpreted as involving 'rituals', although in fact there were no real overtones of satanism, magic or religion. A much-publicised case in 1979 involved a peer of the realm, whose antics with teenage girls included dressing up in his coronet and robes, taking indecent photographs, and telling them stories about ghosts in other parts of the house to frighten them into joining him in his bedroom (*Lord Falkland, Daily Telegraph*, 5 June 1979). In another case, a man (who was incidentally a minister) used 'magic' in the form of conjuring tricks to lure a girl of five to the place where he then raped her (*Scottish Daily Record*, 27 November 1990).

Fifthly, there have been some cases where British courts have been told that the sexual abuse of children was coupled with various 'black magic' antics, and in some of them the courts seem to have accepted these actually happened. In 1991, the Official Solicitor's office announced that allegations of this sort had been made in some 48 cases in which he had been involved, in four of which the judge had eventually accepted that the abuse was of a ritualistic nature (*Social Work Today*, 27 September 1991). In one case, for example, a High Court judge was persuaded that the sexual abuse of the children had been accompanied by the ritual slaughter of a sheep, the blood of which was drunk, and also by the communal drinking of blood taken from the wrist of the children (*In Re F(Minors) (Police Investigation)* [1989] Fam 18). In some other reported wardship cases, however, the 'ritualistic' aspect of the case has been rejected by the judge (as in *Rochdale Borough Council* v *BW* [1991] FCR 705, or found to have been exaggerated (as in *Re C and L* [1991] FCR 351). 'Black magic' details have also adorned certain criminal cases. In some the defendants have pleaded guilty or been convicted (as in *Smith, The Times*, 9 November 1982; *Paul, The Times*, 26 July 1988; *Harris, The Independent*, 1 August 1990). In others, on the other hand, the bizarre details given by the children have discredited their evidence, with the result that prosecutions for sexual abuse have failed: as in the Epping Forest case in England (*The Times*, 20 November 1991), where the prosecution abandoned the case, or as in the famous *McMartin, New York Times*, 24 January 1990 case in California (see page 167 above), where the defendants were eventually acquitted.

Sixthly, if some of the bizarre details of the allegations in these cases are true, there is every reason to be sceptical of those that go as far as murder and human sacrifice. Although the police in Britain and the USA have taken some of these allegations very seriously, they have failed to come up with either evidence of missing children who match the sacrificial victims, or forensic evidence of any such murders (Jones 1991; Lanning 1991). (That said, there are well attested cases of disturbed persons killing children, sometimes horribly, because they believe them to be possessed by the Devil. A Dutch newspaper describes a recent case in Holland where parents, who had been dabbling in the occult, became convinced that their 10-week-old baby was possessed by the Devil—so they burnt him to death with petrol and methylated spirits, using the lavatory pan as a crucible: *De Volkskrant*, 1 February 1989.)

Furthermore, there seems even more reason to doubt the theory, fervently believed in by some people in the USA, and to some extent in Britain, that behind the 'ritual' abuse of children lies a sinister national (or even international) conspiracy of 'satanists' (Bromley 1991) who are preying on children. It is true that some occult writers have written approvingly of bizarre rituals, including sacrifice of children. The best-known example is the satanist Aleister Crowley, in whose 436-page 'Magick in Theory and in Practice' there is a chapter entitled 'Of the Bloody Sacrifice', which talks of using the blood of the participants in the ritual, and also contains the memorable lines:

> A male child of perfect innocence and high intelligence is the most satisfactory and suitable victim. [Note: It appears from the magical records of Frater Perdurabo that he made this particular sacrifice about 150 times every year betwen 1912 and 1928]. (Crowley 1929)

It is also true that some notable child murderers and child molesters have had, or are alleged to have had, an interest in the occult: Gilles de Rais, for example, is said to have acquired his taste for killing children from sacrificing them to the devil whilst trying to practice alchemy (Bossard and De Maulde 1886), and Paisnel, the 'Jersey Monster', a multiple child rapist, was both a dabbler in black magic and an admirer of Gilles de Rais (Paisnel 1972). It is also true that there are in existence various satan worship cults, some of which hold meetings at which unsavoury rituals take place. But nobody has produced any solid evidence whatever that links these groups with child abuse, let alone a national or world-wide conspiracy to organise it (Bromley 1991). Nor do those people who, in Britain at least, have been found guilty of acts of 'ritual' abuse, seem the sort of people who would be capable of helping organise some massive conspiracy.

There is something else which should make us sceptical of any far-reaching conspiracy to sacrifice children, eat foetuses and hold unbridled sexual orgies. It is that over the centuries, in times of moral panic, allegations of just this sort have been made against one suspect group or another, from the early Christians onwards (and possibly before) (Zacharias 1969, Cohn 1975). People see this sort of bizarre behaviour as the very embodiment of evil: and hence a natural accusation with which to make the point that someone else is evil. This does not mean that such behaviour can never happen. Some disturbed and rebellious individuals may be attracted to this sort of thing, just because it is perceived to be so evil. But it does make any kind of large-scale conspiracy to do it seem less likely.

In conclusion it looks as if the 'ritual' abuse of children—in the sense of sexual abuse accompanied by elements of black magic, witchcraft, or devil worship—does occasionally happen; but that it is small-scale, and the work of idiosyncratic individuals, or groups of individuals.

If there is doubt as to what exactly happens, even less is known about the motivation of those who do it. It may be that for some the real interest is black magic or attempted devil-worship, to which the sexual abuse is only incidental. On the other hand, it may be—as judges have said in certain cases—that sometimes the 'black magic' routines were just a callous and cynical trick to scare children into submitting to sexual acts, or to frighten them away from telling. As judge Roy Ward said to one defendant when passing sentence, 'You took the trust and affection of these girls to seduce and corrupt them. You aggravated the matter by seeking to obtain dominance of their minds by the pretence of witchcraft or black magic to continue gratifying your desires' (*Harris, The Independent,* 1 August 1990). Toth and Whalen (1987), two American prosecutors, point out that the more outrageous a child's story, the more sceptical an adult will be, and that some abusers may exploit this scepticism by deliberately including unusual features in their abuse in order to diminish the child's credibility if she or he discloses.

If the size and scale of 'ritual' abuse is only such as we have suggested here, then it follows that what some of what children have said about it—or are said to have said about it—must be false. If so, the question arises as to why such things have been alleged. Several explanations are possible (apart from the obvious one that 'all children are liars').

In the first place, it must be remembered that a lot of the most lurid accounts seem to come, not from child witnesses, but from adult 'survivors' describing what they say happened to them during childhood (see, for example, the BBC programme 'Panorama', 8 December 1992). It is interesting to know why their accounts are false or exaggerated, if they are (Mulhern 1991)—particularly the recurrent allegation about being made pregnant, and then being aborted to provide a foetus for satanic sacrifice; but this issue falls outside the scope of a book on the evidence of children. The explanation of some false and fantastic accounts which allegedly did come from children, as against adult survivors, may also be that children never gave them: their words were misinterpreted or misconstrued by therapists or investigators to fit their preconceptions of what was going on.

Where false and fantastic accounts really did come from children, various explanations are possible. In some cases, the children may indeed have been abused, but their recollections are blurred and confused because they were given alcohol or drugs, or even hypnotised (Jones 1991). Another theory is what has been called 'defensive elaboration'. 'Clinicians have noted that some children appear to cope with overwhelming, noxious past memories by elaborating upon them even further when they recall them at a future date' (Terr 1988). 'Sometimes the memories of sexually abused children and adults contain a fantastic overlay which on investigation by police is readily disproved, rendering the entire account incredible' (Jones 1991). Another theory is 'anxious elaboration', or the tendency to confuse one's fear with reality. 'For example, a 3-year-old child was able to describe in ever increasing detail the sadistic sexual abuse to which she had been exposed. As she shared this during therapy sessions, she obviously experienced an increase in anxiety. She began to talk about other things that were done to her, including "and he made all of my hair fall off". It was known that the abuser had not removed all of her hair. Did her fanciful statement negate everything that she said earlier? The answer is clearly no. As her anxiety became more severe, the child began to confuse actual experiences with threats made by the abuser. The clinical examination clearly indicated that we were dealing with a child who was highly anxious but not psychotic. She was demonstrating an anxiety-based elaboration based on experiences that were emotionally devastating' (Rosenberg 1989).

Another explanation, which some people think accounts for certain cases, is that the children were suggestively questioned, and accidentally led into giving false accounts, by investigators who believed passionately in 'ritual' abuse. (As some investigators clearly do. In a recent study, American clinical psychologists were asked if they had seen a case of 'ritualistic' abuse in the last ten years. 70% said they had seen none; the rest said they had seen one or two each—and 2% reported seeing *more than a hundred* apiece (Bottoms et al. 1991).) This in turn may be related to a phenomenon sometimes called 'social contagion': when a scare about an illness spreads among a group, and anxious parents start reporting symptoms in children who are perfectly well (Jones, in press).

If this is so, there may indeed be a parallel between 'satanic' abuse and witchcraft cases: but it is not the one that is usually made. The common element is not that children fantasise, but the damaging effect of endless questioning by investigators who are convinced that a certain thing is happening, and will not stop until they get confirmation of it.

Children's imagination
Influential child development theories, most notably those of Piaget and Freud, emphasise the role of fantasy and imagination in children's lives (see Lindsay and Johnson 1987). There is no doubt that play and make-believe are an important part of a child's development and these techniques are frequently used in therapeutic interviews (Bannister 1989). But it should be remembered that adults also fantasise and daydream. And the critical issue is not whether children engage in imaginative games, but whether they are unable to distinguish fact from fantasy in the context of a witnessed offence—as Lord Morris of Borth-y-Gest assumed when he said: 'Sometimes it may be that owing to immaturity or perhaps to lively imaginative gifts there is no true appreciation of the gulf that separates truth from falsehood' (*Director of Public Prosecutions* v *Hester* [1973] AC 296).

Relevant laboratory studies (Gordon et al. 1991; Johnson and Foley 1984; Lindsay and Johnson 1987) suggest that children do not show a general tendency to confuse what they have imagined or done with what they have perceived. They did find that children were inferior to adults at discriminating real actions they themselves had performed from their imagined actions. However, the actions which the children performed (e.g., saying a word out loud or touching their elbow) bore little resemblance to the typical events of a crime and this seriously limited the forensic applications of their conclusions, a criticism acknowledged by the researchers. The fact that children were instructed to imagine tells us little about children's spontaneous fantasies, but it may be a useful method for studying children's susceptibility to adult coaching which is considered later in this chapter. Harris et al. (1991) also found that children have a firm grasp of the distinction between fantasy and reality but reported that 4–6 year olds are not always certain that a 'witch, monster or ghost' they have been instructed to imagine cannot become real.

There is certainly no psychological research or medical case study material which suggests that children are in the habit of fantasising about the sort of incidents that might result in court proceedings: for example, observing road accidents or being indecently assaulted. Children's fantasies and play are characterised by their daily experience and personal knowledge, and unusual fantasies are seen by psychiatrists as highly suspicious: 'The cognitive and imaginative capacities of three-year-olds do not enable them to describe anal intercourse and spitting out ejaculate, for instance. Such detailed descriptions from small children, in the absence of other factors, should be seen as stemming from the reality of the past abuse rather than from the imagination' (Vizard et al. 1987, p. 24). As a rule, young children have a very limited knowledge of sexual behaviour (Gordon et al. 1990a, b; Jones and Thompson 1991; Volbert 1992) and this is further discussed in chapter 12. It has been argued however, that children may acquire sexual knowledge from watching adults having sex or from pornographic videos. Here careful interviewing is required, because there seem to be qualitative differences in descriptions of sexual behaviour derived from vicarious knowledge (Conerly, 1986; McCord, 1986). Finally, the suggestion that children are prone to magnifying incidents is not well supported by what clinicians tell us, which is that victims are more likely to under-report the amount and type of abuse, and that exaggeration is rare (Berliner and Barbieri 1984; Boat and Everson 1989; Summit 1983; Wattam 1993).

(E) FALSE ALLEGATIONS

In this section we consider three reasons often given for distrusting children's evidence: (i) children are liable to make false allegations, particularly of sexual crimes; (ii) children are more untruthful than adults; (iii) children can be coached to make fictitious complaints.

False allegations of sexual assault: malice aforethought and Freudian fantasies

> Children sometimes behave in a way evil beyond their years. They may consent to sexual offences against themselves and then deny consent. They may completely invent sexual offences. Some children know that the adult world regards such matters in a serious and peculiar way, and they enjoy investigating this mystery or revenging themselves by making false accusations. (Heydon 1984.)

Women framing innocent men with false complaints of sexual assault has been a recurrent theme in Western literature from Potiphar's wife in the Old Testament (Genesis, 39) to E.M. Forster's Adela Quested in *A Passage to India*. Over the years it has also featured in a number of legal *causes célèbres*: like the case in Hale's *Pleas of the Crown* (1736) of the man accused of a rape he could not have committed because of a rupture 'the size of the crown of a hat' (p. 636), and the case of de la Roncière in 1834 which John Fowles described in his novel *The French Lieutenant's Woman*.

The notion that most sexual complaints by women are false seems to have led to the idea that complaints of sexual offences against children are often false as well. 'There is, however, one case on which medical evidence is of some importance; namely, when a false accusation is made. In some instances, as in respect to rape upon young children, the charge may be founded on mistake; but in others there is little doubt that it is often wilfully and designedly made for motives, into which here it is unnecessary to enquire'. (Taylor 1849.) In the early 19th century it was often said that parents from poor families would falsely accuse respectable men of sexual misbehaviour with their children as a means of blackmail and extortion. This may have been connected with the fact that the deflowering of adolescent virgins was a privilege for which some rich Victorian debauchees would pay huge sums of money, and this may in turn have been connected with the earlier idea that the maidenhead of a young virgin was a cure for venereal disease (Taylor 1957, p. 74). (It was the journalist W. T. Stead's exposure of this trade that led to the age of consent being raised in 1885 to 16: see chapter 1.)

Hence, a major objection to children's evidence has been the widespread belief among lawyers that complaints of sexual assault are often bogus. Judges in criminal cases have voiced this belief when directing juries; Christmas Humphries QC once said: '. . . we who have had long experience of these cases know that the evidence of a girl giving evidence of indecency by a man is notoriously unreliable' (*Gammon* (1959) 43 Cr App R 155 at 159). Judges in civil cases were traditionally of a similar persuasion: 'When one reads the earliest judgments involving allegations of child sexual abuse in civil cases one is struck by the fact that the court dismissed them in *K* v *L* [1984] CAT 878 as "wicked lies" without ordering an investigation of their truth, or that the judge found it hard to believe that a five-year old child could have been sexually abused within the family (*Q* v *Q* [1983] CAT 401)'. (Weyland, 1989.) Barristers may also be tempted to adopt a sceptical approach: 'The experience of the courts has been, over a long period of time, that sexual allegations are very easy to make and very hard to refute and, in the case of children, there are additional dangers—of exaggeration, of outside influence, or collusion or of fantasy' (George Carman QC, BBC 'Panorama', 8 September 1986). In a recent American survey (Brigham and Speir 1992) defence attorneys said that they felt almost one fifth (18.5%) of the child witness cases they had encountered involved children's testimony that was completely inaccurate or fabricated and that in 43% of their cases it was significantly distorted or exaggerated.

This idea that rape complaints are 'easy' to make dates back to Hale (1736) and is reaffirmed in modern judgments (Lord Donaldson of Lymington MR, *Miles* v *Cain* (1989) *The Times*, 15 December 1989; Mr Justice Fennell, *Kyriakou, The Independent*, 10 November 1990). From a legal perspective such an allegation could be regarded as 'easy' because very little evidence needs to be manufactured before the story is plausible, as compared with a fictitious wounding, for example. However, it would be wrong to think that victims find sexual allegations easy to make, and the research into crimes of rape shows clearly that victims who make such complaints find the experience anything but easy (Adler 1987; Chambers and Miller 1983; Temkin 1987).

Sceptical views of the reliability of sexual allegations were also held by certain police officers (Chambers amd Miller 1983; Gorry 1986; Saunders

1987). 'Women and children complainants in sexual matters are notorious for embroidery or for complete fabrication of complaints . . . If a woman walks into a police station and complains of rape with no signs of violence, she must be closely interrogated. Allow her to make her statement to a policewoman and then drive a horse and cart through it.' (Firth 1975, p. 1507.) 'A senior policewoman working on sexual crimes recalls how the police mind has changed during her 20-year career: "The received wisdom about rape used to be: 'It's rubbish, it's always rubbish'." '(Campbell 1988, p. 95.) However, the new specialist units for dealing with sexually assaulted victims are a reflection of an important change in police attitudes regarding the credibility of sexual complainants within the last decade (Kilkerr 1989).

Lawyers' beliefs regarding the general unreliability of women's and children's sexual allegations were bolstered in the 20th century by the promulgation of Sigmund Freud's psychoanalytic theory (Wigmore 1940; Bienen 1983). Freud argued, in an elegantly structured and carefully woven thesis of child development (see Miller 1989; Strachey 1966), that during the 'phallic stage' of development (around three to five years), young children experience powerful sexual urges, characterised by sexual fantasies involving the parent of the opposite sex. (This forms the basis of what he called the Oedipus complex.) These desires are subsequently repressed and 'forgotten' during the 'latency period' (a concept which is now regarded as somewhat dubious: Bentovim and Vizard 1988), until they reappear as a mature interest in the opposite sex at puberty. Thus when Freud's patients reported memories of incestuous acts or sexual abuse during childhood, he said that these were not real physical acts but had only psychological reality, that is, they were only adult recollections of unfulfilled sexual desires from the phallic stage of childhood. With his theory there were now two reasons to dismiss sexual complaints as false, because not only were women and children prone to making malicious allegations for reasons of self-interest, but they may have simply fantasised that they were assaulted or raped because of their uncontrollable erotic desires. As Lord Diplock put it when discussing potentially unreliable testimony: 'as in the case of those alleging sexual acts committed on them by others, because experience shows the danger that fantasy may supplant or supplement genuine recollection' (*Director of Public Prosecutions* v *Hester* [1973] AC 296).

Recently Freud's psychosexual theory has been seriously criticised (Eysenck 1985; Rush 1980). It seems that Freud himself initially believed that his patients' accounts of sexual abuse in childhood were true. A detailed documentation of hitherto unpublished letters reveals his thoughts during the development and subsequent abandonment of the earlier 'seduction theory' (Masson 1984, 1985). Freud's ideas were based on extended analyses of his adult patients, who were predominantly neurotic middle or upper-class women from Viennese society. The first 18 of these patients all reported that they had been sexually abused during childhood and Freud first thought this was probably the source of their neurotic problems. 'The event of which the subject has retained an unconscious memory is a precocious experience of sexual relations with actual excitement of the genitals, resulting from sexual abuse committed by another person, and the period of life at which this fatal event takes place is earliest youth—the years up to the age of eight or ten, before the child has reached sexual maturity' (Freud 1896/1962a, p. 152). In public he stated that servants were the main perpetrators of sexual abuse, while, according to Masson, privately acknowledging, in his letters, that fathers were also responsible. 'The essential point of hysteria is that it results from perversion on the part of the seducer and more and more that heredity is seduction by the father' (Masson 1985, p. 212). Moreover, Freud's initial findings suggested that these assaults were not rare occurrences. 'It seems to me that our children are far more often exposed to sexual assaults than the few precautions taken in this respect would lead us to expect' (Freud 1896/1962b, p. 206). This view would have been endorsed by several contemporary French physicians who had documented enormous numbers of child-abuse cases, but although Freud spent some time in Paris at the end of 1895 and may have been familiar with this literature (e.g., Tardieu's reports, see chapter 1), the prevailing medical opinion at the turn of the century, in both France and Germany, was that children's allegations of sexual assaults were generally false (see Masson 1984 for details).

Freud's original idea that the cause of adult neuroses lay in sexual assaults during childhood proved to be too controversial for the moral climate of the Victorian era. When Freud presented his theory to the medical community it was met with an icy reception. 'I cannot believe that an experienced psychiatrist can read this paper without experiencing genuine outrage. The reason for this outrage is to be found in the fact that Freud takes very seriously what is nothing but paranoid drivel with a sexual content—purely chance events which are entirely insignificant or entirely invented.' (Rieger 1896, see Masson 1984, p. 134). Such reactions resulted in Freud's professional ostracism and a period of painful isolation. By 1905, Freud had reformulated his theory, abandoning his belief in his patients' accounts of childhood sexual trauma, and arguing instead that their accounts were fictitious. He explained that sexual abuse in childhood could not possibly be as frequent as his sample of cases would suggest and therefore he had been mistaken in his original conclusion:

When, however, I was at last obliged to recognise that these scenes of seduction had never taken place, and that they were only phantasies which my patients had made up or which I myself had forced on them, I was for some time completely at a loss. When I had pulled myself together, I was able to draw the right conclusions from my discovery; namely, the neurotic symptoms were not related directly to actual events but to wishful phantasies. (Freud 1924/1959, p. 34.)

For almost a hundred years, Freud's theory provided a 'scientific' basis to medical and legal attitudes that women's and children's allegations of sexual victimisation could simply be fictitious manifestations of their erotic fantasies. But the validity of Freud's conclusions are now disputed, and his critics seem to be vindicated by epidemiological reports of the surprisingly high incidence of sexual offences against children (see chapter 1). It is now widely believed that Freud was correct in his initial conclusion that significant numbers of children are victims of sexual abuse, and that many of these victims will experience emotional problems as a consequence.

The likelihood that Freud 'got it wrong' with regard to sexual fantasy does not, of course, discount the possibility of false allegations which may be made for other reasons. For example, a disturbed child might report psychotic delusions (although delusions of sexual abuse are extremely rare: Nurcombe 1986) or a child could make a false complaint for malicious reasons, for self-protection, or as a result of adult coaching which might result in a conscious collusion, or an unconscious suggestibility effect (see above page 308). The probability of children making fictitious allegations of sexual assault can be estimated by considering reported rates of false allegations.

Incidence of false complaints of sexual offences

Medical opinion regarding the frequency of unfounded sexual allegations has changed during the last hundred years. Taylor's *Medical Jurisprudence* (1849, p. 629) quotes Andrew Amos (a law professor) who allegedly said that false complaints outnumber valid complaints by twelve to one, giving a 92% rate of false complaints. In the late 1880s, Lawson Tait, a gynaecologist advising the Birmingham police on rape prosecutions, only recommended legal action on six out of 100 allegations (i.e., regarding 94% as false or unfounded) (Bristow 1977). Similarly, French doctors such as Brouardel (1907) believed that 60 to 80% of sexual allegations were unfounded. In modern times, estimates have been given of women's allegations of rape made to the police at rates of up to 90% being false or unfounded (Stewart, 1981). Such views about rates of false allegations need to considered against a baseline of ignorance with regard to the real incidence rates of sexual assaults and incest. In the late 19th century, the accepted incidence rates were probably a gross underestimation of the true picture, and modern criminal statistics are also likely to underestimate the size of the problem (see Anthony et al. 1989; Walton 1989). So, what reliable information is there?

Before considering the available survey data, the criteria for labelling an allegation as true or false need to be clearly defined (Corwin et al. 1987). Deciding that an alleged sexual assault on a child did *not* occur is no simple matter, and experienced child psychiatrists acknowledge that there will be a small percentage of cases where it is impossible to reach an unequivocal diagnosis (Green 1986; Jones and Seig 1988). The fact that the accused denies the offence, or the victim denies the offence, or the victim retracts a previous allegation, or the complete absence of medical signs, or the dropping of the case for lack of evidence, are not sufficient grounds for concluding that a sexual offence did not occur, particularly in intra-familial abuse. Although the theory of many lawyers seems to be that a genuine complaint will invariably be made at once (see chapter 6), medical experts point out that delay in reporting the offence, reluctance to give details and recantation of a complaint are very typical of genuine allegations and should not be regarded as indicators of unreliability (Goodwin et al. 1982; Weyland 1989). Prosecuting lawyers' reasons for dismissing cases are also indicative of the criteria they use to evaluate reliability. A new study of American prosecutors' decision-making (Whitcomb et al. 1991) shows that they are less likely to accept child sexual abuse cases involving victims of pre-school age rather than older children. Perpetrator confession, physical evidence, 'fresh complaints' and alleged oral-genital contact were highly related to acceptance for prosecution. (See also Irish Law Reform Commission 1989; McMurray 1987; Wattam, 1992.)

Furthermore, it is also important to distinguish between reported cases where an adult (such as a parent or a concerned professional) makes an allegation on behalf of a child and cases where the child initiates the complaint (i.e., by telling someone the whole or part of the allegation). This is particularly crucial when considering data originating from jurisdictions which have legislation enforcing mandatory reporting (i.e., where it is an offence for a professional not to report a suspicion of child abuse: see chapter 1). In such jurisdictions one would expect a relatively high proportion of reported suspicions to be false alarms, as professionals are likely to err on the side of caution. Consequently, many of these reports will be classified as unfounded as soon as the child is interviewed or after minimal investigation. Jones and McGraw (1987) suggest that unfounded reports usually constitute about 50% of any area's reports. (Eckenrode et al. (1988b) took a sample of 796 sexual abuse cases, 198 physical abuse cases and 880 reports of neglect from a total pool of 84,119 child maltreatment reports made to the New York State Child Abuse and Maltreatment Register in 1985. In their sample they found that the substantiation rates were 48% for physical abuse, 39% for sexual abuse and 28% for the reports of neglect. For each type of report they examined the factors which predicted substantiation (see Eckenrode et al. (1988a) for a detailed examination of sexual abuse reports), and found that in general reports made by professionals were significantly more likely to be substantiated than reports made by non-professionals. (Even among professionals, underlying expectations may influence substantiation rates (see Everson and Boat (1989), discussed below.))

It must be strongly emphasised that in this situation 'unfounded report' means that the report has not been substantiated and does not mean that a child has made an allegation of sexual assault which has subsequently been proven false. One American report by Besharov (1985) stated that 65% of reported suspicions were in fact unfounded, a statistic wildly misrepresented by *Sunday Times* journalist Brian Deer, who concluded, 'Children who do not have to go to court—and who are nevertheless assumed to be telling the truth—have contributed to an epidemic of false allegations. In the last year, 65% of accusations have been found to be untrue in cases affecting 1m families.' (*Sunday Times,* 28 October 1987.) As explained above, unfounded is not necessarily synonymous with untrue; a crucial distinction which appears to have eluded this particular correspondent. There is little doubt that hysterical or careless reporting of child abuse research fuels public anxieties about false allegations and reinforces the mythology of children's unreliability.

It should also be mentioned that there are cases labelled false allegations in which the victim makes a valid complaint of sexual assault but deliberately or unwittingly identifies the wrong person as the perpetrator (as in *Butler* (1987) 84 Cr App R 12; Rosenfield et al. 1979). These cases involving misidentifications should be distinguished from totally fabricated complaints when assessing the incidence of false allegations.

There are actually very few studies which have provided detailed documentation of false allegations of child sexual abuse, making these necessary distinctions. Table 11.1 summarises the available data which form the bases for this discussion. One of the most competent surveys was carried out by child psychiatrists Jones and McGraw (1987), who categorised 576 reports of suspected sexual abuse made to the Social Services Department in Denver, Colorado during 1983. Using six separate categories to classify reports, and a detailed set of validation criteria, they found that of the 439 cases where there was sufficient information to judge whether or not sexual abuse had occurred, only 2% of reports were fictitious allegations made by children (eight allegations made by five children). Four of these children were disturbed female teenagers who had previously been sexually victimised by an adult and the fifth child was a four-year-old boy who, with his mother, produced an account which was judged to be fictitious. A further 6% of allegations ($n = 26$), which were made by adults on behalf of children, were also classified as false. This adult group included parents with major psychiatric disturbances and parents involved in custody or access disputes. (Likewise, Goodwin et al. (1982) reported that, 'The few cases of [incest] hoax that we have seen coincided with psychological evaluations that showed mental retardation, psychosis, and/or extreme anxiety and depression' (p. 9).)

In the second phase of the study, Jones and McGraw examined a further 21 false allegations of child sexual abuse using a carefully designed validation process and compared the characteristics of the false complaints with 696 reliable cases seen in the same three-year period. (Many of the characteristics they used in the validation process are similar to the criteria employed in credibility assessments, e.g., SVA, see chapter 7.) Of the 21 fictitious accounts, five came directly from children (as opposed to adults), by five girls aged between three and nine years, four of whom had been sexually abused prior to the current allegation and who were suffering from untreated post-traumatic stress disorder. When the children's accounts were analysed, a number of common features emerged, such as a lack of accompanying emotion, a lack of detail and an absence of distinguishing features, such as details of surroundings. However, it was emphasised that no one factor alone discriminated reliable from false reports, rather a coexistence of several dubious features was necessary for a diagnosis of fictitious allegation. Jones and McGraw did, however, note that in only two of the 21 fictitious cases could the quality of the initial interview be judged as adequate (cf. Trankell 1958) and that in cases where adults made the initial complaint, a failure to conduct an early interview with the child probably contributed to the confusion about the diagnosis.

Jones and McGraw's conclusion is that 'Fictitious allegations are unusual and that the majority of suspicions of sexual abuse brought to professional attention prove to be reliable cases' (p. 38). This is in accord with the experience of social workers (Faller 1984) and doctors (Mann 1985). The medical profession appears to be in general agreement, for example, Green (1986) states 'False denials, therefore, are common but false disclosures are rare'. Peters (1976) reported that only four out of 64 chilren seen at a hospital emergency room with suspected child sexual abuse were false (i.e., 6%), although it is not clear how many of these allegations were instigated by adults. Psychiatrist Jean Goodwin and her colleagues (1979) found that only one of 46 sexual abuse cases reported to a child abuse agency was a false allegation made by a child (i.e., 2%) and a further two cases from their sample were false accusations made by adults regarding children. Horowitz et al. (1984, cited in Everson and Boat 1989) reported a false allegation rate of 8% from referrals to a sexual abuse programme in Boston, and Faller (1988) observed that 3% of child sexual abuse allegations were untrue, from a sample of 142 cases. Psychologists Everson and Boat (1989) found that in a sample of 1,249 reported cases of child sexual abuse in North Carolina, the estimated rate of false allegations was between 4.7 to 7.6% of all child and adolescent reports. (This ranges from about 2% for children under six years to around 10% for adolescents.) They also examined the specific criteria used to judge an allegation's veracity and assessed the relationship between substantiation rates and professional attitudes about the trustworthiness of child reports of abuse. They concluded that their estimate of false allegations was probably inflated due to some child protection workers being predisposed to doubt children's claims of being sexually abused. 'As a result these workers are likely to interpret ambiguous or inconsistent evidence as proof that the child's report is false, even though a more benign interpretation of the evidence in regard to the child's veracity may be equally compelling' (p. 235). Taken together (see upper section of Table 11.1), these reports suggest that the rate of false complaints of sexual abuse made by children is probably less than 5% of total allegations.

These are all American samples, but despite the dearth of formal research, the indications are that UK figures will be similar. Gorry (1986), in a survey of incest cases reported to the Metropolitan Police (1980 to 1985), found that only 5% of the allegations were false (having been made for a malicious purpose), but this figure includes allegations made by adults. British psychiatrists also believe that the incidence rate of false allegations of child sexual abuse instigated by children is very low.

> When children are eventually able to talk about sexual abuse, it is my experience, that they are virtually all truthful in what they say. I have to date only had direct experience of two or three children whom I am sure have falsely alleged sexual abuse, and all these children have been teenagers, with prior psychiatric disturbance. In the remaining children, over 200 cases, whom I have personally interviewed, if a disclosure emerges, it is nearly always truthful but I would say that in about 25% of the very psychiatrically disturbed and fearful children who I have interviewed, no clear statements have been made truthful or otherwise. (Vizard 1989, p. 24.)

It is important to realise that most false allegations of child sexual abuse are instigated by adults and not by children (Faller 1991a). 'The confirmed incest

Table 11.1 Estimated rates of false allegations of child sexual abuse

Study	Sample	Source	Estimated rate of false allegations
Peters (1976)	64	Hospital emergency room	6% (no separate rates for children and adults)
Goodwin et al. (1979)	46	Child abuse agency	2% (children), 4% (adults)
Horowitz et al. (1984) (see Everson and Boat 1989)	92	Sexual abuse programme	8% (all older than eight years)
Jones and McGraw (1987)	576	Reports to social services	2% (by children), 6% (by adults)
Faller (1988)	142	Child abuse programme	3% (by children)
Everson and Boat (1989)	1,249	Child protective services	2% (younger than six years) 6% (six to 10 years) 10% (older than 10 years)
Thoennes and Tjaden (1988, 1990)	129	Domestic relations courts. Custody and visitation dispute cases	33% (unlikely), 17% (inconclusive) (6% 'consciously false')
Faller (1991a)	120	Child abuse programme Divorce cases	16% (false), 10% (inconclusive) No separate rates for children and adults

Previously estimated rates of false sexual allegation:

93% (Amos c. 1840 quoted in Taylor 1849).
94% (Tait 1889 c. 1880 quoted in Bristow 1977).
60–80% (Brouardel 1907).

hoax is more likely to be the work of a parent than of a child' (Goodwin et al. 1982, p. 7). Likewise, British experts Vizard and Tranter (1988) state:

> The available evidence suggests that false allegations do indeed occur, more often involving older children, frequently in the context of an access dispute, and most frequently when the child is used by one or other parent in dispute to make a false allegation of sexual abuse in order to strengthen their legal case (p. 97).

Jones and McGraw (1987) found that in 16 of their 21 fictitious cases the false allegations were made by adults alone (nine) or were cases where the source of the allegations was unclear (seven). In 12 of these cases, the adult was exhibiting a psychiatric problem, most typically a personality disorder, and in 14 of these cases there were current custody or visitation disputes between the mother and her ex-husband. There is some evidence that the rates of false allegation are higher in custody disputes. Jones and Seig (1988) found that in a small sample of 20 cases involving a child sexual abuse allegation and coexisting parental custody dispute, four cases (20%) were found to be false. They emphasise, however, that 70% of the allegations were reliable and argue strongly 'against the practice of dismissing child sexual abuse allegations in child custody contexts as most likely to be false' (p. 29).

Thoennes and Tjadsen (1988, 1990) found that in a sample of over 9000 American families with custody-visitation disputes which had reached the domestic relations courts, less than 2% of these contested cases also involved an allegation of child sexual abuse. They examined 169 cases where there was an allegation and found that in the opinion of child protection service workers and court custody evaluators that 50% of the cases involved abuse, in 33% no abuse transpired and in the remaining 17% of cases, no determination was reached. (There were 'consciously made false allegations' in 6% of cases, see Faller 1991b for details.) Contested access or custody disputes clearly present a particular constellation of difficulties when a sexual allegation is raised (Hodges 1991; Schuman, 1986), but it should be emphasised that reliable allegations of child sexual abuse do occur in these situations (Schutz et al. 1989) and this may have been the catalyst for the initial marital breakdown. Faller (1991a) analysed possible explanations for child sexual abuse allegations in divorce based on a clinical sample of 120 cases in Michigan, and she identified four 'dynamics': (i) the mother finds out about the sexual abuse and decides to divorce her husband (9%); (ii) long-standing sexual abuse is only revealed during the marital breakup (22%); (iii) sexual abuse has been precipitated by the marital dissolution (43%); or (iv) the allegation is false (16% false plus 10% inconclusive). She advises, 'These findings indicate that mental health professionals who are assessing sexual abuse accusations in divorce contexts should maintain an open mind and an appreciation of the range of potential circumstances and dynamics that might result in such a report' (p. 89).

An equally complex set of dynamics can be found in the sexual abuse allegations raised against foster parents. The National Foster Care Association

(1988) reported that 'accusations are increasingly being made and fewer and fewer cases are being proved'. They suggest that the allegations may be true or false for the following reasons: (i) true—because the child was actually abused; (ii) false—because the child was previously abused and misunderstands an innocent advance; or (iii) false—'The child, or someone close to the child, has a grudge and sees the foster parent as a person to attack. Knowing something of the effect an allegation can have makes it a useful weapon' (pp. 5, 6). Similarly, teachers may also be in a potentially vulnerable position in regard to false allegations of sexual abuse (see Law Society's Gazette 'Postbox', 8 January 1992; HC debate 16.1.92 CD 341 Hansard 1208, 1216).

When all these threads are drawn together, our general conclusions about false complaints in sex cases are these. First, there is no doubt that adults sometimes do make false allegations of sexual crimes (e.g., *Goodwin* (1989) *The Times*, 27 April 1989; *Kyriakou, The Independent*, 10 November 1990). When these cases do reach the courts, the motivations revealed can be a little unusual (4). Given the severity of the penalties for such offences these cases tend to retain a certain notoriety; however, the incidence of such false allegations is now thought to be considerably lower than was once believed (Temkin 1987). (The related issue of whether a false memory of sexual abuse can be 'implanted' by another person (see page 308 above) is at present unresolved. As yet there have been no cases featuring this line of defence in the British courts.)

Secondly, children have also been known to make consciously false sexual complaints; for example, Trankell (1958) documents a famous Swedish case of a five-year-old boy who falsely claimed to have been sexually abused by a window cleaner in order to conceal his own misdemeanours, and Goodwin (1982) describes a number of false allegations of incest; however, the most recent scientific evidence shows that a significant proportion of false allegations are in fact made by adults on behalf of children (e.g., in custody disputes), and that false complaints made by children are rare. This is a consistent finding which has now been replicated across several substantial samples of data. Thirdly, when children do make a false report it is generally for identifiable reasons, and psychologists and psychiatrists are developing a better understanding of the distinguishing characteristics and symptomatology of such cases. It is apparent that interviewing skill is of the utmost importance and lawyers as well as mental health professions require appropriate training to avoid the risk of misinterpreting the indiciators of reliability in a child's statements or behaviours. Fourthly, and ironically, the apparently bigger problem is not the risk of false allegations but is the significant rate of false retractions which are much more common and if undetected can be potentially dangerous for the child (Vizard et al. 1987).

Finally, there is an apparent lack of perspective in the current concern with false allegations of sexual assaults, because no comparison is ever drawn with the proportion of complaints of non-sexual crimes that are fabricated. One might suspect that the incidence rate is not insignificant; take, for instance false reports of theft, of accidental fires that are found to be arson, etc. The 1987 annual report of the Insurance Ombudsman laments, 'I would hazard a guess that many more small claims are exaggerated if not actually false, than the industry realises' (p. 8). In the USA, the National Automobile Theft Bureau estimates that 15% of all vehicle thefts reported are fraudulent (Cook 1989). To put the matter in an even broader perspective, it must be remembered that there is an inevitable risk that any piece of evidence can be false. Even the most convincing forensic evidence can be erroneously labelled, such as a swab taken from another patient, leading to an erroneous accusation of sexual abuse (*G* v *North Tees Health Authority* [1989] FCR 53); false confessions of child abuse are not unknown (for a striking example see *Foster* [1985] QB 115), and children sometimes make false confessions to crimes, even including murder (*X* (1960) *New Law Journal* 207, 15 February 1991).

A decade of research demonstrating that children and women do not habitually make false allegations of sexual assault appears at last to be permeating the legal knowledge base. The Pigot Committee (1989) questioned the necessity of the warning (see chapter 8) which is given to the jury in sexual cases:

> It is true that complainants in sexual cases, like their counterparts in other cases, do sometimes tell entirely false stories. But we know of no evidence whatever which suggests that this takes place on such a scale and in a way so calculated to deceive the jury that a special measure designed to enhance the normal standard of proof is necessary (5.27).

Are children less truthful than adults?

'Only children and fools tell the truth' says the proverb: but Hilaire Belloc warned us of the little girl, Matilda, who 'told such Dreadful Lies, It made one Gasp and Stretch one's Eyes'. So, are children more or less honest than adults? Certainly the belief that 'children in general are thought to lie more frequently than adults' is one of the reasons cited for doubting the veracity of children's testimony (Hedderman 1987, p. 5). As James Morton said:

> in the days of Lord Goddard it was thought that a child under five could not be expected to tell the truth and it is a maxim which has recently been adopted by Ognall J. It is a throwback to the belief that all little boys are thieves, cheats and liars and, if we are totally honest, when we look back over the years it is difficult to deny there is some truth behind that harsh statement (Editorial, *New Law Journal*, 6 October 1989.)

Children and adults do tell lies, but there is no evidence to support the contention that children are more likely to lie than adults (Burton 1976). In fact, the opinion of psychiatrists (Nurcombe 1986) and psychologists (Perry 1987) runs counter to this notion, and a survey of professionals who interviewed child witnesses (e.g., police, social workers, judges, prosecutors) found that 93% of respondents answered no to the question: 'In general have you found children more likely than adults to tell lies?' (Flin et al. 1988). One might almost extend this argument and suggest that children are actually more truthful than adults. Certainly, the research on children's beliefs about court (see chapter 13 and Burton and Strichartz 1991) implies that children may be more cautious about lying in the witness-box than adult witnesses.

Many experts believe that young children's lies are probably easier to detect than those of older children or adults (Morton 1988; Nurcombe 1986) and in fact, this would account for the belief that they lie more frequently (Feldman and White 1980). American college students believe that children under six are highly prone to be liars, second only to politicians (Kintz 1977). Psychological studies of adults' ability to judge the veracity of children's statements have confirmed that the lies of younger children are easier to discern (Westcott et al. 1991) which is probably because effective deception requires sophisticated cognitive and social skills such as reading the listener's mind, and these are skills which undoubtedly improve with age, at least through early childhood (Leekam 1991, 1992; Sodian et al. 1991; Tate et al. 1992; Vasek 1986). (However, it should be noted that the lies in these experiments concerned neutral events and did not recreate any of the emotional or motivational dimensions one might expert to encounter in an investigation of child sexual abuse.)

With the exception of some early psychological interest (e.g., Krout 1931; see Tate et al. 1992 for further examples) there appear to be few studies of children's motivations for lying. Gorphe (1927) quotes a French study from the early years of the century which surveyed teachers' opinions on why children lie, and found they believed in a majority of cases that the primary motive was fear and apprehension. Similarly De Paulo and Jordan (1982) found that the first lies told by children are designed to avoid punishment and when older children lie it seems to be to avoid trouble rather than to create it (Faller 1984; Trankell 1958). Children, like adults, also sometimes lie to obtain rewards, to avoid embarrassment, to protect a loved one and as a social grace (Lewis and Saarni, 1993). A review of new experimental work shows that children can be easily persuaded to lie in order to 'keep a secret' (Pipe and Goodman 1991).

There is actually very little systematic research into the frequency with which child or adult witnesses tell lies. Until recently the psychological studies of lying have tended to concentrate on the development of moral understanding. This is an interesting literature but of limited validity in a forensic context, as moral knowledge does not predict moral behaviour, and only the latter is of interest to the courts (Melton et al. 1987) (although children's competence may be assessed on the basis of the former). Psychiatrists seem to be principally concerned with children's lying as a pathological symptom in disturbed children (e.g., Chagoya and Scholnick 1986) and again this has little relevance for the normal child's behaviour. It is, however, generally agreed that lying at any age is more likely to be a function of situational factors rather than a specific personality trait (Perry 1987). For this reason, SVA is always directed at specific statements and is not regarded as an assessment of the witness's general credibility (see chapter 9). Judgements of credibility must be based on multiple factors including the specific motivations of a given situation. Psychologists are beginning to develop a better understanding of these motivations. (A very interesting collection of articles on the latest psychological research studies into children's lying and deception was edited by Ceci and colleagues in 1992.)

The Pigot Committee (1989) discussing this issue concluded: 'We understand however, that contrary to the traditional view, recent research shows that untruthful child witnesses are comparatively uncommon and that, like their adult counterparts, they act out of identifiable motives' (2.24).

Our courts should be willing to listen to children of all ages and lawyers should be willing to learn what other disciplines can teach them about the features of a child's evidence which suggest that it is true or false, and the circumstances in which false complaints are likely to be made.

Coaching

A further point that Heydon (1984) makes is that child witnesses are unreliable because manipulative adults tend to coach (or in Scotland, tutor) them in what they want them to say: '. . . anxious parents may take a child through a story again and again so that it becomes drilled in untruths'.

This fear, too, is officially recognised by the rules of evidence. Normally, the answers that a witness gives in cross-examination to questions designed to test his creditworthiness are final. There are some exceptional cases where the cross-examiner is nevertheless allowed to prove the answer to such a question was untrue, and one of these exceptions was created in the case of *P illips* (1936) 26 Cr App R 17. At the defendant's trial for incest, the defence asked each of the two girls in cross-examination whether her mother had coached them, to which they answered no. On appeal it was held that the judge should have permitted the defence to lead evidence showing that they had in fact been coached.

As with the theory that children are prone to making false allegations of sexual assault, the idea that children are prone to coaching has a long cultural tradition behind it. A lurid example is given by Voltaire in *Questions sur l'Encyclopédie* (1771, p. 138):

Let me describe a striking case which has just happened before us at Lyon. A woman found her daughter aged 11 did not come home in the evening; she ran everywhere; she suspected her neighbour of having hidden her daughter; she demanded her return; she accused her of having prostituted her. Several weeks later, some fishermen found a girl drowned and decomposing in the Rhône at Condrieux. The woman I am speaking of believed this was her daughter. She was persuaded by her neighbour's enemies that someone had violated her daughter at the neighbour's house, she had been strangled, and thrown into the Rhône. She said it, and everybody was repeating it. A lot of people then claimed to know all the details of the crime exactly. The whole town was in a state of rumour; every mouth cried for vengeance. There is nothing the least surprising about that in a people with no sense or judgment. But here is the thing which really is extraordinary. The neighbour's own son, a child of five and a half, accused his mother of having had the wretched girl found in the Rhône raped before her eyes, and of having had five men hold her down while one had her. He had heard the words the rape victim had said; he described their position; he had seen his mother and these criminals strangle the hapless child immediately afterwards. He had seen his mother and the murderers throw her into a well, pull her out, wrap her in a sheet; he had seen these monsters carry her in triumph in public places, dancing around the dead body, and finally throw her into the Rhône. The judges were obliged to put all those who were said to be involved under lock and key, and witnesses deposed against them. The child was heard first, and with all the innocence of his age reaffirmed everything that he had said about them and about his mother. How could anyone imagine this was not the purest truth? The crime was not a likely one; but it is even more unlikely that a child of five and a half would falsely accuse his mother. How could a child repeat with consistency all the details of an abominable and unheard-of crime, if he has not seen it with his own eyes, unless he has been struck forcibly by the experience, and unless the force of the truth does not compel him to utter? The whole population was waiting to feast its eyes on the execution of the persons accused.

What was the end of this strange prosecution? There was not a word of truth in the accusation. No raped daughter, no youths gathered at the house of the woman accused, no murder, nothing else, nothing else whatever. The child had been suborned, and by whom? An amazing thing, but true!—by two other children who belonged to the accusers. He was on the point of getting his mother burnt alive as the price of a pot of jam.

How commonly, if ever, are children really coached to give false evidence? The studies we described earlier on false allegations in custody disputes suggest that it must happen sometimes, but there is little information available about how far false allegations in custody disputes are made on behalf of children, or through them. In the hope of obtaining more information about coaching, we asked a number of English judges various questions, including whether they thought that child witnesses were ever coached. Of 11 pertinent replies, four said no and seven said yes. Of the majority who thought that deliberate coaching does take place, most said that the problem tends to arise in custody disputes in the civil courts. All but one judge said that it is rather rare. One added that judges sometimes see what looks like carefully rehearsed evidence from child witnesses in criminal cases, but added that the explanation there may not be coaching, but the large number of times the child has had to go through the story at earlier stages in the proceedings. (Similarly, American psychologists Tate et al. (1992) conducted an experiment to test the extent to which three- to seven-year-olds can be coached to give fake descriptions of events. They concluded, 'Our results suggest that children can be coached into making false statements (at least in the context of a harmless trick), but the coaching does not work very well or last very long for the majority of children' (p. 84).)

Significantly, the judges who mentioned coaching usually remarked that when it has taken place it is usually very obvious, and the fact that it has happened gets exposed. If coaching tends to get discovered in court, it does not seem to be a serious reason for being wary of the evidence of children. It is the undetectable flaws in testimony that are dangerous.

The coaching of children is usually discussed in the context of false accusations, but it must be remembered that they are sometimes coached to make false denials. An experienced paediatrician told the authors, 'I see a lot of coached children: ones that have been coached to say that nothing has happened to them. I have had little children tell me "X didn't do such-and-such to me" before I have even had a chance to ask them what is wrong'.

(F) MORAL COMPETENCE

The final reason proferred by lawyers for doubting the reliability of children's evidence is that children are inferior to adults in a moral as well as an intellectual sense; '. . . children often have little notion of the duty to speak the truth, and they may fail to realise how important their evidence is in a case and how important it is for it to be accurate' (Heydon 1984). This bears directly on the competency requirement that the child understands the duty to tell the truth—a criterion which in England until recently effectively prevented the courts hearing the evidence of young children (see chapter 4).

Although there is an extensive psychological literature on children's moral development, most of this is not particularly helpful when considering the question of children's evidence, and the following discussion will concentrate on research studies which have been specifically concerned with child witnesses. There are several components of the moral test of appreciating the duty to tell the truth.

First, at what age do most children understand the difference between truth and falsehood? As suggested earlier (see chapter 4) this will obviously depend on the child's comprehension of the language in which the question is couched.

Certainly by the age of three of four years most children appreciate the essential distinction between truthfulness and lying (Bussey 1991; Myers 1987a), although they may have some difficulty in articulating an appropriate definition of 'truthful'. So of course would a significant percentage of adults. *Chambers Twentieth Century Dictionary* offers the helpfully circular definition of 'truthful' as, 'habitually or actually telling what one believes to be true', having explained 'truth' as 'faithfulness: constancy: veracity: agreement with reality'. Several investigations have shown that children from the age of five or six years generally do appear to know the meaning of terms such as 'truth', 'lie' and 'promise', although they may use different definitions from adults (Bussey et al. 1993; Flin et al. 1989; Saywitz 1989). Young children's concept of truth is based on their perception of factual reality—' "to tell the truth" means to report the facts as they saw them, not modifying their observation by inferences about non-observable intents and beliefs of others' (Strichartz and Burton 1990, p. 218; see also Wimmer et al. 1984).

Secondly, if young children can distinguish between truth and lies, do they appreciate the duty to tell the truth in court? Certainly children often believe there are dire consequences for those who lie in court. Feben (1985) interviewed Australian schoolchildren aged five to 15 years and reported that 'until nine years of age children's reasons for being truthful in court concerned fear of punishment, only older children adopted a less egocentric view and mentioned implications for other parties'. A similar result was found in a Scottish survey (Flin et al. 1989). Children (six to 10 years) were generally found to be aware of the importance of telling the truth in court. The six- and eight-year-olds said that if they lied they would expect to be punished and the majority of children believed that they would be sent to prison if they lied in court. By age 10 years most subjects gave a more adult type of response, stating that the truth was important to avoid the risks of convicting the innocent or acquitting the guilty. In another Scottish study (Flin et al. 1988), a small sample of child witnesses who had actually given evidence in a criminal trial were asked, 'Why is it important to tell the truth in court?' Their responses included the following reasons: 'You might get the wrong person'. 'You would get into trouble'. 'You must get the right account'. 'You get it over and done with'. These data, although preliminary, begin to indicate that children even as young as five and six years do appreciate the importance of telling the truth in court. Moreover, children's apparent fear of imprisonment for dishonesty might lead one to conclude that young child witnesses would be more honest than adults due to their misapprehension of the consequences of lying in the witness-box. With increasing age and intellectual sophistication, the true complexity of moral judgments begins to be appreciated (see Warren-Leubecker et al. 1989). Brian Kearney, a Scottish Judge, tells of his experience of assessing the competence of an eight-year-old girl called to corroborate her ten-year-old brother's evidence that he had been assaulted by their mother.

> In conformity with the latest thinking I had removed wig and gown when the boy was being examined. I had cleared the court to emphasise informality. All was therefore ready for Mary. I asked Mary, as I had asked her brother, what school she went to and what her teacher's name was. She answered appropriately. I then asked her very gently, if she would answer truthfully a few questions which this gentleman (the fiscal) would ask. Up till now all had gone according to plan. The plan was now disrupted when Mary replied 'That depends on the question'. There was silence in court. I suspect the thought passed through some minds that an answer of this degree of frankness proved more than any other form of assurance that this young girl knew truth from falsehood. We proceeded with the trial. (Kearney 1990.)

The underlying purpose of the competency assessment is presumably to determine the likelihood that the child will give honest testimony. But, adult witnesses are not always honest, and no attempt is made to assess their moral understanding prior to admitting their evidence. For good reason, as this would be regarded as a total waste of time; a witness who has a doctorate in moral philosophy is just as likely to lie in the witness-box as any other adult. The legal profession is well aware that moral comprehension does not predict moral behaviour in adults (Stone 1984). Unfortunately, it seems to be less widely appreciated that moral knowledge is equally useless in predicting children's truthfulness (Melton et al. 1987). A four-year-old who has great difficulty in explaining her understanding of 'telling lies' can give wholly honest testimony, while an eight-year-old who can define truthfulness can give totally fabricated evidence. What then is the point of attempting to assess children's moral comprehension if this does not predict their propensity to tell the truth?

Perhaps it is thought that the questions used to assess moral understanding can also act as a gauge of the child's intellectual ability. To some extent this would be true, as the child's comprehension, vocabulary and linguistic development could be judged, at least superficially, from the answers, provided of course that the child was relaxed when the examination took place and the interviewer had the appropriate expertise to conduct such an assessment. However, in terms of judging the child's ability to act as a reliable eyewitness, the competency examination has little to offer (see chapter 4). Feben (1985) compared children's knowledge of the concepts underlying an Australian oath test with their performance on a memory task and found 'that while an increasingly sophisticated understanding of the oath is related to age and basic intellectual cognitive capacity of a witness, it is not directly related to a witness's memory accuracy' (p. 123). These researchers concluded that oath tests or similar competency assessments do not appear to be valid indicators of witnesses' competence. As we saw in chapter 4, many American and Australian jurisdictions have now dispensed with moral assessments for child witnesses, and the Criminal Justice Act 1991 attempts to do the same for England.

For those interested to read more of the relevant psychological research the following may be a useful start: Ceci et al. 1989; Doris, 1991; Dent and Flin 1992; Goodman and Bottoms 1993; Zaragoza (in press).

NOTES

1. In the latest edition of this book (Heydon, 1991), children's evidence is not discussed.

2. The classical literature of the West is full of references to human sacrifice. To take one example out of many, Marlowe's *Dr Faustus*, when thinking about selling his soul to the devil, says

The God thou serv'st is thine own appetite,
Wherein is fix'd the love of Belzebub.
To him I'll build an altar and a church,
And offer lukewarm blood of new-born babes. (Act II, scene 1).

3. Readers in search of further enlightenment will find a survey of views and material in the judgment of Douglas Brown J in *Rochdale Borough Council* v *BW* [1991] FCR 705, in the series of articles collected in (1991) Vol. 15 No. 3 *Child Abuse and Neglect*, and in a recent paper by the child psychiatrist, David Jones (in press). At the time this book goes to press, the anthropologist Jean La Fontaine is conducting a study of the subject for the DSS.

4. In *R* v *Harris* heard at the Central Criminal Court, London in August 1991, a woman who had made a false allegation of rape against three men was found guilty and sentenced to 15 months' imprisonment. Sandra Harris, a 25-year-old lesbian who wished to have a child, persuaded her married

neighbour David Sheedy to have sex with her. Not wishing to jeopardise her relationship with Alison Westcott, her lesbian lover, Harris told her that she had been raped. The police were informed and they took a detailed description of the alleged rapist. The first man to be arrested, Colin Lynch was detained in custody for 24 hours until cleared by forensic tests. A second man, Nigel Kennedy was arrested, he was picked out by Harris at an identity parade and spent 18 days in prison on remand until cleared by DNA genetic fingerprinting tests. The third man to be arrested was David Sheedy, Harris's obliging neighbour and not surprisingly his DNA profile matched, but he denied the accusation of rape. Finally Sandra Harris admitted that the intercourse with Mr Sheedy had been at her request. (See *The Times*, 6 August 1991; Lawrence, letter to the *New Law Journal*, November 1991.)

5.   A very lively but inconclusive debate between Elizabeth Loftus and John Briere took place at the annual conference of the American Psychological Association in Toronto on 22nd August 1993. (This was attended by 800 psychologists and three television crews.) An audio tape of this session, 'Repressed Memory Controversy and Sex Abuse Cases', is available from the American Psychological Association, 750 First Street NE, Washington, DC 20002–4242.

CHAPTER TWELVE

Investigative interviews with children

INTRODUCTION

Children do not normally recite full accounts of their experiences without some degree of prompting, and a central thread of the previous chapter was that the skills of the interviewer can have a significant effect on the quality and reliability of a child's evidence. This chapter opens by examining some recent cases where interviewing techniques have come under scrutiny and then discusses what is now generally regarded by psychologists as best practice for conducting investigative interviews with child witnesses.

For a child to give a complete, relevant, unbiased and accurate account of witnessed events, the interviews (particularly the initial statement and the final examinations) must be conducted with considerable expertise and sensitivity. Interviewing, sometimes described as a 'conversation with a purpose', is not a natural or innate ability, nor is it as easy as this definition implies. Across a broad range of formal interview situations, such as job selection, market research, accident investigation or police interrogation, it is widely acknowledged that the validity of the interview depends on careful preparation, clear objectives and specialised communication skills, including the undervalued ability to listen. (See for example a recent study on videotaping police interviews with suspects, Baldwin 1992.)

Conducting interviews with child sexual abuse victims must rank as one of the most demanding interview situations, due to the sensitivity of the topic, the reticence of victims, prior threats to maintain secrecy and the potential conflict between getting evidence and helping the child. This problem can be particularly acute when the child is a victim of intrafamilial abuse or when the victim is mentally handicapped. Vizard (1987) points out that a significant proportion of abused children seen by psychiatrists could not or would not talk spontaneously about their experiences. The methods used by psychiatrists in diagnostic interviews with child sexual abuse victims have been significantly refined in recent years, partly in response to some very strong judicial criticism (see Douglas and Willmore 1987; chapter 7).

The interviewing skills of professionals who deal with child sexual abuse allegations were scrutinised in the Report into the Cleveland Inquiry by Lord Justice Butler Sloss (DHSS 1988). An entire chapter of the Report is devoted to the problems of 'Listening to Children' and while the professionals who provided evidence to the Inquiry disagreed on the 'desirability of and limits on the facilitative second stage' (12.27), they did agree on the following points to be observed in conducting all interviews.

(1)   The undesirability of calling them 'disclosure' interviews, which precluded the notion that sexual abuse might not have occurred.
(2)   All interviews should be undertaken only by those with some training, experience and aptitude for talking with children.
(3)   The need to approach each interview with an open mind.
(4)   The style of the interview should be open-ended questions to support and encourage the child in free recall.
(5)   There should be where possible only one and not more than two interviews for the purpose of evaluation, and the interview should not be too long.
(6)   The interview should go at the pace of the child and not of the adult.
(7)   The setting for the interview should be suitable and sympathetic.
(8)   It must be accepted that at the end of the interview the child may have given no information to support the suspicion of sexual abuse and the position will remain unclear.
(9)   There must be careful recording of the interview and what the child says, whether or not there is a videorecording.
(10)   It must be recognised that the use of facilitative techniques may create difficulties in subsequent court proceedings.
(11)   The great importance of adequate training for all those engaged in this work.
(12)   In certain circumstances it may be appropriate to use the special skills of a 'facilitated' interview. That type of interview should be treated as a second stage. The interviewer must be conscious of the limitations and strengths of the techniques employed. In such cases the interview should only be conducted by those with special skills and specific training. (para 12.34)

These guidelines are explained in the joint Government departments' inter-agency guide (Department of Health et al. 1991) and have subsequently been mentioned in judgments, sometimes without making explicit mention of the Cleveland Report. For example, in a case that went to the Court of Appeal, H v H [1990] Fam 86, Butler Sloss LJ stressed the importance of video recording interviews and said (at p. 949), 'The conduct of the interviews would inevitably have a marked effect upon the weight to be attached to the evidence adduced. Frequent, repetitive interviews with young suggestible children, reminding them of what they previously said would be likely to have decreasing evidential value'.

In a number of first-instance cases in England, the Cleveland Guidelines have been mentioned explicitly, and the judge has criticised the fact that they were not followed. In Re E [1990] FCR 793, Scott Baker J said, 'At para 12.34 of the [Cleveland] report are set out 12 points with regard to conducting child interviews, on which all of those who provided evidence to the inquiry were agreed. Mr Wall says that every single one of those points was breached during this investigation. I am satisfied that Mr Wall is correct about the vast majority, if not every one'. Scott Baker J specifically criticised the social worker who had carried out the interviews for not doing so with an open mind as to whether any abuse had occurred. He also expressed disappointment that 'several witnesses had either not read the report at all or, if they had, they ignored its conclusions in many respects'.

In *Re A* [1991] 1 WLR 1026, Hollings J (at p. 1029) referred to the Cleveland Guidelines, and then criticised the interviews, the tapes of which he had seen and heard, for the following breaches: (i) untrained and inexperienced interviewers; (ii) failure to approach the interview with an open mind; (iii) leading questions; (iv) too many interviews; (v) taking the interview at the pace of the interviewer, rather than that of the child. Similarly, in *Rochdale BC v BW and others* [1991] FCR 705, Douglas Brown J said that 'the interview work was done with little regard to the Cleveland recommendations'; he singled out the use of leading questions, and the inappropriate use of anatomically correct dolls. In *KVS v GGS* [1992] 2 FCR 23, Thorpe J referred to the Cleveland Guidelines, and criticised joint interviews conducted by a social worker and a police officer because they had used anatomically correct dolls when it was not appropriate to do so, and because the interviews were not properly recorded. The same judge, in *Re C* [1992] 2 FCR 65, mentioned the Cleveland Guidelines again, pointing out that none of the interviews were video-recorded, and saying (at p. 73) that there had been 'far more interviews in this case than good practice recommends'. In two recent cases, the Cleveland Guidelines have been mentioned in criminal proceedings. In *H* [1992] Crim LR 516 and in *Dunphy The Times*, 3 June 1993, the Court of Appeal accepted that if a child had previously been interrogated in breach of the Guidelines this would reduce the weight of any oral evidence he or she later gave at trial—and that if the breaches were serious enough, that the judge might be justified in using the discretion that s. 78 of the Police and Criminal Evidence Act 1984 gives him to exclude unreliable evidence (see page 39 above) to prevent the child giving evidence at all.

Whilst expressing these criticisms, however, the courts have also emphasised that the Cleveland Guidelins are no more than guidelines. In *Re C* [1992] 2 FCR 65, 73, Thorpe J said 'I think in all these cases good practice can never be more than a guide; it cannot be an absolute. Here video interviews were never a practical possibility, since at that stage, the plaintiffs did not have the necessary technical facilities'. And, in *Re A* [1991] 1 WLR 1026, Hollings J said, 'The Cleveland guidelines are, of course, only what they say, guidelines, and there can be variation and flexibility to meet the needs of a particular case provided regard is paid to the principles underlying the guidelines'.

North of the border, the Cleveland Guidelines have also been mentioned in the recent Judicial Inquiry, chaired by Lord Clyde into the Orkney affair (Clyde 1992). In this case nine children aged eight to 15 years from four families, suspected of being the victims of organised sexual abuse were removed from their homes at dawn and were flown with social workers to places of safety on the mainland. Over a period of four weeks, the children were interviewed by social workers and RSSPCC staff but were returned to their homes after Sheriff Kelbie ruled that the Children's Hearings procedures were incompetent and the Reporter to the Children's Panel decided to discontinue the legal proceedings (see chapter 1). In addition to procedural breaches, the Sheriff came to the conclusion that the interview techniques which had been employed were defective and of little or no evidential value (see Bissett-Johnson (1993a) for a detailed account of this case. This author also studied a similar case in Ayr, where the children appear to have been interviewed for 43 days almost continuously (Bissett-Johnson 1993b)). In the 363 page Orkney Inquiry Report (Clyde 1992) 194 recommendations are made, 30 of which (108–137) relate to interviewing. The main issues concern the training of interviewers and the planning, management and recording of the interviews themselves. The following recommendations relate specifically to techniques for conducting investigative interviews with children (pp. 359–360).

109.   The purpose, techniques and course of any interviews should be planned at the outset as well as the need to make an overall assessment of the child.

114.   Where possible interviewers who have dealt extensively with children making allegations about other children should not be involved in interviews of those other children.

115.   Each interviewer should wherever possible have consistent and relevant background information about the child and in particular about his or her emotional, physical and mental development, and an assessment of the child's wider family.

116.   The importance should be recognised of interviewers keeping an open mind on the truth or otherwise of any allegations.

121.   No more than two investigative interviews per interviewer per day should be undertaken and their workloads should be regularly monitored.

122.   Every effort should be made to improve recording techniques and maintain consistent recordings throughout a series of interviews. The standards and practices of recording should be regularly monitored.

124.   Whether or not there is mechanical recording, a full written record must be made as soon as possible after each interview.

125.   Any drawings made during an interview should be labelled at the time of creation to enable the occasion and their creator to be clearly identified.

131.   In general a maximum of two investigative interviews per child per week should be appropriate and the frequency of interviews is a matter for regular review.

133.   An initial series of invesigative interviews should usually not exceed four.

134.   Before embarking on an investigative interview interviewers should consider the matters of denial and retraction by a child, the interviewer's knowledge of information relating to allegations, the interviewer's own agenda, the use of leading questions and the introduction of personal material.

The judicial comments, guidelines and recommendations outlined above are usually based on expert assessors' opinions of what constitutes best practice when children are subject to an investigative interview with a view to subsequent criminal proceedings.

There is, in fact, now a general consensus from psychologists and psychiatrists that research and professional experience support one generic protocol for the conduct of an investigative interview which may be used for evidential purposes. This is a sequential or phased approach and it is described very briefly in the following section with directions for further reading. In the remainder of the chapter, we examine some of the methods used to maximise children's recall (the cognitive interview, dolls and props, facilitative questioning), the problems of interviewing children with special needs and the provision of training for interviewers.

THE PHASED INTERVIEW

In Chapter 11, a review of the psychological research into children's memory indicated that free recall (i.e. an unprompted account) is most accurate and that general questions cause fewer inaccuracies than specific or leading questions. This in fact is the basis of the phased approach and it is the method which was developed by psychiatrists who have revised their diagnostic interview procedures to maximise their evidentiary value. The recommended format for interviewing potentially abused children is to conduct an evaluative assessment which proceeds from an initial open-ended enquiry, then moves gradually to more specific questions and finally to subjective or hypothetical questions if necessary (Kolvin et al. 1988). Within this basic framework there exists a wide range of preferred questioning and play-based techniques (Bentovim et al. 1988; Garbarino and Stott 1989; Wattam 1992). Eileen Vizard (1991), an experienced child psychiatrist, reviewed current clinical practice with children suspected of being sexually abused and she has identified ten different interviewing protocols differentiated according to parameters of structure, evidence gathering and prescriptiveness.

The Home Office Memorandum on video-recorded interviews
As discussed in Chapter 7, the Home Office in conjunction with the Department of Health published in August 1992 a 'Memorandum of Good Practice on Video Recorded Interviews with Child Witnesses for Criminal Proceedings' (1). The introduction states (at p. 1):

> The main purpose of this Memorandum is to help those making a video recording of an interview *where it is intended that the result should be acceptable in criminal proceedings*. Such a recording can spare the child from having to recount *evidence* [meaning evidence-in-chief] to the court in person and provide a highly valuable, early record of the child's account. If handled properly, the video recorded interview will be in the interests of the child and in the interests of justice.

The Memorandum was subject to several revisions before it was finally released and predictably it has not received universal acclaim. However the criticisms voiced frequently attack more than just the Memorandum. Lawyer Jenny McEwan writes (1993 at p. 20):

> The Memorandum comprises an uneasy mixture of legal technicality, sympathy for the child, and advice drawn from the experience of professionals. It might be wondered whether the videotaped interview can be expected to be simultaneously both fish and fowl. It is a witness statement. It replaces oral testimony, and yet the interview process must pay heed to the welfare of the child. There is an obvious risk that, despite the best efforts of interviewers, the process will fall between all three stools and fail to satisfy any of these requirements. If this should happen it will be the fault not of those responsible for drafting this Memorandum, but of the legislators who failed to appreciate the complexities of criminal procedure and to confront directly the impact of participation in its adversarial structure on the vulnerable witness.

A more specific criticism which has been levelled is that the interview protocol suggested in the Memorandum does not encompass the needs of interviewers faced with very reluctant, traumatised and reticent children who may have been abused (Roberts and Glasgow, in press). Wattam (1992) comments that the stepwise method and the Memorandum 'are an ideal approach for a one-off event, particularly perpetrated by a stranger, and are less than ideal for the complex and long-standing repetitive assault cases because they neither acknowledge the child's trauma and the effect this will have on what they say, nor do they acknowledge the consequences' (p. 130). However there is very little psychological research to endorse any one particular approach for dealing with these most difficult of cases. (A related problem concerns interviewing children with special needs which is discussed on page 354 below.)

Provided the Memorandum is treated as a guideline and not as a recipe book, many interviewers will find its contents helpful. The following discussion will examine what we know from psychological research into interviewing children and what the Memorandum has to say on these matters.

Conducting a phased interview
In Part 3A of the Memorandum it suggests (at 3.1) how a video-recorded interview should be 'handled properly' by providing a recommended protocol for interviewing children:

> This treats the interview as a process in which a variety of interviewing techniques are deployed in relatively discrete phases, proceeding from general and open to specific and closed forms of question. What follows is a recommended protocol for interviewing based on a phased approach. It is suggested that this approach is likely to achieve the basic aim of listening to what the child has to say, if anything, about the alleged offence. However, inclusion of a phased approach in this Memorandum should not be taken to imply that all other techniques are necessarily unacceptable or to preclude their development. Neither should what follows be regarded as a check-list

to be rigidly worked through. Nevertheless, the sound legal framework it provides should not be departed from by members of joint investigating teams unless they have fully discussed and agreed the reasons for doing so and have consulted their senior managers.

This protocol was developed as a result of extensive consultation with experienced interviewers (see Bull 1992 for details) and it is very similar to the well respected method advocated by the psychiatrist David Jones (1992) who was a member of the policy steering group. The phased approach shares a number of common features with the semi-structured interview procedure originally developed in Germany by psychologists conducting interviews for the purpose of carrying out the criteria-based content analysis (CBCA) which is used as part of the statement validity analysis (SVA) procedure (see page 243 above).

The interview is structured with regard to principles of cognitive development in children. It is well recognised that free recall increases the likelihood of accuracy of information. The interview format, therefore, is designed to obtain as much information as possible in free narrative style from the child. The interview questions move from broad to specific as is necessary. The design of the questions can be visualised as a funnel, moving from those questions that are designed to produce free-recall information to those requiring specific responses. (Steller and Boychuck 1992, p. 49; see chapter 9 for further details.)

Table 12.1 Investigative interview methods

Video Recording Memorandum (Home Office 1992)	Interview Schedule (Jones 1992)	Step-wise interview (Yuille et al. 1993)	
I Rapport	(a) Gaining rapport	Step 1	Rapport
		Step 2	Discussion of truth
		Step 3	Introducing topics of concern
II Free narrative account	(b) Inquiring about sexual abuse	Step 4	Free narrative

III Questioning
  A. Open ended
  B. Specific yet non leading
		Step 5	Open questions

C. Closed questions D. Leading questions	(c) Facilitation	Step 6	Specific questions
IV Closing the interview	(d) Gathering detail (e) Closing phase	Step 7	Interview aids if if necessary

Canadian psychologist John Yuille also uses this funnelling approach in his step-wise interview method (Yuille et al. 1993) which has been used to train British police and social workers. He has recently carried out an evaluation of the step-wise method following a training programme with police, social workers and prosecutors in British Columbia. The results are encouraging—while 35% of the pre-training interviews were classified as 'useless', only 14% of those conducted after the step-wise training were given this rating. In addition only one of the 156 professionals participating in the study commented negatively on the method (Yuille 1992). Table 12.1 presents a comparison of these three approaches to investigative interviewing.

As Table 12.1 illustrates, these three approaches are very similar. The basic procedure advocated in the Memorandum (Part 3A) is briefly described below with reference to distinctive features of the other two methods. For a detailed discussion of the psychological research which underpins this approach see Bull (1993) and Steward et al. (1993).

Phase One—rapport
The first stage in all three protocols is rapport building which is an essential part of the process as it enables the child to relax and to establish a relationship with the interviewer. In this phase the interviewer should talk to the child about neutral events and with younger children this may involve talking and listening while the child is playing. At this point the interviewer can briefly explain his or her role and the reason for the interview without referring to the alleged offence. Wattam (1992) found in her child protection study that 'children state that despite knowing people's names, and even jobs, this does not adequately explain for them who is involved, at what point, and why' (p. 96). Issues relating to confidentiality and the fact that the interview is being video-recorded should be discussed at this point. There is no legal requirement to administer the oath but it is at this point rather than later in the interview that the child should be made aware of the need to tell the truth. The ground rules for the discussion should now be established, for example the importance of indicating if a question has not been understood and of saying 'I don't know' rather than guessing. The Memorandum suggests (at 3.11):

One form of words would be *'Please tell [us] all you can remember. Don't make anything up or leave anything out. This is very important.'* Or the interviewer could complete an age-appropriate discussion with the child of what is true and false by saying something like: *'You can tell me anything you want. I don't want you to feel you need to hold anything back. All that matters is that you don't make anything up or leave anything out'.*

This opening phase will allow the interviewer to assess the child's intellectual, communication and social skills. In Yuille's step-wise approach, he recommends that the child should be specifically asked to recount two previous events (e.g. a trip or a birthday) as this will allow the interviewer to judge the style and composition of the child's recall of a remembered event.

Phase Two—free narrative account
In the second stage the Memorandum advises (at 3.12) that:

> the child is encouraged to provide *in his or her own words* and at his or her
> own pace an account of the relevant event(s). This is the heart of the
> interview and the interviewer's role is to act as a facilitator not an
> interrogator. Only the most general, open-ended questions should be asked
> in this phase, for example, *'Why do you think we are here today?'; 'Is there
> anything that you would like to tell me?'*

Jones calls this stage 'initial inquiry about sexual abuse'. He acknowledges
that it can be difficult to move from the rapport building phase to inquiring
about sexual abuse. He advises (at p. 33) 'In general the first steps in this phase
will be aimed towards encouraging the child to provide a spontaneous account
. . . The interviewer will need to be careful to avoid altering her demeanour and
style at this point, as this would raise the child's anxiety'.

If the allegations concern repeated abuse over a period of time, Yuille
suggests that it is best first to ask for a description of the general pattern of the
abuse. (This is sometimes called a script memory and it provides the gist of a
familiar and repeated event, e.g., visiting the supermarket.) Once the child has
described the general pattern of the abusive event, this can then be used to help
the child recall specific episodes. The interviewer should demonstrate active
listening, tolerate apparently irrelevant material, remain patient through
silences and pauses and must avoid interrupting the child. Bull (1993) adds
that they should also resist the temptation to speak as soon as the child appears
to finish answering. Tobin (1987) found that teachers obtained fuller replies
from pupils if they were able (which they found difficult) to wait longer than
three seconds before speaking once pupils appeared to stop speaking. As
discussed in chapter 11, psychological experiments have shown that this free
recall stage will often produce limited information from younger children but
that in what they do say they can be as accurate as older witnesses. Certainly
an unprompted account is likely to carry most evidential weight in a court. If
it is necessary to prompt, these should be open-ended, such as 'Did anything
else happen?'. Prompts should not include any details concerning the event
which are known by the interviewer but which have not been mentioned by the
child. Inexperienced interviewers find this stage particularly difficult and
require both training and structured practice to develop these responsive and
yet non-directive techniques (the question of interviewer training is considered below).

Phase Three—questioning
If the interviewer decides to proceed beyond the free narrative, the next stage
is the questioning phase, and this is ordered or funnelled from very general
open-ended questions to more specific questions.

(A)   Open-ended questions   Open-ended questions ask the child to provide
more information but in a way that does not lead or pressurise the child. For

younger children the interviewer may need to state explicitly that he or she does not know what has happened to the child, as young children sometimes believe that adults know all the answers. The Memorandum suggests that for a child who has provided very little relevant information in the first stage a suitable question might be 'Are there some things you are not very happy about?'. When apparently relevant details have been given, then the questions could focus on the information the child has mentioned. If the child becomes distressed then the interviewer should move away from this topic and possibly revert to an earlier phase of the interview e.g., reestablish rapport.

(B)   Specific yet non-leading questions   This stage enables the interviewer to extend and clarify information gathered in the previous stage.

The questions should be kept as simple and as short as possible with one idea per question. Jones suggests that the interviewer should try to avoid 'Why?' questions which may impute guilt and the use of pronouns which may be ambiguous, e.g., 'Did he do anything else?' Question repetition should be avoided as children may interpret this to mean that the interviewer does not accept their first response (see Moston 1987). Bull (1993) warns of the danger that younger children in particular may wish to provide an answer in order to please the interviewer, and the Memorandum stipulates that questions which require a yes or no answer, or ones which allow only one of two possible responses should not be asked. Again this phase should proceed at the child's pace and the interviewer should adopt the vocabulary of the child rather than vice versa, particularly with regard to anatomical or sexual terms. The interviewer also needs to appreciate the level of the child's understanding of sexual behaviour. (There are some useful studies of children's sexual knowledge; see for example: Gordon et al. 1990a, b; Jones and Thompson, 1991; Volbert 1992.)

(C)   Closed questions   If phase B is not sufficiently productive then the interviewer should begin to use closed questions which give the child a limited number of alternative responses, preferably more than two. Thus 'Was the man's jacket blue or brown or black or some other colour? Or can't you remember?'.

The Memorandum cautions (at 3.31) that 'If the answer given to a limited response question contains a fact to be disputed in court, the question may then be considered to be leading'.

(D)   Leading questions   A leading question is one which implies the answer or assumes facts which are likely to be in dispute. There may be a tendency for younger witnesses to respond in the affirmative and if yes/no questions are used they should be phrased so that questions dealing with the same issue sometimes seek a yes and sometimes a no in response. The Memorandum points out (at 3.32) that 'it must be understood that a leading style of questioning may produce replies which are excluded from criminal proceedings'. In a criminal court leading questions are not permitted during the evidence in-chief. This type of questioning should be used only as a last resort and with an appreciation of the limited evidentiary value of this approach.

However, on occasion, leading questions may be facilitative, in that they get a reluctant child to start talking; and if the child's response then contains relevant information not led by the question the interviewer must then refrain from phrasing any further questions in a leading fashion and should revert to one of the neutral modes of questioning.

Phase Four—closing the interview
The final closing phase is used to check that the interviewer has correctly understood the important parts, if there were any, of the child's account. If the interviewer recaps the child's account this should be done in the child's language. This is the time to check whether the child has any questions but the interviewer should be careful when closing the session not to make any promises to the child about what will happen next which cannot be kept. It is normal courtesy to thank the child and good practice to give a contact name and telephone number in case of queries or in case the child decides at a later time that he or she wishes to discuss further matters with the interviewer.

Wattam (1992) in her study of child protection interviews noted that some interviews ended very abruptly. It was almost as if, once the interviewers decided it was over, the whole thing stopped and everyone walked out. Children were sometimes left playing alone in the room. These interviews can be very important events for children, and they might have a mix of feelings to contend with (p. 129). The Memorandum states (at 3.36).

'Every interview should have a closing phase conducted in the interests of the child. It has already been emphasised that it may be appropriate to terminate an interview before sufficient information has been obtained from the child for criminal proceedings. In such circumstances, the child should not be made to feel that he or she has failed, or disappointed the interviewer. The interviewer should be careful to ensure that all interviews end appropriately. Every effort should be made to ensure that the child is not distressed but is in a positive frame of mind.

Accompanying adults
On the question of who else should be present at the interview, the Memorandum states (at 2.27):

Limiting the number of people present at the interview should lessen the possibility of the child feeling overwhelmed by the situation and uncomfortable about revealing information. *A suspected offender should never be present.* The presence of other people may also distract or put pressure on the child. The court in considering whether to admit the recording, may wish to be assured that the witness was not prompted or discouraged during the interview, and to provide a comprehensive record of the words and gestures of more than two persons can be technically demanding. However, such considerations may be outweighed by the benefit of having a supportive accompanying adult available to comfort and reassure a very young or distressed child, particularly if the child requests it. In such cases the accompanying adult will need to be clear that he or she must take no part in the interview.

Clinicians appear to favour interviewing the child alone (Haugaard and Repucci 1988) as this reduces the risk of parental influence, or avoidable embarrassment, or reticence on the part of the child. Jones (1992, p. 23) has found that 'Generally, if the child is given easy access to the parent, and if the interviewer can see the child casually, with the parent, prior to the session, the child will feel comfortable enough to separate from the parent and talk with the interviewer alone. This author often shows the child where the parents will be waiting, and gives the child full permission to find them if necessary'. The issue of the child being supported by an adult in court is discussed further in chapter 13.

The Home Office have now commissioned a psychological study led by Professor Graham Davies at Leicester University which will examine the quality and acceptability of videotaped statements and will evaluate closely how they have adhered to the Memorandum. The researchers will also look at the impact of videotaping interviews on the performance and well being of young witnesses. The findings will be published in September 1994.

Legal effects of not following the Memorandum
Before leaving the Memorandum, something must be said about the legal effects of failing to follow the advice that it contains.

It should be remembered, however, that the Memorandum was drawn up as a guide for obtaining statements for use in criminal, not civil proceedings—and in particular, criminal proceedings in England. It has no official standing north of the Border (though obviously, it may still be relevant in Scotland in so far as it represents a consensus view among professionals as to what good practice requires). As we explained earlier, hearsay statements are now generally admissible in civil proceedings, and the civil courts have no discretion to exclude admissible evidence which is relevant. In civil proceedings, therefore, even in England, an interviewer's failure to follow the guidance contained in the Memorandum may affect the weight a judge is prepared to put upon the statement—but it will not cause him or her to refuse to listen to it. As the Court of Appeal said in Re M (Minors) (Sexual Abuse: Evidence) [1993] 1 FCR 253 at 263:

It is important to draw distinctions between interviews with young children for the purposes of investigation, assessment and therapy. It would be rare, I would assume, that interviews for a specifically therapeutic purpose would be provided for use in court. Generally it is desirable that interviews with young children should be conducted as soon as possible after the allegations are first raised, should be few in number and should have investigation as their primary purpose. However, an expert interview of a child at a later stage, if conducted in such a way as to satisfy the court that the child has given information after acceptable questioning, may be a valuable part of the evidence for consideration as to whether abuse has occurred. No rigid rules can be laid down and it is for the court to decide whether such evidence is or is not of assistance.

In criminal proceedings in England, the judge does have a discretion to exclude a videotape of an interview with a child if he feels the interests of justice require it (page 48 above). But it is important to note that he has a discretion, not a duty. He is not obliged to exclude—and the question is whether the judge will exercise his discretion.

It is suggested that in deciding whether or not to exclude, the judge should not take a mechanical approach, but should consider the purpose behind the guideline which the interviewer is said to have broken. The Memorandum stresses the need for an initial rapport-building phase. This is mainly intended to put the child at ease, and so ease the flow of information. If the child already knows the interviewer and the purpose of the interview, there is no sensible reason for not 'getting down to business': indeed, insisting on a rapport-building phase is likely to cause the confusion it is meant to avoid. So in such a case there should be no question of excluding the videotape for want of a rapport-building phase. The courts should also adopt a purposive approach to leading questions. The risk here is one of producing unreliable answers—in particular, ones which merely take up the suggestions contained in the question. When viewing a tape of an interview, as against presiding over a live examination at a trial, the judge is in a position to see whether the mischief has been produced or not. If the interviewer says 'I think you got that bruise because your daddy got cross with you and hit you', and the child answers 'Yes', it may be wise to exclude both question and answer. If the child replies 'Yes, I went round to X's house where daddy said to never go, and I got back late, and daddy got mad at me and hit me with the poker', the answer goes far beyond the question, and there is less reason to exclude. If the police are able to check the story, and find the child did indeed visit X's house that day, there seems no reason to exclude the statement at all.

MAXIMISING CHILDREN'S RECALL

In this section we examine a range of techniques which can be used to maximise the amount of reliable information reported by child witnesses or to enable reticent children to talk about their experiences using a less direct interview style. The techniques discussed are the cognitive interview, the use of props, drawings and dolls and facilitative questioning.

The cognitive interview
In a study of interview techniques designed to help young children (three to five years) remember a witnessed event, Wilkinson (1988) found that taking the child back to the scene of the event improved the child's recall. This technique, sometimes used by the police, is called 'context reinstatement' and can be achieved either by taking the witness back to the scene of the crime or by asking the witness to think himself back into a particular situation.

Retrieving information from memory is heavily dependent on remembering the context in which the information was originally encountered.

Artificially reinstating context is one of a package of eyewitness interview techniques (derived from scientific studies of memory) which have been developed by the American psychologists Geiselman and Fisher (1989). The cognitive interview is a non-hypnotic memory-enhancing technique, which was originally based on four general retrieval mnemonics: (a) mentally reinstating the environmental and personal context that existed at the time of the crime; (b) reporting everything, regardless of the perceived importance of the information; (c) recounting events in a variety of temporal orders; (d) reporting the events from a variety of perspectives. Their experiments have indicated that the cognitive interview produces better recall than conventional interview techniques, without the suggestibility effects characteristic of hypnotic interviews (see Memon and Bull 1991 for a review of the origins, empirical support and practical implications of the cognitive interview).

The first pilot study using the cognitive interview with children (Geiselman and Padilla 1988) did suggest that the technique looked promising; the only part which children found tricky was being asked to report the events from another person's perspective. Since that time the design of the cognitive interview has been refined (Fisher and Geiselman 1992; Fisher and McCauley in press) and there have been several experimental studies with child witnesses which have reported positive effects (e.g. Saywitz, Geiselman and Bornstein 1992). However not all aspects of the technique appear to work well with children and some studies have failed to find a beneficial effect (Memon et al. 1993). In a recent comprehensive review of the literature on cognitive interviewing with child witnesses, Bull (1993) concluded (at p. 13), 'much more research and development needs to be conducted regarding the possible usefulness of the mnemonic components of the cognitive interview for children, especially the younger ones . . . We should be able to accommodate it into a child centered approach. It encourages listening to, rather than quizzing, the child and it therefore sits well with recent British government reports and recommendations'. (See also Westcott (1992) who discusses the value of this technique for social workers.)

Props, drawings and dolls
David Glasgow (1987), a clinical psychologist, argues that traditional interviews are an entirely inappropriate method of obtaining information from children because of the child's lack of experience with the social conventions of a formal interview and also because of children's reliance on non-verbal communication (facial expressions, gestures, demonstration). Consequently many professionals use an extensive variety of interview materials such as dolls, toys, puppets and drawings in order to facilitate children's communication during diagnostic or therapeutic sessions (Glasgow 1989; Jones 1992; Kendall-Tackett 1992). On the use of dolls and other 'props' the Memorandum takes the following position (see Appendix I, p. 24):

'Props' include dolls, drawings, dolls' houses and small figures which can serve as potentially very useful communication aids in interviews carried out for the purposes of this Memorandum. Young children and those with communication difficulties, may be able to provide clearer accounts when such props are used, compared with purely verbal approaches. For example, drawings or dolls may allow a child to demonstrate body parts or an abusive incident, while a dolls' house may help the child to describe the environment in which an incident took place. All props should be used with caution and without leading questions. The need for their use should be carefully considered before the interview.

There is only a limited amount of empirical evidence on the use of these interview aids but the prevailing view is that they can be helpful if treated with caution. New Zealand psychologist Margaret Pipe has been testing the effects of props and cues in laboratory studies on children's recall. In a recent paper describing this research, she concludes that:

there is now clear evidence that cues and props can help children to provide more complete event reports than they would normally provide in a free-recall account. Cues and props may also help when children are questioned quite specifically if the questions relate directly to cue items. Interviewers must, of course, always be aware of the risk that these retrieval techniques might reduce the accuracy of reports. The effect on accuracy appears to depend on the nature of the cues and props, the way they are presented, and how children are instructed to use them. We are cautiously optimistic that there will be few adverse effects on accuracy when children are interviewed with props in view or when props are used in conjunction with specific questions. (Pipe et al. 1993, p. 43.)

Children are sometimes asked to create drawings in both diagnostic (Goodwin 1982; Sidun and Rosenthal 1987; Yates et al. 1985) and police interviews (Farley 1987) but these have limited diagnostic value and great care needs to be taken in their interpretation. The Pigot Committee (1989) warned (at 4.22) that 'unless these [dolls and drawings] are approached with caution their use will be regarded by the courts as suggestive and prejudicial'. When children do produce drawings during an interview, these must be very clearly labelled. The preservation of evidential drawings formed one of the recommendations in the Orkney Inquiry: 'Drawings undertaken by children during interviews contribute to an overall record of contact with the child. It is important that the way in which drawings were created is also recorded and that drawings themselves are preserved' (Clyde 1992, para. 7.67). For a review of the psychological studies into children's drawings see Cox (1992).

The most controversial of these interview props are the anatomically detailed dolls which allow children to demonstrate sexual touching, intercourse or other acts that the child may not wish to speak about or may lack an appropriate vocabulary or conceptual framework to describe (see Yates and Terr 1988 for two opposing psychiatric opinions on their use). The dolls are manufactured in a range of designs and there is no standard interview protocol for their use. The guidance provided in the Memorandum states (at Appendix I, p. 24):

> Particular care is necessary when genitalled dolls are used, where it is important the the interviewer is skilled and trained in their use and misuse. A combination of leading questioning style and the use of genitalled dolls can be particularly error prone, and is unlikely to produce evidence which could be used in criminal proceedings. In the main genitalled dolls should only be used as an adjunct to the interview to establish the meanings of terms used by the child *once the child has finished his or her free narrative account, and the general substance of his or her evidence is reasonably clear.*

This is a somewhat limited application of the dolls and in the hands of a specialist interviewer it is said that they can have other facilitative effects. Boat and Everson (1993) explain that the dolls could have a variety of potentially useful functions:

(a)   as an 'icebreaker' to help focus the child on broad sexual issues;
(b)   as an anatomical model to visually cue the child when determining her sexual knowledge and vocabulary;
(c)   as a 'memory stimulus' and
(d)   as a diagnostic test if abused children interacted with the dolls in a different way from non-abused children.

A key question is whether or not the use of genitalled dolls really does create a risk of leading and suggestion—at any rate, when they are used for any purpose other than merely enabling a child to give a more precise account of an incident he or she has previously described without them. A related question is their possible use for purpose (d) above. If children are allowed to play with them, is their behaviour any reliable guide to whether or not they have been abused?

There have now been a considerable number of evaluation studies on young children's behaviour with these dolls, and in some studies the sample includes children who are known to have been abused (e.g. Goodman and Aman 1990; Kendall-Tackett and Watson 1992; Maan 1991; White et al. 1986). Their experiments have consistently reported that non-abused children do not generally show the sexually explicit doll play characteristic of abused children, even under conditions of suggestive questioning (Goodman and Aman 1990). Absence of sexualised play of course cannot be taken as confirmation of non-abuse. Morever, there are indications that a minority of 'non-suspected' children do exhibit reticence, refuse to touch the dolls or demonstrate sexual behaviours and care must be taken in interpreting such reactions. Boat and Everson (1989) conducted a follow-up study 16 months after observing an original sample of 209 non-suspected two- to five-year-olds. They were interested in the small percentage of children who had shown unusual behaviour during the initial test session (8% avoiders; 5% demonstrators) and they re-interviewed 10 of the children who had refused to touch the unclothed dolls and 10 who had demonstrated clear intercourse positions with the dolls and compared their behaviour at the second session with matched controls. No differences were found between the experimental and control groups; thus children who had previously demonstrated sexual acts did not do so when they were 16 months older and the avoiders had become more comfortable with the dolls over the same period. They concluded that the avoiders were sexually more naive, and their initial behaviour may have reflected family norms of modesty, and that the demonstrators tended to come from lower social backgrounds, more cramped housing conditions and had had greater potential exposure to sexual behaviour (e.g., videos). The authors concluded (at p. 5): 'Although sexualised demonstrations by non-abused children with the dolls are rare, they do occur and therefore are not definitive markers of abuse'.

One insurmountable difficulty in such studies is ensuring that the 'non-abused' group does not in fact contain abuse victims. Glaser and Collins (1989) observed 91 children aged three to six years who had no history of abuse and found that the majority of children did not demonstrate unusual play, while, like Boat and Everson's sample, five children refused to touch the dolls and a further five did demonstrate explicit sexual behaviour. Three of those children who demonstrated sexual acts were later found to have been exposed to explicit sexual behaviour. Interestingly, an American study by Britton and O'Keefe (1991) found that children (aged 2–10 years) 'referred for medical evaluation of sexual abuse will use sexually explicit behaviour to demonstrate what has happened to them with *non-anatomical* dolls as frequently as when they are interviewed with anatomically detailed ones' (p. 567).

Boat and Everson (1993) have recently reviewed the available research findings in relation to the four applications of the dolls listed above and they advise (at p. 65), 'The preponderance of research supports the use of anatomical dolls as an interview tool but not as a litmus test for sexual abuse. It is important that we remember that the effectiveness of any tool is contingent upon the skill of its user'. This view is shared by the medical profession who believe that 'there are too many questions about the validity and reliability of anatomically correct dolls to recommend their use as a first stage diagnostic aid' (Kolvin 1988, p. 58), but they suggest that the dolls can be of facilitative value in the later stages of an interview. (See Glanville Williams 1987a for a legal view, and Vizard and Tranter 1988 for guidelines on the conduct and interpretation of doll interviews.) The major conclusion that can be drawn on the doll question is that they should only be used by trained professionals and that considerable expertise is also required to interpret the resulting video-tapes, particularly when they are being used in evidence. Vizard et al. (1987) underline the importance of this by pointing out that doctors who take X-rays into court do not expect the judge and jurors to interpret them by themselves.

Facilitative techniques

In the Cleveland report (DHSS 1988) the potential evidential problems of using facilitative interview techniques, such as posing hypothetial questions were discussed (12.27–12.33) and it was emphasised that such methods should only be adopted by those with specific training. This issue is also addressed in Appendix II to the Memorandum (at p. 24):

A facilitative style of questioning may be used with children who are particularly reticent. This can involve asking the child about nice/nasty things, good/bad people, what the child would like to change in his or her life, or similar techniques. For those children who have been put under pressure not to disclose certain matters an open-ended discussion of secrets may be introduced.

Such methods may be very successful for those trained in such particular styles of questioning. If the interviewer avoids any suggestive questioning and succeeds in encouraging the child to give a spontaneous account there should be no reason why evidence gained in this way should not be acceptable to the courts. However, such techniques should not be used without prior discussion and agreement with senior managers.

Given the difficult circumstances in which these facilitative techniques are employed, it would be extremely difficult to design a psychological test of their impact on the reliability of the child's statements. (See Jones (1992, chapter 5) for examples of this type of question.)

CHILDREN WITH SPECIAL NEEDS

Very few of the child witness researchers have studied children who have special needs caused by mental or physical disability. One notable exception is the psychologist Helen Dent who has undertaken a number of studies to identify the best methods of interviewing children with learning difficulties (Dent 1986; 1992). Another psychologist who has been studying the problems facing child victims and witnesses with many different types of special needs is Helen Westcott, a Research Officer for the NSPCC. In a recent review of over twenty studies she found that children with differing disabilities are at increased risk of abuse, perhaps by as much as 50% (Westcott 1991). This unpalatable statistic is compounded by the difficulties that then may occur when allegations involving disabled children must be investigated and subsequently tested in court. Part of the problem also lies with adult understanding of and attitudes to disability. Westcott (1993a) cites the example of a case where social workers investigating sexual abuse of an able bodied daughter did not even question her blind sister even though she too had been physically and sexually abused by the father. Many professionals are aware of these problems and are eager to develop more sophisticated interview techniques to use with disabled children. In 1992 the Scottish Crown Office commissioned psychologists Ray Bull and Chris Cullen to produce a booklet to help procurators fiscal interview 'witnesses who may have mental handicaps'. Helen Westcott has written a section (Reading 7) relating to disabled children in the new Open University (1993) materials on investigative interviewing. The National Resource Center on Child Sexual Abuse in Huntsville, Alabama recently devoted an entire issue of its newsletter to the special needs of sexually abused children with disabilities, and their families. (NRCCSA, December 1992). (For a fuller discussion of child witnesses with special needs, see Bull (1993).) The Memorandum mentions the question of children with disabilities:

If the child has any disabilities, for example a speech or hearing impediment, or learning difficulties, particular care should be taken to develop effective strategies for the interview to minimise the effect of such disabilities. The use of dolls and other 'props' as communication aids should be considered. In some cases it may be necessary for communication to pass through an appropriately skilled third party, for example a person who can use sign language. In others it might be necessary to consider asking such people to conduct the interview. As when any other language is used, a translation will need to be made available to the court. (2.10, p. 10).

Westcott (1993b) has commented that the real problems facing children with disabilities are not acknowledged in the Memorandum. This criticism is accepted by Ray Bull (1993, at p. 20) who was one of the authors; he agrees but explains that the reason that the Memorandum contains so little specific advice on how to interview children with special needs is because 'so little is known on the topic, particularly in terms of procedures whose effectiveness has been researched and evaluated'.

TRAINING

This chapter has highlighted the considerable demands placed on professionals who must conduct investigative interviews with child witnesses. Psychological studies which have examined interviewers' techniques in detail provide confirmation of the need for specialist training, even for those who may be proficient at other kinds of interviewing.

Dent (1982) analysed the transcripts of both experienced and inexperienced interviewers who questioned nine-year-olds about a staged event, and found a mixture of both productive (e.g., setting a context) and unproductive techniques (e.g., forming preconceptions or over-structuring). Experienced interviewers were not notably different in their success rates from inexperienced interviewers, and the quality of recall was primarily related to the level of rapport established between the adult and child. Flexibility and sensitivity were found to be important and Dent concluded that interviewers must have a range of strategies at their disposal and be able to recognise which approach will suit a particular child. In a study of real criminal investigations, Aldridge and Cameron (1989) recorded and analysed videotapes of interviews with alleged child sexual abuse victims, and concluded that, 'Without training, experienced police officers and social workers perform inadequately on a wide range of interview behaviours' (p. 198). Fisher et al. (1987) in a study of adult witnesses, characterised the differences between effective and ineffective police interviewers. ('Ineffective' being defined by the quality of the final statements.) The effective interviewers asked more open-ended questions and allowed the witness to control the flow of information. In contrast, ineffective interviewers sought direct, short answers from a haphazard sequence of questions, they tended to interrupt the witness, and gave themselves a more central role in the interview.

Again, the similarity of the 'ineffective' techniques and those that lawyers use in court to cross-examine witnesses is striking. Not only the reliability of the evidence but also the jurors' judgments of the witness's credibility are influenced by the advocate's style of questioning. 'If the lawyer constrained the witness by asking many questions that called for only brief answers (as opposed to few questions that called for expansive answers) the lawyer was perceived to have little faith in that witness. Accordingly, the subject-jurors rated that witness as less competent, less intelligent and less assertive.' (Loftus and Goodman 1985, p. 274). Thus, if the interviewer's aim is to discredit the witness rather than to elicit a reliable report, then these so called 'ineffective' techniques may, in fact, be highly effective.

The need for those conducting investigative interviews with child witnesses to be properly trained permeates every article, judicial guideline and government publication on this subject. (There is also a training need for those who are required to evaluate and interpret video tapes of recorded interviews.) Evidential interviews which are carried out by inexperienced and inadequately trained interviewers will be justifiably challenged in court by defence lawyers. To date the training provision has been inadequate and under-funded with predictable results (Aldridge 1992; Fielding and Conroy 1992; Moran et al. 1991; Westcott 1993). In other countries where children's evidence may be taken out of court, such as Israel which has a youth interrogator system (described in chapter 14), these professionals are trained and retrained on a continuing basis (Israel, Ministry of Labour and Social Affairs, 1990).

With admission of videotaped interviews as evidence in-chief in England and Wales, some attempts have been made to improve national interviewing skills. The initial Home Office response was to provide a $2\frac{1}{2}$ day training course for one policeman from each force and one social worker from each authority. The chosen ones were supposed to 'cascade' their expertise through their organisations. By all accounts this training programme was not a resounding success. The Open University has now launched (February 1993) a teach-yourself-to-interview-children pack called 'Investigative Interviewing with Children' (K501). These materials have been prepared in conjunction with a number of experts with funding provided by the Department of Health, the Scottish Office and the Home Office. The multi-media training pack is designed 'to help professionals to become more child-centred in their approach to investigations, more skilful in planning and decision-making as well as in interviewing itself and more competent to contribute to legal proceedings in which children's evidence is involved'. (One is tempted to ask: 'How much more?' and 'From what baseline?') The pack is available from the Open University (2), price £162. We await market feedback with interest.

Another new initiative is the development of award-bearing University courses on gathering evidence from children (3). Given the national enthusiasm for vocational qualifications and certificates of competence, it seems entirely sensible that those entrusted to obtain evidence from children should be as well trained and qualified as professionals in other positions of responsibility.

NOTES

1.   Our request to reproduce the Memorandum of Good Practice as an appendix to this book was refused.

2.   *'Investigative Interviewing with Children'* Training Pack (K501) is available from the Department of Health and Social Welfare, The Open University, Walton Hall, Milton Keynes, MK7 6AA.

3.   Leicester University's Diploma in Child Protection includes a five day programme on *'Theory and Practice of Children's Testimony'*. Contact Professor Graham Davies, Department of Psychology. The Universities of Portsmouth, Leeds and Liverpool are developing an award-bearing course *'Interviewing Children for Legal Purposes'*. Contact Professor Ray Bull, Department of Psychology, Portsmouth University.

CHAPTER THIRTEEN
Stress

Since 1989, there have been major changes in the rules and procedures for hearing children's evidence. These reforms resulted from the inescapable fact that some child witnesses were being exposed to an unjustifiable degree of stress at the hands of our legal system. This could obviously create emotional problems for the child, but it was also creating problems for justice when children were so traumatised by their court appearance that their testimony was incomplete, incoherent or totally worthless.

> The child may be so overcome as to be incapable of giving any evidence or any coherent evidence or may only come out with part of what he or she would like to say, and therefore, in that case, justice may well not be done. A person may be acquitted because the child just cannot give the details required. (Judge Pickles, BBC 'Panorama', 8 September 1986.)

There was also concern that witnesses' fears of appearing in court were increasing both the non-reporting of criminal offences and the frequency of accepting guilty pleas to reduced charges in order to prevent the child having to testify. An experienced English judge, discussing child victims, commented:

> For various reasons many cases do not even reach the courts and when they do, they are often abruptly terminated by the inability or unwillingness of a witness to recall painful events. In our search for justice it is often forgotten that when a guilty person is not charged or if charged, the court case does not reach its proper conclusion but is terminated abruptly because of the failure of a key witness to give evidence or come up to proof, that can be as much a failure or miscarriage of justice as if an innocent person had been convicted. (Judge Pigot 1990.)

Thus although exposing child witnesses to the potential stress of open court might be advantageous for child molesters, it was clearly not in the interests of justice, nor in the interests of the child victim or the other children in our society who might also be at risk.

Evidence that child witnesses were experiencing stress in court could be marshalled from three principal sources:

(a)   Anecdotal accounts of witnesses traumatised by their court appearance are legion: there are adult victims' accounts (Victim Support 1988); adults' memories of giving evidence as child victims (see chapter 5); and media reports of children exhibiting extreme distress in court by crying or collapsing in the witness-box. For example, in a High Court rape trial in Inverness, an eight-year-old girl was unable to give her evidence. The judge directed the jury not to accept the accused's guilty plea and as a result he was only convicted on two lesser charges of assault and indecent assault. The child's mother said:

> How can anyone expect a young girl to describe things that happened to her while the person she is most frightened of stands and watches. In this day and age of modern technology why couldn't my daughter have given evidence on video or from a separate room? There was no microphone to help her be heard and she didn't want to shout out words she has always understood to be bad to a courtroom full of strangers. She was so frightened by the boy that she couldn't hold her head up. She stood alone for an hour giving evidence. I wasn't allowed to stand with her or give her any kind of support and all the statements gathered by the police at the time of the attack weren't allowed to be presented in court. (*Scotland on Sunday,* 24 December 1989.)

While the videolink system is now installed in a number of English courts, its use is not mandatory and it may be deployed only on the basis of an advance application and at the discretion of the presiding judge (see chapter 5). In Scotland, videolink facilities have been installed for a trial period in Glasgow and Edinburgh courts. Another recent trial in Aberdeen provided a powerful demonstration that without the videolink provision, children are still being traumatised in open court with very unsatisfactory results. 'Demand for an explanation follows the scrapping of a case after a vital 12-year-old girl witness broke down while giving evidence. The girl was alleged to have been raped by a 46-year-old offshore worker who faced seven charges alleging sexual offences against young girls. The young witness was unable to continue giving evidence and recount details of the alleged assault when she broke down in tears in the courtroom. It was subsequently revealed that the trial was originally supposed to have taken place in Glasgow where close circuit TV facilities to reduce the trauma for child witnesses were available'. (*Aberdeen Evening Express,* 12 November 1992.)

(b)   The majority of professionals who work with child witnesses believe that involvement in a criminal investigation and a civil or criminal trial is a significant source of stress for children. Some experts have complained that this process constituted 'a revictimisation' or 'a second rape' for the child victim. Jane Wynne, a paediatrician, when discussing incest cases, is reported as saying, 'The court appearance is child abuse in itself' (*The Times,* 17 April 1986). Surveys of experts in the United States (Whitcomb et al. 1985) and in Britain (Flin et al. 1988) show that such opinions are widely endorsed.

(c)   These personal reports are complemented by a growing body of social science research which provides a more objective perspective on the question of witnesses' stress. Goodman et al. (1992) found that of 40 American children observed during preliminary hearings, 20 showed some distress or appeared to be very distressed. In actual trials, 11 out of 17 children were judged to be distressed. However, it is not only children who are affected. Recent research indicates that many adults find attending court to be unacceptably stressful (Stafford and Asquith 1991), especially victims in rape trials (Adler 1987; Brown et al. 1992; Chambers and Miller 1986; Temkin 1987). Police officers rate attending court and giving evidence as a principal source of occupational stress (Alexander et al. 1991). Even expert witnesses find the prospect daunting and many professionals are taught how to cope with the 'anxiety-provoking business' of giving expert evidence (Carson 1990; Livesey 1988; Mitchels and Meadow 1989). Other studies show that, in fact, the stress probably begins long before the witness even reaches court. Flin et al. (1988) interviewed a small sample of child witnesses waiting in court to give evidence in criminal trials, and found that most children said they felt nervous or anxious. On more than one occasion child victims were observed to be crying in the waiting-room prior to trials for sexual offences. Both experts and the parents of child witnesses have identified the months of waiting and the resulting apprehension as a significant cause of stress (see below). Again adult witnesses may be similarly distressed. Gregory (1989) found that many applicants at industrial tribunals without legal representation found the process too stressful to face on their own. Murch et al. (1987) discovered that even the prospect of going to a county court or magistrates' court can cause anxiety for adults. When asked how they felt when they knew they had to go to court, the litigants frequently used words such as 'frightening', 'terrified', 'nerve-racking' (p. 55).

Prosecuting lawyers are certainly aware of the difficulties facing child witnesses; the opinions of defence lawyers are rather more difficult to gauge: and judges' private thoughts are usually deemed out of bounds to researchers (although Davies and Noon 1991 is a notable exception, and their report reveals that judges are very sensitive to the problems experienced by child witnesses). Traditionally, the question of witnesses experiencing stress does not seem to be an issue that has overly concerned the Bar (Mullins 1943): although the Bar has furnished a few notable exceptions, such as the Scottish barrister Archibald Crawford who wrote of child sexual abuse trials, 'Not only counsel, but all concerned are harassed almost beyond endurance. It is as if all in court were in conspiracy to rape the child again.' (Crawford 1938, p. 127.)

Despite the attempts of such enlightened lawyers to address this problem, for many years no significant changes were enacted. Thirty years later, the Scottish Thomson Committee (Scottish Home and Health Department and Crown Office 1975, 43.31 to 32) considered whether children who have been the victims of sexual offences should be required to give evidence in court. But they concluded, 'that while the present procedure is not ideal and children are inevitably caused a certain amount of distress by having to give evidence in court, we are not aware of any alternative procedure that would satisfy the interests of justice and be fair to accused persons' (p. 165). Again no formal changes ensued.

Obviously, the legal profession as a body did not see any pressing need for change. Perhaps ungenerously, one might surmise that lawyers were simply unaware of the anxiety experienced by victims in courts, or if they were sensitive to this problem, perhaps (like Sir James Stephen, see chapter 5) it was felt that upsetting witnesses was an unavoidable price to pay for the protection of the defendant. Lord McCluskey, a senior Scottish judge, said at an RSSPCC conference entitled 'The Child: Victim of the Legal Process?' in 1985, that 'he could find no clear evidence that the child suffered unnecessary trauma and distress other than of a temporary nature and what one would normally expect of a witness before a court. His verdict on whether or not the child was a victim of the legal process was one of not proven.' (Irvine and Dunning 1985, p. 265.) Some legal practitioners may believe that the courts should not pander to the needs of child witnesses:

> On occasions I have sometimes felt that I have been part of what may appear to some as an all-round conspiracy to make things so easy for the complaining child that the interests of the accused and the fundamental presumption of innocence have been completely forgotten. While I accept that in most prosecutions the child has indeed genuinely complained, the fact is that the interests of the accused cannot be completely ignored just because the complainer is of tender years. Perhaps the above is unhelpful but, while I have every sympathy with the position of child witnesses, I sometimes wonder if too much concern is shown for them. Children are resilient creatures and are often better able to look after themselves than many adults. It has been my experience that an innocent child can much more readily give an account of an incident and apparently remain emotionally stable throughout than can a grown woman. (Respondent to RSSPCC Discussion Paper 1988, p. 10.)

However, by the late 1980s a significant wind of change could be felt. Giving the opening address to an international conference on children's evidence in June 1989, the Lord Chancellor said:

> Today there is a growing recognition by all those involved that, where a child has suffered or is witness to a serious, violent or sexual attack, to appear in court, seeing the perpetrator again, and facing cross-examination can cause anguish, may often be terrifying, and can sometimes have traumatic effects. Unnecessary stress in such a situation cannot be in the interests of the unfortunate children involved and it certainly does nothing to further the interests of justice. (Lord Mackay 1990.)

Lord Mackay's comments reflected a general acceptance by the legal profession that courts are unnecessarily stressful for child witnesses. By 1990, proposals for reform had been published in both Scotland and England with the aim of adapting the system to accommodate the needs of a child witness, without threatening the rights of the accused, and by 1992 a number of these proposals had been enacted, most significantly the provisions for videolinked and videotaped evidence.

Attempting to reduce stress for child witnesses obviously needs to be based on an accurate knowledge of the causes and effects of stress on child witnesses. Unfortunately, there is very little research into the experiences of victims and witnesses in court and in the case of children, there have only been a handful of studies which have attempted to identify both the causes (stressors) and the effects of stress relating to the prosecution process. The methodology of these investigations is briefly outlined below and is followed by a résumé of their principal findings and conclusions.

One way to identify the sources of stress for child witnesses is to ask the various professionals who work with children involved in legal proceedings. Burgess and Holmstrom (1978) examined case study material and provided a useful summary of factors relating to the American court process which would increase or decrease stress for child abuse victims. Their findings were later confirmed by Whitcomb et al. (1985), who conducted the first full-scale survey of American professional attitudes. They questioned prosecutors, defence attorneys, victim/witness advocates, child protection workers, police and judges in order to examine prosecutorial practices used with child witnesses, and identified several principal causes of stress. Their research was developed into a very large-scale project which examined the prosecution process for child sexual assault cases in four American states (Whitcomb et al. 1991). In the UK, there have been several similar investigations, for example, a small pilot study was conducted by Flin et al. (1988), who used a postal questionnaire to survey 200 professionals, the 103 respondents included Scottish judges, procurators fiscal, police officers, social workers and psychologists. These experts were asked about their attitudes to children's evidence, preferred interviewing techniques and the aspects of a criminal trial which they considered to be potentially stressful for child witnesses. Morgan and Zedner (1992) identified some of the particular difficulties encountered by child victims in the English legal system on the basis of interviews with over 250 personnel from all agencies which respond to child victimisation.

It cannot be assumed, however, that adults really know how child witnesses feel before, during or after their appearance in court. The first British study actually to interview child witnesses during their involvement in the legal process was carried out by psychologists in Aberdeen (Flin et al. 1988). The researchers were informed when a child under the age of 16 years was sent a citation (summons) to appear in a criminal trial. Within a 12-month period 226 children were cited for 121 criminal trials. Many of these children did not actually attend court on the day set for the trial, due to postponements, guilty pleas, because they were not required or because they did not turn up. From a subsample of 72 children who did attend court, pre-trial and/or post-trial interviews were conducted with 46 children and their parents or guardians. In addition, observations were made of 22 children while they were giving evidence. This pilot study was subsequently developed into a larger-scale investigation which recorded details of child witnesses cited for criminal trials in Glasgow (in total 1800 children aged between 3 and 15 years cited for 1058 trials in a 15-month period between 1988 and 1989), and which conducted systematic observations of 89 children giving evidence (Flin et al. 1993). The observation schedule they used was based on an instrument developed by Goodman et al. (1992) for a study of child victims in American courts (3). Using this rating schedule, they conducted observations during trials in Denver as well as obtaining pre- and post-trial interviews and assessments with child sexual abuse victims in order to assess the effects of testifying on child complainants. Davies and Noon (1991) also used a version of this rating scale for their evaluation of the live video link in English courts. They observed 154 children (4–13 years) giving evidence in physical and sexual abuse cases via the live video link and they also obtained reports from a small sample of police officers and social workers on their impressions of the effects of the trials on the child witnesses. The only other courtroom observations of child witnesses were carried out by Morgan and Zedner (1992) who watched a number of teenagers who gave evidence in English courts. (See also Cashmore and De Haan (1992) for a study of Australian children giving evidence via video link.)

As a preface to this examination of the causes and effects of stress on child witnesses, the main findings of these investigations have been summarised in figure 13.1. This model is designed as a descriptive framework for the following discussion and is not intended to demonstrate or chart precise causal relationships. It should also be noted that there are marked individual differences in child witnesses' reactions to their involvement in the legal process, and whether a child's exposure to a particular set of stressors actually causes anxiety will depend on a number of intervening variables, labelled as 'mediating factors'.

CAUSES OF STRESS (STRESSORS)

The causes of stress for child witnesses can be divided into three categories which are temporally distinct as shown in figure 13.1. The first source of stress relates to the observation or experience of the crime itself, and while this is not caused by the legal process, its presence must be acknowledged (see, for example Greenberg and Ruback's (1992) analysis of victim decision making, also Morgan and Zedner's (1992) study of child victims. In any assessment of the effects of stress on the child witness, an attempt must be made to disentangle psychological reactions due to the crime from effects caused by the investigation and trial. In the period following the crime possible stress factors can be divided into (a) those relating to the pre-trial investigation and (b) those factors attributable to the trial process. While the admission of a videotaped interview in place of the child's evidence in-chief, and the possible use of videolink for the cross-examination do solve one of the major problems for child witnesses (i.e., confronting the accused), they do not adequately deal with other stress factors (e.g., pre-trial delays) (Flin 1993). This issue will be discussed further below.

The pre-trial period
Whitcomb et al. (1985; see also Whitcomb 1990; Sas et al. 1991) identified a number of factors relating to the pre-trial period, namely: (a) repeated interviews; (b) time taken to dispose of the case; (c) repeated schedule changes;

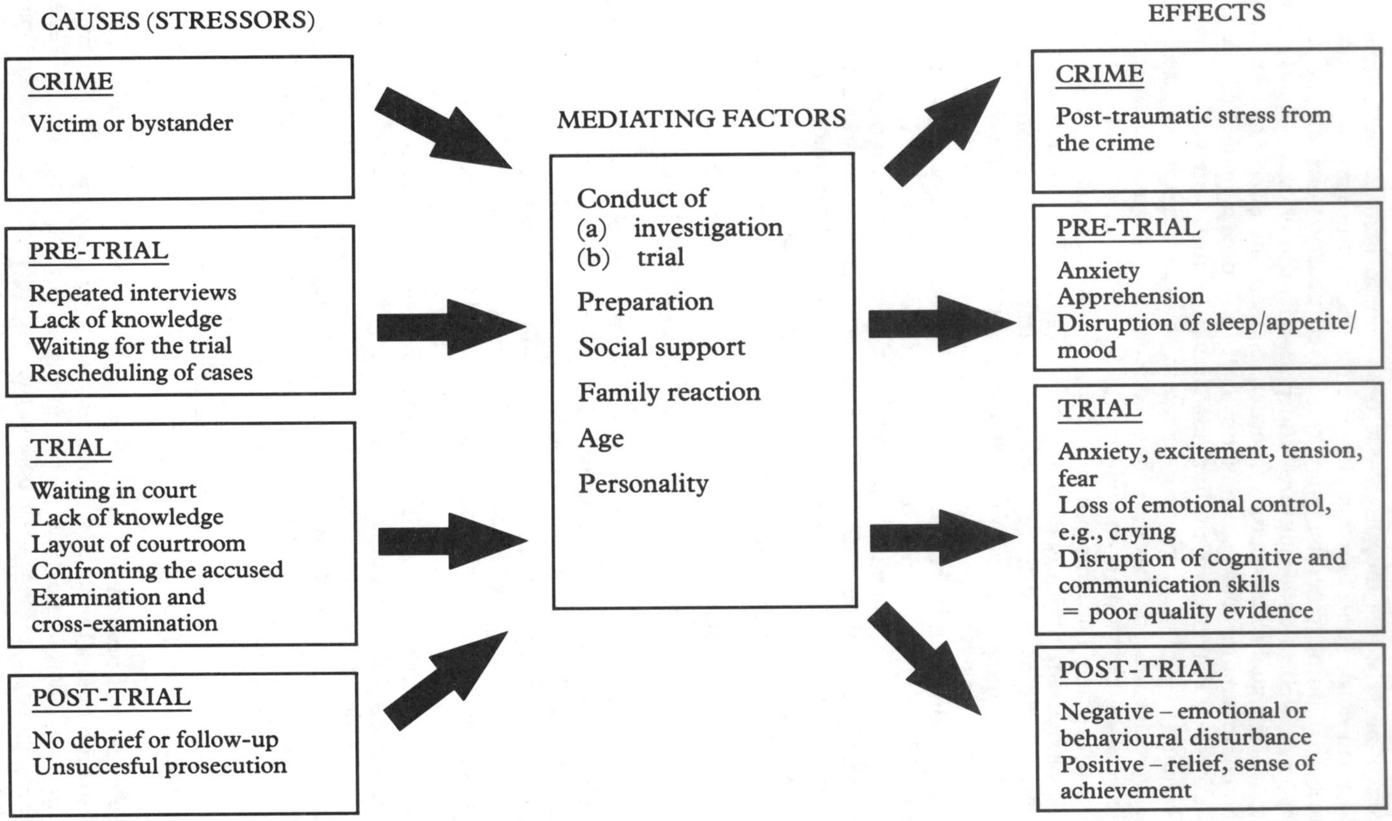

EFFECTS

CRIME
Post-traumatic stress from
the crime

PRE-TRIAL
Anxiety
Apprehension
Disruption of sleep/appetite/
mood

TRIAL
Anxiety, excitement, tension,
fear
Loss of emotional control,
e.g., crying
Disruption of cognitive and
communication skills
= poor quality evidence

POST-TRIAL
Negative – emotional or
behavioural disturbance
Positive – relief, sense of
achievement

MEDIATING FACTORS

Conduct of
(a) investigation
(b) trial
Preparation
Social support
Family reaction

Age
Personality

CAUSES (STRESSORS)

CRIME
Victim or bystander

PRE-TRIAL
Repeated interviews
Lack of knowledge
Waiting for the trial
Rescheduling of cases

TRIAL
Waiting in court
Lack of knowledge
Layout of courtroom
Confronting the accused
Examination and
cross-examination

POST-TRIAL
No debrief or follow-up
Unsuccesful prosecution

Figure 13.1   *Model of Stress Factors for Child Witnesses*

(d) removal of child from home; (e) retaliation; (f) fear of the unknown; (g) victim/family exposed in media. This is North American research into child sexual abuse victims but the results would seem to be applicable in a British context. Some of the factors they identified for child victims, such as lack of knowledge or delays, also apply to child bystanders, particularly those who have witnessed murders, serious assaults and fatal accidents.

Repeated interviews

The problems of repeated interviews conducted by an assortment of professionals, with different agendas, have been officially acknowledged (DHSS 1991). Whitcomb (1990) argues that repeated interviewing is not only stressful but jeopardises the quality of the child's evidence by increasing the likelihood of leading questions and confusing the child. There is also a risk that this will diminish the child's motivation and cooperation. By the time the child reaches the courtroom she may be reluctant to repeat her evidence yet again, and in addition, over-rehearsed evidence may diminish the child's credibility in the eyes of the court. Developmental psychologists (e.g., Brainerd and Ornstein 1991) have argued that multiple interviews can preserve children's memory, but although this may occur in the sterile conditions of a laboratory, great care must be taken in attempting to generalise from such data to the real problem of ensuring the quality of children's evidence (Flin 1991). Recent experimental studies (Poole and White 1991; Tucker et al. 1990) which have tested interview repetition on children's memory one week after a witnessed event have not shown any clear facilitative effect of repeated interviews. Tucker et al. concluded (at p. 117), 'The findings support the current trend towards early interviewing of child witnesses after a crime, followed by minimal reinterviewing'.

Lack of legal knowledge

Children's lack of legal knowledge may cause additional anxiety during the months preceding the trial. Even the delivery of a formal notification to attend court as a witness (which threatens prosecution for non-attendance), can heighten witnesses' fears (Shapland et al. 1985; Victim Support 1988), particularly as these documents are generally written in unintelligible jargon. This specific problem has recently been dealt with by the Home Office 'Victims' Charter' (1990) and the instruction leaflet for adult witnesses (*Witness in Court*, HMSO) designed by Victim Support (1988) and adopted by the Home Office as part of the notification procedure for witnesses. A new Child Witness Information Pack has been developed by the Home Office, the NSPCC, Childline and the Department of Health and, from 10 May 1993 has been available routinely to all child witnesses. The pack consists of three parts: 'Let's Get Ready for Court' is designed for children of nine years or younger; 'Tell Me More About Court' is aimed at children over the age of nine, and there is also a leaflet 'Your Child is a Witness—Information and Advice for Parents and Carers' (1). In Scotland, due principally to the efforts of the procurators fiscal in Glasgow, a colourful explanatory leaflet (*Going To Court*, Crown Office, Edinburgh, 1989) is now sent to child witnesses along with their citation to attend a criminal trial. Techniques for preparing children for court are discussed in more detail below.

Waiting for the trial

In many jurisdictions, there are backlogs of cases awaiting trial and offences involving child victims may take months to reach the courts (Plotnikoff 1990). Such delays can prolong the child's anxiety. 'One mother whose daughter had been sexually assaulted said 'the wait for the case to come up [10 months] was interminable'. Another put it more strongly still: 'the worst thing about the whole affair at present for my daughter was thinking about having to go to court and the wait. If she'd known it would be like this she would never have reported it'. (Morgan and Zedner 1992, p. 143). Flin et al. (1988) found that both experts and parents believed that the long interval between the child witnessing the offence and the trial was a significant cause of stress—one father talked of 'the long stressful wait'. In their Aberdeen sample, some children waited from one to 17 months between witnessing the incident and the date of the trial; the average delay period was six months. In a Glasgow sample, the average waiting period for child witnesses was seven months (Flin et al. 1993). Davies and Noon (1991) reported that in England child abuse victims were faced with delays ranging from four months to 26 months (average 10.5 months) between the defendant being charged and the final trial date. Joyce Plotnikoff at Birmingham University is currently carrying out a study of delays in child abuse prosecutions funded by the Nuffield Foundation. Her preliminary results show that of 200 cases involving 394 children, those cases which finished at the Crown Court took 182 days from committal to final hearing. Cases heard in the magistrates' courts took 78 days on average from first to last appearance. (Plotnikoff, 1993.)

Psychiatrists and psychologists argue that these delays can hamper attempts to treat the child by postponing therapy to avoid accusations of contaminating the child's evidence (see Glaser and Spencer 1990; Sas et al. 1991) although this might be alleviated by the use of videotapes, see chapter 7. As discussed in chapter 5, attempts to expedite cases involving child victims have generally been unsuccessful. This is unfortunate because as discussed in chapter 11, young children's memories seem to be disproportionately sensitive to long delays.

Rescheduling of cases

Delays are often caused by trial dates being rearranged due to requests from the defence or the pressure on court facilities. Whitcomb et al. (1985) found that in America schedule changes, where trials are repeatedly postponed, were usually an additional source of stress for child victims and their families. 'Continuances [adjournments] can sometimes benefit the prosecution, for example, when the child is recanting. But more often, the effect of repeated continuances is devastating, both to child victims and the quality of their testimony.' (Whitcomb et al. 1985, p. 105.) They quote psychiatrists Pynoos and Eth (1984) who concluded from their study of children who watched a parent being murdered, that 'Each trial postponement can cause renewed anxiety until, perhaps, anxiety related to the original memories of the event is shifted to the court proceedings' (p. 103). Trial postponements are not uncommon in British courts and while they are often unavoidable, attempts should be made not only to expedite the processing of cases involving child victims, but also to minimise rescheduling as far as possible. Davies and Noon (1991) found that the trials of 40% of the child victims in their sample were rescheduled and Morgan and Zedner (at p. 139) describe a case in Oxford where 'A trial involving a child witness was put back from February until the next visit of the High Court judge in July. The child was at court expecting to testify on the day in February when this occurred and was greatly distressed by the news of the delay'. A Court of Appeal judgment indicates judicial sensitivity to the stress caused by rescheduling. In an incest case, the defence counsel were criticised for raising an objection on the day of the trial which delayed hearing the child's evidence. 'As it was the child was brought to court on November 22nd 1989, only to be sent away, because the quashing of the indictment was being argued, and having to return the next day. This must have added to the strain that she felt in giving evidence against her father on such a charge. This court feels bound to say that it deplores the tactics that were adopted by the defence in this case.' (*H* (1991) 155 JP 561). Flin et al. (1993) found that in a sample of 89 child witnesses in Glasgow 36% were not called to give their evidence the first day they were asked to attend court. Davies and Noon (1991) reported that 31% of their sample of 154 child victims were not called on the first day they attended court.

The child witness in court

Waiting in court
Flin et al. (1988) interviewed child witnesses while they sat in the court waiting-room. The children were asked how they felt that morning about coming to court and the majority replied that they felt worried, scared or nervous. Not all children expressed negative emotions, but those who did were asked why they felt that way. The factors mentioned by the children confirmed the experts' opinions. Facing the accused and fear of retribution from the accused were sources of concern for child bystanders as well as for child victims. Children were worried about giving evidence, and having to speak out in front of an audience of strangers. Parents were sometimes concerned about their child's ability to cope with the cross-examination but it was impossible to assess how many children knew that this would happen.

The period of waiting in the court building appeared to increase witnesses' anxiety and a number of parents were concerned about the lack of information while waiting and the fact that they had not been forewarned about delays on the day of the trial. It appeared that many families arrived in the waiting-room and expected to be called almost immediately. In fact witnesses in this sample waited between one and two hours on average but in some cases they waited for an entire day and were then told to return the following day. Davies and Noon (1991) found that child victims scheduled to give evidence by live video link waited on average $2\frac{1}{2}$ hours before testifying (range: 5 minutes to $6\frac{1}{2}$ hours). Waiting facilities vary enormously from court to court, but sometimes children are waiting in unsuitable surroundings, with the risk of seeing the accused and the presence of uniformed police officers and begowned lawyers who can appear rather intimidating to a young child. These sources of stress for witnesses are not peculiar to children and are also encountered by adult witnesses in criminal trials (Shapland et al. 1985; Stafford and Asquith 1991) and adult litigants in civil trials (Murch et al. 1987). Raine and Smith (1991) in a study for Victim Support found that 60% of victims and witnesses in English courts had to wait in the same area as defendants and their supporters; most felt worried, frightened or upset; lack of information about what was happening or what to expect increased their anxiety. Some of the more modern court buildings (e.g., Glasgow Sheriff court) have special facilities for child witnesses, but at older courts child witnesses should at least be allowed to wait in a room separate from the main waiting area and out of contact with the defendant.

Lack of knowledge
One of the major factors contributing to children's anxiety at court appears to be fear of the unknown. Child witnesses did not know what would happen in the courtroom, they did not comprehend the roles of the various professionals involved in the trial and they did not always understand their own role in the proceedings (Flin et al. 1988). The majority of children had not been briefed or prepared for court and a significant number of parents reported having great difficulty in explaining to their child what would happen in the courtroom due to their own lack of knowledge. One five-year-old boy (observed by the second author) who was in tears as he waited to give evidence, repeatedly asked his mother if he would be able to go home afterwards, and when she enquired what he meant, he replied, 'I don't want to go to the jail'. An eight-year-old girl involved in the same case said anxiously, 'I don't like the witches', indicating a coven of begowned defence agents (lawyers) who were cackling at the other end of the waiting-room. These findings, which showed that child witnesses were ill-informed, are confirmed by anecdotal reports; a social worker told us of a four-year-old girl who had just given evidence and said on leaving the courtroom 'Who were all those big children?' (the jury); another social worker recalled a small boy who was very distressed in the witness-box because he thought the jury were the defendant's friends.

These children are not unusual in their ignorance of court proceedings. Flin et al. (1989) interviewed six-, eight- and 10-year-old schoolchildren (90 non-witnesses) and adults to measure their knowledge of legal terminology and court proceedings. The researchers found that children under the age of 10 years have a very limited comprehension of legal vocabulary and court procedures. (Older children and adults do not always perform much better.) Children sometimes say that they know what a legal term means, but in fact misunderstand its true meaning. For example, a consistent misapprehension was that if a person was to be prosecuted this meant that the individual would be 'badly hurt', 'hung', 'killed' or 'jailed'. One eight-year-old in response to 'What happens to you if you are prosecuted?' replied, 'You get put in prison, pay fines and when you come out of jail, you don't get a job usually, unless you sell drugs'. Children also find the roles of the various legal professionals and the jury difficult to comprehend. A six-year-old thought that judges 'teach people dancing' and a 10-year-old said of a jury, 'They ask the criminal questions, then he gives up and they sit down'. An eight-year-old thought that a lawyer is 'A guy who keeps money—he helps people save it. He's got a briefcase and pens and everything. He gives money to the poor.' Freshwater (1991) in a similar study reported three common misunderstandings in teenagers and adults: (a) that the victim is the defendant; (b) that the prosecution gives out punishments; (c) that the death penalty can be given. She found that even teenagers do not understand what cross-examination is—e.g., 'they put a cross on their head and ask questions' (15 years); 'they are examined by medical people, e.g., in a rape victim' (14 years); who the jury is—'people who saw the crime are in the jury or the person's family who is being prosecuted' (11 years); 'the jury consists of policemen and solicitors' (12 years); or the role of the defence—'a defence lawyer defends the wronged person' (35 years). In an American study, some children believed that a lawyer 'loans money', 'sits around', 'plays golf' or 'lies' (Warren-Leubecker et al. 1989), and a 10-year-old Canadian girl thought that a subpoena was 'a male's private part' (Sas et al. 1991). (See also Cashmore and Bussey (1990), Saywitz (1989) and Saywitz et al. (1990), who have found the same patterns of results in Australia and the USA, respectively.)

Flin et al. (1989) also asked their sample of schoolchildren how they would feel if they had to go to court, and found that a majority of children said that they would be worried, nervous or scared. Their expectations of experiencing negative emotions seemed to be related to the idea that courts were for bad people (a belief also reported by children in Feben 1985 and Warren-Leubecker et al. 1989), and that they might not be believed and consequently sent to jail. Other reasons they offered were: (a) not being able to understand or answer the questions correctly; (b) not knowing what to do; (c) fear of being on their own in the courtroom; (d) having to speak up in front of a large adult audience, and (e) fear of seeing the accused or of retribution from the accused. Typical responses were, 'They might believe you were a bad person and you could go to prison' (10-year-old) or, 'I would be scared because people might think I did it' (eight-year-old) or, 'I'd be unhappy, I've never been before and I don't know what it's about' (eight-year-old). The only child (eight years) in this sample who had been to court as a witness in a criminal trial, said that she did not like it 'because they had horrible hair'. A comparison group of 15 adults who were interviewed in the same study also said that they would feel nervous at the prospect of giving evidence. They were more concerned with their conduct or performance as a witness, and with the necessity of having to recount unpleasant events. However, they also referred to the unfamiliarity of the surroundings and their lack of relevant knowledge as reasons for their anticipated anxiety.

There is little doubt that misconceptions about the role of a witness or the purpose of a trial will contribute to pre-trial anxiety during the months of waiting for a case to come to court. Children's lack of legal vocabularly means that great care must be taken when conversing with child witnesses before and during the trial, and it is not enough to say 'Do you know what a jury is?' because many children who reply in the affirmative will not in fact possess the requisite knowledge. Very little is taught in schools about our law and children acquire much of their legal knowledge from television, which tends to portray over-dramatised scenes in American courts.

Those who work regularly in criminal courts, such as lawyers, police officers and court officials, may sometimes fail to appreciate how unfamiliar and intimidating our courts can appear to witnesses and jurors alike. It must be said, however, that many professionals are now aware of this problem and do attempt to prepare child witnesses as carefully as possible (see below).

Layout of the courtroom

Courtrooms are deliberately designed to be user-unfriendly places in order to ensure a suitable degree of respect for the seriousness of the proceedings. Whatever effect the formality and ceremony have on the criminal fraternity (and our rates of recidivism give some indication), the design of most courtrooms tends to intimidate innocent witnesses, particularly child victims. Predictably the resulting anxiety diminishes the quality of their evidence (Saywitz and Nathanson in press). Flin et al. (1988) asked the professionals they surveyed to state anything about the layout or design of the courtroom that might be especially stressful for child witnesses. The majority felt that the layout was indeed a source of stress; over half mentioned the large size of the room, the elevated position of the judge and the isolation of the witness-box as being the principal causes of anxiety. One respondent said that the practice of putting children in the witness-box made the child feel as if she was on trial. A small child's perception and interpretation of these surroundings may be quite different from an adult's view and younger children will have no experience of taking the leading role in formal proceedings of this nature. Several respondents suggested that the child should be placed at the table in the well of the court and that the judge and lawyers should sit with the child when conducting their examinations. In some courtrooms there are no suitable chairs for small children to sit on, although we have heard of recent cases where children's chairs were brought into the courtroom.

Other factors mentioned included poor lighting and bad acoustics, with many courts lacking voice amplification facilities. Finally, the large 'audience' present to hear the child's testimony may intimidate the child, for example, a crowded press bench or a gallery filled with gawping members of the public or the defendant's supporters. Judges do have the power to exclude the public when a child victim is giving evidence, but even if they choose to apply this provision (and not all do), the courtroom can still contain as many as 20 or 30 unfamiliar adults (the judge, the defendant/s, the lawyers, court officials, 12 or 15 jurors and the press). Many of these 'environmental' difficulties can only be alleviated by removing the child from the courtroom, an option that is provided by the live video link. However Davies and Noon (1991) caution that even when this is used, serious consideration should be given to clearing the courtroom as the child may be aware that there is an unnecessary audience listening to her evidence.

Confronting the accused

When witnesses are required to give evidence from the courtroom, seeing the accused and fear of retribution from him are major causes of stress for adults

(Asquith and Stafford 1991; Raine and Smith 1991) as well as for children (Sas et al. 1991).

Flin et al. (1988) found that facing the defendant is a significant source of concern for child bystanders as well as for child victims, and fear of retaliation is heightened when he lives in the same neighbourhood as the child. There are reports of cases where the accused has attempted to scare the child by making threatening faces or gestures and in some cases children may actually fear that they will be attacked while giving evidence. Awareness of this problem led to the use of the video link, or more simply the introduction of screens in court which are placed to block the child's view of the defendant while allowing the jury to see the child. The use of screens seems to be of variable effectiveness, and as discussed earlier, the options which remove the child from the presence of the accused are clearly preferable.

Examination and cross-examination

The examination of a child witness during a criminal trial is not governed by any special rules or procedures and a child's evidence can be tested in exactly the same way as that of an adult. While cross-examination is generally regarded as more stressful than direct examination, for a child witness the whole business of being interviewed in the alien environment of a court is likely to be most intimidating. Lawyers are not trained to interview children and may lack the necessary sensitivity and requisite skills to elicit a coherent account from the child. As Walker (1993) complains, 'There is no reciprocal test that a questioner must meet, however, that measures his or her competency to ask intelligent, easily understood, and unambiguous questions' (p. 59). Several specific difficulties can be identified in the examination process.

First, the formality of the questioning procedure is likely to be unusual and potentially threatening for the child who may never have been interviewed in this way before. Barristers are skilled at projecting their voices and may stand some distance from the child when speaking, thus requiring the child to raise her voice in reply. The child may not fully understand the purpose of the trial, and having told her story several times already, the point of repeating it yet again may be far from clear. The aim of the cross-examination may be even more obscure, particularly if the child is directly accused of dishonesty, by statements such as, 'I put it to you that you are not telling the truth'. It is interesting to note that 'Telling the truth but no one believing me' is regarded by children as one of life's most stressful occurrences (Yamamoto et al. 1987). Yet in child sexual abuse prosecutions this is likely to be the principal line of attack during cross-examination. 'The cross-examination by counsel for the abuser will be aimed at only one thing, to destroy the child's credibility in the eyes of the jury. The defence will not be based on mistaken identity or alibi but, most commonly, that the child's allegation is either malicious or fantastic.' (Ferguson 1985, p. 15.)

Secondly, both the semantics and syntax of the language used in court are likely to be at best unfamiliar to a child and at worst totally incomprehensible. Legal terminology (your lordship, objection, learned friend, recess, adjourn etc.) has the effect of accentuating formality but may also serve to baffle a child witness. Children's legal vocabulary is very restricted (Flin et al. 1989) and studies of child offenders have shown that they frequently do not understand the language used during their own trials (Cavenagh 1959). Children can also be wrong-footed even unintentionally, by unfamiliar expressions, such as: 'What is your position in relation to . . .?' 'Did he appear to take offence?' 'Did he try to resist?' And prosecuting lawyers have to be just as careful with their choice of vocabulary as defence agents. Flin et al. (1993) observed that while 80% of direct examinations were carried out using vocabulary rated as 'virtually all age appropriate', only 58% of cross-examinations fell into this category. Davies and Noon (1991) observing children on the live video link concluded (at p. 122) 'Interview techniques were a major source of concern for the research team. Basic principles of opening and rapport building were frequently ignored and questions were often pitched at the wrong level for the child. Moreover, the way in which delicate subjects were approached was often far from sensitive'. Euphemisms are especially perilous even if they do spare barristerial blushes. In an experiment in the United States, Goodman found that pre-school children pointed to their ears and arms when asked to indicate their 'private parts' (Goodman and Clarke-Stewart 1990). Any discussion of body parts and sexual behaviour should adopt the child's terminology to avoid the risk of confusion.

Psychological and linguistic analyses of British (Woodbury 1984), American (Loftus and Goodman 1985) and Australian (Brennan and Brennan 1988; Open University 1993, Reading 6) trials reveal that courtroom lawyers like to use grammatical devices, such as prosodic questions, tag questions, double negatives and embedded clauses, which can confuse witnesses and thereby damage the credibility of their evidence. In the Brennans' study of the language used to communicate with children in Australian courts, they found an alarming catalogue of incomprehensible questions. For example, a magistrate attempted to clarify the purpose of cross-examination to a distraught 11-year-old, thus:

'Now he is suggesting some other things to you that might I suppose remind you that might have happened now I suppose it is hard to understand why he says these things to you when you say it didn't happen, that's hard to understand isn't it, but he is allowed to do these things and if you say it didn't happen, all you have to do is say no, okay or if it did say yes, now do you follow that?' (Brennan and Brennan 1988, p. 88.)

In a detailed study of the transcripts of a five-year-old giving evidence in an American murder trial, Walker (1993) found 'three chief sources of communicative mischief in (a) age-inappropriate vocabulary, (b) complex syntax, and (c) general ambiguity' (p. 59).

In order to retain tight control over a witness's testimony, advocates and barristers often use short closed questions and will frequently interrupt the witness's natural flow of speech in order to restrict the witness's account and to obtain specific answers. Carson (1990) presents (at p. 34) an illuminating description of techniques (such as pinning out, focussing on peripheral issues and making suggestive remarks) that lawyers use when cross-examining expert witnesses. He explains 'pinning out' as follows: 'The object is by a series of preliminary questions, to fix the witness—as if by pins to a board—into a position from which she or he cannot move when the critical question—directed at the heart eventually comes. Witnesses are often caught because the preliminary questions can appear to be so innocent, indeed complimentary to them. Also the questions can be framed so that only one answer is really possible'. (See also Myers (1992) for a useful description of cross-examination techniques and Brigham and Spier (1992) for attorneys' views on preferred tactics for dealing with a child's evidence in an opponent's case.)

This highly structured interrogation is often accompanied by repeated requests to amplify certain answers, which can prevent the child recounting a series of events in what she remembers as their natural order. As discussed in chapters 10 and 11, these interviewing techniques are not only difficult for children to comprehend, but they also maximise the chances of contaminating the child's memory (see Cashmore 1991). The various linguistic and behavioural tactics which can be used to constrain a witness's evidence, particularly during cross-examination, are obviously of enormous advantage to the defence in their attempt to discredit a hostile witness. American lawyers actually advise a comprehensive range of strategies for the deliberate manipulation of children's testimony during cross-examination (see Myers 1987b; Lees-Haley 1988).

Thirdly, irrespective of the child's level of comprehension, the experience of being examined in court can cause stress and be physically exhausting. The process of examining a witness may take hours in a serious trial, and in cases where a witness has given evidence incriminating more than one defendant, it is likely that each defendant's lawyer will wish to cross-examine the witness. Scottish trials have been observed where a child has been cross-examined eight times by different lawyers—resulting in a total of 10 examinations including two by the prosecution (Flin et al. 1993). In American trials children have suffered gruelling experiences in abuse trials. During the notorious McMartin case in California, one child was on the witness stand for 16 days (Crewsdon 1988). At the Crookham Court School trial in England, the transcript of which we have read, the examinations in-chief cover 7 to 16 pages, the cross-examinations 24 to 107 pages: the longest one, of a boy aged 15, lasting for a day and a half (2).

There have been several assessments by psychologists of the duration of children's examinations and cross-examinations. In the first of these studies, Goodman et al. (1992) measured the time spent on the stand by 17 American child sexual abuse victims. In preliminary hearings this ranged from 4–90 minutes (average 27 minutes), in competence examinations 4–21 minutes (average 10 minutes) and in trials 13–270 minutes (average 69 minutes). Sas et al. (1991) reported that in their study of 71 Canadian child victims the children spent on average (25 minutes) maximum 95 minutes) on the stand during examinations in-chief and an average of 32 minutes (maximum 130 minutes) during cross-examinations. Flin et al. (1993) observed 89 Scottish criminal trials and reported examinations in-chief lasted from 3–92 minutes (average 16 minutes), cross-examinations lasted from 1–59 minutes (average 10 minutes), and re-examinations lasted from 1–18 minutes (average 4 minutes). Observing 154 child victims in England testifying via the live video link, Davies and Noon (1991) found that examinations in-chief lasted from 2–88 minutes (average 18 minutes), cross-examinations lasted from 2–95 minutes (average 25 minutes) and re-examinations ranged from 1–42 minutes (average 6 minutes). Thus there is some indication that cross-examinations take longer with the live video link system than with face to face examinations, but these are preliminary findings.

It has also been noticed that interruptions and adjournments during a child witness's evidence can be extremely difficult for the witness, and during these breaks they are sometimes left in the witness-box with minimal explanation of why the proceedings have been halted. We have been told of cases where this has happened. In a murder trial, a child (eight years), who was giving an extremely competent account of the accuseds' farcical attempts to dispose of a wailing burglar alarm, had her evidence completely disrupted when the defence advocate suddenly requested an adjournment in the middle of her testimony. The child, who was left alone in the witness-box during this interruption, became very distressed and only managed to complete her evidence with the greatest of difficulty when the proceedings were eventually resumed. Whether advocates ever deliberately restort to disruptive techniques is obviously a matter for conjecture (Harvey 1958).

For a child victim who may already be frightened by his courtroom appearance, the cross-examination may simply destroy rather than test his evidence.

An excerpt from the Crookham Court School trial (2) is illustrative:

(To a witness aged 15, who has repeatedly broken down in tears when giving evidence)
Q   During your school career, as you have told the jury, there were occasions when you have not told the truth?
A   Yes.
Q   Sometimes you were caught out, sometimes not, I expect?
A   Sometimes . . .
Q   And times when people caught you out, they would make you feel guilty about telling a lie?
A   Yes—and I'd get punished for it.
Q   And when you felt guilty for telling a lie at school, you would often cry, would you not?

Defence lawyers have told us that they try to avoid upsetting child witnesses as, apart from any ethical considerations, this would produce the counter-effect of antagonising the jury. This is a disingenuous argument, as cross-examination need not be vicious to traumatise an innocent victim or to ruin an honest child's testimony. Psychiatrist Eileen Vizard says:

Clever arguments put forward by defence counsel, that it is not in their best interests to be hostile to vulnerable looking children, in front of juries, are not very convincing. Children can be discredited much more readily through a process of engaging their trust, in the initial cross-examination, and then implanting suggestions about their capacity to tell lies in their minds later. All this can be done in a pleasant charming way, by a skilled defence counsel, who does not wish to alienate the jury. However, this sort of cross-examination in my opinion, needs looking at very carefully, since it is likely to have a major negative impact on a child with existing low self-esteem. (Vizard 1989, p. 30.)

For many witnesses, the experience of being cross-examined is traumatic and adult witnesses have described it as a frustrating, humiliating and distressing ordeal. In the words of Auberon Waugh,

The [rape] victim's suffering might be reduced if our courtoom procedure did not resemble something between a Pontifical High Mass in the Tridentine Rite and a comic opera. In a British courtroom, an ordinary act such as eating a sausage can be made under cross-examination, to sound like some bizarre perversion. (*Sunday Times*, 23 September 1984.)

If mature and socially experienced adults who comprehend the meaning and purpose of the judicial process, can find their experience in the witness-box to be distressing (see chapter 5), one can only conjecture what it might feel like for a small child to be interviewed in this fashion.

Anecdotal accounts suggest that judges, who have the responsibility for the witness's well-being while giving evidence, can be sometimes insensitive to the needs of victims in court. Some judges have not only refused applications for screens in court, but insist that the child stands alone in the witness-box without any psychological support from a parent or supportive professional. Requests from the prosecution that a child be permitted to take a break during examination have also been denied. Whatever the legal merits of such decisions, they remain highly questionable on ethical grounds.

The examination and cross-examination processes present three particular areas of difficulty for children: (a) their inexperience with the demands of this type of interaction, (b) the unfamiliar language used in court, (c) the physical and mental stress which cross-examination can cause. The Scottish Thomson Committee in 1975 pointed out 'that a great responsibility rests on the legal profession in this matter, and prosecution and defence counsel should never be aggressive in their examination or cross-examination of children' (43.32). Judges do have the power to intervene if they feel that an advocate's line of questioning is unfair, but this may not always happen in practice and more specific guidelines would be helpful.

In summary, the major stress factors for child witnesses attending trials appear to be associated with (a) the long delays waiting for the trial, (b) lack of legal knowledge resulting in misunderstanding and fear of the unknown, (c) repeated pre-trial interviews, (d) rescheduling of trials, (e) delays and the lack of adequate waiting facilities and information in courts, (f) unsuitable design of courtrooms, (g) confronting the accused, (h) insensitive interviewing techniques used in cross-examination, (i) inadequate protection of the child during cross-examination, (j) lack of social support for the child giving evidence.

After giving evidence
It is important that the child's contribution to the trial process is formally acknowledged, by the judge or the prosecuting lawyer. However this has recently become something of a contentious issue and it appears that great care must be taken in the phrasing of any such acknowledgement. In *Hogg* v *Normand* 1992 SCCR 26 the High Court quashed a conviction for lewd and libidinous behaviour because the trial judge congratulated the mother on her children after they gave evidence. In contrast, Lord Lane, Kennedy and Pill JJ dismissed an appeal following a conviction of indecent assault based on the judge telling a 12-year-old girl that she had done very well, and saying at the close of the appellant's evidence, 'So this 12-year-old girl has made wicked lies about you?' The grounds of dismissal stated that there was nothing wrong in the judge issuing a word of comfort to a witness who had gone through an unpleasant ordeal (*Wilson* [1991] Crim LR 838). The Criminal Law Review commentary suggests that (at p. 838) 'it would surely be better if the judge were to postpone any words of commendation till after the verdict had been given'. Witnesses also benefit from being 'debriefed' after a trial has ended when the reasons for the verdict can be explained more carefully (Morgan and Zedner 1992). However, in practice witnesses are not always informed of the result of the trial and the Home Office Victims' Charter (1990) states (at p. 19) 'The victim can expect to be told of the result of the court case if he or she is not there to hear it. It may be practical for the police—who need the information for their own purposes—to pass it on to the victim. There have been difficulties over communicating the outcomes of court cases. Work is being done to tackle these problems'. Families may be very distressed if the prosecution is unsuccessful and may require professional counselling at this time.

Summary
The obvious conclusion to be drawn from the extant research is that the best way of alleviating stress for child witnesses is to keep them out of the court-room forum whereever possible. The options available range from:

(a) Making a videotape of a pre-trial deposition so that the child need not attend court at all.

(b) Admitting a previously videotaped interview in place of the child's examination-in-chief.

(c) Using the live video link for children who are required to give evidence at trial.

However, the problem of hostile or inappropriate interviewing still remains. As psychiatrist Leona Terr (1986) points out, 'Television would not protect the youngster against child-ignorant or tricky cross-examination' (p. 469); however some judges surveyed by Davies and Noon (1991) thought the live video link gave them more control of the examinations. It seems necessary to underline that the judge is responsible for safeguarding the rights of the witness while giving evidence and should be held accountable if the witness is made to suffer unnecessary stress. Finally, the features of the prosecution process which children find stressful can also cause stress for adult witnesses, particularly those who have been victimised and attempts to instigate procedural reforms for all vulnerable witnesses are long overdue.

MEDIATING FACTORS

In any analysis of the impact of stress on human performance or on mental health, the precise relationship between cause and effect is difficult to chart due to the influence of *mediating variables*. In the case of child witnesses, whether or not a child finds the experience of a criminal investigation and trial to be stressful will depend on the individual's personality; the type of offence in question; the relationship of the child to the defendant; the reaction of the parents; the manner in which the investigation and the trial are conducted; the degree of support given to the child, and the outcome of the trial. These variables may be more important in determining the likelihood of negative effects than age *per se*, which may not be a particularly useful predictor of the child's psychological reaction to the demands of the witness role. In terms of improving our present systems we can virtually disregard factors such as personality or the crime itself, over which we can have no control (although a better understanding of these factors would also improve professional responses to the needs of witnesses). Of more immediate importance is the need to analyse the function of mediating factors which can be controlled, for instance, the conduct of the investigation and trial, the availability of social support and the preparation of child witnesses for the trial. These 'system variables' are procedures which can be improved to ensure that the child is exposed to a minimum of stress before and during the trial and that the child's evidence is not diminished by the legal process itself.

Conduct of the investigation and trial

Studies of child victims in the criminal justice system suggest that the conduct of the investigation and the trial have a significant impact on the individual's ability to cope with the process (Morgan and Zedner 1992; Victim Support 1988). Many police forces have now established specialist units for dealing with female and child victims and some prosecutors' offices allocate these cases to staff with relevant experience. In 1991 the Crown Office in Scotland issued procurators fiscal with guidance notes for the investigation and prosecution of cases involving child witnesses and we understand that a similar manual has been prepared for the English Crown Prosecution Service.

When a case comes to trial, the presiding judge now has considerable discretion regarding the manner by which the child's evidence should be presented to the court. Where children are required to give evidence in open court, there are a number of simple modifications to standard trial procedure which may make the court appear less frightening to the child. In Scotland, the Lord Justice General (the most senior judge) issued a practice direction to judges in July 1990 which offered guidance as to the use of discretionary measures in cases where children are witnesses. (See chapter 5 for details and Nicholson and Murray 1992 for a copy of the memorandum.)

In our experience, most judges are concerned about the impact of trial procedures on children and are sensitive to their responsibilities to minimise unnecessary stress on vulnerable child witnesses in their courtrooms. The issue of judicial training on children's ability to provide eyewitness evidence has been addressed by the Judicial Studies Board who have included speakers on child evidence in their programme of training seminars for English judges. An extremely well-written and valuable manual for Californian judges has been prepared by attorney Ellen Matthews and psychologist Karen Saywitz. This contains a wealth of advice on the management of cases relating to children and it is properly founded on a critical review of the relevant psychological research and practice (Matthews and Saywitz 1992).

Preparing the child witness for court
In the last five years there has been a growing realisation that preparing child witnesses for their court appearance can produce tangible benefits by reducing unnecessary anxiety and thereby improve the quality of the child's evidence. (It has been known for a decade that psychological preparation for hospital surgery produces benefits in terms of post-operative recovery, Ridgeway and Matthews, 1982). In England and Wales, if not in Scotland too, this continues to be of real importance given that the full version of the Pigot recommendations was not implemented and therefore children still have to attend court. Recent research has also examined specific cognitive training techniques to enhance children's memory and communication skills in the courtroom. There are at least five critical competencies for a child witness in court which may be improved by participation in a pre-trial preparation programme.

(a) Recall information completely and accurately.
(b) Understand the lawyers' questions, and indicate non-comprehension.
(c) Resist complying with leading questions.
(d) Cope with anxiety.
(e) Understand the trial procedures.

In the UK there has been an improvement in pre-trial preparation for child witnesses, most notably attempts to familiarise children with the court room and to explain the trial process using visits and booklets. The new Courts' Charter for England and Wales (Lord Chancellor's department 1992) states (at p. 9) 'If you are worried about appearing in court, we will show you a courtroom before the case starts. You may then familiarise yourself with the layout'. In Scotland this responsibility rests with the prosecutor, and the Scottish Law Commission (1990) recently endorsed the importance of 'careful and sympathetic pre-trial preparation'. They acknowledged (at 2.10) 'that a very great deal is already being done in this regard by the Crown Office and by procurators fiscal around the country. It is obvious that great attention is now being given to this, and we understand that the results are already being perceived as beneficial in that many children are thought to have been better able to cope with the experience of giving evidence than would otherwise have been the case'. As mentioned above, an explanatory leaflet 'Going to Court', is now sent to all Scottish children who are called to court as witnesses.

In England and Wales the position appears to be rather less satisfactory, because the responsibility for pre-trial preparation has not been allocated to a single agency and at present tends to be provided by women police officers and social workers who may have limited time available for this task and little experience of this type of preparation (Morgan and Zedner 1992; Plotnikoff 1990). There are no offical guidelines (although the Home Office Child Witness Information Pack contains some advice) and there are no recognised training packages or programmes. Davies and Noon (1991) reported that 40% of the children in their videolink study were given the opportunity to visit the court prior to trial but that only 21% were given a practical demonstration of the equipment.

This problem was addressed at the end of 1992 when each Crown Court Centre equipped with the live video link equipment was asked to appoint a Child Liaison Officer. The functions of this post are to promote the welfare of the child witness at the Crown Court; to co-ordinate arrangements and facilities at court for the child, and to provide a focal point for liaison with other criminal justice agencies.

> The Child Liaison Officer is responsible for liaising with the Crown Prosecution Service on the practical arrangements for the child's attendance at court. This will include ascertaining who will accompany the child; sending out information about the location of the court; arranging for the child to enter the court by an entrance separate from the general public (where possible); ensuring that a separate waiting area is available for the child and his/her supporters; arranging for the child to have a familiarisation visit to the court prior to the day of the trial (if desired) and to have a demonstration of the live TV link equipment; liaising with the court Listing Officer to ensure that the adult supporter is given a reasonable time for arrival at court in order to minimise the child's waiting time prior to giving evidence; ensuring that the TV link equipment is fully operational; ensuring that arrangements have been made for an usher to accompany the child witness in the separate TV link room (if directed by the judges); and organising toilet facilities and lunch arrangements. Furthermore, the Child Liaison Officer is responsible for liaising with the Resident Judge and Listing Officer to ensure, as far as possible, that any case involving a child witness progresses within the time limits laid down for each stage in the relevant Rules of Court.

(Explanatory letter sent out with Child Witness Pack, May 1993). The Lord Chancellor's Department intend to review the effectiveness of the Child Liaison Officers in the near future.

It is not customary for English barristers to meet their witnesses before the trial, and very few children (4%) were introduced to their counsel before they gave evidence on video link. Davies and Noon commented (at p. 36), 'it is reasonable to suppose that a child who had been introduced to a supportive and friendly prosecution counsel may be more at ease during the examination-in-chief than a child confronted with a stranger on a screen'. Morgan and Zedner (1992) also comment on this (at p. 133), 'One of the most curious features of the court system in England and Wales is surely the convention that the prosecutor should not speak to any witness before the trial begins. In practice a number of prosecutors are now introducing themselves to the child before the trial in order to try to create rapport with the child concerned. However they remain conscious of the need to exercise extreme care when speaking to witnesses prior to trial'. This unsociable behaviour has recently been criticised by the Royal Commission on Criminal Justice (1993) pp. 80–81. It is not found in Scotland where the procurator fiscal will often have precognosced (officially interviewed) the child before the trial as well as examine him in court. Scottish prosecution barristers (advocates depute) will routinely introduce themselves to prosecution witnesses on the day of the trial. By way of contrast, however, another notable cultural difference in pre-trial practice is that in England it is permissible to refresh the witness's memory with previous statements or video recordings but this would not be done in Scotland (*Richardson* [1991] 2 QB 484; Blackstone's *Criminal Practice* 1993, para. F6.12. The position in Scotland is discussed in Macphail (1987) at 8.50).

There are booklets available for child witnesses in England and Wales; for example, 'Susie and the Wise Hedgehog go to Court' is an illustrated story book which was written by social worker Madge Bray (1989) and 'Going to Court' is a cartoon leaflet prepared by West Yorkshire Police. The Children's Legal Centre in London has produced two information sheets: 'Being a Witness' for children and 'The Child Witness' for families, police officers, social workers and prosecutors. These were written by Joyce Plotnikoff, a research fellow in the Faculty of Law, Birmingham University. The new English Child Witness Information Pack, described earlier, was launched on 10 May 1993. In other jurisdictions some excellent materials have also been produced, such as booklets, videos and activity books which can be usefully adapted for British children (1).

Given the limitations of pre-trial familiarisation for child witnesses in Britain, it is not surprising that there has been virtually no research into the efficacy of these procedures (a pilot study by Freshwater (1991) is one of exception; see Aldridge and Freshwater 1993). Simply providing the child with some legal knowledge and giving her a tour of the courtroom may not be enough to reduce her stress and to improve her testimony (Saywitz and Snyder 1993). Sisterman-Keeney et al. (1992) in Alabama point out (at p. 203) that traditional procedures used to familiarise children with the courtroom do not necessarily prepare them for the impact of the actual experience. 'Children who had seen the courtroom, and who knew the roles and positions of the court personnel, still froze when they had to testify at trial.' Proper preparation of child witnesses may also need to provide them with the appropriate communication skills for the formal examination procedure and anxiety management techniques to enable them to cope with stress.

Results from recent North American studies suggest that systematic preparation of child witnesses in this way can yield significant benefits. Psychologist Louise Sas and her colleagues at the Family Court Clinic in Ontario have completed a three year demonstration project designed to reduce the traumatisation of child witnesses in the Canadian criminal justice system. Their aim was to develop a successful model of intervention for child sexual abuse victims testifying in court—the specific goals were (a) to demystify the courtroom through education and (b) to reduce the fear and anxiety related to testifying through stress reduction techniques. Their court preparation protocol assessed the needs of each child victim and designed a tailored preparation programme to meet those needs. The preparation programme typically included work with a courtroom model and dolls, role play and the use of booklets, as well as a court tour to familiarise the child with a courtroom and court procedures. Stress reduction techniques such as breathing exercises, muscle relaxation, and cognitive restructuring were taught to each child to help them cope with the physiological and psychological effects of anxiety. The researchers evaluated the effectiveness of this programme by taking a series of measurements of knowledge, fears and mental health of 144 child victims during their involvement in the preparation sessions and the trial process. Precise measurement of effects was problematic given the heterogeneity of cases, but their most significant finding was that 'the Child Witness Project's court preparation served to mitigate the effects of a documented major stressor, "length of time in the criminal justice system", and resulted in better adjustment in some of the psychological measures of fear, increased knowledge of court, and better performance (i.e. testimony) by child witnesses as rated by crown attorneys'. (Dezwirek-Sas 1992; see Sas et al. 1991 for a detailed report of the project).

Similar preparation techniques can be used with groups of child witnesses, such as the 'court schools' in Los Angeles, San Diego and Philadelphia (Whitcomb 1992) or the programmes developed by the National Children's Advocacy Center in Tennessee and Alabama (Sisterman-Keeney et al. 1992).

One of the most interesting research endeavours in this area has been established by a team of psychologists in Los Angeles, led by Professor Karen Saywitz. They believe that if we wish to maximise the quality of children's testimony, we need to improve the communication skills of the adult examiners as well as the child witnesses. 'At times, child witnesses appear to be confused and inconsistent. In many instances, this has more to do with the competence of adults to relate to and communicate with children than with children's abilities to accurately relate their experiences. The problem is a function of the discrepancy between the typical process by which evidence is elicited and the developmentally sensitive process that is needed to elicit accurate information from young children. Consequently, children may not testify at the optimal level of which they are capable, and they may experience higher levels of system-related stress than is necessary.' (Saywitz and Snyder 1993, p. 117.)

They have been carrying out a series of laboratory experiments using school children with the aim of developing training techniques which could be taught to child witnesses to improve the quality of their testimony. The first study examined techniques designed to maximise the amount of information children will provide on free recall about a witnessed event. This employed simple instructions and a memory prompt card with schematic drawings to remind the child to report full details of participants, setting, actions, conversations and feelings. The results which were based on 132 subjects interviewed about a staged event in their classroom two weeks earlier, indicate that the completeness of 7- to 11-year-olds' eyewitness memory can be increased by this technique, without any increase in error rate. In their second study, an attempt to train seven-year-olds to resist misleading questions produced mixed results. Giving instruction on the problems of suggestibility and encouraging the children to respond 'I don't know' rather than agreeing or guessing when they did not know the answer, produced a reduction in compliance with misleading questions but also fewer correct responses to non-leading questions: that is, the children gave more 'I don't know' responses. As discussed in chapter 11, suggestibility is a complex social and cognitive phenomenon and the results of this experiment highlight the necessity for rigorous laboratory testing of preparation techniques before they are used with child witnesses.

Their third experiment focussed on comprehension monitoring, that is children's ability to monitor whether they fully understand another's questions. The training programme instructed six- and eight-year-old children how to detect incomprehensible questions and taught them to tell the interviewer when they did not understand by saying, 'I don't get it. What do you mean?'. When the children were interviewed about an event witnessed two weeks earlier, those children who had been taught the comprehension monitoring techniques performed significantly better than a control group who attempted to answer questions that they were unlikely to have understood. These are obviously preliminary results from laboratory studies of children witnessing neutral events, however they do illustrate the potential benefits of applying the fruits of developmental psychology to the practical problem of improving young children's communication skills in the courtroom. It may well be possible through this type of preparation to enhance the quality of a child's testimony without threatening the rights of the accused.

As pre-trial preparation techniques increase in sophistication, the need to control and monitor their application becomes more pressing. Concern about coaching or contamination of the child's evidence is not unjustified and underlines the need for a proper understanding of evidentiary requirements. The Scottish Law Commission (1990) considered the issue of coaching in the context of pre-trial preparation and concluded (at 2.11) that, 'Prosecutors will be aware of this risk and will, we are sure, guard against anything untoward being said to the child prior to trial. In the circumstances we do not consider that existing practices should be disturbed for this reason'. Where preparation is not undertaken by a prosecuting lawyer, these risks may have to be guarded against by the use of a more systematic approach.

Social support
One important factor known to reduce stress in a range of situations is the availability of support and comfort from other people (Cox 1978; Saywitz and Nathanson in press). Moston (1992) found that children provided more information in an interview when they were allowed some degree of social support, e.g., the presence of a non-involved friend. Thus child witnesses may derive not only emotional comfort from the presence of a support person but the consequent reduction in anxiety may ultimately improve the quality of their evidence (see Moston and Engelberg 1992 for a review of this issue). Child witnesses will normally receive social support from parents, friends, and professionals involved in the case, as well as from specialist agencies such as Victim Support. In an intrafamilial abuse case, the child may lack an adequate personal support network and additional professional resources may be required during the investigation and after the trial. (See Runyan 1993 for a discussion of maternal support in sexual abuse cases.) On the day of the trial, the child can be accompanied by a support person when giving evidence. Davies and Noon (1991) found that when children gave evidence on live video link, they were usually accompanied by one adult, typically ushers (45%), but sometimes social workers, parents and police officers. They argue that the accompanying person should, if possible, be familiar to the child, but they also questioned (at p. 122) 'whether the presence of a parent or teacher in the Livelink room assists the witness during evidence, particularly with evidence of an intimate nature, unless the child has requested their support'. As discussed in chapter 5, a practice guideline has now been issued stating that the support person should normally be an usher.

These three factors: (i) the conduct of the investigation and trial; (ii) the preparation of the child for giving evidence; and (iii) the presence of social support, are all instrumental in reducing the impact of stress in children. In the final section in this chapter we consider the possible effects of stress on child witnesses.

THE EFFECTS OF STRESS ON CHILD WITNESSES

There is a fairly extensive literature on the subject of stress in children (Arnold 1990; Garmezy and Rutter 1983; Goodyer 1988; Udwin, 1993) much of which deals with bereavement, illness and divorce. This is a complex topic, but one consistent finding is that there are marked differences in children's reactions and ability to cope with such events. One explanation is that in a given circumstance, the degree of stress experienced (by children or adults) is a function of the individual's personal appraisal of the situation (i.e., how threatening it is thought to be) and of the individual's assessment of his or her own coping resources (Cox 1978; Rossman 1992).

When attempting to evaluate the degree of stress experienced by child witnesses, it is obviously necessary to distinguish between the psychological effects attributable to witnessing or being the victim of a crime, and those caused by the child's involvement in the investigation and trial. This is undoubtedly easier said than done. Nevertheless mental health professionals now have a far greater understanding of the effects of being exposed to traumatic events, such as disasters (Yule 1989) and violent crimes (Black et al. 1993; Morgan and Zedner 1992).

It is now generally accepted that many children suffer serious emotional and developmental harm as a result of sexual abuse (Draucker 1992; Oates 1992; Wyatt and Powell 1988). The direct psychological effects are usually classified as a post-traumatic stress disorder (Bentovim and Boston 1988) or as 'a sexual abuse accommodation syndrome' (Summit 1988). (That it was harmful was not always the prevailing view; for example, Burton (1968) (at p. 169) argued 'that sexual assault of children by adults does not have particularly detrimental effects on the child's subsequent personality development'.)

The diagnosis of post-traumatic stress disorder (PTSD) has now achieved official status and is listed in the American Psychiatric Association's Diagnostic and Statistical Manual of Mental Disorders (1987). PTSD is an intense psychological reaction which occurs as a result of being the victim of a traumatic event, such as an accident, a disaster or a disease. Diagnostic criteria include re-experiencing the trauma by intrusive thoughts, dreams or memories, a numbing of responsiveness and the presence of associated symptoms, for example, feelings of guilt or sleep disturbances (see chapter 9). Victims of stressful events caused by their fellow human beings, e.g., violent crimes, are particularly likely to suffer from this anxiety disorder (Janoff-Bulman 1988). Pynoos et al. (1987) point out that there is a need for more empirical research with child victims in order to establish a consistent set of symptoms for PTSD in children. However, their own study of 159 children who experienced a fatal sniper attack on their school provided strong evidence that acute PTSD symptoms occur in school-age children, with a notable correlation between proximity to the violence and type and number of PTSD symptoms. (See also Scott and Stradling 1992; Yule 1989.)

When it comes to the psychological effects of a witness's involvement in the criminal investigation and the trial, however, there is very little research. This is hardly surprising, bearing in mind the public concern about victims and witnesses is comparatively recent, and that this kind of research is particularly difficult and time-consuming. There are obvious practical problems in gaining access to courts and witnesses, in collecting the information from children, parents and others, and in analysing the resulting data, which is likely to contain all sorts of complicated variables.

In figure 13.1 we summarise the possible effects of the child's involvement in the legal process based on anecdotal and professional accounts (see above and chapter 5), and on the available research data which are briefly outlined below.

Pre-trial effects
As discussed earlier, many witnesses, both children and adults, report that the long delay before the trial and their lack of knowledge about the legal process cause them to feel anxious and apprehensive. Such emotions may well produce symptoms such as sleep or appetite disturbances, mood changes or disruption of concentration or even more severe effects. At present there are insufficient

data available to define or to permit quantification of incidence rates or specific symptoms, but cases occur where the results are clearly serious. When the Epping Forest ritual abuse case was dropped the prosecution were reported as saying, 'The case has dragged on largely owing to the ill health of Mr. Linge. As a result the victim has found it impossible to cope with the strain of waiting to give evidence'. (*The Independent*, 2 March 1992.) For victims of serious crimes it is almost impossible to disentangle post-traumatic effects attributable to the crime itself from pre-trial anxiety. Bystander witnesses, too, can also experience anxiety as the following excerpt from a letter to the television programme 'That's Life!' illustrates:

> Court proceedings are something totally outside my experience but last year I was asked to give evidence regarding a child in my care. I cannot express how terrified I felt, and I did not think I would be able to do this. After many sleepless night I even contemplated asking my doctor for a tranquilliser to get me through the ordeal. This I obviously did not do and I did survive the experience. I have talked to many foster-parents who had the same feelings as myself and we try to support one another. I just wanted to say that I am a 36-year-old woman. I did not have to face an abuser and have what I said discredited. I cannot imagine a child coping with that and being articulate enough in their evidence, especially after feeling the stress I felt and I certainly was not in their position.

We have also had reports from jurors who admitted to being extremely worried about their forthcoming duty (again this seems to be partly due to inadequate information), and from expert witnesses who describe feeling apprehension while waiting for trial.

The question of children's stress during the pre-trial period is extremely significant because prosecutors may decide whether to proceed with a case on the basis of a child's emotional fitness to testify (see page 323 for other factors taken into consideration). McMurry (1987) examined prosecutorial decision-making for a random sample of 87 cases of child sexual abuse referred to a Massachusetts district attorney's office. He found that 'cases involving young victims were more likely to result in screening attrition and non-prosecution than cases with older victims. For these young victims, concerns about the competency (and credibility) of the child as a witness, the risk of psychological harm resulting from criminal court involvement, and the child's relative dependence upon parents or guardians may all be sources of potential problems for formal prosecution' (p. 16). Debra Whitcomb and her colleagues examinined the prosecution process for child sexual abuse cases in four States: New York; Iowa; Minnesota; and California and considered how the child's level of trauma relates to prosecutorial decision-making and case management (Whitcomb et al. 1991). An interesting study in Ireland by Simon O'Leary of the reasons for not prosecuting 90 cases from a total sample of 203 child sexual abuse complaints shows that the likely effect on the child of giving evidence was a factor taken into consideration (Irish Law Reform Commission 1989). Sas et al. (1991) reported that in 10% of cases when sexual abuse charges were not laid by Canadian police the reason given was the child's fear of testifying. There do not appear to be any comparable British data from either the police, the Crown Prosecution Service or the Procurator Fiscal Service although Morgan and Zedner (1992) provide a useful description of the English process and the new study of videotaped evidence at Leicester University may be instructive. This would appear to be an important area for research, both in terms of understanding how children's fitness to withstand the trial is evaluated and also to quantify the percentage of cases screened out at this stage of the prosecution process because the child is judged unable to cope with the demands of testifying in open court.

The effect of stress on the day of the trial

Waiting at court

Many child witnesses (bystanders and victims) report feeling worried or anxious while waiting in the court building (Flin et al. 1988; Morgan and Zedner 1992). Goodman et al. (1992) interviewed 110 child victims of sexual abuse who were waiting to testify for either preliminary hearings, competency examinations or full trials in Denver. (The majority of the sample, 91%, were waiting for preliminary hearings.) They found that children expressed negative feelings about testifying, about talking to the defence attorney and especially about having to see the defendant again. Children reported generally positive feelings about talking to the prosecutor and having their mother with them. There was a mixed response when children were asked how they felt about talking to the judge. Older children tended to report more negative emotions, perhaps due to a better understanding of the process and its implications.

It appears that waiting for a significant period of time before being called to the witness-box can have a disastrous effect on the quality of a child's evidence. We have been told by both prosecuting barristers and procurators fiscal of cases which have collapsed because the child was unable to give coherent evidence because she or he had become too tired or over-anxious while waiting several hours to be called.

Giving evidence

It is almost impossible to measure the degree of stress experienced by witnesses while they are giving evidence in court, unless the witness displays an unambiguous physical reaction such as crying, shaking or fainting. Certainly there have been decisions from the civil courts which have explicitly acknowledged that giving evidence might be harmful for the child (Re K (Minors) (Wardship: Criminal Proceedings) [1988] Fam 1; Re S (Minors) (Wardship: Police Investigation) [1987] Fam 199; Northamptonshire County Council v H [1988] QB 205). The precise impact of stress on witnesses' ability to recall and recount events is also uncertain, although an alarming number of anecdotal reports indicate that many witnesses believe that the quality of their evidence was diminished by their anxiety in the witness-box.

Last year I was raped, it took me two days to pluck up enough courage to actually go to the police station. [At the magistrates' court] . . . It was the most horrific day of my life. First of all . . . we were made to sit in the same waiting-room as the man and it had been the first time I had seen him since it happened and I just cannot describe how I felt. I had to stand up in court for two hours and tell the court what he did to me with him in the court I was crying and shaking and so scared. . . . When it came round to Crown Court once again [four months later] I was very frightened and nervous. Again I had to stand up in court for many hours, what I couldn't see the point of was that I had to say all over again what he did to me, why couldn't they just have read out my statement, because under pressure and because of nerves and because it happened about six months ago, you do get muddled up and his barrister helps that by cross-questioning you, firing questions at you and trying to make you say something you don't want to say or that's not true. (Letter to BBC 'That's Life!' from an 18-year-old.)

Saywitz and Nathanson (in press) tested the ability of eight- and ten-year-old children to recall an event they had participated in two weeks earlier, when they were interviewed in a classroom or in a mock courtroom at a Californian University law school. Their results showed that the children who were interviewed 'at court' demonstrated poorer recall than children questioned at school. 'Children interviewed in the courtroom identified certain court-related experiences as more stressful than peers who were interviewed at school. Also children's perceived anxiety was negatively correlated with correct free recall'. These are interesting data which, if replicated, will provide empirical support for witnesses' anecdotal reports that their memories were impaired by anxiety in the witness box.

Goodman et al. (1992) observed a sample of 57 child sexual abuse victims giving evidence at preliminary hearings (40) or criminal trials (17) in Denver. Using a specially designed behavioural rating scale they recorded details of the children's reactions during their testimony. Of the children giving evidence at preliminary hearings, 17 were judged to be showing some distress and three to be very distressed. During cross-examination younger children, compared with older, showed more faltering speech, provided less detail and appeared to be less credible. For the 17 children giving testimony in full trials, 11 were rated as experiencing some distress or being very distressed. Goodman's data indicated that children who had been rated as showing a greater degree of behavioural disturbance 48 hours prior to the trial (as assessed by the parents) were less able to answer the prosecutor's questions. The children who were most worried about confronting the defendant (from pre-trial interview responses) had more difficulty in answering the prosecutor's questions. Her findings clearly suggest that children experience distress in the courtroom and that the effect of this may be to interfere with their evidence.

The first British research study to observe the children giving evidence reported similar findings to Goodman et al. (1992). Flin et al. (1993) recorded systematic observations of 89 child witnesses (23 victims, 66 bystanders, aged 5–15 years) giving evidence in criminal trials in Glasgow. They used 'The

Courtroom Observation Schedule' (a specially adapted version of Goodman's scale) and found that although only five children (6%) were moved to tears when giving evidence, 50% of the children were rated as being (i) unhappy or very unhappy and (ii) tense or very tense during the examination-in-chief and the cross-examination.

Children's demeanour when giving evidence via the live video link was rated by Davies and Noon (1991) who also used a version of Goodman's scale. They observed 154 child abuse victims aged 4–13 years and found that while 26% were judged to be unhappy or very unhappy, 55% were rated as tense or very tense and 24% cried at some point whilst giving evidence. In order to evaluate the effect of the live video link they compared the behaviour of their sample with 28 children in Flin et al.'s study who had given evidence in physical or sexual abuse cases. The children who gave evidence via the live video link appeared to be less unhappy and more self confident, but as Davies and Noon point out, the diversity of the samples effectively limits the interpretation that can be drawn from this comparison. Nevertheless, there appears to be a degree of consistency across these three studies based in different adversarial legal systems. The pooled research data show that many child witnesses experience anxiety during the examinations and while this may be alleviated to a certain degree by the live video link, great care must still be taken to support children giving evidence and to protect their psychological wellbeing. Two new investigations are underway which will record observations of children giving evidence. Graham Davies, Professor of Psychology at Leicester University is continuing his observational study of children giving evidence via the live video link in English courts and Kathleen Murray a psychologist from Glasgow University, is undertaking a similar evaluation of the Scottish live video link system (Murray 1992).

One major source of bias in all such assessments is that those children who reach the witness-box to give their evidence represent a subgroup of the total sample of child witnesses, comprised only of those who have been judged capable of coping with the demands of the trial. We do not know how many cases have not made it to the courts because the child would not have been able to handle the stress of facing the defendant and being examined in court.

The long-term effect of giving evidence
While there appears to be little doubt that many witnesses, particularly victims, do experience stress before and during the trial, the psychological after-effects of having to give evidence are much less clear. As indicated in figure 13.1, the long-term effects will be dependent on a host of variables relating to the circumstances of the crime, the conduct of the investigation and trial, the witness's personality and the final verdict.

In 1963 Gibbens and Prince analysed a set of 82 cases of child sexual abuse referred to the Federation of Committees for the Moral Welfare of Children in England; 46 of which were involved 'in some way' in a prosecution. They concluded that those children who were involved in criminal proceedings showed a greater degree of behavioural disturbances and appeared to show a slower rate of recovery than the control group. Unfortunately the data are highly ambiguous and the researchers were unable to determine how many children actually attended court or gave evidence. Oates and Tong (1987) interviewed the non-offending parent or guardian of 21 Australian children who were involved in court proceedings, as victims of sexual abuse. Although only six children gave evidence, 18 parents reported that their child was 'distressed' after the hearing and 12 parents said that their child was still upset about the court hearing two years later.

There have been a number of similar American surveys of child abuse victims' reactions to the investigation and litigation. The first of these reports (De Francis 1969) indicated that children found the legal process to be stressful, but as Goodman et al. (1992) point out, no control group was included so it is difficult to know how much of the children's stress was caused by the assault as opposed to the investigation or trial. Tedesco and Schnell (1987) suggested that the interview and litigation process were not necessarily harmful to children, but of their very small sample of 49 sexual abuse victims (aged four to 22 years) only nine testified in court. Of these nine subjects, two rated the investigation and litigation process as helpful, two thought it was harmful and five were ambivalent. A somewhat larger study by Runyan et al. (1988) designed to assess the impact of legal intervention on 79 child sexual abuse victims (12 of whom testified in the juvenile (youth) court and five of whom had completed criminal trials), concluded, 'Testimony in juvenile court may be beneficial for the child, whereas protracted criminal proceedings may have an adverse effect on the mental health of the victim' (p. 647). Their findings were extended in a new study which tracked 256 child victims involved in sexual abuse prosecutions in four States. The children were interviewed and given psychological tests when the case was referred for prosecution and again seven to nine months later. Their preliminary results indicate that, 'Testifying in itself does not appear to produce significant changes in the child victim's mental health. However, measures of stressful testimony which include testifying more than once and enduring long and/or harsh cross-examination, do appear to have significant adverse effects. This finding is limited to children over the age of eight, who were more likely than the younger children to experience more stressful testimony . . . preliminary results suggest that testifying is less stressful for younger children (than older children) and may even be helpful. Yet our case data suggest that prosecutors are reluctant to pursue cases involving pre-school children'. (Whitcomb, Runyan et al. 1991, p. 139.) Sas et al. (1991) in their study of 144 Canadian child abuse victims stated (at p. 115) that the involvement in the prosecution may indirectly impair children's wellbeing. 'Although court involvement does not necessarily cause more emotional disturbance in all child victims, it does appear to prevent children from healing. Our experiences confirm these earlier findings in that the majority of our child witnesses frequently verbalized their inability to get on with their lives until the court was over. Unfortunately this "in limbo" state often stretched to two years.'

Goodman et al. (1992) compared the emotional responses and psychological adjustment of 46 child sexual abuse victims who were involved in court proceedings with a matched sample of cases who did not have to testify. They collected data from children, parents and teachers (a) when the case was referred for prosecution; (b) when the child attended court (before, during and after testimony, if possible); (c) three months after the child first testified; (d) seven months after the child first testified; and (e) after the prosecution closed. Within this sample of 46 children, 35 first testified in preliminary hearings, 7 in trials, 2 at motions hearings, 1 at a competency examination and 1 at a sentencing hearing. They found that at seven months after the initial testimony, the children who testified showed greater behavioural disturbance than the children who did not testify, especially if the 'testifiers' gave evidence multiple times, were deprived of maternal support and lacked corroboration of their claims. However, once giving evidence was safely behind them (an average 11 months after first testifying) the adverse effects of testifying were diminished. Interviews conducted with a subsample of children after they had testified showed a variable response in terms of the children's opinions about their experience. Flin et al. (1988) found the same mixed reaction for a small number of children they spoke to who had just given evidence. Both research teams noted that this is a biased sample favouring children who are least distressed by the experience of giving evidence, because parents (quite understandably) rarely give permission to interview children who are visibly upset.

There are significant differences between American and British legal proceedings and it is difficult to determine to what extent Goodman's conclusions can be applied in a British context. Moreover, only a very small number of children (17) actually testified in 'open trials' in Goodman's sample and a detailed breakdown into type of proceedings (e.g. grand jury) for the 65 children who testified is not given in the Whitcomb et al. (1991) study. It may be that fewer American child victims are required to give testimony at a full trial. Rogers (1982) tracked 261 police cases of child sexual abuse between 1978 and 1979 in Washington and discovered that only three cases involving adult suspects and five cases involving juvenile suspects actually went to trial. In order to evaluate properly new techniques for hearing and testing evidence in the UK, longitudinal data should be collected to monitor children's mental health during and after the prosecution process. Unfortunately research psychologists have encountered strong resistance from the judiciary to interviewing children pre-trial despite (or possibly because of) the fact that a plethora of other professionals will have been allowed to talk to the child.

It is also important to remember that most children do not live in isolation and the impact of the prosecution process on the family needs to be considered. Regehr (1990) in a study of extra-familiar child sexual assault reported, 'The experience of the Mississauga Hospital team is that 'many families who go through the court process feel so damaged by it that they are adamant that they would not put their child through such an investigation again' (p. 115).

The view that attending court and giving evidence produce negative effects after the trial has to be balanced against the opinions of some North American professionals who believe that the process of giving testimony can, in the long term, be empowering or therapeutic for child victims (Rogers 1982; Berliner and Barbieri 1984; Melton 1987; Sas et al. 1991). This optimistic conclusion is always qualified by a proviso which states that such positive effects will only ensue if (a) the child is properly prepared; (b) the investigation and trial are conducted with care and sensitivity; and (c) the child is provided with adequate support before, during and after the experience. Psychological case study reports of child victims who have to testify in court generally draw the same conclusion (Claman et al. 1986; Freshwater 1991; Hurley et al. 1988; Jaffe and Wilson 1987; Weiss and Berg 1982).

Conclusion

It is still far from clear whether children experience long-term psychological disturbance as the result of attending court and giving evidence. Child and adult victims of serious crimes frequently suffer from post-traumatic stress disorders for months or years following the offence, and it is particularly difficult to attribute identifiable causes to specific effects in these cases. Our survey of the available literature on this topic suggests that some children do experience negative effects for several months after, and probably as a result of the trial, but it is also apparent that such reactions can be minimised by attention to particular features of the trial process which are known to cause stress in the short term.

It appears to be generally accepted that child witnesses, especially those who have been abused, find the long wait and inadequate preparation before the trial to be significant sources of stress. For many children, the experience of attending court, confronting the accused and giving evidence will at best cause anxiety and, at worst, result in such severe fear or distress that they are unable to provide coherent testimony. This is not an insurmountable problem. We know that child witnesses can give competent evidence by modifying conventional trial procedures to minimise the risk of unnecessary stress. Typically this necessitated hearing the evidence of the child in his or her absence. In chapter 14 we look at how this is achieved by foreign jurisdictions, and in chapter 15 we discuss further changes that might help matters.

NOTES

1.   Court preparation materials:
Child Witness Information Pack. NSPCC, 67 Saffron Hill, London EC1N 8RS.
Going to Court. Crown Office, 5/7 Regent Road, Edinburgh.
Castell-McGregor, S. et al. (1989) '*Tell It Like It Is*'. Booklet. Children's Interests Bureau, 68 Grenfell Street, Adelaide, Australia.
Castell-McGregor, S. et al. '*Tell It Like It Is*'. Video. South Australian Child Protection Council, P.O. Box 39, Rundle Mall, Adelaide, South Australia 5000.
Gaitskell, S. (ed) (1989) '*What's My Job In Court?*'. Activity book. Witness Assistance Program, Ministry of the Attorney General, 720 Bay Street, Toronto, Ontario, M5G 2K1.
Harvey, W. and Watson-Russell, A. (1988) '*So You Have To Go To Court!*', 2nd ed. Booklet. Toronto: Butterworths.

2.   Cadman and Printer, Reading Crown Court, 19 June–10 July 1990. It was the subject of a BBC1 programme 'The Scandal of Crookham Court School' on 13 February 1991.

3.   Gail Goodman's willingness to share the court observation measure developed by her team provided an important contribution to this cross-cultural exercise and her help is gratefully acknowledged by the British research groups.

CHAPTER FOURTEEN
The evidence of children in other legal systems

Although the subject is a large one, this chapter will be fairly short. Our knowledge of the position in other legal systems does not extend to all the countries of the world; much of what we know about it has been said in the earlier parts of this book; more is said in the collection of essays which we and others edited after the international conference on children's evidence in legal proceedings at Selwyn College, Cambridge in June 1989 (Spencer et al. 1990); and in a recent article by the first author (Spencer 1993b), and in a series of papers from a symposium organised by Professor Max Steller at a conference in Nuremberg in 1990 (Lösel et al. 1992).

The countries of which we have some knowledge are the USA, Canada, Australia, New Zealand, the Republic of Ireland, France, Germany, Italy, Holland, the Scandinavian countries, Japan and Israel. This covers a much larger number of jurisdictions than at first appears, because the USA and Australia are made up of different States, each with the power to make its own rules of procedure and evidence, and a federal government with criminal jurisdiction as well. Fortunately the task of describing the position in the USA is made easier because several American writers have already done so. Those who seek more information than is to be found here should look at Myers (1987a), or Whitcomb (1992). Kate Warner has recently described the position in the different States of Australia and in New Zealand (Warner 1990), and another useful account appears in the recent report of the Law Reform Commission of Western Australia (LRC of Western Australia 1991).

In other countries of the English-speaking world, as in Britain, there has been a general move to reform the law of children's evidence in recent years. This has produced a number of official reports. The reports of the Law Commissions, and Law Reform Commissions, of Ireland and of a number of jurisdictions in Australia are mentioned in the list of references at the end of this book. In New Zealand there has been the Geddis Report (1988), and in Canada the Badgley Report (1984). Most of these reports have led to legislative changes.

This chapter is largely about children's evidence in criminal proceedings. It is arranged by topic rather than by jurisdiction, and where the position in other jurisdictions has been examined earlier in the book we have resorted to cross-references.

THE HEARSAY RULE—ALTERNATIVES TO
LIVE EVIDENCE AT TRIAL

In chapter 5 we examined the differences between the accusatorial and inquisitorial systems (and the cross-fertilisation that has taken place between the two).

France, Belgium and Holland adhere fairly closely to the inquisitorial idea, and have neither the hearsay rule as it is understood in England and Scotland, nor the traditional veneration for oral evidence. Witnesses (and defendants) are almost invariably interrogated ahead of trial, and the written minutes of these interviews—called *procès-verbaux* in French and *processen-verbaal* in Dutch—are part of a dossier which (to put it in common lawyers' terms) forms part of the evidence in the case. If the witness testifies at the eventual trial, the court has the *procès-verbaux* to supplement his oral evidence, and if he does not, they can usually replace it. The *procès-verbaux* will almost invariably include statements made to the police in the early stages of the investigation. If the case is a serious or difficult one—as a case where a child is a victim usually is—a further round of pre-trial questioning will then take place before a judicial officer called a *juge d'instruction* in French (or *rechter-commissaris* in Dutch). This official is a professional judge, and he has certain limited powers to delegate the questioning to others. In the busier parts of France he may even be one who specialises in questioning children. He or she sits in private, but with a clerk and those lawyers who have a right to be present. His interrogations are recorded in writing: as yet there is no question of tape-recording, whether audio or video. Where young children are witnesses the court of trial will usually read the *procès-verbaux* instead of hearing from the child as a live witness, and the same is sometimes done with older children. Indeed, so completely does this system insulate the child from the need to appear at trial that in France there is actually some concern about children who wish to make a live appearance and are not allowed to do so (Hamon 1990)—exactly the opposite of what people are currently worried about in Britain.

If these systems successfully protect the child from the need to appear in open court, the French system is less efficient at protecting him or her from the trauma of a confrontation with the defendant. Although the *juge d'instruction* is not obliged to do so, it is a strong tradition for him to arrange *une confrontation* between the defendant and his accusers at some point in the investigations (Crétin 1992). In the words of a French judge, 'confronting a minor with an adult perpetrator of sexual abuse requires particularly careful handling' (Hamon 1990). At these sessions child witnesses not infrequently retract; but that does not necessarily mean the case collapses, because French judges seem to be well aware that such a retraction may be false (Hamon 1990). Confrontations can be arranged in Holland too, but in the Dutch system there is less of a tradition of doing so.

What safeguards do these systems provide for the defendant?

The first is a number of procedural rules which regulate the way in which the pre-trial interrogation is conducted. An official clerk is present at the interview, the statement is recorded in writing, each page must be read by (or read back to) the witness, and signed by all parties present: and the defence are given access to the statements in advance of trial.

The second is that the defendant (and of course the prosecutor) has the right to require any witness—including one who has previously been examined—to give live evidence at trial. There is not necessarily much mileage in this for the defence, however, because traditionally the witness will be examined not by counsel but by the judge; and if the witness is cited and does not turn up, as not infrequently happens, the presiding judge may allow the case to go ahead on the basis of the *procès-verbaux*—at any rate where there has been an earlier confrontation.

The third safeguard is the practice of confrontation, previously mentioned. As we explained in chapter 5, the result of a series of decisions of the European Court of Human Rights has been to enable defendants in this group of legal systems to insist on a confrontation at some stage in the proceedings—either before the *juge d'instruction*, or if none took place at that stage, at trial.

A big difference between the German inquisitorial system and the French is that the German system operates on a 'principle of personal examination' (*Grundsatz der Persönlchen Vernehmung*) (*Strafproceßordnung*, art. 251), which usually requires witnesses to give evidence orally at the trial. Unlike the hearsay rule in England, which it at first sight resembles, the German rule does not mean that witness A is banned from telling the court what was said about the incident by witness B: but it does mean that if B's evidence is important the court must also hear direct evidence from B, and, unlike a court in France or Holland, may not use a transcript of an earlier official interview with B as substitute for B's live evidence. However, under the German system the process of giving evidence at trial seems to be much less harrowing for the child than it is under the adversarial system in Britain. Offences against children are tried before the special courts that also deal with juvenile offenders, and hence before a tribunal with experience of communicating with chidren. In some circumstances the child has a right to refuse to give evidence, and the parents can sometimes refuse on his or her behalf. Juvenile witnesses must be interrogated by the judge, so avoiding the trauma of adversarial examination and cross-examination. When hearing witnesses under the age of 16 the court has the power not only to exclude the public, but also to exclude the defendant himself if his presence is thought likely to be harmful for the witness: so avoiding the need for screens, live links, and other devices. And where the witness is the victim of the offence the court may permit him or her to have a 'support person' present when testifying, and must allow the witness to be legally represented.

Although the German system depends mainly on first-hand oral testimony, it does have a mechanism by which the evidence of a child can sometimes be taken in advance of trial. Where there are 'insurmountable impediments' to the live appearance of a witness at trial, the court may read a record of an earlier judicial interrogation of the witness, if there was one; and where this difficulty is foreseen, the court has power to conduct a judicial examination of the witness in advance of the trial. Where children are concerned, 'insurmountable impediments' can include the risk of serious psychological harm from appearing at trial (Frehsee 1990).

The position is similar in Japan. The Japanese system, like the German system, usually requires evidence to be given orally at trial. However, as in Germany, the Code of Criminal Procedure gives the court power to hold the examination of a witness out of court and in advance of trial in certain circumstances, including where the age of the witness makes it necessary (art. 158), and where it is feared that a prosecution witness will be put under pressure to retract a statement he has previously given (art. 227). In addition, formal statements made to the police are sometimes admissible as documentary evidence. Our Japanese informants tell us that the courts avoid a situation in which children are required to give evidence in court by using a combination of these provisions (1).

To the accusatorial tradition belong the jurisdictions of the English-speaking world, together with some others that have copied them: notably the Scandinavian countries, Israel, and Italy.

In the systems which follow the accusatorial tradition there is a strong tradition in favour of hearing oral evidence. In the English-speaking world, in particular, the 'orality principle' is bolstered up by the two rules which we examined in chapter 6: the hearsay rule, and the rule against narrative, alias the rule against self-corroboration. Taken together, these mean that if a party wishes to prove that a person saw, heard, did or experienced something, he must produce that person to recount his experiences orally to the court—and having got the witness there, may not supplement his oral evidence by reference to any previous account the witness may have given: though the other side may make use of his previous statement, if it differs from his courtroom evidence, in order to undermine his credibility.

As we explained in chapter 5, the insistence on oral evidence at trial creates acute problems where child witnesses are concerned, and other countries besides England and Scotland have been forced to create exceptions to the normal rules to cope with the evidence of children. These exceptions are of three different types.

The first is simply to create an exception to the hearsay rule, so that adult witnesses can repeat to the court what an absent child told them. As we saw in chapter 6, this is what has been done for civil proceedings in both England and Scotland. In adopting this approach in civil cases, Britain followed the lead given earlier in other common law jurisdictions, notably in the United States (Myers 1987a, p. 293 et seq.). As we saw in chapter 6, some common law jurisdictions, notably the State of Washington, have gone further and have created a major exception to the hearsay rule for use in criminal cases. But if hearsay exceptions are justifiable in civil proceedings where the dominant aim is the welfare of the child, they cause serious difficulties of principle in criminal proceedings which are brought to punish, because they conflict with the generally held idea that it is unjust to punish someone without giving him the opportunity to put his side of the case to his accuser—as we explain above (page 162).

The second line of approach has been to knock a dent, not in the hearsay rule, but in the 'rule against narrative': in other words, to change the rules of evidence so that if a child testifies his evidence in court can be supplemented by his previous statements. As we saw in the previous chapter, there is a strong case for abolishing the 'rule against narrative' in its entirety, and official committees have proposed this both in England and in Scotland. A limited exception to the rule against narrative in relation to child witnesses only is, of course, what has been enacted in England in the provisions of the Criminal Justice Act 1991 that allow videotapes of earlier interviews with children to be used as evidence, provided the child comes to court to undergo a live cross-examination (see chapter 7). This scheme was not original to England, because as we saw above (pages 166–169) the idea originated in North America, notably Canada as part of the package of reforms enacted in 1987 in the wake of the Badgley Report in 1984. Canadian informants tell us, however, that very little use has actually been made of the Canadian videotape evidence provisions: which makes it all the stranger that in England the Home Office put an identical scheme forward with such vigour, and in opposition to the carefully thought-out proposals of the Pigot Committee (page 90 above).

Supplementing the child's courtroom testimony in this way gives the courts more evidence to work on, and is obviously fairer to the defence than allowing what the child told someone else to be repeated to the court by an adult under a straightforward exception to the hearsay rule. But it does little for the child, who still has the stress of waiting to give evidence at trial, and of giving it having got there.

Partly for this reason, many legal systems within the accusatorial tradition have gone further, and have introduced a third type of modification to the oral tradition. This is a scheme under which a child can be examined, with due formality, before a judge or other official person ahead of trial—the resulting formal record of the examination, or *deposition*, then replacing the appearance of the child as a live witness. As we saw in chapter 5, some such laws already exist in Britain. England has the apparently moribund scheme for sick or severely traumatised child witnesses contained in ss. 42 and 43 of the Children and Young Persons Act 1933 (pages 83–86 above), and in Scotland there is the recent s. 33 of the Prisoners and Criminal Proceedings (Scotland) Act 1993. In the same pattern was the scheme proposed by the Pigot Committee in 1989 (page 88 above).

In principle, schemes of this sort fall into two distinct types. In the first, a designated official examines the child on behalf of the court, without any input from the defence. The defence has some safeguard in the quality of the person who conducts the questioning, and under the Israeli scheme (discussed below) the additional safeguard of a corroboration requirement: but it has no right to put questions to the child, or even to require the examiner to put them. In the second and more developed model—to which the British legislation and the Pigot proposal all belong—the defence are allowed to watch the examination, and to put their questions to the child.

The Israeli scheme (Harnon 1988, 1990; David 1990) is one of the most radical innovations to have been adopted to cope with the evidence of children. In 1955, in response to growing concern about the sufferings of child witnesses under the adversarial system, the Knesset passed the Law of Evidence

Revision (Protection of Children) Law, which set up the system of child examiners—or 'youth interrogators', as the English text of the statute rather formidably calls them.

At first the child examiners were often police officers, but nowadays they are specially designated and trained members of the youth probation service. Their main function is to collect evidence from children for use in court; in the past there was a tendency for them to combine this task with a social worker role, but the current attitude is for them to see themselves as primarily collectors of evidence. They interview the children at the request of the police, on behalf of whom they act. The interview takes place in private; at one time it was the practice to interview the child at home, but nowadays this is usually done in a special office. The interview is recorded: at first this was done in writing, but audiotaping was introduced in 1989, and there is now some pressure for videotaping to be introduced. Following the interview, the child examiner makes a decision about whether the child shall be called to give live evidence at any subsequent trial. If not—and it is usually not—the child examiner goes to court and gives evidence in place of the child. In giving evidence, the child examiner provides the court with a factual account of what the child said at the interview, and is also permitted to give his or her opinion on the credibility of the child.

The big objection that is usually levelled against the Israeli system is that it enables the defendant to be convicted on hearsay evidence, and without being given the chance to put their version of events to the accuser. Two features are built into the system in an attempt to overcome these difficulties. Where the defendant raises new matters which the child examiner did not put the child, the examiner can be asked to conduct a supplementary interview (but he or she may lawfully refuse). And in addition there is an overriding rule that the court may not convict where the child examiner has given evidence in place of the child unless there is corroboration. Thus although the defendant may be convicted partly on the hearsay evidence of a witness to whom he cannot put his version of events, he cannot be convicted on such evidence alone.

The child examiner scheme operates only in trials for sexual offences, and is limited to cases where the child is under the age of 14.

At the time of writing there is a certain amount of controversy in Israel about the child examiner scheme. There seems to be general agreement that it works well to protect the child, but it is nevertheless attacked from two directions. On the one hand, some Israeli lawyers complain that it is unfair to the defendant, and on the other, some people involved in child protection say that the corroboration requirement causes prosecutions brought using the scheme to fail in cases where the defendant is clearly guilty. Certain Israelis to whom we have spoken have expressed interest in reforming the scheme to give the defence a right to have their questions put to the child—as under the Pigot scheme unsuccessfully proposed for England (2).

Sweden and Norway also have schemes for taking children's evidence ahead of trial by deposition, and like the Israeli scheme they do not give the defence the right to put questions to the child (3).

The Swedish scheme provides the fewest safeguards for the defence. The Swedish Code of Procedure gives the court of trial a discretion as to whether or not to call a witness under 15 years of age, and also a general right to admit in evidence statements taken from potential witnesses by the police if the circumstances of the case require it. In recent years it has become usual for the courts to use these provisions in combination, so enabling a videotape of a police interview with the child to be used as evidence as a substitute for calling the child to give live evidence.

In Norway the scheme is rather more formal (Haivik 1992). A special system for child witnesses was introduced in 1926, in response to pressure from a women's organisation, which was concerned about the sufferings of child witnesses under the existing system. Where a witness is under 14, the evidence can be taken in advance of trial by an examining magistrate, whose report the interview normally replaces the appearance of the child at trial. The examiner is allowed to use specialist help in questioning the child—for example, a child psychologist, policewoman, or social worker—and the court can go to where the child is as an alternative to bringing the child to court. Nowadays the interview must usually be recorded on audiotape—and it is increasingly common for it to be videotaped. In Norway, unlike in Sweden, the defence have the further safeguard that the examination is judicially controlled, but they do not have the right to be represented and put questions at the time of the examination. A change on these lines was proposed when the Code of Criminal Procedure was revised in 1981, but the public reaction was negative and the idea was dropped.

The other type of pre-trial deposition, where the defence are given the opportunity to put questions to the child—or to have questions put to him—is something which is possible under the codes of criminal procedure in a number of jurisdictions in the USA. It was under such a provision in the State of Colorado that Drs. Jones and Krugman took a video-deposition from the three-year-old girl who had been abducted, sexually assaulted, and put into a cess-pit to drown (Jones and Krugman 1986; Jones 1987). The precondition for using this kind of procedure is that the child should be 'unavailable' to give oral evidence in the traditional fashion. As far as we can gather these procedures are not greatly used: prosecutors fear objections based on the 'Confrontation Clause' in the US Constitution (page 77 above), and tend to steer clear of them. In 1989 changes were enacted to the New Zealand Evidence Act which make such an examination—which is recorded on video-tape—one of a range of options which a judge can use to facilitate a child's evidence being put before a criminal court. Similar changes have been made, or are currently under discussion, in a number of jurisdictions in Australia (Law Reform Commission of Western Australia 1991).

Such a scheme has been in operation for a while in Denmark. In that country there is no special procedure for the examination of child witnesses, but their evidence is usually taken in advance of trial under general provisions in the Danish Code of Procedure which permit this to be done with a witness of any age if necessary. The hearing usually takes place in a local court, before a judge in chambers.

In recent years the technique of video-recording has increasingly been taken into use . . . A method which seems to become usual is that a qualified police officer undertakes the questioning, while the judge, the prosecution, the accused and the defence counsel follow the interrogation on a TV in another room. Afterwards the defence counsel may put additional questions. This could be said to be something in between a police hearing and a judicial hearing. It seems to me that this method combines as far as possible consideration for the child with safeguards for the defence. (Andenaes 1990.)

From one Danish informant we gather that there have been certain difficulties with this procedure. The standard of interviewing has not always been high, and because the combined police-interview-cum-cross-examination takes place early, the defence sometimes do not know enough about the case to put pertinent questions to the child. In consequence there have been cases where, although this procedure was originally followed, it was eventually necessary to make the child come to court for a live examination. (Under the Pigot proposal, by contrast, the defence questioning session would have taken place some time after the initial interview. And under the Scottish Law Commission proposal, now enacted, the whole of the child's examination will usually take place after the defence know the nature of the case.)

In broad terms, it can be said that in civil proceedings the problems involved in making children give oral evidence are commonly avoided by allowing others to repeat to the court what the child has said: and that in criminal proceedings they are reduced by a number of devices—notably a pre-trial examination, held in private before a judicial officer, at which the defence are given the chance to put their side of the story to the child.

NON-ADVERSARIAL EXAMINATION

As we saw earlier in chapter 5, one of the things which young children tend to find distressing and confusing about giving evidence is the process of adversarial examination, in which they are pulled first in one direction and then the other. In many jurisdictions this ordeal for children is avoided.

In the continental systems, the tradition is for all witnesses to be non-adversarially examined by the presiding judge—who then allows the parties to put further questions to the witnesses themselves, or puts their questions for them, in his discretion. The potential drawback with this system is that it sometimes puts the defending lawyer into conflict with the judge, and with this in mind the law has been changed in some jurisdictions so that the prosecutor and the defence lawyer now examine the witnesses adversarially. However, in these jurisdictions it seems to be widely accepted that non-adversarial examination is still preferable where the witness is a child. In Germany, for example, witnesses are usually examined by the judge, but adversarial examination is also permitted—though article 241(a) of the *Straf-prozeßordnung* (Code of Criminal Procedure) requires all witnesses under 16 to be examined by the judge. Adversarial examination is now the rule under the new Italian Code of Criminal Procedure of 1988—but by article 498(a), witnesses who are minors are still to be examined by the judge. In France, one of the last acts of the socialist government was to vote through Parliament a reform of the Code of Criminal Procedure, including—in the name of the rights of man in general and of defendants in particular—adversarial examination. No exception is made for fragile witnesses of any kind. The change provoked bitter opposition (Pradel 1993), not least among French judges. Before it came into force there was a change of government in France, and the new law looks like being repealed before it comes into force.

In the common law world, by contrast, there is increasing interest in making an exception to the usual rule of adversarial examination where the witness is a child. In England, the Pigot Committee proposed this for cases where the child was young or severely traumatised. This was one of its proposals which, predictably, the government did not adopt. But the following provision was inserted in the New Zealand Evidence Act in 1989:

> Where the complainant is to give his or her evidence (by CCTV [live link] or behind screens) the judge may direct that any questions to be put to the complainant shall be given through an appropriate audio link to a person, approved by the judge, placed next to the complainant, who shall repeat the question to the complainant.

A rather similar provision was recently enacted in the Republic of Ireland (Criminal Evidence Act 1992, s. 14).

COMPETENCY AND CORROBORATION

In chapter 4 we examined the competency requirement: the body of rules which require (or formerly required) the court to reject the evidence of a child who had not reached a certain level of moral development.

In the Western world, competency requirements of this sort seem to be unknown, at least in modern times, outside the common law systems. Some continental jurisdictions have rules allowing children to refuse to give evidence against their parents—but these do not affect their ability to do so if they wish: as, for example, s. 52 of the German Code of Criminal Procedure. In those jurisdictions where witnesses generally give evidence on oath, children under a certain age are usually forbidden to take the oath. But this does not prevent the court from hearing the child, because the court is always allowed to hear unsworn evidence from those who are not qualified to take an oath. In France, for example, article 108 and other articles of the Code of Criminal Procedure provide that children under the age of 16 shall give their evidence unsworn, but there is no formal age limit or competency test before a child under that age may be heard as a witness, and the fact that the child's evidence is not given on oath in no way prevents the court from acting on it if it believes it. In West Germany the position is the same. By section 60(1) of the Code of Criminal Procedure persons under the age of 16 give their evidence unsworn, but:

> There is no formal age limit to be a witness. It depends only on the 'natural capacity for testimony' in any individual case, i.e. whether the child has

reached a mental and cognitive stage to make evidential perceptions, to understand questions, and to give a comprehensible report of facts. All this is dependent on the kind of facts to be manifested. The factual limit is usually set at four to five years of age. There is no formal requirement of corroboration of the child's testimony by any additional means of evidence either. (Frehsee 1990.)

Another German writer tells us that children as young as three have given evidence (Volbert 1992b).

The position in the Scandinavian countries is similar. Insofar as these systems still retain oaths for adults, children give evidence unsworn (Andenaes 1990). But the courts are prepared to listen to the evidence of children however young and immature, giving it what weight they think it deserves. In 1988 a court in Sweden convicted two doctors of murdering a prostitute partly on the evidence of a little girl of five, in which she described seeing the dead woman's body being dismembered when she was little more than a baby (*Daily Telegraph*, 9 March 1988); (but the conviction was eventually quashed when an appeal court found the totality of evidence in the case did not point to guilt beyond reasonable doubt).

In all these jurisdictions, the basic rule is that any person is competent to be a witness; a rule that is an unspoken premise in some of them, but which in others—like Italy—is explicitly spelt out (CPP 1988, art. 198).

As we saw in chapter 4, an attempt was made in England to abolish the competency requirement for children with the Criminal Justice Act 1991. This move is in accordance with what has been happening elsewhere in the common law world, where everywhere the competency requirement now seems to be in full retreat. In the United States it was attacked by Wigmore (page 56 above), in Canada it was criticised by the Badgley Committee (Badgley 1984, pp. 371–2), and various law reform bodies have also attacked it in Australia and New Zealand. Legislative changes have followed. In the USA, Rule 601 of the Federal Rules of Evidence now provides that 'Every person is competent to be a witness except as otherwise provided in these rules'—and makes no exception in the case of children. As the next rule, rule 602, requires a witness to declare that he will testify truthfully, some minimum knowledge of the duty to speak truthfully is still implicit in these provisions: but some State laws go further and allow children to give evidence even when they do not reach this level of understanding (Myers 1987a, para. 3:11). The same has been done in a number of jurisdictions in Australia: in South Australia, for example, a statute of 1988 allows the court to receive the evidence of a child who is unable to promise to tell the truth, provided there is corroboration. In 1992, s. 27(1) of the Criminal Evidence Act was enacted in the Republic of Ireland, which is as follows:

Notwithstanding any enactment, in any criminal proceedings the evidence of a person under 14 years of age may be received otherwise than on oath or affirmation if the court is satisfied that he is capable of giving an intelligible account of events which are relevant to those proceedings.

Throughout the common law world, the modern trend seems to be to allow children to give evidence however young or immature they are, their age and immaturity affecting the weight of their evidence, but no longer making it inadmissible.

Most of those parts of the world which borrowed their criminal procedure from England also borrowed the English rules about corroboration and children's evidence which were explained in chapter 8. The rest of the common law world has been ahead of England in abolishing them. The move began in the USA in the 1970s (Myers 1987a, para. 4:21), and rapidly spread to other jurisdictions. In Canada, New Zealand and the Australian State of Victoria, the new law does not merely relieve the judge of the duty to warn against believing the evidence of cerain categories of witness: it actually forbids him to do so (page 214 above). Although corroboration requirements are clearly on the wane in the common law world, there is still a tendency to fall back on them when enacting legislation that extends the competency of children, or which otherwise lets in evidence that was previously unavailable. Thus, as we saw, corroboration is required under the Israeli child examiner scheme, and is also required in South Australia before the court can convict on the evidence of a child too young to promise to tell the truth (Evidence Act 1929, s. 12(1), as amended).

Corroboration requirements specific to the evidence of children seem to be unknown outside the world of the common law. At one time the Continental legal systems, like Scotland today, usually had a rule requiring two witnesses—or one witness and a confession—before anyone could be convicted of anything. Certain jurisdictions, like Holland, have kept them (page 235, n. 4 above). But these corroboration rules were mainly purged in the period of modernisation that followed the French Revolution. (Napoleon himself is said to have influenced the matter, arguing that with a corroboration requirement an honourable man could not prove a single rascal guilty, but the word of two rascals would suffice to convict an honourable man (7 Wigmore, Evidence, sect. 2033, n. 3).) When doubts arise about the credibility of children's evidence, the reaction of the Continental legal systems is to call for expert assistance to advise on the credibility of the child in question, rather than to shelter behind a corroboration requirement that denigrates the evidence of children generally. We saw in chapter 9 how psychological experts are used in Germany, Austria and Sweden. The French courts also widely resort to expert help (Bardet 1990).

OTHER MATTERS

For further information about the position of experts in the continental systems, readers are referred to chapter 9. What we have to offer on the methods used by other legal systems to make life easier for those children who have to give their evidence live in court is also set out elsewhere; readers are referred to chapter 5.

Before leaving the question of children's evidence in other systems there are two further points we should mention.

The first concerns the position of the victim generally. In criminal proceedings in England and in Scotland—and generally in the common law world—the victim of a criminal offence has no particular status. Victims have certain rights to institute criminal prosecutions: but they get no official help to do so, and the public prosecutor usually has the power to intervene to bring the proceedings to an end. In a public prosecution the victim, broadly speaking, is just a witness like any other, with no particular status or rights. This is not the case in some legal systems outside the common law world. In France in particular, the victim of the offence has always had a particular status. He or she has the right to institute a prosecution, and where this course is taken, only the court can bring the proceedings to a stop. In a public prosecution the victim has a right to intervene as what is called a *partie civile*. The *partie civile* is entitled to counsel at the trial to protect his interests: his counsel can examine witnesses, make representations on sentence, and ask for damages—and for the victim who is poor, legal aid is available for this purpose (Merle and Vitu 1989, chapter 2; Spencer 1993c).

The second matter concerns the position of juries. In chapter 10 we identified jury trial as the cause of a number of difficulties where child abuse cases are concerned. To what extent is jury trial the norm in other jurisdictions?

In the common law world the jury is often regarded as something almost sacred. The right to jury trial is guaranteed by the United States Constitution, and even in parts of the common law world where the constitution does not entrench it, proposals to curtail the right to jury trial for child abuse cases would probably cause an outcry.

Yet the common law veneration for the jury is not shared by the whole of the rest of the Western world. Although Lord Devlin, in a famous phrase, called the jury 'the lamp by which we know that freedom lives' (Devlin 1956), a number of spectacularly free and liberal countries have never had trial jury, and show no signs of wanting it: the Netherlands, for example (4). Some of the countries of Europe which introduced juries under English or American influence have modified them heavily—like France, where the jury now consists of a panel of nine randomly-selected laymen sitting together with three professional judges—and there are others, like Germany, which have abolished it altogether. In Germany, there are now mixed tribunals that consist of judges sitting together with a group of specially selected laymen (Frehsee 1990). Although guaranteed by the US Constitution, the right to jury trial is not one of the minimum rights for defendants decreed by the United Nations Convention on Civil and Political Rights of 1966, or by the European Convention on Human Rights.

NOTES

1. We are grateful to Professor Yukiko Matsushima and Miss Masumi Matsushima who took considerable trouble to find this out for us.

2. We learnt this at a conference in Israel, organised by the National Council for the Child and the Law Faculty of the Hebrew University of Jerusalem, in December 1991.

3.   Our information about Scandinavia is largely based on a paper by the distinguished Norwegian professor, Johannes Andenaes (Andenaes 1990).

4.   To be strictly accurate, Holland had jury trial for a short period under French occupation during the Napoleonic wars. It was abolished as soon as the Dutch regained their freedom.

CHAPTER FIFTEEN

Proposals for reform—future directions for research

In this final chapter we review the most recent developments in the law and psychology of children's evidence, and try to point the way ahead.

On the legal side, perhaps the most significant changes in recent years have been those affecting children's evidence in civil proceedings. In rapid succession, the law of civil evidence has been changed, first in Scotland and then in England, to allow a child's account of what happened to be put before the court at second-hand: either by a videotape of an interview with the child, or by allowing an adult who has spoken to the child to repeat what the child has said. At the same time, official recognition has been given to the idea that the views of children are important, and must be considered by courts that have to make decisions affecting their future—a position prominently taken in the opening provisions of the Children Act 1989 in England. Both of these matters have been discussed in some detail earlier in the book (pages 146–159 and 96–97 above).

As regards children's evidence in criminal proceedings, the main legal debate has centred around the official reports on children's evidence that were published on each side of the Border during the winter of 1989–90, and the subsequent moves to get the proposals they contained put into effect. The first of these was the report of the Home Office Advisory Group on Video Evidence, alias the Pigot Committee, which was published in December 1989 (Home Office 1989), and the second was the Report of the Scottish Law Commission on the Evidence of Children and Other Potentially Vulnerable Witnesses (S.L.C. No: 125), which came out in February 1990.

The Scottish Law Commission began work on children's evidence in 1986, under terms of reference which did not limit their enquiries to any particular aspect of the subject. They floated their provisional views in a discussion paper which they published together with a research study in June 1988 (Scottish Law Commission 1988a), and were able to consider a range of responses to those proposals before producing their final report. The Pigot Committee was a one-off advisory group set up by the Home Secretary in June 1988, with restricted terms of reference: 'to look in greater depth than has so far been possible at the idea that video recordings of interviews with child victims (and possibly other victims of crime) should be readily admissible as evidence in criminal trials'. Although they interpreted their terms of reference quite widely, they were unable to consider as many aspects of the evidence of children as the Scottish Law Commission. They had a tight timetable to work to, and did not produce a working paper. They consulted widely, however: so it was a little surprising when the Home Office, having taken several months to publish the report, then announced that there would be a period of public consultation under Home Office direction (the results of which were never officially released).

The issues that the two bodies considered were similar, and to a large extent they identified the same areas of the law as candidates for reform. Both also pointed out that these areas of the law cause problems for other fragile witnesses, and said that the reforms they proposed for child witnesses could usefully be applied to other vulnerable groups as well. However, there was a noticeable difference between them as to how the law should be reformed. Broadly speaking, the Scottish Law Commission took a cautious line. They assumed that most of the problems for child witnesses could be accommodated within the existing system under which evidence is given orally at trial, and mainly concentrated on ways of making the existing trial procedure more 'child friendly'. The Pigot Committee, on the other hand, was more radical, and proposed a completely new system under which child witnesses in serious cases would give their evidence in advance, and so be relieved of the need to appear at trial.

In several important matters, however, the Scottish Law Commission went further than the Pigot Committee. They considered that their proposals should apply to child witnesses in general, whereas the Pigot Committee limited its main proposals to those who are witnesses at trials for crimes of sex and personal violence. With their wider terms of reference, too, they were able to put forward changes that were to be applicable in civil as well as in criminal proceedings. The Scottish Law Commission also proposed a general change in the law of evidence that would enable the court to know the contents of any previous statement by a person (child or adult) who gives evidence.

In the earlier chapters of this book we identified the following features of the law of evidence in Britain as causing serious problems with the evidence of children, particularly in criminal cases:

(a) the competency requirement;

(b) the conditions under which evidence must be given: in particular, the requirement that all evidence be given live, in open court, in the presence of the defendant, and under a system of adversarial examination;

(c) the hearsay rule: the rejection as evidence of what any person said outside the court, including previous statements made by people who are called as witnesses in the case;

(d) corroboration requirements;

(e) reluctance in the legal system to make intelligent use of expert help from those with specialist knowledge in dealing with children.

We shall analyse the recommendations of the Scottish Law Commission and of the Pigot Committee under these headings, explaining as we go how far their proposals have now been put into effect.

THE PROPOSALS OF THE SCOTTISH LAW COMMISSION

(a) Competency

The Scottish Law Commission thought the law of Scotland was satisfactory on this point, and proposed no change. Accordingly no change has taken place.

At the time, there seemed to be no striking cases where the Scots courts refused to listen to child witnesses because of the competency requirement. The evidence of little children was in practice much more willingly received in Scotland than it was in England (see chapter 4), and there was general satisfaction with the position. This could now change. One recent case where a Scottish judge's decision to reject a young child as a witness because of the competency requirement attracted the attention of the newspapers (page 55 above). The Criminal Justice Act 1991, as we saw, attempts to abolish the competency requirement for child witnesses in criminal proceedings in England (page 62 above), and, as we saw in the previous chapter, competency requirements appear to be under attack throughout the English-speaking world.

(b) How children are to give evidence: live evidence at trial or evidence taken in advance?

On this, the Commission stated their position early in the report:

> In the majority of cases—and provided that there has been careful and sympathetic pre-trial preparation of the child—we anticipate that children will be able to give evidence at trial by conventional means without suffering undue trauma and distress (para. 1.8).

With this in mind, they proposed a number of changes designed to make the appearance of the child in court less stressful than at present, and more likely to result in the child communicating his evidence effectively.

Dealing with their proposals in the order in which a criminal case comes before the courts, the first thing they suggested was that more should be done to prepare the child witness for what lies ahead. Then they proposed that waiting facilities at courts should be improved; where possible, there should be special waiting-rooms in courts for children and their families, with toys and books to keep children amused while waiting, as in doctors' surgeries. Children cited by the Crown should never have to share a waiting-room with the defendant and his family. Cases involving child witnesses should be heard in a small courtroom wherever possible, and sound amplification should be provided so that the child is audible without having to shout.

Where a child is likely to be intimidated by the usual trappings and methods of justice, the Commission proposed that the judge should have discretion to order a number of different measures, either singly or in combination. They endorsed the practice—already in occasional use—of judges and lawyers sometimes removing wigs and gowns, of allowing children to give evidence from the well of the court rather than from the witness-box, of a supporting adult to be permitted to sit with the child, and of having the public gallery cleared. The Commission recognised that particular problems are caused for child witnesses who are confronted in court with adult defendants of whom they are afraid, and recommended the discretionary use of both screens and the live television link. A particular problem about the possible use of screens and live television links arose from the practice in Scotland—long ago abandoned in serious cases in England—of holding 'dock identifications': where the witness is asked if he or she sees the attacker present in court, and predictably points to the man in the dock. Obviously there can be no 'dock identification' where the witness and the defendant do not see each other, and the Commission proposed that dock identifications should be replaced (as in England) by evidence that the defendant was the person whom the witness had earlier picked out at an identification parade.

Whilst believing that these changes would enable most children to give evidence effectively and without undue stress, the Commission recognised that there were some particularly vulnerable children for whom this would not be so. With that in mind, they proposed that as an alternative to live evidence, the possibility of using what is called in North America a 'video deposition'—under which the whole of the child's evidence, including the cross-examination, takes place in private ahead of trial, is videotaped, and the tape is then played to the court. These are already used in various parts of the world (see pages 397–400 above).

Of the possible variants on offer the Commission rejected the more radical ones, where (as in Denmark: see page 399 above) the deposition is taken at an early stage. Instead they opted for a conservative model, in which the child would usually be examined some time after the initial questioning by the police, and where the child would be examined in the traditional way by the lawyers for the prosecution and defence—but privately, and with the defendant watching by means of a television link rather than as at present in the flesh. An examination later rather than earlier, they felt, was necessary because at an earlier stage the defence would often not have enough information to put their case to the child in an effective way. The Commission added, however, that

> There may be exceptional cases where the use of the procedure at an earlier stage might be advantageous, and we do not wish to exclude that possibility (para. 4.13).

A considerable part of this section of the Commission's proposals has since come into effect—though in a very piecemeal fashion. Removal of wigs and gowns, altering the place from which the child gives evidence, allowing the child a support person and clearing the court were all the subject of an official directive to the Scottish judges which was issued by the Lord Justice General, Lord Hope, in July 1990 (page 117 above). The possibility of using the live television link was created by the Law Reform (Miscellaneous Provisions) (Scotland) Act in 1990—although so far it is only available for trials in the High Court, and the only courtrooms with the equipment are in Edinburgh and Glasgow (page 107 above). The same Act made a limited change to the rules about in-court identification (page 99 above). Screens, already in occasional use without any particular statutory authority to use them, were officially sanctioned by the Prisoners and Criminal Proceedings (Scotland) Act 1993 (page 101 above). This Act also carried out the recommendation of the Scottish Law Commission about enabling the whole of a child's evidence to be taken ahead of trial by means of video depositions: a procedure which the legislation calls 'taking evidence on commission'.

(c) The hearsay rule and evidence of the witness's previous statements

We argued the case for making the previous statements of a witness admissible to supplement his evidence in court in chapter 10 (pages 268–269 above). The Scottish Law Commission had issued a separate discussion paper on this subject in 1988 (No. 77), and after considering the responses to this as well as to the discussion paper on children's evidence, they came down firmly in favour of the idea, although subject to three limitations. First it should not cover *precognitions*—which are approximately the same as 'proofs of evidence' in England, and are formal statements, prepared by lawyers, using their words rather than the witness's, recording what their witness has indicated that his evidence will be. Secondly, it should be limited to statements 'in written form and signed by the witness, in the form of an audio recording or a video recording, or in some other permanent form from which it can be reasonably inferred that it accurately and completely records what was said by the witness on the previous occasion'; thus it would not extend, for example, to the words a child casually uttered to a parent when describing what so-and-so had done to him. And thirdly, 'the witness must, in the course of his or her evidence, indicate by appropriate means that the statement (or any part of the statement) was made and that its contents (or any part of its contents) are true'. If the previous statement was made in response to leading questions, this in their view should affect is weight, but not render it inadmissible. They said that this change should not be restricted to children, but should cover previous statements of witnesses of any age.

As far as child witnesses are concerned this would be a change of very great significance, and a very welcome one. It would means that a previous interview with the child preserved on tape, or recorded in writing, would be admissible to flesh out the child's live evidence at trial, instead of merely being a stick for the other side to beat the child with when he or she says something different in court. The court would only get to hear it where the child gives evidence. But where the child gives evidence orally at trial, or does so 'on commission' under the procedure described in the previous section, that evidence could in some cases presumably consist of little more than the child being shown the videotape of a previous interview, adopting what was said there, and then answering the questions put about it by the defence. When used in conjunction with the provision about taking evidence ahead of trial on commission, it would enable the Scots courts, in exceptional cases, to follow much the same sort of procedure as was recommended for England in the Pigot report.

So far, however, this provision has not been enacted. Thus, as we explained earlier (page 173), the Scottish courts are at present in the opposite position in relation to videotapes in criminal proceedings to the courts in England: they can receive the whole of a child's evidence on tape by what amounts to a video deposition, but cannot in general refer to a videotape (or any other kind of record) of a previous interview with the child to supplement his fractured utterances in court.

The Commission did not propose any exceptions to the hearsay rule that would have let in the statements of children who do not themselves give evidence, either live or on commission. But this question—and presumably the related question of making records of earlier interviews available to supplement the testimony of children who do give evidence—is not closed for ever; because the Commission is at present engaged in a general study of the hearsay rule in criminal cases.

(d) Corroboration

As we explained in chapter 8, the Scottish corroboration rule, as applied to criminal cases, seems to have attracted little of the anger that the English rules have had vented upon them. In response to the discussion paper, hardly anyone wanted to make an exception to the general requirement of corroboration in Scotland to deal with the particular problem of crimes against children, and the Commission did not propose one. Nor did they propose to alter the existing Scottish rule that generally forbids the prosecution to put in evidence the fact that the defendant has previous convictions, or has a tendency to commit crimes against children.

(e) Expert evidence

As mentioned in chapter 9, no changes are proposed in the present Scottish rules on expert evidence.

THE PROPOSALS OF THE PIGOT COMMITTEE

(a) Competency

This, as interpreted in England, they regarded as a major stumbling-block, to be removed if any of their other proposals were to work:

In principle it seems wrong to us that our courts should refuse to consider any relevant understandable evidence. If a child's account is available it should be heard. We have already looked at ways in which video recording could be used to obtain such evidence where this might now present insuperable difficulties. Once this evidence is admitted juries will obviously weigh matters such as the demeanour of the witness, his or her maturity and understanding and the coherence and consistency of the testimony, in deciding how much reliance to place upon it. We think that this would be a much more satisfactory proceeding and one far better attuned to the principle of trial by jury, modern psychological research and the practice in other jurisdictions than the present approach which appears to us to be founded upon the archaic belief that children below a certain age or level of understanding are either too senseless or too morally delinquent to be worth listening to at all. It follows that we believe the competence requirement which is applied to potential child witnesses should be dispensed with and that it should not be replaced. (Paragraphs 5.12 to 5.13).

They also said that all children under the age of 14 should give evidence unsworn (para. 5.14).

This reasoning convinced the Home Office. But alas, as we saw in chapter 4 (pages 62–64 above) the section of the Criminal Justice Act 1991 which they drafted with the aim of abolishing the competency requirement is so obscure that it may actually achieve the effect of making it more exacting—and even if it does what it was meant to do, the competency requirement survives intact in civil procedings.

(b)   Live evidence or evidence in advance of trial?
Instead of trying to improve existing trial procedures, the Pigot Committee put forward a radical scheme under which children under the age of 14 (or 17 in a sex case) are examined in advance and a videotape of the examination is shown to the court in place of a live appearance by the child. In principle, this would have been similar to the scheme for taking children's evidence on commission proposed by the Scottish Law Commission, but with important differences. First, the Pigot Committee envisaged the child's evidence being taken early, rather than shortly before trial, and secondly, this system would have been routine in cases serious enough to go to the Crown Court, rather than an alternative for use in exceptional cases. In their view, children:

> ought never to be required to appear in public as witnesses in the Crown Court, whether in open court or protected by screens or closed-circuit television, unless they wish to do so. This principle, we believe, is not only absolutely necessary for their welfare, but is also essential in overcoming the reluctance of children and their parents to assist the authorities. It would create a certainty which, we suggest, would enable many more prosecutions to be pursued successfully and therefore enhance the protection afforded to the very young by the courts. (Paragraph 2.26.)

The details of the scheme were given in chapter 5, where it was explained with the aid of a diagram (page 89). To summarise very briefly what was said there, the Pigot scheme provided for the main examination of the child to be conducted by a trained examiner, and videotaped. The defence would later have a chance to cross-examine the child, in chambers, before a judge, this session too being videotaped. And at trial the tape of the first interview would replace the child's live examination-in-chief, the tape of the second interview would replace the child's live cross-examination.

Such a scheme, said the Pigot Committee, would get around the twin problems that arise from making the child deliver his evidence live at trial: stress both in waiting to give evidence and in giving it, and the fact that memories fade with time.

Going further, a majority of the committee proposed that where the child is very young or highly disturbed, the judge should have a discretion to order the 'relaying of questions through a paediatrician, child psychiatrist, social worker or person who enjoys the child's confidence' (para. 2.32). The committee:

> recognise that this would be a substantial change and realise that there will be unease at the prospect of interposing a third party between advocate and witness. Clearly some of the advocate's forensic skills, timing, intonation and the rest, would be lost, and it is, of course, possible that a child might be confused by being subjected to testing questioning from someone regarded as a friend. Nevertheless we do not find these objections conclusive. Where it is absolutely impossible for counsel to communicate successfully with a child there is, in our view, no great difference of principle between the use of someone who can do so and the employment of an interpreter where a witness cannot speak English. Neither technique is entirely satisfactory but both can prevent the loss of crucial evidence without which the court cannot do justice. (Paragraph 2.33.)

This proposal provoked the sole dissent of any committee member from any of the proposals. Ann Rafferty, a barrister, thought the problem could be overcome by allowing counsel to establish rapport with the child before the hearing takes place.

Whilst thinking that their new scheme for children's evidence should become the normal method, the Pigot Committee thought that the possibility of giving evidence in the traditional way ought to remain. In principle, the decision about the method of giving evidence should be the child's; but the prosecution should have the right to insist on the new method if it thought the child was 'manifestly unsuitable' to give evidence in the traditional manner (para. 2.25).

(c) The hearsay rule and the admissibility of previous statements

As we saw, an important proposal of the Scottish Law Commission was to make the previous statements of a witness admissible to supplement the evidence he or she gives directly to the court. This did not feature among the recommendations of the Pigot Committee. They were not opposed to this idea: indeed they expressed some muffled sympathy for it (para. 2.8). But they felt inhibited in dealing with the point, because it raised a point of principle about the previous statements of witnesses of any age, and took them beyond their terms of reference. Thus there is nothing in the Pigot Report upon which to base the idea of making a new exception to the 'rule against narrative' (see page 137 above) to enable videotapes of earlier interviews with children to be put in evidence where they come to court and testify live—the essence of the reform effected by the Criminal Justice Act 1991.

In chapter 5 we explained what happened next.

Although the Pigot scheme attracted widespread approval it was too radical for the government—in reality, probably for the officials in the Home Office. Instead the government put forward the scheme, which we examined in detail in chapter 7, under which a child has to come to court as a live witness—but if he does so, the party calling him can put in evidence a videotape of an earlier interview: and where the videotape is put in evidence, this replaces the child's evidence in-chief as regards any matters 'dealt with' in the video interview.

Having rejected the central element of the Pigot scheme, and opted for a scheme under which the child is still obliged to come to court, the government tried to sweeten the pill with various changes designed to make involvement as a live witness a less daunting prospect for the child. The government's proposals abolished the right of the defendant to insist on a child witness giving live evidence at committal proceedings as well as at the trial, and curtailed the right of unrepresented defendants to cross-examine child witnesses in person (page 87 and 95–96 above). They also extended the live television link to a slightly wider range of child witnesses (pages 104–105 above). These proposals formed part of the Criminal Justice Bill which the government introduced in the autumn of 1990.

In chapter 5 we examined the factors that seem to have persuaded the government to take the line it did. We also explained there how supporters of the Pigot scheme campaigned to get the Bill amended so that it provided what was originally proposed, and how these attempts were narrowly defeated. The idea of taking the whole of the child's evidence ahead of trial was something to which the Home Office was resolutely opposed: even to the extent of blocking an attempt to amend the rarely-used provisions of the Children and Young Persons Act 1933, which permit the evidence of sick children to be taken ahead of trial, to enable such evidence to be reported to the court of trial in the form of a video deposition instead of a deposition in writing (which is what the law at present requires—see page 189 above). Which makes it surprising that the Home Office circular (SP/1992), which explains the children's evidence provisions of the Criminal Justice Act 1991, says they 'follow the recommendations of the Advisory Group on Video Evidence; chaired by His Honour, Judge Thomas Pigot'.

In forcing through the Home Office scheme, the government did however promise to monitor its working, with a view to thinking further about the Pigot scheme if the provisions of the 1991 Act do not work well. A team of researchers is already at work (page 185 above).

(d-e) Corroboration; evidence of bad character

As we saw in chapter 8, the Pigot Committee condemned the present English corroboration rules resoundingly, and recommended that what is left of them should be abolished (paras 5.30 to 5.31). They did not consider the question of evidence of bad character, which they thought was too far outside their terms of reference (para. 7.13). No doubt for the same reason, they did not take up the question of expert evidence.

As we saw earlier (page 218 above) the Law Commission later also recommended that the existing rules about corroboration in England should be abolished. But the recommendation came too late to be included in the Criminal Justice Act 1991, and the rules about corroboration and expert evidence remain much as they were at the time the Pigot Committe reported. The House of Lords' decision in *DPP* v *P* [1991] 2 AC 447, however, has gone a long way to change the law on the admissibility of evidence of previous misconduct in child abuse cases—and in doing so, meets some of the criticisms of the existing law which were made in the first edition of this book (page 225 above).

(f) Children's evidence in civil proceedings
The evidence of children in civil proceedings fell outside their terms of reference; but they did propose that evidence recorded on videotape for criminal proceedings should then be made available to the civil courts, in order to reduce the number of times that children have to repeate distressing evidence (para. 7.12). As we saw in chapter 6, the Children (Admissibility of Hearsay) Order 1993 meets this point by abrogating the hearsay rule in civil proceedings concerned with the upbringing, maintenance or welfare of a child (page 147 above).

WHAT NOW?

Where are we now as far as reforming the law is concerned?

On the one hand what has happened is vexing and frustrating. Both the Scottish Law Commission and the Pigot Committee thought deeply, and consulted widely, to produce coherent schemes designed to put the law relating to children's evidence into a decent state. But in each case the government, like a fussy child confronted with an elaborate dish his mother has laboured to prepare, has picked out the bits it fancies and left the rest congealing on the plate: and Parliament has tamely voted for what the government has proposed. An essential part of the Scottish Law Commission scheme was the proposal to enable the previous statement of a witness to be put before the court to supplement his oral evidence—but as we saw, this has not so far been enacted. Similarly, an essential part of the Pigot scheme was to make it possible for the whole of a child's evidence to be taken in advance of trial—and this has not been enacted either. There is something perverse, too, about the way the government has exercised its choice. When reforming the law of England, as we saw, it resolutely opposed any suggestion that the child be relieved of the duty to undergo a live cross-examination at the trial; yet with its kilt rather than its trousers on, this is exactly the change that it has promoted in the Prisoners and Criminal Proceedings (Scotland) Act 1993. Is this an interesting experiment in comparative law; or is it just a case of the left hand not knowing what the right hand is doing?

On the other hand, real progress has been made, even in the thorny area of children's evidence in criminal proceedings. The live video link, screens, and the willingness of the English courts to listen to the evidence of little children are advances which seemed impossible when the authors of this book first became involved in the evidence of children in the mid-1980's.

In the first edition of this book we concluded with some facts and figures to show how badly the law was operating at that time. Drawing together figures from various English sources, we said that of the allegations of child sexual abuse that get as far as the police, the police think the overwhelming majority are genuine. Yet despite this there was no prosecution in something like 80%

of them. If some of these were cases where the police could have prosecuted with a prospect of success but chose not to do so, it was the rules of evidence which usually made a prosecution impossible. If some of these were cases where a prosecution would have done more harm than good, they included others which were very serious indeed, and where leaving the offender at large involved a serious risk to children (1). There were also evidential problems in prosecuting for physical violence to children. From figures given to the Pigot Committee (para. 1.6), it seems that prosecutions were planned in only 9% of the physical abuse cases which the NSPCC considered in the whole period from 1983 to 1987.

The United Nations Convention on the Rights of the Child imposes various duties on contracting states, including provision for any child capable of forming his own views to be heard in any judicial or administrative proceedings that affect him, measures to protect children from all forms of sexual exploitation and abuse, and appropriate measures to ensure the physical and psychological recovery of children who are victims of neglect, or sexual exploitation or abuse (Van Buren 1991). In 1990, we expressed our doubts as to whether as the law then stood this country could ratify this Convention with a clear conscience.

Since 1990 it has become easier for the courts (particularly in England) to hear the views of children in civil proceedings. And our impression from discussions with police officers, prosecutors, judges, barristers, social workers and others makes us think that in the last few years, changes in the laws of criminal evidence have indeed made it rather easier for offences against children to be prosecuted. We have no facts and figures to back up this impression: but perhaps the study that the Home Office has commissioned on the working of the children's evidence provisions of the Criminal Justice Act 1991 will eventually show whether our impression is correct.

Meanwhile, the following matters surely need to be addressed, irrespective of what impact has been made by the changes that have already come about. First, we should provide, in England, some workable procedure by which the evidence of children can be taken in its entirety ahead of trial—if only for use in exceptional cases. Secondly, for Scotland, we need to enable the courts to hear an account of what a child witness previously said as a supplement to his oral evidence. And thirdly, we need to improve the preparation of children who are required to give their evidence live in court. This is particularly important in England. Despite the welcome introduction of the child Witness Pack and of child liaison officers at court (see chapter 13), there is still doubt about how far a child may be prepared for a court appearance without accusations of coaching, and about whose job it is to do the preparation.

DEVELOPMENTS IN PSYCHOLOGY

On the psychology of children's evidence there have been some developments since the first edition of this book appeared in 1990.

First, as we explained in chapter 12, there have been serious attempts to think about the most effective ways of interviewing children: effective, that is, in the sense of getting information out of them without distorting it in the process. Secondly, psychologists, who as a group have tended in the past to concentrate their efforts on discovering how accurate children can be when they are trying to tell the truth, have now started to address the much harder question of deliberate lies: how often children lie, why they lie, and how good they are at persuading adults that they are telling the truth. Some of this work is discussed in chapter 11. Thirdly, researchers have begun to realise that the question of suggestibility in children is more complicated than they once thought. In the earlier years of this century, as we explained in chapter 11, psychologists and lawyers tended to think that children were highly suggestible in comparison with adults. By the time the first edition of this book appeared in 1990 they had demonstrated that children were considerably less suggestible than first thought—and adults substantially more so. But psychologists are now becoming aware that the issue of suggestibility can arise in legal proceedings in a number of rather different situations. Not only is there the question, much studied by experimental psychologists in the 1980s, as to whether a child who witnesses a single event and is then questioned about it once, can be readily induced to give false information about it if the questioning is suggestive. There is the further question, more complex to study, as to whether by repeated 'brain washing' over a period of time it is possible to implant a completely false memory in a child's (or an adult's) mind: a question which might be a relevant issue in a certain type of custody dispute, for example. This is another issue we have tried to address in chapter 11. Lastly, there is the question of stress in children who have to give evidence, and how far this can be alleviated by preparing them for court. Some recent work in this area is discussed in chapter 13.

Children's evidence remains an area, clearly, where lawyers and social scientists need to keep talking to one another: not only to find answers to their own questions, but also to formulate the questions which their own discipline could usefully address.

NOTE

1. In Parliamentary debate Sir Eldon Griffiths MP quoted the following figures given to him by the police in Lancashire:

> During the first 12 weeks of [1988] . . . one police station had reported to it no fewer than 42 child abuse cases, and 14 of them led to court proceedings. Of the 28 cases that in the end had to be marked 'no further action', the police are convinced that at least 17, of which 12 were very serious—11 of them committed against babies—could and would have been placed before the courts if video recordings had been admissible. (HC Deb, vol. 135, col. 836–7, 20 June 1988.)

Statistics given in the Bexley report suggest that sexual abuse had taken place in at least three-quarters of the cases they investigated; 78% of suspects were not charged with any criminal offence (Metropolitan Police and Bexley

London Borough 1987). In 1986, one Metropolitan Police station received 43 allegations of various forms of child sex abuse, of which only seven resulted in criminal proceedings (personal information). In P. J. Gorry's study of incest cases in the Metropolitan Police area between 1980 and 1985, only some 5% of which were thought to be false accusations, no proceedings were taken in 28.4% of cases because of problems with the evidence. The police prosecuted in over half the cases in Gorry's sample (which were all incests—and thus were all serious) but in only 26.3% was the suspect eventually convicted of the crime of incest (Gorry 1986).

References

Adler, Z. (1987) *Rape on Trial.* London: Routledge and Kegan Paul.

Aldridge, J. (1992) The further training of professionals dealing with child witnesses. In H. Dent and R. Flin (eds.) *Children as Witnesses.* Chichester: Wiley.

Aldridge, J. and Cameron, S. (1989) The evaluation of training in evidential interviewing. In *Research into the Use of Video in the Investigation of Child Abuse.* West Yorkshire Police.

Aldridge, J. and Freshwater, K. (1993) The preparation of child witnesses. *Tolley's Journal of Child Law,* 5, 25–27.

Alldridge, P. (1992) Recognising Novel Scientific Techniques: DNA as a test case [1992] Criminal Law Review, 687–698.

Allen, A. and Morton, A. (1961) *This is Your Child: the Story of the N.S.P.C.C.* London: Routledge and Kegan Paul.

Alexander, D., Innes, G., Irving, B., Sinclair, S. and Walker, L. (1991) *Health, Stress and Policing: A Study in Grampian Police.* London: The Police Foundation.

American Psychiatric Association (1987) *Diagnostic and Statistical Manual of Mental Disorders (DSM III–R)* (3rd edn). (revised) Washington D.C.: American Psychiatric Association.

Andenaes, J. (1990) Evidence of children in legal proceedings: the Scandinavian countries. In J. Spencer, G. Nicholson, R. Flin and R. Bull (eds.) *Children's Evidence in Legal Proceedings: an International Perspective.* Cambridge Law Faculty, Old Syndics Building, Cambridge CB2 1RX.

Andersen, J.P. (1985) The anonymity of witnesses—a Danish development. [1985] *Criminal Law Review,* 363.

Anonymous (1985) The testimony of child victims in sex abuse prosecutions: two legislative innovations. *Harvard Law Review* 98, 806.

Anthony, G., Jenkins, J. and Watkeys, J. (1989) Child sexual abuse. In A. Levy (ed.), *Focus on Child Abuse.* London: Hawksmere.

Archbold, J.F. (1992) *Criminal Pleading, Evidence and Practice* (44th edn). London: Sweet & Maxwell.

Argyle, M. (1989) *The Social Psychology of Work* (3rd edn). Harmondsworth: Penguin.

Aries, P. (1962) *Centuries of Childhood: A Social History of Family Life.* New York: Alfred Knopf.

Armstrong, J.J. (1976) The criminal videotape trial: serious constitutional questions. *Oregon Law Review,* 55, 567–85.

Arnold, L.E. (1990) *Childhood Stress*. Chichester: Wiley.

Ashley, B. (1985) *A Stone on the Mantelpiece* (Centenary Volume of the RSSPCC). Edinburgh: Scottish Academic Press.

Ashworth, A. and Pattenden, R. (1986) Reliability, hearsay evidence and the English criminal trial. *Law Quarterly Review*, **102**, 292–331.

Baddeley, A. (1983) *Your Memory. A User's Guide*. Harmondsworth: Penguin.

Badgley Committee, (1984) *Sexual Offences Against Children: Report of the Committee on Sexual Offences against Children and Youths*. Canadian Government Publishing Centre.

Bailey, V. and Blackburn, S. (1979) The Punishment of Incest Act 1908: a case study of law creation. [1979] *Criminal Law Review*, 708-18.

Bainham, A. (1990) The Children Act 1989, The Future of Wardship, July [1990] *Family Law* 270–73.

Bainham, A. (1993) *Children—the Modern Law*. Bristol: Jordan.

Baker, A.W. and Duncan, S.P. (1985) Child sexual abuse: a study of prevalence in Great Britain. *Child Abuse and Neglect*, **9**, 457–467.

Baker, E.V. (1990), Psychological expert testimony on a child's veracity in child sexual abuse prosecutions. *Louisiana Law Review*, **50**, 1039–56.

Baldwin, J. (1985) The police and tape recorders. [1985] *Criminal Law Review*, 695–704.

Baldwin, J. (1992) Videotaping police interviews with suspects—an evaluation. Police Research Series: Paper No. 1. London: Home Office Police Department.

Bankton, Andrew MacDouall, Lord (1751-3) *An Institute of the Laws of Scotland in Civil Rights*. 3 vols. Edinburgh: R. Fleming.

Bannister, A. (1989) Healing action—action methods with children who have been sexually abused. In C. Wattam, J. Hughes and H. Blagg (eds.) *Child Sexual Abuse. Listening, Hearing and Validating the Experiences of Children*. London: NSPCC/Longman.

Bardet, C. (1990) The place of the expert in the French legal system. In J. Spencer, G. Nicholson, R. Flin and R. Bull (eds.). *Children's Evidence in Legal Proceedings: an International Perspective*. Cambridge: Cambridge Law Faculty.

Baxter, J. (1988) *Children as Eyewitnesses: A Developmental Study*. Unpublished PhD Thesis. University of Aberdeen.

Baxter, J. (1990) The suggestibility of child witnesses: a review. *Applied Cognitive Psychology*, **4**, 393–408.

Bays, J. and Chadwick, D. (1993) Medical diagnosis of the sexually abused child. *Child Abuse and Neglect*, **17**, 91–110.

Beaumont, M. (1987) Confessions, cautions, experts and the subnormal after *R v Silcott and Others*. *New Law Journal*, **137**, 807-14.

Beaumont, M. (1988) Psychiatric evidence: over-rationalising the abnormal. [1988] *Criminal Law Review*, 290-4.

Behlmer, G.K. (1982) *Child Abuse and Moral Reform in England 1870-1908*. Stanford: Stanford University Press.

Bentham J. (1790) *Draught for the Organisation of the Judicial Establishment in France. Works* (ed. J. Bowring) vol. 4. Edinburgh: Tait, 1843.

Bentham, J. (1825) *A Treatise on Judicial Evidence* ed. Dumont, transl. into English. London: Baldwin, Cradock & Joy.

Bentham, J. (1827) *Rationale of Judicial Evidence*. Edition cited is in *Works* (ed. J. Bowring), vols 6 & 7. Edinburgh: Tait, 1843.

Bentovim, A. and Boston, P. (1988) Sexual abuse—basic issues—characteristics of children and families. In A. Bentovim et al. (eds.) *Child Sexual Abuse within the Family*. Bristol: John Wright.

Bentovim, A. and Tranter, M. (1988) The sexual abuse of children and the courts. In G. Davies and J. Drinkwater (eds.) *The Child Witness: do the Courts Abuse Children?* Leicester: British Psychological Society.

Bentovim, A., Elton, A., Hildebrand, J., Tranter, M., and Vizard, E. (eds.) (1988) *Child Sexual Abuse within the Family: Assessment and Treatment*. Bristol: John Wright.

Bentovim, A. and Vizard, E. (1988) Sexual abuse, sexuality and childhood. In A. Bentovim, A. Elton, J. Hildebrand, M. Tranter and E. Vizard (eds.) *Child Sexual Abuse within the Family*. Bristol: John Wright.

Berents, D.A. (1982) *Gilles de Rais: de moordenaar en de mythe*. 's-Gravenhage: Nijhoff.

Berliner, L. and Barbieri, M.K. (1984) The testimony of the child victim of sexual assault. *Journal of Social Issues*, **40**, 125-37.

Besharov, D. (1985) Doing something about child abuse: The need to narrow the grounds for state intervention. *Harvard Journal of Law and Public Policy*, **8**, 539-89.

Bevan, H.K. (1989) *Child Law*. London: Butterworths.

Bexley Report (1987): see Metropolitan Police.

Bienen, L.B. (1983) A question of credibility: John Henry Wigmore's use of scientific authority in section 934a of the treatise on evidence. *California Western Law Review*, **19**, 235-68.

Birch, D. (1992) The Criminal Justice Act 1991: Children's evidence. [1992] *Criminal Law Review*, 262–276.

Birch, D. (1989) Documentary evidence. [1989] *Criminal Law Reveiw*, 15-31.

Birchall, E. (1989) The frequency of child abuse—what do we really know. In O. Stephenson (ed.) *Child Abuse, Professional Practice and Public Policy*. London: Harvester.

Bissett-Johnson, A. (1993a) The Orkney Report—Key issues for lawyers. *Journal of Child Law*, **5**, 1–6.

Bissett-Johnson, A. (1993b) Family violence—Investigating child abuse and learning from British mistakes. *Dalhousie Law Journal*, **16**, 1–62.

Black, D., Kaplan, T. and Harris-Hendriks, J. (1993) *When Father Kills Mother*. London: Routledge.

Blackstone's Criminal Practice (1993) Murphy, P. (ed.). London: Blackstone Press.

Boat, B. and Everson, M. (1989) Anatomical doll play among young children: a follow-up of sexual demonstrators and doll avoiders. Paper presented at the American Psychological Association Conference, New Orleans, August.

Boat, B. and Everson, M. (1993) The use of anatomical dolls in sexual abuse evaluations: Current research and practice. In Goodman, G. and Bottoms, B. (eds.) *Child Victims, Child Witnesses*. New York: Guildford Press.

Bodin, J. (1593) *De la Demonamie des Sorcières, de nouveau reveu & corrigé*. Anvers [Antwerp]: Arnould Conix.

Booth, W. (1890) *In Darkest England and the Way Out*. London: Salvation Army.

Borgida, E., Gresham, A.W., Kovera, M.B., and Regan, P.C. (1992) Children as witnesses in court: the influence of expert psychological testimony. In Burgess, A.W. (ed.), *Child Trauma—Issues and research*, 131–165. New York: Garland.

Bossard et Maulde (1886) *Gilles de Rais maréchal de France dit Barbe-Bleue (1404-1440)* (2nd edn). Paris: H. Champion.

Bottoms, B.L. and Shaver, P.R. and Goodman, G.S. (1991) Profile of Ritualistic and Religion-Related Abuse Allegations Reported to Clinical Psychologists in the United States. Paper presented at the American Psychological Association Conference, San Francisco, August 1991.

Boyer, P. and Nissenbaum, S. (1977) *The Salem Witchcraft Papers*. New York: Da Capo Press.

Boyle, R. (1989) *Medical Evidence in Cases of Child Abuse*. Guidance written for the British Paediatric Association.

Brainerd, C. and Ornstein, P. (1991) Children's testimony: the developmental backdrop. In J. Doris (ed.) *The Suggestibility of Children's Recollections*. Washington: American Psychological Association.

Bray, M. (1989) *Susie and the Wise Hedgehog go to Court*. London: Hawksmere.

Brennan, M. and Brennan R. (1988) *Strange Language* (2nd edn). Wagga Wagga: Riverina Murray Institute of Higher Education.

Briere, J. and Conte, J. (1993) Self-reported amnesia for abuse in adults molested as children. *Journal of Traumatic Stress*, **6**, 21–31.

Brigham, J. and Spiers, S. (1992) Opinions held by professionals who work with child witnesses. In H. Dent and R. Flin (eds.) *Children as Witnesses*. Chichester: Wiley.

Brigham, J., Vanverst, M. and Bothwell, R. (1986) Accuracy of children's eyewitness identifications in a field setting. *Basic and Applied Social Psychology*, **7**, 295-306.

Brigham, J. and Wolfskeil, M. (1983) Opinions of attorneys and law enforcement personnel on the accuracy of eyewitness identifications. *Law and Human Behaviour*, **7**, 337-49.

Bristow, E. (1977) *Vice and Vigilance. Purity Movements in Britain since 1700*. Dublin: Gill and Macmillan.

British Medical Association and Magistrates' Association (1949) *The Criminal Law and Sexual Offenders*. London: British Medical Association.

Britton, H. and O'Keefe, M. (1991) The use of non-anatomical dolls in the sexual abuse interview. *Child Abuse and Neglect*, **15**, 567-73.

Bromley, D.G. and Best, J. and Richardson, J.T. (ed.) (1991) *The Satanism Scare*. New York: Aldine de Gruyter.

Bronfenbrenner, U. (1974) Developmental research, public policy and the ecology of childhood. *Child Development*, **45**, 1-27.

Brouardel, P. (1907) Les attentats au moeurs faussement allégués. *Annales d'Hygiène Publique et de Médecine Légale*. 4 ser. XIII, 221-42.

Brown, B., Burman, M. and Jamieson, L. (1992) *Sexual History and Sexual Character Evidence in Scottish Sexual Offence Trials*. Edinburgh: Scottish Office, Central Research Unit Papers.

Brown, R. (1988) *Group Processes—Dynamics Within and Between Groups*. Oxford: Basil Blackwell.

Bulkley, J.A. (1989) The impact of new child witness research on sexual abuse prosecutions. In S. Ceci, D. Ross and M. Toglia (eds.) *Perspectives on Children's Testimony*. New York: Springer.

Bull, R. (in press) Innovative techniques for the questioning of child witnesses especially those who are young and those with learning disability. In M. Zaragoza (ed.) *Memory and Testimony in the Child Witness*. New York: Sage.

Bull, R. (1989) Can Training Enhance the Detection of Deception? In J.C. Yuille (ed.) *Credibility Assessment*. Dordrect: Kluwer.

Bull, R. (1992) Obtaining evidence expertly: the reliability of interviews with child witnesses. *Expert Evidence*, **1**, 5–12.

Burgess, A. (1983) Rape trauma syndrome. *Behavioural Science and Law*, **1**, 97–100.

Burgess, A. and Holmstrom, L. (1974) Rape trauma syndrome, *American Journal of Psychiatry*, **131**, 981–86.

Burgess, A. and Holmstrom, L. (1978) The child and family during the court process. In A. Burgess, A. Groth, L. Holmstrom and S. Sgroi. *Sexual Assault of Children and Adults*. Lexington, Mass: Lexington Books.

Burton, L. (1968) *Vulnerable Children*. London: Routledge.

Burton, R. (1976) Honesty and dishonesty. In T. Lickona (ed.) *Moral Development and Behaviour*. New York: Holt, Rinehart and Winston.

Burton, R. and Strichartz, A. (1991) Children on the stand: the obligation to speak the truth. *Developmental and Behavioural Pediatrics*, **12**, 121–28.

Bussey, K. (1992) Lying and truthfulness: children's definitions, standards and evaluative reactions. *Child Development*, **63**, 129–37.

Bussey, K., Lee, K. and Grimbeek, E. (1993) Lies and secrets: implications for children's reporting of sexual abuse. In G. Goodman and B. Bottoms (eds.) *Child Victims. Child Witnesses*. New York: Guildford.

Butler, J., Glasgow, D. and Ucrel, A.M. (1991) Child testimony—the potential of forensic linguistics and computational analysis for assessing the credibility of evidence. [1991] *Family Law* 34-37.

Butler-Sloss Report: See Department of Health and Social Security (1988).

Calcutt (1990) *Report of the Committee on Privacy and Related Matters* (Chairman David Calcutt QC); Cm 1102. London, HMSO.

Campbell, B. (1988) *Unofficial Secrets*. London: Virago.

Campbell, Lord (1849) *Lives of the Chief Justices*. London: John Murray.

Carson, D. (1990) *Professionals and the Courts. A Handbook for Expert Witnesses*. Birmingham: Venture Press.

Carson, D. (1992). Beyond the Ultimate Issue. In F. Lösel, D. Bender and T. Bliesener, *Psychology and Law*: International Perspectives: De Gruyfer.

Cashmore, J. (1990) The use of video technology for child witnesses. *Monash University Law Review*, **16**, 228–50.

Cashmore, J. (1991) Problems and solutions in lawyer-child communication. *Australian Criminal Law Journal*, **15**, 193–202.

Cashmore, J. and De Haas, N. (1992) The use of closed-circuit television for child witnesses in the ACT. Research Paper 1. Sydney: Australian Law Reform Commission.

Cashmore, J. and Bussey, K. (1990) Children's conceptions of the witness role. In J. Spencer, G. Nicholson, R. Flin and R. Bull (eds.) *Children's Evidence in Legal Proceedings: an International Perspective*. Cambridge: Cambridge Law Faculty.

Cavenagh, W.E. (1959) *The Child and the Court*. London: Victor Gollancz.

Cecchettini-Whaley, G.D. (1992) Children as witnesses after *Maryland* v *Craig*. *Southern California Law Review*, **65**, 1993–2037.

Ceci, S.J. and Bruck, M. (1993b) Child witnesses: translating research into policy. Society for Research in Child Development, Social Policy Report, Volume XX, number X (Fall 1993).

Ceci, S. and Bruck, M. (1993a) Suggestibility of the child witness: A historical review and synthesis. *Psychological Bulletin*, **113**, 403–439.

Ceci, S., Leichtman, M. and Putnick, M. (1992) (eds.) *Cognitive and Social Factors in Early Deception*. New Jersey: Lawrence Erlbaum Associates.

Ceci, S., Leichtman, M. and White, T. (in press) Interviewing preschoolers: The remembrance of things planted. In Peters, D. (ed.) *The Child Witness in Cognitive, Social and Legal Context*. Netherlands: Kluwer.

Ceci, S., Ross, D. and Toglia, M. (1989) *Perspectives on Children's Testimony*. New York: Springer.

Ceci, S., Toglia, M. and Ross, D. (1987) *Children's Eyewitness Memory*. New York: Springer.

Ceci, S.J., Ross, D.F. and Toglia, M.P. (1987) Suggestibility of children's memory: psycho-legal implications. *Journal of Experimental Psychology: General*, **116** (1), 38-49.

Cecil, H. (1972) *Brief to Counsel*. London: Michael Joseph.

Cecil, H. (1975) *Just Within the Law*. London: Hutchinson.

Chagoya, L. and Scholnick, T. (1986) Children who lie: a review of the literature. *Canadian Journal of Psychiatry*, **31**, 665-9.

Chambers, G. and Miller, A. (1983) *Investigating Sexual Assault*. Edinburgh: HMSO.

Chambers, G. and Miller, A. (1986) *Prosecuting Sexual Assault*. Edinburgh: HMSO.

Chaney, S. (1985) Videotaped interviews with child abuse victims: the search for truth under a Texas procedure. In *Papers from a National Policy Conference on Legal Reforms in Child Sexual Abuse Cases*. American Bar Association.

Chi, M. and Ceci, S. (1986) Content knowledge and the reorganisation of memory. In H.W. Reese and L. Lipsitt (eds.) *Advances in Child Development and Behaviour*, **20**, 1-37.

CIBA Foundation (1984) *Child Sexual Abuse within the Family*. London.

Claman, L., Harris, J., Bernstein, B. and Lovitt, R. (1986) The adolescent as a witness in a case of incest: assessment and outcome. *Journal of the American Academy of Child Psychiatry*, 25, 457-61.

Cleveland Inquiry: See Department of Health and Social Security (1988).

Clyde, Lord (1992). *The Report of the Inquiry into the Removal of Children from Orkney in February 1991*. HC 195, Edinburgh: HMSO.

Cocks, D., QC. (1989) *Misplaced Criticism of the Advocate*. Paper presented at the Bar Conference, 30 September and 1 October 1989.

Cohn, N. (1975) Europe's Inner Demons: an Enquiry Inspired by the Great Witch-hunt. London: Chatto-Heinemann, for Sussex University Press.

Cole, C. and Loftus, E. (1987) The memory of children. In S. Ceci, M. Toglia and D. Ross (eds.) *Children's Eyewitness Memory*. New York: Springer.

Conerly, S. (1986) Assessment of suspected child sexual abuse. In K. MacFarlane et al. (eds.) *Sexual Abuse of Young Children*. New York: Guildford Press.

Cook, P.J. (1989) The economics of criminal sanctions. In M. Friedland (ed.) *Sanctions and Rewards in the Legal System*. Toronto: University of Toronto Press.

Corwin, D., Berliner, L., Goodman, G., Goodwin, J. and White, S. (1987) Child sexual abuse and custody disputes. No easy answers. *Journal of Interpersonal Violence*, 2, 91–105

Cousins, G., Child's evidence: Specific issue order, [1992] *Family Law* 278.

Cox, M. (1991) *The Child's Point of View* (2nd edn). Hemel Hempstead: Harvester Wheatsheaf.

Cox, M. (1992) *Children's Drawings*. London: Penguin.

Cox, T. (1978) *Stress*. London: Macmillan.

Crawford, A. (1938) *Guilty as Libelled*. London: A. Barker Ltd.

Creighton, S.J. and Noyes, P. (1989): See National Society for the Prevention of Cruelty to Children.

Cretin, T. (1992) La preuve impossible? De la difficulté d'administrer la preuve des infractions dont sont victimes les mineurs: attentats à la pudeur, violences et mavais traitements. [1992] *Revue de Science Criminelle et de Droit Pénal Comparé*, 53–58.

Crewdson, J. (1988) *By Silence Betrayed*. Boston: Little, Brown and Co.

Criminal Law Revision Committee (1972) *Eleventh Report, Evidence (General)* (Cmnd 4991). London: HMSO.

Crombag, H.F.N., Van Koppen, P.J., and Wagenaar, W.A. (1992) *Dubieuze Zaken*. Amsterdam: Contract. (English version in preparation: Anchored Narratives. Harvester Wheatsheaf (in press)).

Cross, Sir Rupert (1967) *Evidence* (3rd edn). London: Butterworths.

Cross, Sir Rupert (1985) *Cross on Evidence* (6th edn). London: Butterworths.

Cross, R, and Tapper, C. (1990) *Cross on Evidence* (7th edn). London: Butterworths.

Crowley, A. (1929) *Magick in Theory and Practice*, by the Master Therion. Privately, Paris: Lecram Press.

Cutler, B., Fisher, R. and Chicvara, C. (1989) Eyewitness identification from live versus videotaped line-ups. *Forensic Reports*, 2, 93-106.

Cutshall, J. and Yuille, J. (1989) Field studies of eyewitness memory of actual crimes. In D. Raskin (ed.) *Psychological Techniques in Law Enforcement*. New York: Springer.

Dale, P.S., Loftus, E.F. and Rathbun, L. (1978) The influence of the form of the question on the eyewitness testimony of preschool children. *Journal of Psycholinguistic Research*, 7, 269-77.

David, H. (1990) The role of the youth interrogator. In J. Spencer, G. Nicholson, R. Flin and R. Bull (eds.) *Children's Evidence in Legal Proceedings: an International Perspective*. Cambridge: Cambridge Law Faculty.

Davies, G. (1981) Face recall systems. In G. Davies, H. Ellis and J. Shepherd (eds.) *Perceiving and Remembering Faces*. London: Academic Press.

Davies, G. (1991) *Children on trial? Psychology, videotechnology and the law. The Howard Journal of Criminal Justice*, 30, 177–191.

Davies, G. (1991) Child abuse evidence abused? In Underwager and Wakefield's Training Manual. *Child Abuse Review*, 2, 7–9.

Davies, G.M. (1993) Children's memory for other people: An integrative review. In C. Nelson (ed.) *Memory and Affect in Development*. The Minnesota Symposium on Child Psychology, 26, 123–158. New Jersey: Lawrence Erlbaum.

Davies, G.M. (in press) Children's identification evidence. In S. Sporer, R. Malpass and G. Koehnken (eds.) *Psychological Issues in Eyewitness Identification*. New Jersey: Lawrence Erlbaum.

Davies, G. and Drinkwater, J. (1988) *The Child Witness—Do the Courts Abuse Children?* (Issues in Criminological and Legal Psychology No. 13). Leicester: British Psychological Society.

Davies, G.M. and Noon, E. (1991) *An Evaluation of the Live Link for Child Witnesses*. London: Home Office.

Davies, G. and Robertson, N. (1993) Recognition memory for automobiles: A developmental study. *Bulletin of the Psychonomic Society*, 31, 103–106.

Davies, G., Stevenson, Y. and Flin, R. (1988) Telling tales out of school: children's memory for an unexpected event. In M. Grueneberg, P. Morris and R. Sykes (eds.) *Practical Aspects of Memory*. Chichester: Wiley.

Davies, G., Tarrant, A. and Flin, R. (1989) Close encounters of the witness kind: children's memory for a simulated health inspection. *British Journal of Psychology*, 80, 415-29.

Dawson, J. and Johnston, C. (1989) When the truth hurts. *Community Care*, 30 March, 11-13.

De Francis, V. (1969) *Protecting the Child Victim of Sexual Crimes Committed by Adults*. Denver: American Humane Association.

De Mause, L. (1974) *The History of Childhood*. London: Harper.

De Paulo, B. and Jordan A. (1982) Age changes in deceiving and detecting deceit. In R. Feldman (ed.) *Development of Non-Verbal Behaviour in Children*. New York: Springer.

Deffenbacher, K. (1983) The influence of arousal on reliability of testimony. In B. Clifford and S. Lloyd Bostock (eds.) *Evaluating Witness Evidence*. Chichester: Wiley.

Dennis, I. (1984) Corroboration requirements reconsidered. [1984] *Criminal Law Review*, 316-36.

Dent, H.R. (1977) Stress as a factor influencing person recognition in line-up parades. *Bulletin of the British Psychological Society*, **30**, 339-40.

Dent, H. (1982) The effects of interviewing strategies on the results of interviews with child witnesses. In A. Trankell (ed.) *Reconstructing the Past*. Deventer: Kluwer.

Dent, H.R. (1986) An experimental study of the effectiveness of different techniques of questioning mentally handicapped child witnesses. *British Journal of Clinical Psychology*, **25**, 13-17.

Dent, H.R. (1991) Interviewing. In J. Doris (ed.) *Suggestibility of Children's Recollections*. Washington: American Psychological Association.

Dent, H. (1992) The effects of age and intelligence on eyewitnessing ability. In H. Dent and R. Flin (eds.) *Children as Witnesses*. Chichester: Wiley.

Dent, H. and Flin, R. (1992) (eds.) *Children as Witnesses*. Chichester: Wiley.

Dent, H.R. and Stephenson, G.M. (1979a) Identification evidence: experimental investigations of factors affecting the reliability of juvenile and adult witnesses. In D. Farrington, K. Hawkins and S. Lloyd-Bostock (eds.). *Psychology, Law and Legal Processes*. Atlantic Highlands NJ: Humanities Press.

Dent, H.R. and Stephenson, G.M. (1979b) An experimental study of the effectiveness of different techniques of questioning child witnesses. *British Journal of Social and Clinical Psychology*, **18**, 41-5 1.

Department of Health and Social Security (1974) *Report of the Committee of Enquiry Set up to Enquire into the Care and Supervision Provided in Relation to Maria Colwell*. London: HMSO.

Department of Health and Social Security (1985) *Review of Child Care Law*. London: HMSO.

Department of Health and Social Security (1987) *The Law on Child Care and Family Services* (Cm 62). London: HMSO.

Department of Health and Social Security (1988) *Report of the Inquiry into Child Abuse in Cleveland 1987* (Cm 412). London: HMSO.

Department of Health and Social Security (1988) *Diagnosis of child sexual abuse: guidance for doctors*. London: HMSO.

Department of Health and Social Security and Welsh Office (1991) *Working Together Under the Children Act 1989. A Guide to Arrangements for Inter-Agency Co-operation for the Protection of Children from Abuse*. London: HMSO.

Departmental Committee on Evidence of Identification in Criminal Cases (Devlin Committee) (1976) *Report*. London: HMSO.

Departmental Committee on Sexual Offences against Young Persons (1925) *Report* (Cmd 2561). London: HMSO.

Devlin Report: see Departmental Committee on Evidence of Identification.

Devlin, P. (1956) *Trial by Jury*. London: Stevens.

Devlin, P. (1979) *The Judge*. Oxford: Oxford University Press.

Dezwirek-Sas, L. (1992) Empowering child witnesses for sexual abuse prosecution. In H. Dent and R. Flin (eds.) *Children as Witnesses*. Chichester: Wiley.

DHSS see Department of Health and Social Security.

Dickson, W.G. (1864) *A Treatise on the Law of Evidence in Scotland,* 2nd ed. by J. Skelton. Edinburgh: Bell and Bradfute.

Dickson, W.G. (1887) *A Treatise on the Law of Evidence in Scotland,* 3rd ed. by P.J. Hamilton Grierson. Edinburgh: T. & T. Clark.

Dickson, W.K.L. and Dickson, A. (1894) *The Life and Inventions of Thomas Alva Edison.* London: Chatto and Windus.

Directors of Social Work in Scotland (1992) Child Protection Policy Practice and Procedure: an overview of child abuse issues in social work departments in Scotland. Edinburgh: HMSO.

Donaldson, M. (1992) *Human Minds.* London: Allen Lane, Penguin.

Donaldson, M. (1978) *Children's Minds.* London: Fontana.

Donaldson, M., Grieve, R. and Pratt, C. (eds.) (1983) *Early Childhood Development and Education.* Oxford: Basil Blackwell.

Doob, A.N. and Kirshenbaum, H.M. (1972) Some empirical evidence on the effect of s. 12 of the Canada Evidence Act upon an accused. *Criminal Law Quarterly,* **15,** 88-96.

Doris, J. (ed.) (1991) *The Suggestibility of Children's Recollections.* Washington: American Psychological Association.

Douglas, G. and Willmore, C. (1987) Diagnostic interviews as evidence in cases of child sexual assault. [1987] *Family Law,* 151-4.

Draucker, C.B. (1992) *Counselling Survivors of Childhood Sexual Abuse.* London: Sage.

Du Cann, R. (1964) *The Art of the Advocate.* Harmondsworth: Penguin.

Dziech, B.W. and Schudson, C.B. (1991) *On Trial.* Boston: Beacon Press.

East, Sir Edward (1803) *A Treatise of the Pleas of the Crown.* London: Butterworth.

Eatman, R. and Bulkley, J. (1986) *Protecting Child Victim/Witnesses: Sample Laws and Materials.* Washington DC: American Bar Association. National Center for Child Advocacy and Protection.

Eckenrode, J., Munsch, J., Powers, J. and Doris, J. (1988a) The nature and substantiation of official sexual abuse reports. *Child Abuse and Neglect,* **12,** 311-19.

Eckenrode, J., Powers, J., Doris, J., Munsch, J. and Bolger, N. (1988b) Substantiation of child and abuse and neglect reports. *Journal of Consulting and Clinical Psychology,* **56,** 9-16.

Edwards, S. (1986) Evidential matters in rape prosecutions from "first opportunity to complain" to corroboration. *New Law Journal,* **136,** 291-3.

Ekman, P. (1986) *Telling Lies: Clues to Deception in the Marketplace, Marriage and Politics.* New York: W.W. Norton.

Elliott, D.W. (1993) The young person's guide to similar fact evidence. [1993] *Criminal Law Review,* 284-296, 352-364.

Ellis, H. (1992) The development of face processing skills. *Philosophical Transactions for the Royal Society of London,* **335,** 105-11.

Ellis, H., Shepherd, J., Flin, R. and Davies, G. (1989) Identification from a computer-driven retrieval system compared with a traditional mug-shot album search: a new tool for police investigations. *Ergonomics,* **32,** 167-77.

Emmins, C.J. (1992) *Emmins on Criminal Procedure* (5th edn). Sprack, J. (ed.). London: Blackstone Press.

Erskine, J. (1773) *An Institute of the Law of Scotland.* J.B. Nicholson (ed.). Edinburgh: Bell and Bradfute, 1871.

Everson, M. and Boat, B. (1989) False allegations of sexual abuse by children and adolescents. *Journal of American Academy of Child and Adolescent Psychiatry,* **28**, 230-5.

Eysenck, H. (1985) *The Decline and Fall of the Freudian Empire.* Harmondsworth: Penguin.

Faller, K. (1984) Is the child victim of sexual abuse telling the truth? *Child Abuse and Neglect,* **8**, 473-81.

Faller, K. (1988) *Child Sexual Abuse.* London: Macmillan.

Faller, K. (1991a) Possible explanations for child sexual abuse allegations in divorce. *American Journal of Orthopsychiatry,* **61**, 86–91

Faller, K. (1991b) The parent-child interview. Use in evaluating child allegations of sexual abuse by the parent. *American Journal of Orthopsychiatry,* **61**, 552–57.

Farley, R.H. (1987) 'Drawing interviews': an alternative technique. *The Police Chief,* April, 37-8.

Farrar, M. and Goodman, G. (1992) Developmental changes in event memory. *Child Development,* **63**, 173–87.

Farrington, R. (1981) The prevalence of convictions. *British Journal of Criminology,* **21**, 173.

Feben, D.J. (1985) *Age of Witness Competency: Cognitive Correlates.* Honours Thesis: Monash University, Australia.

Feldman, R. and White, J. (1980) Detecting deception in children. *Journal of Communication,* **30**, 121-8.

Ferguson, P. (1985) Child sexual abuse—can the legal system cope? *The Scottish Child,* **6**, 13-16.

Field, D. (1988) *The Law of Evidence in Scotland.* Edinburgh: W. Green & Son.

Fielding, N. and Conroy, S. (1992) Interviewing child victims: Police and Social Work investigations of child sexual abuse. *Sociology,* **26**, 103–24.

Finkelhor, D. (1979) *Sexually Victimised Children.* New York: The Free Press.

Finkelhor, D. (1984) *Child Sexual Abuse: New Theory and Research.* London: Collier Macmillan; New York: The Free Press.

Finkelhor, D., Williams, L. and Burns, N. (1988) *Nursery Crimes. Sexual Abuse in Day Care.* California: Sage.

Firth, A. (1975) Interrogation. *Police Review,* **28**, November, 1507.

Fisher, R. and Geiselman, R.E. (1992) *Memory-enhancing Techniques for Investigative Interviewing. The Cognitive Interview.* Springfield, Illinois: C. C. Thomas.

Fisher, R. and McCauley, M. (in press) Improving eyewitness testimony with the cognitive interview. In M. Zaragoza (ed.) *Memory and Testimony in the Child Witness.* California: Sage.

Fisher, R., Geiselman, E. and Raymond, D. (1987) Critical analysis of police interview techniques. *Journal of Police Science and Administration,* **15**, 177-85.

Flavell, J., Miller, P. and Miller, S. (1993) *Cognitive Development* (3rd ed.). New York: Prentice Hall.

Flin, R.H. (1993) Hearing and testing children's evidence. In G. Goodman and B. Bottoms (eds.) *Child Victims. Child Witnesses*. New York: Guildford.

Flin, R.H. (1991) A grand memory for forgetting: commentary on Brainerd and Ornstein. In J. Doris (ed.) *Suggestibility of Children's Recollections*. Washington: American Psychological Association.

Flin, R., Bull, R., Boon, J. and Knox, A. (1993). Child witnesses in Scottish criminal trials. *International Review of Victimology*, 2, 319–339.

Flin, R.H. and Bull. R. (1990) Child witnesses in Scottish prosecutions. In J. Spencer, G. Nicholson, R. Flin and R. Bull (eds.) *Children's Evidence in Legal Proceedings: an International Perspective*. Cambridge: Cambridge Law Faculty.

Flin, R.H., Boon, J. and Knox, A., Bull, R., (1992) The effects of a five month delay on children's and adults' eyewitness memory. *British Journal of Psychology*, 83, 323–36.

Flin, R.H., Davies, G. and Tarrant, A. (1988). *The Child Witness*. Final Report to the Scottish Home and Health Department. Grant 85/9290.

Flin, R.H. and Dzurawiec, S. (1989) Developmental factors in face processing. In A. Young and H. Ellis (eds.) *Handbook of Research on Face Processing*. Amsterdam: North-Holland.

Flin, R., Markham, R. and Davies, G. (1989) Making faces: on the relative competence of children and adults at constructing police photofit composites. *Journal of Applied Developmental Psychology*, 10, 123-37.

Flin, R.H. and Shepherd, J.W. (1986) Tall stories: Eyewitness' ability to judge height and weight characteristics. *Human Learning*, 5, 29-38.

Flin, R.H., Stevenson, Y. and Davies, G.M. (1989) Children's knowledge of court proceedings. *British Journal of Psychology*, 80, 285-97.

Foss, E. (1870) *A Biographical Dictionary of the Judges of England. From the Conquest to the Present Time (1066-1870)*. London: John Murray.

Frauds Trials Committee (Roskill Committee) (1986) *Report*. London: HMSO.

Freeman, M.D.A. (1989), Cleveland, Butler-Sloss and beyond—How are we to react to the sexual abuse of children? *Current Legal Problems*, 42, 85–133.

Frehsee, D. (1990) Children's evidence within the German legal system. In J. Spencer, G. Nicholson, R. Flin and R. Bull (eds.) *Children's Evidence in Legal Proceedings*. Cambridge: Cambridge Law Faculty.

Freshwater, K. (1991) *Preparing Child Witnesses for Court*. Unpublished MSc Thesis, University of Leeds.

Freud, S. (1896/1962a) Heredity and the aetiology of the neuroses. In J. Strachey (ed. and transl.) *The Standard Edition of the Complete Psychological Works of Sigmund Freud*, vol. 3. London: Hogarth Press.

Freud, S. (1896/1962b) The aetiology of hysteria. In J. Strachey (ed. and transl.) *The Standard Edition of the Complete Psychological Works of Sigmund Freud*, vol. 3. London: Hogarth Press.

Freud, S. (1924/1959) An autobiographical study. In J. Strachey (ed. and transl.) *The Standard Edition of the Complete Psychological Works of Sigmund Freud*, vol. 20. London: Hogarth Press.

Friedman, W.J. (1991) The development of children's memory for the time of past events. *Child Development*, **62**, 139–55.

Fundundis, T. (1989) Children's memory and the assessment of possible child sex abuse. *Journal of Child Psychology and Psychiatry*, **30**, 337-46.

Garbarino, J. and Stott, F. (1989) *What Children Can Tell Us*. San Francisco: Jossey Bass.

Garmezy, N. and Rutter, M. (eds.) (1983) *Stress, Coping and Development in Children*. New York: McGraw-Hill.

Geddis, D. (1988) *A Private or Public Nightmare: Report of the Advisory Committee on the Investigation, Detection and Prosecution of Offences against Children*. New Zealand.

Geddis, D.C., Taylor, N.J. and Henaghan, R.M. (1990) Child sexual abuse. [1990] *New Zealand Law Journal*, 371–75, 388–94, 425–31.

Gee, D.J. (1987) The expert witness in the criminal trial. [1987] *Criminal Law Review*, 307-14.

Geis, G. and Bunn, I. (1981) Sir Thomas Browne and witchcraft—a cautionary tale for contemporary law and psychiatry. *International Journal of Law and Psychiatry*, **4**, 1-11.

Geiselman, E. and Fisher, R. (1989) The cognitive interview technique for victims and witnesses of crime. In D. Raskin (ed.) *Psychological Methods in Criminal Investigation and Evidence*. New York: Springer.

Geiselman, E. and Padilla, J. (1988) Interviewing child witnesses with the cognitive interview. *Journal of Police Science and Administration*, **16**, 236–42.

General Council of the Bar (1973) *Evidence in Criminal Cases. Memorandum on the Eleventh Report of the Criminal Law Revision Committee: Evidence (General)*. London.

Gibbens, T.C. and Prince, J. (1963) *Child Victims of Sex Offences*. London: Institute for the Study and Treatment of Delinquency.

Gillham, B. (1991) *The Facts About Child Sexual Abuse*. London: Cassell Educational.

Glaser, D. and Collins, C. (1989) The response of young, non-sexually abused children to anatomically correct dolls. *Journal of Child Psychology and Psychiatry*, **30**, 547-60.

Glaser, D. and Frosh, S. (1988) *Child Sexual Abuse*. London: Macmillan.

Glaser, D. and Spencer, J. (1990) Sentencing, children's evidence and children's trauma. [1990] *Criminal Law Review*, 371-82.

Glasgow, D. (1987) *Responding to Child Sexual Abuse*. Liverpool: Mersey Regional Health Authority.

Glasgow, D (1989) Play based investigative assessment of children who may have been sexually abused. In C. Wattam, J. Hughes and H. Blagg (eds.). *Child Sexual Abuse*. London: NSPCC/Longman.

Glasgow, D., Roberts, H. and Horne, L. (1993) Child protection prosecution and the evidence: A case of egocentricity of adults. *Expert Evidence*, **2**, 13–18.

Goetze, H.J. (1980) *The Effect of Age and Method of Interview on the Accuracy and Completeness of Eyewitness Accounts*. Unpublished PhD thesis. Hofstra University.

Goodman, G. (1984) Children's testimony in historical perspective. *Journal of Social Issues*, 40, 9-3 1.

Goodman, G. (1991) On stress and accuracy in research on children's testimony. Commentary on Peters. In J. Doris (ed.) *The Suggestibility of Children's Recollections*. Washington: American Psychological Association.

Goodman, G. and Aman, C. (1990) Children's use of anatomically detailed dolls to recount an event. *Child Development*, 61, 1859–71.

Goodman, G., Aman, C. and Hirschman, J. (1987) Child sexual and physical abuse. In S. Ceci, M. Toglia and D. Ross (eds.) *Children's Eyewitness Memory*. New York: Springer.

Goodman, G.S. and Bottoms, B.L. (1993) (eds.) *Child Witnesses, Child Victims*. New York: Guilford.

Goodman, G.S., Bottoms, B.L., Schwartz-Kenney, B.M. and Rudy, L. (1991a) Children's testimony about a stressful event: Improving children's reports. *Journal of Narrative and Life History*, 1, 69–99.

Goodman, G. and Clarke-Stewart, A. (1991) Suggestibility in children's testimony: implications for child sexual abuse investigations. In J. Doris (ed.) *The Suggestibility of Children's Recollections*. Washington: American Psychological Association.

Goodman, G.S. and Helgeson, V.S. (1985) Child sexual assault: children's memory and the law. *University of Miami Law Review*, 40, 181.

Goodman, G.S. and Helgeson, V.S. (1988) Children as witnesses: what do they remember? In L. Walker (ed.) *Handbook on Sexual Abuse of Children*. New York: Springer.

Goodman, G.S., Hepps, D. and Reed, R.S. (1986) The child victim's testimony. In A. Haralambie (ed.) *New Issues for Child Advocates*. Phoenix, Arizona: Arizona Council of Attorneys for Children.

Goodman, G., Hirshman, J., Hepps, D. and Rudy, L. (1991b) Children's memories for stressful events. *Merrill-Palmer Quarterly*, 37, 109–58.

Goodman, G. and Reed, R. (1986) Age differences in eyewitness testimony. *Law and Human Behaviour*, 10, 317-32.

Goodman, G., Rudy, L., Bottoms, B. and Aman, C. (1990) Children's concerns and memory: ecological issues in the study of children's eyewitness testimony. In R. Fivush and J. Hudson (eds.) *What Young Children Remember and Why*. Cambridge: Cambridge University Press.

Goodman, G.S. and Schwartz-Kenney, B. (1992) Why knowing a child's age is not enough. Influence of cognitive, social and emotional factors on children's testimony. In H. Dent and R. Flin (eds.) *Children as Witnesses*. Chichester: Wiley.

Goodman, G., Taub, E., Jones, D., England, P., Port, L., Rudy, L. and Prado, L. (1992) Testifying in Criminal Court: Emotional effects on child sexual assault victims. *Monograph of the Society for Research in Child Development*, 57, 5. (Serial Number 229.)

Goodman, J. (ed.) (1973) *The Trial of Ian Brady and Myra Hindley—the Moors Case*. Newton Abbott: David & Charles (Celebrated Trials Series).

Goodwin, J., Sahd, C. and Rada, R. (1979) Incest hoax: false accusations, false denials. *Bulletin of the American Academy of Psychiatry and Law*, 6, 269-76.

Goodwin, J., Sahd, D. and Rada, R. (1982) False accusations and false denials of incest: clinical myths and clinical realities. In J. Goodwin. *Sexual Abuse, Incest Victims and their Families*. Bristol: John Wright.

Goodyer, I. (1988) Stress in childhood and adolescence. In S. Fisher and J. Reason (eds.) *Handbook of Life Stress, Cognition and Health*. Chichester: Wiley.

Gordon, B., Jens, K., Shaddock, A. and Watson, T. (1991) Children's ability to remember activities performed and imagined: Implications for testimony. *Child Psychiatry and Human Development*, **21**, 301–14.

Gordon, B., Schroeder, C., and Abrams, J. (1990a) Age and social class differences in children's knowledge of sexuality. *Journal of Clinical Child Psychology*, **19**, 33–43.

Gordon, B., Schroeder, C. and Abrams, M. (1990b) Children's knowledge of sexuality: A comparison of sexually abused and non-abused children. *American Journal of Orthopsychiatry*, **60**, 250–57.

Gorphe, F. (1927) *La Critique du Témoignage*, 2nd ed. Paris: Dalloz.

Gorry, P. (1986) *Incest: The Offence and Police Investigation*. MPhil thesis. Cambridge University.

Graham, C.F. (1990) Sequestration screens for young complainants, early developments in Canada. *Criminal Law Quarterly*, **32**, 227–52.

Graham, M.H. (1985) Child abuse prosecutions: the current state of the art. *University of Miami Law Review*, **40**, 1.

Graham Hall, J. and Martin, D.F. (1987) *Child Abuse: Procedure and Evidence in Juvenile Courts*, 2nd ed. Chichester: Barry Rose.

Graham Hall, J. and Smith, G.D. (1992) *The Expert Witness*. Chichester: Barry Rose.

Green, A.M. (1986) True and false allegations of sexual abuse in child custody disputes. *Journal of American Academy of Child Psychiatry*, **25**, 449–56.

Green, R. (1992) *Sexual Science and the Law*. Cambridge (Mass): Harvard University Press.

Greenberg, M.S. and Ruback, R.B. (1992) *After the Crime, Victim Decision Making*. New York: Plenum.

Gregory, J. (1989) *Trial by Ordeal. London:* EOC/HMSO.

Grindrod, H. (1992) Preparing the defence in child sexual abuse cases [1992] *Solicitors Journal*, 310–311.

Groth, A.N. and Birnbaum, B. (1987) Adult sexual orientation and attraction to underage persons. *Archives of Sexual Behaviour*, **7**, 175–81.

Gudjonsson, G. (1992) *The Psychology of Interrogations, Confessions and Testimony*. Chichester: Wiley.

Gudjonsson, G.H. and Gunn, J. (1982) The competence and reliability of a witness in a criminal court: a case report. *British Journal of Psychiatry*, **141**, 624–7.

Gwynn, P. (1988) Investigating child abuse: the Bexley project. In G. Davies and J. Drinkwater (eds.) *The Child Witness: do the Courts Abuse Children?* Leicester: British Psychological Society.

Hain, P. (1976) *Mistaken Identity*. London: Quartet.

Hale, Sir Matthew (1736) *Historia Placitorum Coronae. The History of the Pleas of the Crown.* In Sollom Emlyn (ed.). London: Nutt and Gosling.

Hamon, H. (1990) The testimony of the child victim of intra-familial sex abuse. In J. Spencer, G. Nicholson, R. Flin and R. Bull (eds.) *Children's Evidence in Legal Proceedings: an International Perspective.* Cambridge: Cambridge Law Faculty.

Hansen, J.K. (1990) Danish criminal procedure—a comparison with English law. (Dissertation for the Diploma in Legal Studies, Cambridge.)

Hanson, R.S. (1989) James Alphonzo Frye is 65-years-old; should he retire? *Western State University Law Review,* **16**, 357–459.

Harnon, E. (1988) The examination of children in sexual offences—the Israeli law and practice. [1988] *Criminal Law Review,* 263-74.

Harnon, E. (1990) Children's evidence in the Israeli criminal justice system: with special reference to sexual offences. In J. Spencer, G. Nicholson, R. Flin and R. Bull (eds.) *Children's Evidence in Legal Proceedings: an International Perspective.* Cambridge: Cambridge Law Faculty.

Harris, P., Brown, E., Marriott, C., Whittall, S. and Harmer, S. (1991) Monsters, ghosts and witches: Testing the limits of the fantasy-reality distinction in young children. *British Journal of Developmental Psychology,* **9**, 105–123.

Harvey, C.P. (1958) *The Advocate's Devil.* London: Stevens.

Haugaard, J. and Reppucci, N. (1988) *The Sexual Abuse of Children.* San Francisco: Jossey Bass.

Havik, T. (1992) Official ideals and correct practice in work with child witnesses in sexual abuse cases in Norway. In Lösel et al. (eds.) *Psychology and Law: International Perspectives.* Berlin: Walter de Gruyter.

Haward, L. (1981a) *Forensic Psychology.* London: Batsford.

Haward, L. (1981b) The psychologist as expert witness. In J. Shapland (ed.) *Lawyers and Psychologists—The Way Forward.* (Issues in Criminological and Legal Psychology No. 1) British Psychological Society.

Hedderman, C. (1987) *Children's Evidence: The Need for Corroboration,* Home Office Research and Planning Unit Paper 41 (London: Home Office).

Heger, A. (1990) Physical examination. In D. Gough and K. Murray (eds.) *Intervening in Child Sexual Abuse.* Edinburgh: Scottish Academic Press.

Hernandez, L. (1921) Le procès inquisitorial de Gilles de Rais, maréchal de France avec on essai de réhabilitation. Paris: Bibliothèque des Curieux.

Heydon, J. (1984) *Evidence. Cases and Materials,* 2nd edn. London: Butterworths.

Hill, P.E. and Hill, S.M. (1987) Videotaping children's testimony: an empirical view. *Michigan Law Review,* **85**, 809.

Hobbs, C. and Wynne, J. (1986) Buggery in childhood, a common syndrome of child abuse. *Lancet,* 4 October 1986, 792-6.

Hobbs, C.J. and Wynne, J.M. (1987a) Management of sexual abuse. *Archives of Disease in Childhood,* **62**, 1182-7.

Hobbs, C.J. and Wynne, J.M. (1987b) Child sexual abuse—an increasing rate of diagnosis. *Lancet* (10 October 1987), 837-41.

Hobbs, C.J. and Wynne, J.M. (1989) Sexual abuse of English boys and girls: the importance of anal examination. *Child Abuse and Neglect,* **13**, 195-210.

Hodges, W. (1991) *Interventions for Children of Divorce* (2nd ed) New York: Wiley.

Hodgkinson, T. (1990) *Expert Evidence: Law and Practice*. London: Sweet and Maxwell.

Hoggett, B. (1986) Family courts or family law reform—which should come first? *Legal Studies*, **6**, 1.

Home Office (1960) *Report of the Committee on Children and Young Persons* (Ingleby Committee) (Cmnd 1191) London: HMSO.

Home Office (1987) *The Use of Video Technology at Trials of Alleged Child Abusers*. London: Home Office. (Not a HMSO publication.)

Home Office (1988) Circular 52/1988. The Investigation of Child Sexual Abuse.

Home Office (1989) *Report of the Working Group on the Right to Silence*.

Home Office (1989) *Report of the Advisory Group on Video Evidence* (Chairman Judge Thomas Pigot QC). London: Home Office.

Home Office (1990) *Victim's Charter. A Statement of the Rights of Victims of Crime*. London: Home Office.

Home Office (1990) Circular No. 61/1990. Use of screens in magistrates' courts.

Home Office (1991) Circular No. 84/1991. Child Abuse.

Home Office, Department of Health, Department of Education and Welsh Office (1991) *Working Together under the Children Act 1989*. London: HMSO.

Home Office and Department of Health (1992) *Memorandum of Good Practice on Videorecording Interviews with Child Witnesses for Criminal Proceedings*. London HMSO.

Honoré, T. (1981) The primacy of oral evidence? In Tapper (ed.) *Crime, Proof and Punishment: Essays in Memory of Sir Rupert Cross*. London: Butterworths.

Horne, L., Glasgow, D., Cox, A., and Calam, R. (1991) Sexual abuse of children by children. *Tolley's Journal of Child Law*, **3**, 4, 147.

Horneck, Anthony (translator) (1682) *A Relation of the Strange Witchcraft Discovered in the Village of Mohra in Swedeland*. In Glanvil, *Saducismus Triumphatus*. London: T. Newcomb, for S. Lownds.

Howe, M. and Brainerd, C. (1989) Development of children's long term retention. *Developmental Review*, **9**, 301–40.

Hudson, J. (1990) Constructive processing in children's event memory. *Developmental Psychology*, **26**, 180–87.

Hudson, J. and Fivush, R. (1991) As time goes by: Sixth graders remember a kindergarten experience. *Applied Cognitive Psychology*, **5**, 347–60.

Hughes, M. and Grieve, R. (1980) On asking children bizarre questions. *First Language*, **1**, 149–60.

Hume, D. (1844) *Commentaries on the Law of Scotland, Respecting Crimes. With a Supplement by Benjamin Robert Bell*. Edinburgh: Bell and Bradfute.

Humphreys, T. (1946) *Criminal Days*. London: Hodder and Stoughton.

Hurley, P., Sas, L. and Wilson, S. (1988) Empowering children for abuse litigations. *Preventing Sexual Abuse*, **1**, 8-12.

Hutchinson, F. (1720) *An Historical Essay Concerning Witchcraft*. London: Knaplock and Midwinter.

Ingleby Committee: see Home Office (1960).

Insurance Ombudsman, Annual Report 1987. London: Insurance Ombudsman Bureau.

Irish Law Reform Commission (1989) *Consultation Paper on Child Sexual Abuse*. Dublin: Irish Law Reform Commission.

Irvine, R. and Dunning, N. (1985) The child and the criminal justice system. *Journal of the Law Society of Scotland*, **30**, 264-6.

Israel Ministry of Labour and Social Affairs (1990) *Interrogation of Children Involved in Sexual Offences: Victims, Witnesses and Suspects*. Jerusalem Juvenile Probation Service. Annual Report.

Jackson, J.D. (1984) The ultimate issue rule: one rule too many. [1984] *Criminal Law Review*, 75-86.

Jackson, J.D. (1989) Recent developments in criminal evidence. *Northern Ireland Law Quarterly*, **40**, 105–130.

Jackson, J.D. (1991). Curtailing the Right of Silence: lessons from Northern Ireland. [1991] *Criminal Law Review*, 404–415.

Jackson, R.M. (1988) *Jackson's Machinery of Justice* (8th edn). by J.R. Spencer. Cambridge: Cambridge University Press.

Jaffe, P. and Wilson, S. (1987) Court testimony of child sexual abuse victims: emerging issues in clinical assessments. *Canadian Psychology*, **28**, 291-5.

Janoff-Bulman, R. (1988) Victims of violence. In S. Fisher and J. Reason (eds.). *Handbook of Life Stress, Cognition and Health*. Chichester: Wiley.

Jessop, A. (1988) Children as witnesses: the Glasgow experience. Paper presented at the RSSPCC Study Day, Edinburgh, October.

Johnson, M. and Foley, M. (1984) Differentiating fact from fantasy: The reliability of children's memory. *Journal of Social Issues*, **40**, 33-50.

Johnson, P. (1990) *Child Abuse—Understanding the Problem*. Marlborough: Crowood Press.

Jones, D.N., Picket, J., Oates, M.R. and Barbor, P. (1987) *Understanding Child Abuse*, 2nd ed. London: Macmillan.

Jones, D.P.H. (1987) The evidence of a three-year-old child. [1987] *Criminal Law Review*, 677-81.

Jones, D.P.H. (1989) Some reflections on the Cleveland affair. *Association of Child Psychology and Psychiatry Newsletter*, 13.

Jones, D.P.H. (1991) Commentary: Ritualism and child sexual abuse. *Child Abuse and Neglect*, **15**, 163–70.

Jones, D.P.H. (1992) *Interviewing the Sexually Abused Child* (4th edn.). London: Gaskell.

Jones, D.P.H. (in press) Child sexual abuse and satanism. *Newsletter of the Association of Child Psychology and Psychiatry*.

Jones, D.P.H. and Krugman, R.D. (1986) Can a three-year-old child bear witness to her sexual assault and attempted murder? *Child Abuse and Neglect*, **10**, 253-8.

Jones, D.P.H. and McGraw, J.M. (1987) Reliable and fictitious accounts of sexual abuse to children. *Journal of Inter-personal Violence*, **2**, 27-45.

Jones, D.P.H. and Seig, A. (1988) Child sexual abuse allegations in custody or visitation disputes: a report of 20 cases. In E. Nicholson and J. Bulkely (eds.) *Sexual Abuse Allegations in Custody and Visitation Cases*. Washington DC: American Bar Association.

Jones, D.P.H. and Thompson, P.J. (1991) Children's sexual experience—normal and abnormal. In J. Eyre and R. Boyd (eds.) *Paediatric Speciality Practice 1991*. London: Royal College of Physicians.

Kail, R., and Wicks Nelson, R. (1993) *Developmental Psychology* (5 edn). New York: Prentice Hall.

Kearney, B. (1987) *Children's Hearings and the Sheriff Court*. London and Edinburgh: Butterworths.

Kearney, B. (1990) The evidence of children—the Scottish dimension. In J. Spencer, G. Nicholson, R.H. Flin and R. Bull (eds.) *Children's Evidence in Legal Proceedings: an International Perspective*. Cambridge: Cambridge Law Faculty.

Kelly, L. (1992) The connections between disability and child abuse: a review of the research evidence. *Child Abuse Review*, 1, 157–167.

Kempe, H. et al. (1962) The battered child syndrome. *Journal of the American Medical Association*, 181, 1:17-22.

Kendall-Tackett, K. (1992) Beyond anatomical dolls: Professionals' use of other playtherapy techniques. *Child Abuse and Neglect*, 16, 139–42.

Kendall-Tackett, K. and Watson, M. (1992) Use of anatomical dolls by Boston professionals. *Child Abuse and Neglect*, 16, 423–28.

Kilbrandon Report: see Scottish Home and Health Department and Scottish Education Department (1964).

Kilkerr, A (1989) The police response. In C. Wattam, J. Hughes and H. Blagg (eds.) *Child Sexual Abuse. Listening, Hearing and Validating the Experiences of Children*. London: NSPCC/Longman.

King, M.A. and Yuille, J.C. (1986) An investigation of the eyewitness abilities of children. Unpublished manuscript.

King, M.A. and Yuille, J.C. (1987) Suggestibility and the child witness. In S.J. Ceci, M.P. Toglia and D.F. Ross (eds.) *Children's Eyewitness Memory*. New York: Springer.

Kingham, J. and Latham, C.T. (1992) Child Cases—confidential information. [1992] 1 *Family Court Reporter*, 221–22.

Kinsey, R. and Loader, I. (1990) Myth of the mindless hooligan. *Scotland on Sunday*, 14 January.

Kintz, B. (1977) College students' attitudes about telling lies. *Bulletin of the Psychonomic Society*, 10, 490–92.

Köhnken, G. (1989) Behavioural correlates of statement credibility: themes, paradigms and results. In H. Wegener, F. Losel and J. Haisch (eds.) *Criminal Behaviour and the Justice System: Psychological Perspectives*. New York: Springer.

Köhnken, G. (1990) The evaluation of statement credibility: social judgment and expert diagnostic approaches. In J. Spencer, G. Nicholson, R. Flin and R. Bull (eds.) *Children's Evidence in Legal Proceedings: an International Perspective*. Cambridge: Cambridge Law Faculty.

Köhnken, G. and Steller, M. (1988) The evaluation of the credibility of child witness statements in the German procedural system. In G. Davies and J. Drinkwater (eds.) *The Child Witness: Do the Courts Abuse Children?* Leicester: British Psychological Society.

Kolvin I. et al. (1988) Child sexual abuse: principles of good practice. *British Journal of Hospital Medicine*, **39**, 54-62.

Krout, M. (1931) The psychology of children's lies. *Journal of Abnormal and Social Psychology*, **26**, 1-27.

La Fontaine, J. (1990) *Child Sexual Abuse*. Cambridge: Polity Press.

La Fontaine, J. (1993) Concepts of evil, witchcraft and the sexual abuse of children in modern England. ETNOFOOR, **2**, 6-20.

Langbein, J.H. (1978) The criminal trial before the lawyers. *University of Chicago Law Review*, **45**, 263-316.

Langbein, J.H. (1983) Shaping the eighteenth-century criminal trial: a view from the Ryder sources. *University of Chicago Law Review*, **50**, 1-136.

Lanning, K.V. (1991) Commentary: Ritual abuse: A law enforcement view or perspective, *Child Abuse and Neglect*, **15**, 171-73.

Larner, C. (1981) *Enemies of God: the Witch-hunt in Scotland*. London: Chatto & Windus.

Latham, C. (1989) *Care Proceedings—An Outline of the Law and Practice*. Chichester: Barry Rose.

Latham, C.T. (1991) Local authorities acting fairly towards suspected child abusers. A review of recent decisions. [1991] *Family Court Reporter*, 677-84.

Latham, M. (1987) *Evidentiary and Procedural Trends in Child Sexual Assault Litigation in USA*. Report to the New South Wales Law Foundation.

Law Commission (1988) *Family Law. Review of Child Law. Guardianship and Custody* (Law Com. No. 172). London: HMSO.

Law Commission (1991) Criminal law—corroboration of evidence in criminal trials; Law Com, No. 202, Cm 1620. London: HMSO.

Law Reform Advisory Committee for Northern Ireland (1990). *Hearsay Evidence in Civil Proceedings* (Discussion Paper No. 1).

Law Reform Commission of Australia (1987), *Evidence* Report No. 38.

Law Reform Commission of Australia (1989) *Children's Evidence by Video Link* (Discussion Paper No. 40).

Law Reform Commission of Australia (1992) *The use of closed-circuit television for child witnesses in the ACT*. Children's evidence Research Paper 1 by Cashmore and De Haas, Sydney, Australian Law Reform Commission.

Law Reform Commission of Western Australia (1991) *Report on Evidence of Children and Other Vulnerable Witnesses* (Project No. 87); Perth: Law Reform Commission of Western Australia.

Law Commissioner of Tasmania (1989) *Draft Report on Child Witnesses*.

Lawrence, K. (1988) Let the child be heard. *Police Review*, 20 May, 1074-5.

Lazoritz, S. (1990) 'Whatever happened to Mary Ellen?'. *Child Abuse and Neglect*, **14**, 143-49.

Leach, T. (1815) *Cases in Crown Law* (4th edn). London: Butterworths.

Leekam, S. (1991) Jokes and lies. Children's understanding of intentional falsehood. In A. Whiten (ed.) *Natural Theories of Mind. The Evolution Development and Simulation of Everyday Mindreading.* Oxford: Blackwell.

Leekam, S. (1992) Believing and deceiving: Steps to becoming a good liar. In S. Ceci, M. Leichtman and M. Putnick (eds.) *Cognitive and Social Factors in Early Deception.* New Jersey: Lawrence Erlbaum Assoc.

Lees-Haley, P. (1988) Innocent lies, tragic consequences. *Trial*, April, 37–41.

Lehrman (1988) The psychoanalytic legacy: from whence we came. In L. Walker (ed.) *Handbook on Sexual Abuse of Children.* New York: Springer.

Leippe, M., Brigham, J., Cousins, C. and Romanczyk, A. (1989) The opinions and practices of criminal attorneys regarding child eyewitnesses. A survey. In S. Ceci, D. Ross and M. Toglia (eds.) *Perspectives on Children's Testimony.* New York: Springer.

Leippe, M., Romanczyk, A. and Manion, A. (1991) Eyewitness memory for a touching experience: Accuracy differences between child and adult witnesses. *Journal of Applied Psychology*, 76, 367–97.

Levy, R.J. (1989) Using 'scientific' testimony to prove child sexual abuse. *Family Law Quarterly*, 13, 383–409.

Lewis, M. and Saarni, C. (1993) *Lying and Deception in Everyday Life.* New York: Guildford.

Libai, D. (1969) The protection of the child victim of a sexual offence in the criminal justice system, *Wayne Law Review*, 15, 977–1032.

Lickona, T. (ed.) (1976) *Moral Development and Behaviour.* New York: Holt, Rinehart and Winston.

Lindsay, D.S. and Johnson, M.K. (1987) Reality monitoring and suggestibility: children's ability to discriminate among memories from different sources. In S.J. Ceci, M.P. Toglia and D.F. Ross (eds.) *Children's Eyewitness Memory.* New York: Springer.

Livesey, B. (1988) *Giving Evidence in Court.* London: British Association for the Study and Prevention of Child Abuse and Neglect.

Loftus, E.F. (1979) *Eyewitness Testimony.* Cambridge, Mass: Harvard University Press.

Loftus, E.F. (1993) The reality of repressed memories. *American Psychologist*, 48, 518–537.

Loftus, E.F. and Goodman, J. (1985) Questioning witnesses. In S. Kassin and L. Wrightsman (eds.) *The Psychology of Evidence and Trial Procedure.* San Mateo, Calif: Sage.

Loftus, E.F., Korf, N. and Schooler, J. (1989) Misguided memories: sincere distortions of reality. In J. Yuille (ed.) *Credibility Assessment.* Dordrecht: Kluwer.

Loftus, E.F., Weingardt, K. and Hoffman, H. (in press) Sleeping memories on trial: Reactions to memories that were previously repressed. *Expert Evidence.*

Lord Chancellor's Department (1988) *Improvements in the Arrangements for Care Proceedings.*

Lord Chancellor's Department (1992) *The Courts Charter.* London: HMSO.

L.S.E. Jury Project (1973): see Sealy.

Luft, J. (1984) *An Introduction to Group Dynamics*. Palo Alto: Mayfield.

Luus, E. and Wells, G. (1992) The perceived credibility of child eyewitnesses. In H. Dent and R. Flin (eds.) *Children as Eyewitnesses*. Chichester: Wiley.

McCord, D. (1986) Expert testimony about child complaints in sexual abuse prosecutions: a foray into the admissibility of novel psychological evidence. *Journal of Criminal Law and Criminology*, 77, 1-68.

McCormack, G. (1985) The admissibility of tracker dog evidence. [1985] *Criminal Law Review*, 202.

McCrystal, J.L. (1977) The promise of prerecorded videotape trials. *American Bar Association Journal*, 63.

MacDouall (1751-3): see Bankton.

McEwan, J. (1988) Child evidence: more proposals for reform. [1988] *Criminal Law Review*, 813-22.

McEwan, J. (1989) Documentary hearsay evidence—refuge for the vulnerable witness? [1989] *Criminal Law Review*, 629-42.

McEwan, J. (1992) *Evidence and the Adversarial Process*, Oxford: Blackwell.

McEwan, J. (1993) Where the prosecution witness is a child: The Memorandum of Good Practice, *Tolley's Journal of Child Law*, 5, 16–20.

Macfarlane, A. (1970) *Witchcraft in Tudor and Stuart England, A Regional and Comparitive Study*. London: Routledge & Kegan Paul.

McFarlane, K. (1985) Diagnostic evaluations and the use of videotapes in child sexual abuse cases. *University of Miami Law Review*, 40, 135-65.

MacFarlane, K. and Elias, H. (1990) Legal and clinical issues in videotaping. In K. Murry and D. Gough (eds.) *Intervening in Child Sexual Abuse*. Edinburgh: Scottish Academic Press.

MacLean, H. (1993) *Once Upon a Time. A True Story of Memory, Murder and a Trial*. New York: Harper Collins.

Mackay, J. (Lord Mackay of Clashfern) (1988) *The Child: A View across the Tweed*. The Child & Co. Lecture 1988. Inns of Court School of Law, London.

Mackay, J. (Lord Mackay of Clashfern) (1990) Opening address to the International Conference on Children's Evidence. In J. Spencer, G. Nicholson, R. Flin and R. Bull (eds.) *Children's Evidence in Legal Proceedings*. Cambridge: Cambridge Law Faculty.

MacKenna, Sir Brian (1974) Discretion. *Irish Jurist*, 9, 1.

McMurray, B. (1987) Criminal decision making for child sexual abuse: important factors in initial screening judgements by prosecutors. Paper presented at the American Society of Criminology, Montreal, November.

Macphail, I.D. (1987) *Evidence*. Edinburgh: Law Society of Scotland.

Macphail, I.D. (1988) *Sheriff Court Practice*. London: Sweet & Maxwell.

Macphail, I.D. (1991) *Evidence, Stair Memorial Encyclopaedia*, vol. 10. Edinburgh: Law Society of Scotland, and Butterworths.

Maan, C. (1991) Assessment of sexually abused children with anatomically detailed dolls: A critical review. *Behavioral Sciences and the Law*, 9, 43–51.

Magistrates' Association (1962) *Memorandum on Criminal Procedure and Child Victims of Sexual Offences*.

Maher, G. (1983) Jury trials and the presumption of innocence. *Legal Studies*, 3, 146-58.

Mann, E. (1985) The assessment of credibility of sexually abused children in criminal court cases. *American Journal of Forensic Psychiatry*, 15, 9-15.

Marin, B., Holmes, D., Guth, M. and Kovac, P. (1979) The potential of children as eyewitnesses. *Law and Human Behaviour*, 3, 295-306.

Martin, F.M., Fox, S.J. and Murray, K. (1981) *Children Out of Court*. Edinburgh: Scottish Academic Press.

Martin, F.M. and Murray, K. (eds.) (1982) *The Scottish Juvenile Justice System*. Edinburgh: Scottish Academic Press.

Mason, J.M. (1992) The official solicitor as the Child's Guardian *ad litem* under the Children Act 1989. *Tolley's Journal of Child Law* 1992, 4, 58-62.

Masson, J. (1988) The role of the judge in children's cases. *Civil Justice Quarterly*, 7, 141-55.

Masson, J.M. (1984) *The Assault on Truth: Freud's Suppression of the Seduction Theory*. Harmondsworth: Penguin.

Masson, J.M. (1985) (ed. and transl.) *The Complete Letters of Sigmund Freud to Wilheim Fliess 1887-1904*. Cambridge, Mass: Harvard University Press.

Matthews, E. and Saywitz, K. (1992) *Child Victim Witness Manual*. California Center for Judicial Education and Research Journal, 12, 5-81.

Mayes, G.M., Currie, E.F., Macleod, L., Gilles, J.B. and Warden, D.A. (1992) *Child sexual abuse—a review of literature and educational materials*. Edinburgh: Scottish Academic Press.

Melton, G.B. (1987) Children's testimony in cases of alleged sexual abuse. In M. Wolraich and D. Routh (eds.) *Advances in Developmental and Behavioural Pediatrics* vol. 8, 179-203. California: Jai Press.

Melton, G.B., Petrilia, J., Poythress, N. and Slobogin, C. (1987) *Psychological Evaluations for the Courts*. New York: Guilford Press.

Memon, A., Cronin, O., Eaves, R. and Bull, R. (1993) The cognitive interview and child witnesses. In *Children, Evidence and Procedure*. Leicester: British Psychological Society, Division of Criminological and Legal Psychology.

Memon, A., and Bull, R. (1991) The cognitive interview: Its origin, empirical support, evaluation and practical implications. *Journal of Community and Applied Social Psychology*, 1, 291-307.

Memorandum of Good Practice. See Home Office 1992.

Merle, R. and Vitu, A. (1989) *Traité de droit criminel—Procédure pénale*, 4th edn. Paris: Cujas.

Mertin, P. (1989) The memory of young children for eyewitness events. *Australian Journal of Social Issues*, 24, 23-32.

Metropolitan Police and Bexley London Borough (1987) *Child Sexual Abuse. Joint Investigative Programme. Bexley Experiment. Final Report*. London: HMSO.

Miller, G.R. and Fontes, N.E. (1979) *Videotape on Trial*. Beverly Hills, California: Sage.

Misener, M. (1991) Children's hearsay evidence in child sexual abuse prosecutions: a proposal for reform. *Criminal Law Quarterly*, 33, 364-84.

Mitchels, B. and Meadow, R. (1989) ABC of child abuse—about courts. *British Medical Journal*, 299, 9 September.

Moran, J., Conroy, S., Fielding, N. and Tunstall, J. (1991) *Investigation of Child Sexual Abuse*. ESRC Grant Report (No. R00231467).

Morey, R. (1985) The competency requirement for the child victim of sexual abuse: must we abandon it? *University of Miami Law Review*, 40, 245.

Morgan, J. and Plotnikoff, J. (1990) Children as victims of crime: procedure at court. In J. Spencer, G. Nicholson, R. Flin and R. Bull (eds.). *Children's Evidence in Legal Proceedings: an International Perspective*. Cambridge: Cambridge Law Faculty.

Morgan, J. and Zedner, L. (1992) *Child Victims*. Oxford: Clarendon Press.

Morris, A. and Giller, H. (1987) *Understanding Juvenile Justice*. London: Croom Helm.

Morton, J. (1988) When can lying start? In G. Davies and J. Drinkwater (eds.) *The Child Witness—Do the Courts Abuse Children?* Leicester: British Psychological Society.

Moston, S. (1987) The suggestibility of children in interview studies. *First Language*, 7, 67-78.

Moston, S. (1992) Social support and the quality of children's eyewitness testimony. In H. Dent and R. Flin (eds.) *Children as Witnesses*. Chichester: Wiley.

Moston, S. and Engelberg, E. (1990) The effects of social support on children's eyewitness testimony. *Applied Cognitive Psychology*, 6, 61–72.

Mrazek, D. and Mrazek P. (1985) Child maltreatment. In M. Rutter and L. Hersov (eds.) *Child and Adolescent Psychiatry*, 2nd ed. Oxford: Basil Blackwell.

Mulhern, S. (1991) Satanism and psychotherapy: A rumor in search of an inquisition. In D.G. Bromley, J. Best, and J.T. Richardson (eds.) *The Satanism Scare*. New York: Aldine de Gruyter.

Mullins, C. (1943) *Crime and Psychology*. London: Methuen.

Munday, R. (1991) Hostile witnesses and the admission of witness statements under section 23 of the Criminal Justice Act 1988 [1991] *Criminal Law Review* 349–60.

Muram, D. (1989) Child sexual abuse: relationship between sexual acts and genital findings. *Child Abuse and Neglect*, 13, 211-16.

Murch, M., Borkowski, M., Copner, R. and Griew, K. (1987) *The Overlapping Family Jurisdictions of Magistrates' Courts and County Courts*, vols 1 and 2. Bristol: Socio-Legal Centre for Family Studies, University of Bristol.

Murphy, P. (1992) *A Practical Approach to Evidence* (4th edn). London: Blackstone Press.

Murray, K. (1992) Children's evidence and the use of live television links in Scotland. Paper presented at the Children's Evidence and Technology Conference, University of Glasgow, 25 September.

Murray, K. (1993) *Interviews with Child Witnesses for Criminal Proceedings. Video Recordings—the Findings of a Colloquium on Ethical Issues*. Pamphlet published by the Local Government Management Board, Luton LU1 2TS.

Murray, K. (1988) *Research Paper on Evidence from Children: Alternatives to In-Court Testimony in Criminal Proceedings in the United States of America*. Edinburgh: Scottish Law Commission.

Murray, K. and Gough, D. (1990) *Intervening in Child Sexual Abuse*. Edinburgh: Scottish Academic Press.

Myers, J.E.B (1987a) *Child Witness Law and Practice*. New York: Wiley.

Myers, J.E.B. (1987b) The child witness: techniques for direct examination, cross-examination and impeachment. *Pacific Law Journal*, 18, 801-942.

Myers, J.E.B. (1990) Expert testimony in child sexual abuse litigation—the American experience. In K. Murray and D. Gough (eds.) *Intervening in Child Sexual Abuse*. Edinburgh: Scottish Academic Press.

Myers, J.E.B. (1992) *Legal Issues in Child Abuse and Neglect*. London: Sage.

Myers, J.E.B., Bays, J, Becker, J., Berliner, L., Corwin, D.L. and Saywitz, K.J. (1989) Expert testimony in child sexual abuse litigation. *Nebraska Law Review*, 68, 1-145.

National Foster Care Association (1988) *Child Abuse: Accusations Against Foster Parents Report*, January. London: NCFA.

National Society for the Prevention of Cruelty to Children (1989). Child Abuse Trends in England and Wales 1983-87. London: NSPCC.

Nicholson, G., and Murray, K. (1992) The child witness in Scotland, in H. Dent, and R. Flin (eds.) *Children as Witnesses*. Chichester: Wiley.

Nurcombe, B. (1986) The child as witness: competence and credibility. *Journal of the American Academy of Child Psychiatry*, 25, 473-80.

Oates, R.K. (1992) The effects of child sexual abuse. *Australian Law Journal*, 66, 186-93.

Oates, R. and Shrimpton, S. (1991) Children's memories for stressful and non-stressful events. *Medicine, Science and the Law*, 31, 4-10.

Oates, R. and Tong, L. (1987) Sexual abuse of children: an area with room for professional reforms. *Medical Journal of Australia*, 147, 544-48.

Ochsner, J.E. and Zaragoza, M.S. (1988) The accuracy and suggestibility of children's memory for neutral and criminal eyewitness events. Paper presented at the American Psychology and Law Association Meeting, Miami.

Ockleton, M. (1992) Documentary hearsay in criminal cases. [1992] *Criminal Law Review* 15-21.

Open University (1993) *Investigative Interviewing with Children*. K501. Milton Keynes: Open University.

Ornstein, P., Gordon, B. and Larus, D. (1992) Children's memory for a personally experienced event: Implications for testimony. *Applied Cognitive Psychology*, 6, 49-60

Paisnel, J. (1972) *The Beast of Jersey, by his Wife*. London: Robert Hale.

Pattenden, R. (1991) Should confessions be corroborated? *Law Quarterly Review*, 107, 317-39.

Parry, E.A. (1922) *What the Judge Thought*. London: T. Fisher Unwin.

Perry, N. (1987) Child and adolescent development: a psycholegal perspective. In J. Myers. *Child Witness Law and Practice*. New York: Wiley.

Peters, D. (1987) The impact of naturally occurring stress on children's memory. In S.J. Ceci, M.P. Toglia and D.F. Ross (eds.) *Children's Eyewitness Memory*. New York: Springer.

Peters, D. (1991) The influence of stress and arousal on the child witness. In J. Doris (ed.) *The Suggestibility of Children's Recollections*. Washington: American Psychological Association.

Peters, D. (ed.) (in press) *The Child Witness in Context: Social and Legal Perspectives*. Dordrecht: Kluwer.

Peters, J. (1976) Children who are victims of sexual assault and the psychology of offenders. *American Journal of Psychotherapy*, 30, 398-421.

Piaget, J. (1965) *Insights and Illusions of Philosophy* (translated from French by Wolfe Mays (1972)). London: Routledge and Kegan Paul.

Pigot, Judge T., QC. (1990) Women and children first. In J. Spencer, G. Nicholson, R. Flin and R. Bull (eds.) *Children's Evidence in Legal Proceedings: an International Perspective*. Cambridge: Cambridge Law Faculty.

Pigot Committee: See Home Office 1989.

Pipe, M., Gee, S. and Wilson, C. (1993) Cues, props and context: Do they facilitate children's event reports? In G. Goodman and B. Bottoms (eds.) *Child Victims, Child Witnesses*. New York: Guilford.

Pipe, M. and Goodman, G. (1991) Elements of secrecy: implications for children's testimony. *Behavioral Sciences and the Law*, 9, 33–41.

Pitcairn, R. (1833) *Criminal Trials in Scotland 1488–1624*. Edinburgh: William Tait.

Plotnikoff, J. (1990a) Support and preparation of the child witness: Whose responsibility? *Journal of Law and Practice*, 1, 21–31.

Plotnikoff, J. (1990b) Delay in child abuse prosecutions. *Criminal Law Review*, 645–47.

Plotnikoff, J. (1993) Delay in child abuse prosecutions (1991–1993). Paper presented at the Michael Sleff Foundation Conference, September.

Poole, D. (1992) The impact of a long delay on the eyewitness testimony of children and adults. Paper presented at the NATO Advanced Studies Institute: The Child Witness in Context. Italy, May.

Poole, D. and White, L. (1991) Effects of question repetition on the eyewitness testimony of children and adults. *Developmental Psychology*, 27, 975–86.

Pradel, J. (1993) Observations brères sur une loi à refaire. *Recueil Dalloz Sirey*, 1993, chronique, 39–40.

Price, D. and Goodman, G. (1990) Visiting the wizard. Children's memory for a recurring event. *Child Development*, 61, 664–80.

Pynoos, R. et al. (1987) Life threat and post-traumatic stress in school-age children. *Archives of General Psychiatry*, 44, 1057-63.

Pynoos, R.S. and Eth, S. (1984) The child as witness to homicide. *Journal of Social Issues*, 40, 87-108.

Pynoos, R.S. and Nader, K. (1988) Children who witness the sexual assaults of their mothers. *Journal of the American Academy of Child and Adolescent Psychiatry*, 27, 567-72.

Pynoos, R.S. and Nader, K. (1988) Children's memory and proximity to violence. *Journal of the American Academy of Child and Adolescent Psychiatry*, 28, 236-41.

Raine, J. and Smith, R. (1991) *The Victim in Court*. Report available from Victim Support, 39 Brixton Road, London SW9 6D7.

Regehr, C. (1990) Parental responses to extra familial child sexual assault. *Child Abuse and Neglect*, **14**, 113–120.

Remy, N., *Demonolatry* (translated by E.A. Ashwin, 1595, ed. M. Summers 1929).

Renton, R.W. and Brown H.H. (1984) *Criminal Procedure According to the Law of Scotland*, 5th ed. Edinburgh: Green & Son.

Ridgeway, V. and Matthews, A. (1982) Psychological preparation for surgery: A comparison of methods. *British Journal of Clinical Psychology*, **21**, 271–280.

Roberts, M. and Glasgow, D. (in press) Gathering evidence from children: A systematic approach. *Issues in Criminological and Legal Psychology*, **20**.

Roe, R.J. (1985) Expert testimony in child sexual abuse cases. *University of Miami Law Review*, **40**, 97–113.

Rogers, C.M. (1982) Child sexual abuse and the courts: preliminary findings. *Journal of Social Work and Human Sexuality*, **1**, 145–53.

Rosenberg, L.A. Interviewing children: Psychological considerations, In Wissow, L.S. (ed.) *Child Advocacy for the Clinician; An Approach to Child Abuse and Neglect*. London: Williams & Wilkins.

Rosenfield, A., Nadelson, C. and Krieger, M. (1979) Fantasy and reality in patients' reports of incest. *Journal of Clinical Psychiatry*, **40**, 159–64.

Ross, Lord Justice-Clerk (1991) Family conciliation—The child's view and confidentiality [1991] *Journal of the Law Society of Scotland*, 20–22.

Rossman, B. (1992) School age children's perceptions of coping with distress. *Journal of Child Psychology and Psychiatry*, **33**, 1373–1397.

Royal College of Physicians (1991) Physical signs of sexual abuse in children. London: Royal College of Surgeons.

Royal Commission on Criminal Justice (1993) *Report* (Cm 2263).

Royal Commission on Criminal Procedure (1981) *Report* (Cmnd 8092). London: HMSO.

RSPCC (1988) *Children as Witnesses. Discussion Paper*. Edinburgh.

Rudy, L. and Goodman, G. (1991) Effects of participation on children's reports. *Developmental Psychology*, **27**, 527–38.

Runyan, D. (1993) The emotional impact of societal intervention into child abuse. In G. Goodman and B. Bottoms (eds.) *Child Victims, Child Witnesses*. New York: Guilford.

Runyan, D., Everson, M., Edelsohn, G., Hunter, W. and Coulter, M. (1988) Impact of legal intervention on sexually abused children. *Journal of Pediatrics*, **113**, 647–53.

Rush, F. (1980). *The Best Kept Secret: Sexual Abuse of Children*. Englewood Cliffs NJ: Prentice-Hall.

Russell, D. (1983) The incidence and prevalence of intrafamilial sexual abuse of female children. *Child Abuse and Neglect*, **7**, 133–46.

Russell, D. (1986) *The Secret Trauma: Incest in the Lives of Girls and Women*. New York: Basic Books.

Sargant, T. and Hill, P. (1986) *Criminal Trials: The Search for Truth* (Fabian Research Series No. 348). London: Fabian Society.

Sas, L., Hurley, P., Austin, G. and Wolfe, D. (1991) *Reducing the System-Induced Trauma for Child Sexual Abuse Victims through Court Preparation, Assessment and Follow-up*. Ontario: London Family Court Clinic.

Saunders, E. (1987) Police officers' attitudes toward child sexual abuse: an exploratory study. *Journal of Police Science and Administration*, **15**, 186-91.

Saywitz, K. (1989) Children's conceptions of the legal system: 'Court is a place to play basketball'. In S. Ceci, D. Ross and M. Toglia (eds.) *Perspectives on Children's Testimony*. New York: Springer.

Saywitz, K., Geiselman, R. and Bornstein, G. (1992) Effects of cognitive interviewing and practice on children's recall performance. *Journal of Applied Psychology*, **77**, 744–56.

Saywitz, K., Goodman, G., Nicholas, E. and Moan S. (1991) Children's memories of a physical examination involving genital touch: Implications for reports of child sexual abuse. *Journal of Consulting and Clinical Psychology*, **59**, 682–691.

Saywitz, K., Jaenicke, C. and Camparo, L. (1990) Children's knowledge of legal terminology. *Law and Human Behaviour*, **14**, 523–35.

Saywitz, K. and Nathanson, R. (in press) The effects of environment on children's testimony and perceived stress. *International Journal of Child Abuse and Neglect*.

Saywitz, K. and Synder, L. (1993) Improving children's testimony with preparation. In G. Goodman and B. Bottoms (eds.) *Child Victims, Child Witnesses*. New York: Guilford.

Scheer, H.P. (1993) Publicity and the presumption of innocence. [1993] *Cambridge Law Journal*, **37**, 39.

Schneikert, Hans (1904) Die Zeugenvernehmung im Lichte der Strafprozeßreform. *Beiträge zur Psychologie der Aussage*, **4**, 1.

Schuman, D. (1986) False accusations of physical and sexual abuse. *Bull. AM. Acad. Psychiatry Law*, **14**, 5–21.

Schutz, B., Dixon, E., Lindenberger, J. and Ruther, N. (1989) *Solomon's Sword. A Practical Guide to Conducting Child Custody Evaluations*. San Francisco: Jossey Bass.

Scott, M. and Stradling, S. (1992) *Counselling for Post-Traumatic Stress Disorder*. London: Sage.

Scottish Home and Health Department (1985) *The Tape Recording of Police Interviews with Suspected Persons in Scotland*. Edinburgh: Scottish Home and Health Department.

Scottish Home and Health Department and Crown Office (1975) *Criminal Procedure in Scotland (Second Report)* (Thomson Committee) (Cmnd 6218). Edinburgh: HMSO.

Scottish Home and Health Department and Scottish Education Department (1964) *Children and Young Persons, Scotland* (Cmnd 2306). Edinburgh. HMSO.

Scottish Law Commission (1986) *Evidence, Report on Corroboration, Hearsay and Related Matters* (SLC No. 100).

Scottish Law Commission (1988a) *The Evidence of Children and Other Potentially Vulnerable Witnesses* (Discussion Paper No. 75).

Scottish Law Commission (1988b) *Criminal Evidence—Affidavit Evidence, Hearsay and Related Matters in Criminal Proceedings* (Discussion Paper No. 77).

Scottish Law Commission (1990) *Report on the Evidence of Children and Other Potentially Vulnerable Witnesses* (SLC No. 125).

Scottish Law Commission (1990) Dicussion Paper No. 88 *Parental Responsibilities and Rights, Guardianship and the Administration of Children's Property,* October 1990.

Scottish Law Commission (1992). Evidence: *Report on Documentary Evidence and Proof of Undisputed Facts in Criminal Proceedings.* SLC No. 137, Edinburgh: HMSO.

Scottish Office (1990) *Review of Child Care Law in Scotland.* Edinburgh: HMSO.

Scottish Office (1992) *The Report of the Inquiry into the Removal of Children from Orkney in February 1991.* Edinburgh: HMSO. (Clyde Report.)

Seale, S.M.G. (1984) *Children in Divorce. A Study of Information Available to the Scottish Courts on Children Involved in Divorce Actions.* Central Research Unit, Scottish Office.

Sealy, A.P. and Cornish W.R. (1973) Juries and the rules of evidence. [1973] *Criminal Law Review,* 208, 220.

Seth, D. (1969) *Children Against Witches.* New York: Taplinger.

Shapland, J., Willmore, J. and Duff, P. (1985) *Victims in the Criminal Justice System.* Aldershot: Gower.

Sharp, F. (1989) Live TV-links in child abuse trials. *Brief* (Anglia Higher Education College School of Law), 98.

Sheehan, A.V. (1975) *Criminal Procedure in Scotland and France.* Edinburgh: HMSO.

Sheehan, A.V. (1990) *Criminal Procedure.* Edinburgh: Butterworths.

Shepherd, J. (1983) Identification after long delays. In S. Lloyd-Bostock and B. Clifford (eds.) *Evaluating Witness Evidence.* Chichester: Wiley.

Shutkin, J.A. (1973) Videotape trials: legal and practical implications. *Columbia Journal of Law and Social Problems,* 9, 363.

Sidun, N. and Rosenthal, R. (1987) Graphic indicators of sexual abuse in draw-a-person tests of psychiatrically hospitalised adolescents. *The Arts in Psychotherapy,* 14, 25-33.

Simpson, K. and Knight, B. (1985) *Forensic Medicine,* 9th ed. London: Edward Arnold.

Sisterman-Keeney, K., Amachev, E. and Kastankis, J. (1992) The court prep group: A vital part of the court process. In H. Dent and R. Flin (eds.) *Children as Witnesses.* Chichester: Wiley.

Skolnick, A. (1975) The limits of childhood: conceptions of child development and social context. *Law and Contemporary Problems,* 39, 38-77.

Smith, P. and Cowie H. (1991) *Understanding Child Development* (2nd edn) Oxford: Blackwell.

Social Trends 16 (1986). Central Statistical office. London: HMSO.

Sodian, B., Taylor, C., Harris, P. and Perner, J. (1991) Early deception and the child's theory of mind: False trails and genuine markers. *Child Development*, **62**, 468–83.

Soppe, H. (1986) Children's recognition of unfamiliar faces: Developments and determinants. *International Journal of Behavioural Development*, **9**, 219-33.

Southall, D.P., Stebbens, V.A., Rees, S.V., Lang, M.H., Warner, J.O. and Shinebourne, E.A. (1987) Apnoeic episodes induced by smothering: two cases identified by covert video surveillance. *British Medical Journal*, **294**, 1637-41.

Spencer, J.R. (1982) Lies, damned lies, and corroboration. *Cambridge Law Journal*, **41**, 27.

Spencer, J.R. (1987a) Child witnesses, video technology and the law of evidence. [1987] *Criminal Law Review*, 76.

Spencer, J.R. (1987b) Child witnesses and the Criminal Justice Bill. *New Law Journal*, **137**, 1031.

Spencer, J.R. (1987c) Child witnesses—a further skirmish. *New Law Journal*, **137**, 1127.

Spencer, J.R (1987d) Child witnesses and video technology: thoughts for the Home Office. *Journal of Criminal Law*, **51**, 444.

Spencer, J.R. (1988) How not to reform the law. *New Law Journal*, **138**, 497.

Spencer, J.R. (1990) Children's evidence and the Criminal Justice Bill. *New Law Journal*, **140**, 1750–51.

Spencer, J.R. (1991) Reformers despair. *New Law Journal*, **141**, 787.

Spencer, J.R. (1992) Court experts and expert witnesses. Have we a lesson to learn from the French? *Current Legal Problems*, **45**, 213–236.

Spencer, J.R. (1993a) Hearsay, relevance and implied assertions. [1993] *Cambridge Law Journal*, 40–42.

Spencer, J.R. (1993b) The law on children's evidence: an international overview. In D. Peters (ed.) *The Child Witness in Context*.

Spencer, J.R. (1993c), French and English criminal procedure—a brief comparison. In B.S. Markesinis, (ed.) *The Gradual Convergence—Foreign Ideas, Foreign Influences and English Law on the Eve of the 21st Century.* Oxford: Oxford University Press.

Spencer, J.R., Nicholson, G., Flin, R.H. and Bull, R. (1990) *Children's Evidence in Legal Proceedings: an International Perspective.* Cambridge University Law Faculty.

Spencer, J.R. and Tucker, P. (1987) The evidence of absent children. *New Law Journal*, **137**, 816-17.

Sprack, J. (1992) *Emmins on Criminal Procedure* (5th edn). London: Blackstone Press.

Stafford, A. and Asquith, S. (1991) The Witness in the Scottish Criminal Justice System. Edinburgh: Scottish Office, Central Research Unit Papers.

Stainton Rogers, R. and W. (1992) *Stories of Childhood.* London: Harvester Wheatsheaf.

Stair, J. (1693) *Institutions of the Law of Scotland.* D.M. Walker (ed.). Edinburgh and Glasgow: University Presses of Edinburgh and Glasgow, 1981.

Steller, M. (1989) Recent developments in statement analysis. In J.C. Yuille (ed.) *Credibility Assessment*. Dordrecht: Kluwer.

Steller, M. and Boychuck, T. (1992) Children as witnesses in sexual abuse cases: Investigative interviews and assessment techniques. In H. Dent and R. Flin (eds.) *Children as Witnesses*. Chichester: Wiley.

Steller, M. and Köhnken, G. (1989) Criteria-based statement analysis. Credibility assessment of children's testimonies in sexual abuse cases. In D. Raskin (ed.) *Psychological Techniques in Law Enforcement*. New York: Springer.

Steller, M., Raskin, D. and Yuille, J. (1990) *Sexually Abused Children: Interview and Assessment Techniques*. New York: Springer.

Stephen, J.F. (1876) *Digest of the Law of Evidence*. London: Macmillan.

Stephen, J.F. (1883) *A History of the Criminal Law of England*. London: Macmillan.

Steward, M. (1989) The development of a model interview for young child victims of sexual abuse: Comparing the effectiveness of anatomical dolls, drawings and videographics. Grant Report 90CA1332. Washington DC: National Center on Child Abuse and Neglect, USA.

Steward, M., Bussey, K., Goodman, G. and Saywitz, K. (1993) Implications of developmental research for interviewing children. *Child Abuse and Neglect*, 17, 25–37.

Stewart, A.L. (1990) *The Scottish Criminal Courts in Action*. Edinburgh: Butterworths.

Stewart, C. (1981) A retrospective study of alleged sexual assault cases. *Police Surgeon*, November, 28-32.

Stone, M. (1984) *Proof of Fact in Criminal Trials*. Edinburgh: W. Green & Son.

Stone, M. (1988) *Cross-examination in Criminal Trials*. London: Butterworth.

Strachey, J. (ed. and transl.) (1966) *The Standard Edition of the Complete Psychological Works of Sigmund Freud*. London: Hogarth Press.

Strichartz, A. and Burton, R. (1990) Lies and truth: A study of the development of the concept. *Child Development*, 61, 211-20.

Summit, R. (1988) Hidden victims, hidden pain. In G. Wyatt and G. Powell (eds.) *Lasting Effects of Child Sexual Abuse*. San Mateo, California: Sage.

Summit, R.C. (1983) The child abuse accommodation syndrome. *Child Abuse and Neglect*, 7, 177-92.

Tardieu, A (1857) *Étude médico-légale sur les attentats aux moeurs*. Paris: Baillère.

Tardieu, A. (1860) Étude médico-légale sur les sévices et mauvais traitements exercés sur des enfants. *Annales d'hygiène publique et de médicine légale*, 2nd series, 13, 361-98.

Tate, C., Warren, A. and Hess, T. (1992) Adults' liability for children's 'lie-ability': Can adults coach children to lie successfully? In S. Ceci, M. Leichtman and M. Putnick (eds.) *Cognitive and Social Factors in Early Deception*. New Jersey: Lawrence Erlbaum Associates.

Taylor (1849) *Medical Jurisprudence* (3rd edn). London: Churchill.

Taylor, A.S. (1957) *Taylor's Principles and Practice of Medical Jurisprudence*, volume II; (11th edn), by Smith, Sir S., and Simpson, K. London: Churchill.

Tedesco, J. and Schnell, S. (1987) Children's reactions to sex abuse. Investigation and litigation. *Child Abuse and Neglect,* 11, 267-72.

Temkin, J. (1987) *Rape and the Legal Process.* London: Sweet and Maxwell.

Terr, L. (1980) The child as witness. In D. Schetky and E. Benedek (eds.) *Child Psychiatry and the Law.* New York: Bruner/Mazel.

Terr, L. (1986) The child psychiatrist and the child witness: travelling companions by necessity if not by design. *Journal of the American Academy of Child Psychiatry,* 25, 462-72.

Terr, L. (1988) What happens to early memories of trauma? A study of twenty children under age five at the time of the documented traumatic events. *Journal of the American Academy of Child and Adolescent Psychiatry,* 27, 96-104.

Thayer, J.B. (1898) *A Preliminary Treatise on Evidence at the Common Law.* London: Sweet & Maxwell.

Thoennes, N., Pearson, T. and Tadjen, P. (1988) Allegations of sexual abuse in custody and visitation cases: an empirical study of 169 cases from 12 states. Denver: Association of Family and Conciliation Courts.

Thoennes, N. and Tjaden, P. (1990) The extent, nature and validity of sexual abuse allegations in custody visitation disputes. *Child Abuse and Neglect,* 14, 151-63.

Thomas, K. (1971) *Religion and the Decline of Magic.* London: Weidenfeld & Nicholson; Penguin (1991).

Thomson Committee (1975): see Scottish Home and Health Department and Crown Office (1975).

Thomson, J.M. (1987) *Family Law in Scotland.* London: Butterworths.

Thorpe, Mr. Justice (1990) Court intervention in child abuse. Protecting children and protecting families. [1990] *Family Law* 390–93.

Thrupp, J. (1862) *The Anglo-Saxon Home.* London: Longman.

Tobey, A.E., Goodman, G.S., Batterman-Faunce, J.M. and Orcutt, H. (in press) Effects of closed-circuit testimony on children's accuracy and factfinders' perceptions of child witnesses. In Zaragoza, M. (in press) (ed.) *Memory and Testimony in the Child Witness.* California: Sage.

Tobey, A. and Goodman, G. (in press) Children's eyewitness memory: Effects of participation and forensic context. *Child Abuse and Neglect.*

Tobin, K. (1987) The role of wait time in higher level cognitive learning. *Review of Educational Research,* 57, 69–95.

Tong, L. and Oates, R.K. (1990). Long term effects of child sexual abuse. In R.K. Oates (ed.) *Understanding and managing child sexual abuse.* Sydney: W.B. Saunders/Baillière Tindall.

Toth, P. and Whalen, M. (1987) *Investigation and Prosecution of Child Abuse.* Alexandria Va: American Prosecutors Research Institute National Center for the Prosecution of Child Abuse.

Trankell, A. (1958) Was Lars sexually assaulted? A study in the reliability of witnesses and of experts. *Journal of Abnormal and Social Psychology,* 56, 385-95.

Trankell, A. (1972) *Reliability of Evidence.* Stockholm: Beckmans.

Trollope, A. (1858) *The Three Clerks.* London.

Tucker, A., Mertin, P. and Luszcz, M. (1990) The effect of a repeated interview on young children's eyewitness memory. *Aust. and NZ. Journal of Criminology*, **23**, 117–24.

Udwin, O. (1993) Children's reactions to traumatic events. *Journal of Child Psychology and Psychiatry*, **34**, 115–27.

Undeutsch, U. (1982) Statement reality analysis: In A. Trankell (ed.) *Reconstructing the Past*. Deventer: Kluwer.

Undeutsch, U. (1984) Courtroom evaluation of eyewitness testimony. *International Review of Applied Psychology*, **33**, 51-67.

Undeutsch, U. (1989) The development of statement reality analysis. In J.C. Yuille (ed.) *Credibility Assessment*. Dordrecht: Kluwer.

Vaillancourt, D.K. (1990) *State v Thomas*: Face to face with *Coy* and *Craig*—Constitutional Invocation of Wisconsin's Child-Witness Protection Statute. [1990] *Wisconsin Law Review*, 1613–53.

Van Bueren, G. (1991) The UN Convention on the Rights of the Child. *Journal of Child Law*, 63–66.

Vandermass, M., Hess, T. and Baker-Ward, L. (1993) Does anxiety affect children's memory for a stressful event? *Applied Cognitive Psychology*, **7**, 109–127.

Varendonck, J. (1911) Les témoignages d'enfants dans un procès retentissant. *Archives des Psychologie*, **11**, 129–171.

Vasek, M. (1986) Lying as a skill. The development of deception in children. In R. Mitchell and N. Thompson (eds.) *Deception: Perspectives on Human and Non-human Deceit*. Albany: SUNY Press.

Victim Support (1988) The Victim in Court. *Working Party Report*. London: Victim Support.

Vizard, E. (1987) Interviewing young, sexually abused children—assessment techniques. [1987] *Family Law*, 28-33.

Vizard, E. (1988) Child sexual abuse—the child's experience. *British Journal of Psychotherapy*, **5**, 77-91.

Vizard, E. (1989) Video recorded evidence and the implications for the child. Submission (Paper 2) to the Pigot Committee.

Vizard, E. (1991) Interviewing children suspected of being sexually abused. A review of theory and practice. In C. Hollin and K. Howells (eds.) *Clinical Approaches to Sex Offenders and Their Victims*. Chichester: Wiley.

Vizard, E., Bentovim, A. and Tranter, M. (1987) Interviewing sexually abused children. *Adoption and Fostering*, **11**, 20-7.

Vizard, E. and Tranter, M. (1988) Helping children describe experiences of child sexual abuse—a guide to practice. In A. Bentovim, A. Elton, J. Hildegrand, M. Tranter and E. Vizard (eds.) *Child Sexual Abuse within the Family, Assessment and Treatment*. Bristol: John Wright.

Vizard, E., Wiseman, M., Bentovim, A. and Leventhal, J. (1989) Child Sexual Abuse Videos—Is Seeing Believing? Paper given to the British Paediatric Association, 11-14 April.

Volbert, R. (1992a) Statements about sexual abuse and sexual knowledge of pre-school children. Paper presented at the European Law and Psychology Conference, Oxford, September.

Volbert, R. (1992b) Child Witnesses in Sexual Abuse Cases: the juridical situation in Germany. In Lösel, F., Bender, D. and Bliesener, T. (eds.) *Psychology and Law: International Perspectives*. Berlin: Walter de Gruyter.

Voltaire, F. (1771-72) Questions sur L'Encyclopédie, distribuées en forme de dictionnaire. Par des amateurs. London.

Vulliamy, C.E. (1931) *John Wesley*. London: G. Bles.

Walker, A.G. (1993) Questioning young children in court. A linguistic case study. *Law and Human Behavior*, 17, 59–81.

Walker, A.G. and Walker, N.M.L. (1964) *The Law of Evidence in Scotland*. Edinburgh: Hodge & Co.

Walker, D.M. (1981) *The Scottish Legal System* (5th edn). Edinburgh: W. Green & Son.

Walton, M. (1989) What use are statistics—policy and practice in child abuse. In C. Wattam, J. Hughes and H. Blagg (eds.) *Child Sexual Abuse: Listening, Hearing and Validating the Experiences of Children*. London: NSPCC/ Longman.

Warner, K. (1990) Child witnesses—developments in Australia and New Zealand. In J. Spencer, G. Nicholson, R. Flin and R. Bull (eds.) *Children's Evidence in Legal Proceedings: an International Perspective*. Cambridge: Cambridge University Law Faculty.

Warren, A., Hulse-Trotter, K. and Tubbs, E. (1991) Inducing resistance and suggestibility in children. *Law and Human Behavior*, 15, 273–85.

Warren-Leubecker, A., Tate, C., Hinton, I. and Ozbek, N. (1989) What do children know about the legal system and when do they know it? In S. Ceci, D. Ross and M. Toglia (eds.) *Perspectives on Children's Testimony*. New York: Springer.

Wasik, M. and Taylor, R.D. (1991) *Blackstone's Guide to the Criminal Justice Act 1991*. London: Blackstone Press.

Wattam, C. (1993) *Making a Case in Child Protection*. London: Longman.

Waugh, R. (1913) *The Life of Benjamin Waugh*. London: T. Fisher Unwin.

Wegener, H. (1989) The present state of statement analysis. In J.C. Yuille (ed.) *Credibility Assessment*. Dordrecht: Kluwer.

Weinberg, S.G. (1955) *Incest Behaviour*. Secaucus NJ: Citadel Press.

Weiss, E. and Berg, R. (1982) Child victims of sexual assault: impact of court procedures. *Journal of the American Academy of Child Psychiatry*, 21, 513-18.

Wellborn, O.G. (1991) Demeanor. *Cornell Law Review*, 76, 1075–1105.

Wells, G. and Loftus, E. (1991) Is the child fabricating? Reactions to a new assessment technique. In J. Doris (ed.) *The Suggestibility of Children's Recollections*. Washington: American Psychological Association.

West, D. (1985) *Sexual Victimisation: Two Recent Researches into Sex Problems and Their Social Effects*. Aldershot: Gower.

West, D.J. (1977) *Homosexuality Re-examined*. London: Duckworth.

West Yorkshire Police (1989) *Research into the Use of Video in the Investigation of Child Abuse*. West Yorkshire Police.

Westcott, H. (1991) The abuse of disabled children: A review of the literature. *Child Care, Health and Development*, 17, 243–58.

Westcott, H. (1992) The cognitive interview—a useful tool for social workers? *British Journal of Social Work*, 22, 519–33.

Westcott, H. (1993a) Investigative interviewing and children with disabilities: Meeting whose needs? Paper presented at the Investigative Interviewing Conference, Leicester, February.

Westcott, H. (1993b) The Memorandum of Good Practice and Children with Disabilities. *The Journal of Law and Practice*.

Westcott, H., Davies, G. and Clifford B. (1989b) The use of anatomical dolls in child witness interviews. *Adoption and Fostering*, 13, 6-14.

Westcott, Davies, G. and Clifford, B. (1991) Adult's perceptions of children's videotaped truthful and deceptive statements. *Children and Society*, 5, 123–35.

Weyland, I. (1989) The response of civil courts to allegations of child sexual abuse. [1989] *Family Law*, 240-7.

Whitcomb, D. (1990) When the victim is a child: past hope, current reality, and future promise of legal reform in the United States. In J. Spencer, G. Nicholson, R. Flin and R. Bull (eds.) *Children's Evidence in Legal Proceedings: an International Perspective*. Cambridge: Cambridge University Law Faculty.

Whitcomb, D. (1992) *When the Victim is a Child* (2nd edn). Washington DC: National Institute of Justice.

Whitcomb, D., Runyan, D. et al. (1991) *Child Victim as Witness. Research and Development Program*. Final Report to US Department of Justice. Grant 87-MC-CX-0026.

Whitcomb, D., Shapiro, E.R. and Stellwagen, C.D. (1985) *When the Victim is a Child: Issues for Judges and Prosecutors*. Washington DC: National Institute of Justice.

White, R. (1990) Children and hearsay evidence. *New Law Journal*, 140, 300–301.

White, S., Strom, G., Santilli, G. and Halpin, B. (1986) Interviewing young children with anatomically correct dolls. *Child Abuse and Neglect*, 10, 519-29.

Wigmore, J.H. (1940) *Evidence in Trials at Common Law*. Boston: Little, Brown & Co.

Wigmore, J.H. (1979) *Evidence in Trials at Common Law*, revised by J.H. Chadbourn. Boston: Little, Brown & Co.

Wilkinson, A.B. (1982) The rule against hearsay in Scotland. [1982] *Juridical Review*, 213-36.

Wilkinson, A.B. (1986) *The Scottish Law of Evidence*. London and Edinburgh: Butterworths/Law Society of Scotland.

Wilkinson, J. (1988) Context effects in children's event memory. In M. Gruneberg, P. Morris and R. Sykes (eds.) *Practical Aspects of Memory: Current Research and Issues*. Chichester: Wiley.

Williams, G. (1960) Questioning by the police: some practical considerations. [1960] *Criminal Law Review*, 325-46.

Williams, G. (1963) *The Proof of Guilt* (3rd edn). London: Stevens.

Williams, G. (1979) The authentication of statements to the police. [1979] *Criminal Law Review*, 6-23.

Williams, G. (1987a) Child witnesses. In P. Smith (ed.) *Criminal Law: Essays in Honour of J. C. Smith*. London: Butterworths.

Williams, G. (1987b) Videotaping children's evidence. *New Law Journal*, 137, 108-112.

Williams, G. (1987c) The corroboration question. *New Law Journal*, 137, 131.

Williams, G. (1987d) More about videotaping children. *New Law Journal*, 137, 351-70.

Williams, G. (1989) Which of you did it? *Modern Law Review*, 52, 179.

Wilson, G.J. (1990) A perspective on the Canadian position. In J. Spencer, G. Nicholson, R. Flin and R. Bull (eds.) *Children's Evidence in Legal Proceedings: an International Perspective*. Cambridge: Cambridge University Law Faculty.

Wimmer, H., Gruber, S. and Perner, J. (1984) Young children's conception of lying: lexical realism—moral subjectivism. *Journal of Experimental Child Psychology*, 37, 1-30.

Wiseman, M.R., Vizard, E., Bentovim, A. and Leventhal, J. (1992) Reliability of videotaped interviews with children suspected of being sexually abused. *British Medical Journal*, 304, 1089–91.

Wolchover, D. (1987) Criminal trials: Proof by missing witnesses—an election issue. *New Law Journal*, 137, 525–28; A postscript on proof by missing witnesses, *ibid.*, 805–86, 833–34.

Wolchover, D. (1988) Proof by missing witnesses: a safeguard restored. *New Law Journal*, 138, 202–03, 242–43, 261–62, 461–63.

Wolfe, V., Sas, L. and Wilson, S. (1987) Some issues in preparing sexually abused children for courtroom testimony. *Behaviour Therapist*, 10, 107-13.

Woodbury, H. (1984) The strategic use of questions in court. *Semiotica*, 48, 197-228.

Woodcraft, E. (1988) Child sexual abuse and the law, *Feminist Review*, 28, 124.

Wyatt, G. and Powell, G. (eds.) (1988) *The Lasting Effects of Child Sexual Abuse*. San Mateo, California: Sage.

Wyld, N. (1991) Children's participation—myth or reality? [1991] *Journal of Child Law*, 83–86.

Wynne, J. (1989) Medical aspects of child abuse. In A. Levy (ed.) *Focus on Child Abuse*. London: Hawksmere.

Yamamoto, K., Soliman, A., Parsons, J. and Davies, O. (1987) Voices in unison: stressful events in the lives of children in six countries. *Journal of Child Psychology and Psychiatry*, 28, 855-64.

Yang Cheng (1988) Criminal procedure in China: some comparisons with the English system. *International and Comparative Law Quarterly*, 37, 190.

Yates, A., Beutler, L. and Crago, M. (1985) Drawings by child victims of incest. *Child Abuse and Neglect*, 9, 183-9.

Yates, A. and Terr, L. (1988) Anatomically correct dolls—should they be used as the basis for expert testimony? *Journal of the American Academy of Child and Adolescent Psychiatry*, 27(2), 254-57; 27(3), 387-8.

Younts, D. (1991) Evaluating and admitting expert opinion testimony in child sexual abuse prosecutions. *Duke Law Journal*, 41, 691–739.

Yuille, J. (1988) The systematic assessment of children's testimony. *Canadian Psychology,* **29**, 247-62.

Yuille, J.C. (1989) Expert evidence by psychologists: sometimes problematic and often premature. *Behavioural Sciences and the Law,* **7**, 181-96.

Yuille, J. (1992) Investigative interviewing with children. Seminar presented to the National Children's Bureau, London, 21st July.

Yuille, J.C., Cutshall, J.L. and King, M.A. (1986) Age related changes in eyewitness accounts and photo-identification. Unpublished manuscript.

Yuille, J., Hunter, R., Joffe, R. and Zaparnink, J. (1993) Interviewing children in child sexual abuse cases. In G. Goodman and B. Bottoms (eds.) *Child Victims, Child Witnesses.* New York: Guilford.

Yule, W. (1989) The effects of disasters on children. *Association for Child Psychology and Psychiatry Newsletter,* **11** (6), 1-6.

Yun, J. (1983) A comprehensive approach to child hearsay in sex abuse cases. *Columbia Law Review,* **83**, 1745.

Zacharias, G. (translated by Trollope, C.) (1969). *The Satanic Cult.* London: Allen & Unwin.

Zaragoza, M. (in press) (ed.) *Memory and Testimony in The Child Witness.* California: Sage.

Index